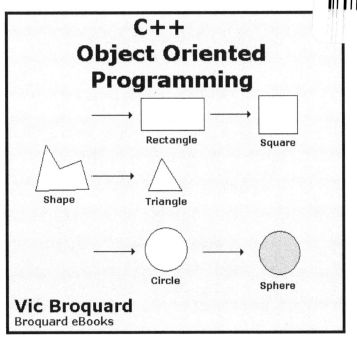

C++ Object Oriented Programming
4th Edition

Vic Broquard

C++ Object Oriented Programming
4th Edition
Vic Broquard
Copyright 2006, 2014 by Vic Broquard

ISBN: 978-1-941415-56-6

Broquard eBooks
103 Timberlane
East Peoria, IL 61611
author@Broquard-eBooks.com

To all of my dedicated, persevering students,
and to L. Ron Hubbard, who taught me to "Simplify"

Table of Contents

Preface

This book assumes you have had an introduction to C++ or C programming course as well as a beginning course in data structures. Specifically, you should be familiar with array and structure processing algorithms. In other words, this text can be used by those who already know C programming but have yet to learn the new features that C++ added to the language.

If you discover your array processing or structure work is weak, please see the Appendix A—A Review of Array and Structure Processing.

On the other hand, if you discover your basic C++ is weak, please see Appendix B—A Review of Basic C++ which is in ebook format, available at the link below, along with the samples.

Each chapter in some manner builds upon the previous material. One or more complete programming examples accompany each chapter. The book comes with a self-extracting zip file containing all of the sample programs in the book along with all of the test data required for the programming assignments. Download them at:
http://www.Broquard-eBooks.com/pb/cppoop and use the link there.

At the end of each chapter are **Review Exercises**, **Stop Exercises,** and **Programming Problems**. Before you tackle any programming assignments, you should do both the Review and Stop exercises. The Review Exercises are paper and pencil activities that assist in solidifying the basic design principles covered in the chapter. The Stop Exercises cover the new syntax of the language and the new principles of data structures. These illustrate many of the more common errors beginners make in coding or using the chapter's information. In some chapters, the Stop Exercises develop additional ways that the data structure can be applied or designed. If you dutifully do these two sets of exercises **before** you start in on your programming assignments, you will have a much better chance of success with drastically lower frustration level.

If you find any errors or have any suggestions or comments, please email me at author@Broquard-eBooks.com

Chapter 1—An Overview of OOP and a Review of Basic C++

Introduction

Welcome to Object-Oriented Programming (OOP). An object is "a thing," an entity. You are studying an approach toward programming that is centered upon objects and how they interact. This viewpoint is in contrast to C-style procedural type programming in which programs were primarily defined by functional decomposition which outlined the steps necessary to solving a problem, such as IPO (Input, Process, and Output). Functional decomposition is not discarded. Rather, it is expanded by the introduction of objects. However, here at the beginning we must define the common starting point.

For some, your background consists of pure C programming in which case, I assume that you have some skill in the use of pointers and structure processing. For others, you have already had an elementary introduction to C++ programming and data structures. In this case I assume that you are already well versed in the new C++ features that were added to the C language along with structure processing. A few may have been exposed to writing some simple object-oriented classes. Readers' backgrounds vary widely. Thus, the first three chapters are designed to ensure that everyone has acquired the necessary fundamental building blocks of the C++ language which are then utilized heavily in the subsequent object-oriented programming chapters.

For some of you, these first three chapters will serve as a solid review of that with which you are already conversant. For others, much of this will be new. If you should find yourself a bit weak in array and structure processing, please study Appendix A as you study these first three chapters. If you are weak on the C++ input and output operations, please study Appendix B. The starting point is the definition of the key terms used in object-oriented programming.

C++, as its name implies, in an enhanced, improved C language. One does not just forget all of the C language that one knows. Rather the opposite. C++ encompasses all of C and adds many new features in an attempt to improve the short comings of C, and it adds support for object-oriented programming. Since C++ was invented to support object-oriented programming, many of its features are related to OOP. Thus, the chapter begins with a brief outline of what OOP is all about. The next three chapters cover the many improvements to the C language. With these new basics known, we can delve into OOP proper.

C++ has its own OOP run-time library, but it also supports all of the C run-time functions as well. C++ uses the same control structures as C and includes all of the same basic built-in data types.

1

Object-Oriented Terminology

Consider a computer emulation of a car object. It has **properties** associated with it; these are often called **data members** similar to structure members. Some car object properties might be the number of doors, its color, the engine size, its mpg, gas tank gallons, whether the motor is turned on, and its current speed. A car object also has capabilities known as **member functions**. It may have the capabilities of start, stop, drive, speed up, slow down, and turn.

A **class** is a model for the compiler to follow to create an object; it is very similar to a structure template. A class usually has data members that define its various properties and has member functions that perform requested actions. When one creates a specific instance of the car class in memory, one has then a real object. This is called **instantiating an object**. The actions and nomenclature parallel that of a structure. Given an instance of a car, we can then request it to perform various actions, such as starting up and driving.

Encapsulation means to enclose in a capsule. The data members and the functions to operate on those data are joined into an inseparable whole. The outside world can utilize the object through its provided member functions. How those actions are actually implemented are totally **hidden** from the outside world. Internally, the object itself knows how to carry out those actions. Hence, we have the idea of a black box. Ideally, one should be able to completely rework the internal algorithms and never touch the user's coding.

With the car, the user might invoke a **StartCar()** function. How the car is actually started is **never** known nor is it ever a concern to the user. The benefit of encapsulation is large. Perhaps the biggest is code reusability.

The member data and functions have a user **access attribute**: **public**, **private**, and **protected**. Specifying **public** access on a data item or function allows the user to use and refer to it. Only public data and functions can be accessed by the user of the object. Sometimes we do not wish the user to be able to access some of the class data and function members; these are given either **protected** or **private** access; these are for our own internal use within our class.

For example, the manner in which we wish to keep track of whether the car is started or not is our own business. The user should not be given public access to that member; instead we give him a function **IsStarted()** which returns **true** or **false**. If we do not like the way we are internally storing the started state, we can change it without affecting the user's code. It is unwise to make data members public, for that allows the user to be able to change object state directly; doing so removes a bit of the black box. We then cannot change these public data members without impacting the users of our class. Member functions are often public so the user can perform actions with the object.

Polymorphism means having many forms. Polymorphism allows one name to be used to handle a set of similar actions. For example in C, we have the three conversion functions: **atoi()**, **atol()**, and **atof()**:

```
int    x = atoi (string);
```

```
long    y = atol (string);
double z = atof (string);
```

Polymorphism permits us to create one function name, say **convert()**, and then based on the actual arguments passed, determine which conversion process is needed:

```
void convert (const char* string, int&    ansr);
void convert (const char* string, long&   ansr);
void convert (const char* string, double& ansr);
```

This is also called **function overloading**. We use one function name but have several versions of that function to carry out the similar actions.

Inheritance is an extremely powerful concept denoting a hierarchical relationship of classes where one class builds upon another. If we have written a great Car class, then it might be extended or reused. What is a truck but a car that can haul cargo? What is a taxi or a limousine but a car with some extras? Our Car class can serve as the base class or parent class. We could create a Truck class derived from the Car class. The Truck class would inherit everything in the Car class. That is, the Truck would have all the Car's properties such as **is_moving**, **speed**, **weight**, and **color**. The Truck would also have all of the Car's member functions such as **IncreaseSpeed()**, **Start()**, and **Stop()**. In turn, the Truck class might wish to add some additional members such as cargo capacity and might wish to add some new functions to work with the cargo.

With inheritance, you write the code for moving the Car base class, and then in the Truck and Taxi classes, you do not have to reinvent the wheel, just use the inherited data and functions. Of course, if the Car function does not do what is needed, it can be completely overridden in the Truck class. Inheritance, then, allows one to build hierarchies of classes dependent upon one another.

Let's begin with a review of the basics. Structures evolved into classes, so this is not wasted effort. However, if you need to review even more basic C++, see the additional materials in ebook format.

C++ Programming Changes Caused by the new Microsoft Visual Studio .NET 2005

Release executables now by default require three MS dll files in order to actually execute. Thus, if you intend to run a DOS C++ program on a machine that does not have .NET 2005 installed on it, you must install the three dlls. However, there is a way to avoid this and have a DOS C++ program that can execute on its own. In the Project Settings, C++ tab, Code Generation tab, Runtime Libs set this one to Multi Threaded /MT and rebuild. See Appendix B for details and screen shots of this setting.

At the beginning C++ level, and thus impacting all other courses, is Microsoft's re-write of the C Library. Their purpose is to make these basic functions "secure." However, their changes have not yet gotten ANSI standards approval, and are hence Microsoft only at this point. However, if you ignore this, compiles will generate tons of "function call is deprecated. Please use. . ." The area that impacts a beginning data structure's student is the string functions only. Yes, there are many other functions that have changed, but they will be covered in this course in the appropriate chapter.

First, let me explain the reasoning behind Microsoft's re-write of the standard C Library. A couple quick examples illustrate why. Suppose you had the following coding.

```
char string[5];
strcpy (string, "Hello World from Vic");
strcat (string, ". I forgot the .");
strcpy (0, "Hi");
strcpy (string, 0);
```

The first two instructions perform a core-override or a buffer overrun (to be politically correct), with wildly unpredictable results, potentially including a program crash. The last two instructions wipe out or read as a string the beginning part of the program's data segment where the C runtime globals are stored, equally disastrous.

With Microsoft's new library functions, all four of these instructions cause a program abort and do not wipe out any memory. No more security breaches is the idea. Over four hundred library functions have either been rewritten or replaced with new functions. It is my hunch that most all of these changes will eventually find their way into the ANSI standard for C++, given time.

Here is a summary of the changes at the beginning level of coding. The "big three" functions that most directly impact us are: string compare, string concatenation, and string copy.

```
Name-new: strcmp and _stricmp
Meaning: string compare, case sensitive and case insensitive
Prototype: int strcmp (const char* string1, const char* string2);
        int _stricmp (const char* string1, const char* string2);
Action done: strcmp does a case sensitive comparison of the two
        strings, beginning with the first character of each
        string. It returns 0 if all characters in both
        strings are the same. It returns a negative value if
```

4

```
                    the different character in string1 is less than that
                    in string2. It returns a positive value if it is
                    larger. Both functions abort the program if the
                    memory address is NULL or 0.
Example: char s1[10] = "Bcd";
         char s2[10] = "Bcd";
         char s3[10] = "Abc";
         char s4[10] = "Cde";
         char s5[10] = "bcd";
         strcmp (s1, s2) yields 0 - stings are equal
         _stricmp (s1, s5) yields 0 - strings are equal
         strcmp (s1, s3) yields a + value—s1 > s3
         strcmp (s1, s4) yields a - value—s1 < s4
```

```
Name-new: strcat_s
Meaning: string concatenation
Prototype: strcat (char* desString, size_t maxDestSize,
                 const char* srcString);
Action done: The srcString is appended onto the end of the
           desString. Aborts the program if dest is too small or
either pointer is NULL.
Example: char s1[20] = "Hello";
         char s2[10] = " World";
       strcat_s (s1, sizeof(s1), s2); yields "Hello World" in s1.
```

```
Name-new: strcpy_s
Meaning: string copy
Prototype: char* strcpy (char* desString, size_t maxDestSize,
                        const char* srcString);
Action done: All bytes of the srcString are copied into the
            destination string, including the null terminator.
            The function returns the desString memory address.
            It aborts the program if destination is too small or
            either pointer is NULL.
Example: char s1[10];
         char s2[10] = "Sam";
         strcpy_s (s1, sizeof (s1), s2);
When done, s1 now contains "Sam".
```

```
Name-new: strlwr_s
Meaning: string to lowercase
Prototype: char* strlwr (char* string, size_t maxSizeOfString);
Action done: All uppercase letters in the string are converted
            to lowercase letters. All others are left untouched.
            Aborts the program if the pointer is NULL.
```

```
Example: char s1[10] = "Hello 123";
         strlwr_s (s1, sizeof (s1));
         Yields "hello 123" in s1 when done.
```

Name-new: **strupr_s**
Meaning: convert a string to uppercase
Prototype: char* strupr_s (char* string, size_t maxSizeOfString);
Action done: Any lowercase letters in the string are converted
             to uppercase; all others are untouched.
             Aborts the program if the pointer is NULL.

```
Example: char s1[10] = "Hello 123";
         strupr_s (s1, sizeof(s1));
         When done, s1 contains "HELLO 123"
```

Name-new: **_strrev**
Meaning: string reverse
Prototype: char* _strrev (char* string);
Action done: Reverses the characters in a string. **It aborts the program if the memory address passed is null or 0.**

```
Example: char s1[10] = "Hello";
         _strrev (s1);
         When done, string contains "olleH"
```

Finally, when we pass a string to a function, we often encounter this situation.

```
void Fun (char* string) {
    strcpy_s (string, sizeof (string), "Hello World!");
    // error sizeof(pointer) is 4 bytes

    // use the const int that was used to define the string
    // in the first place.
    strcpy_s (string, MAXARRAYSIZE, "Hello World!");
```

The Input and Output of Character Strings

The input of character strings is often misunderstood, yet they play a vital role in object oriented programming. The method used to input a character string varies depending upon the data to be input itself. Let's examine some of the more common methods.

A. Using the Extraction Operator >> (a severely limited technique)

The extraction operator can be used to input character strings. The specific rules of string extraction follow those for the other data types. It skips over whitespace to the first nonwhite space character, inputs successive characters storing them into successive bytes in the array until:

      1. the extraction operator encounters whitespace or

      2. the end of file is reached.

Lastly, it stores the null terminator. There are two aspects of this input operation that frequently make the use of the extraction operator completely useless.

Notice that the extraction operator does not permit a blank to be in the string. Suppose that you prompted the user to input their name and age and then used **cin** to input them as follows. `cin >> name >> age;`

What results if the user enters the following data?

```
Sam Spade   25
```

The input stream goes into the bad or fail state. It inputs the characters "Sam" and stores them along with the trailing null terminator into the **name** field. It skips over the blank and attempts to input the character S of Spade into the **age** integer and goes immediately into the fail state. If you reflect upon all the different kinds of strings that you might encounter in the real world of programming (names, product descriptions, addresses, cities), the vast majority may have embedded blanks in them. This rules out the extraction operation as a method of inputting them.

The other part of the extraction operator rules is quite destructive, especially if you are running on the earlier Windows platforms. It inputs all characters until it finds whitespace or EOF. Now suppose that the field **name** is defined to be an array of 21 characters. What happens if in response to the prompt to enter a name, the user enters the following name.

```
Rumplestillskinchevskikov
```

The computer attempts to store 26 characters into an array that is only 21 characters long. Four bytes of memory are now overlain. What happens next is unpredictable. If another variable in your program occupies that overlaid memory, its contents are trashed. If that memory is not even part of your program, but is part of some other program, such as a Windows system dll, it is overlain; even wilder things can happen! Under Windows NT/2000/XP Pro, if you attempt to overlay memory that is not part of your data segment, the program is aborted instead. This is one reason for so many system crashes under Windows 95/98.

The get() and getline() Functions

Either the **get()** or **getline()** function provides another way to input strings. These two functions can be used in one of two ways. Note: while I am using **cin** in these examples, any **ifstream** instance can be used as well.

```
cin.get (string variable, sizeof (string variable),
            delimiter character);

cin.getline (string variable, sizeof (string variable),
                delimiter character);
```

The delimiter character defaults to a new line code, if the third parameter is not coded.

Both functions input all characters from the current position in the stream until:
1. the maximum number of characters including the null terminator has been read or
2. It reaches the end of the file or
3. the delimiter is found.

By default the delimiter is a new line code.

The major difference between these two functions is that with **get()**, the delimiter is **not** extracted but remains in the input stream, while with **getline()**, the delimiter is removed, but not stored in the string.

How these functions are used to input strings depends upon the actual character data to be input.

Method B—All Strings Have the Same Length

This is a common situation, particularly when the data has been ported from a main frame computer. In the input set of data or file, all character strings are the same length, the maximum. Shorter strings have blanks added onto the end of the character series to fill out the maximum length. Assume that a cost record input set of data contains the item number, quantity, description and cost fields. The program defines the input fields as

```
const int DescrLimit = 21;
long    itemnumber;
long    quantity;
char    description[DescrLimit];
double cost;
```

The **description** field can hold up to twenty characters plus one for the null terminator. The input set of data would appear as

```
12345    10 Pots and Pans         14.99
34567   101 Cups                   5.99
45667     3 Silverware, Finished 10.42
```

8

Notice how the shorter strings are padded with blanks so that in all circumstances the **description** field is 20 characters long.

The data is then input this way.
```
infile >> itemnumber >> quantity >> ws;
infile.get (description, sizeof (description));
infile >> cost;
```
Observe that the first line ends by using the **ws** manipulator function to skip over whitespace to position the input stream to the first character of the description field. The **sizeof()** always returns the defined number of bytes that the variable occupies. In the case of the **description** field, it yields twenty-one. If one used **sizeof(quantity)**, it would return four bytes, since longs occupy four bytes. One could also use the constant integer **DescrLimit** instead of the **sizeof()**; this subtle difference will be important shortly.

Many company input data files are set up in this manner. What is input and stored in the **description** field when the second line of data above is input? The **description** contains "Cups "—that is, the characters C-u-p-s followed by sixteen blanks and then the null terminator.

There is one drawback to this method. The blanks are stored. If we compared this description to the literal "Cups," the two would not be equal. The inputted description contains sixteen blanks that the literal does not contain! Thus, if the trailing blanks are going to present a problem to the processing logic of the program, they need to be removed. On the other hand, if the description field is only going to be displayed, the presence of the blanks is harmless.

With a few lines of coding, the blanks can be removed. The idea is to begin at the end of the string and if that byte contains a blank, back up another byte until a byte that is non-blank is found. Then place a null terminator in the last blank position. Since the length of all strings must be twenty characters (after the **get()** function is done, the null terminator is in the twenty-first position), the location of the last byte that contains real data must be subscript 19. The null terminator must be at subscript 20. The following coding can be used to remove the blanks at the end, if any.
```
int index = DescrLimit - 2; // or 19
while (index >= 0 && description[index] == ' ') index--;
index++; // index=subscript of the first non-blank char
description[index] = 0; // insert a null terminator
                        // over last blank
```
If the **description** contains all blanks or if the string contains a non-blank character in the 20th position, this coding still works well.

The main problem to consider when inputting strings with the **get()** function is handling the detection of the end of file properly. We are used to seeing coding such as
```
while (cin >> itemnumber >> quantity) {
```
But in this case, the input operation cannot be done with one chained series of extraction operators. Rather, it is broken into three separate statements. Later in this chapter we will see an alternate method of handling this.

Method B, where all strings are the same length, also applies to data files that have more than one string in a line of data. Consider a customer data line, which contains the customer number, name, address, city, state and zip code. Here three strings potentially contain blanks, assuming the state is a two-digit abbreviation. Thus, Method B is commonly used.

Method C—String Contains Only the Needed Characters, But Is the Last Field on a Line

In certain circumstances, the string data field is the last item on the input data line. If so, it can contain just the number of characters it needs. Assume that the cost record data were reorganized as shown (<CR> indicates the enter key).

```
12345    10 14.99 Pots and Pans<CR>
34567   101  5.99 Cups<CR>
45667     3 10.42 Silverware, Finished<CR>
```

This data can be input more easily as follows.

```
infile >> itemnumber >> quantity >> cost >> ws;
infile.get (description, sizeof (description));
```

Alternately, the **getline()** function could also be used. The difference is **get()** leaves the current position in the stream pointing to the <CR> while **getline()** removes it. There are no excess blanks on the end of the descriptions to be removed. It is simpler. However, its use is limited because many data entry lines contain more than one string and it is often impossible to reorganize a company's data files just to put the string at the end of the data entry lines.

Method C works well when prompting the user to enter a single string. Consider the action of asking the user to enter a filename for the program to use for input.

```
char filename[_MAX_FNAME];
cin.get (filename, sizeof(filename));
ifstream infile;
infile.open (filename, ios::in);
```

When dealing with filenames, one common problem to face is just how many characters long should the **filename** array actually be? The compiler provides a #**define** of **_MAX_FNAME** that contains the platform specific maximum length a complete path could be.

Method D—All strings Are Delimited

The problem that we are facing is knowing where a string actually ends because a blank is not usually a good delimiter. Sometimes quote marks are used to surround the string data. Here a double quote mark begins and ends a string. Suppose that the input data appeared as follows.

```
12345   10 "Pots and Pans" 14.99
34567  101 "Cups" 5.99
45667    3 "Silverware, Finished" 10.42
```

When a string is delimited, the data can be input rather easily if we use the alternate form of the **get()** function, supplying the delimiter `'\"'`.

```
char junk;
infile >> itemnumber >> quantity >> junk;
infile.get (description, sizeof (description), '\"');
infile >> junk >> cost;
```

Notice that we must input both the beginning and ending quote marks. The **get()** function leaves the delimiter in the input stream, so we must extract it before continuing on with the next field, **cost**.

On the other hand, the **getline()** function removes the delimiter. Coding becomes simpler.

```
char junk;
infile >> itemnumber >> quantity >> junk;
infile.getline (description, DescrLimit, '\"');
infile >> cost;
```

Sometimes when the data has been exported from a database, a comma is used to delimit each field of data. Suppose that the lines looked this way.

```
12345, 10, Pots and Pans, 14.99
34567, 101, Cups, 5.99
45667, 3, Silverware Finished, 10.42
```

We could input the fields this way. Note the different delimiter to the **get()** function.

```
char junk;
infile >> itemnumber >> junk >> quantity >> junk;
infile.get (description, sizeof (description), ',');
infile >> junk >> cost;
```

The restriction must be that the strings cannot contain an embedded delimiter character, a comma in this case. **Note**: there is a bug in the .NET2005 compiler. If an integer is being extracted and it is followed by a comma, the integer is not input and the stream goes into the fail state! One way around this bug is to input into a double and then assign the double into the integer variable.

Outputting Character Strings

Outputting strings presents a different set of problems, one of spacing and alignment. In most all cases, the insertion operator handles the output of strings quite well. In the most basic form one might output a line of the cost record as follows

```
cout << setw (10) << itemnumber
     << setw (10) << quantity
     << description
     << setw (10) << cost << endl;
```

If the entire program output consisted of one line, the above is fine. Usually, the output consists of many lines, columnar aligned. If so, the above fails utterly because of the different lengths of the strings.

With a string, the insertion operator outputs all of the characters up to the null terminator. It does not output the null terminator. With strings of varying length, there is going to be an unacceptable jagged right edge in the description column. On the other hand, if Method A was used to input the strings and all strings are of the same length, all is well until the **setw()** function is used to define the total field width. Suppose that the **description** field should be displayed within a width of thirty columns. One might be tempted to code

```
cout << setw (10) << itemnumber
     << setw (10) << quantity
     << setw (30) << description
     << setw (10) << cost << endl;
```

The default field alignment of an **ostream** is right alignment. All of our numeric fields display perfectly this way. But when right alignment is used on character strings, the results are usually not acceptable as shown below

```
12345    10                      Pots and Pans 14.99
34567   101                              Cups  5.99
45667     3           Silverware, Finished 10.42
```

Left alignment must be used when displaying strings. Right alignment must be used when displaying numerical data. The alignment is easily changed by using the **left** and **right** manipulator functions.

```
cout << setw (10) << itemnumber
     << setw (10) << quantity
     << left << setw (30) << description
     << right << setw (10) << cost << endl;
```

Finally, the insertion operator displays all characters in a string until it encounters the null terminator. What happens if by accident a string is missing its null terminator? Simple—the insertion operator displays all bytes until it finds a null terminator. I often refer to this action as a "light show." Yes, one sees the contents of the string appear, but "garbage" characters follow that. If a line gets full, DOS line wraps and continues on the next line. If the screen fills, DOS scrolls. All of this occurs at a blazing speed. Sit back and relax; don't panic if this happens to you. It is harmless. Enjoy the show. It will stop eventually when it finds a byte with a zero in it.

Constant Character Strings

Sometimes we need a constant string. Suppose that we needed to store a string that contains "Apple" or "Apples." There are several easy ways to handle this situation where the strings are constant.

```
const char singleProduct[6] = "Apple";
const char pluralProduct[7] = "Apples";
```

The liability of this approach is accurate counting of the number of characters in the string. Don't forget to allow for the null-terminator.

Another approach is to let the compiler determine the actual length of the strings at compile time by omitting the array size.

```
const char singleProduct[] = "Apple";
const char pluralProduct[] = "Apples";
```

Finally, a third possibility is to recognize that a string is an array of char, or the memory address of the first element and store it that way.

```
const char* singleProduct = "Apple";
const char* pluralProduct = "Apples";
```

The Fill Character and Inputting Numbers with Leading 0's

The fill character for output is a blank by default. This is usually desired since we use **setw()** to force columnar alignment and we wish these leading positions to be blank. However, when outputting dates, sometimes we desire to see leading 0's appear. For example, the following represents unacceptable dates.

```
1/8/2001
10/9/2001
1/20/2001
```

What is desired is the following.

```
01/08/2001
10/09/2001
01/20/2001
```

The **setfill()** function is used to install a new fill character. Once set, it remains in effect for all future output operations until it is reset to another value. The function is passed the character to be used as the fill. To output the dates shown above, one codes

```
cout.setfill ('0');
cout << setw(2) << month << "/" << setw(2) << day
     << "/" << setw(4) << year;
cout.setfill (' ');
```

When displaying a check amount, an asterisk (*) is sometimes used.

13

The input extraction of numbers with leading zeros presents another problem. To input a date in the form above, one would expect the following to work, assuming that variable **c** is a character.

```
infile >> day >> c >> month >> c >> year;
```
or
```
cin >> day >> c >> month >> c >> year;
```

However, when the **istream** encounters numbers with leading zeros, it assumes these numbers are octal or base 8 numbers. In octal, the 8 and 9 digits are illegal and thus the input of dates can fail when there is a month or day that is 08 or 09. The **dec** manipulator function should be called one time to set the default to decimal instead of octal. This needs to be done only one time per stream. The correct version is

```
infile >> dec >> day >> c >> month >> c >> year;
```
or
```
cin >> dec >> day >> c >> month >> c >> year;
```

Usually, it is done one time often when the coding to setup floating point output is done on the output stream. Be alert for this problem as it will appear throughout this text in the programming examples and problems.

Structures and the iostreams

Structure members can also be input and output using the **iostream**s. Let's say that we have defined a **COSTREC** structure to store a customer's purchase. This is called the structure **template**, or blueprint or model for the compiler to follow when it makes actual instances of it.

```
const int DESCRLEN = 21;
struct COSTREC {
  long    itemNumber;
  char    description[DESCRLEN];
  int     quantity;
  double cost;
};
```

Here **COSTREC** is the structure **tag** which is used as a data type in C++. We can create instances in **main()** as follows.

```
int main () {
  COSTREC crec;
  COSTREC oldrec;
  ...
```

crec and **oldrec** are structure variables, instances of the **COSTREC** structure in memory.

Remember that only five actions are possible with a structure variable. The address of the instance can be taken, as in **&crec** which returns the memory location of **crec**. A function can be passed a structure variable and a function can return a structure variable. One structure variable can be assigned to another as long as they both have the same structure tag; for example

```
oldrec = crec;
```

And the individual structure members of an instance can be accessed using the dot (.) operator.

```
crec.quantity
```

```
crec.description
oldrec.cost
```

Since a structure variable can neither be inputted or outputted, we must use this last action to input or output the individual structure members. To input a **COSTREC** we can code

```
infile >> crec.itemNumber >> crec.quantity;
infile.get (crec.description, sizeof (crec.description));
infile >> crec.cost;
```

Notice that this coding assumes that all descriptions are 20 characters long.

To output **crec**, assume that floating point output formatting has been already set.

```
cout << setw (10) << crec.itemNumber  << " " << left
     << setw(25)  << crec.description << right << "    $"
     << setw (12) << crec.cost << endl;
```

However, very often a pair of functions are written to encapsulate a structure instance's input and output. For example, we might have the functions **InputCostRec()** and **OutputCostRec()** or **DisplayCostRec()**. But before we can examine how these functions are written, we need another new feature of the language.

Reference Variables

A **reference variable** is a pointer or the address of something, in which the compiler is responsible for all of the implementation details. To define a reference variable, we use the & token within the data definition. The **Swap()** function to switch the contents of two integers uses reference variables.

```
void Swap (int& num1, int& num2) {
   int temp = num1;
   num1 = num2;
   num2 = temp;
}
```

Here **num1** and **num2** are reference variables. Each contains the memory address of an integer. However, it is the compiler that handles all of the details for us. The invocation of **Swap()** could be done this way in say the main function.

```
int itemNumber1;
int itemNumber2;
...
Swap (itemNumber1, itemNumber2);
```

The compiler examines the prototype of **Swap()** and discovers that two references to integers are required. The compiler then passes a copy of the memory locations for these two numbers for us. In C++ all functions must have a prototype or the compiler issues an error message.

Consider the implementation of a function to convert the long total seconds in a day back into three integers, hours, minutes, and seconds. Since a function can only return a single value or no value, we must pass either three pointers to the three answer integers in the calling function or pass three references. Here is how the function could be implemented using reference variables.

15

```
void TotSec_to_HMS (long totsec, int& hours, int& min,
                    int& sec) {
  hours = (int) (totsec / 3600);
  min = (int) (totsec % 3600 / 60);
  sec = (int) (totsec % 60);
}
```

Here the parameters **hours**, **min**, and **sec** are reference variables. These three parameters contain the memory locations of the caller's three answer integers. It might be invoked this way.

```
int elapsedHours;
int elapsedMinutes;
int elapsedSeconds;
long totalSeconds = 3642;
TotSec_to_HMS (totalSeconds, elapsedHours, elapsedMinutes,
               elapsedSeconds);
```

If **totsec** contained 3642 seconds, then 1 would be stored in the caller's **elapsedHours** field. 0 is stored in **elapsedMinutes** and 42 stored in **elapsedSeconds**.

Reference variables are critical when passing an I/O stream to a function.

Passing iostream Instances to Functions

Commonly, an instance of the **iostream**s must be passed to a function to encapsulate the input or output operations of a program. Since the streams are being updated by the I/O operations performed within these functions, a reference to them must be passed.

Rule: Always pass an iostream by reference and return a reference to the iostream. Never pass a copy of the stream.

Rule: When passing a file stream to a function, always pass a reference to its base class, istream or ostream whenever possible. This way, the function can handle both situations. It could be passed a file or passed **cin** or **cout**. Only pass the **ifstream** or **ofstream** when you need specific file-only functions, such as **open()** or **close()**.

Why should a function return a reference to the stream that it was given? Users prefer to chain operations and test the results of I/O operations. To see this effect, consider how a **GetData()** function could be written to input a set of cost data. In the calling function, it is invoked this way.

```
while (GetData (infile, itemnumber, quantity,
                description, cost, DescrLimit)) {
```

Notice how the caller desires to test the goodness of the stream after the input operation has finished. If the **GetData()** function did not return a reference to the stream it was passed, the caller could not test the stream in the same line of coding.

The function is coded this way. Notice that the fields to fill up are passed by reference as well. However, the character string description is not because it is an array of characters; remember that the name of an array is always the memory address of the first element.

```
istream& GetData (istream& infile, long& itemnumber,
                  long& quantity, char description[],
                  double& cost, int descrLimit) {
  infile >> itemnumber >> quantity >> ws;
  if (!infile) return infile;
  infile.get (description, descrLimit);
  if (!infile) return infile;
  infile >> cost;
  if (!infile) return infile;
  int index = descrLimit - 1;
  while (index >= 0 && description[index] == ' ') index--;
  description[++index] = 0;
  return infile;
}
```

Vitally important is that the number of bytes to use in the **get()** function this time is not **sizeof(description)**. Why? Within the function, the **description** is the memory address of where the first element of the array of characters is located. Memory addresses are always four bytes in size on a 32-bit platform. Thus, had we used **sizeof(description)**, then 4 bytes would have been the limit!

Notice also that the caller passed an instance of **ifstream** to the **GetData()** who defined it as an **istream&**. This magic is made possible by the rules of class inheritance which we will examine in great detail in a later chapter. Why is this important? It gives the user more flexibility. The user can also invoke **GetData()** this way.

```
while (GetData (cin, itemnumber, quantity,
                description, cost, DescrLimit)) {
```

We write one input function, but the user can call it using keyboard input or a real file!

The Vital Role of the const Qualifier

The **const** qualifier plays a vital role in OOP. Let's examine just how the use of constant applies to what we know at this point. Suppose that we had written a **CalcTax()** function to calculate the tax based upon a particular sales. The structure that contains the information is defined this way.

```
const int DESCRLEN = 21;
struct COSTREC {
  long    itemNumber;
  char    description[DESCRLEN];
  int     quantity;
  short   stateCode;
  double  cost;
};
```

Initially, we can propose a prototype such as this.

```
double CalcTax (COSTREC crec);
```

The function then calculates and returns the total tax based upon **crec**'s quantity, cost and the state code.

However, we know that it is very inefficient to pass duplicate copies of structures to functions. So we can pass a reference to **crec**.

```
double tax = CalcTax (crec);
```
with the prototype
```
double CalcTax (COSTREC& crec);
```

Here is the crucial detail. Within **CalcTax()**, should any of **crec**'s data be altered in any way while finding the tax? No, in no way should the calculation of the tax on this order change any of the order information. Thus, good OOP design insists and demands that we indicate that the passed data is to be constant so no changes can ever be made to it within **CalcTax()** itself. The prototype must be changed to the following.

```
double CalcTax (const COSTREC& crec);
```
The **const** qualifier is saying that the data pointed to by the reference variable is itself constant.

Specifically, if we use the above prototype, then the compiler will error any attempt we might accidentally make that would alter the caller's data.

```
double CalcTax (const COSTREC& crec) {
 crec.quantity = 42; // error - data is not constant
```

I cannot stress enough just how vitally important it is to make constant those data items that are not being altered within a function. It is a major source of frustration to those OOP programmers who have not grasped this principle. Let's look at another example. Suppose that we wished to write a **DisplayCostRec()** function to display nicely formatted a **COSTREC** instance.

The caller intends to invoke **DisplayCostRec()** as follows.

```
DisplayCostRec (cout, crec) << setw (12) << CalcTax (crec)
                            << endl;
```
Ok. I purposely made this an overly complex one-liner. It could also be coded this way with more clarity.

```
DisplayCostRec (cout, crec);
double tax = CalcTax (crec);
cout << setw (12) << tax << endl;
```

What would the prototype for **DisplayCostRec()** be? We know that the stream should be passed by reference and that the function must return that same stream reference. But what about the **COSTREC** instance? It should also be passed by reference. However, should any function whose purpose is to display a record ever, under any circumstances, alter the data it is to display? Of course not! Thus, we must make it constant. Here is the prototype.

```
ostream& DisplayCostRec (ostream& os, const COSTREC& crec);
```

Warning. If you do not get into the slavish habit of making things that need to be constant constant, you will shortly become burned in OOP programming.

Consider the following structure to store properties of a race car.

```
struct RACECAR {
```

```
  int number;
  char name[21];
  float speed;
};
```

The **main()** function then defines the pace car which sets the initial pace at the start of the race along with an array of cars that are in the race.

```
const RACECAR paceCar = {42, "Pace Car", 80.00};
RACECAR cars[100]; // the racers
int numCars;
...
DisplayCar (cout, paceCar);
for (j=0; j<numCars; j++) {
  DisplayCar (cout, cars[j]);
}
```

What would occur if the prototype for **DisplayCar()** was coded this way?

```
ostream& DisplayCar (ostream& os, RACECAR& car);
```

When the function is called with the constant pace car, the compiler issues the error "Cannot convert const RACECAR& to RACECAR&." The prototype must be

```
ostream& DisplayCar (ostream& os, const RACECAR& car);
```

As you begin doing the programming assignments in this text, some of you will get burned by this constant qualifier, sometimes many times. One does not just start making everything in the universe constant! Consider the use of const in the following prototype.

```
void Fun (const int x, const int y);
```

Here what is being made constant? The parameter copies of the passed integers are now constant. This is regarded as silly coding in the industry. Why is it silly? Under what circumstances could a line of code in the **Fun()** function change the caller's two integers? None. Copies of the caller's data are made. What this is actually doing is preventing assignments to the parameters **x** and **y** as shown below.

```
void Fun (const int x, const int y) {
  x = 42; // error: x is constant
```

From the calling function's point of view or the user of your function's point of view, changing your copy of their passed values is just "shooting yourself in the foot." The caller could care less if you should desire to "shoot yourself in the foot." What they **do** care about is your function "shooting them in the foot," that is, changing their data.

Passing Arrays and Array Elements

When an array is passed to a function and that function is not going to alter any of the array data, it should be passed as a constant as well.

Consider passing an array of **COSTREC** structures to a function called **PrintArray**. Its prototype should be the following.

```
ostream& PrintArray (const COSTREC arec[], int numRecs,
                     ostream& os);
```

19

The main function defines **arec** and calls **PrintArray** this way, where **numRecs** contains the number of elements currently in the array.

```
COSTREC arec[MAXRECS];
int numRecs;
 . . .
PrintArray (arec, numRecs, cout);
```

By using the **const** keyword in the prototype, we guarantee that compiler will generate error messages should we accidentally attempt to alter any of the data in the **COSTREC** array.

However, at other times, perhaps only the ith element of the array should be passed. For example, suppose that the function was **PrintRec** and not **PrintArray**. Here the **PrintRec** function should display a single **COSTREC** and should not alter any of the passed data. Its prototype is coded this way. Again, notice the use of the **const** keyword.

```
ostream& PrintRec (const COSTREC& crec, ostream& os);
```

The main function now calls **PrintRec** this way.

```
COSTREC arec[MAXRECS];
int numRecs;
 . . .
PrintRec (arec[i], cout);
```

Application Section

Pgm01a—The Cost of Goods Sold Program

The Cost of Goods Sold Program ties all of these new features together into a complete program. It is actually a very simple program. It must load an array of cost records and produce the cost report. While technically we do not need to actually store all of the records in an array, I chose to do so to illustrate array processing to help you review basic C++ operations. Here is the output of three text runs.

```
 Three Output Runs of the Cost of Goods Sold Program

 1 Test Run #1:
 2                   Acme Cost of Goods Sold
 3
 4   Item  Qty  Description              Unit        Tax          Total
 5 Number  Sold                          Cost
 6
 7  12345   42  Pots and Pans          $ 14.99  $ 45.64  $   675.22
 8  23456   10  Silverware, Brahms     $ 20.49  $ 14.86  $   219.76
 9  34567   29  Coffee #10 lb can      $  5.99  $ 12.59  $   186.30
10  45678    1  Cup and Saucers xxxx   $  4.25  $  0.31  $     4.56
11  56789    4  Soap                   $  1.22  $  0.35  $     5.23
12  67890    1                         $  1.00  $  0.07  $     1.07
13                                                       ---------
```

```
14                                                         $ 1092.15
15
16 Test Run #2:
17                     Acme Cost of Goods Sold
18
19   Item  Qty  Description              Unit      Tax      Total
20 Number Sold                           Cost
21
22 Error: too many cost records in the file
23
24
25 Test Run #3:
26                     Acme Cost of Goods Sold
27
28   Item  Qty  Description              Unit      Tax      Total
29 Number Sold                           Cost
30
31 Error: bad data in the file on line 4
```

What does the input data look like? Here is the small test file. Notice that the strings are delimited by double quote marks. Also notice that I included a string of maximum length as well as a string with no characters in it. To produce the other two test runs, I lowered the maximum number of elements in the array to 3 and inserted a letter in place of an item number.

```
The Input File for Pgm01

1 12345 42 "Pots and Pans" 14.99
2 23456 10 "Silverware, Brahms" 20.49
3 34567 29 "Coffee #10 lb can" 5.99
4 45678  1 "Cup and Saucers xxxx" 4.25
5 56789  4 "Soap" 1.22
6 67890  1 "" 1.00
```

As you look over the coding solution below, notice my use of comments. The first comment block identifies the program and with twenty-five words or less its purpose. Every function has a block comment preceding it outlining its purpose and return values, as needed. I also inserted instruction comments where I felt they would enhance a reader's overall understanding of the coding. Using the visually strong block comments before each function body makes it very easy to find the start of functions when reading the code.

I have made liberal use of functions to break the problem down into very small, manageable units. Next, observe the function prototypes and be certain you understand each occurrence of the use of the **const** qualifier.

I also tend to define my variables as I need them rather than define them all at the start of **main()**. A word on my coding style. I capitalize the names of functions. The names of variables all begin with a lowercase letter. If the variable name is a compound one, the second and subsequent

21

words of the name are capitalized, Java style. Global constant data items and structure tags are uppercased. I use one space for indentation so that I have plenty of room on lines for comments. I believe in placing the begin { on the line that is launching the block of coding, indenting all lines within the block and aligning the end } with the line that launched the block. Whatever style you choose, be consistent in its use.

The only coding that really needs an explanation is the handling of error situations within the **LoadArray()** function. Notice that I verify that the array bounds has not yet been exceeded before the call **GetData()**.

```
int i = 0;
while (i<limit && GetData (infile, arec[i])) {
 i++;
}
```

When the loop has ended, first I check for too many records or exceeding the array size. I attempt to input another character by skipping over whitespace and inputting a character. If that was successful and **i** is at the limit, then there are too many records in the file for the given array bounds. After displaying the error message to **cerr**, I close the file and use the **exit()** function to abort the program.

```
char c;
if (i == limit && infile >> c && infile.good()) {
 cerr << "Error: too many cost records in the file\n";
 infile.close ();
 exit (2);
}
```

If array size was not exceeded, then I check for bad data in the input, such as a letter where a digit should be in numeric fields. If it is not at EOF and the fail bit is on, then bad data is indicated. When I display the error message, I also gave the user the line number on which the bad data is located.

```
else if (!infile.eof() && infile.fail()) {
 cerr << "Error: bad data in the file on line " << i+1 << endl;
 infile.close ();
 exit (3);
}
// here all is ok
infile.close ();
return i;           // returns the number of records input
```

Look over the complete coding and see how the new C++ **iostream**s are handled. Here is the complete program.

```
Pgm01a - Cost of Goods Sold Program

 1 #include <iostream>
 2 #include <iomanip>
 3 #include <fstream>
 4 using namespace std;
 5
```

```
 6 /**************************************************************/
 7 /*                                                          */
 8 /* Pgm01a: Cost of Goods Sold Program                       */
 9 /*                                                          */
10 /**************************************************************/
11
12 const int DESCRLEN = 21;        // maximum length of description
13
14 struct COSTREC {
15  long    itemNum;              // the item number purchased
16  int     quantity;            // the quantity purchased
17  char    description[DESCRLEN]; // the description of the item
18  double  cost;                // the cost of one of these items
19 };
20
21 const int MAX = 100;            // maximum number of COSTRECs
22 const double TAXRATE = .0725;   // sales tax rate
23
24 // function prototypes
25 int      LoadArray (const char* filename, COSTREC arec[],
26                       int limit);
27 istream& GetData (istream& is, COSTREC& crec);
28 double   CalcTax (const COSTREC& crec);
29 ostream& Headings (ostream& os);
30 ostream& PrintRec (ostream& os, const COSTREC& crec, double tax,
31                     double total);
32
33 int main () {
34  // setup floating point output to show dollars and cents
35  cout << fixed << setprecision (2);
36
37  Headings (cout);      // display the headings of the report
38
39  COSTREC arec[MAX];   // the array of cost records
40  // load the array of cost records saving the number input
41  int numRecs = LoadArray ("costrecs.txt", arec, MAX);
42
43  double tax;          // the tax on this sale
44  double total;        // the total cost of this order
45  double gtotal = 0;   // the grand total sales
46
47  // print the report
48  for (long i=0; i<numRecs; i++) {
49    tax = CalcTax (arec[i]);
50    total = arec[i].quantity * arec[i].cost + tax;
51    gtotal += total;
52    PrintRec (cout, arec[i], tax, total);
53  }
54  // print grand total
55  cout << setw (53) << " " << "---------\n";
56  cout << setw (54) <<  "$" << setw (8) << gtotal << endl;
57
58  return 0;
```

```
 59  }
 60
 61  /*****************************************************************/
 62  /*                                                               */
 63  /* LoadArray: loads a file of cost records                       */
 64  /*            returns the number input or aborts the program     */
 65  /*            if bad data is encountered or array size exceeded*/
 66  /*                                                               */
 67  /*****************************************************************/
 68
 69  int LoadArray (const char* filename, COSTREC arec[], int limit) {
 70   // attempt to open the file
 71   ifstream infile (filename);
 72   if (!infile) {
 73    cerr << "Error: cannot open the input file " << filename
 74         << endl;
 75    exit (1);
 76   }
 77
 78   // input all cost records
 79   int i = 0;
 80   while (i<limit && GetData (infile, arec[i])) {
 81    i++;
 82   }
 83
 84   // guard against too many records in the file
 85   char c;
 86   if (i == limit && infile >> c && infile.good()) {
 87    cerr << "Error: too many cost records in the file\n";
 88    infile.close ();
 89    exit (2);
 90   }
 91
 92   // guard against bad data in the input file
 93   else if (!infile.eof() && infile.fail()) {
 94    cerr << "Error: bad data in the file on line " << i+1 << endl;
 95    infile.close ();
 96    exit (3);
 97   }
 98   // here all is ok
 99   infile.close ();
100   return i;           // returns the number of records input
101  }
102
103  /*****************************************************************/
104  /*                                                               */
105  /* GetData: input a single cost record                           */
106  /*                                                               */
107  /*****************************************************************/
108
109  istream& GetData (istream& is, COSTREC& crec) {
110   char c;
```

```
111  is >> crec.itemNum >> crec.quantity >> c;
112  if (!is) return is;
113  is.getline (crec.description, sizeof (crec.description), '\"');
114  is >> crec.cost;
115  return is;
116  }
117
118  /****************************************************************/
119  /*                                                              */
120  /* CalcTax: calculates the tax on this order ignoring state cd */
121  /*                                                              */
122  /****************************************************************/
123
124  double CalcTax (const COSTREC& crec) {
125   return crec.quantity * crec.cost * TAXRATE;
126  }
127
128  /****************************************************************/
129  /*                                                              */
130  /* Headings: prints the heading and column heading lines       */
131  /*                                                              */
132  /****************************************************************/
133
134  ostream& Headings (ostream& os) {
135   os << "                    Acme Cost of Goods Sold\n\n";
136   os << "  Item  Qty  Description                 Unit       Tax"
137      << "      Total\n"
138      << "Number Sold                           Cost \n\n";
139   return os;
140  }
141
142  /****************************************************************/
143  /*                                                              */
144  /* PrintRec: displays a detail line on the report             */
145  /*                                                              */
146  /****************************************************************/
147
148  ostream& PrintRec (ostream& os, const COSTREC& crec, double tax,
149                     double total) {
150   os << setw (6) << crec.itemNum << setw (5) << crec.quantity
151      << "  " << left << setw (22) << crec.description << right
152      << "$" << setw(6) << crec.cost << "  $" << setw (6) << tax
153      << "  $" << setw (8) << total << endl;
154   return os;
155  }
156
```

Review Questions

1. What is a class? How does encapsulation apply to a class?

2. What is meant by the term polymorphism? Give an example of polymorphism.

3. What is meant by the term inheritance? How can inheritance be a valuable aspect of OOP? How does inheritance apply to **cin** and an **ifstream** instance?

4. What is the difference between the New Style and Old Style C++?

5. What is the difference between the two **ostream**s **cout** and **cerr**? When would you use **cerr** instead of **cout**?

6. What is meant by the term manipulator function? Give two examples of a manipulator function.

7. What are the two ways a new line code can be inserted into an output stream?

8. What is meant by the term chaining? Give an example of chaining with **cout** and **cin**.

9. When extracting a number, character or a string, what are the rules that the extraction operator function follows to extract the indicated value?

10. What kinds of things can be inserted to an output stream?

11. What is the purpose of the **setw()** function? If one passes it a value of 7, to what does the width of 7 apply?

12. Why must floating point output be "setup" for dollars and cents? What would happen to the output if it was not setup this way?

13. What is the purpose of the **setprecision()** function? If a programmer passes it a value of 2, to what does it apply? How is this function's scope of application different than the scope of a **setw()** function?

14. What is the difference between the behavior of the Old Style and New Style **ifstream** class when opening a file?

15. Why does one always need to check on the "goodness" of a file stream after first opening the file?

16. What are the four states that any **iostream** can be in? How can the specific state of a stream be checked?

17. How can we tell when an input file stream has reached the end of file?

18. Why should all opened files be closed by the program before it terminates?

19. What is a sentinel controlled loop? Philosophically why is it a better design to have the program detect EOF automatically instead of looking for a sentinel value?

20. What is the difference between using the extraction operator to extract a character of data versus using the **get()** function? Under what circumstances would a **get()** function be a better choice?

21. Under what circumstances would the extraction of a person's name be acceptable and work properly?

22. What is the difference between the way that **get()** and **getline()** operate when inputting a character string?

23. When making a columnar aligned report, why is setting the width of character strings insufficient to produce acceptable output? What other step(s) should be taken?

24. When printing a check dollar amount, how can a program guarantee there are no blanks between the dollar sign and the first digit of the check amount?

25. What must be done to the input stream in order to input a person's id number which appears as 008192934 in the input data set? Why?

26. What is a reference variable? How do they differ from a pointer? Why are reference variables less error prone than using a pointer?

27. Why must all **iostream**s be passed to functions by reference?

28. Why should a function that is passed a reference to an **istream** return that same reference?

29. Why should an **InputData()** function be passed an **istream&** instead of an **ifstream&** if it is to input from a file?

30. When a function is passed a reference or a pointer to an item that this function is not going to alter, why should that item be made constant?

Stop! Do These Exercises Before Programming

1. Show the output of the following sequence of instructions. Be sure to indicate with a 'b' all of the blanks in the output.

```
cout << fixed << setprecision (2);
double a(42.425);
double b(-123.4567);
int x = 10;
int y (99);
char z ('A');
char msg[80] = "Hello there";
```

A.) Show the output.
```
cout << a << b << x << endl;
cout << setw (6) << a << setw (8) << b << endl;
```

B.) Show the output.
```
cout << setw(3) << x << y << endl;
```

C.) Show the output.
```
cout << setw (3) << z << x << endl << setw (3) << z << setw(4)
     << x << endl;
cout << setw (4) << y << setw (15) << msg << setw (4) << y
     << endl;
```

D.) Show the output.
```
cout << setw (4) << y;
cout << left << setw(15)  << msg << setw (4) << y << endl;
```

E.) Show the output.
```
cout right << setw (4) << y;
cout left  << setw(15) << msg;
cout right << setw (4) << y << endl;
```

F.) Show the output.
```
cout << setprecision(3) << setw(8) << a << setw(8) << b << endl;
```

2. Given the following definitions, what is input by each of these operations? The data entered at the keyboard is shown below the code line. I show blanks in the input line by the 'b' character. Also indicate the state that the stream is in when the action is finished.

```
double x;
int     k;
char    c;
char    string[21];
short   month, day, year;
```

A.) Show the input and stream state.
```
cin >> x >> k >> c;
b1234.55b42bZ<CR>
```

B.) Show the input and stream state.
```
cin >> x >> k >> c;
1b1b1<CR>
```

C.) Show the input and stream state.
```
cin >> k >> x >> c;
10.5 A<CR>
```

D.) Show the input and stream state.
```
cin >> k >> c >> x;
10.5 A<CR>
```

E.) Show the input and stream state.
```
cin >> month >> day >> year;
10/10/2001
```

F.) Show the input and stream state.
```
cin >> month >> day >> year;
10 10 2001
```

G.) Show the input and stream state.
```
cin >> month >> c >> day >> c >> year;
10/10/2001
```

H.) Show the input and stream state.
```
cin >> month >> c >> day >> c >> year;
08/09/2001
```

I.) Show the input and stream state.
```
cin >> dec >> month >> c >> day >> c >> year;
08/09/2001
```

J.) Show the input and stream state.
```
cin >> string;
Sam Spade<CR>
```

K.) Show the input and stream state.
```
cin >> string >> c;
Sam Spade<CR>
```

L.) Show the input and stream state.
```
cin.get (string, sizeof(string));
Sam Spade<CR>
```

M.) Show the input and stream state.
```
cin.getline (string, sizeof(string));
Sam Spade<CR>
```

N.) Show the input and stream state.
```
cin >> c;
cin.getline (string, sizeof(string), '\"');
"Sam Spade"<CR>
```

O.) Show the input and stream state.
```
cin >> c;
cin.get (string, sizeof(string), '\"');
cin >> c;
"Sam Spade"<CR>
```

3. Given the following definitions, write the output instruction(s) to display the data on the screen. There is to be three spaces between each field plus three spaces as a left margin. Integer fields are to be shown with five digits. Floating point fields are to be shown with a width of eight and a precision of two decimals. Display the fields in the order they are defined below.
```
long    policyNumber;
char    name[21];
int     numCars;
char    coverageCode;
double  premium;
```

4. A program to input the five fields as defined in question 4 above is to be written. The input file, **policies.txt**, contains many records whose fields are in the same order as the above fields are defined. All policy holders' names are padded with sufficient blanks to reach twenty characters long. At least one blank separates all fields. Write the coding to define and open the input file. Call it **infile**. The program should terminate with an appropriate error message should the file not be found.

5. Write a loop that would input all of these policy records and count them. When the loop ends, close the file and display the total number of records in the file.

6. Next, a **POLICY** structure is defined as follows.
```
const int LEN = 21;
struct POLICY {
   long    policyNumber;
   char    name[LEN];
   int     numCars;
   char    coverageCode;
   double  premium;
};
```
In the **main()** function, an array is defined and a loop is written to load the array.
```
const int MAX = 100;
int main () {
 POLICY array[MAX];
```

```
long j = 0;
while (j<MAX && GetPolicy (infile, array[i])) {
 ... // Point B
}
// Point A
```

Based upon the **GetPolicy()** function usage in the above **while** statement, code its prototype and then code the function. Assume the fields on each line are the same as in question 6.

7. At Point A in question 6, write the needed coding to close the file and guard against the array size being exceeded as well as encountering bad data in the input file.

8. At Point B in question 6, a call to a function called **PrintPolicy()** is to be done. It is passed the ith instance and an instance of an **ofstream** on which to display the data. Write the prototype for this function.

9. Within the **PrintPolicy()** function, display all of the fields in the same order as they are defined within the structure. Leave three blanks between each field. The policy number field should always be shown with seven digits and should contain as many leading 0 digits as required. The number of cars should be limited to two digits on output. The premium field should be in dollars and cents format and occupy ten total spaces. Write the body of this function.

Programming Problems

Problem Pgm01-1—The Coin Changer

Write a program that computes the minimum number of dollars, half-dollars, quarters, dimes, nickels and pennies that are contained within a specified amount of money. For example, given $1.18, the answer would be 1 dollar, 1 dime, 1 nickel and 3 pennies. Use the following structure to define a single coin type.

```
struct COIN {
  int denom;          // 1, 5, 10, 25, 50, 100 - the number of pennies
                      // int this type of coin
  long count;         // the number of this coin in the amount
  const char* single;   // text for a single coin, ie "penny"
  const char* multiple; // text for more than 1 coin, ie "pennies"
};
```

In **main()**, create an array of 6 **COIN** structures and initialize them to their starting values. Then, create a loop that prompts the user to enter a new amount until a -1 is entered. The amount variable should be a **long** containing the number of pennies. For example, to enter $1.18, the user would enter 118.

For each amount entered by the user, create a **for** loop that traverses the array of **COIN** objects and for each element in the **COIN** array, calls the **Change()** and **Print()** functions passing that single element in the **COIN** array.

The **Change()** function takes two parameters. First is the amount of money passed as a **long** reference. The second is a reference to the current element in the **COIN** array. The **Change()** function computes the number of this type of coin in the amount and removes their value from the amount. This can be done in just 2 lines of code. In the example of 1.18, if change is passed the **COIN** reference to the dollar object, it would store a count of 1 and lower the amount to 18 pennies.

The **Print()** function is passed a single constant reference to a **COIN** object. It should print out the number of this coin and the appropriate text message. For example, "1 dollar" would be printed when print is passed the dollar's **COIN** object. Do not print any output for a coin whose count is zero. However, it the total amount is originally zero, then do print "0 pennies."

For both the **Change()** and **Print()** functions, do **not** pass the entire array of coin objects. Do not use a global array of coin objects. Pay particular attention to the use of the **const** keyword in these functions.

Problem Pgm01-2—The Great Car Race Results

The Great American Car Race has finished. A report must be created displaying all contestants' final elapsed times. The input file consists of the car entry number, the name of the racer (20 characters maximum), the name of the car (20 characters maximum), the start time and the finish time—both of the form hh:mm:ss.ss. Note on input, every time must contain two digits for the hours and minutes and four digits and a decimal point for the seconds. Create a **RACER** structure that contains these fields along with the elapsed time (hours, minutes, and seconds). Create an array of 100 **RACER** structures.

The main() function then calls **LoadRacers()** whose purpose is to load the array from the input file. Guard against too many elements in the array as well as bad data on input. The function should return the number of race entries loaded into the array. If anything has gone wrong, the program should abort.

Next, the **main()** function should call **CalcElapsedTime()** for each element in the array. This function calculates the elapsed time from the start and finish times, storing the result in the elapsed time members of the structure.

Finally, **main()** should open an output file called **RaceResults.txt** and call **DisplayResults()** for each element in the array. It is passed the output file and the current element in the array. It displays the current contestant's information in a nicely formatted manner. Display the fields in the same order as they are in the structure instance, namely entry number, name, car name, start time, finish time, and the elapsed time. All times should be displayed in hh:mm::ss.ss format, such as 01:08:42.42 or 10:51:04.56.

Do not use any global variables in the program. Pass only a single element of the array to the **CalcElapsedTime()** and **DisplayResults()** functions. Pay particular attention to the use of the **const** keyword in these functions.

Chapter 2—Mechanics of Larger Program Creation

Introduction

When writing larger programs, some new considerations and mechanics arise that are not present necessarily when one writes smaller programs. One consideration that cannot be ignored is the likelihood of several programmers working together on the large application. When the program is your sole province, since you know what you are doing and coding, you can often get away with anything you can make work to meet the program specifications. However, when several programmers are working together on a project, communication between the programmers via the actual code becomes vital.

How often I have heard the lament "But I thought you said that Accounting was department number . . ." Mis-communication and misunderstood coding can wreak havoc on a project. Internal program comments certainly can go a long way to easing the task of code comprehension. However, there are some C++ features that also greatly facilitate code readability and hence reduce errors. These new features are examined first.

When an application becomes large, C++ provides some mechanical features that provide a tremendous boost in productivity. These include user written header files and the ability to have many separate cpp files make up the actual programming project. Individual programmers on the project can work on separate cpp files that form the entire program. These aspects are discussed later in the chapter in detail for they form the basis of OOP programs. An OOP program virtually never consists of a single cpp file.

Let's begin with a review of the enumerated data type. This feature of the language is heavily used in OOP.

Enumerated Data Types

Many integer variables hold key values that a program checks within **while**, If-Then-Else and Do Case statements. Suppose that a company has five departments that are identified by values ranging from one to five. Throughout a program, one might see these numbers appearing for various processing needs. However, these abstract numbers bear little relation to what they represent. For example, it is not obvious to anyone that department number 1 represents the Appliance department; 2, the Automotive department and so on. To make the program clearer, one can add comments such as these.

```
case 1: // appliance department
if (deptno == 2) { // the automotive department
```

A better approach would be to make a set of **#define** symbols or constant **int**s such as these two versions.

```
#define Appliances 1
#define Automotive 2
...
case Appliances:
if (deptno == Automotive) {
```

or

```
const int Appliances = 1;
const int Automotive = 2;
...
case Appliances:
if (deptno == Automotive) {
```

The **#define** creates a symbolic name that represents the value that comes after the name. It is a preprocessor directive. The preprocessor handles all the lines that begin with a # sign. It includes the various header files. In the case of **#define**s, it does a text substitution. That is, the preprocessor looks for all occurrences of **Appliances** within the program and replaces that symbol with its corresponding value, 1. Because the **#define** is just a simple text substitution, the **const int** approach is preferred because the **Appliances** is actually an instance of the integer data type.

Please note that although **Appliances** is a "variable" it really is a constant integer. The values on the **case** statements cannot be variables. That is, the following is invalid because, in this case, **appliances** is a variable, not a constant.

```
int appliances = 1;
...
case appliances: // error not a constant value
```

For many uses, using either a **const int** or a **#define** to create a more meaningful name is extremely important for readability. However, when there are more than just a few possibilities, errors can occur with this approach. What would result if the user coded the following and then used these as the values in a Do Case statement?

```
const int Appliances = 1;
const int Automotive = 2;
const int Housewares = 3;
const int Toys = 3;
const int Accounting = 5;
```

Because **Toys** was accidentally given the wrong value, incorrect results will occur that are difficult to find. There is a better way.

An **enumerated data type** allows us to create a "new" data type and specify precisely what possible values that variables of this new type can contain. The syntax is

```
enum new_data_type {enumerator-1, enumerator-2,
                  ..., enumerator-n };
```

where the form of the enumerators is

```
identifier = integer value
```

35

Usually the new data type is capitalized as are the enumerator identifiers. If the integer values are not coded, the first one is given the value 0, the next one is given a value of 1, and so on. Specifically, to handle these department numbers, an **enum** is a terrific way to proceed. Consider this version.

```
enum DeptNum {Invalid, Appliances, Automotive,
              Housewares, Toys, Accounting};
```

This creates a new data type known as **DeptNum**. Variables of this type can only have the six indicated values represented by **Invalid**, **Appliances** and so on.

Actually, an **enum** is implemented as an **int**, so you can look upon an **enum** as a "disguised int." By default, the first value the **enum** can hold is given the value 0. Thus, in the above definition, **Invalid** represents a 0; **Appliances**, a 1; **Automotive**, a 2; and so on. That is, the compiler from the point of definition of this **enum** now knows to replace all occurrences of **Appliances** with its value 1.

Where are most all **enum** definitions placed within a program? They, like **#define**s and **const int**s, must be defined before their first use. They are usually placed after the **#include**s and before the prototypes of functions.

How do we create an instance of a **DeptNum**? One is created precisely the same way we create an instance of a **double** or a **long**. The following creates several instances of the **enum DeptNum**.

```
DeptNum deptnum;
DeptNum previousDeptNum;
DeptNum x;
```

Given these new variables, then the following are valid.

```
if (deptnum == Appliances)
if (x == Automotive)
case Toys:
```

But these are invalid because specific integer values are being used.

```
if (deptnum == 1)
if (x == 2)
case 3:
```

An **enum** can be passed to a function and one can be returned by a function. The prototypes require a data type and that is simple to code.

```
DeptNum someFunction (DeptNum z);
```

In other words, we use our new **enum** just as if it were any other intrinsic or built-in data type.

Here is the total view of how the **enum** fits into the program. The function **GetAlternativeDept()** returns an alternative department number; perhaps the item desired is located in that department, and so on.

```
#include <iostream>
using namespace std;
enum DeptNum {Invalid, Appliances, Automotive,
              Housewares, Toys, Accounting};
```

```
DeptNum GetAlternativeDept (DeptNum thisDept);

int main () {
 DeptNum thisDept;
 ...
 switch (thisDept) {
  case Appliances:
    ...
    break;
  case Automotive:
    ...
    break;
 }
 DeptNum altDept = GetAlternativeDept (thisDept);
 ...
}

DeptNum GetAlternativeDept (DeptNum thisDept) {
 switch (thisDept) {
  case Appliances:
    return Housewares;
  case Automotive:
    return Appliances;
  ...
 }
 ...
}
```

As you look this rather contrived example over, notice one major feature. No where in it are the actual numerical values that would have had to be there if **enum**s were not used! Also note that since the first **enum** symbol has the value 0 by default and since no department number can have the value 0, I chose to place another identifier to represent the value 0, **Invalid**. Thus, **Appliances** has the value 1 as required.

Here is another example of an **enum**. This time, I use convenient names for the month.
```
enum Month {Invalid, Jan, Feb, Mar, Apl, May, Jun,
            Jul, Aug, Sep, Oct, Nov, Dec};
```
Then within **main()** an instance can be created and used.
```
Month month;
...
if (month == Jun || month == Jul || month == Aug)
  cout << "Vacation Time!\n";
```
An **enum** can be very useful in the right circumstance. A store might use an **enum** to represent its products:
```
enum ProductId {Coffee, Tea, Milk, Soda};
```
Or a pet shop program could define an **enum** to help identify all the animals it has for sale:
```
enum Pets {Cat, Dog, Hamster, Snake, Goldfish, Bird};
```

The bottom line is simple: an English identifier that is easily read replaces abstract numerical values. The result is far fewer errors in such programs! Enumerated data types greatly ease the communication between programmers working on the same project.

There must be a catch you say. Well, yes, there is a catch. **enum**s are implemented as an integer data type internally. No I/O operations use **enum**s directly; instead, all I/O operations read and write the integer value. Using the **Pet enum** above, if one coded

```
Pets myNewPet;
cin >> myNewPet; // error
```

The compiler issues the error message "no operator defined which takes a right-hand operand of type 'enum Pets'." Likewise, if you tried to output

```
cout << myNewPet; // error
```

a similar compile error results. (Note that the Old Style **iostream**s do not give the compiler error message on the above lines. They actually expect the user to enter or display a numerical value)

For clear output, there is an easy way around the **enum** problem. Use a Do Case statement and display the appropriate string. This is really what is desired in most cases anyway. Think about it. You want to display the pet type. What good would it do for the user of the report to see columns of numbers? They would not easily know that a 1 meant a dog.

```
switch (myNewPet) {
  case Cat:
    cout << "Cat"; break;
  case Dog:
    cout << "Dog"; break;
  ...
}
```

This is very commonly done for output. It makes the output very readable.

How can the input operation be accomplished and still be readable? The worst approach is to input the data as an integer and then, using a typecast, make the assignment to the **enum** instance.

```
int   num;
Pets myNewPet;
cin >> num;
myNewPet = (Pets) num;
```

Why is this disasterous? There is nothing to prevent the user from inputting 42 when asked to enter the new pet number!

Instead of inputting the enumerated value directly, input something more meaningful and use a Do Case to assign the correct **enum** value. One way would be to use a single letter for the pet type, 'D' for Dog, 'C' for Cat and so on. Here is a way it can be written. Note the different header files for the character C built-in functions. The header file for character functions is **<cctype>**; math functions are in file **<cmath>**; string functions are in **<cstring>**.

```
#include <iostream>
#include <cctype>
using namespace std;
```

```
enum Pets {Cat, Dog, Hamster, Snake, Goldfish, Bird};

istream& GetPet (istream& is, Pets& newPet);

int main () {
 Pets thePet;
 while (GetPet (cin, thePet)) {
  ... here we have a valid thePet
 }
 ...
 return 0;
}

istream& GetPet (istream& is, Pets& newPet) {
 char c;
 bool validEntry = false;
 while (is && !validEntry) {
  cout << "Enter Pet type - C (for cat), D (for dog),\n"
      << "H (for hamster), S (for snake), G (for goldfish)\n"
      << "B (for bird)\n";
  is >> c;
  if (!is)
   return is;
  c = toupper (c);
  switch (c) {
    case 'C':
      newPet = Cat;
      validEntry = true;
      break;
    case 'D':
      newPet = Dog;
      validEntry = true;
      break;
    case 'H':
      newPet = Hamster;
      validEntry = true;
      break;
    case 'S':
      newPet = Snake;
      validEntry = true;
      break;
    case 'G':
      newPet = Goldfish;
      validEntry = true;
      break;
    case 'B':
      newPet = Bird;
      validEntry = true;
      break;
```

```
    default:
       cout << "Invalid entry - try again\n";
   }
 }
 return is;
}
```

In the **GetPet()** function, the boolean variable **validEntry** is initialized to **false**. If the user ever enters a valid pet character, then the **validEntry** is set to **true**. The **while** loop repeats the sequence as long as **infile** is still in the good state and a valid entry has not yet been made. After prompting the user and getting their input, if the end of file has been reached, the function returns at once. Otherwise, the character is converted to uppercase and a Do Case sorts out the possibilities. If the user entry matches one of the valid characters, the reference parameter **enum newPet** is assigned the corresponding value and **validEntry** is set to **true**. If no match occurs, then after an error message is displayed, the loop repeats until the user enters a proper pet code.

If the pet store also had horses, then the single character scheme tends to lose its effectiveness. One could use 'O' for horse, of course. Another alternative is to input descriptive strings and sort them out using **_stricmp()** comparisons. However, forcing the user to enter strings is a lot of extra input typing and should be avoided if possible.

Thus we have ways of inputting and outputting these enumerated values in a much more readable, user-friendly manner than just a set of abstract numbers.

Suppose that a program must deal with coins at a financial institution. Here is another way the **enum** can be setup in which each identifier is given its value instead of taking the default.
```
enum CoinAmt {Penny = 1, Nickel = 5, Dime = 10,
              Quarter = 25, HalfDollar = 50,
              Dollar = 100};
```
Given these values, one can now use them anywhere an integer data type could be used. For example
```
long totalAmount = 124; // total pennies

// the number of quarters in the change
int numQuarters = totalAmount / Quarter;

// remaining change
totalAmount %= Quarter;
```

Once one stops providing unique values, the next enumerator's values go up by one from the previous ones. With the department number **enum**, if one did not wish to have **Invalid** be a part of the enumerated values, then it could have been coded this way.
```
enum DeptNum {Appliances = 1, Automotive, Housewares, Toys,
              Accounting};
```
Likewise, the month **enum** could have been done this way.
```
enum Month {Jan = 1, Feb, Mar, Apl, May, Jun,
            Jul, Aug, Sep, Oct, Nov, Dec};
```

In these two cases, **Automotive** and **Feb** are given the value of 2; **Housewares** and **Mar**, 3; and so on.

Finally, if no instances of the enumerated data type are ever going to be created, the name can be omitted. This is called an **anonymous enum**. Of course, the enumerated values can be used wherever an integer type can be used. In the coin amount example above, I did not create any instances of **CoinAmt**. I did, however, make use of the enumerated values. It could have been defined this way.

```
enum {Penny = 1, Nickel = 5, Dime = 10, Quarter = 25,
      HalfDollar = 50, Dollar = 100};
```

Anonymous enums are often used to create good symbolic names for numerical values.

When an application has need of a series of numerical values that are used for some form of identification purposes, consider making those values as part of an enumerated data type to increase readability of the program and lessen the chance for errors.

The Use of Default Arguments

Another new feature of C++ that can help ease the task of programming is the use of default arguments to a function. Suppose that our program made extensive use of rectangles and had a RECTANGLE structure defined as follows.

```
struct RECTANGLE {
  int top;
  int left;
  int bottom;
  int right;
};
```

Obviously one ever-present need within the program is the ability to initialize an instance. Thus, the **InitializeRect()** function is written this way.

```
void InitializeRect (RECTANGLE& r, int top, int left,
                     int bottom, int right);
void InitializeRect (RECTANGLE& r, int top, int left,
                     int bottom, int right) {
  r.top = top;
  r.left = left;
  r.bottom = bottom;
  r.right = right;
}
```

The calling functions then invoke it as follows.

```
RECTANGLE r;
RECTANGLE s;
InitializeRect (r, 0, 0, 0, 0);
InitializeRect (s, 1, 10, 42, 55);
```

In the first call to **InitializeRect()**, the rectangle r is being initialized to 0. If one thinks about the situation of initializing many rectangles in a program, initializing to 0 is likely to be the single most common function call. In such a case, the use of default arguments greatly eases coding.

When coding the prototype (never in the actual function header), one can provide a default value for the compiler to pass should that parameter not be coded in the function call. Here is what the **InitializeRect()** prototype would look like if we chose to use default values of zero.

```
void InitializeRect (RECTANGLE& r, int top = 0, int left = 0,
                     int bottom = 0, int right = 0);
```

Now when the function is called and some of the parameters are omitted, the compiler supplies the missing ones using the indicated values in the prototype.

```
InitializeRect (r);
InitializeRect (s, 1, 1);
InitializeRect (t, 0, 1);
InitializeRect (u, 1, 10, 42);
```

All of the above are valid. Rectangle **r** uses zeros for all four integers. Rectangles **s** and **t** use zeros for their bottom and right integers. Rectangle **u** uses a zero for its right integer.

Rule: in a prototype, when a specific argument is given a default value, all remaining arguments must also be given a default value.

Rule: when invoking a function which has default arguments and you let a specific parameter use its default value, all remaining parameters must use their defaults as well.

The following prototype violates the first rule.

```
void InitializeRect (int top = 0, int left = 0, int bottom = 0,
                     int right = 0, RECTANGLE& r); // error
```

This is why I chose to pass the rectangle reference as the first parameter. The rectangle structure to initialize really cannot be defaulted—what would it default to? Thus, when using default arguments, make sure you place the arguments that cannot have any default values first in the parameter list.

The second rule impacted the coding of the initialization of rectangle **t** in the above coding. While it might be "nice" to be able to code the following, the rule invalidates this coding.

```
InitializeRect (t, , 1); // error - cannot omit and resume
```

Function Overloading and the istrstream and ostrstream Classes

Another new feature of C++ is the ability to have several different versions of the same function. This is known as polymorphism. Polymorphism allows one name to be used to handle a set of similar actions. Polymorphism permits us to create one function name, say **Convert()**, and then based on the actual arguments passed, determine which conversion process is needed:

```
bool Convert (const char* string, int&    ansr);
```

```
bool Convert (const char* string, long&   ansr);
bool Convert (const char* string, double& ansr);
```

This is also called **function overloading**. We use one function name but have several versions of that function to carry out the similar actions.

The istrstream Class

These functions could be implemented using the standard C functions that convert an ASCII string into an integer, long or double. However, C++ provides a much easier method. We now know just how easy it is to input data using an input stream instance such as **cin**. C++ provides two additional **iostream** derived classes, **istrstream** and **ostrstream**. The needed header files are **<strstream>**.

The **istrstream** inputs data from a character string. Thus, everything we know about inputting data from say **cin** applies totally to **istrstream**. We have nothing new to learn, except how to create the stream. To create the stream, pass it the character string from which the data is to be extracted.

```
istrstream is (string);
```

Then one can use the stream **is** in any way that you can use the **cin** stream. Here is how one of the **Convert()** functions could be implemented. Note that the string passed to the **istrstream** constructor cannot be constant, hence the typecast.

```
bool Convert (const char* string, int& ansr) {
  istrstream is ((char*) string);
  is >> ansr;
  return is ? true : false;
}
```

However, the return statement could be shortened to just

```
return is;
```

When we get to the chapter on inheritance, we will see just how this magic can come about. How would you implement the other two overloaded functions? With exactly the same coding!

Now we have a consistent set of string to number conversion functions for use throughout the larger application. Instead of trying to remember several different functions for conversion, we only need to remember the single name **Convert()**. Even though there are three different versions and different prototypes, they all take the same number of parameters and in the same order: the string and the receiving number field.

Rule: two or more functions can have the same name as long as their prototypes differ in the number of parameters, the data types of the parameters, and order.

Rule: the return data type is never sufficient to distinguish between overloaded functions.

The following are all valid overloaded functions.
```
bool Convert (const char* string, int&    ansr);
bool Convert (const char* string, long&   ansr);
bool Convert (const char* string, double& ansr);
bool Convert (int& ansr, const char* string);
```

```
bool Convert (char* string, long* ptransr);
int  Convert (double& ansr, const char* string);
int  Convert (const char* string);
```
In the above, they all differ in the types and order of the parameters or in the number of parameters.

The following create compile time errors because they violate the above rules.
```
int    Convert (const char* string);
long   Convert (const char* string);
double Convert (const char* string);
```
Why? Remember that the compiler sees these prototypes. Suppose that we wrote in the calling function the following.
```
double x = Convert (string);
```
Which version would the compiler call? It could call any one of the three safely, since an **int** or a **long** can be converted safely to a **double**. Since the compiler is responsible for data conversions anyway, it cannot use that as a deciding factor. It must use the parameters instead.

The **istrstream** also has terrific use when writing data editing type programs in which the program must check upon the validity of each data item as it is being input. We know that an invalid character input into a numeric type causes the **istream** to go into the fail state and lock up at that point. This makes it a bit difficult to process the entire file pointing out all of the data entering errors. While there are some ways of resetting the stream flags to resume, an **istrstream** provides an easy way around that complexity. For example, the **main()** function inputs entire lines of data from the file.
```
char string [1000];
while (infile.getline (string, sizeof (string))) {
  CheckData (string);
}
```

Now the **CheckData()** function can wrap an **istrstream** instance around the passed string and see if the correct data can be extracted. If not, it can display appropriate error messages. In this way, the entire file can be edited in a single run of the program. Indeed, we will make good use of this class when writing OOP programs; in the right circumstances it is very handy indeed.

The ostrstream Class

There is a corresponding output string stream class, **ostrstream** which outputs data into a string. In Windows programming, there is only one text output function available to display data in a window. And that function can only display a character string. Thus, all numeric values to be displayed in a Windows application must be converted into strings. One easy way is to use an **ostrstream**. However, we are not writing Windows programs, only DOS console applications.

Still there are times that this class is very useful for us. Suppose that we needed to provide the calling function with a string version of a date that we are storing for the user. The date consists of three integers for the month, day, and year. An instance of the **ostrstream** class can be created by providing it with the string to fill up and the maximum length of that string. The **ostrstream** instance will never overlay core. Any attempt to output more characters than there are characters in the string causes the stream to go into the fail state. Here is how this can be done.

```
char string[11];
ostrstream os (string, sizeof (string));
os << setfill('0') << setw(2) << month << '/'
    << setw(2) << day << '/' << setw (4) << year << ends;
```

If the date was January 12, 2001, then the string contains "01/12/2001". There is also one small detail. The string we create must be null terminated. The **ends** manipulator function appends that null terminator for us but only if there is room in the string for the null terminator.

We must make sure the string is sufficiently large enough to hold the results. If **string** in the above example was defined to be only 6 bytes long, then it would hold "01/12/" and there would be no null terminator!

Function Ambiguity and Default Arguments

Be careful in your use of default values. When you have overloaded functions that have default values, you can introduce "function ambiguity." Consider the following two versions of function **Fun()**.

```
long Fun (long I) {
 return I/42;
}

int  Fun (int I) {
 return I/10;
}
```

If the caller codes the following, what occurs?

```
long  a = 50;
int   b = 22;
short c = 55.;
cout << Fun (a); // calls the long version of Fun
cout << Fun (b); // calls the int version of Fun
cout << Fun (c); // ambiguous function call error
```

On the last one, the compiler cannot determine how to convert the **short**. It can safely convert it to an **int** or a **long**. Thus, both versions are valid. Whenever the compiler has a choice to make between equally possible versions of a function, it refuses to choose and issues the ambiguous function call error message.

When one or more variables are passed by reference, function ambiguity can be introduced. Consider these two functions.

```
// these two are inherently ambiguous
int MoreFun (int a, int b) {
 return a*b;
```

```
}

int MoreFun (int a, int&b) {
 return a/b;
}
```

Why? Consider these two lines:

```
int a = 5, b = 10;
int c = MoreFun (a, b);
```

Which version of **MoreFun()** is called? Since both **a** and **b** are of type **int**, it could call the first version. However, since the compiler is responsible for handling references, it could equally call the second version. Hence, the compiler generates the function ambiguity error message.

Also, using default arguments can accidentally cause ambiguity as well. Consider these two versions.

```
int MoreFun (int a);
int MoreFun (int a, int b = 1);
```

The caller does the following.

```
int a = 5, b = 10;
int c = MoreFun (a, b); // is ok - calls second version
int d = MoreFun (a);    // error which morefun??
```

In the first call to **MoreFun()** there is only one possible choice, since two parameters are being passed. However, when an attempt is made to call **MoreFun()** with only one parameter, both versions are equally valid for the compiler to use, thus the error message. When using default arguments with overloaded functions, be alert for inadvertent function ambiguity.

Multiple Cpp Files Project

Larger programs make use of the ability of a project to handle multiple cpp files. Microsoft's Visual C++ compiler requires a project file in order to build a program. The project file contains the compiler options required to make the program. It contains also what files make up the program. We know that to make a new project, we select File—New and then Project and select the Win32 Console Application type. We also know that once the empty project has been built, we do another File—New and choose cpp file. The compiler adds this file to the project. But what about multiple cpp files?

To add additional cpp files to the project, just continue to choose File—New cpp file and each of these are added to the project. Similarly with user header files, choose File—New and choose C++ header file. If you have the various files on a floppy disk and wish to build the program, as usual, copy the files to a program folder on the hard disk and make a new project. Then right click on the Program Files label in the File View tab window and choose Add Files to Project as you normally would do. However, when the File Open dialog appears, multi-select all the cpp and header files desired. Click Okay. You should then see all of the cpp and header files listed in the tree view.

The first time you choose Build the program, all of the individual cpp files must be compiled into their corresponding obj files. Then, the Linker joins all the pieces, the obj files, into the single program exe file.

There are many benefits to having many cpp files making up the whole project. Indeed, it is hard to envision how code can be reused in other applications if that code is buried in a huge single cpp file. When splitting a large program into smaller cpp files, several key benefits occur at once. After the initial build of the project in which the compiler creates an obj file (object file of machine instructions) for each of the cpp files, subsequent Builds only recompile those cpp files that have changed or are dependent upon other files, such as headers, that have changed. In this way, compilation times for larger programs are speeded up.

With multiple cpp files, it is much easier for a team of programmers to work on the same project. The aggravation and hassle of working with a huge single file is gone.

Additionally, with multiple files, you can have several editor windows open at the same time. This allows you to look at the place in one file where a function that is contained in another file is actually called, while viewing that called function in another source window. This allows you to see how you are calling the function as you examine the function coding itself. And finally, the tendency for errors to creep in is reduced. I've observed over my many years of programming that the number of errors in coding goes up exponentially as the number of lines in the cpp file goes up. Or programmers make fewer errors when they can see the entirety of the coding of a function on the screen without any scrolling.

Beginning with this chapter, all programs will consist of multiple cpp files. Indeed, when we begin to write our classes in chapter 4, a program will always have at least three files making it up, the class definition, the class implementation, and the client or user program.

User Written Header Files

You have been using system header files since you coded your first C++ "Hello World" program. We code

```
#include <iostream>
```

The # sign indicates a command to the preprocessor. The **include** means to copy the contents of the following file and place them at this location in the source file. The <> signifies that this is a system header file and to look for this file in the **\include** folders located in the folder in which the compiler has been installed. The actual filename is coded between the angle brackets. Typically a header file has no extension or an extension of .h. If you look in the **\include** folder under the folder in which you installed the compiler, you will see files **iostream.h** (older style headers) and **iostream** (current style headers).

A header file is a definition type of file. That is, it contains definitions of things such as constant integers, #defines, structure templates, function prototypes, includes for other header files and so on. A header file ideally should contain **no** actual coding—coding is implementation and should be in the cpp files.

To illustrate header files, let's examine the situation at Acme Hardware Stores, Inc. Acme owns a chain of stores. Each store has the potential to stock any number of company sanctioned items. The definition of one of these items is shown using the following structure template.

```
const int DESCRLEN = 21;
struct INVREC {
    long    itemNum;
    char    description[DESCRLEN];
    int     qtyOnHand;
    double  unitCost;
};
```

The **main()** function could create an instance of this structure by coding

```
INVREC invRec;
```

If a program for a single store wished to input all of the stock records that that store had, the program would define an array of **INVREC**s, where **MAXITEMS** contains the maximum number of possible items.

```
INVREC stock[MAXITEMS];
```

A subscript is then used to access the specific item in the array, such as

```
stock[i].itemNum, stock[i].description, stock[i].qtyOnHand.
```

However, if Acme Corporate Headquarters wished to have a program that inputted the stock contained in all four stores, a two-dimensional array would be defined.

```
INVREC stock[NUMSTORES][MAXITEMS];
```

Now two subscripts are needed to access a specific store's specific item data

```
stock[store][i].itemNum, stock[store][i].description,
stock[store][i].qtyOnHand.
```

With these basics in mind, here is the problem facing the Acme company. Obviously, many of their programs are going to use the inventory data. So many programs are going to have to define this **INVREC** structure. For example, Acme may find that a total of twenty programs are going to need this structure. Certainly, it could be defined within each of the programs. However, if that were done, consider what would happen if management decided tomorrow to add a new field to the record, such as **retailCost**? What would happen if the length of the item description was increased to 31 characters? The programming staff would have a miniature nightmare on their hands. They would have to find all the various definitions of the structure among all of the hundreds of programs in production and make the same change to every one of them. This is a tedious and very error prone task indeed. Think what would result if they forgot to change it in one or more programs? A disaster at production run time occurs.

Instead, suppose that Acme created a single header file that defined this **INVREC** structure and had all twenty programs simply include this single header file. If changes occur, one programmer can change the single header file and simply recompile the programs to implement the changes in all programs. What a difference in quality control! No more nightmares. Placing the definitions of items in header files and then including them in one or more programs goes a long way toward the "reuse of coding" that is so important in today's programming environment.

Mechanics of Header File Construction

The contents of the header file for the inventory records would be as shown.
file: InvRec.h

```
const int DESCRLEN = 21; // length of the description

/*************************************************/
/*                                               */
/* Acme Stock Inventory Record                   */
/*                                               */
/*************************************************/

struct INVREC {
  long    itemNum;                  // Acme stock number
  char    description[DESCRLEN];    // product description
  int     qtyOnHand;               // store's qty on hand
  double  unitCost;                // Acme's cost of the item
};
```

The next question is how would other cpp files include this new header file? The answer depends upon where the **InvRec.h** file is actually stored on disk. One will certainly **not** code the following.

```
#include <InvRec.h>
```
This is saying to look for **InvRec.h** in the **\include** folders where the compiler is installed!

Never place user header files into the **include** folders of the compiler. Compilers get updated, replaced and moved. User-written header files are never ever placed into the compiler include folders. Thus, we cannot use the < > notation. Instead we surround the filename with double quote marks.

```
#include "InvRec.h"
```
The " " tells the compiler that this is a user header file located in the user's folders.

Specifically, if no path information is included, the compiler looks for **InvRec.h** in the current project folder where the project cpp files are located. For most student programs this is precisely where the header files belong.

The compiler allows for an absolute or relative path as well. In the case of the Acme structure, since each of the twenty programs that need to use this header file would be located in its own separate project folders, the above technique needs to be refined. Otherwise, we would have to make twenty copies of that header file and put on into each of the twenty project folders, thereby losing most of the benefits of coding it once and reusing it twenty times! Instead, there should be one single company production header file folder, say **D:\AcmeProduction\Includes**. Now the **#include**

49

would be coded in this manner.
```
#include "d:\\AcmeProduction\\Includes\\InvRec.h"
```
Don't forget the double \\; a single \ starts an escape sequence in C++.

Relative paths could also be used. Suppose that Pgm1 needs to use this header file and it is located in the **D:\AcmeProduction\Pgm1** folder. One could code a relative path as follows.
```
#include "..\\Includes\\InvRec.h"
```

All of the remaining examples in this text assume that user header files are located in the project folder with the cpp files that make up the program.

Placement of Header File Includes in a Cpp File

With the header file created and located in the project's folder. Let's see how to include it in the **main()** function's cpp file. Normally, any given cpp file begins with one or more **#include** statements that bring in the definitions and prototypes of the language elements and functions, such as **iostream.h**.

Rule: One should always include one's own personal header files after including the any needed system headers.

Thus, the coding for the **main()** function's cpp file begins
```
#include <iostream>
#include <iomanip>
#include <cmath>
using namespace std;

#include "InvRec.h"

int main () {
```

One should not include one's own header files before including those for the system definitions. Why? Namespace collisions can occur. To illustrate this, let us suppose that Acme began an **I**nternet **O**nline **S**ervice and our program decided to store the data in a structure. We store that structure definition in a personal header file called **ios.h** in our project's folder. The file looks like this.
File: ios.h
```
struct ios {
  ... // various member fields are defined here
};
```
Now we code the **main()** function's cpp file as follows, placing our header file first.
```
#include "ios.h"
#include <iostream>
using namespace std;
```

```
int main () {
```

What results? A huge number of compiler errors result, complaining about the **ios iostream** class. All the errors are on lines contained in the various system header files, like **iostream**. These are occurring because of a misfortunate choice of a structure name. There is an object-oriented **iostream** class called **ios** that is included and it is a part of all the **iostream** classes. Since we included our definition first, it overrides the C++ system header definitions and thus all of the subsequent **iostream** uses of **ios** end up referring to our new **ios** structure. Piles of errors result, giving the appearance that something is horribly wrong with our system header files! I have had students decide that their compiler must have some how gotten corrupted and totally reinstalled the compiler. Of course, it did not fix anything.

If you include your personal headers before the system header files, then any conflicts are reported as error messages within the system header files, not your header file. This makes tracking down the real cause very difficult indeed.

If we include our headers after the system headers, then the errors are reported within our coding. The real source of the error is then more readily found. Here is the proper way to handle the above example.

```
#include <iostream>
using namespace std;
#include "ios.h"
int main () {
```

All the errors point to our structure redefinition of the **ios** symbol.

#ifndef/#define or #pragma once Logic

So far, making our own header files to contain definitions of things looks straight forward. However, there is another vital detail that must be understood and circumvented. To see this problem in action, consider this situation of multiple structure definitions.

Acme uses dates frequently throughout their collections of programs. To standardize the way that dates are stored, the following header file has been created and used by all programs.
File: date.h

```
struct Date {
  int month;
  int day;
  int year;
};
```

Next, a customer record structure is defined, but it needs to use an instance of the **Date** structure as one of its members. Oops. Thus, the **customer.h** file must include the **date.h** file. Also, since there can be some function prototypes in the customer header file, any needed system headers must be included. Here, the input and output functions are using references to the iostreams; thus

<iostream> must be included. We have then the following for **customer.h**.

File: customer.h

```
#include <iostream>
using namespace std;
#include "date.h"

struct Customer {
  Date serviceLaunchDate;
  Date warrantyExpirationDate;
  ... // many other field definitions
};

// needed function prototypes
istream& InputCustomer (istream& in, Customer& customer);
ostream& OutputCustomer (ostream& out, const Customer& cus);
```

Notice that the **iostream** header must be included because the function prototypes are using references to the streams. If you do not include the system **iostream** header, the compiler does not know what **istream** and **ostream** are and generates error messages. Likewise, without the inclusion of **date.h**, the compiler does not know what a **Date** object is that is. Finally, notice that the **OutputCustomer()** defines the customer as a constant reference to a **Customer** structure instance. Remember, an "output" function should not under any circumstances alter the contents of the data that it is to output.

Next, the company defines a service call structure which is generated in response to a technician visiting the customer and performing the needed repairs. The definition is stored in the **service.h** header file.

File: service.h

```
#include <iostream>
using namespace std;
#include "date.h"

struct ServiceCall {
  Date servicedDate;
  ... // many other field definitions
};

// needed function prototypes
istream& InputServiceCallData (istream& in,
                               ServiceCall& sc);
ostream& OutputServiceCallData (ostream& in,
                               const ServiceCall& sc);
```

Again, notice that the **date.h** header file must be included here because of the use of a **Date** instance in the **ServiceCall** structure.

Now let's look at the **main()** function of the Process Service Call Program. The coding begins as follows.

```
#include <iostream>
using namespace std;
#include "customer.h"
#include "service.h"

int main () {
  Customer    customer;
  ServiceCall serviceCall;

  InputCustomer (cin, customer);
  InputServiceCallData (cin, serviceCall);
  ...
```

As it stands, it looks well designed. However, it will not compile. Follow what the compiler does as it attempts to build the program. First, it is instructed to include the **customer.h** file. It does so, but that file instructs it to subsequently bring in the **date.h** file. It does so and now the compiler sees a **Date** structure definition and then a **Customer** structure definition. All is well. Next, the compiler is instructed to include the **service.h** file. It does so, but that file also instructs it to bring in the **date.h** file and it does that action. Now the compiler has the following structure definitions:

```
struct Date
struct Customer
struct Date
struct ServiceCall
```

And the compiler generates the error message that **Date** already exists: "error C2011: 'Date' : 'struct' type redefinition."

This situation occurs quite frequently in larger programs. So we must know how to deal with it. The solution is to instruct the compiler to only bring in one copy of the actual definition of the **Date** structure per cpp file. This is accomplished by using some additional preprocessor directives.

The directive **#ifndef** is a conditional if-then-else type logic command. It works with both versions of the compiler. It is saying if the following symbol is not yet defined and known to you, compiler, please include all of the following lines until you reach the **#endif** statement, and in any case, include all lines coded after the **#endif**. Thus, the **#ifndef** and **#endif** occur in pairs. If you forget your ending **#endif**, the compiler eats lines until it finds one. The symbol to be found is coded after the **#ifndef**. That symbol must be a unique one—one which would never conflict with any other name in the entire file. By convention, most programmers use a name that is some variation of the header file name using all uppercase letters. Thus, the **date.h** file must be rewritten as follows.
File: date.h

```
#ifndef DATE_H
#define DATE_H
struct Date {
  int month;
  int day;
  int year;
```

```
};
#endif
```

Notice the vitally important second line, **#define DATE_H**. This is the first line that is actually included if the compiler has not yet seen the symbol **DATE_H**. This **#define** line then actually defines the symbol we are checking. Normally, we provide some value after the name such as **#define MAX 100**. Here, we give the symbol no value; however, the compiler provides a simple "true," the symbol is defined.

To understand better how this works, let's examine how compilers operate. When a compiler begins the compilation of a file, it creates a "**symbol dictionary**" whose entries contain the name of the symbol and other pertinent details. Initially, as it starts to compile **main.cpp** in this example, it is empty. The second line includes **customer.h**. The compiler copies that file into the program, but then discovers the include for **date.h**. It then copies in the **date.h** file contents. Now it sees, the **#ifndef** logic. It looks at its symbol table, which thus far has only the **iostream** definitions in it from the first line that included **iostream.h**. The symbol **DATE_H** is not there, so it places all of the contents of **date.h** down through the **#endif** statement along with any lines that come after the **#endif** into the main program for compilation. However, the second line in **date.h** tells the compiler to now define that symbol, **DATE_H**. So it makes an entry in its symbol dictionary for **DATE_H**. Next, it sees the include for **service.h** and copies that file into the program. Finally, it copies in the **date.h** file as instructed within **service.h**. However, the **#ifndef** logic is then processed. The **#ifndef** causes the compiler again to look to see if the symbol **DATE_H** is in its symbol dictionary. It is there this time. Thus, the compiler only includes all coding found in **date.h** after the **#endif**. Of course, there is no coding after that point. The result: only one copy of the structure definition for **Date** is included in the compilation.

With header files, you often do not know all of the uses that a specific header file may have when you first write it. Thus, the following rule applies always.

Rule: The contents of every header file should be wrapped with #ifndef/#define logic.

Why? Imagine a large program with many header files and source cpp files. If the header files are not protected against multiple inclusions, then it is highly likely that multiple inclusions will occur. The resultant bombardment of compiler error messages can be terrific. It is no fun at all to try to guess long after writing the header files which ones absolutely must have the **#ifndef/#define** logic in them and then go back and put it in.

Thus, from this point forward in this text, all header files will be wrapped with **#ifndef/#define** logic. Then, there cannot be any surprises waiting at compile-time, no matter how the header files are included. Yes, in the above example, the customer and service header files should also be wrapped. Here is what they should be.

File: customer.h

```
#ifndef CUSTOMER_H
```

```
#define CUSTOMER_H
#include <iostream>
using namespace std;
#include "date.h"
struct Customer {
  Date serviceLaunchDate;
  Date warrantyExpirationDate;
 ... // many other field definitions
};
// needed function prototypes
istream& InputCustomer (istream& in, Customer& customer);
ostream& OutputCustomer (ostream& out, const Customer& cus);
#endif
```

File: service.h

```
#ifndef SERVICE_H
#define SERVICE_H
#include <iostream>
using namespace std;
#include "date.h"
struct ServiceCall {
  Date servicedDate;
 ... // many other field definitions
};
// needed function prototypes
istream& InputServiceCallData (istream& in,
                               ServiceCall& sc);
ostream& OutputServiceCallData (ostream& in,
                                const ServiceCall& sc);

#endif
```

With Version 7.0, a new Microsoft-only compiler directive can be used to accomplish all this in an even simpler manner, the **#pragma once**, which replaces this older scheme. Here is how it looks this way.

File: customer.h

```
#pragma once
#include <iostream>
using namespace std;
#include "date.h"
struct Customer {
  Date serviceLaunchDate;
  Date warrantyExpirationDate;
 ... // many other field definitions
};
// needed function prototypes
istream& InputCustomer (istream& in, Customer& customer);
ostream& OutputCustomer (ostream& out, const Customer& cus);
```

File: service.h

```
#pragma once
#include <iostream>
using namespace std;
#include "date.h"
struct ServiceCall {
  Date servicedDate;
  ... // many other field definitions
};
// needed function prototypes
istream& InputServiceCallData (istream& in,
                                  ServiceCall& sc);
ostream& OutputServiceCallData (ostream& in,
                                  const ServiceCall& sc);
```

Now let's examine how a larger program implements most all of the features discussed in both chapter 1 and 2.

Application Section

Pgm02a—Acme Pets 'R Us Inquiry/Update Program

Acme Pets company has a master file of the pets that they have in stock. They need a program that can display the pets that they have in stock, add new pets to the inventory as new ones are purchased and remove a pet from stock when it is sold. Thus, it is basically doing inquiry and update actions.

First, let's examine the initial master file and see what kinds of data are being stored for a pet. Here is the inventory.txt file.

```
inventory.txt input file for Pgm02a

 1 123456 C F 6 "Pussy Cat" 12.50 20.00 01/12/2001
 2 234567 c m 7 "Sylvester" 11.75 20.00 02/08/2001
 3 001245 D m 3 "Fido" 100 200 02/09/2001
 4 456800 d f 4 "Lady Hawk" 75.50 150.00 02/07/2001
 5 234344 h m 2 "" 5.99 19.99 02/02/2001
 6 344223 s f 6 "" 2.50 5.00 01/01/2001
 7 485833 g m 1 "" 1.00 2.00 02/02/2001
 8 238848 g f 1 "" 1.00 2.00 02/02/2001
 9 485834 g m 1 "" 1.00 2.00 02/02/2001
10 238849 g f 1 "" 1.00 2.00 02/02/2001
11 010203 B f 2 "Polly" 50.00 100.00 01/15/2001
12
```

The data consists of a unique stock number that has leading zeroes to pad to a length of six digits. Next comes a character pet type code: c for cat, d for dog, h for hamster, s for snake, g for gerbil, and b for bird. The pet's sex comes next followed by the pet's age in months. The name of the pet, where known, is enclosed in double quote marks. This is followed by the wholesale and retail costs and the date that the pet was acquired.

Here is a sample execution of the program. Note that I had to manually squeeze some blank spaces out of the longer report lines in order to make the line width fit within the box below.

```
Output from a Test Run of Pgm02a

 1
 2
 3
 4      Acme Pets 'R Us - Main Menu
 5
 6      1. List All Pets of a Specific Type
 7      2. Make a Report of All Pets in Stock
 8      3. Add a New Pet to Inventory
 9      4. Remove a Pet from Inventory
10      5. Save New Inventory File
11      6. Exit Program
12
13 Enter the number of your choice: 2
14
15  Stock    Pet       Sex Age Pet's      Wholesale    Retail     Acquired
16 Number    Type              Name         Cost        Cost         Date
17
18 123456   Cat        F    6  Pussy Cat  $ 12.50    $ 20.00    01/12/2001
19 234567   Cat        M    7  Sylvester  $ 11.75    $ 20.00    02/08/2001
20 001245   Dog        M    3  Fido       $100.00    $200.00    02/09/2001
21 456800   Dog        F    4  Lady Hawk  $ 75.50    $150.00    02/07/2001
22 234344   Hamster    M    2             $  5.99    $ 19.99    02/02/2001
23 344223   Snake      F    6             $  2.50    $  5.00    01/01/2001
24 485833   Goldfish   M    1             $  1.00    $  2.00    02/02/2001
25 238848   Goldfish   F    1             $  1.00    $  2.00    02/02/2001
26 485834   Goldfish   M    1             $  1.00    $  2.00    02/02/2001
27 238849   Goldfish   F    1             $  1.00    $  2.00    02/02/2001
28 010203   Bird       F    2  Polly      $ 50.00    $100.00    01/15/2001
29
30
31 Enter C to continue c
32
33
34
35      Acme Pets 'R Us - Main Menu
36
37      1. List All Pets of a Specific Type
38      2. Make a Report of All Pets in Stock
39      3. Add a New Pet to Inventory
40      4. Remove a Pet from Inventory
41      5. Save New Inventory File
42      6. Exit Program
```

```
43
44 Enter the number of your choice: 1
45
46 The Types of Pets We Have in Stock
47
48    C    Cat
49    D    Dog
50    H    Hamster
51    S    Snake
52    G    Goldfish
53    B    Bird
54 Enter the letter of your choice: d
55
56
57
58  Stock   Pet        Sex Age Pet's    Wholesale    Retail      Acquired
59  Number  Type               Name       Cost        Cost          Date
60
61 001245  Dog        M   3   Fido      $100.00    $200.00   02/09/2001
62 456800  Dog        F   4   Lady Hawk $ 75.50    $150.00   02/07/2001
63
64
65 Enter C to continue c
66
67
68
69      Acme Pets 'R Us - Main Menu
70
71      1. List All Pets of a Specific Type
72      2. Make a Report of All Pets in Stock
73      3. Add a New Pet to Inventory
74      4. Remove a Pet from Inventory
75      5. Save New Inventory File
76      6. Exit Program
77
78 Enter the number of your choice: 1
79
80 The Types of Pets We Have in Stock
81
82    C    Cat
83    D    Dog
84    H    Hamster
85    S    Snake
86    G    Goldfish
87    B    Bird
88 Enter the letter of your choice: r
89
90 Please enter a single letter choice - try again
91    C    Cat
92    D    Dog
93    H    Hamster
94    S    Snake
95    G    Goldfish
```

```
 96   B    Bird
 97 Enter the letter of your choice: b
 98
 99
100
101  Stock    Pet      Sex Age Pet's     Wholesale   Retail    Acquired
102  Number   Type             Name          Cost     Cost        Date
103
104 010203   Bird      F   2   Polly     $ 50.00   $100.00   01/15/2001
105
106
107 Enter C to continue c
108
109
110
111     Acme Pets 'R Us - Main Menu
112
113     1. List All Pets of a Specific Type
114     2. Make a Report of All Pets in Stock
115     3. Add a New Pet to Inventory
116     4. Remove a Pet from Inventory
117     5. Save New Inventory File
118     6. Exit Program
119
120 Enter the number of your choice: 3
121
122 Add Another Pet to Stock List
123 Enter Stock Number (6 digits): 444444
124
125 Enter the Type of Pet
126
127    C    Cat
128    D    Dog
129    H    Hamster
130    S    Snake
131    G    Goldfish
132    B    Bird
133 Enter the letter of your choice: d
134
135 Enter Pet Sex - M or F: f
136 Enter the Pet's Age in Months: 3
137 Enter the name of the pet (16 characters) surrounded by
138  double quote marks.
139 For example, "Rover"
140 "Fifi Bleu"
141 Enter the Wholesale Cost: 100.00
142 Enter the Retail Cost: 200.00
143 Enter the Acquired Date (mm/dd/yyyy): 04/01/2001
144
145 Added:
146 444444   Dog       F   3   Fifi Bleu $100.00   $200.00   04/01/2001
147
148
```

```
149 Enter C to continue c
150
151
152
153     Acme Pets 'R Us - Main Menu
154
155     1. List All Pets of a Specific Type
156     2. Make a Report of All Pets in Stock
157     3. Add a New Pet to Inventory
158     4. Remove a Pet from Inventory
159     5. Save New Inventory File
160     6. Exit Program
161
162 Enter the number of your choice: 4
163 Enter the stock number to remove: 123456
164 Pet with stock number 123456 removed
165
166
167 Enter C to continue c
168
169
170
171     Acme Pets 'R Us - Main Menu
172
173     1. List All Pets of a Specific Type
174     2. Make a Report of All Pets in Stock
175     3. Add a New Pet to Inventory
176     4. Remove a Pet from Inventory
177     5. Save New Inventory File
178     6. Exit Program
179
180 Enter the number of your choice: 2
181
182  Stock    Pet        Sex Age Pet's    Wholesale    Retail    Acquired
183 Number    Type              Name        Cost       Cost       Date
184
185 234567   Cat        M   7   Sylvester $ 11.75   $ 20.00   02/08/2001
186 001245   Dog        M   3   Fido      $100.00   $200.00   02/09/2001
187 456800   Dog        F   4   Lady Hawk $ 75.50   $150.00   02/07/2001
188 234344   Hamster    M   2             $  5.99   $ 19.99   02/02/2001
189 344223   Snake      F   6             $  2.50   $  5.00   01/01/2001
190 485833   Goldfish   M   1             $  1.00   $  2.00   02/02/2001
191 238848   Goldfish   F   1             $  1.00   $  2.00   02/02/2001
192 485834   Goldfish   M   1             $  1.00   $  2.00   02/02/2001
193 238849   Goldfish   F   1             $  1.00   $  2.00   02/02/2001
194 010203   Bird       F   2   Polly     $ 50.00   $100.00   01/15/2001
195 444444   Dog        F   3   Fifi Bleu $100.00   $200.00   04/01/2001
196
197
198 Enter C to continue c
199
200
201
```

```
202        Acme Pets 'R Us - Main Menu
203
204        1. List All Pets of a Specific Type
205        2. Make a Report of All Pets in Stock
206        3. Add a New Pet to Inventory
207        4. Remove a Pet from Inventory
208        5. Save New Inventory File
209        6. Exit Program
210
211 Enter the number of your choice: 4
212 Enter the stock number to remove: 444444
213 Pet with stock number 444444 removed
214
215
216 Enter C to continue c
217
218
219
220        Acme Pets 'R Us - Main Menu
221
222        1. List All Pets of a Specific Type
223        2. Make a Report of All Pets in Stock
224        3. Add a New Pet to Inventory
225        4. Remove a Pet from Inventory
226        5. Save New Inventory File
227        6. Exit Program
228
229 Enter the number of your choice: 4
230 Enter the stock number to remove: 456800
231 Pet with stock number 456800 removed
232
233
234 Enter C to continue c
235
236
237
238        Acme Pets 'R Us - Main Menu
239
240        1. List All Pets of a Specific Type
241        2. Make a Report of All Pets in Stock
242        3. Add a New Pet to Inventory
243        4. Remove a Pet from Inventory
244        5. Save New Inventory File
245        6. Exit Program
246
247 Enter the number of your choice: 4
248 Enter the stock number to remove: 666666
249 Error: stock number 666666 is not in the inventory - please retry
250
251
252 Enter C to continue c
253
254
```

```
255
256       Acme Pets 'R Us - Main Menu
257
258       1. List All Pets of a Specific Type
259       2. Make a Report of All Pets in Stock
260       3. Add a New Pet to Inventory
261       4. Remove a Pet from Inventory
262       5. Save New Inventory File
263       6. Exit Program
264
265 Enter the number of your choice: 6
266 Caution: The Inventory File has been altered and not saved.
267 Do you wish to exit without saving the changes?
268 Enter Y or N: n
269
270
271 Enter C to continue c
272
273
274
275       Acme Pets 'R Us - Main Menu
276
277       1. List All Pets of a Specific Type
278       2. Make a Report of All Pets in Stock
279       3. Add a New Pet to Inventory
280       4. Remove a Pet from Inventory
281       5. Save New Inventory File
282       6. Exit Program
283
284 Enter the number of your choice: 5
285 File has been saved in inventorynew.txt
286
287 Enter C to continue c
288
289
290
291       Acme Pets 'R Us - Main Menu
292
293       1. List All Pets of a Specific Type
294       2. Make a Report of All Pets in Stock
295       3. Add a New Pet to Inventory
296       4. Remove a Pet from Inventory
297       5. Save New Inventory File
298       6. Exit Program
299
300 Enter the number of your choice: y
301
302
303
304       Acme Pets 'R Us - Main Menu
305
306       1. List All Pets of a Specific Type
307       2. Make a Report of All Pets in Stock
```

62

```
308      3. Add a New Pet to Inventory
309      4. Remove a Pet from Inventory
310      5. Save New Inventory File
311      6. Exit Program
312
313 Enter the number of your choice: 6
```

Here we have pet types in use throughout the program. So an **enum** is a good choice for pet type. It is also a good choice for the sex field. I also used an **enum** to represent the valid menu choices. I used six header files in my solution. First, is the header file that defines a **DATE** structure.

Date.h

```
1 #pragma once
2
3 struct DATE {
4   short month;
5   short day;
6   short year;
7 };
```

I defined the pet type enumerated values in **PetEnum.h**.

PetEnum.h

```
1 #pragma once
2
3 enum Pets {Cat, Dog, Hamster, Snake, Goldfish, Bird};
4
5 const int MAXPETTYPES = 6;  // the number of Pets in the enum
```

As you look over the output, at some locations, the program needs the corresponding letter either for proper input operations or for picking a pet type to list. On the listings, the string name of the pet type is used, such as "Dog." Thus, an array of **PETTYPE** structures whose members contain the **enum** value, its corresponding letter code, and its corresponding string name will make the process much more convenient and less error prone.

PetType.h

```
1 #pragma once
2 #include "PetEnum.h"
3
4 const int PETSTRINGLEN = 9;
5
6 struct PETTYPE {
7   Pets petEnumValue;         // the enum value
8   char petLetter;            // the input letter
9   char petString[PETSTRINGLEN]; // the output display string
10 };
```

63

```
11
12 const PETTYPE petConversion[MAXPETTYPES] = {
13 {Cat, 'C', "Cat"}, {Dog, 'D', "Dog"}, {Hamster, 'H', "Hamster"},
14 {Snake, 'S', "Snake"}, {Goldfish, 'G', "Goldfish"},
15 {Bird, 'B', "Bird"}
16 };
```

Now the actual **Pet** structure can be defined. Here is the **Pet.h** file. Notice the **Gender enum** definition. This header must include the **PetEnum.h** and **Date.h** header files since the structure contains an instance of a date and the pet type **enum**.

```
Pet.h

 1 #pragma once
 2 #include "PetEnum.h"
 3 #include "Date.h"
 4
 5 enum Gender {Female, Male};
 6
 7 const int NAMELEN = 16;
 8
 9 struct Pet {
10   long    stockNum;       // id number - 6 digits
11   Pets    type;           // enum pet type
12   Gender  sex;            // m or f
13   short   age;            // age in months
14   char    name[NAMELEN];  // pet's name, if any
15   double  wholesaleCost;  // our cost
16   double  retailCost;     // customer's cost
17   DATE    purchasedDate;  // purchased date
18 };
```

The menu choice **enum** is defined in the file **MenuChoices.h**.

```
MenuChoices.h

 1 #pragma once
 3
 4 enum Choices {Invalid, ListSpecific, ListAll, Add, Remove,
 5               Save, Exit};
```

The final header file is used for convenience. It is called an **application header file** to distinguish it from header files that are shared between many applications. It gets its name from the idea that its usefulness is only for this program or application. We often make use of an application-specific header file for our convenience. Since there are quite a few cpp files in the program, rather than try to figure out which specific headers must be included and which prototypes need to be defined for each cpp file, I created one master program header that includes everything that the entire program needs. This is commonly done. Here is the **Pgm02a.h** header file that all of the various cpp files include.

```
Pgm02a.h

 1 #pragma once
 2 #include <iostream>
 3 #include <iomanip>
 4 #include <strstream>
 5 #include <cctype>
 6 #include <fstream>
 7 using namespace std;
 8
 9 #include "Pet.h"
10 #include "PetType.h"
11 #include "MenuChoices.h"
12
13 // load file prototypes
14 int       LoadPetsArray (const char * filename, Pet pets[],
15                              int limit);
16 istream& InputPet (istream& is, Pet& pet);
17
18 // menu prototypes
19 Choices GetValidMenuChoice ();
20 void     ShowMenu ();
21
22 //process menu choices prototypes
23 void    ProcessChoice (Choices& c, Pet pets[], int& numPets,
24                          bool& modifiedData);
25 void    ListSpecificPetType (const Pet pets[], int numPets);
26 void    ListAllPets (const Pet pets[], int numPets);
27 void    DisplayListHeader ();
28 void    DisplayAPet (const Pet& pet);
29 void    AddAPet (Pet pets[], int& numPets, bool& modifiedData);
30 Pets    GetPetType (const char* msg);
31 void    RemovePet (Pet pets[], int& numPets, bool& modifiedData);
32 void    SaveFile (const Pet pets[], int numPets,
33                     bool& modifiedData);
34 void    SaveCheck (Choices& c, bool& modifiedData);
```

With larger programs, the Top-Down Design that is used greatly aids understanding of the overall processing. The design I use is shown in Figure 2.1. The **main()** function is very streamlined. It loads the pets array and then loops through successive calls to Get a Valid Menu Choice and Process the Menu Choice until the user chooses to quit. Many of the detailed menu processing steps call the same lowest level functions, such as Display a List Heading and Display a Pet. I tried to reuse as much coding as possible.

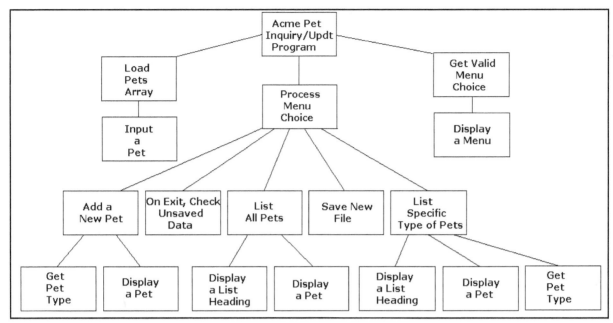

Figure 2.1 Top-Down Design Pet Inquiry/Update Program

Next, examine the streamlined coding for **main()**. It holds the array of pets, the number of pets currently in the array, and the modified flag. It then enters the main processing loop which consists of getting a valid menu choice and then carrying out that action. Notice the menu choice is an **enum** value for program clarity in these functions.

```
Pgm02a - Acme Pet Inquiry/Update Processing Program

 1 #include "Pgm02a.h"
 2
 3 const int MAXPETS = 100;
 4
 5 /****************************************************************/
 6 /*                                                            */
 7 /* Acme Pet Store Processing Program - Inquiry and Update     */
 8 /*                                                            */
 9 /****************************************************************/
10
11 int main () {
12   cout << fixed << setprecision (2);
15   Pet pets[MAXPETS];
16   int numPets = LoadPetsArray ("inventory.txt", pets, MAXPETS);
17   bool modifiedData = false;
18   Choices choice = Invalid;
19   while (choice != Exit) {
20     choice = GetValidMenuChoice ();
21     ProcessChoice (choice, pets, numPets, modifiedData);
22   }
23   return 0;
```

```
24 }
```

LoadPetsArray() is typical array loading code. It handles the higher level operations, delegating the actual input actions to the **InputPet()** function. However, **InputPet()** does have some interesting coding to input the pet type. After a simple input of the basic data, the pet type is a letter. By having the **petConversion** array of **PETTYPE** structures that contain the **enum** value, the corresponding letter and the string description, the validation becomes simple. Loop through all possible letters. If a match is found, set the **bool matched** to **true** and break. If the loop ends with no match, display the error message. If it was found, then store in the pet instance the corresponding **enum** value.

LoadPetsArray.cpp

```
 1 #include "Pgm02a.h"
 2
 3 /*****************************************************************/
 4 /*                                                             */
 5 /* LoadPetsArray: load the pets from the input data base       */
 6 /*               returns number of pets in the array           */
 7 /*                                                             */
 8 /* aborts if there is bad data or array size exceeded          */
 9 /*                                                             */
10 /*****************************************************************/
11
12 int LoadPetsArray (const char * filename, Pet pets[], int limit){
13  // attempt to open the master file of pets
14  ifstream infile (filename);
15  if (!infile) {
16   cerr << "Error: cannot open pets input file: " << filename
17        << endl;
18   exit (1);
19  }
20  infile >> dec; // set for leading 0's in dates and stock numbers
21
22  // main input loop - try to input all pets in the file
23  int i = 0;
24  while (i<limit && InputPet (infile, pets[i])) {
25   i++;
26  }
27
28  // now check to array size exceeded
29  char c;
30  if (!infile.eof () && infile && infile >> c) {
31   cerr << "Error: pet array size of " << limit
32        << " has been exceeded\n";
32.5 infile.close ();
33   exit (4);
34  }
35
36  // now check for bad data in the input file
```

67

```
37  else if (!infile.eof() && infile.fail ()) {
38    cerr << "Error: bad data encountered on input on line "
39          << i + 1 << endl;
39.5 infile.close ();
40    exit (5);
41  }
42
43  infile.close ();
44  return i; // the number of pets in the array
45 }
46
47 /**************************************************************/
48 /*                                                          */
49 /* InputPet: inputs a set of Pet data from a stream         */
50 /*                                                          */
51 /**************************************************************/
52
53 istream& InputPet (istream& is, Pet& pet) {
54  char petchar;
55  char sex;
56  char c;
57  // attempt to input the basic data
58  is >> pet.stockNum >> petchar >> sex >> pet.age >> c;
59  if (!is) return is;
60  is.getline (pet.name, sizeof (pet.name), '\"');
61  if (!is) return is;
62  is >> pet.wholesaleCost >> pet.retailCost
63     >> pet.purchasedDate.month >> c
64     >> pet.purchasedDate.day >> c
65     >> pet.purchasedDate.year;
66  if (!is) return is;
68  // convert the two letters to upper case for convenience
69  petchar = toupper (petchar);
70  sex = toupper (sex);
72  // convert the pet letter code into the proper Pets enum
73  int i = 0;
74  bool matched = false;
75  while (i < MAXPETTYPES) {
76   if (petchar == petConversion[i].petLetter) {
77    matched = true;
78    break;
79   }
80   i++;
81  }
82  // check for no match = invalid pet letter code
83  if (!matched) {
84   cerr << "Error: invalid pet letter code in the input file\n"
85        << "Letter was: " << petchar << " on pet number: "
86        << pet.stockNum << endl;
87   exit (2);
88  }
89  pet.type = petConversion[i].petEnumValue;
91  // verify sex field is correct
```

```
 92  if (sex == 'M')
 93   pet.sex = Male;
 94  else if (sex == 'F')
 95   pet.sex = Female;
 96  else {
 97   cerr << "Error: invalid pet sex code in the input file\n"
 98        << "Letter was: " << sex << " on pet number: "
 99        << pet.stockNum << endl;
100   exit (3);
101  }
102  return is;
103 }
```

The **ShowMenu()** function displays a simple menu. In this sample, I needed to capture all of the screen output for display purposes. However, in an actual menu processing program, another function greatly improves the DOS window. That function call is

```
system ("cls");
```

This system call clears the DOS window. The string parameter is a DOS command CLS which in a DOS window clears the screen. The **system()** function allows a program to issue DOS commands. Ideally the **ShowMenu()** function could have been coded this way.

```
system ("cls");
cout << "\n\n\n";
cout << "       Acme Pets 'R Us - Main Menu\n\n"
     << "       1. List All Pets of a Specific Type\n"
     << "       2. Make a Report of All Pets in Stock\n"
     << "       3. Add a New Pet to Inventory\n"
     << "       4. Remove a Pet from Inventory\n"
     << "       5. Save New Inventory File\n"
     << "       6. Exit Program\n\n"
     << "Enter the number of your choice: ";
```

Make this single line change, rebuild the program and run it to see the effect. In fact, one could insert this call into many of the other lower level functions that also prompt and input user data. It makes a cleaner interface for the user.

If a stream goes into the fail state because of inputting a letter for a number, one can reset the state to good and then input the offending letter. The **clear()** function resets a stream back to the good state.

```
cin.clear ();
infile.clear ();
```

One can input the single character using a **get()** function call or one can choose to ignore all the remaining characters on a line using the **ignore()** function.

```
infile.ignore (100, "\n");
```

This skips all characters until it finds the newline code or 100 chars, whichever occurs first.

In **GetValidMenuChoice()** the user enters an integer for the menu choice. Notice how I typecast that integer into the **Choices enum** and check to see that it is within range. This trick can be used to convert an integer into an **enum** value. However, always use error checking to ensure the resulting **enum** is within range. Finally, notice how readable the Do-Case statement is in the **ProcessChoice()** function. That is why I used it, readability of the coding.

```cpp
GetAndProcessMenu.cpp

 1 #include "Pgm02a.h"
 2
 3 /*****************************************************************/
 4 /*                                                             */
 5 /* ShowMenu: Display a menu on screen                          */
 6 /*                                                             */
 7 /*****************************************************************/
 8
 9 void ShowMenu () {
10  cout << "\n\n\n";
11  cout << "     Acme Pets 'R Us - Main Menu\n\n"
12       << "       1. List All Pets of a Specific Type\n"
13       << "       2. Make a Report of All Pets in Stock\n"
14       << "       3. Add a New Pet to Inventory\n"
15       << "       4. Remove a Pet from Inventory\n"
16       << "       5. Save New Inventory File\n"
17       << "       6. Exit Program\n\n"
18       << "Enter the number of your choice: ";
19 }
20
21 /*****************************************************************/
22 /*                                                             */
23 /* GetValidMenuChoice: get and return a valid menu choice      */
24 /*                                                             */
25 /*****************************************************************/
26
27 Choices GetValidMenuChoice () {
28  Choices choice = Invalid;
29  while (choice <= Invalid || choice > Exit) {
30   ShowMenu ();
31   int num;
32   cin >> num;
33   // guard against invalid number entered
36   if (cin.fail()) { // non-numeric data, locked up stream
37    cin.clear ();     // clear the flags back to good state
38    char c;           // and input the offending character
39    cin >> c;
40   }
41   choice = (Choices) num;
42  }
43  // return only a valid menu choice here
44  return choice;
45 }
46
47 /*****************************************************************/
48 /*                                                             */
49 /* ProcessChoice: Process the different menu choices,          */
```

70

```
50 /*                  displaying a pause message                */
51 /*                                                            */
52 /**************************************************************/
53
54 void ProcessChoice (Choices& choice, Pet pets[], int& numPets,
55                     bool& modifiedData) {
56  switch (choice) {
57   case ListSpecific:
58     ListSpecificPetType (pets, numPets);
59     break;
60   case ListAll:
61     ListAllPets (pets, numPets);
62     break;
63   case Add:
64     AddAPet (pets, numPets, modifiedData);
65     break;
66   case Remove:
67     RemovePet (pets, numPets, modifiedData);
68     break;
69   case Save:
70     SaveFile (pets, numPets, modifiedData);
71     break;
72   case Exit:
73     SaveCheck (choice, modifiedData);
74     break;
75  };
76
77  // display a pause message unless it is Exit time
78  if (choice != Exit) {
79   cout << "\n\nEnter C to continue ";
80   char c;
81   cin >> c;
82  }
83 }
```

The **GetPetType()** function is called from both **AddPet()** and **ListSpecificPetType()** functions. Here I used a Do Until loop to input a valid pet type. A little menu of all possible letters and the string pet descriptions is shown and the user must enter the corresponding letter. Once the letter is input and converted to uppercase, I then try to match the entered letter with the valid choices. Although there is some duplicate coding with the matching, it is not much. However, one could create a **MatchType()** function to common this duplicate coding out as well. If no match is found, an error message is shown so that the menu is redisplayed until the user enters a proper letter. The function returns only the corresponding pet type **enum** value.

```
GetPetType.cpp

 1 #include "Pgm02a.h"
 2
 3 /**************************************************************/
 4 /*                                                          */
```

```
 5 /* GetPetType: Prompt and get the pet letter to choose which   */
 6 /*             type of pet is desired                          */
 7 /*             Returns only a valid Pets enum value            */
 8 /*                                                             */
 9 /*************************************************************/
10
11 Pets GetPetType (const char* msg) {
12  char c;
13  int i;
14  bool matched = false;
15  cout << endl << msg << endl << endl;
16
17  do {
18   // show the possible choices
19   for (i=0; i<MAXPETTYPES; i++) {
20    cout << setw (3) << petConversion[i].petLetter << "    "
21         << petConversion[i].petString << endl;
22   }
23   // get user's letter choice and upper case it
24   cout << "Enter the letter of your choice: ";
25   cin >> c;
26   cout << endl;
27   c = toupper (c);
28
29   // verify it is one of the valid pet letter choices
30   matched = false;
31   i=0;
32   while (!matched && i<MAXPETTYPES) {
33    if (c == petConversion[i].petLetter)
34     matched = true;
35    else i++;
36   }
37   // if not matched, show a reprompt message and try again
38   if (!matched)
39    cout << "Please enter a single letter choice - try again\n";
40  } while (!matched);
41
42  // return only a valid Pets type enum value
43  return petConversion[i].petEnumValue;
44 }
```

The **AddPet()** function is very straightforward at this point. Notice how it uses **GetPetType()**. Also, once the data for a pet has been entered and stored in the array, I also call **DisplayAPet()** to display what has been entered; make your users happy.

```
AddPet.cpp

 1 #include "Pgm02a.h"
 2
 3 /*************************************************************/
 4 /*                                                             */
```

```
 5 /* AddAPet: add a new pet into the inventory                    */
 6 /*                                                               */
 7 /****************************************************************/
 8
 9 void AddAPet (Pet pets[], int& numPets, bool& modifiedData) {
10  Pet p;
11  char c;
12  cout << "\nAdd Another Pet to Stock List\n"
13      << "Enter Stock Number (6 digits): ";
14  cin >> p.stockNum;
15  p.type = GetPetType ("Enter the Type of Pet");
16  cout << "Enter Pet Sex - M or F: ";
17  cin >> c;
18  c = toupper (c);
19  p.sex = (c == 'M') ? Male : Female;
20  cout << "Enter the Pet's Age in Months: ";
21  cin >> p.age;
22  cout << "Enter the name of the pet (" << NAMELEN
23      << " characters) surrounded by double quote marks.\n"
24      << "For example, \"Rover\"\n";
25  cin >> c;
26  cin.getline (p.name, NAMELEN, '\"');
27  cout << "Enter the Wholesale Cost: ";
28  cin >> p.wholesaleCost;
29  cout << "Enter the Retail Cost: ";
30  cin >> p.retailCost;
31  cout << "Enter the Acquired Date (mm/dd/yyyy): ";
32  cin >> p.purchasedDate.month >> c >> p.purchasedDate.day
33      >> c >> p.purchasedDate.year;
34
35  // display here's what was added message
36  if (cin) {
37   pets[numPets] = p;
38   numPets++;
39   modifiedData = true;
40   cout << endl << "Added:\n";
41   DisplayAPet (pets[numPets-1]);
42  }
43 }
44
```

The two list functions that are to display either all pets or only all pets of a specific type share similar coding. Namely, a set of column headings is needed in each case as well as coding to display a single pet. Thus, a pair of helper functions reduces the duplicate coding. If you are shaky on your use of the formatting of output lines, look over this coding carefully.

```
ListingFunctions.cpp

 1 #include "Pgm02a.h"
 2
 3 /****************************************************************/
```

```
 4 /*                                                             */
 5 /* ListAllPets: display a report of all pets in the array     */
 6 /*                                                             */
 7 /****************************************************************/
 8
 9 void ListAllPets (const Pet pets[], int numPets) {
10   DisplayListHeader ();
11   for (int i=0; i<numPets; i++) {
12     DisplayAPet (pets[i]);
13   }
14 }
15
16 /****************************************************************/
17 /*                                                             */
18 /* ListSpecificPetType: Make a report of all pets in stock of  */
19 /*                      one specific type                      */
20 /*                                                             */
21 /****************************************************************/
22
23 void ListSpecificPetType (const Pet pets[], int numPets) {
24   // get the type of pet on which to report
25   Pets type = GetPetType ("The Types of Pets We Have in Stock");
26   cout << endl;
27
28   // display a report of all those pets in stock
29   DisplayListHeader ();
30   for (int i=0; i<numPets; i++) {
31     if (type == pets[i].type)
32       DisplayAPet (pets[i]);
33   }
34 }
35
36 /****************************************************************/
37 /*                                                             */
38 /* DisplayListHeader: display column headings for report       */
39 /*                                                             */
40 /****************************************************************/
41
42 void DisplayListHeader () {
43   cout << "\n Stock  Pet       Sex Age Pet's          Wholesale"
44        << "    Retail     Acquired\n"
45        <<" Number  Type               Name            Cost"
46        << "      Cost        Date\n\n";
47 }
48
49 /****************************************************************/
50 /*                                                             */
51 /* DisplayAPet: display one pet nicely formatted on the report */
52 /*                                                             */
53 /****************************************************************/
54
55 void DisplayAPet (const Pet& pet) {
56   const char sex[2] = {'F', 'M'};
```

74

```
57  cout << ' ' << setfill('0') << setw(6) << pet.stockNum
58        << setfill (' ') << "  " << left << setw (9)
59        << petConversion[pet.type].petString << right << setw (2)
60        << sex[pet.sex] << setw (4) << pet.age << "  " << left
61        << setw (NAMELEN) << pet.name << right << '$' << setw (6)
62        << pet.wholesaleCost << "   $" << setw(6) << pet.retailCost
63        << "  " << setfill ('0') << setw (2)
64        << pet.purchasedDate.month << '/' << setw(2)
65        << pet.purchasedDate.day << '/'
66        << setw (4) << pet.purchasedDate.year
67        << setfill (' ') << endl;
68  }
```

When a pet is sold, it must be removed from the inventory. **RemovePet()** accomplishes this. In this case, I have the user enter the pet's stock number. A simple search for that number results in the subscript of the matching pet in the array. If it is not found, I display an error message and abort the deletion. Alternatively, one could make a loop and re prompt for a valid stock number. However, if you choose that route, then also allow a means for the user to abort the addition process completely for they may need to go re-list the data to find the stock number to remove. The actual removal operation is simple. Copy all elements below the one to be deleted into the row above it.

```
RemovePet.cpp

 1  #include "Pgm02a.h"
 2
 3  /**************************************************************/
 4  /*                                                            */
 5  /* RemovePet: delete a pet from inventory based on stock number*/
 6  /*                                                            */
 7  /**************************************************************/
 8
 9  void RemovePet (Pet pets[], int& numPets, bool& modifiedData) {
10   // get the stock number of the desired pet
11   long stockNum;
12   cout << "Enter the stock number to remove: ";
13   cin >> stockNum;
14
15   // now find this specific pet in the array
16   int i = 0;
17   bool found = false;
18   while (!found && i < numPets) {
19    if (pets[i].stockNum == stockNum) {
20     found = true;
21     break;
22    }
23    i++;
24   }
25
26   // abort the deletion if the stock number was not found
27   if (!found) {
```

```
28    cerr << "Error: stock number " << stockNum
29        << " is not in the inventory - please retry\n";
30    return;
31  }
32
33  // copy all pet elements below this point up one row
34  int j;
35  for (j=i+1; j<numPets; j++) {
36   pets[j-1] = pets[j];
37  }
38
39  // dec number of pets in the array and set the modified flag
40  numPets--;
41  modifiedData = true;
42  // display a short success message
43  cout << "Pet with stock number " << stockNum << " removed\n";
44 }
```

Finally come the save operations. Recall that **SaveCheck()** is called only when the user has chosen to exit the program and the data has been modified. If the user chooses not to exit the program, then the menu choice is reset back to Invalid to permit the main loop to continue. Notice that only a correct response to the Yes-No prompt is permitted. I dislike programs that check only for 'Y' and assume all other letters equal 'N'. The **SaveFile()** function is also very simple.

```
SaveFunctions.cpp

 1 #include "Pgm02a.h"
 2
 3 /***********************************************************/
 4 /*                                                         */
 5 /* SaveCheck: On Exit, if data has changed, prompt user    */
 6 /*                                                         */
 7 /***********************************************************/
 8
 9 void SaveCheck (Choices& c, bool& modifiedData) {
10  char yn;
11  if (modifiedData) {
12   cout << "Caution: The Inventory File has been altered and "
13        << "not saved.\n"
14        << "Do you wish to exit without saving the changes?\n"
15        << "Enter Y or N: ";
16   cin >> yn;
17   yn = toupper(yn);
18   while (yn != 'Y' && yn !='N') {
19    cout << "Enter Y or N: ";
20    cin >> yn;
21    yn = toupper (yn);
22   }
23
24   // if the user does not want to quit with the modified data
25   // not saved, replace the Exit menu choice with Invalid
```

```
26    if (yn == 'N')
27      c = Invalid;
28   }
29 }
30
31 /****************************************************************/
32 /*                                                            */
33 /* SaveFile: saves the pets array to a new disk file          */
34 /*                                                            */
35 /****************************************************************/
36
37 void SaveFile (const Pet pets[], int numPets,
38                 bool& modifiedData) {
39  // attempt to open the new output file
40  ofstream os ("inventorynew.txt");
41  if (!os) {
42   cerr << "Error: cannot open pets output file: "
43        << "inventorynew.txt\n";
44   // instead of aborting and risk loosing the changes,
45   // just return and let the user fix the disk
46   return;
47  }
48
49  // setup floating point output for dollars and cents
50  os.setf (ios::fixed, ios::floatfield);
51  os.setf (ios::showpoint);
52  os << setprecision (2);
53
54  const char sex[2] = {'F', 'M'};
55
56  // output all pets in the array to the new file
57  for (int i=0; i<numPets; i++) {
58   os << setfill ('0') << setw (6) << pets[i].stockNum
59      << setfill (' ') << setw (2)
60      << petConversion[pets[i].type].petLetter
61      << setw (2) << sex[pets[i].sex] << setw (3) << pets[i].age
62      << " \"" << pets[i].name << "\" "
63      << pets[i].wholesaleCost << " " << pets[i].retailCost
64      << " " << setfill ('0') << setw (2)
65      << pets[i].purchasedDate.month << '/' << setw(2)
66      << pets[i].purchasedDate.day << '/'
67      << setw (4) << pets[i].purchasedDate.year
68      << setfill (' ') << endl;
69  }
70  os.close();
71  // reset the modified flag now that the save is successful
72  modifiedData = false;
73  cout << "File has been saved in inventorynew.txt\n";
74 }
```

The last thing to observe about this larger program is how I chose to break the actual functions into separate cpp files. Notice that I did not place every function into its own separate cpp file. Rather, I placed similar or related functions into the same cpp file. Figure 2.2 shows what the Project View window looks like using Microsoft's Visual Studio 2005. If you have uncertainties about how to create such a project as this one, please consult the appendices on how to use the Microsoft compiler.

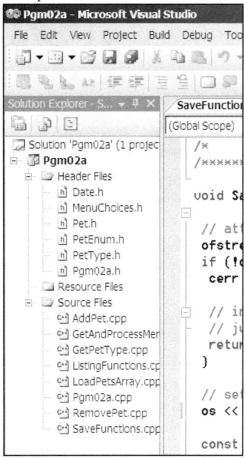

Figure 2.2 The Pgm02a Project

Review Questions

1. What are the benefits of using a **bool** for a data type instead of the traditional **int**?

2. What is the purpose of an enumerated data type? Give an example not in this chapter in which an enumerated data type aids program readability.

3. How can using an enumerated data type help reduce the possibilities of errors creeping into a program?

4. If a programmer wishes to define an enumerated data type for department numbers such that this new type is available anywhere within the entire program, where should the definition of the **enum** be located? Why?

5. When coding an **enum**, what is the default integer value that is assigned to the first enumerated value if one is not explicitly coded?

6. When coding an **enum**, the first value was assigned the value of 42. If the programmer then takes the defaults, what would the next value's numerical value be?

7. What is an anonymous **enum**? Could any instance of that anonymous **enum** ever be allocated? Why would a program ever use an anonymous **enum**? Give an example of such.

8. If an instance of an **enum** cannot be output to an **ostream**, how can such information be displayed? Give an example.

9. If an **enum** instance cannot be directly input from an **istream**, how can its value be inputted? Show three different methods of inputting the data. Which form is more optimum? Why?

10. Why are default arguments used? What benefit is their use to the client program?

11. Why are default argument values never coded in the actual function header?

12. A programmer has given the third argument to a function a default value of 1. What must be done to the remaining two arguments that follow the third argument? Why?

13. The function prototype for function **Fun()** is coded this way.
```
    double Fun (int a=42, int b=5, int c=84, int d=0);
```
Show all of the possible ways this function could be called from a client program.

14. What is meant by "function ambiguity?" Give an example of function ambiguity that was not shown in this chapter.

15. What is meant by function overloading? Give an example of function overloading that was not shown in this chapter.

16. Why does the use of default arguments on several overloaded functions sometimes lead to function ambiguity?

17. Why does the use of reference variables and default arguments on overloaded functions also sometimes lead to function ambiguity?

18. On a #include statement, how does the compiler distinguish between system header files and user written header files?

19. What kinds of things belong in a user header file? What kinds of things should never be coded in a user header file?

20. What is the purpose of using **#ifndef/#define** logic in a header file?

21. Why should every user written header file be wrapped with **#ifndef/#define** logic?

22. Why should larger programs be broken down into one or more user header files and multiple cpp files? What are the benefits of doing so?

23. What is the purpose of an **istrstream**? Of an **ostrstream**?

Stop! Do These Exercises Before Programming

1. Convert the following function coding to a proper utilization of **bool** variables.
```
int    Compare (double x, double y) {
  int yn = x == y ? 1 : 0;
  if (yn == 1)
    cout << "X and Y are equal\n";
  return yn;
}
```

2. Acme Department Store has new product information stored in a file whose lines consist of product id, product type and cost. The product id is a **long** integer while the cost is a **double**. The product type is a letter code indicating the category of merchandise, such as A (automotive), C (clothing), S (sports) and so on. A typical line looks like this with one blank on either side of the product type letter.
```
23455 A 4.99
```

However, since these are new items, sometimes the type of product has not yet been determined and that field is blank in that line. Code an enumerated data type to represent the product type.

3. Using your **enum** created in question 2 above, the programmer wrote the following input function to input a new product. It does not work. Why? What can be done to fix it up so that it properly inputs the data whether or not the product type is temporarily blank?
```
istream& getData (istream& infile, long& id, char& type,
                  double& cost) {
  infile >> id >> type >> cost;
  return infile;
}
```

4. Using your new **enum** created in question 2 above, change the coding of question 3. The parameter **type** should be a reference to your **enum** type. Correct the coding to properly fill **type** with the correct enumerated value.

5. The programmer wanted to setup an enumerated data type to handle the employee's shift. However, the following coding fails. Why? How can it be repaired?

```
Enum ShiftType = First, Second, and Third;
```

6. A programmer setup the following enumerated data type to handle the product types.

```
enum ProductTypes {Games, Auto, Clothing, Appliances};
```

In the input a set of data function, the user is instructed to enter a letter for the product type: G, A, C or A. What is the design flaw and why does not the following input coding work? How can it be repaired?

```
ProductTypes prodType;
infile >> prodType;
```

7. In question 6 above, the programmer got frustrated and then did the following which does not compile. Why? Can this coding be repaired?

```
ProductTypes prodType;
char c;
infile >> c;
if (c == 'A')
 prodType = 1;
if (c == 'G')
 prodType = 0;
```

8. Anonymous **enums** are often used to store numerical flag values that can be ORed together to form the final set of flags. For example, the binary values of the following decimal numbers work well: 1, 2, 4, and 8. Their respective binary bit values are 0001, 0010, 0100, and 1000. When these are ORed together, they produce the following in binary: 1111.

A company wishes to have an anonymous **enum** setup to provide well-documented flags for their update variable. The update can be done in any combination of the following ways: weekly, monthly, quarterly, semiannually and annually. Create the anonymous **enum** for these flags.

9. A **POINT** structure contains two double members, **x** and **y**. In a graphics program that uses many instances of this structure, initialization becomes messy. Create an **InitializePoint()** function that takes a reference to the point to be initialized and two additional parameters for the **x** and **y** values. Use default values of 0 for the two additional arguments. Show the function prototype and the

function header and function body. Then, show three different ways that a client program could invoke the **InitializePoint()** function.

10. In the graphics application that uses the **POINT** structures, the user wishes to be able to easily perform additions. They wish the following **Add()** functions to be written.

```
POINT p, q, r;
double x, y, number;
Add (p, x, y);   // adds x and y to p's x and y respectively
Add (p, q);      // adds q's x and y values to p's and stores
                 // the result in p's x and y values
Add (p, number);// adds the number to p's x and y values
```

Code the three **Add()** function prototypes and function headers and function bodies. Use default values of 1 for x and y and number. Then show all of the different ways that a client program can call these **Add()** functions.

11. A programmer decided to create the following overloaded **Add()** functions to partially solve question 10 above. The idea is to pass a reference to the second parameter thereby avoiding making duplicate copies of the point.

```
void Add (POINT& p, const POINT& q);
void Add (POINT& p, POINT q);
```

What is inherently wrong with this design? Show an example of client coding that would produce the troubles you suggest.

12. A programmer fell in love with the concept of default arguments. He coded the following prototypes and eventually the corresponding function bodies. When he created a tester client program, he got numerous error messages. What do you suppose most of those messages concerned? How could these prototypes be repaired so that they would work?

```
long Add (long num, long x=1);
long Add (long num, short x=1);
long Add (long num, char x=1);
long Add (long num, long& x);
long Add (long num, short& x);
long Add (long num, char& x);
```

13. A function **StoreDate()** is passed a date as a character string and a reference to a **DATE** structure with members: **month**, **day**, and **year**. It is to extract the three numerical values and store them in the structure. The date string has the form of mm/dd/yyyy. Write the coding for the **StoreDate()** function.

14. A function **FormatDate()** is passed a DATE structure instance that contains the members: **month**, **day**, and **year**. It is also passed a character string and that string's length in bytes. It is to store in the string the date as "mm/dd/yyyy" with leading 0's as needed. However, if the user's string is not long enough to store the entire date, store only those characters that will fit along with a null terminator. Always leave the passed string with a valid null terminator and do not wipe out memory beyond the length of the string. The prototype for the **FormatDate()** function is

```
void FormatDate (const DATE& d, char* string,
                      unsigned int maxlength);
```

15. The programmer created the following header file.
Rectangle.h

```
struct RECTANGLE {
  int top;
  int left;
  int bottom;
  int right;
};
```

This header file will be included in many other headers and cpp files in the large graphics application program. Code the required lines to guard against multiple structure definition inclusion in all of these other files.

16. The programmer coded the following for the **PetEnum.h** header file. What is wrong with it and how can it be fixed?

```
#ifndef PETENUM_H

    enum Pets {Cat, Dog, Hamster, Snake, Goldfish, Bird};

#endif
```

17. The programmer coded the following for the **PetType.h** header file. What is wrong with it and how can it be fixed?

```
#ifndef PETTYPE
#define PETTYPE
    enum PETTYPE {Cat, Dog, Hamster, Snake, Goldfish, Bird};
```

Programming Problems

Problem Pgm02-1—Cost Record Processing

Make a structure whose tag is **COSTREC**; it contains a pair of short integers for quantity and item number, a double cost member, an enumerated food type member, and a character string containing the item description. Use a **const int** to provide the maximum length of the description, 31 characters which includes the null terminator. The enumerated food type member can contain Food, NonFood, or Magazine. You may have the members in any order you choose.

Place the **COSTREC** structure definition in a header file, **costrec.h**. The enumerated data type and the **const int** string length should precede the structure definition in the header file. Wrap the entire contents of the header file with a #ifndef – #endif arrangement.

Write a function, **ReadRec()**, to input a **COSTREC**. It should be passed two parameters: a reference to an **istream** and a reference to a **COSTREC** structure. The function should return that same **istream** reference it was given. On input, the **enum** food type value should be inputted as a character, F, N, or M. This function should display appropriate error messages should the data on input not be correct. The description string should be enclosed within double quote marks and at least one blank separates the fields. The order of the input fields in the input file is: item number, quantity, description, food type, and cost. Place the **ReadRec()** function in its own cpp file.

Write a function, **CalcRec()**, that takes a constant **COSTREC** reference and returns the total cost (quantity times cost) as a **double** with the tax added into the total. Assume the tax to be added to the total cost is based on the food type: food 2%, non-food 7%, magazines 0%. Place the **CalcRec()** in its own cpp file.

Write a function, **PrintRec()**, to display in columnar form a cost record and its total cost. It should be passed a reference to an **ostream**, a reference to a constant **COSTREC** and the **double** total cost. It returns the **ostream** it was given. Display the fields in this order: item number, quantity, food-type, description, cost, and total cost. You may display the fields with any reasonable field width. Display the enumeration with the appropriate English: Food, Non-Food, Magazine. The output is displayed on the passed **ostream** reference. Place the **PrintRec()** function in its own cpp file.

Finally, write a main program in its own cpp file to input and calculate and print a series of user entered cost records. Include the needed function prototypes in this cpp file; the other cpp files do not need them. You will need to use an input file for the input data. The output can either go to the screen with output DOS redirection to obtain the printed report or the output can be written directly to an output file.

Make up some test data (at least 10 records) and THOROUGHLY test the program. Grading is also based upon how thoroughly you are actually testing the program. Display error messages for bad input data along with the line number on which the bad data was found. Also, document the program. You will lose some credit if the program has no internal documentation.

Problem Pgm02-2—The Acme News Feeds Accounts Processing

Acme Usenet News Feeds stores their online user information in an account file. Each line of the account file contains the user name (a string of up to 20 characters), their password (a string of up to 20 characters, the account activation date (stored as mm/dd/yyyy), the account duration in months, and a character that indicates what type of news group account they purchased.

Acme offers three types of news group accounts, Silver, Gold, and Platinum. Create an enumerated data type for the account type. The fixed annual cost of these accounts are: $75, $100, and $130 respectively.

Make a structure whose tag is **ACCOUNT**; it contains the user name and password, the account activation date, an instance of the account type **enum**, and a cost field. Note the cost field is not in the input file. Store the **const int** string lengths, the enum definition, and the structure definition in a header file called **Account.h**.

Write a **ReadAccount()** function that takes an **istream** reference and a reference to an **ACCOUNT** structure and returns the same **istream** reference it was given. It should set the cost member to 0 and input another account from the input stream. Specifically, the user name and password strings are surrounded by double quote marks. All fields are separated by a single blank in the input lines. The account type is a single character. Guard against bad data being input. Place the **ReadAccount()** function in a separate cpp file.

Write a **FindCost()** function which is passed a reference to an **ACCOUNT** structure. Based upon the account type **enum**, assign the correct cost value to the structure member. Place this function in its own separate cpp file.

Write a **PrintAccount()** function which is passed a reference to an **ostream** and a constant reference to an **ACCOUNT** structure; it returns the same **ostream** reference it was given. It outputs the account record to the passed stream nicely formatted. The fields to display are from left to right, the user name, the password, the activation date, the account type as a string such as "Gold", and the cost. Place the function in its own cpp file.

Write the **main()** function to input a file of account records, find the cost of each account and display the accounts to a report. Place the **main()** function and any other functions you choose to have **main()** call other than the ones above (such as a **PrintHeading()**) in its own cpp file. Use an input file stream for the input operations. However, the output may go either to the screen (use DOS redirection to make printed copies to hand in) or the output may be written directly to an output file.

Make up an input file of test data that thoroughly tests the program. Grading emphasis is in part upon how thoroughly you test the program. Also, be sure to include internal program documentation.

Chapter 3—Pointers and Dynamic Memory Allocation

Introduction

A **pointer** is nothing more than the memory address of something, where in memory the item or thing begins. Addresses are essentially unsigned long numbers. The first byte of memory is given the number 0. Each byte's address is sequentially one larger than the previous byte's. On a Win32 platform, the maximum address is 4G. An address cannot be negative.

In actual fact, we have been using pointers already when we pass references to variables and arrays. However, with these data types, the compiler is responsible for their operation. When you use a pointer directly, you, the programmer must manually do the actions that the compiler does for you when you use a reference variable. Pointers are a powerful feature of the C++ language.

Until this point, the exact amount of memory a program required at any point in its execution is known at compile time. The compiler knows exactly the total amount of memory it must create as it enters each block of coding. Array bounds are fixed at constant, unchangeable values. Automatic and parameter variables are created and stored on the stack by the compiler upon block entry. Local static variables go into the static portion of the data segment of the program along with global variables that go into the global portion. However, the C++ language is far more flexible than this. It supports a method by which we can allocate some additional memory while the program is executing.

This is called **dynamic memory allocation** which is the action of allocating some additional memory that was not specifically specified as needed at compile time. Dynamic memory allocation allows a program to have a variable array bounds! That is, the number of elements in an array is not known until the program actually executes to some point in the program and determines then the array size. For example, the program asks the user how many elements they wish in an array. Then an array of that dimension is allocated. This removes the arbitrary upper limit to the number of items that can be input into an array! Arrays can be as big as they need to be at run time. This ability to dynamically allocate needed memory as the program is executing along is extremely important. In larger programs, a large percentage of variables are dynamically allocated as the program needs the space. It forms the basis for many of the OOP solutions that we will be studying in the later chapters of this text.

Pointer Basics

Defining Pointer Variables

The topic of pointers in general is the most difficult portion of the C++ language to learn and program well. It is error prone. Right from the start, I am going to name my pointer variables in a special way. Then, as we see how to use pointers, I will show you the tremendous benefit this naming convention has.

A pointer variable is defined by placing a * after the data type and before the variable name. The following all define pointer variables.
```
int*    ptrqty;
double* ptrcost;
char*   ptrstring;
```
The * in a data definition means "is a pointer to" whatever data type is involved.

These data definitions read backwards—**ptrqty** is a pointer to an **int**; **ptrcost** is a pointer to a **double**; **ptrstring** is a pointer to a **char**. Since a pointer is essentially an **unsigned long** on a 32-bit platform (they are an **unsigned int** or 2 bytes long under old DOS), a pointer takes up 4 bytes of memory.

The placement of the * in the definition is not critical from a syntax view point. These could have been defined this way.
```
int    *ptrqty;
double *ptrcost;
char   *ptrstring;
```
However, when the * is placed up against the variable name, the * tends to visually disappear from the reader's gaze. There is a huge difference between a **double** and the memory address of a **double**! Thus, I try to always place the * right after the data type where it is more prominently visible and not so easily missed.

More than one pointer can be defined on a single line. However, observe the syntax that is needed.
```
int *ptrqty, quantity, *ptrcount, count, *ptrtally;
```
Three pointers are defined along with two integers. The following would not yield the definition of two pointers.
```
int* ptrqty, ptrcount;
```
Here, **ptrcount** is assumed to be an integer.

A pointer can be of automatic storage type or it can be a parameter pointer or it can be a static pointer or even a global pointer. The following are all valid pointer definitions.
```
int    *ptrqty; // global pointer to an int
int main () {
   double *ptrcost;        // automatic storage pointer
```

```
static char *ptrstring; // static storage pointer
...
double* Fun (double* ptrdata) {
        // parameter pointer and
        // a returned pointer from a function
...
```

Notice that every pointer is defined to point to some specific type of data, such as an **int**, **double,** or even an **INVREC** structure instance from the last chapter. When we use pointers, the compiler is very conscientious about making sure that our pointers match the kind of data to which they are supposed to be pointing. It does not allow one to access a **double** by using a pointer to an **int**, for example. There is one special kind of pointer that has no data type associated with it, a **void***. In order to make use of a **void*** type pointer, usually one must typecast it to the type of data to which it actually points or use the **mem**xxx string functions.

Ok. So we can define a pointer variable. But what is its starting value, its contents? At the moment, core garbage. The next step is vital. A pointer must be initialized with the memory address of the data to which it is supposed to point!

Initializing Pointers

Pointers must contain the address of what they are supposed to be pointing. How this is done depends upon the circumstances. The address operator, &, is sometimes used to obtain the memory address of the item that comes after it. So taking the address of something is one way to get the initial value for a pointer.

> Suppose that we have defined the following variables.
> ```
> int    qty;
> double cost;
> int* ptrqty;
> double* ptrcost;
> ```
We could initialize these two pointers by coding
> ```
> ptrqty = &qty;
> ptrcost = &cost
> ```
Or they could be initialized as they are defined as follows.
> ```
> int* ptrqty = &qty;
> double* ptrcost = &cost;
> ```

However, the above is rather a contrived example. Why would one want an alternative way to access the function's **qty** and **cost** variables? In reality, you would not code the above two pointers. More frequently, the pointers are parameter variables. Suppose that we wanted to write a **Swap()** function that swapped two integers. Until now, how would you pass those two integers? Why by reference variables, of course. Here is how they could also be passed by pointers instead.
main()
```
    int x;
```

```
      int y;
      Swap (&x, &y);
```
Swap()
```
      void Swap (int* ptrx, int* ptry) {
```

Notice that we must manually pass the addresses of **x** and **y**, Again, while we could write **Swap()** this way, pointers are not really often used where a reference variable could and should be used. The reason pointers do not replace reference variables is that their use is more error prone in many ways. Reference variables are designed to remove many of the common causes of errors when pointers were used. What would have happened if **main()** had called **Swap()** this way?
```
      Swap (x, y);
```
The compiler generates an error message, "cannot convert int to int*"—that is it cannot convert an integer into a memory address. In fact, this conversion error is one of the most common errors programmers new to pointers get—"cannot convert double to double*", "cannot convert long* to long", "cannot convert INVREC to INVREC*".

A pointer variable can also be initialized to the name of a single dimensioned array. Suppose that a function defined the following array.
```
      double grades[20];
```
What is the data type of the name of the array, in this case, **grades**? The name of an array is always a constant pointer to the first element. In this case, the symbol **grades** is a constant pointer to a **double**. Using this one can define and initialize **ptrthisgrade** as follows.
```
      double* ptrthisgrade = grades;
```
Here, **ptrthisgrade** now points to the first element of the array **grades**, that is, it contains the address of **grades[0]**. One could have also initialized **ptrthisgrade** this way.
```
      double* ptrthisgrade = &grades[0];
```

Dereferencing a Pointer

How can the contents of what the pointer points to be accessed? This is done by using the dereference operator, also a *. Assuming that **ptrqty** contains the address of the function's **qty** variable, then the following places a 42 into the **qty** variable.
```
      *ptrqty = 42;
```
The * means go to the address pointed to by the pointer and access what is there. When it is on the left-hand side, it copying the right-hand value into the location pointed to by the pointer. When it is on the right-hand side, the compiler is accessing or reading the contents of the memory location pointed to by the pointer. Here **cost** is being multiplied by the **qty** field.
```
      totalCost = *ptrqty * cost;
```
The dereference operator is needed to implement the **Swap()** function. It can be done as follows.
```
      void Swap (int* ptrx, int* ptry) {
        int temp = *ptrx;
        *ptrx = *ptry;
        *ptry = temp;
      }
```

Here the contents pointed to by **ptrx** are copied into the temporary integer, **temp**. Then the contents pointed to by **ptry** are stored in the memory location pointed to by **ptrx**. And finally, the temporary value in **temp** is copied into the memory location pointed to by **ptry**.

The Rules of Pointer Arithmetic

Pointer variables can be used in simple arithmetic expressions. Indeed, much of their benefits arise from these special abilities. But before we launch into these rules, let's see how a simple program could be written using all subscripts. Then, let's see how all subscripts could be completely replaced by pointers. Consider the following program to input an unknown number of grades, compute their average, and then print out the grades.

```cpp
const int LIMIT = 5;
int main() {
  double grades[LIMIT];
  int j = 0;
  double sum = 0;
  while (j<LIMIT && cin >> grades[j]) {
    sum += grades[j];
    j++;
  }
  if (j == LIMIT && cin >> ws && cin.good()) {
    cerr << "Array bounds exceeded\n"
    return 1;
  }
  else if (!cin.eof() && cin.fail()) {
    cerr << "Error: bad data entered\n"
    return 2;
  }
  int numGrades = j;
  cout << "Average grade: " << sum / numGrades << endl;
  for (j=0; j<numGrades; j++) {
    cout << grades[j] << endl;
  }
  return 0;
}
```

Ok. Pointer notation and subscript notation can be interchanged. The goal is to eliminate all subscripts and counters in the above program. To do so, two pointers are needed, here called **ptrthisgrade** and **ptrlastgrade**. The **ptrthisgrade** always points to the current element to be utilized, either to be filled by an input operation or to be accessed in summing operations or displaying actions. The **ptrlastgrade** is used to point to the first byte that comes after the last element in the array. Thus, if the memory address in **ptrthisgrade** is strictly less than the memory address in **ptrlastgrade**, then there is still another element in the array that we can use. If **ptrthisgrade** ever becomes equal to or larger than **ptrlastgrade**, then the array bound is exceeded. Figure 3.1 illustrates this initial setup with these pointers.

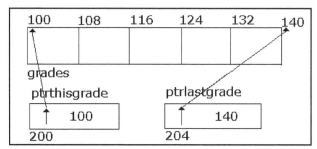

Figure 3.1 The Initial Pointer Setup

Assuming that the array **grades** begins at memory location 100 and that a double is 8 bytes in size, then if there are 5 elements in the array, memory address 140 marks the first byte that is not in the array **grades**. The two pointers are located at memory addresses 200 and 204 respectively. The initial state must have **ptrthisgrade** containing the address of the first element of the array, the address 100. The **ptrlastgrade** must contain the address of the first byte not in the array, the address 140 as shown above in Figure 3.1.

Recall that the name of an array is a constant pointer to the first element. Thus, we can define and initialize **ptrthisgrade** as follows.
```
const int LIMIT = 5;
int main() {
   double grades[LIMIT];
   double* ptrthisgrade = grades;
```
But how do we get the address 140 into **ptrlastgrade**?

An integer can be added to or subtracted from any pointer. However, that value is scaled by the **sizeof** the data type being pointed to, that is multiplied by the **sizeof** the data type. Thus, we can write
```
   double* ptrlastgrade = grades + LIMIT;
   double sum = 0;
```
To the right of the = sign, the symbol **grades** is really the memory address of the first element or 100. **LIMIT** has been defined to be 5. Thus, the equation appears as
```
   ptrlastgrade = 100 + 5;
```
However, if the compiler just added five bytes to 100, yielding 105, disaster would result since we would now be 5/8's of the way thru a **double**! Instead the compiler does the following.
```
   ptrlastgrade = 100 + 5 * sizeof (double);
```
or
```
   ptrlastgrade = 100 + 5 * 8;
```
or
```
   ptrlastgrade = 140;
```

Next, two pointers can be compared as long as they both point to the same type of data. Using this we can rewrite the **while** statement as follows.
```
   while (ptrthisgrade < ptrlastgrade
          && cin >> *ptrthisgrade) {
```

91

Notice also that the extraction operator needs a variable to fill and by dereferencing **ptrthisgrade**, we get it. Similarly, we can accumulate the score just inputted by coding

```
sum += *ptrthisgrade;
```

Again, dereferencing the pointer gets to the value contained in this element in the array.

Then, **ptrthisgrade** must be incremented to point to the next element in the array or address 108. This is done by coding

```
ptrthisgrade++;
```

Remember that an integer can be added to a pointer. The increment operator is adding 1, well, really 1 * sizeof (the data type) or 8 bytes in this case. However, the sum and the pointer increment lines are often combined into a single statement as shown below.

```
sum += *ptrthisgrade++;
}
```

The postfix inc and dec operators have a higher precedence than the dereference operator. So the above expression reads, increment **ptrthisgrade** after any use is made of its current contents. If one wanted to actually increment the grade being pointed to by the pointer, one would have to use () such as

```
sum = sum + *(ptrthisgrade++);
```

This would add one grade point to the person's grade and add that new grade value into the sum.

Most of the coding to check for errors when the loop is done is exactly the same. The only difference in coding is how to check if we are at the end of the array. That is handled by comparing the two pointers:

```
if (ptrthisgrade == ptrlastgrade &&
    cin >> ws && cin.good()) {
cerr << "Array bounds exceeded\n"
return 1;
}
else if (!cin.eof() && cin.fail()) {
cerr << "Error: bad data entered\n"
return 2;
}
```

Next, a most important step must be done. With subscripts, we set the integer **numGrades** to the actual number of elements or grades that was input on this run. When using a pure pointer version, we reset **ptrlastgrade** to now point to the real end of the array on this run. The **ptrthisgrade** is pointing to the next available element that was not yet used. So we have

```
ptrlastgrade = ptrthisgrade;
```

The next action is to display the average, **sum / numGrades**. But wait, we do not know the number of grades that was input! We can easily calculate that value by subtraction of two pointers. Two pointers can be subtracted as long as they both point to the same type of data; the resulting integer is scaled by the **sizeof** the data type, divided by the **sizeof** the data type, in this case. To see this in operation, let's assume that three grades were input on this run. Figure 3.2 shows the state of our program at this point in its execution.

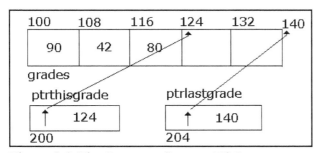

Figure 3.2 The Program State at EOF

If we write the expression,
ptrthisgrade - grades
this yields
        124 - 100 => 24
But it is then scaled by the size of a **double**
        24 / 8 => 3
This gives us the number of elements actually in the array on this run.

The way to think about what subtracting two pointers gives you is this: when you subtract the two pointers, it gives you the number of elements between these two points in the array. A pointer is just that a way of marking some point in an array in this case. So the program line becomes:
```
cout << "Average grade: " << sum /(ptrthisgrade - grades)
        << endl;
```

The final operation of the program is to display all of the grades as entered. That is, we must begin at the beginning of the array and move sequentially through all elements that were input accessing each one in turn. This is perhaps the most common coding found with array processing. The **for** loop is rewritten this way.
```
for (ptrthisgrade=grades; ptrthisgrade<ptrlastgrade;
        ptrthisgrade++) {
    cout << *ptrthisgrade << cndl;
}
```
The working pointer, **ptrthisgrade**, is reinitialized back to the start of the array, it is tested each time through the loop to see that it is less than **ptrlastgrade** which marks the first element not actually used on this run. And it is incremented to get to the next element after each pass through the loop. Remember, to access the value that the pointer is pointing to, the dereference operator is needed.

For your reference, here is the complete pointer replacement program.
```
const int LIMIT = 5;
int main() {
  double grades[LIMIT];
  double* ptrthisgrade = grades;
  double* ptrlastgrade = grades + LIMIT;
  double sum = 0;
```

```
    while (ptrthisgrade < ptrlastgrade
          && cin >> *ptrthisgrade) {
      sum += *ptrthisgrade++;
    }
    if (ptrthisgrade == ptrlastgrade &&
        cin >> ws && cin.good()) {
      cerr << "Array bounds exceeded\n"
      return 1;
    }
    else if (!cin.eof() && cin.fail()) {
      cerr << "Error: bad data entered\n"
      return 2;
    }
    ptrlastgrade = ptrthisgrade;
    cout << "Average grade: " << sum /(ptrthisgrade - grades)
         << endl;
    for (ptrthisgrade=grades; ptrthisgrade<ptrlastgrade;
         ptrthisgrade++) {
      cout << *ptrthisgrade << endl;
    }
    return 0;
}
```

Table 3.1 summarizes all of the rules for pointer arithmetic.

`ptrthisgrade = grades;`	The name of an array is a constant pointer to the first element.
`grades + 5 => 140,` `if grades contains 100 and points to doubles`	An integer can be added to or subtracted from any pointer. That integer is scaled by the sizeof the data type the pointer is pointing to, that is, multiplied by the sizeof the data type
`ptrthisgrade++`	Any pointer can be incremented or decremented. This is a variation of adding or subtracting an integer to/from a pointer.
`ptrthisgrade < ptrlastgrade`	Two pointers can be compared as long as they both point to the same type of data.
`ptrthisgrade - grades` `if ptrthisgrade contains 124 and grades has 100, this yields 24 / 8 => 3`	Two pointers can be subtracted as long as they both point to the same type of data. The resulting integer is scaled by the size of the data type, or divided by the size of the data type. Thus, when you subtract two pointers, you get the number of elements between these two points in the array.

`ptrthisgrade * n`	Pointer variables cannot be multiplied or divided.
`ptrthisgrade + 1.2345`	No floating point operations are allowed.
`*ptrthisgrade or *grades`	Any pointer can be dereferenced.
`grades[i] or ptrthisgrade[i]`	Any pointer can be subscripted.

Table 3.1 Summary of the Rules for Pointer Arithmetic

It is obvious that no multiplication or division is allowed. They would make no sense, such as **ptrthisgrade** * 100 for this would yield 100 * 100 or 10000! No floating point values can be used for obvious reasons. Pointers point to discrete locations, not fractional locations. Any pointer can be dereferenced. But look at this unusual one

```
*grades
```

Since the symbol **grades** is a constant pointer to the first element, it is a pointer and can be dereferenced. This accesses the first element in the array and is synonymous with writing

```
grades[0]
```

Even more peculiar is any pointer can be subscripted. No problem with writing

```
grades[i]
```

But what about

```
ptrthisgrade[i]
```

This unusual coding considers the origin point of the array to be at the location given by **ptrthisgrade**.

The Impact of Pointers on a Program

Why are pointers widely used with array processing instead of the more familiar subscript notation? Coding that uses pointers to process an array executes faster than coding that uses subscripts. Coding that uses subscripts generally requires fewer machine instructions and thus the program exe size is a bit smaller. Why?

To understand why there is a difference in execution speed, we need to examine how the computer actually does these actions. Let's say that we wrote

```
x = grades[i];
```

The compiler generates the following series of machine instructions to carry out this statement. I also show how many clock cycles that machine instruction might take. A clock cycle is the smallest unit of time in which a particular computer can perform units of work.

  1. Look up the contents of variable **i** in memory, say it holds 1 => 1 clock cycle

  2. Multiply that value by the size of the data type, 1 * 8 => 30+ clock cycles

  3. Look up the contents of **grades**, 100 => 1 clock cycle

4. Add the 100 and the offset of 8, to get the memory address needed, 108 => 2 clock cycles

5. Go to that location and retrieve its contents, the grade of 42 in this case => 1 clock cycle

Total time is about 35 clock cycles.

For the pointer version

```
x = *ptrthisgrade;
```

we have the following machine instructions.

1. Look up the contents of the variable **ptrthisgrade**, say 108 => 1 clock cycle

2. Goto that location and retrieve its contents, the **grade** of 42 => 1 clock cycle

And the total time is about 2 clock cycles.

The difference between these two is 35 – 2 or 33 clock cycles. How fast is a clock cycle? In general it depends, in an overly simplified case, on the speed in MHZ of your computer. To find the approximate clock speed of your computer, divide 1000 nanoseconds by the MHZ speed rating of your computer. Suppose your machine had a speed rating of 500 MHZ. Then a clock cycle would be 2 nanoseconds. A nanosecond is 10^{-9} of a second or one-trillionth of a second. Ok. So is this difference in speed of 33 clock cycles significant? The answer is that it all depends. If you had a single subscript access contained inside a loop that was executed 100 times, then the difference is minuscule. If you blink, you missed the difference in speed between these two versions of the program. On the other hand, if that single access was located within a loop that was done 100 times and that whole loop was within another loop done 10000 times, then you would certainly be able to observe the difference in run time speed between these two versions of the program.

Thus, pointers are widely used with array processing to gain speed of execution. But what about the pointer increment statement that must be part of such processing?

```
ptrthisgrade++;
```

The increment is always adding one to the pointer and the compiler knows at compile time what the size of the data type actually is. Hence, the compiler does not generate any multiply instructions, rather it generates an add instruction. The above expression becomes

```
ptrthisgrade + 8;
```

And speed of execution is maintained.

The Use of Hybrids and Dual Incrementing

There are two ways a programmer can misuse the pointer approach and thus lose much or all of the inherent speed benefits. The first of these is called using a hybrid expression—hybrid, in that both subscripts and pointers are used.

```
ptrthisgrade[i] = ptrthisgrade[i+1];
```

Here, although pointers are being used, a subscript is inserted. All speed benefits are lost as the slower subscript coding must be generated. Faster execution would be had by writing

```
*ptrthisgrade = *(ptrthisgrade + 1);
```

where **ptrthisgrade** is pointing to the ith element. The compiler handles the +1 term by simply generating +8 bytes to the pointer.

The second way to lose speed is to use a dual incrementing algorithm. Here is an example.

```
ptrthisgrade = grades;
for (i=0; i<numGrades; i++) {
  cout << *ptrthisgrade++ << endl;
}
```

Here, the pointer is dereferenced and dutifully incremented to get to the next element. However, the programmer cannot figure out how to terminate the loop and so uses another counter, **i** in this case. The program is incrementing the pointer and variable **i**—a dual increment.

Arrays of Pointers

Thus far, we have looked at various aspects of a pointer variable. But how about making an array of pointers? This is actually a very versatile type of an array as we will explore in this chapter and subsequent ones. Suppose that we wished to store an array of day name strings. If the user enters a day of 1, we can display the string "Sunday" on the screen. Here is how the array of pointers can be defined and initialized.

```
char* days[8] = {"", "Sunday", "Monday", "Tuesday",
                 "Wednesday", "Thursday", "Friday",
                 "Saturday"};
```

Each element of the array **days** contains the memory address of a null-terminated string. Figure 3.3 shows what this array looks like.

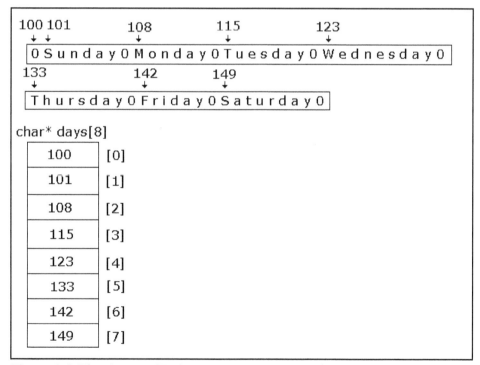

Figure 3.3 The Array of Pointers to Day Name Strings

To use our array, one could code the following, ignoring the possibility of day values being out of range.

```
int day;
cin >> day;
cout << days[day];
```

If the user enters 1 for **day**, then **days[day]** is the element whose value is 101 which is the memory address of the string "Sunday."

It is just such a data layout that is used to pass the DOS command line parameters into the **main()** function of a program.

Handling Command Line Parameters in the main() Function

When the **main()** function is called by the C runtime start up code, it is passed an array of **char*** items. Each **char*** element of the array points to one of the strings from the command line. As with any array, the number of items in the array is also passed. Here are the actual parameters that every **main()** function is passed.

```
int main (int argc, char* argv[]) {
```

The first parameter is the argument count or the number of items in the array. The second parameter an array of pointers, each pointer is the address of a string.

Let's review how a program can be launched. Assuming that the name of the program is pgm1.exe and that it is located in the \UserApps folder, the following represent various ways the program could be run.

```
      C:\>cd \UserApps
1     C:\UserApps>Pgm1
2     C:\UserApps>Pgm1 test.txt
3     C:\UserApps>Pgm1 test.txt result.txt
4     C:\UserApps>Pgm1 test.txt result.txt 10/12/2000
```

In the example on line 1, there are no parameters. However, since you cannot have an array with no elements in it, C++ always passes the full path to the program being run in element 0. Thus the content of **argv[0]** is always the program path that is being executed. In this case, **argv[0]** contains "C:\UserApps\Pgm1.exe" and the **argc** variable contains a 1, one item in the array.

In the example on line 4, the **argc** parameter contains 4 since there are 4 items in the **argv** array. The four strings contain:

argv[0] contains "C:\UserApps\Pgm1.exe"

argv[1] contains "test.txt"

argv[2] contains "result.txt"

argv[3] contains "10/12/2000"

Remember that on a command line, blanks are used to separate things. C++ places each item into a string for us.

This also is what happens if you create an icon from which to double click and launch the program. Remember that if you right click on the new icon and choose Properties, you can set a default path and also items to be on its command line.

Suppose that the program expected to be passed the input and output filenames from the command line. The following coding opens the two files.

```
int main (int argc, char* argv[]) {
   if (argc != 3) {
      cerr << "Error: program is expecting the input and "
              "output filenames on the command line\n"
           << "Usage: Pgm1 infile.txt outfile.txt\n"
      return 1;
   }
   ifstream infile (argv[1]);
   ofstream outfile (argv[2]);
```

The Use of the const Keyword with Pointers

The **const** keyword when used with pointers and reference variables can have two meanings, depending upon its location within the data definition.

When the **const** precedes the data type, the data pointed to by that pointer or reference variable is constant. That is, the data itself cannot be changed. Consider the following definitions of functions.

```
void Fun1 (long* array, int numItems);
void Fun2 (const long* array, int numItems);
void Fun3 (long* const array, int numItems);
void Fun4 (const long* const array, int numItems);
```

In **Fun1()** one could say
```
array[0] = 42;
```
and one could say
```
array = new long[42];
```
This is because nothing is considered constant.

In **Fun2()**, the array data has been made constant. Thus if one coded
```
array[0] = 42;
```
it would generate a compile error. However, one could still say
```
array = new long[42];
```
This is because the parameter pointer is not considered constant.

In **Fun3()**, the parameter pointer is constant. Thus, one could say
```
array[0] = 42;
```
because the array has not been made constant. However, if you tried to do the following

```
array = new long[42];
```
This creates a compile error since the parameter pointer is constant.

In **Fun4()** both the array and the parameter pointer have been made constant. Thus both of the following would generate an error.
```
array[0] = 42;
array = new long[42];
```
Normally, only the array data is made constant to those functions that should not be granted rights to alter the array data.

Dynamic Memory Allocation

During program execution, C++ provides a mechanism for a program to ask for additional memory for items. This is done with the **new** function. Of course, when the program is finished using that memory, it needs to free it up by using the **delete** function.

The **new** function is coded a bit differently. The basic syntax is
```
new datatype_desired
```
The **new** function returns a pointer to the dynamically allocated memory if it is available. If there is no more memory with which to carry out the request, then **new** returns the null pointer, 0.

Here in lies the difference between Version 6.0 and the newer .NET versions of Microsoft's compilers. In Version 6.0, if **new** fails to allocate the memory, it returns a 0 or null pointer. It can be made to throw one of the new C++ run time exceptions which are covered in a much later chapter. However, when using any of the .NET versions, Microsoft changed **new** to throw the exception if it cannot allocate the memory. In order to get the .NET version's **new** function to return the 0 or null pointer, we must pass it a parameter: **std::nothrow**.

Suppose that we wished to allocate memory for a new **double** that represents a total. One could code
```
double* ptrtotal = new (std::nothrow) double;
```
The **new** function allocates 8 bytes of memory (the size of a **double**) and returns its memory address which is then assigned to the automatic storage pointer variable, **ptrtotal**.

These are all valid.
```
int* ptrtally = new (std::nothrow) int;
// allocates space for a new int

long* ptrlong = new (std::nothrow) long;
// allocates space for a new long

char* ptrtype = new (std::nothrow) char;
// allocates space for a new char
```

These four new variables can then be used in anyway a **double**, **int**, **long** or **char** could be used, just remember to use the dereference operator. One could code

```
*ptrtotal = 0;    // set the total to 0
*ptrtotal += cost * qty; // accumulate total of orders
*ptrtally = 0;    // set tally counter to 0
(*ptrtally)++;    // increment tally counter
*ptrlong = 42;    // assign 42 to the long
*ptrtype = 'F';   // place the letter F into the char
```

Finally, when the program is finished with the memory, the **delete** function is called.

```
delete ptrtotal;
delete ptrtally;
delete ptrlong;
delete ptrtype;
```

Deleting these then returns the memory back into the free pool of available memory for applications to use.

Now in practice, seldom does one dynamically allocate a new **double**, **int** or **long**. Much more frequently, one allocates a new instance of a structure. Suppose the program defined the following **INVREC** structure.

```
const int DESCRLEN = 21;
struct INVREC {
   long    itemNum;
   char    description[DESCRLEN];
   int     qtyOnHand;
   double  unitCost;
};
```

One could now code a far more interesting allocation.

```
INVREC* ptrrec = new (std::nothrow) INVREC;
```

And the corresponding freeing of the memory would be

```
delete ptrrec;
```

The Location of the Heap

From where does the memory that is being allocated come? It is acquired from the local heap, which is, as its name indicates, a large pile of unallocated memory that is available for this use. Figure 3.4 shows the layout of memory of a C++ program and where the heap is located.

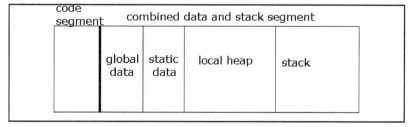

Figure 3.4 The Memory Layout of a Program

101

The heap is located between the static data section and the top of the stack section. On a Win32 platform, such as Windows 95/98/NT/2000/ME, if the stack section becomes full and more stack space is needed, Windows temporarily halts the program and resizes these areas making the stack larger. The same is true if the amount of memory needed on the heap exceeds the current size of the heap. Windows reallocates the heap larger dynamically on the fly as the program is running. How much can the stack and the heap grow? Any Win32 application can have a total memory usage of about 2G. However, being just a bit more practical since most of us do not have 2G of memory installed on our computers at this time, it is really the size of the Windows swap or paging file (virtual memory) plus the amount of unused memory that determines the maximum size that the entire program can occupy. For example, on my programming machine that runs Win2000, I have a dedicated 500M swap file. Thus, no single application can use more than 500M + the amount of the free128M memory available on the machine.

Do We Need to Check for Successful Allocation?

Ideally, one should check the returned pointer for 0 and handle appropriately. That is, if the returned pointer is 0, the computer does not have sufficient memory to satisfy this request. Theoretically, one should code

```
double* ptrtotal = new (std::nothrow) double;
if (!ptrtotal) {
  cerr << "Error: out of memory\n";
  return 1;
}
*ptrtotal += cost * qty; // accumulate total of orders
```

In practice, this check is often not done. Consider the status of the Windows system itself if it cannot allocate a **double** for us. Long before we ever arrive at running totally out of memory so that it cannot even allocate 8 additional bytes, Windows has been displaying its famous message: "The system is dangerously low on resources; shut down some applications." In a simple allocation such as all of these are, most programmers do not even bother to check that returned pointer, figuring that if there is not sufficient memory left, Windows would already have told the user many times that it was running out of memory. By design, address 0, which would be the value returned if the computer was out of memory, actually is the very first byte of the global section of the data-stack segment. So they figure there is memory there somehow. Ah, mostly working programs arise from this. But with small amounts as the above four allocations are, it is probably a reasonable way to go, if the program was not a critical application.

If the program is a critical application, such as customer billing, a real-time spaceflight simulator, an intensive-care health monitoring program, then **always** check on the success of the request for more memory. Also, if you are asking for a larger amount of memory as we will do here shortly, such as a new array or space to hold a graphical image, then by all means check that returned pointer for 0. These are often the two guidelines that seem to be followed by most working programmers on a Windows platform. However, to avoid mostly working software, one should always check that returned pointer for 0.

Dynamic Allocation of Arrays

Far more commonly an entire array of items is allocated. Suppose that the user has entered the number of points, **numPoints**, that they needed for a pair of x and y value arrays. We know that the following coding cannot compile.

```
int numPoints;
cin >> numPoints;
long x[numPoints];
long y[numPoints];
```

Remember, array bounds must be a constant known at compile time and are often **const int**s or **#define** symbols for ease of program maintenance. In the past, the only recourse was to make the array bounds sufficiently large to hold the worst case the programmer expected would arise. And if that limit was exceeded, the program would produce an array size exceeded message and abort.

Dynamic memory allocation totally removes this restriction on array limits. However, to dynamically allocate a single dimensioned array, changes must be made to both the **new** and **delete** function syntax.

```
new datatype_desired [arraysize];
delete [] arraypointer;
```

Thus, to handle the user inputting the number of points they need and then allocating a pair of **x** and **y** arrays sufficiently large, one could code the following.

```
int numPoints;
cin >> numPoints;
long* x = new (std::nothrow) long [numPoints];
long* y = new (std::nothrow) long [numPoints];
```

The **arraysize** parameter can be a constant, variable or integer expression. Here it is a variable. When the allocation is completed, memory appears as shown in Figure 3.5.

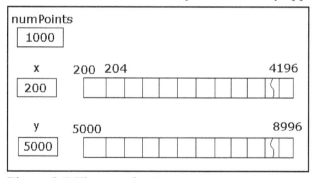

Figure 3.5 The x and y Arrays

Notice that **x** contains the address of the first element of the 1000 **long**s. Since each long is 4 bytes in size, the total array size is 4000 bytes, making the address of **x[999]** 4196. The array **y** begins at memory address 5000. Thus, the address of element **y[0]** is 5000. The address of **y[999]** is 8996.

103

Notice a subtle difference in the naming convention I have used with the two arrays. They are not called **ptrx** and **ptry** as have all of the other pointers. Why? I intend to use subscripts to access the elements in these arrays. Thus, one might expect to next see a sequence such as this.

```
for (int j=0; j<numPoints; j++) {
  cin >> x[j] >> y[j];
}
```

The following are all valid array allocations.

```
double*  totals = new (std::nothrow) double [maxTotals];
char* name = new (std::nothrow) char [currentNameLength];
INVREC* arec = new (std::nothrow) INVREC[maxInventoryItems];
```

What about passing these dynamically allocated arrays to a function? The prototype could be either of these two.

```
void DoCalcs (long x[], long y[], int numPoints);
void DoCalcs (long* x, long* y, int numPoints);
```

In either case, the function would be called this way.

```
DoCalcs (x, y, numPoints);
```

Remember, the name of an array is a pointer to the first element. Hence, there is no difference between coding **long x[]** and **long* x**; they are the same thing, the memory address of the first element. However, the reader of your program will naturally expect to see subscripts being used to access the elements when you use **long x[]**. Likewise, they will expect to see pointer notation being used when you use **long* x**.

Thus, dynamically allocated arrays open up vast new possibilities with array processing programs!

However, the deletion of dynamically allocated arrays is special too. Consider these two allocations.

```
long* ptrlong = new (std::nothrow) long;
long* x = new (std::nothrow) long [numPoints];
```

Notice one crucial, vital fact. Both **ptrlong** and **x** contain the memory address of a **long**. As far as the compiler is concerned, there is no difference whatsoever between these two pointers. They both point to the memory address of a **long**. However, there are also 999 more **long**s after that first one to which **x** points! And here is where a programmer can get into trouble with the **delete** function. These two dynamically allocated items must be deleted differently. The compiler must be told that pointer **x** is pointing to a whole array of **long**s!

```
delete ptrlong;
delete [] x;
```

What would happen if the programmer goofed and coded just

```
delete x;
```

The **delete** function would just free up storage occupied by one **long**, leaving the remaining 999 **long**s still marked as in use! This is called a memory leak. A **memory leak** means that some dynamically allocated memory has not been freed when the program terminates.

Memory Leaks

Failure to free up dynamically allocated memory is known as a memory leak. Is it serious? Well, it all depends. Under the Windows platform, when any application terminates, Windows automatically frees any and all memory that that program has ever allocated. In other words, Windows cleans up after you; it does not trust you.

However, being lazy and not freeing up dynamically allocated memory can sometimes get you and your program into deep trouble. Suppose that every time a new transaction was entered your program did something like

```
TRANSACTION* ptrtrans = new (std::nothrow) TRANSACTION;
```

Suppose that you forgot to free up the memory allocated when you were done processing that transaction. Suppose that an instance of this structure occupied 100 bytes. When the program is finally done processing today's transactions, suppose that it handled 100,000 of them. How much memory did the program ultimately consume and then leak? 10,000,000 or just under 10M.

Ah, but suppose your program in production is run on the company's network server. Servers are seldom rebooted for obvious reasons. And programs often run for days on servers. What do you suppose would happen after your program ran for 20 days consecutively? Now you have asked for 200M of server memory! You are going to eventually run the server completely out of memory, causing operations to have to deal with many "The server is dangerously low on resources; please shut down some applications." Once they discover which application has used up all of the server's memory, you will be asked not so politely to fix your program!

If you go on into Windows programming, you often need to allocate instances of Windows' system resources, such as brushes, pens, fonts, and so on. There are a limited, finite number of these items. If you ask for a new brush and do not give it back when you are done with it, eventually Windows runs out of brushes and crashes.

Thus, a program should never go into production with memory leaks. Period!

How can you tell if a program has a memory leak? Careful design aids along with verifying that every **new** has a corresponding **delete**. But there is another way. The Visual C++ compiler has an automatic way it can check for memory leaks and notify you of them if they occur.

Checking for Memory Leaks with Visual C++

The methods used to check for memory leaks are left up to the compiler manufacturer. Microsoft has developed a fairly easy way to check for them. To check for leaks, first include the header file **<crtdbg.h>**. Then, just before you return to DOS, call the **_CrtDumpMemoryLeaks()** function. This function takes no parameters but does two actions. It returns a **bool**; **true** if there are leaks, **false** if there are no leaks. Secondly, if there are leaks, then it dumps the memory addresses and contents of all memory that was leaked. The display is in the Output window after the program has terminated.

Common coding of this function is in **main()** just before the "return 0 instruction" as shown below.

```
      if (_CrtDumpMemoryLeaks())
       cerr << "Memory leaks occurred!\n";
      else
       cerr << "No memory leaks.\n";
      return 0;
}
```

There is one major caution here. Please note that the New Style **iostream** classes that are used with **namespace std;** contain internal memory leaks as of VC6.0 Service Pack 4! This "design feature" was fixed in Version 7.0 (.Net). Thus, if you use VC 6 and the **namespace std;** you are guaranteed to get memory leaks. Try using the Old Style **iostream** classes with VC 6. They do not leak memory. Mostly working software, grrr.

Checking for Memory Leaks with Borland C++ 5.0

Borland does not have such a built-in method to check for leaks. Instead, we must provide a helper function to assist us in detecting leaks. Here is some coding that works for a Win32 Console application under BC5.0.

```
#include <alloc.h>

long HeapSize () {
 int result;
 if ((result = heapcheck ()) != _HEAPOK) {
  cout << "Corrupted heap: " << result << endl;
  return 0;
 }
 long hsize = 0;
 heapinfo info;
 info.ptr = 0;
 while (heapwalk (&info) == _HEAPOK)
  hsize += info.size;
 return hsize;
```

106

```
}

int main () {
 long beginsize =HeapSize  (), endsize = 0;
 ... now go allocate stuff
 ... now go free stuff
 endsize = HeapSize ();
 if (beginsize != endsize) cout << "Memory Leaks\n"
 else cout << "No Memory Leaks\n";
 return 0;
}
```

This coding and another version that can handle memory leak checking on other Borland platforms than just Win32 console applications are located in a BorlandOnly subfolder of Chapter03 folder in the sample programs for this chapter.

Dynamically Allocating Strings

Suppose that a description field that is entered for our **INVREC** structures could contain up to 50 characters. Further, suppose that most of the descriptions only contained around 15 characters or less. Until now, we are forced to define our structure this way.

```
const int DESCRLEN = 51;
struct INVREC {
   long    itemNum;
   char    description[DESCRLEN];
   int     qtyOnHand;
   double unitCost;
};
```

And suppose that we needed to reserve space for an array of 1000 inventory records. How many bytes are thus allocated for all of the description fields? 1000 times 51 or 51,000 bytes. Yet if on the average only 15 characters are used, we really need to use only 15,000 of those bytes, wasting 36,000 bytes!

In situations such as this, the **INVREC** structure is defined differently so that the actual description string is dynamically allocated.

```
struct INVREC {
   long    itemNum;
   char*  description;
   int     qtyOnHand;
   double unitCost;
};
...
INVREC invrec[1000];
```

We turn **description** into a pointer to **char**.

How do we allocate and store the needed data? In the input inventory record function, we still define the one and only **real** array of char that is 51 bytes long and input into the real string.

```
char desc[51];
char c;
infile >> c; // get leading quote
infile.get (desc, sizeof (desc), '\"');
infile >> c; // get trailing quote
```

Next, we can allocate the new string. Assume that **invrec** is the passed reference to the **INVREC** we are to fill with the input data.

```
invrec.description=new (std::nothrow)char[strlen(desc) + 1];
strcpy_s (invrec.description, strlen(desc) + 1, desc);
```

Why did I use **strlen(desc) + 1**? Do not forget to leave room for the null terminator. One common error is to code

```
invrec.description = new char [strlen(desc + 1)];
```

If we do this, we are then short 2 bytes and the string copy wipes out memory!

Don't forget to delete [] invrec.description; when the program is finishing up.

Arrays of Pointers and Turning a Pointer Back into a Reference

One can also have an array of pointers. Suppose that instead of creating an array of 1000 inventory records, we create an array of 1000 pointers to inventory records. Then, as a new record is needed, we allocate a new record and store its address in the array of pointers. The main structure now is defined this way.

```
INVREC* invrec[1000];
int      numRecs = 0;
```

We now have an array of 1000 pointers to inventory records.

How do we get a real instance to pass to the **InputRecord()** function? Let's use a primed loop for the input. Thus, we need to initially allocate an **INVREC** and store it in the next slot in the array.

```
invrec[numRecs] = new INVREC;
while (numRecs<1000 && InputRecord(infile, *invrec[numRecs])){
    . . .
    numRecs++;
    invrec[numRecs] = new INVREC;
}
delete invrec[numRecs];
```

There is a lot going on in this small block of coding. First, a new **INVREC** is allocated and is stored in the next slot in the array. Then as long as the array size is not yet exceeded and **InputRecord()** is successful at inputting this inventory record, within the loop's body, the number

108

of records is incremented and another **INVREC** is allocated. When the loop finally ends, the currently allocated **INVREC** has no information in it since the end of file occurred (or bad data on input). This last one is now unneeded. Thus, it is deleted when the loop ends.

However, all of the other functions in the program are most likely expecting a reference to the current inventory record to be passed, not the entire array. Thus, the prototype for **InputRecord()** is likely to be this.

```
istream& InputRecord (istream& infile, INVREC& invrec);
```

We cannot pass it **invrec[numRecs]** because this is a pointer to an inventory record, not a reference. Actually, what we want passed is just the memory location of this current inventory record. Both a pointer and a reference variable contain the memory address of the item. Yet, the compiler will generate an error if we try to pass just **invrec[numRecs]** to **InputRecord()** complaining that an **INVREC*** cannot be converted to an **INVREC&**.

The solution is to dereference the pointer, which yields the actual structure instance which the compiler in turn retakes its address. Hence, we must pass it as ***invrec[numRecs]**.

This situation occurs with some frequence all throughout OOP programming. At some point in our coding, we have a pointer to something but we must convert it to a reference to something. This is easily done by just dereferencing the pointer.

Also, do not forget that before the program terminates, each of these inventory records must be deleted.

A Complete Example Using Dynamic Memory Allocation

Pgm03a, Normal Body Temperatures, illustrates the use of dynamic memory allocation of an array. A health research institute has gathered a collection of the normal body temperatures for a large number of people. The first number in the file contains a count of the number of temperatures contained in that file. The program displays the average body temperature, the maximum and minimum temperatures, the mean temperature and the standard deviation from the mean. The program should accept the names of the input and output files from the command line.

Looking over the problem, we obviously need to dynamically allocate an array of **float**s to hold the temperatures. To get the mean, the one in the middle, the array must be sorted. To calculate the standard deviation from the mean, we must sum the square of the difference of each temperature from the mean temperature, divide that sum by the number of temperatures – 1, and finally take the square root of that result.

As usual, the first step is to design a solution. Figure 3.7 shows the Top-Down Design I chose.

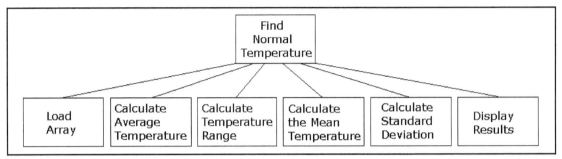

Figure 3.7 Top-Down Design for Normal Temperatures Program

I have decided to use the C built-in **qsort()** function to handle the sorting aspect. However, there is one significant detail that this design has upon the array processing. And that is the **LoadArray()** function. For obvious reasons, I prefer to encapsulate the inputting of an array thereby streamlining the **main()** function. In this situation, within **LoadArray()**, the first number in the data represents the actual array bounds. If I then dynamically allocate an array of that dimension, how do I get the address of that array back into a variable in the **main()** function? Here is what we have done up to this point.

```
int main () {
  float temps[MAX];
  int numValues = LoadArray (temps, MAX);
```
with
```
int LoadArray (float x[], int limit) {
```

LoadArray()'s **x** parameter is a pointer that contains a **copy** of the memory location of the first element of **main()**'s array **temps**. In this case where **LoadArray()** actually allocates the memory for the array, the following cannot possibly work!

```
int main () {
  float* temps;
  int numValues = LoadArray (temps);
```
with
```
int LoadArray (float x[]) {
  int num;
  cin >> num;
  x = new float [num];
  ...
```

This is a very common error that programmers new to dynamic memory allocation make. What is wrong with this approach? Certainly, **LoadArray()** is allocating the needed array properly. But where does that address of the array get stored? It is placed into **LoadArray()**'s parameter **copy** of the contents of **main()**'s **temps** variable (which is initially core garbage). So what is in **main()**'s **temps** pointer when **LoadArray()** returns? The same initial core garbage!

There are a number of ways this can be fixed. An easy one is to have the **LoadArray()** function simply return the pointer to the dynamically allocated memory. Here is the way I chose to handle this.

```
int main () {
```

```
int numTemps;
float* temps = LoadArray (numTemps);
```
with
```
float* LoadArray (int& numTemps) {
 float* temps;
 cin >> numTemps;
 temps = new (std::nothrow) float [numTemps];
 ...
 return temps;
}
```

The alternative is to pass the array as a reference to the address.
```
int main () {
 float* temps;
 int numValues = LoadArray (temps);
```
with
```
int LoadArray (float*& x) {
 int num;
 cin >> num;
 x = new (std::nothrow) float [num];
 ...
}
```
We allocate the new array but **x** is really a reference to main's **temps** pointer and the compiler stores the address of the new array back into main's **temps** variable.

C++ has a built-in function, **qsort()**, that can sort any array. Its simplified prototype is
```
qsort (array, number of elements, size of one element,
        the comparison function to use);
```
The array is obviously the memory address of the first element. The second parameter is the integer number of elements in the array. The third parameter is the integer size of one element. However, the function depends on the user to tell it which of two particular elements is the smaller. The fourth parameter is the memory address of a function, our comparison function that we provide. The comparison function must have this prototype:
```
int compare (const void* ptritem1, const void* ptritem2);
```
And the return value is
```
0 if the two items are equal
1 if the first item is larger than the second item
-1 if the first item is smaller than the second item
```
Of course, when we implement the comparison function, the first action must be to typecast the **void** pointers back into usable pointers. In this case, the array is of type **float**; thus, a pointer to a specific element would be a **float***. So we can handle the conversion similar to this.
```
float* ptrt1 = (float*) ptritem1;
```

Here is the test1 input file and the results that the program produced.

```
Temps.txt - First Set of Test Data
```

```
 1 11
 2 98.6
 3 98.5
 4 98.7
 5 98.8
 6 98.4
 7 98.9
 8 98.3
 9 98.6
10 98.6
11 98.4
12 98.6
```

Results.txt - The Output of the Program on the First Test Set

```
1 Acme Health Studies - Average Body Temperatures
2
3 Number   Average  Maximum  Minimum  Median Standard
4  Temps   Temp     Temp     Temp     Temp   Deviation
5
6    11     98.6     98.9     98.3     98.6     0.2
```

Pgm03a.h - Includes and Prototypes

```
 1 #pragma once
 2 #include <iostream>
 3 #include <iomanip>
 4 #include <fstream>
 5 #include <cmath>     // for sqrt
 6 using namespace std;
 7 #include <crtdbg.h> // for memory leak checking
 8
 9 float* LoadArray (int& numTemps, const char* infileName);
10 float  CalcAvgTemp (const float temps[], int numTemps);
11 void   CalcTempRanges (const float temps[], int numTemps,
12                      float& minTemp, float& maxTemp);
13 float  CalcMeanTemp (const float temps[], int numTemps);
14 float  CalcStdDev (const float temps[], int numTemps, float avg);
15 void   DisplayResults (int numTemps, float avgTemp,
16                      float minTemp, float maxTemp,
17                      float meanTemp, float stdDev,
18                      const char* outfileName);
19 int    CmpTemps (const void* ptrtemp1, const void* ptrtemp2);
```

Pgm03a.cpp main() - Produce the Body Temperature Report

```
 1 #include "Pgm03a.h"
 2
 3 /*****************************************************/
 4 /*                                                 */
```

```
 5 /* Pgm03a: Compute the Average Body Temperature        */
 6 /*                                                      */
 7 /*****************************************************/
 8
 9 int main (int argc, char* argv[]) {
10
11  // verify we have the correct number of cmd line parms
12  if (argc != 3) {
13   cerr << "Error: the names of the input and output files "
14           "must be given\n"
15        << "Usage: Pgm03a temps.txt results.txt\n";
16   return 1;
17  }
18
19  int numTemps; // to store the number of temps in the array
20
21  // load the array, we are responsible for its deletion
22  float* temps = LoadArray (numTemps, argv[1]);
23
24  // find the average, maximum and minimum temperatures
25  float  avgTemp = CalcAvgTemp (temps, numTemps);
26  float  minTemp;
27  float  maxTemp;
28  CalcTempRanges (temps, numTemps, minTemp, maxTemp);
29
30  // sort the array so we can find the mean temperature
31  qsort (temps, numTemps, sizeof (float), CmpTemps);
32
33  // find the mean and standard deviation from that mean
34  float  meanTemp = CalcMeanTemp (temps, numTemps);
35  float  stdDev = CalcStdDev (temps, numTemps, avgTemp);
36
37  // produce the final report
38  DisplayResults (numTemps, avgTemp, minTemp, maxTemp,
39                  meanTemp, stdDev, argv[2]);
40
41  // remove the dynamically allocated array
42  delete [] temps;
43
44  // check for memory leaks
45  if (_CrtDumpMemoryLeaks())
46   cerr << "Memory leaks occurred!\n";
47  else
48   cerr << "No memory leaks.\n";
49
50  return 0;
51 }
```

LoadArray.cpp - Dynamically Allocates the Array and Inputs It

```
 1 #include "Pgm03a.h"
 2
```

```
 3 /********************************************************/
 4 /*                                                      */
 5 /* LoadArray: dynamically allocates an array of         */
 6 /*            numTemps floats and inputs the array       */
 7 /*            if successful, returns the addr of the    */
 8 /*              array                                    */
 9 /*            if it fails, array is removed and pgm      */
10 /*              is aborted                               */
11 /*                                                      */
12 /********************************************************/
13
14 float* LoadArray (int& numTemps, const char* infileName) {
15  ifstream infile (infileName);
16
17  if (!infile) {
18   cerr << "Error: cannot open input file: "
19        << infileName << endl;
20   exit (2);
21  }
22
23  infile >> numTemps; // input the number of temps in the file
24
25  if (!infile) {
26   cerr << "Error: cannot input the number of temperatures\n";
27   infile.close();
28   exit (3);
29  }
30
31  // abort if the number is not at least 1
32  if (numTemps <= 0) {
33   cerr << "Error: the number of temperatures cannot be 0 or less"
34        << "\nIt was: " << numTemps << endl;
35   infile.close();
36   exit (4);
37  }
38
39  // dynamically allocate the array to store the temperatures
40  float* temps = new (std::nothrow) float [numTemps];
41
42  // abort if out of memory
43  if (!temps) {
44   cerr << "Error: cannot allocate the memory for the array\n";
45   infile.close();
46   exit (5);
47  }
48  char junk;
49
50  // input the entire array of temperatures
51  for (int i=0; i<numTemps && infile >> temps[i]; i++) ;
52
53  // eof should not have occurred yet
54  if (infile.eof()) {
55   cerr << "Error: premature EOF - too few temperatures in the "
```

```
56             << "file\nAborting the program\n";
57   delete [] temps;
58   infile.close();
59   exit (6);
60  }
61  else if (!infile) { // check for bad data on input
62   cerr << "Error: bad data in the input file\n"
63        << "Aborting the program\n";
64   delete [] temps;
65   infile.close();
66   exit(7);
67  }
68  else if (infile >> junk) { // check for extra temps remaining
69                            // in the file
70   cerr << "Error: there appears to be additional temperatures "
71        << "in the input file.\nCheck the count.\n"
72        << "Aborting the program\n";
73   delete [] temps;
74   infile.close();
75   exit(8);
76  }
77  infile.close();
78
79  // all went as planned, so return the address of the array
80  return temps;
81 }
```

CalcAvgTemp.cpp - Find the Average Temperature

```
 1 #include "Pgm03a.h"
 2
 3 /**********************************************************/
 4 /*                                                        */
 5 /* CalcAvgTemp: find the average temperature from         */
 6 /*              an array of numTemps which as at least    */
 7 /*              one element in it                         */
 8 /*                                                        */
 9 /**********************************************************/
10
11 float  CalcAvgTemp (const float temps[], int numTemps) {
12  float sum = 0;
13  for (int i=0; i<numTemps; i++) {
14   sum += temps[i];
15  }
16  return sum / numTemps;
17 }
```

CalcTempRanges.cpp - Find the Max and Min Temperatures

```
 1 #include "Pgm03a.h"
 2
```

115

```
 3 /***********************************************/
 4 /*                                             */
 5 /* CalcTempRanges: find the maximum and minimum temps */
 6 /*                 from an array of numTemps which    */
 7 /*                 has at least one element in it     */
 8 /*                                             */
 9 /***********************************************/
10
11 void   CalcTempRanges (const float temps[], int numTemps,
12                          float& minTemp, float& maxTemp) {
13  minTemp = maxTemp = temps[0];
14  for (int i=1; i<numTemps; i++) {
15   if (minTemp > temps[i])
16    minTemp = temps[i];
17   if (maxTemp < temps[i])
18    maxTemp = temps[i];
19  }
20 }
```

CmpTemps.cpp - qsort() Helper - Compares Two Temperatures

```
 1 #include "Pgm03a.h"
 2
 3 /***********************************************/
 4 /*                                             */
 5 /* CmpTemps: qsort comparison function         */
 6 /*           compares two temperatures         */
 7 /*           returns 0 if temp1 = temp2        */
 8 /*                   1 if temp1 > temp2        */
 9 /*                  -1 if temp1 < temp2        */
10 /*                                             */
11 /***********************************************/
12
13 int    CmpTemps (const void* ptrtemp1, const void* ptrtemp2) {
14  float* ptrt1 = (float*) ptrtemp1;
15  float* ptrt2 = (float*) ptrtemp2;
16  if (*ptrt1 < *ptrt2)
17   return -1;
18  if (*ptrt1 > *ptrt2)
19   return 1;
20  return 0;
21 }
```

CalcMeanTemp.cpp - Find the Mean Temperature

```
 1 #include "Pgm03a.h"
 2
 3 /***********************************************/
 4 /*                                             */
 5 /* CalcMeanTemp: find the median temperature from an */
 6 /*               array of temps that is sorted into  */
```

```
 7 /*                   increasing value order - numTemps    */
 8 /*                   is at least 1                        */
 9 /*                                                        */
10 /**********************************************************/
11
12 float  CalcMeanTemp (const float temps[], int numTemps) {
13  if (numTemps % 2) // odd number of temps
14   return temps[numTemps/2];
15  else // even number of temps
16   return (temps[numTemps/2] + temps[(numTemps-1)/2])/2;
17 }
```

CalcStdDev.cpp - Find the Standard Deviation

```
 1 #include "Pgm03a.h"
 2
 3 /**********************************************************/
 4 /*                                                        */
 5 /* CalcStdDev: find the standard deviation from the       */
 6 /*             Average by summing the squares of the      */
 7 /*             difference of each temp from the avg       */
 8 /*             and taking the sqrt of that over n-1       */
 9 /*                                                        */
10 /**********************************************************/
11
12 float  CalcStdDev (const float temps[],int numTemps, float avg) {
13  float sum = 0;
14  for (int i=0; i<numTemps; i++) {
15   float x = temps[i] - avg;
16   sum += x * x;
17  }
18  return (float) (sqrt (sum / (numTemps-1)));
19 }
```

DisplayResults.cpp - Print the Report

```
 1 #include "Pgm03a.h"
 2
 3 /**********************************************************/
 4 /*                                                        */
 5 /* DisplayResults: prints the final results               */
 6 /*                                                        */
 7 /**********************************************************/
 8
 9 void   DisplayResults (int numTemps, float avgTemp,
10                        float minTemp, float maxTemp,
11                        float meanTemp, float stdDev,
12                        const char* outfileName) {
13  ofstream outfile (outfileName);
14  if (!outfile) {
15   cerr << "Error: cannot open the output file whose name"
```

117

```
16              << " was: " << outfileName << endl;
17    exit (7);
18   }
19
20   outfile << fixed << setprecision (1);
22
23   outfile << "Acme Health Studies - Average Body Temperatures"
24           << endl << endl
25           << "Number    Average   Maximum   Minumum   Median  Standard"
26           << endl
27           << " Temps     Temp      Temp      Temp      Temp   Deviation"
28           << "\n\n";
29
30   outfile << setw(5) << numTemps << setw(9) << avgTemp
31           << setw(9) << maxTemp  << setw(9) << minTemp
32           << setw(8) << meanTemp << setw(8) << stdDev
33           << endl;
34
35   outfile.close();
36 }
```

Notice that I placed all of the needed **#includes** in the program header file along with all of the function prototypes. Then, this header is included in all of the cpp files.

Notice that most all of the functions are indeed very short. Indeed, we could have coded the whole program within the **main()** function. However, I did it this way for several reasons. One, we need more practice in seeing how a program can be composed of multiple cpp files. Two, by using many functions, the **main()** function becomes streamlined and shows the overall program flow or logic much better. Three, by developing larger programs in this fashion, stub testing becomes a breeze. That is, we can write **main()** and the **LoadArray()** functions and stub out the other functions and then run and test the program, guaranteeing that we have the array loaded properly. Then one by one, we can supply the missing function bodies and test each as we go along. The whole process of program development becomes much easier to handle this way.

What about test oracles? Notice that in the initial block comments of the functions, I outlined the incoming specifications. We can easily construct several testing oracles to verify all is working to specifications. However, I left a potential crash error in the program for you to find. The testing oracles that I created are as shown.

temps.txt	11 temperatures should work ok
temps-even.txt	10 temperatures should work ok
temps-baddata.txt	contains a letter where there should be a number
temps-extratemp.txt	contains an extra temperature, count is off
temps-missingdata.txt	lacking one temperature, count is off
temps-outmemory.txt	asks for too much memory

118

temps-zero.txt	asks for 0 elements in the array

There is still one situation, which if it occurs, will crash the program. Look over the coding and the testing oracles and create another testing oracle that would produce that error. The run the program with that oracle and prove that it does crash. Then, revise the program to be able to detect and handle that error.

Review Questions

1. If you have not yet done so, find the remaining error(s) in **Pgm03a** and create a testing oracle that would crash the program. Then sketch a fix that would allow the program to detect and handle that circumstance.

2. Assume that variable **x** is located at memory location 100 and that **ptrx** is located at address 104. Fill in the data types and value of the following expressions.

```
int x = 42;
int* ptrx = &x;
```

Expression	Data Type	Value
x		
&x		
* x		
ptrx		
&ptrx		
*ptrx		

3. A program defined the following.

```
double x;
double y;
double z;
double* prtx;
double* ptry;
double* ptrz;
```

Assume that the memory address of x is 100, y is 108, z is 116, ptrx is 124, ptry is 128 and ptrz is 132. Suppose that the following statements are executed sequentially in order so that their effects are cumulative. Show the new value of any expression whose value is changed by each assignment statement.

	Statement	x	ptrx	y	ptry	z	ptrz	*ptrx	*ptry	*ptrz
1	x = 1.23;									
2	ptry = & y;									
3	y = 42.5									
4	ptrx = &x;									
5	z = 99;									
6	ptrz = &z;									
7	z = *ptrx;									
8	*ptrx = y;									
9	*ptry = *ptrz;									
10	z = y;									
11	*ptrz = 0;									

4. Dynamically allocate memory for each of these and then delete that memory.
   A. a char
   B. an int
   C. an unsigned long
   D. a double
   E. an array of 100 longs
   F. an array of maxStore of doubles
   G. an array of count + 2 characters

5. What advantages are there for dynamically allocating strings within a program? At what point in the program would such strings be deleted?

6. Review the dynamic allocation of the **INVREC** structures which were stored in the array of 1000 pointers example in the text.

```
INVREC* invrec[1000];
int      numRecs = 0;
```

Recall that they were created and filled in this manner.

```
invrec[numRecs] = new INVREC;
while (numRecs<1000 && InputRecord(infile, *invrec[numRecs])){
   ...
   numRecs++;
   invrec[numRecs] = new INVREC;
}
delete invrec[numRecs];
```

Just before the return to DOS instruction, write the instructions that must be done to delete the dynamically allocated inventory records.

Stop! Do These Exercises Before Programming

1. A programmer coded the following function. What is wrong with it and how would you fix it? Careful, there is quite a lot wrong with it.

```
double fun (double x, int num) {
   double* array;
   array = new double [num];
   for (int j=0; j<num; j++) {
      array[j] = x + j;
      sum += array[j] / j;
   }
   return sum;
}
```

2. A program must be written to input all of the cash register sales receipts and perform some statistical studies on them. The first line in the input file contains the number of receipts that this file contains. The input file is produced as the output from another program and can be counted upon to contain no errors or discrepancies, such as missing a receipt.

The programmer began the **main()** function by trying to create the array. The following does not compile. Why? How can it be fixed so that it works?

```
int main () {
   int count;
   double receipts = new double [count];
   cin >> count;
```

3. Frustrated by the failure of only 4 lines of code, the programmer then tried the following.

```
int main () {
   int count;
```

121

```
    cin >> count;
    double receipts = new double;
```
Likewise this did not compile. Why? How can it be repaired so that it would work?

4. Undaunted, the programmer guessed at his error and then tried the following coding. Memory became corrupted and the program did strange things and crashed. Why? How can it be repaired?
```
    int main() {
        int count;
        cin >> count;
        double* receipts = new double;
        for (int k=0; k<count; k++)
          cin >> receipts[k];
```

5. Grateful for your assistance and with the idea of using modular development and stub testing, the programmer next decided to have a **FindAverageReceipt()** function. He created the prototype and a stub body. However, it did not work either. Why? How can it be fixed?
```
    double FindAverageReceipt (double x[], int num);
    int main () {
        int count;
        ...
        double* receipts;
        ...
        double avg = FindAverageReceipt (receipts[count], count);
```

6. Having learned a great deal from your assistance, the programmer successfully implemented several other functions. Now, however, he decided he should check for memory leaks. Sure enough, his program leaked memory. Where is the leak and how can this be repaired?
```
    int main () {
        int count;
        ...
        double* receipts = new double [count];
        ... // loads it
        double avg = FindAverageReceipt (...
        SortIt (receipts, count);
        double mean = FindMean (receipts, count);
        DisplayResults (avg, mean, ...
        return 0;
    }
```

Programming Problems

Problem Pgm03-1—Revised Cost Record Processing (Pgm02-1)

This program revises Problem Pgm02-1—Cost Record Processing. In this version, the main program is to input all the cost records in a file and store them in an array. The object is to allocate no more memory than is needed to hold the data. Two major ways are used to reduce the total memory requirements.

The first way to reduce memory requirements, instead of having an array of 100 **COSTREC** structures, define the array as
```
COSTREC* costRecs [100];
int      numRecs = 0;
```
(Of course, use a **const int** for the limit of 100.) Notice that this is an array of pointers. Each time the main program needs a new **COSTREC** to pass to the **ReadRec()** function to be filled up, dynamically allocate one using:
```
new COSTREC;
```
If **ReadRec()** inputs a record, then **main()** must save the pointer into the next slot in the array of **costRecs** pointers. If it is the end of file, then delete this extra cost record.

The second way memory requirements can be reduced is to avoid wasting memory on the item description strings. Before they were all 31 bytes long whether or not that many characters were actually needed. In this program, modify the **COSTREC** structure's item description member to now be a **char*** and remove the **const int limit** of 31 characters from the header file—place it in the **ReadRec()** cpp file. We are going to store just the number of characters that are entered plus one for the null terminator. In other words, once we know how big this particular item description is, we wish to allocate space to hold it. In this way, we will only be storing the minimum number of characters for each item description.

However, since we are now dynamically allocating memory for the structure which itself contains a dynamically allocated character string, great care must be taken to ensure the character string (description pointer) is initialized. Why, because we must eventually delete all memory we allocate. If a pointer is not initialized and you then try to delete memory using that pointer, a program crash ensues.

Thus, add a new function, **InitRec()**, which is passed first a reference to a **COSTREC** structure followed by a string description (ie, a **char***), followed by the short integers item number and quantity, the **TaxType enum** and lastly the **double** cost. Provide a default value for the description string (or pointer) of NULL or 0. Also, provide default values of 0 for the other items. Now in **InitRec()**, if the passed item description argument is 0, the function sets the passed **COSTREC**'s item description pointer to 0 and sets the other structure member values to 0. This is the initialization step that ensures the pointer has a value. However, if the passed item description in not 0, the function allocates a new string of just the required length to hold the string passed. Use something like

```
new char [len];
```
Don't forget to allow for the null terminator in your length calculations. Then, copy the passed description into this new structure member string along with the other passed values.

InitRec() is going to be called from two locations. First, in the main program loop, after you allocate a new **COSTREC** to be passed to **ReadRec()**, call **InitRec()** to have that structure instance initialized. Then call **ReadRec()** to input the real data. The sequence in **main()** may be something like this:

> open an ifstream in main, pointing it to your test data file (pass it to readRec)
> set the count to 0
> allocate a new COSTREC, storing it in the array at subscript count
> call InitRec to initialize this one
> while the file is still good and ReadRec (passed this new COSTREC) returns the stream
>> in the good state, do the following
>> increment the count
>> allocate a new COSTREC, storing it in the array at the subscript count
>> call InitRec to initialize it
> end while
> delete the extra unneeded COSTREC instance

The **ReadRec()** function still must define a real char string of length 31 in which to input the item description. **ReadRec()** inputs all the data for one **COSTREC** into temporary fields. Then, **ReadRec()** also calls **InitRec()** passing these temporary fields to **InitRec()**. It is **InitRec()**, then, that will actually place all data into this structure instance. **ReadRec()** should not directly input any data directly into this **COSTREC** instance via the file input operation; instead input into temporary fields and call **InitRec()**.

Since we are trying to minimize the memory requirements, if you read in the description string as always 30 characters, you must remove all trailing blanks before you call **InitRec()**. Only store the actual number of characters that are in the actual description with no trailing blanks.

Next, create a **DeleteRec()** function which is passed a reference to a **COSTREC** structure. If the **char* description** member is not NULL or 0, then it will free the string's memory. Then, back in the **main()** function, once the end of file is reached, write a second loop to go through the array and call both **CalcRec()** and **PrintRec()** to produce the same report as before as in Problem 2-1.

Finally, in the main program before you return to DOS, insert as third loop to go through the array once more calling the **DeleteRec()** function passing each instance in the array. This will free the memory allocated by the string description. Then delete each **COSTREC** structure in the array of **COSTREC** pointers.

From this point onward in your programing assignments, you will loose points if you have a memory leak. That is, if you allocate memory and do not free it when you terminate. How you check depends on which compiler you are using. If you are using the Visual C++ compiler, insert a line just before the return to DOS in the main function:

```
if (_CrtDumpMemoryLeaks ())
  cout << "Memory Leaks\n";
else
  cout << "No Memory Leaks\n";
```

Place each of the functions in their own separate cpp file. Thoroughly test your program as usual.

Problem Pgm03-2—Name Processing

A commonly entered field is a person's name. However, names vary greatly in their total length. Commonly, a program that needs to store names dynamically allocates a string that is exactly the right length to hold the current person's name. Often that string is a member of a structure. However, in this problem we are going to concentrate on the mechanics of how to construct the string in the first place.

Write a function **InputName()** that takes an **istream&** and returns a **char***. It defines a character string that is 100 characters long and inputs the next person's name into that string. The name in the input file is delimited by double quote marks. For example, "John Jones." Now, with the name inputted into the string that is fixed at 100 characters, dynamically allocate a new string that is sufficiently large enough to hold this new name. In this case, the new string's array size would be 11—don't forget space for the null terminator. Then, copy the name into the new string and return the address of that new string.

Write a **main()** function that opens the file that I have given you called **names.txt**. Now write a loop that calls **InputName()** to retrieve the next name and then display's that name as shown below along with its **strlen()** value. When the end of file is reached, check for memory leaks.

```
string name
 len
  10    John Jones
  19    Samuel Addison, Jr.
```

Problem Pgm03-3—Customer Order Statistics

Acme wishes a program to perform a statistical study of their customer orders. Input the **orders.txt** file that I have provided and use the following structure.

```
struct ORDERS {
    long custNumber;
    char* name;
    double sales;
};
```

Each line of the data file gives the customer number (a 9-digit number), the customer's name surrounded by double quote marks (" ") and then that order's total sales.

Define an array that can hold 1000 orders. Then call a **LoadArray()** function to load the array from the data file, returning the number actually input on this run. When **LoadArray()** is ready to input the person's name, call the **InputName()** function from Pgm03-2 above. Store the returned pointer to the person's name string in the **name** variable of the current element in the array of orders.

Next, find the average sales, minimum sales, maximum sales, mean sales, and the standard deviation from the mean. Display the results similar to the following.

```
Acme Sales Analysis Report

Average    Minimum  Maximum          Mean  Standard
  Sales      Sales    Sales         Sales  Deviation
$1234.55  $   1.99  $2222.55   $ 500.50     1.22
Highest Sales: John Jones
Lowest Sales: Besty Smith
```

Finally, do not forget to delete all dynamically allocated memory. Before returning to DOS, check for memory leaks. Place each function in its own separate cpp file.

Chapter 4—An Introduction to Classes I

Introduction

Recall from chapter 1, an object is "a thing," an entity. In this chapter we begin our study of programming that is centered upon objects and how they interact. Consider a computer emulation of a car object. It has **properties** associated with it, the **data members**. Some car object properties might be the number of doors, its color, the engine size, its mpg, gas tank capacity, a flag representing whether or not the motor is running, and its current speed. A car object also has **member functions** to perform actions on the car object, such as, start, stop, drive, speed up, slow down, and turn.

Similar to a structure template, a **class** is a model for the compiler to follow to create an object. A class usually has data members that define its various properties and has member functions that perform requested actions. When one creates a specific instance of the car class in memory, one has then a real object. This is called **instantiating an object**. The actions and nomenclature parallel that of a structure. Given an instance of a car, we can then request it to perform various actions, such as starting up and driving.

Recall that the data members and the functions to operate on those data are joined into an inseparable whole, encapsulation. The outside world can utilize the object normally only through its provided member functions. How those actions are actually implemented is totally hidden from the outside world. With this black box approach, ideally one should be able to completely rework the internal algorithms and never touch the client's coding.

With the car, the user might invoke a **StartCar()** function. How the car is actually started is never known nor is it ever a concern to the user. The benefit of encapsulation is large with perhaps the biggest being code reusability.

The member data and functions have a user **access attribute**: **public**, **private**, and **protected**. Specifying **public** access on a data item or function allows the user to use and refer to it. Only public data and functions can be accessed by the user of the object. Sometimes we do not wish the user to be able to access some of the class data and function members; these are given either **protected** or **private** access; these are for our own internal use within our class.

For example, the manner in which we wish to keep track of whether the car is started or not is our own business. The user should not be given public access to that member; instead we give him a function **IsStarted()** which returns **true** or **false**. If we do not like the way we are internally storing the started state, we can change it without affecting the user's code. It is unwise to make data members public for that allows the user to be able to change object state directly; doing so removes a bit of the black box. For then we cannot change these public data members without impacting the users of our class. Member functions are often public so the user can perform actions with the object.

Class Syntax

A class is normally composed of a definition file and an implementation file—that is, a header file and a cpp file. In a later chapter, we will examine alternatives. The definition of a class begins with the keyword **class** which is followed by the name of the class and the begin brace. Class names are usually capitalized while the data member names it contains are usually lowercase. An end brace and semicolon end the definition.

Here is the basic syntax of a class definition.

```
/**********************************************/
/*                                            */
/* name: purpose, etc.                        */
/*                                            */
/**********************************************/

class name {

   /**********************************************/
   /*                                            */
   /* class data                                 */
   /*                                            */
   /**********************************************/

   public:
   protected:
   private:
    data definitions

   /**********************************************/
   /*                                            */
   /* class function                             */
   /*                                            */
   /**********************************************/

   public:
   protected:
   private:
    function prototypes
};
```

Notice that I usually group all of the member data into one area and all of the member functions into another portion. This enables the reader to rapidly find things. If you intersperse data definitions and function prototypes, it becomes more difficult to rapidly find items of interest.

Suppose that we wanted to create a class to encapsulate a simple vehicle, such as a wagon or cart. We can code the following.

```
class Vehicle {
 // here the default access is private unless qualified
};
```

This definition is located in the file **Vehicle.h**; its implementation is in **Vehicle.cpp**.

The Three Access Qualifiers

Every data member and member function has an access qualifier associated with it: **public:** or **protected:** or **private:**.

Rule: By default, everything after the begin brace of the class definition is private.

Public items can be accessed directly by everyone, including the client programs. Certainly the class user interface (member functions) should be public. This represents the main user interface to the object. However, most all of the member data should not be given public access.

Private access is the most restrictive. No client program can ever access private items. Furthermore, if we derive a **Car** class from the **Vehicle** class, the **Car** class inherits all of the member data and functions of the **Vehicle** class. However, those items that are private cannot be accessed from the new derived **Car** class. In general this is way too restrictive. The whole idea of OOP is to create a good hierarchical collection of classes. Thus, one should really make private only those really critical items that even a derived class should not have access to.

If one were creating a linked list of items, the pointer to the head of the list should likely be given private access because if that pointer to the entire list should get messed up, the list is irrevocably corrupted. A reference count is sometimes maintained by a class, tracking how many instances of the class have been created. When that count becomes zero, the class may take special actions. For example, dynamic link libraries (dlls) and ActiveX controls often maintain a reference count so that when no applications are using them, they can unload themselves from memory. Reference counts, in my opinion, should be private in nature.

The third access qualifier is **protected**. Protected items are not accessible by client programs. However, a derived class does have direct access to them. Nearly all of my examples in this text use protected for data member access. Why? If one has done a great job creating a class, then someone else is highly likely to wish to extend it to help handle their situation, that is, to derive another class from it. Private items make the derived class very awkward to implement; the designer must find ways and means to work around the inability to access their own inherited members.

This is one fallacy that is rampant in the OOP textbook arena as well as many magazine articles. One frequently sees all of the data members having private access! Time and time again, I have seen this occur. It is terrible practice because if you have done your programming task well, someone else will want to reuse your class extending it to solve their problem. Private items become

129

a real bane to class derivations as we will see in a later chapter. Thus, right here from the onset, I will make my data members protected, reserving private access for those items I really do not want even a derived class to have access.

For a **Vehicle**, what data members could be defined? Let's keep this simple and track whether or not the vehicle is in motion and how fast it is traveling. We have then the following.
vehicle.h

```
class Vehicle {

  protected:
    bool isMoving;
    int  speed;

  public:

};
```

Now we need some functions. Function fall roughly into three broad categories: constructors/destructor functions, access functions, and operations functions.

Constructors and Destructors

Generally, a class has one or more **constructor** functions and one and only one **destructor** function. The constructor function is called by the compiler when the object is being created and its job is usually to give initial values to this instance's data members. Think of the constructor as getting the object all ready for operations. The destructor function is called by the compiler when the object is being destroyed. Its purpose is to provide clean up actions, such as removal of dynamically allocated memory items or reference count decrementing. Both functions have the same name as the class, except that the destructor has a ~ character before its name.

Neither a constructor nor a destructor function can ever return any value of any kind, not even **void**. A destructor function cannot ever be passed any parameters, ever, and thus cannot ever be overloaded with multiple versions. However, the constructor function can have as many parameters as desired and often is overloaded so that the class can be initialized in a variety of ways. Note that "constructor" is often abbreviated as "**ctor**." Likewise, "destructor" is often called "**dtor**."

> **Rule: All classes must have at least one constructor function whose job is to initialize this instance's member data. It can be overloaded and is always called by the compiler.**

> **Rule: All classes must have a destructor function whose job is to perform cleanup activities. It is called by the compiler when the object goes out of scope and must be deleted.**

Rule: If a class has either no constructor or destructor function, the compiler provides a default constructor or destructor function for you. The provided constructor and destructor do nothing but issue a return instruction.

Remember that overloaded functions are functions whose names are the same but differ in the number and types of parameters being passed to the function. Return data types do not count. Here in the **Vehicle** class the constructor function and destructor function prototypes could be

```
Vehicle ();
~Vehicle ();
```

When designing the constructor functions, give some thought to how the user might like to create instances of your class. With a **Vehicle**, the user might want to create a default vehicle or they might like to create a specific vehicle that is moving down the road at 42 miles an hour. Thus, we should provide two different constructor functions in this case. Here is the class definition with the new functions added. Note that since there is no dynamic memory allocation involved in this class, there is no need to code the destructor function. Let the compiler create a default one which does nothing because there is nothing to delete.

vehicle.h

```
class Vehicle {

  protected:
   bool isMoving;
   int  speed;

  public:
        // creates a default Vehicle
        Vehicle ();

        // creates a specific Vehicle
        Vehicle (bool move, int sped);
};
```

The **default constructor** is a constructor that takes no parameters.

Rule: A class should always provide a default constructor as a matter of good practice.

This default constructor is called when the user wishes to create a default instance. Hence, this is most likely to be the most frequently invoked function in a client program.

Notice the comment lines just above the function prototype. Any comments above the prototypes will be shown by Intellisense! This is a very nice feature of the new compilers! Hence, in the actual coding, I will insert appropriate comments into the definition files. However, in the text portion, I will omit them for brevity.

The Implementation File

These functions are actually implemented in the **Vehicle.cpp** file; they are only defined in the header file. Think about the default constructor's implementation. What should it do? Suppose that in the **Vehicle.cpp** file we coded the following.

vehicle.cpp

```
#include "Vehicle.h"
Vehicle () {           // error
 isMoving = false;
 speed = 0;
}
```

How does the compiler know that this function **Vehicle()** is the constructor that is defined in the header file? As it is coded, it does not know this. The compiler thinks that this is an ordinary C function whose name is **Vehicle**! It does not know that this function actually belongs to the **Vehicle** class. Further, no return data type is coded, so it assumes it returns an **int**.

To show that a data member or a member function is part of a class, we use the **class qualifier** which is the name of the class followed by a double colon—**classname::** To notify the compiler that this function belongs to the **Vehicle** class, we code

```
Vehicle::Vehicle () {
...
}
```

Rule: When you define the member function body, include the classname::

```
returntype   classname::functionname (parameter list) {
 ....
}
```

Rule: any member function has complete access to all member data and functions.

Outside that class, only public members are available (except with derived classes and friend functions). Here is how we could implement the two constructor functions of the **Vehicle** class.

vehicle.cpp

```
#include "Vehicle.h"

Vehicle::Vehicle () {
 isMoving = false;
 speed = 0;
}

Vehicle::Vehicle (bool move, int sped) {
 isMoving = move;
 speed = sped;
}
```

Of course, the implementation in the second constructor function is a bit shaky. Suppose that the caller passed **false** and 42 miles per hour. We are then storing a vehicle that is not moving at 42 miles an hour. Or suppose that the user passed **true** and 0? Ok. We could check on the speed and override the user's request so that the object was not in some silly state. But for simplicity, I am overlooking this situation.

Notice how that within the member functions, we have complete access to all of the member data.

One must be a bit careful of parameter variable names. Suppose that we had coded it this way. We run into a scope of names situation. Specifically, a parameter name hides member names of the same exact name.

```
Vehicle::Vehicle (bool isMoving, int speed) {
  isMoving = isMoving; // error
  speed = speed;       // error
}
```

What is happening is that the parameter variables hide the class member variables of the same name. These two lines are saying to copy the contents of the parameter **speed** and put it into the parameter **speed**. One way around this conflict is to use different names for the parameters as I originally did. However, you can also use the class qualifier to specify which variable is desired.

```
Vehicle::Vehicle (bool isMoving, int speed) {
  Vehicle::isMoving = isMoving;
  Vehicle::speed = speed;
}
```

Since this is a lot of extra coding, the simpler solution is to ensure the parameter names do not conflict with member names.

Access Functions

Because we do not want the user directly accessing any of the protected data members, we must provide some means for the user to access this protected data that we are storing for them. Functions that permit the user to retrieve and change protected data members are called **access functions**. Such functions commonly begin with the prefixes Get . . . and Set . . . If a class is encapsulating a lot of data, then there are a large number of these access type functions.

Consider our **Vehicle** class. What access functions do we need to provide? What data that we are storing would a user need to retrieve or change? In this example, a user of a **Vehicle** object probably needs to access the **isMoving** state and the vehicle's **speed**. Thus, the definition is expanded to include four more functions.

vehicle.h

```
class Vehicle {

protected:
  bool isMoving;
```

```
    int speed;

 public:
        Vehicle  ();
        Vehicle  (bool move, int sped);

   // the access functions
   bool IsMoving ();
   void SetMoving(bool move);

   int  GetSpeed ();
   void SetSpeed (int sped);
};
```

These four new functions are implemented as follows.
vehicle.cpp:

```
#include "Vehicle.h"

bool Vehicle::IsMoving () {
 return isMoving;
}

void Vehicle::SetMoving(bool move) {
 isMoving = move;
}

int Vehicle::GetSpeed () {
 return speed;
}

void Vehicle::SetSpeed (int sped) {
 speed = sped;
}
```

Again, the implementations are oversimplified with respect to the interrelationship between **isMoving** and **speed**. One could also overload the **SetSpeed()** and pass two parameters. The definition and implementation are as follows.

```
void SetSpeed (bool move, int sped);

void Vehicle::SetSpeed (bool move, int sped) {
 is_moving = move;
 speed = sped;
}
```

Finally, have you noticed anything rather unusual about OOP coding? Quite frequently, the implementation of a class consists of a rather large number of extremely short functions, many of which are one-liners!

Instantiating Classes

How are instances of a class instantiated or created in client programs? An instance is defined just like any other data type—just like you would create an instance of a structure. Objects can be of automatic storage type, static, constant and even dynamically allocated. Arrays can be created as well.

main.cpp
```cpp
#include "vehicle.h"
int main () {
 Vehicle a;                  // calls the default constructor
 Vehicle b (true, 42); // calls the overloaded version to create
                        // a vehicle that is moving at 42 mph

 const Vehicle c (true, 55);  // a constant vehicle
 static Vehicle d (true, 60); // a static vehicle

 Vehicle e[100];         // creates an array of 100 vehicles

 // dynamically allocate a vehicle calling the default ctor
 Vehicle* ptrv;
 ptrv = new (std::nothrow) Vehicle;
 delete ptrv;

 // dynamically allocate a vehicle and call the second ctor
 ptrv = new (std::nothrow) Vehicle (true, 42); delete ptrv;

 // allocate an array of Vehicles
 Vehicle* array = new Vehicle [number];
 delete [] array;
```

The next action is to access public data members and call public member functions. The syntax parallels that of structures. How is a member of a structure accessed? By using the dot (.) operator or the pointer operator (->) in the case of a pointer to a structure. The same is true with classes. We use

```cpp
        object_instance.function
```
or
```cpp
        object_instance.data_item
```
If one has a pointer to the object, use
```cpp
        ptr->function
```
or
```cpp
        ptr->data_item
```

The client program can now perform the following actions on its newly created vehicle **a** by coding the following.

```cpp
        a.SetSpeed (100);       // get the car moving
        a.SetMoving (true);     // at 100 miles per hour
        cout << a.GetSpeed (); // display a's speed
```

135

Or if using the vehicle that was dynamically allocated

```
ptrv->SetSpeed (100);      // get the car moving
ptrv->SetMoving (true);    // at 100 miles per hour
cout << ptrv->GetSpeed (); // display a's speed
```

Or if using element j of the array of 100 vehicles

```
e[j].SetSpeed (100);      // get the car moving
e[j].SetMoving (true);    // at 100 miles per hour
cout << e[j].GetSpeed (); // display a's speed
```

Or if using element j of the dynamically allocated array of vehicles

```
array[j].SetSpeed (100);      // get the car moving
array[j].SetMoving (true);    // at 100 miles per hour
cout << array[j].GetSpeed (); // display a's speed
```

Pointer operations for array accessing also work, yielding a faster execution. Define a pointer to the current vehicle and one that points to the last vehicle.

```
Vehicle *ptrThisVehicle = &e[0];
```

or

```
Vehicle *ptrThisVehicle = e; // name of array is const ptr to
                             // the first element as usual
Vehicle *ptrLastVehicle = e + 100;
```

Pointer arithmetic works as normal. Here **ptrLastVehicle** is given the address of the beginning of the array of **e** plus 100 * **sizeof** a **Vehicle** object. Similarly, the ++ and -- operators work as expected. The following sets all vehicles in the array moving at 50 miles per hour.

```
while (ptrThisVehicle < ptrLastVehicle) {
  ptrThisVehicle->SetMoving (true);
  ptrThisVehicle->SetSpeed (50);
  ptrThisVehicle++;
}
```

Only one of the many vehicles created in the **main()** function above causes problems. Have you spotted which one it is? Look at the definition of vehicle **c** once more. This vehicle is defined to be a constant vehicle. If we coded these same function calls, compile time errors result.

```
c.SetSpeed (100);      // error trying to alter a const obj
c.SetMoving (true);    // error trying to alter a const obj
cout << c.GetSpeed (); // error trying to alter a const obj
```

The error message says that the compiler cannot convert a **const Vehicle** to a **Vehicle**. That is, it cannot call a function that may change the member data of an instance when that instance is supposed to be a constant instance. Certainly the compiler is correct on the first two calls above. If vehicle **c** is defined to be constant, then we should not be allowed to change its speed or moving state. However, we also cannot even access in a read-only manner the speed so that we can display it. This factor is addressed and handled below in the Constant Functions section.

Initializing Arrays of Objects

The client program can allocate an array of objects. In the example a few pages above, the **main()** function created an array called **e** as follows.

```
Vehicle e[100];    // array of vehicles
```
In a similar manner, one can create arrays of structures or intrinsic data types, such as **temps** shown below.
```
double temps[100];
```
However, there is a significant difference between these two allocations. What is the content of each element in the array **temps** after it is defined above? No initialization is done and so all elements contain core garbage. Instances of classes behave differently.

> **Rule: When the compiler allocates each instance of a class, it also calls that instance's constructor function to permit that instance to initialize itself!**

Thus, when the compiler allocates the memory for the array **e** above, it then calls the default **Vehicle()** constructor 100 times, once for each instance in the array. Whenever an instance of a class is created, the compiler always gives it a chance to initialize itself.

The same is true when we dynamically allocate an array. Consider the allocation of the array of a variable number of vehicles. We had above
```
Vehicle* array = new Vehicle [number]; // allocate an array
```
Once the compiler has allocated space for **number** of **Vehicle** objects, it then calls the default constructor for each of the **Vehicles** in the array.

It is also possible to specify which constructor function is to be called during array initialization. **Vehicle** has a second constructor that allows the user to specify the initial state. The syntax is shown below.
```
Vehicle d[3] = {Vehicle(false,0), Vehicle(true,50),
                Vehicle(true,30)};
```
Within braces {}, one specifically invokes the desired constructor function passing it the desired parameters. However, if one had a large array to initialize, the syntax would be cumbersome to say the least.

Assigning Instances

Just as one structure instance can be assigned to another structure instance as long as they both have the same structure tag, objects can be assigned as long as they are instances of the same class. Thus, the client program could make a copy of **Vehicle b** as follows.
```
a = b;
```

When an assignment is done, the compiler looks to see if we have provided an assignment operator function. If not, then the compiler itself copies all data members as is. The compiler does a byte-by-byte copy of all of **b**'s data into instance **a**, replacing all of the data stored in object **a**. In the case of the **Vehicle** class, this is just what is desired. This is called a **shallow copy**.

However, if a class has dynamically allocated memory, such as an array, then catastrophic trouble arises, because only the pointer to the memory is copied, not the array itself. Be extra careful when the constructor allocates memory and a destructor frees that memory. Consider this class called **Trouble** which stores a dynamically allocated character string as its member data.

Trouble.h
```
class Trouble {

protected:
 char *ourString;

public:
  Trouble (char* string);
 ~Trouble ();
};


Trouble.cpp
#include "Trouble.h"

Trouble::Trouble (char* string) {
 ourString = new (std::nothrow) char [strlen (string) + 1];
 strcpy (ourString, string);
}

Trouble::~Trouble () {
 delete [] ourString;
}
```

Now consider what happens in **main()** when the assignment operator is required.

main.cpp
```
 . . .
 Trouble s1 ("hello");
 Trouble s2 ("hi");
 s2 = s1;
 return 0;
} // here bad trouble
```
The assignment copies the contents of **s1**'s **ourString** and places it in **s2**'s **ourString**, without freeing **s2**'s initial string. Thus, it leaks all memory allocated by the original **s2** instance. Next, as **main()** ends, both objects go out of scope and are destroyed in the reverse order they were created (both objects are automatic storage instances on **main()**'s stack). The destructor for **s2** is called which deletes the memory to which **ourString** points, which is really the string held in object **s1**. Then, when the compiler calls the destructor for **s1**, it attempts to delete the memory pointed to by **ourString** which has already been deleted; a program crash results.

When dynamic memory allocations are part of class member data, we must provide an assignment operator to handle the situation. Obviously, our new assignment operator function will have to make a duplicate copy of the string. This is called a **deep copy**. We will examine this in great detail later on.

Objects (Instances of a Class) Can Be Passed to Functions and Returned

A function can return an instance of a class. A function can be passed a copy of a class instance. This is exactly the same as structures. We saw with structures, that returning a structure instance or passing a copy of a structure to a function is inherently inefficient in terms of both speed of execution and of memory usage. The same holds true when passing or returning class instances. With structures, we removed these inefficiencies by passing pointers or references to a structure instance. The same is true when passing instances of classes to functions.

Consider the following client C function. Notice how it is passed a copy of a **Vehicle** object and also returns a copy of a **Vehicle** object.

```
Vehicle fun (Vehicle a) { // Vehicle a is a copy of the
                          // object that was passed
  Vehicle b = a;    // copy Vehicle a
  b.SetSpeed (42); // and change its speed
  return b;        // return a copy of b on the stack
}
```

And the **main()** function might call **fun()** as follows.

```
Vehicle newvehicle = fun (b);
```

> **Rule: When passing objects to functions, always pass them by reference whenever possible. Further, if that function is not going to alter the member data of a passed object, pass a constant reference to it.**

In the above example, function **fun()** does not change the passed vehicle **a**. Thus, the function should have been coded this way.

```
Vehicle fun (const Vehicle& a) {
```

> **Rule: When possible, a function should return a reference to an object instead of a copy of the object.**

Again, returning a reference to an object avoids making a duplicate copy of the object to return. However, it is not always possible to return a reference. Consider what would result if this was done in the preceding example.

```
Vehicle& fun (const Vehicle& a) {
  Vehicle b = a;
  b.SetSpeed (42);
  return b;
}
```

And the **main()** function might call **fun()** as follows.

```
Vehicle newvehicle = fun (b);
```

139

When the return is executed, the compiler returns the memory address of the automatic storage instance of **fun()**'s vehicle **b**. But when the end brace of **fun()** is reached, the compiler then deletes all of the automatic storage for function **fun()**. Specifically, vehicle **b** is destroyed. When the compiler next reaches the assignment portion, the reference it has now points to a destroyed, nonexistent vehicle. This rule of returning a reference to an object must be applied to objects that do not go out of scope when the function terminates.

Constant Member Functions

Consider the Get . . . type of access functions. A Get . . . function's purpose is simply to return the value of the indicated property that the class is encapsulating for the user. Under what circumstances could such a Get . . . type access function ever change the data that it is retrieving for the user? None!

> **Rule: Those member functions that do not in any way alter the data being stored in this class instance must be made constant member functions.**

Only member functions can be constant. They are so indicated by placing the keyword **const** after the end of the parameter list. In the **Vehicle** class, the **GetSpeed()** and **IsMoving()** functions should be constant functions. I have highlighted the new keyword in the header file below.
vehicle.h

```
class Vehicle {

 protected:
  bool isMoving;
  int speed;

 public:
        Vehicle  ();
        Vehicle  (bool move, int sped);

   // the access functions
   bool IsMoving () const;
   void SetMoving(bool move);

   int  GetSpeed () const;
   void SetSpeed (int sped);
};
```

Also, these functions must be specified as constant in the implementation file. I have highlighted this addition below.

```
bool Vehicle::IsMoving () const {
  return isMoving;
}

int Vehicle::GetSpeed () const {
```

140

```
 return speed;
}
```

Why do they have to be made constant functions? Users sometimes create constant objects whose properties are supposed to be held constant under all situations. In the case of a **Vehicle** class, suppose the user has created the "pace car" at a race track. Its properties are to be constant, since it is setting the initial launching of the race. The user might code

```
const Vehicle paceCar (true, 80);
cout << paceCar.GetSpeed();
```

If the user now calls **GetSpeed()** on this object, the compiler generates an error unless this **GetSpeed()** member function has been made constant.

If one does not specify **const** in the prototype (and function header), it does not matter whether or not you actually change any member data in the actual implementation file. Remember that when compiling the client program, the compiler sees only the **Vehicle** definition file with the prototype; it cannot look ahead into another cpp file to see if you are really not changing anything; it must depend upon the class function prototype.

Another way a constant object occurs is when the client program passes a constant reference (or pointer) to an object to a function that should not be altering that passed object. For example, suppose that the client race track program had an array of **Vehicle** objects and wanted to call a function, **CalcAverageSpeed()**. It might do so as follows.

```
Vehicle array[100];
int numCars; // current array bounds
double avgSpeed = CalcAverageSpeed (array, numCars);
```

The function is coded as follows.

```
double CalcAverageSpeed  (const Vehicle* array,
                          int numCars) {
 double sum = 0;
 if (!numCars) return 0;
 for (int j=0; j<numCars; j++) {
  sum += array[j].GetSpeed();
 }
 return sum / numCars;
}
```

Here the call to **GetSpeed()** is made on a series of constant objects. If **GetSpeed()** was not a constant function, the compiler would issue an error message about this.

Default Arguments

Suppose that we chose to overload the Vehicle **SetSpeed()** function with another version that allowed for modification of the moving state as well as the speed. We would have

```
void SetSpeed (int sped);
void SetSpeed (bool move, int sped);
```

A very powerful feature is the ability to specify default values for arguments should none be specified. One could also use default arguments on the second version as follows.

```
void SetSpeed (int sped);
void SetSpeed (bool move=false, int sped = 0);
```

Now, when this specific **SetSpeed()** function is called, it can be invoked three ways:

```
a.SetSpeed ();
a.SetSpeed (true);
a.SetSpeed (true, 55);
```

But what would happen if we chose to use default arguments with both functions?

```
void SetSpeed (int sped = 0);
void SetSpeed (bool move=false, int sped = 0);
```

If **main()** chose to call it passing two parameters, all is well, since there is only one overloaded function that takes the two parameters.

```
a.SetSpeed (true, 55);
```

But consider what happens at compile time for this one.

```
a.SetSpeed ();
```

Which function does the compiler invoke? Both versions are equally possible. Thus, an ambiguous function error message results.

Default arguments can also be used with the constructor functions. I could have coded them this way.

```
Vehicle  ();
Vehicle  (bool move = false, int sped = 0);
```

Had I done so, then I would have introduced function ambiguity with the default constructor that takes no parameters. Sometimes, a class designer deletes the default ctor function and uses another ctor function whose arguments are all defaulted. I could have used only this one ctor function.

```
Vehicle  (bool move = false, int sped = 0);
```

It would then serve dual duty, so to speak.

Operations Functions—Handling I/O Operations—A First Look

Under the category of operations functions come all those functions that client programs can use to manipulate the object. I/O operations are often the foremost actions that are usually needed. Comparison functions are frequently required so the client program can compare two instances. In addition, there can be a large number of specialized operations. If one created a Rectangle class, one might need a **GetArea()** function and maybe even a **GetPerimeter()** function.

How can an object be input or output to/from a text file? The insertion and extraction operators are certainly convenient with intrinsic data types, such as longs. However, those operators are discussed in a later chapter on operator overloaded functions. There is an alternate approach that is often used in place of and/or in addition to the insertion/extraction operators. Such member functions are commonly called **Input()** and **Output()**. Please don't despair, learning how to code these functions is actually quite vital; they play a prominent role in inheritance and in getting the insertion and extraction operators to function properly in call such cases!

An **Input()** member function has access to all of the member data. Thus, if it is passed the **istream&** from which to input the data, it can do so, filling up all the member data. Likewise, for the **Output()** function. If it is passed the **ostream&** on which to display, it can display the data members as desired. However, would any output type function ever alter the member data being displayed? No. Thus, the **Output()** function must be made constant.

For our **Vehicle** class, here are the two new prototypes in the header file.
vehicle.h
```
class Vehicle {
 protected:
  bool isMoving;
  int speed;

 public:
        Vehicle  ();
        Vehicle  (bool move, int sped);

   // the access functions
   bool IsMoving () const;
   void SetMoving(bool move);

   int  GetSpeed () const;
   void SetSpeed (int sped);

   istream& Input (istream& is);
   ostream& Output (ostream& os) const;
};
```

The implementation of **Input()** has the additional problem of how to input the **bool isMoving**. The best way is not to input it at all, but input only the **speed** and then set **isMoving** based upon whether or not the vehicle is moving.

Rule: An input function should always leave the object in a stable state, even if bad data is entered!

```cpp
istream& Vehicle::Input (istream& is) {
 is >> speed;
 if (!is) {
  cerr << "Error on inputting vehicle's speed\n";
  // now leave object in a stable state
  speed = 0;
  isMoving = false;
  return is;
 }
 isMoving = speed ? true : false;
 return is;
}
```

An alternative is to input into temporary variables. If all is okay, then assign the temporary variables to the member variables.

```cpp
istream& Vehicle::Input (istream& is) {
 int s;
 is >> s;
 if (!is) {
  cerr << "Error on inputting vehicle's speed\n";
  // now leave object in a stable state
  return is;
 }
 // here all is fine, so make the assignments
 speed = s;
 isMoving = speed ? true : false;
 return is;
}
```

The **Output()** function can be written to match the form of display that the client desires. Let's say that the user wishes to see output similar to the following.

```
The vehicle is not moving.
The vehicle is moving at 42 miles per hour.
```

Then, the **Output()** function would be as shown below.

```cpp
ostream& Vehicle::Output (ostream& os) const {
 if (isMoving)
  os << "The vehicle is moving at " << speed
     << " miles per hour.\n";
 else
  os << "The vehicle is not moving.\n";
```

```
   return os;
}
```

Practical Example 1—The Class Rectangle (Pgm04a)

Let's encapsulate a rectangle. First, we must decide upon what properties we should store. I have chosen to save the length and the width as **double**s. It also stores the user's choice for a name of this rectangle in a character string.

Next, examine how a user might wish to construct an instance of a **Rectangle** class. Certainly, there must be a default constructor that takes no parameters. But also we should provide one that is passed the length and the width the user desires.

Now examine what user access functions should be provided to allow the client to retrieve and alter the length and width we are storing for them. I have chosen to create Get/Set functions for both the length and the width. And I also chose to allow the user to change them both by providing **GetDimensions()** and **SetDimensions()** functions.

Additionally, a rectangle's length and width cannot be negative. Rather than code that verification code in many places, I have opted to create a protected helper function to do that **VerifyNumber()** which can be called to verify both the length and width. Since an error message about negative dimensions must contain which item is incorrect, I pass a character string to it which contains either "length" or "width." Further, the actual class member to be filled with the correct value if all is okay is passed by reference.

The character string poses another problem. Anytime a function is passed a **char***, that pointer could be 0 or null. Also, since there is a maximum number of characters that the class member string can hold, we must guard against too long a user name. This is handled in the **VerifyName()** helper function.

Some means must be provided for I/O operations. Thus, I have an **Input()** and **Output()** pair of functions. However, the client also wishes to have a fancier form of output that looks like this: [10.5, 22.5]. This function I called **OutputFormatted()**.

Finally, what operations would you expect a user to wish to do with a rectangle? Most likely they wish to find the area or the perimeter of the rectangle. Hence, I added **GetArea()** and **GetPerimeter()**.

The next step is to code the **Rectangle** definition file. When all of the function prototypes have been coded, look them over and decide which functions must be made constant member functions and add that **const** keyword to them. Here is the **Rectangle** definition file from **Pgm04a**.

```
Class Rectangle Definition
```

145

```
 1 #pragma once
 2 #include <iostream>
 3 using namespace std;
 4
 5 /*********************************************************/
 6 /*                                                       */
 7 /* Rectangle: encapsulates a rectangle                   */
 8 /*                                                       */
 9 /*********************************************************/
10
11 const int MAXNAMELEN = 21;
12
13 class Rectangle {
14
15   /*********************************************************/
16   /*                                                       */
17   /* class data                                            */
18   /*                                                       */
19   /*********************************************************/
20
21 protected:
22   double length;
23   double width;
24   char   name[MAXNAMELEN];
25
26   /*********************************************************/
27   /*                                                       */
28   /* class function                                        */
29   /*                                                       */
30   /*********************************************************/
31
32 public:
33   // makes a default rectangle
34   Rectangle ();
35   // makes a specific rectangle
36   Rectangle (double len, double wid,
37             const char* nam = "Rectangle");
38
39   ~Rectangle ();
40
41   // Access Functions
42
43   // returns the name of this rectangle as a string
44   const char* GetName () const;
45   // change the name of this rectangle
46   void   SetName (const char* nam);
47
48   // returns the length of this rectangle
49   double GetLength () const;
50   // change the length of this rectangle
51   void   SetLength (double len);
52
53   // returns the width of this rectangle
```

```
54  double GetWidth () const;
55  // change the width of this rectangle
56  void   SetWidth (double wid);
57
58  // returns both the length and width of this rectangle
59  void   GetDimensions (double& len, double& wid) const;
60  // change both the length and width of this rectangle
61  void   SetDimensions (double len, double wid);
62
63  // Operational Functions
64  // returns the area occupied by this rectangle
65  double GetArea () const;
66  // returns the perimeter of this rectangle
67  double GetPerimeter () const;
68
69  // I/O Functions
70  // inputs a rectangle from any input stream
71  istream& Input (istream& is);
72  // outputs the rectangle in a formatted manner
73  ostream& OutputFormatted (ostream& os) const;
74  // outputs the rectangle
75  ostream& Output (ostream& os) const;
76
77 protected:
78   // helper functions
79   // verifies that a length or width is valid and stores it
80   void VerifyNumber (double& number, double val, const char* who);
81   // verifies the new string name is valid and stores it
82   void VerifyName (const char* newname);
83 };
84
```

Next, start the cpp file by copying all of the prototypes into the **Rectangle.cpp** file and removing the semicolons and inserting { } braces. Do not forget to add the **Rectangle::** qualifier to all functions. In this implementation, I chose to log an error message to **cerr** whenever I encountered a negative length or width. And I inserted a value of zero in its place in the corresponding data member. All of the coding is very simple and quite straightforward. Here is the **Rectangle.cpp** file.

```
Class Rectangle Implementation

 1 #include <iostream>
 2 #include <iomanip>
 3 using namespace std;
 4
 5 #include "Rectangle.h"
 6
 7 /**********************************************************/
 8 /*                                                        */
 9 /* Rectangle: default constructor - sets all to 0         */
10 /*                                                        */
11 /**********************************************************/
```

```
12
13 Rectangle::Rectangle () {
14  length = width = 0;
15  name[0] = 0;
16 }
17
18 /***************************************************************/
19 /*                                                           */
20 /* VerifyNumber: helper function to verify val is not        */
21 /*               negative - displays error msg if so         */
22 /*                                                           */
23 /***************************************************************/
24
25 void Rectangle::VerifyNumber (double& number, double val,
26                               const char* who) {
27  if (val >= 0)
28   number = val;
29  else {
30   number = 0;
31   cerr << "Error: a rectangle's " << who
32        << " cannot be less than 0\n";
33  }
34 }
35
36 /***************************************************************/
37 /*                                                           */
38 /* VerifyName:  helper function to verify new name string*/
39 /*              is not 0 or too long - fills up name        */
40 /*                                                           */
41 /***************************************************************/
42
43 void Rectangle::VerifyName (const char* newname) {
44  if (!newname) {
45   cerr << "Error: a null pointer was passed for the name"
46        << " instead of a character string\n";
47   name[0]  = 0;
48   return;
49  }
50  if (strlen (newname) > MAXNAMELEN - 1) {
51   cerr << "Error: name exceeds " << MAXNAMELEN -1
52        << " characters - truncation occurred\n";
53   strncpy_s (name, sizeof(name), newname, MAXNAMELEN -1);
54   name[MAXNAMELEN-1] = 0;
55   return;
56  }
57  strcpy_s (name, sizeof (name), newname);
58 }
59
60 /***************************************************************/
61 /*                                                           */
62 /* Rectangle: makes a rectangle from user's data            */
63 /*            displays error if either is < 0               */
64 /*                                                           */
```

```
 65 /************************************************************/
 66
 67 Rectangle::Rectangle (double len, double wid,
 68                       const char* nam) {
 69  VerifyNumber (length, len, "length");
 70  VerifyNumber (width, wid, "width");
 71  VerifyName (nam);
 72 }
 73
 74 /************************************************************/
 75 /*                                                        */
 76 /* ~Rectangle: destructor - does nothing                  */
 77 /*                                                        */
 78 /************************************************************/
 79
 80 Rectangle::~Rectangle () { }
 81
 82 /************************************************************/
 83 /*                                                        */
 84 /* GetName: returns the name property                     */
 85 /*                                                        */
 86 /************************************************************/
 87
 88 const char* Rectangle::GetName () const {
 89  return name;
 90 }
 91
 92 /************************************************************/
 93 /*                                                        */
 94 /* SetName: sets our name property to a new string        */
 95 /*                                                        */
 96 /************************************************************/
 97
 98 void Rectangle::SetName (const char* nam) {
 99  VerifyName (nam);
100 }
101
102 /************************************************************/
103 /*                                                        */
104 /* GetLength: returns the length of a rectangle           */
105 /*                                                        */
106 /************************************************************/
107
108 double Rectangle::GetLength () const {
109  return length;
110 }
111
112 /************************************************************/
113 /*                                                        */
114 /* SetLength: sets the length, displays error if < 0      */
115 /*                                                        */
116 /************************************************************/
117
```

```
118 void   Rectangle::SetLength (double len) {
119  VerifyNumber (length, len, "length");
120 }
121
122 /**********************************************************/
123 /*                                                        */
124 /* GetWidth: returns the width of the rectangle           */
125 /*                                                        */
126 /**********************************************************/
127
128 double Rectangle::GetWidth () const {
129  return width;
130 }
131
132 /**********************************************************/
133 /*                                                        */
134 /* SetWidth: sets the width - displays error if < 0       */
135 /*                                                        */
136 /**********************************************************/
137
138 void   Rectangle::SetWidth (double wid) {
139  VerifyNumber (width, wid, "width");
140 }
141
142 /**********************************************************/
143 /*                                                        */
144 /* GetDimensions: updates user's fields with length/width*/
145 /*                                                        */
146 /**********************************************************/
147
148 void Rectangle::GetDimensions (double& len, double& wid) const {
149  len = length;
150  wid = width;
151 }
152
153 /**********************************************************/
154 /*                                                        */
155 /* SetDimensions: sets the length and width - errors are */
156 /*                displayed if either is < 0             */
157 /*                                                        */
158 /**********************************************************/
159
160 void   Rectangle::SetDimensions (double len, double wid) {
161  VerifyNumber (length, len, "length");
162  VerifyNumber (width, wid, "width");
163 }
164
165 /**********************************************************/
166 /*                                                        */
167 /* GetArea: returns the area of a rectangle               */
168 /*                                                        */
169 /**********************************************************/
170
```

```
171 double Rectangle::GetArea () const {
172  return length * width;
173 }
174
175 /**********************************************************/
176 /*                                                        */
177 /* GetPerimeter: returns the perimeter of a rectangle    */
178 /*                                                        */
179 /**********************************************************/
180
181 double Rectangle::GetPerimeter () const {
182  return length * 2 + width * 2;
183 }
184
185 /**********************************************************/
186 /*                                                        */
187 /* Input: "name" len wid is the format expected          */
188 /*                                                        */
189 /**********************************************************/
190
191 istream& Rectangle::Input (istream& is) {
192  char nam[MAXNAMELEN];
193  char c;
194  double val1, val2;
195  is >> c;
196  if (!is) return is;
197  is.get (nam, sizeof (nam), '\"');
198  is >> c >> val1 >> val2;
199  if (!is) return is;
200
201  VerifyName (nam);
202  VerifyNumber (length, val1, "length");
203  VerifyNumber (width, val2, "width");
204
205  return is;
206 }
207
208 /**********************************************************/
209 /*                                                        */
210 /* OutputFormatted: displays as name [length, width]     */
211 /*                                                        */
212 /**********************************************************/
213
214 ostream& Rectangle::OutputFormatted (ostream& os) const {
215  os << fixed << left << setw (MAXNAMELEN + 2) << name << right
217    << " [" << setprecision (2) << length << ", " << width << "]";
218  return os;
219 }
220
221 /**********************************************************/
222 /*                                                        */
223 /* Output: displays the name surrounded with " " and     */
224 /*         the length and width with 2 decimals           */
```

```
225 /*          separated by a blank                         */
226 /*                                                       */
227 /******************************************************/
228
229 ostream& Rectangle::Output (ostream& os) const {
230  os << fixed << '\"' << name << "\" " << setprecision (2)
231     << length << " " << width;
232  return os;
233 }
```

The last step is to design a testing program to **thoroughly** test the class before placing it into production by giving it to the user. A testing oracle is highly desirable. Ideally, one should test out all circumstances of the class usage. Specifically, this means at least testing every one of the member functions. In the case of those functions which can report an error or run into execution errors, such as inputting bad data from the input stream, several tests are needed. Please carefully examine the output from the tester program and the tester program (**Pgm04a.cpp**) and see if I did indeed test all of the possibilities. (In actual fact, I did not; I failed to thoroughly test this one. However, that is the topic of a Stop Exercise below.)

```
Pgm04a Rectangle Class Tester Program

 1 #include <iostream>
 2 #include <iomanip>
 3 #include <fstream>
 4 #include <strstream>
 5
 6 #include "Rectangle.h"
 7
 8 using namespace std;
 9
10 int main () {
11  Rectangle a;                    // test default ctor
12  cout << "Default ctor (0,0): " << a.GetLength() << " "
13     << a.GetWidth() << endl;
14
15  Rectangle b (42.42, 84.84); // test overloaded ctor
16  cout << "b's overloaded ctor (should be 42.42, 84.84): "
17     << b.GetLength() << " " << b.GetWidth() << endl << endl;
18
19  double l, w;                    // test GetDimensions
20  b.GetDimensions (l, w);
21  cout << "GetDimemsions: should be the same: "
22     << l << " " << w << endl;
23
24  Rectangle c;                    // test assignment
25  c = b;
26  cout << "Rectangle c should be as b: " << c.GetLength()
27     << " " << c.GetWidth() << endl;
28
29  Rectangle d (1, 2);             // test integers
```

```
30  cout << "Rectangle d should be 1,2: " << d.GetLength()
31       << " " << d.GetWidth() << endl << endl;
32
33  Rectangle e (-1., 4);        // test error length
34  Rectangle f (1, -4.4);       // test error width
35  Rectangle g (-2, -4);        // test error both
36  a.SetLength (-1.1);          // test error length
37  a.SetWidth (-2);             // test error width
38  a.SetDimensions (-1, -2);    // test error both
39  cout << endl;
40
41  a.SetLength (4);             // test SetLength and SetWidth
42  a.SetWidth (8);
43  cout << "SetLen and width check (should be 4,8): "
44       << a.GetLength() << " " << a.GetWidth() << endl;
45
46  a.SetDimensions (9, 10);     // test SetDimensions
47  cout << "SetLen and width check (should be 9,10): "
48       << a.GetLength() << " " << a.GetWidth() << endl << endl;
49
50  // test GetArea and GetPerimeter
51  cout << "Check area (should be 90): " << a.GetArea()
52       << endl;
53  cout << "Check perimeter (should be 38): "
54       << a.GetPerimeter() << endl << endl;
55
56  // test Input function for good and bad data
57  char string[] = "\"Test Input 1\" 10.10 20.20   ";
58  istrstream is (string);
59  a.Input (is);
60  if (!is) {
61   cerr << "Oops: input should be good\n"
62        << a.GetName () << " " << a.GetLength() << " "
63        << a.GetWidth() << endl;
64  }
65  cout << "Input test (should be Test Input 1 10.1 20.2):\n "
66        << a.GetName () << " " << a.GetLength() << " "
67        << a.GetWidth() << endl;
68
69  // test bad input
70  char stringbad[] = "\"Test Input 2\" 30 A";
71  istrstream isbad (stringbad);
72  if (a.Input (isbad).fail()) {
73   cout << "bad data was correctly found\n";
74  }
75  else {
76   cerr << "Oops - bad data not detected in Input function\n"
77        << a.GetName () << " " << a.GetLength() << " "
78        << a.GetWidth() << endl;
79  }
80
81  // testing Output function
82  cout << "\nTest Output: ";
```

153

```
 83  b.Output (cout) << endl;
 84
 85  // testing OutputFormatted function
 86  cout << "Test OutputFormatted: ";
 87  b.OutputFormatted (cout) << endl << endl;
 88
 89  Rectangle m (42,42, "Test name");
 90  m.Output (cout) << endl;
 91
 92  Rectangle n (42, 42, "too long a nameeeeeeeeeeeeeeeee");
 93  n.Output (cout) << endl;
 94
 95  cout << "n's truncated name is |" << n.GetName () << "|" <<endl;
 96  n.SetName (0);
 97  cout << "Should have seen null pointer for name error\n";
 98  n.SetName ("A new Name");
 99  cout << "n's new name is |" << n.GetName () << "|" << endl;
100
101
102  // test file operations
103  cout << "\nTest reading a file\n";
104  ifstream infile ("RectangleTest.txt");
105  while (a.Input (infile)) {
106   a.OutputFormatted (cout) << endl;
107  }
108  infile.close ();
109  cout << "tests done\n";
110
111  return 0;
112 }
```

```
Pgm04a Output Results

 1 Default ctor (0,0): 0 0
 2 b's overloaded ctor (should be 42.42, 84.84): 42.42 84.84
 3
 4 GetDimemsions: should be the same: 42.42 84.84
 5 Rectangle c should be as b: 42.42 84.84
 6 Rectangle d should be 1,2: 1 2
 7
 8 Error: a rectangle's length cannot be less than 0
 9 Error: a rectangle's width cannot be less than 0
10 Error: a rectangle's length cannot be less than 0
11 Error: a rectangle's width cannot be less than 0
12 Error: a rectangle's length cannot be less than 0
13 Error: a rectangle's width cannot be less than 0
14 Error: a rectangle's length cannot be less than 0
15 Error: a rectangle's width cannot be less than 0
16
17 SetLen and width check (should be 4,8): 4 8
18 SetLen and width check (should be 9,10): 9 10
19
```

```
20 Check area (should be 90): 90
21 Check perimeter (should be 38): 38
22
23 Input test (should be Test Input 1 10.1 20.2):
24   Test Input 1 10.1 20.2
25 bad data was correctly found
26
27 Test Output: "Rectangle" 42.42 84.84
28 Test OutputFormatted: Rectangle                    [42.42, 84.84]
29
30 "Test name" 42.00 42.00
31 Error: name exceeds 20 characters - truncation occurred
32 "too long a nameeeeee" 42.00 42.00
33 n's truncated name is |too long a nameeeeee|
34 Error: a null pointer was passed for the name instead of a charac
35 Should have seen null pointer for name error
36 n's new name is |A new Name|
37
38 Test reading a file
39 Rectangle 1             [1.00, 2.00]
40 Rectangle 2             [3.00, 4.00]
41 Rectangle 3             [5.00, 6.00]
42 Rectangle 4             [0.50, 0.50]
43 Rectangle 5             [123.00, 45.00]
44 Rectangle 6             [678.00, 99.00]
45 tests done
46 Press any key to continue . . .
```

Practical Example 2—The Interval Timer Class (Pgm04b)

Suppose that we wished to time how long some action took to execute. The C Standard Library has built-in support for timing. The function **clock()** returns the number of clock cycles that have taken place since the computer was started. The returned data type is **clock_t** which is a **typedef** name for a **long**. The library also provides a constant, **CLOCKS_PER_SEC**, which, if divided into a **clock_t** value, converts it into seconds. The header files are **ctime** or **time.h**.

To construct an interval timer class, what data items are required? It should store the start and ending **clock_t** times. The class constructor can initialize these to 0 or perhaps the current time. The operational functions are **StartTiming()**, **EndTiming()**, and **GetInterval()**. The idea is to invoke **StartTiming()** to initialize the start time member. Then, do the processing we wish to time. When it is finished, invoke **EndTiming()** to set the end time. And call **GetInterval()** to obtain the number of seconds the process required. With these functions, one only needs to allocate a single instance of the **Timer** class in order to be able to time many events.

Here are the **Timer** class definition and implementation files. It is a very simple class but highly useful for timing things.

```
Timer Class Definition

 1  #pragma once
 2
 3  #include <ctime>
 4  using namespace std;
 5
 6  /******************************************************/
 7  /*                                                    */
 8  /* Timer: encapsulates an elapsed time in clock cycles */
 9  /*                                                    */
10  /******************************************************/
11
12  class Timer {
13
14  protected:
15    clock_t startTime;    // the starting time of the interval
16    clock_t endTime;      // the ending time of the interval
17
18  public:
19    Timer();              // initializes the two times to 0
20
21    // reset the starting time value to begin monitoring
22    void StartTiming ();
23
24    // resets the ending time value at the end of the interval
25    void EndTiming ();
26
27    // returns the measured interval in seconds
28    double GetInterval () const;
```

```
29
30 };
31
```

```
Timer Class Implementation

 1 #include "Timer.h"
 2
 3 /*****************************************************************/
 4 /*                                                             */
 5 /* Timer: ctor that sets the two times to 0 clock cycles       */
 6 /*                                                             */
 7 /*****************************************************************/
 8
 9 Timer::Timer() {
10   startTime = endTime = 0;
11 }
12
13 /*****************************************************************/
14 /*                                                             */
15 /* StartTiming: sets startTime to the current time at the      */
16 /*              beginning of the interval to monitor           */
17 /*                                                             */
18 /*****************************************************************/
19
20 void Timer::StartTiming () {
21   startTime = clock ();
22 }
23
24 /*****************************************************************/
25 /*                                                             */
26 /* EndTiming: sets endTime to the current time at the end      */
27 /*            of the interval to be monitored                  */
28 /*                                                             */
29 /*****************************************************************/
30
31 void Timer::EndTiming () {
32   endTime = clock ();
33 }
34
35 /*****************************************************************/
36 /*                                                             */
37 /* GetInterval: returns the interval just timed in seconds     */
38 /*                                                             */
39 /*****************************************************************/
40
41 double Timer::GetInterval () const {
42   return ((double) (endTime - startTime)) / CLOCKS_PER_SEC;
43 }
```

Next, we need something to time. I have chosen to find out just how much faster it is to use a pointer to access the elements in an array of objects than using the traditional subscript approach. The objects are rectangles. I have simply copied the **Rectangle** class definition and implementation files from **Pgm04a** into this new project folder, **Pgm04b**. No changes are required in the **Rectangle** class.

The code to time consists of setting the dimensions of 1000 **Rectangle** objects and outputting the resultant area. The first version uses subscripts to access each element in the **Rectangle** array. The second version uses a pointer to point to each successive element; to move to the next element in the array, I use **ptrThis++**.

I create a single instance of the **Timer** class and invoke the **StartTiming()** method. After the subscript processing loop is finished, I call the **EndTiming()** method to set the ending time and invoke **GetInterval()** to acquire the total elapsed time for the loop in seconds. Then, the process is repeated for the pointer version. When that loop has finished and its interval acquired, the program then prints a short report of the results.

Here is **Pgm04b** and a sample output run that is abbreviated showing the last few lines. Are the results what you expected?

```
Pgm04b - Timing Subscript Versus Pointer Array Access

 1 #include <iostream>
 2 #include <iomanip>
 3 using namespace std;
 4
 5 #include "Timer.h"
 6 #include "Rectangle.h"
 7
 8 /*************************************************************/
 9 /*                                                         */
10 /* Pgm04b: measure the difference in execution speed       */
11 /*         between using subscript array accesses and      */
12 /*         using pointer array accessing methods           */
13 /*                                                         */
14 /*************************************************************/
15
16 const int MAXRECTS = 1000; // maximum number of rectangles
17
18 int main () {
19   Rectangle array[MAXRECTS];
20   int i;
21
22   Timer timer;            // the single Timer object
23   timer.StartTiming ();   // begin timing the subscript version
24
25   for (i=0; i<MAXRECTS; i++) {
26    array[i].SetDimensions (i, i);
27    cout << array[i].GetArea() << endl;
```

```
28  }
29
30  timer.EndTiming ();       // mark the end of the subscript timing
31  double subscripts = timer.GetInterval (); // get its duration
32
33  timer.StartTiming ();     // begin timing the pointer version
34
35  i = 0;
36  Rectangle* ptrThis = array;
37  Rectangle* ptrEnd = array + MAXRECTS;
38  while (ptrThis < ptrEnd) {
39   ptrThis->SetDimensions (i, i);
40   cout << ptrThis->GetArea () << endl;
41   ptrThis++;
42   i++;
43  }
44
45  timer.EndTiming ();       // mark the end of the pointer timing
46  double pointers = timer.GetInterval (); // get its duration
47
48  // display a simple report of the results
49  cout << endl << "Release Build Run Timings\n";
50  cout << "Subscripts version total time: " << subscripts
51       << " seconds\n";
52  cout << "Pointers version total time:  " << pointers
53       << " seconds\n";
54  cout << "Elapsed time difference:      " << subscripts-pointers
55       << " seconds\n";
56
57  return 0;
58 }
```

```
Results of Timing Subscript Versus Pointer Array Access 1.6GHz CPU

 1 ...
 2 996004
 3 998001
 4
 5 Release Build Run Timings
 6 Subscripts version total time: 0.34 seconds
 7 Pointers version total time:   0.16 seconds
 8 Elapsed time difference:       0.18 seconds
 9
10 For a 3 GHz CPU:
11 Subscripts version total time: 0.469 seconds
12 Pointers version total time:   0.25 seconds
13 Elapsed time difference:       0.219 seconds
```

Review Questions

1. Reflecting upon member data and member functions, how do member data obviate the need for global variables or the passing a large amounts of data to a series of functions?

2. Why should most member data have the protected (or private) access qualifier?

3. How does encapsulation impact class design? What is its benefit to the programmer of a class and to the client of the class?

4. What is meant by polymorphism? Of what use is it in class function design?

5. What are the parallels in coding syntax between **struct CostRec** and **class CostRec**?

6. What is a constructor function? What is its purpose? How many constructors can a class have?

7. What is a destructor? What is its purpose? How many destructors can a class have? Why?

8. Why is the class qualifier, such as **Vehicle::**, needed in the implementation file?

9. What is the purpose of access type member functions? Give an example. Why are they needed?

10. What is the purpose of operation type member functions? Give an example.

11. Ignoring the initialization aspect, compare how a client program can create instances of a structure called **CostRec** and a class called **InventoryRec**.

12. Why is the use of default arguments useful? What problems does the use of default arguments pose when such functions are overloaded?

13. What is the difference between the two uses of the **const** key word shown below?
```
class Point {
protected:
  int x;
  int y;
public:
  Point ();
  long AvgPoints (const Point& p);
  long SumPoints () const;
};
```

14. What happens if a class has no constructor functions? What happens if it has no destructor functions?

160

15. What is meant by a default constructor? For a class **Dog**, write the prototype for the default ctor. Why should every class have a default ctor?

16. If the parameter names being passed to a member function are the same as member data names, how can that function access its members with the same names as the parameters?

17. Assuming **Dog** is a class, the **main()** function codes the following.
```
Dog dogs[1000];
```
Is any ctor called? If so, how many times is the ctor called?

18. Assuming the array of dogs in question 17, is the following legal, assuming the subscripts are within range? If so, what does it do?
```
dogs[i] = dogs[i+1];
```

19. What is the difference between a shallow copy and a deep copy operation when assigning objects?

20. Why is it preferable to always pass a reference or a constant reference to an object to a function instead of passing a copy of that object?

21. What is a constant member function? Why do some member functions need to be constant? Could not all member functions be made constant?

Stop! Do These Exercises Before Programming

1. Look over the **Pgm04a** testing program. What major feature covered in this chapter concerning the use of instances of objects did I fail to test in any way whatsoever? What about constant objects? Sketch out some additional tests and perhaps a client function call that would guarantee that **Rectangle** is properly supporting constant objects.

2. A programmer decided to encapsulate a geometric point object by writing a class called **Point**. He began with the following design. There are several design flaws with what has been actually coded thus far. Point out these flaws and show a more optimum way to code the definition.
Point.h
```
Class Point {
  int x;
  int y;
public:
  Point ();
  Point (int x, int y);

  Point GetPoint ();
  void  SetPoint (int x, int y);
  void  SetPoint (Point& p);
}
```

3. The programmer decided to add the ability to I/O a point. He added the following two member function prototypes. What is wrong with them and how should they be corrected?

```
class Point {
...
  void InputPoint (istream infile, int x, int y);
  void OutputPoint (ostream outfile, Point& p);
```

4. The programmer decided to use overloaded functions with default arguments. He added the following member prototypes. What is inherently non-optimum with these new functions as coded? Could they be repaired to be productive?

```
class Point {
...
  void SetPoint (int xx, int yy);
  void SetPoint (int xx, int yy = 0);
  void SetPoint (int xx = 0, int yy = 0);
```

5. The programmer created two tester functions to be called from the **main()** function. What is non-optimum about the coding? How can it be repaired?

```
void SumPoints (Point& p, long& totalX, long& totalY,
                long& count) {
  totalX += p.x;
  totalY += p.y;
  count++;
}

Point MakePoint (int x, int y) {
  Point p (x+42, y+42);
  return p;
}
```

6. The programmer gave up on overloaded functions and wrote the following implementations. What is wrong with the coding and how can it be fixed?
Point.cpp

```
void SetPoint (int xx, int yy) {
  x = xx;
  y = yy;
}

void GetPoint (int xx, int yy) const {
  xx = x;
  yy = y;
}
```

7. Next the programmer attempted to implement the constructors but failed. How can they be corrected so that the constructors work fine?
Point.cpp

```
void Point::Point (int x, int y) {
```

162

```
  x = x;
  y = y;
}

void Point::Point () {
  x = y = 0;
}
```

Programming Problems

Problem Pgm04-1 —A Date Class—I

The objective is to construct a class to encapsulate a calendar date. I provide the interface that you must meet; the internal details of how you wish to support that interface are completely up to you. However, do not store the date as three integers. In future chapters, you will be asked to modify this beginning problem to add new features. Eventually, the **Date** class will be able to handle addition and subtraction of a number of days from the date and so on. If you store the data as three integers, future programs will be very hard to implement. It is highly recommended that you store the date as a long serial date; see below.

The Interface for the Date Class

The name of the class is **Date** and it is to store and manipulate a calendar date. The user creates a **Date** object as follows. (Note in the next chapter, other alternate methods of constructing a **Date** will be added.) There are no constructor or destructor functions in the class at this time.

```
      Date date;
```
or
```
      Date *ptrdate = new Date;
```

Provide the Following Public Member Functions

```
      void SetDate (int month, int day, int year);
```
SetDate() should set your internal date to the passed date. If the year is less than 100, then add 1900 to the year; thus, a year of 97 would really be 1997. (It is not "year 2000" compliant.)

```
      void GetDate (int &month, int &day, int &year);
```
GetDate() should return the current date you are storing converted into month, day and year filling up the three reference parameters. The year should be a 4-digit number.

```
      void FormatDate (char *string, unsigned int max_string_len);
```
FormatDate() fills the string with a formatted date, such as " 01/10/1997". The parameter, **max_string_len**, contains the maximum length of the caller's string including the null terminator. If the string is too small to hold the formatted date, place as much as will fit including a null terminator. The idea is to avoid overwriting memory should the user give the function too small a

163

string to fill. There are a number of ways you can handle this. However, the easiest method is to utilize an instance of **ostrstream** wrapped around the user's string.

```
long DateToSerial (int month, int day, int year);
```
DateToSerial() returns the number of days since November 25, 4713 BC.

```
void SerialToDate (int &month, int &day, int &year);
```
SerialToDate() fills up the month, day and year from a long serialized date which is assumed to be a class member.

Serialized Dates

When comparing, adding a number of days to a date, and finding the number of days between two dates, it is very convenient to convert the date into a long integer number of days from some given point in time. In this case I use November 25, 4713 BC as the starting point. I am providing two C style helper functions that you may use as models for your above two member functions. You may cannibalize them as you see fit. The C functions are located in the **TestDataForAssignments Pgm04-1** folder.

Additional Requirements for the Date Class

Create two files: **Date.h** and **Date.cpp**. Cannibalize the **datehlpr.cpp** file—do not include this file nor its C style functions in your project. Rework them into your two member functions.

You may assume that all dates are correct so no error checking need be done. You may write any additional helper functions to simplify the main interface actions and to avoid repetitious coding.

Make sure you use the **const** keyword where appropriate. That is, make all parameter pointers or references that are not changed constant. Make all member functions that do not alter the object constant as well. This means the above prototypes I have given you could be changed by adding in **const** where you deem appropriate.

Write a Main Program Tester Application

Also, located in the **TestDataForAssignments Pgm04-1** folder is the testing file, **dates1.txt**. Write a main program that thoroughly tests your class. You may add additional test lines to the testing file. The **dates1.txt** file consists of one date per line in month, day and year order, separated by a blank. Assuming that you read in the date 1 2 1601, for each of these dates printout the following.

```
date            date from    date from    date to      date from
input           GetDate      FormatDate   serial       serial

 1   2 1601     01/02/1601   01/02/1601   9999999      01/02/1601
```
Note: in the date to serial column, the 99999's represent whatever that number should be.

You may add in any additional testing as you deem appropriate to thoroughly test your class. When using **cin** or an **ifstream** instance to input an integer that can have leading 0's as in 02 or 08 month numbers, one time only do

```
cin >> dec;
```

or

```
infile >> dec;
```

This tells the input stream class that the data with leading zero's are really decimal numbers. The default is leading 0's imply octal numbers.

Additionally, the date to serial column in the main program is problematical. **main()** should not have access to the protected/private data members. You may handle this in any way you see fit. You could temporarily make that data member public or provide a constant member function that just returns that long value.

Here is the C style coding to convert dates to and from the long serial date. It has been adapted from FORTRAN coding *Communications of the ACM*, Vol 11, No 10 October 1968, page 657 by Fliegl and Van Flanders.

```
/*********************************************************************/
/*                                                                   */
/* date2serial: converts a calendar date to a serial number that may be  */
/*              used in date arithmetic.                             */
/*                                                                   */
/* Arguments:   a month, a day, and a year (in that order, all int's).  */
/*                                                                   */
/* Returns:     a long int representing the same calendar date as   */
/*              the number of days elapsed since November 25, 4713 B.C.  */
/*                                                                   */
/*********************************************************************/

long    date2serial (int mo, int day, int yr) {
 return day - 32075L + 1461L * (yr + 4800 + (mo - 14L) / 12L) / 4L
       + 367L * (mo - 2L - (mo - 14L) / 12L * 12L) / 12L
       - 3L * ((yr + 4900L + (mo - 14L) / 12L) / 100L) / 4L;
}


/*********************************************************************/
/*                                                                   */
/* serial2date: converts a date serial number to the date's         */
/*              month, day, and year.                                */
/*                                                                   */
/* Arguments:   a date serial number (long int) and pointers to     */
/*              month, day, and year variables (int*)                */
/*                                                                   */
/* Results:     the month, day, and year variables are assigned      */
/*              the calendar date corresponding to the date serial number */
/*                                                                   */
/*********************************************************************/

void    serial2date (long serial, int *ptrmo, int *ptrday, int *ptryr) {
 long t1, t2, m, y;

 t1 = serial + 68569L;
 t2 = 4L * t1 / 146097L;
```

```
t1 = t1 - (146097L * t2 + 3L) / 4L;
y  = 4000L * (t1 + 1) / 1461001L;
t1 = t1 - 1461L * y / 4L + 31;
m  = 80L * t1 / 2447L;
*ptrday = (int)(t1 - 2447L * m / 80L);
t1 = m / 11L;
*ptrmo = (int)(m + 2L - 12L * t1);
*ptryr = (int)(100L * (t2 - 49L) + y + t1);
}
```

Problem Pgm04-2 —A Circle Class

Design, implement, and test a class that encapsulates a **Circle** object. It should have three data members: its radius and the integer x, y coordinates of its center. There should be a default constructor and a constructor that takes the necessary three parameters to define a circle object. Provide proper access functions for the user to retrieve and modify the three properties. **Circle** operations include obtaining the area of the circle, its circumference, and the ability to input and output a **Circle** object.

The input stream containing a **Circle** object consists of two integers for the coordinates (x, y) followed by a **double** representing the radius. The output is more formalized. It should appear as follows:
```
Circle at [xxx, yyy] of radius rrrr.rr
```
Always show two decimals in the radius.

Next, add a function, **CompareRadius()**, which returns an **int** as follows.
    0 means the two circles have the same radius
    + value means the member circle has a larger radius than the passed circle
    – value means the member circle has a smaller radius than the passed circle
Its prototype is
```
int CompareRadius (const Circle& c) const;
```
Now write a tester program to thoroughly test the **Circle** class.

Problem Pgm04-3 —An Employee Class

Acme Corporation wishes a class to encapsulate their employee workforce. The **Employee** class contains the employee first and last name strings which should include a maximum of 10 and 20 characters respectively. The date that he or she was hired should be stored as three **short**s. His/her job title is a string of up to 20 characters. His/her age and sex should be stored as **char** fields. His/her pay rate is stored in a **double** and the pay type is a **char** containing an H or S for hourly or salaried. If he or she is an hourly worker, the pay rate is the hourly rate. If he or she is a salaried worker, the pay rate is the uniform amount that he or she is paid each week. Finally, his or her employee id number is stored as a **long**.

The class should have a default constructor and a constructor that is passed all of the relevant data needed to initialize an employee object. Provide access functions for all of the data members.

Write an **Input()** function that is passed a reference to an **istream** from which to input the data. One blank separates each field on input. All strings are padded with blanks to the maximum length of that particular string. That is, if the first name was Sam, on the input it would appear as Sambbbbbbb where the b represents a blank. The order of the fields on input is as follows.

id number, first name, last name, job title, mm/dd/yyyy, age, sex, pay rate, pay type

Note that there are / separating the elements of the hired date.

Write a **Pay()** function that calculates and returns the employee's weekly pay. Its prototype should be

```
double Pay () const;
```

Write a tester program to thoroughly test the class functions.

When that is working properly, then write the client Weekly Pay Program. Use the file that came with the book called **Problem4-3-WeeklyPay.txt** as the input file. The pay program inputs all of the employee records into an array of **Employee** objects. Allow for a maximum of 50 employees in the array. Then, for each employee in the array, calculate and print their pay as shown below.

```
                    Acme Weekly Payroll Report
Employee   First       Last                    Date        Weekly
    Id     Name        Name                    Hired       Pay

 1123123   John        Jones                   05/12/1994  $9999.99
...
Total Payroll --------------------------------> $999999.99
```

The last line represents the total amount that all of the employees are paid.

Problem Pgm04-4 —A Bank Account Class

Acme First National Bank wishes a new basic **BankAccount** class to be written. The class contains a long account number, the current balance and the accumulated total fees for this month.

Provide a default constructor and one that takes the three parameters necessary to properly initialize an account. Create access functions to get and set each of the three properties. Create input and output functions to handle I/O of a bank account. On input, the account number comes first, followed by the balance and fees. On output, display the fields in the same order, but with each field 10 columns wide and separated by five blanks.

The operations member functions consist of **Deposit()** and **Withdrawal()**. We are ignoring any possible interest in this overly simplified problem. The **Deposit()** function is passed a positive amount to be added to the current balance and it returns the new balance.

The **Withdrawal()**function is more complicated; it is passed the withdrawal amount and a reference to the service charge that will be applied to the account for this transaction. The function returns **true** if the withdrawal was successful or **false** if there are insufficient funds for this transaction. The service charge is $0.10 per withdrawal as long as the balance is below $500.00. There is no service charge if the balance is $500.00 or above. If the withdrawn amount plus any service charge would take the balance below $0.00, then the withdrawal is not made; instead a service charge of $25.00 is applied to the account and the function returns false. Note that the service charges are always applied to the balance with each transaction. They are accumulated as well for later monthly display. The service charge for this transaction is stored in the passed reference variable for the client program's use.

Next, write a tester program to thoroughly test the new class.

When you are satisfied that the class is working correctly, write the client program to process a day's transactions. There are two files provided with this text. The first file, **Problem4-4-BankAccounts.txt**, contains the initial bank accounts at the start of the day. The program should load these into an array of up to 50 bank account objects. Next, the program should input the transaction's file, **Problem4-4-Transactions.txt**. Each line in the transaction's file contains a character, D for deposit or W for withdrawal. This letter is followed by the account number and then the monetary amount to be deposited or withdrawn. For each transaction, attempt to process it. Display the results in a report as shown below. When the end of the file is reached, then output a new version of the bank accounts for use in the next day's processing.

```
Account   Type  Amount      Status   Service Charge
1234567    W    $ 100.00    Okay        $ 0.10
1234546    D    $  50.00    Okay        $ 0.00
1234556    W    $1000.00    Failed      $25.00
```

Problem Pgm04-5 —A Distance Class – I

Write a **Distance** class to encapsulate linear distances. You may store the distance in any format you choose. For example, you might save the distance as a **double**, the total distance in millimeters. The header file should be called **Distance.h** and the implementation file **Distance.cpp**.

Provide the Following Constructors
a default constructor with no parameters, use 0 as the distance
accept a **long** number of millimeters
accept a trio of **long**s containing meters, centimeters, and millimeters
accept a pair of **int**s containing feet first and inches second
accept a **double** representing miles
There is no destructor.

Create Public Member Functions as Follows
GetDistance() returns a **double** which is the distance you are storing converted to millimeters

SetDistance() which accepts a **double** millimeters – set the stored distance accordingly

MtoE() which returns a **double** representing the feet that this distance represents
EtoM() which is given two **int**s, feet and inches, and returns the **double** millimeters
EtoM() which is given a **double** miles and returns the **double** millimeters
Paint() which is given a **char** which is used to determine how to print the distance
> display the distance as "Distance is nnn units\n"
> ```
> M or m -> print in millimeters
> F or f -> print in feet
> I or i -> print in meters and millimeters
> L or l -> print in miles
> ```
> for example:
> ```
> cout << "Distance is = " << mm << " millimeters\n";
> ```

Unless you have an alternative, use the following to convert meters to feet
```
const double MTF = 3.280833;
```

The Main Testing Program

Create a main program to thoroughly test the **Distance** class. Include at least the following tests as well as your additional ones:
```
Distance a;
Distance b (1000.);
Distance c (100L, 50L, 8L)
Distance d (10, 11);
Distance f (1.23);
a.SetDistance (1234.);
```

169

```
cout << "1234 mm equals " << a.MtoE () << " feet\n";
cout << "Testing GetDistance for object a - 1234 mm = "
     << a.GetDistance () << " mm\n";
```

Now use these 5 objects and thoroughly test the **Paint()** function. Next, test assignment:

```
a = b;
cout << "a should now be the same as b:\n"
a.Paint ('M');
b.Paint ('M');
```

Now test passing and returning objects to functions.

```
a = fun (c);
cout << "a should now be the same as c:\n"
a.Paint ('M');
c.Paint ('M');
```

Use the following for the function.

```
Distance  fun  (const Distance &x) {
 Distance y, z;
 cout << "fun: passed value: ";
 x.Paint ('M');
 y = z = x;
 y.SetDistance (1234.);
 cout << "fun: altered value: ";
 y.Paint ('M');
 return z;
}
```

Chapter 5—An Introduction to Classes II

Introduction

First we examine how a class can use an instance of another class as a data member. Back in chapter 2 we discovered the need for **#ifndef-#define** or **#pragma once** logic in header files. This same need is carried forward into class definition files as well. We must examine the impact of having a class which includes an instance of another class versus one which uses a reference or pointer to an instance of another class. Next, we must examine just how a member function can actually find the member data on which to operate.

Enumerated data types are extremely useful for adding clarity to a program. An **enum** can be physically a part of a class definition. That is, the **enum** itself may belong to a class and is called a **class enum**. In OOP programming, the use of **class enums** is widespread and becomes a very powerful feature. We will see how an ordinary C style nonmember function can be granted the ability to access a class's private member data.

Classes may have constant data members as well as static data members and reference variables to other items. However, their usage imposes some restrictions upon class initialization. A class may also have static member functions which can utilize the static data members.

We examine how short member functions can have their execution speed increased. The compiler does perform some amazing implicit type conversions when classes are involved. In the practical example, all of the new principles are put to use as an operational dice rolling set of classes are built. Finally, we explore how production libraries of operational classes can be built.

Using Instances of Another Class as Data Members in Another Class

Commonly, one class may use an instance of another class as one of its data members. A class to encapsulate a circle would certainly have a radius data member, but it might also have an instance of a **Point** class which is used to mark the origin or center of the circle in a two-dimensional space.

For example, the definition file of the **Point** class might be as follows.

Point.h

```
class Point {
protected:
 int x;
 int y;

public:
```

```
Point ();
...
};
```

If the **Circle** class desires to have an instance of the **Point** class as one of its members, then the **Circle** definition file must include the **Point** class definition file so that the compiler knows how much memory a **Point** object requires.
Circle.

```
#include "Point.h"
class Circle {
protected:
  double radius;
  Point origin;

public:
  Circle ();
...
};
```

Notice that the **Circle** class is actually a client of the **Point** class just as the **main()** function has been a client of the classes discussed thus far.

Using #ifndef-#define or #pragma once Logic in Class Header Files

Back in chapter 2, we discovered the need to guarantee that a specific definition, then of a structure, was copied only one time into a given cpp implementation file. The same is even more true when dealing with class definitions. A very common practice in OOP is to include instances or references to instances of other classes or structures within a given class definition.

Consider for example, designing an **Employee** class. One of its data members would likely be a date, such as their hired date. Very often, a company already has an existing **Date** class to encapsulate a date and provide standardized support for date operations. Notice that the **Employee** class is now considered a client of the **Date** class, just like the **main()** function has been the client program thus far. However, duplicate **Date** class definitions can very easily occur when **#ifndef** logic is not used. Consider the following skeletal class coding.
Date.h

```
class Date {
...
};
```

Employee.h

```
#include "Date.h"
class Employee {
...
  Date hiredDate;
```

172

```
      ...
      };
payroll.h
      #include "Date.h"
      class Payroll {
      ...
       Date payrollDate;
      ...
      };
main.cpp
      #include "Date.h"
      #include "Employee.h"
      #include "Payroll.h"
      int main () {
       Date today;
       Employee employee;
       Payroll payroll;
      ...
      }
```

As you can see, in **main.cpp**, three copies of the definition of the **Date** class are brought in by the compiler which results in a compile-time error. Okay, in this overly simplified example, **main()** does not need to include **Date.h** because it is coming in from **Employee.h**. True. But then **Payroll.h** also needs it and must include it or that header will not compile. However, let's add another class to **main.cpp**, **YTDPay** (year to date pay), which encapsulates the yearly accumulated pay of the employees. This class would also have one or more **Date** instances as data members and would be also including **Date.h** in its header. The situation just gets worse and worse. As you know by now, the solution is to use **#ifndef** logic around the entire class definition or the **#pragma once** statement.

> **Rule: Always wrap a class definition with #ifndef logic or #pragma once to avoid any future possibility of duplicate definitions.**

Thus, the above example should have been coded as follows.

Date.h
```
      #pragma once
      class Date {
      ...
      };
```
Employee.h
```
      #pragma once
      #include "Date.h"
      class Employee {
      ...
       Date hiredDate;
      ...
      };
```

payroll.h
```
#pragma once
#include "Date.h"
class Payroll {
...
 Date payrollDate;
...
};
```
main.cpp
```
#include "Date.h"
#include "Employee.h"
#include "Payroll.h"
int main () {
 Date today;
 Employee employee;
 Payroll payroll;
...
}
```
Now only one copy of the **Date** class definition is included by the compiler in **main.cpp**.

The this Pointer

Suppose I had four instances of the **Vehicle** class from chapter 4 called, **a**, **b**, **c** and **d**. There is only one code area for each of the member function; the machine instructions of the functions are the same for every instance of the class. However, there must be four separate member data areas, one for each of the four **Vehicle** objects. It does not make sense to carry along a copy of constant code (member functions) with each object instance. Figure 5.1 shows the layout of memory for these four **Vehicle** objects.

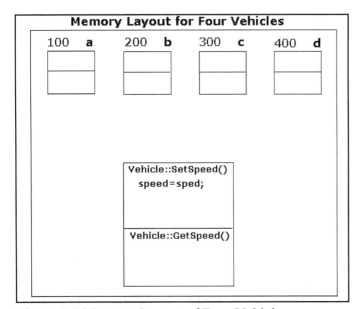

Figure 5.1 Memory Layout of Four Vehicles

Here **Vehicle a** is located at memory location 100. Its two member data, **isMoving** and **speed**, are shown. Similarly the other three vehicles are at locations 200, 300 and 400. Consider what happens when the **main()** function does

```
a.SetSpeed (50);
```

How does that common code, the **SetSpeed()** member function in this case, know where to find the data for object **a**—that is to set **a**'s **speed**? Without some help, it cannot know where object **a** is located and thus cannot place a new value into **a**'s **speed**!

The C++ language handles this situation by defining and passing a very special constant pointer that contains the memory location of the object in question. The pointer is called **this** and it is automatically passed to any member functions by the compiler. Actually, it is a hidden first parameter to member functions. When we code

```
a.SetSpeed (50);
```

The compiler obtains the address of **Vehicle a**, here location 100, and passes that address into the **this** parameter of the **SetSpeed()** function. Our prototype for this function is

```
void SetSpeed (int sped);
```

But when the compiler compiles the class, it modifies our prototypes of member functions to include the **this** parameter. What the compiler actually creates is shown below with the additions by the compiler in bold/italics.

```
void SetSpeed (Vehicle* const this, int sped);
```

Now in the implementation of **SetSpeed()**, we code

```
void Vehicle::SetSpeed (int sped) {
 speed = sped;
}
```

But the compiler alters our coding as follows.

```
void Vehicle::SetSpeed (Vehicle* const this, int sped) {
 this->speed = sped;
}
```

This clever scheme allows the compiler to automatically access the member data of any object from within member functions. In fact, the **this** parameter is also available for our use as well, when the need arises. We could also have implemented the function this way.

```
void Vehicle::SetSpeed (int sped) {
 this->speed = sped;
}
```

But why do the compiler's work for it? However, suppose that we had called the parameter **speed** instead of **sped**? We saw in the last chapter that we cannot just code

```
void Vehicle::SetSpeed (int speed) {
 speed = speed;
}
```

But now we have two ways to specify the member data **speed**. Either of the following is correct.

```
void Vehicle::SetSpeed (int speed) {
 Vehicle::speed = speed;
 this->speed = speed;
}
```

When the situation of conflicting parameters and member names occur, programmers use either one of these methods to avoid the name conflict. However, the major use of the **this** pointer occurs when we implement operator overloading.

When Classes Contain References or Pointers or Instances of Other Classes—Forward References

Classes can be interrelated and contain instances of other classes or pointers or references to other classes. With the **Employee** class, an actual **Date** instance is being used. Thus, the **Employee** header file **must** also include the **Date** header file so the compiler knows how to create the needed **Date** member. However, in other circumstances, only a reference or pointer to another class is used. And this brings up additional considerations.

We already have a class to encapsulate vehicles. Suppose that we also needed some kind of class to monitor the traffic flow of vehicles. Consider this additional class, **Monitor**, whose job is to track counts of moving and nonmoving vehicles.

In this example, a pointer to a **Vehicle** object is being passed to the **AddVehicle()** function. In the **Monitor.h** file, the compiler must know what the identifier **Vehicle** is. True, the actual parameter is just a pointer, but the compiler still must know that **Vehicle** is a class. With pointers and references to other classes, all that is really required by the compiler is notification that this identifier is a class. This can be done by using a **forward reference** to the class. A forward reference is just the keyword class followed by the name of the class and a semicolon.
Monitor.h

```
class Vehicle; // forward reference to class that's not
               // defined at this point
class Monitor {
 protected:
  int moving;
  int stationary;

 public:
      Monitor ();
 void  AddVehicle (const Vehicle* ptrv);
};
```

On the other hand, if this **Monitor** class contained an actual instance of the **Vehicle** class, then in the **Monitor** header file, the **Vehicle** class definition must be included so that the compiler can determine how much memory must be reserved for this **Vehicle** instance within a **Monitor** instance.

When only a reference or a pointer to another class is used within another header file, a forward reference suffices. However, one could also include the actual other class header file instead of the forward reference.

In all cases, in the implementation file, the other class header file must be included. So in **Monitor.cpp**, we must include **Vehicle.h,** unless it has already been included in **Monitor.h**. Monitor.cpp

```
#include "Monitor.h"
#include "Vehicle.h"

void Monitor::AddVehicle (const Vehicle* ptrv) {
 if (ptrv->IsMoving ()) moving++;
 else stationary++;
}
```

Notice that a forward reference in **Monitor.h** is required so that the identifier **Vehicle** is known to be a class. However, in **Monitor.cpp**, the actual **Vehicle** header file must be included so code can be created.

Now examine the **Vehicle** class once more. In the **SetSpeed()** function and **Vehicle()** constructors, a call to the monitor class **AddVehicle()** is needed. We must add an additional parameter as follows.
Vehicle.h

```
class Monitor;   // forward reference

class Vehicle {
 protected:
  bool is_moving;
  int  speed;

 public:
        Vehicle ();
        Vehicle (bool move, int sped, Monitor* ptrm);
  bool IsMoving  () const;
  void SetMoving ();
  int  GetSpeed  () const;
  void SetSpeed  (bool, int, Monitor* ptrm);
};
```

In the **Vehicle.cpp** file, we must add an include for the **Monitor** class. Now a new problem arises. In the **Vehicle()** ctor, the **Monitor**'s **AddVehicle()** function must be called passing the address of this new **Vehicle** object. How can the ctor pass the address of this object to **AddVehicle()**? Remember that member functions are always passed the hidden **this** parameter which is a pointer to this object. Notice how the **this** parameter is used.
Vehicle.cpp

```
#include "Monitor.h"
#include "Vehicle.h"

Vehicle::Vehicle (bool move, int sped, Monitor* ptrm) {
 is_moving = move;
```

```
  speed = sped;
 ptrm->AddVehicle (this);
}

void Vehicle::SetSpeed (bool move, int sped, Monitor* ptrm){
 is_moving = move;
 speed = sped;
 ptrm->AddVehicle (this);
}
```

So far so good. But now we have the potential for the common C++ header file—circular class definitions problem. The compiler creates a complete class definition whenever the class is included in the cpp files. Consider the **main()** function, for here is where the problem occurs; **main()** must include both class headers. If only forward references were used, no problem. However, if the actual header files were used instead of a forward reference, then **main()** would wind up with multiple class definitions.

```
#include "Vehicle.h"
#include "Monitor.h"

Monitor m;
Vehicle a, b, c (true, 50, &m);
a.SetSpeed (true, 50, &m);
b.SetSpeed (false, 0, &m);
```

Notice how the address of the **Monitor** class instance is passed to the **Vehicle()** constructor and member function **SetSpeed()**.

To be totally safe in all circumstances, always use **#ifndef/#define or #pragma once** logic in all class definition files. Here is a far better way to define the two classes.
Monitor.h

```
#pragma once
class Vehicle; // forward reference to class that's not
               // defined at this point
class Monitor {
 protected:
  int  moving;
  int  stationary;
public:
      Monitor ();
 void  AddVehicle (const Vehicle* ptrv);
};
```

Vehicle.h

```
#pragma once
class Monitor;  // forward reference

class Vehicle {
 protected:
```

```
  int  is_moving;
  int  speed;
 public:
      Vehicle ();
      Vehicle (int move, int sped, Monitor* ptrm);
  int  IsMoving  ();
  void SetMoving ();
  int  GetSpeed  ();
  void SetSpeed  (int, Monitor* ptrm);
};
```

In OOP programming, references are preferred to pointers wherever possible. If I had used references, the **Vehicle** class would appear as follows

```
#include "Monitor.h"

Vehicle::Vehicle (bool move, int sped, Monitor& m) {
 is_moving = move;
 speed = sped;
 m.AddVehicle (this); // in error
}

void Vehicle::SetSpeed (bool move, int sped, Monitor& m) {
 is_moving = move;
 speed = sped;
 m.AddVehicle (this); // in error
}
```

Further, suppose that in the **Monitor** class, I wanted a reference to the **Vehicle** instance. Monitor.cpp

```
#include "Vehicle.h"
void Monitor::AddVehicle (const Vehicle& v) {
 if (v.IsMoving ()) moving++;
 else stationary++;
}
```

Ah, now I have added an error to the **SetSpeed()** function and the **Vehicle()** constructor. Can you spot it?

I used the **this** parameter to pass this instance of the **Vehicle** class to **AddVehicle()**. Yet the function requires a reference! I would now have to recode the **Vehicle** functions using ***this** to convert the pointer to a reference.

```
Vehicle::Vehicle (bool move, int sped, Monitor& m) {
 is_moving = move;
 speed = sped;
 m.AddVehicle (*this);
}
void Vehicle::SetSpeed (bool move, int sped, Monitor& m) {
 is_moving = move;
```

179

```
speed = sped;
m.AddVehicle (*this);
}
```

Rule: When a reference to the current object is needed, use *this.

This conversion from a pointer to a reference and vice versa is found with great frequency in OOP programming situation.

Using Class enums

Suppose that we desired to make a class to encapsulate pets for a pet store. One of the data members would have to be the pet's type, such as dog, cat, snake, hamster or mouse. While one could use **#define**s or **const int**s to create good identifiers for the pet types, we know that an **enum** is a much better approach. We could easily define **PetType** as follows.

```
enum PetType {Dog, Cat, Snake, Hamster, Mouse};
```

From a design point of view, this new **PetType** really belongs with our new **Pet** class. It does not likely make any sense if used outside of the **Pet** class and such operations. So if we just defined the **enum** as above, then there is nothing to show that it really is used in conjunction with **Pet** objects.

A **class enum** is an enumerated data type that is defined within the class definition and thus belongs to the class. As such, all uses outside the class require the class qualifier. Usually, a **class enum** has the **public** access qualifier so that it can be broadly used. Here is how the **Pet** class could be defined.

Pet.h

```
#pragma once
class Pet {
 public:
   enum PetType {Dog, Cat, Snake, Hamster, Mouse};
   enum Gender {Male, Female};
 protected:
   PetType type;
   Gender  sex;
 public:
   Pet ();
   Pet (PetType t, Gender g);
   PetType GetPetType () const;
   Gender  GetPetGender () const;
};
```

And here is how it could be implemented. Notice how the **Pet::** class qualifier is used with both the return data types and with actual **enum** values.

Pet.cpp

```
Pet::Pet () {
 type = Dog;
 sex = Female;
}

Pet::Pet (PetType t, Gender g) {
 type = t;
 sex = g;
}

Pet::PetType Pet::GetPetType () const {
 return type;
}

Pet::Gender Pet::GetPetGender () const {
 return sex;
}
```

Notice that within the **Pet** class member functions, the **Pet::** qualifier is not needed on the two class **enum** variables or values. However, when class **enums** are used as a return value, we must use the class qualifier as shown in bold face above.

Here is how a client program may use the class **enum**s. Since the **enum** is **public**, it can even allocate instances of the **enum**. However, it must use the **Pet::** class qualifier for both instances of the **enums** and for the values.

```
int main () {
 Pet::PetType t = Pet::Cat;
 Pet p (Pet::Dog, Pet::Male);
 if (p.GetPetGender() == Pet::Male &&
     P.GetPetType() == Pet::Cat) {
```

Class **enum**s are widely used in class designs. All of the **ios::** identifiers you have been coding are class **ios enum**s! Try opening up the **ios.h** header file and there you will find all of the **ios::** identifiers you are familiar with—all are **ios** class **enum**s.

Friend Functions

A friend function is not a member of the class of which it is a friend, but it is granted the rights to access private member data as if it were. Its primary use is to aid operator overloading and I/O streaming as discussed later on. It also is a means for a function to be able to access member data of several classes to be able to do its work.

For example, we could add a friend function to Vehicle, **Compare()** as follows
```
class Vehicle {
  ...
```

181

```
public:
  friend int Compare (const Vehicle &a, const Vehicle &b);
};
```

The keyword **friend** appears only in the class definition on the function prototype. It never is present in the actual cpp file. Here, **Compare()** is not a member function, rather it is an ordinary C style function. However, because it is a friend function, it can access all **Vehicle** data and functions, independent of access qualifiers.

We could implement the **Compare()** function as follows. Notice that friend functions also are located in the class implementation file along with member functions.

Vehicle.cpp
```
int Compare (const Vehicle &a, const Vehicle &b) {
  return a.speed>b.speed ? 1 : a.speed==b.speed ? 0 : -1;
}
```
We would invoke it in **main()** this way.
```
if (Compare (a, b) > 0) // is vehicle a faster than b?
```

Note that inside a friend function, all references to data members and functions must be qualified by which object instance, such as **a.speed**. It is a separate function outside of the class. It is meaningless to refer to data member without a reference to a specific object. That is, this would be a compile time error: **speed**. Whose speed is being referred to?

Friend functions offer us a way to handle several situations that arise in OOP design that otherwise would have no possible solution. Frequently these occur in operator overloading as we will see in the next chapter.

In this specific case there is no real reason to make **Compare()** a friend function. In fact, it is more awkward for the client programs when it is a friend function. Here is how it could have been written as a member function.

Vehicle.h
```
class Vehicle {
  . . .
public:
  int Compare (const Vehicle &b) const;
};
```
Vehicle.cpp
```
int Vehicle::Compare (const Vehicle &b) const {
  return speed>b.speed ? 1 : speed==b.speed ? 0 : -1;
}
```
We would invoke it in **main()** this way.
```
if (a.Compare (b) > 0) // is vehicle a faster than b?
```

182

Creating a Deck of Cards Using Enums

Suppose that we wanted to encapsulate a deck of playing cards. Certainly enumerated data types would greatly aid the design and implementation. We might use the following.

```
enum Suit {Clubs, Diamonds, Hearts, Spades};
enum Rank {Ace, Deuce, Trey, Four, Five, Six, Seven, Eight,
           Nine, Ten, Jack, Queen, King};
```

If we now create a **Card** class to encapsulate a single playing card, a new problem in design arises. Suppose that this card is created to be the **Ace** of **Spades**. That is, the class contains an instance of both **Suit** and **Rank**. Once created, this card instance cannot ever be changed. It cannot suddenly become the **King** of **Hearts**. That is otherwise known as "cheating." Once a card instance has been created or initialized, its **Suit** and **Rank** data members can never be changed. These are called **constant data members**.

Constant Data Members

A class may desire certain data members to be constant. Once these items have their initial values, they can never be changed. To indicate that a class data member is to be held constant, simply prefix the data definition with the const **keyword**. Here is how the **Card** class can be partially defined.
Card.h
```
#pragma once

class Card {
public:
  enum Suit {Clubs, Diamonds, Hearts, Spades};
  enum Rank {Ace, Deuce, Trey, Four, Five, Six, Seven, Eight,
             Nine, Ten, Jack, Queen, King};

protected:
  const Suit suit;
  const Rank rank;

public:
  Card (Suit s, Rank r);
  ...
};
```

When we try to implement the class, a new problem arises. Consider this attempt to implement the constructor. It fails utterly.
Card.cpp
```
#include "Card.h"
Card::Card (Suit s, Rank r) {
  suit = s;
  rank = r;
}
```

183

Rule: Upon block entry of the constructor, all constant data members must already have their values.

When the compiler reaches the begin brace of the ctor for **Card**, the **suit** and **rank** constant members must already have their values. They cannot ever be assigned their values within the block of coding. This leaves only one single location at which constant data members can be assigned their values. Recall the scope of parameter variables and when they come into existence. Their scope is from their point of definition within the function header to the end of the defining block of coding, the end of the function. Parameter variables are given their values as the function is called and before reaching that actual function body. Thus, parameter variables can be utilized after the parameter list and before the begin brace of the function body. This is shown at "x" marks the spot below.

```
Card::Card (Suit s, Rank r) x {
```

C++ allows a new style of initialization not only for class instances but also for all of the intrinsic built-in data types. The initialization parallels that of constructor invocation. The following are legal.

```
int x (0);     // define x and initialize it to 0
double z (42); // define a double z and set it too 42
```

This new form produces identical and is interchangeable with the following with which you are familiar.

```
int x = 0;
double z = 42;
```

If **main()** was creating the Ace of Spades, we have as expected the following.

```
Card ace (Card::Spades, Card::Ace);
```

How does this help us in providing the proper initialization of the constant data members?

C++ provides the **base class and member initialization list mechanism**. After the parameter list and before the begin brace of the function body, code a single colon. This says here comes the base class and member initialization list. Base class initialization refers to derived classes and inheritance and is covered in a later chapter. Here we are after member initialization. We must use the new form of initialization. Separate each member initialization with a comma. Here is how we must code the Card constructor. It is the only way to initialize constant data members.

```
Card::Card (Suit s, Rank r) : suit (s), rank (r) {}
```

Notice that now there is nothing left in the actual function body.

This member initialization list can be used for any data member's initialization, not just constant members.

Rule: All constant data members must be initialized in the constructor function by using the base class and member data initialization mechanism.

Consider the **Rectangle** class from the last chapter. The default ctor could have been coded this way.

```
Rectangle::Rectangle () : length(0), width(0) { }
```

Likewise, the Timer class ctor could have been written this way.

```
Timer::Timer() : startTime(0), endTime (0) { }
```

The ctor for a Point could be done this way.

```
Point::Point (int xx, int yy) : x (xx), y (yy) { }
```

Certainly, this base class and member initialization mechanism can shorten the normal coding for constructor functions besides providing the only method for initializing constant data members.

The Copy Constructor and How to Forbid Certain Constructors

There is one very special constructor function. It is called the copy constructor. As its name implies, it is used by the compiler to create copies of an object.

> **Rule: The copy constructor is a constructor that is passed a constant reference to this same class.**

The copy constructor for the **Card** class would be given by the following.
```
Card (const Card& c);
```
The copy ctor for a **Rectangle** class is
```
Rectangle (const Rectangle& r);
```
The copy ctor for a **Point** class is
```
Point (const Point& p);
```
The copy ctor for the **Timer** class is
```
Timer (const Timer& t);
```

When does the compiler call the copy constructor? It is called whenever the compiler must make a duplicate copy of an instance. Here are the possibilities.

```
Point Fun (Point w); // assume this prototype
. . .
Point p;            // default ctor
Point q (p);        // copy ctor
Point r = p;        // copy ctor, not the assignment operator
Point e;            // default ctor
e = p;              // the assignment operator, not copy ctor
Point s = Fun (p);  // copy p into parameter w
                    // then copy the returned value into s
Point Fun (Point w) {
  Point t;
  return t;         // copy t as the return value
}
```

In general, just as a class should always define a default constructor, it should also define a copy constructor. In fact, a copy constructor is mandatory when the class has dynamic memory allocation of member data. This is examined in detail in the next chapter.

How is the copy constructor implemented? It only has to copy the passed object's data. Here is the implementation for the **Point** copy constructor.

```
Point::Point (const Point& p) {
  x = p.x;
  y = p.y;
}
```

Alternatively, it could be implemented this way using the base class and member initialization method.

```
Point::Point (const Point& p): x(p.x), y(p.y) { }
```

It is a lot shorter this way.

For the **Circle** class, the copy constructor can be implemented this way.

```
Circle::Circle (const Circle& c) {
  radius = c.radius;
  origin = c.origin;
}
```

Or it may be done this way.

```
Circle::Circle (const Circle& c) :
radius(c.radius),origin(c.origin){}
```

Now, what has all this to do with our **Card** class? Ah, let's examine some **main()** function coding.

```
#include "Card.h"
int main () {
  Card ace (Card::Hearts, Card::Ace);
  Card anotherAce (ace);
  Card moreAce = ace;
  Card whatIsIt;
```

At this point, we now have three aces of hearts! Oops. Cheating again. With a deck of cards, a single card must not be allowed to be duplicated. How can we prevent this from happening?

When you wish to prevent a specific function from being called by the client programs or the compiler, simply make it a protected or private function. The compiler cannot call protected or private constructor functions. We can protect against accidental copying of a card by defining a private copy constructor.

Card.h

```
#pragma once
class Card {
public:
  enum Suit {Clubs, Diamonds, Hearts, Spades};
  enum Rank {Ace, Deuce, Trey, Four, Five, Six, Seven, Eight,
            Nine, Ten, Jack, Queen, King};
```

```
protected:
  const Suit suit;
  const Rank rank;

public:
  Card (Suit s, Rank r);

private:
  Card (const Card& c);
  Card ();
...
};
```

Notice that I also took care of another illegal detail, the creation of a card with no rank or suit defined. In the **main()** function above, the last instance called **whatIsIt** should also not be allowed, for it would have no suit or rank specified. There cannot be a "default" card when creating a deck of cards. Thus, I made that ctor also private.

When a function has been made private or protected and the client or the compiler (in the case of the constructors) attempts to invoke it, the compiler generates an error message stating that "cannot call a protected or private function." Here is an implementation of the **Card** copy ctor function that cannot be called because its access is private.

```
Card::Card (const Card& c) : suit(c.suit), rank(c.rank) {
  cerr << "Error cannot call the copy constructor\n";
}
```

Reference Variables as Data Members

A class can also have **reference variables** as data members. To see why we might need reference variables as class members, let's continue developing the playing card example. The next step is to create the actual deck of cards class.

Class **Deck** contains the number of cards in the deck along with an array of the remaining cards in the deck. Exactly how the cards are created, stored,and used is very specific to the intended use. Here, I just want to illustrate some basic actions. Thus, I store the cards in an array of Card pointers so that I can individually dynamically allocate and initialize each card.

```
Deck.h
#pragma once
class Card;    // forward reference to the Card class

class Deck {
protected:
  Card* *cards; // going to be single dim array of pointers to the
                // card objects
  int    numcards;

public:
```

187

```
Deck (int number_of_cards = 52);
~Deck ();

private:
 Deck (const Deck& d); // do not permit duplicate decks
};
```

Notice that I have provided a default of 52 cards in the deck since this is very often the correct number. I have disallowed making duplicate decks by making the copy constructor private. Obviously the next step is to add some action functions to the deck class, such as deal cards and so on. However, here is what I have for the basic implementation. Notice, a much better method for card creation should be devised, since the method I use here is really only satisfactory for a 52-card deck.

Deck.cpp
```
#include <iostream>
using namespace std;
#include "Deck.h"
#include "Card.h"

Deck::Deck (int number_of_cards) {
 numcards = number_of_cards;
 if (numcards <= 0) {
  cerr << "Error in Deck: you cannot create an empty deck\n";
  cards = 0;
  ret;
 }
 cards = new (std::nothrow) Card* [numcards];
 if (!cards) {
  cerr << "Error - out of memory in Deck\n";
  exit (1);
 }
 int i = 0;
 for (int j=0; j<4 && i<numcards; j++) {
  for (int k=0; k<13 && i<numcards; k++) {
   cards[i] = new(std::nothrow)Card((Card::Suit)j,(Card::Rank)k);
    if (!cards[i]) {
     cerr << "Error - out of memory in Deck - making cards\n";
     exit (2);
    }
   i++;
  }
 }
}

Deck::~Deck () {
 if (!cards) return;
 for (int i=0; i<numcards; i++) {
  delete cards[i];
```

```
 }
 delete [] cards;
}

Deck::Deck (const Deck& d) {
 cards = 0;
 numcards = 0;
}
```

Finally we need a **Player** class. However, the **main()** function will create the one and only actual **Deck** instance. Each **Player** instance should have a reference to this single deck. So here is the start of the **Player** class.

```
#pragma once
class Deck;        // forward reference to the Deck

class Player {
protected:
 Deck& thisdeck;

public:
 Player (Deck& deck);
};
```

So here is an example of a class that has a reference variable as member data. How can the constructor be implemented?

> **Rule: Upon block entry of the constructor, all reference data members must already have their values.**

> **Rule: All reference data members must be initialized in the constructor function by using the base class and member data initialization mechanism.**
> Here is the only way that the constructor can be implemented.

Player.cpp
```
#include "Player.h"
#include "Deck.h"

Player::Player (Deck& deck) : thisdeck (deck) {}
```

Finally, to tie these three classes together, here is a simple **main()** function that creates the single deck and allocates some players. This shell coding can be found in the sample programs under the **Pgm05Cards** folder.

Main.cpp
```
#include <iostream>
using namespace std;
#include "Card.h"
#include "Deck.h"
```

```
#include "Player.h"

int main () {
 Deck thedeck;
 Player player1 (thedeck);
 Player player2 (thedeck);
 Player player3 (thedeck);

 return 0;
}
```

Static Data Members and Static Member Functions

Static Member Data

A **static member variable** belongs to the entire class. It acts as if it were a global variable to this entire class. Only **one** instance of the static member exists and it is independent of whether or not any actual instances of the class have ever been or are or ever will be allocated. They are often used as a "reference count" tracking the number of class instances that are currently allocated.

But why do we need static data members? Consider the design of a **Circle** class to encapsulate a circle object. As soon as we begin to add operational functions, such as **GetArea()** or **GetCircumference()**, we need **PI**. So we might code the following for the **Circle** class.
Circle.h
```
#pragma once
class Circle {
protected:
 double radius;
 const double PI;
public:
 Circle (double rad = 0);
 double GetArea () const;
 double GetCircumference () const;
};
```

Notice that I made **PI** be a constant member. Then, we proceed to implement the **Circle** as follows.
Circle.cpp
```
#include <cmath> // for acos() function for PI
using namespace std;
#include "Circle.h"

Circle::Circle (double rad) : PI(acos(-1.)), radius(rad) {}

double Circle::GetArea () const {
```

```
 return PI * radius * radius;
}

double Circle::GetCircumference () const {
 return 2 * PI * radius;
}
```

I cleverly initialized **PI** to the most accurate value of **PI** that can fit in a **double**. Geometrically, the arc cosine of –1 is, by definition, **PI**. All works fine, until you think about memory requirements. Suppose that the drawing program allocates 1,000 **Circle** objects. How many **PI** instances are created? 1,000! That is 999 PI's too many! We only need a single **PI** to service all of these instances.

Now one could insert a global constant in the **Circle.cpp** file this way.
Circle.cpp
```
#include <cmath> // for acos() function for PI
using namespace std;
#include "Circle.h"
```

const double PI = acos (-1.); // a global PI

```
Circle::Circle (double rad) : radius(rad) {}
...
```

However, when we define global items, we run the risk of collision with other globals defined in other cpp files. A way around this is to use the **static** keyword on the global item. A **static global item** is global in scope within this cpp file. It is not known beyond this cpp file. So a somewhat better approach is this way.
Circle.cpp
```
#include <cmath> // for acos() function for PI
using namespace std;
#include "Circle.h"
```

const static double PI = acos (-1.); // a PI for this cpp file

```
Circle::Circle (double rad) : radius(rad) {}
...
```

But a class can have a **static data member**. So here is a far better OOP way of handling **PI.**
Circle.h
```
#pragma once
class Circle {
protected:
 double radius;
 const static double PI;
public:
 Circle (double rad = 0);
```

191

. . .

When new instances of the class that contains the static data members are allocated, no additional instances of the static members are created. In fact, the compiler, at compile time, allocates and initializes the static data members. However, since the compiler must reserve space for the static variables in the program, they must appear in the cpp file. Hence, we must include the definitions there as well. Although it looks like we are redefining **PI**, we are not: we are just providing a place holder for the compiler and perhaps to initialize it as well. But we must use the class qualifier so the compiler recognizes this as the same variable that is defined in the class definition

Circle.cpp
```
#include <cmath> // for acos() function for PI
using namespace std;
#include "Circle.h"

const double Circle::PI = acos (-1.); // a static PI member

Circle::Circle (double rad) : radius(rad) {}
```
. . .

Reference counting is another example of static data members. Suppose that a class needs to know how many instances of that class are in existence at any point. A static counter can be added as a data member. It is incremented in the constructor functions and decremented in the destructor.

tally.h
```
class Tally {
protected:
static int count;
public:
  Tally ();
 ~Tally ();
};
```
tally.cpp
```
int Tally::count = 0;  // initialize count

Tally::Tally () {
 count++;
}

Tally::~Tally () {
 count--;
}
```

Static Member Functions

Static member functions operate similarly. Only **one** instance of the function exists and it can operate on **no** class instance! That is, it applies to the entire class independent of whether or not any objects of the class are yet allocated. It has no **this** parameter, hence no instance data. It is often used for global class initializations. What static functions can operate on are static member data.

Static member data and functions provide the OOP way to handle having some data available application-wide.

For example, suppose our application needed access to the running full path location of several folders so that it could automatically save report files in the **Reports** folder, update some accounting files located in the **Accounts** folder, and file some notices in the **Pending** folder. These folders are assumed to be located beneath the folder wherever the user has installed our program and we do not have control over where the user has installed us. Assume that the user installed our application to the **SuperApp** folder located on **D:** drive under the folder **Program Files**. It would be very convenient if one time only, our application constructed these paths and had them readily available for all the functions that needed to use them. This is an ideal application for a special **SysInfo** class which contains only static data members and static member functions.

We can define the **SysInfo** class this way.

```
SysInfo Class Definition

 1 #pragma once
 2 #include <iostream>
 3 using namespace std;
 4
 5 class SysInfo {
 6 public:
 7   static char reports[_MAX_FNAME];
 8   static char accounts[_MAX_FNAME];
19   static char notices[_MAX_FNAME];
10
11   static bool InitSysInfo (const char* exePath);
12 };
```

Notice that the class has no instance data, only static data. It does not even have a constructor, however, the compiler will supply one for us that does nothing. No function is ever going to allocate any instances of this class. Instead, all of our program functions are just going to use the data. The purpose of the single static member function, **InitSysInfo()** is to initially construct these three paths for us. The define **_MAX_FNAME** contains the maximum length a path can be on the platform for which you are compiling. For a Win32 platform, this is 256 bytes. I made the three strings public so that the users could have direct access to them.

If you wish additional protection since anyone can not only get at these but also modify them, then make these three protected and provide three static access functions, such as
```
static const char* GetReportPath () const;
```

Next, in SysInfo.cpp, we must define these three static strings.

```
char SysInfo::reports[_MAX_FNAME];
char SysInfo::accounts[_MAX_FNAME];
char SysInfo::notices[_MAX_FNAME];

bool SysInfo::InitSysInfo (const char* exePath) {
  ...
}
```

The real question is how can we actually implement **InitSysInfo()**? Recall that the first string that is passed to the **main()** function always contains the full drive and path and filename of the program itself. Thus, if we remove the program name and exe extension, we have the installed path of our application. We only need to append the three subfolders. Thus, one time only in **main()** before our application really begins its work, we need to invoke **InitSysInfo()** to fill up these three strings.

```
Main Function to Test SysInfo Class

 1 #include <iostream>
 2 using namespace std;
 3 #include "SysInfo.h"
 4
 5 void Tester ();
 6
 7 int main (int argc, char* argv[]) {
 8
 9  // initialize the three application path strings
10  if (!SysInfo::InitSysInfo (argv[0])) {
11     cerr << "Initialization failure:\n"
12        << "Unable to create needed report subfolders\n";
13   return 1;
14  }
15
16  // go write a sample test file
17  Tester ();
18
19  return 0;
20 }
21
```

Now any function anywhere within the entire application can have direct access to the paths simply by including the **SysInfo.h** header file! Here is the **Tester()** function that writes a test file. The concatenation assumes that the **reports SysInfo** string ends with a backslash.

```
Tester Function to Write a Test File

 1 #include <fstream>
 2 #include <string>
```

```
 3 using namespace std;
 4 #include "SysInfo.h"
 5
 6 void Tester () {
 7  char file[_MAX_FNAME];
 8
 9  // construct the file name
10  strcpy_s (file, sizeof(file), SysInfo::reports);
11  strcat_s (file, sizeof(file), "TestFile.txt");
12
13  // attempt to open the output file
14  ofstream outfile (file);
15  if (!outfile) {
16   cerr << "Error - unable to open test file: "
17        << file << endl;
18   return;
19  }
20
21  // write a test message
22  outfile << "This is a test message.\n";
23  outfile.close ();
24 }
```

The only really remaining question is how to actually implement the **InitSysInfo()** function. A C library function, **_splitpath_s()** takes a fully qualified path with filename and extension and splits it into four strings: the drive string, the path, the filename and the extension. Once that is done, we merely have to rejoin the drive and path strings to obtain the full path to the folder in which our application executable is installed. We can then append the three various subfolders that the application requires to this full path.

Another C library function, **_mkdir()**, makes a directory. It is passed the character string containing the full path to make. If it is not successful, it returns a –1. One reason it could fail is that the folder already exists. The function automatically sets a global error field, **errno**, if it fails. If we test **errno** for the value **EEXIST**, we can rule out that the folder already exists. Here is the complete **SysInfo** implementation.

```
Class SysInfo Implementation

 1 #include <iostream>
 2 using namespace std;
 3 #include <io.h>
 4 #include <string>
 5 #include <direct.h>
 6 #include <errno.h>
 7
 8 #include "SysInfo.h"
 9
10 char SysInfo::reports[_MAX_FNAME];
11 char SysInfo::accounts[_MAX_FNAME];
```

```
12 char SysInfo::notices[_MAX_FNAME];
13
14 /*******************************************************************/
15 /*                                                                 */
16 /* InitSysInfo: build the three application subfolders             */
17 /*              beneath the exe folder, if not already there       */
18 /*                                                                 */
19 /*******************************************************************/
20
21 bool SysInfo::InitSysInfo (const char* exePath) {
22
23   char drive[_MAX_DRIVE];
24   char dir [_MAX_DIR];
25   char file[_MAX_FNAME];
26   char ext[_MAX_EXT];
27
28   // split the exe path into its parts - pitch the file.exe parts
29   _splitpath_s (exePath, drive, sizeof(drive), dir, sizeof(dir),
30                 file, sizeof(file), ext, sizeof(ext));
31   // form up the drive and path parts
32   strcpy_s (file, sizeof(file), drive);
33   strcat_s (file, sizeof(file), dir);
34
35   // copy to each of the needed folder strings and append the
36   // appropriate subfolder name
37   strcpy_s (reports, sizeof(reports), file);
38   strcat_s (reports, sizeof(reports),"Reports");
39   strcpy_s (accounts,sizeof(accounts), file);
40   strcat_s (accounts,sizeof(accounts), "Accounts");
41   strcpy_s (notices, sizeof(notices), file);
42   strcat_s (notices,sizeof(notices), "Pending");
43
44   // attempt to make the reports folder
45   if (_mkdir (reports) == -1) { // was there an error?
46    if (errno == EEXIST); // folder already there? yes do nothing
47    else {                    // no, so display error message
48     cerr << "Error: The desired folder cannot be created\n";
49     cerr << "The path was: " << reports << endl;
50     return false;
51    }
52   }
53
54   // attempt to make the accounts folder
55   if (_mkdir (accounts) == -1) { // was there an error?
56    if (errno == EEXIST); // folder already there? yes do nothing
57    else {                    // no, so display error message
58     cerr << "Error: The desired folder cannot be created\n";
59     cerr << "The path was: " << accounts << endl;
60     return false;
61    }
62   }
63
64   // attempt to make the notices Pending folder
```

196

```
65  if (_mkdir (notices) == -1) { // was there an error?
66   if (errno == EEXIST); // folder already there? yes do nothing
67   else {                  // no, so display error message
68    cerr << "Error: The desired folder cannot be created\n";
69    cerr << "The path was: " << notices << endl;
70    return false;
71   }
72  }
73
74  // for later convenience, append the trailing backslash
75  strcat_s (reports, sizeof(reports), "\\");
76  strcat_s (accounts, sizeof(accounts), "\\");
77  strcat_s (notices, sizeof(notices), "\\");
78
79  return true;
80 }
```

In the right circumstances, static data and static functions are quite handy. They obviate the need for anything global/external in your OOP programming!

Inline Functions

An **inline** function is a function for which the compiler actually substitutes the function body in the calling program and does not actually create a function of that name in the resulting program. In other words, the compiler bypasses all of the function calling overhead by placing what would have been the function's body directly in the client's code at the point the function would have been invoked. The idea is to speed up the client program by reducing the function calling overhead of that function. However, please use caution with inline functions. In the client program, wherever that inline function is used, the compiler places another copy of the function body. Thus, if the client calls an inline function from 100 locations, then there are 100 copies of that function's body in the client program. Its exe size has grown but it runs faster.

Inlining should only be used on very short functions, such as constructors. Inlining is only a request of the compiler. If the compiler feels it is not worth it or is too complex a body to inline, it will not inline that function.

A function can be inlined in one of two ways. One is to code its body right there in the header file. In the industry, this **automatic inlining** is frowned upon because the clients of the class are going to have a copy of the header file. Thus, part of the actual class implementation is visible to the customers of the class. Inlining by coding the body directly in the header file is found in short magazine articles, academic areas and book examples. It is not done in the real world of production. Circle.h

```
#pragma once
class Circle {
protected:
```

197

```
 double radius;
 const static double PI;
public:
 Circle (double rad = 0) : radius(rad) {}
...
```
Circle.cpp
```
#include <cmath> // for acos() function for PI
using namespace std;
#include "Circle.h"

const double Circle::PI = acos (-1.); // a static PI member
...
```

The preferred, second method of inlining still has the function coded in a separate **.inl** file (short for inline), but uses the inline identifier on the function prototype in the class definition file. Here is an example of how inlining can be requested in a header file. Notice the use of the **inline** identifier.

Circle.h
```
#pragma once
class Circle {
protected:
 double radius;
 const static double PI;
public:
 inline Circle (double rad = 0);
...
};
#include "Circle.inl"
```

Circle.inl
```
#include "Circle.h"
Circle::Circle (double rad) : radius(rad) {}
...
```
Circle.cpp
```
#include <cmath> // for acos() function for PI
using namespace std;
#include "Circle.h"
const double Circle::PI = acos (-1.); // a static PI member
...
```
Note that the **inline** keyword is not found in the implementation file nor in the inl file.

If you want to use inline functions, first get the entire class fully operational and error free. Then simply add the **inline** keyword before the function prototypes that you wish to inline (in the header file). However, when debugging, one cannot step into inline functions to examine things. There is no function there to step into! Thus, debugging inline functions is best done before they are actually inlined.

Implicit Type Conversions

The compiler does implicit type conversions fully utilizing all of your class member functions in an attempt to build the client program. To see just how this works, let's examine a **Circle** class once again, adding a **Compare()** function. To keep the illustration short, I have automatically inlined all functions.

Circle.h
```
class Circle {
protected:
 double radius;
public:
 Circle() : radius (0) {}
 Circle (const circle& c) : radius(c.radius) {}
 Circle (double rad) : radius (rad) {}
 bool Compare (const Circle& c) {return radius == c.radius;}
};
```

Here is a client program.

Main.cpp
```
#include "Circle.h"
int main () {
 Circle a, b (42.0), c (b); // uses all three ctors
 if (a.Compare (b))
  cout << "Circle a equals circle b\n";
 if (b.Compare (42.0))
  cout << "Circle b has a radius of 42.\n";
 return 0;
}
```

The first invocation of the **Compare()** function calls our member function passing a constant reference to **Circle b**. But what about the second call to **Compare()**? The parameter is a double. We have **not** written a **Compare()** function with the necessary prototype:

```
     bool Compare (double r);
```

Nevertheless, this not only compiles fine, but also executes properly outputting the fact that **Circle b** does have a radius of 42! How can this be?

The compiler first examines our **Circle** class looking for a **Compare()** function that takes a double. It does not find one. Then, it sees that if it somehow had another **Circle** object, there is a **Compare()** function it could call. So the compiler now asks is there any way to turn a **double** into a **Circle** object? Yes, there is a constructor function that is passed a single **double** parameter. The compiler then constructs a temporary **Circle** object, calls the **double** ctor function to initialize it, calls the **Compare()** function passing a reference to this temporary **Circle** object, calls the **Circle** destructor for this temporary **Circle** object, and finally deletes the memory occupied by the temporary **Circle** object. This is what is meant by implicit type conversion. It is a very powerful capability of OOP compilers.

199

Summary of Constructor and Destructor Functions

A constructor (ctor) is a special nonstatic member function whose purpose is to initialize this instance's member variables.

1. It is automatically called by the compiler whenever an instance of the class comes into existence, whether it is on the stack (automatic or parameter), in the data segment (static or global), on the heap (dynamically allocated with **new**), or contained inside another class.

2. It is not invoked when the compiler is creating a pointer or a reference to an instance; these are memory addresses, not instances that the compiler is creating.

3. It must be the same name as the class.

4. It can have no return value, not even **void**.

5. It cannot be static or constant.

6. It may be public, protected or private. The compiler can only call public ctors.

7. If there is no constructor for a class, the compiler makes a default one which does nothing but issue a return instruction.

8. It can be overloaded and very often is overloaded.

9. The default constructor is one that has no parameters.

10. The copy constructor is one that is passed only a constant reference to another instance of the same class.

11. It is never called directly by programs.

The destructor (dtor) is a special member function that is called by the compiler whenever an instance of a class goes out of existence. Its purpose is to provide clean up actions, such as deleting dynamically allocated memory.

1. It is a function with the same name as the class but with a ~ prefix.

2. It can have no return value, not even **void**.

3. It cannot be static or constant.

4. It cannot be overloaded.

5. It cannot have any parameters.

6. It must have public access. A destructor cannot be protected or private.

7. If a class has no destructor, the compiler supplies one; it only issues a return instruction.

8. If a function aborts the program by calling exit (1); only global objects' dtors are called.

Practical Example 1—Dice and Die Rolling

Many games involve the rolling of one or more dice. Imagine that you hold a group of dice of various number of sides in your hand. You shake them and roll them. Each time you roll the dice, you get a "random" set of results. This is what we wish to simulate with a series of classes.

The starting point is the generation of random numbers. The C library has two functions to assist us in creation of random numbers: **rand()** and **srand()**. Each time **rand()** is called, it returns a random integer. Well, the value is not really random. It begins with a seed integer and generates a pseudo random sequence of integers from that seed value. Given the same seed, **rand()** produces the same sequence of random numbers. **srand()** is used to provide the initial seed value. For debugging, it is helpful if the same sequence of numbers is generated. However, from a game playability point of view, we need to generate very different sequences of numbers each time the application starts. This is commonly done by using the current time as the seed value.

```
srand ((unsigned) time (0));
```

The **Random** class is very simple. It has a constructor that initializes the seed value and a **GetRandom()** function to obtain a die roll for a die. The number must be between 1 and the passed number of sides of the die. However, if you are debugging a game which uses this class, you need a repeatable sequence of "random" numbers. Hence, I provided a second constructor which is passed the seed value to use.

```
Class Random Definition

 1 #pragma once
 2 /*******************************************************/
 3 /*                                                     */
 4 /* Random: obtain a random number between 1 and the number of  */
 5 /*         die sides passed                            */
 6 /*                                                     */
 7 /*******************************************************/
 8
 9 class Random {
10
11 public:
12         // seeds the random number generator with current time
13         Random ();
14
```

```
15          // for debugging, seed with a specific repeatable sequence
16          Random (unsigned int x);
17
18             // gets a random number between 1 and num_sides
19  unsigned GetRandom (int num_sides) const;
20
21  };
```

The **Random** class implementation is also very simple.

```
Class Random Implementation
```

```
 1 #include <ctime>
 2 #include <iostream> // for the random number functions
 3 using namespace std;
 4 #include "Random.h"
 5
 6 /*****************************************************************/
 7 /*                                                             */
 8 /* Random: initialize the random number generator             */
 9 /*         using the current time as the seed value           */
10 /*                                                             */
11 /*****************************************************************/
12
13          Random::Random () {
14  srand ((unsigned) time (0)); // use the current time as the seed
15 }
16
17 /*****************************************************************/
18 /*                                                             */
19 /* Random: for debugging, use the passed seed value           */
20 /*                                                             */
21 /*****************************************************************/
22
23          Random::Random (unsigned int x) {
24  srand (x); // use the passed repeatable seed value
25 }
26
27 /*****************************************************************/
28 /*                                                             */
29 /* GetRandom: obtain a random number between 1 and numsides    */
30 /*                                                             */
31 /*****************************************************************/
32
33 unsigned  Random::GetRandom (int num_sides) const {
34  return (rand () % num_sides) + 1;
35 }
```

Next, we must encapsulate a **Die** object. A die has a fixed number of sides. Once the number of sides is known, that die cannot ever change its number of sides. So the number of sides should be a constant. Further, the minimum number of sides is 4, but 6-sided dice are more commonly found. The two instance data members are the constant number of sides and the current die roll of the die. In order to actually roll the die, an instance of the Random class is needed. But notice only a single instance of the **Random** class is needed to service all instances of the die class. Hence, the instance of **Random** is a static data member.

```
Class Die Definition

 1 #pragma once
 2 #include "Random.h"
 3
 4 /**************************************************************/
 5 /*                                                          */
 6 /* Die: encapsulates the behavior of one die-sides must be >=4 */
 7 /*                                                          */
 8 /* Toss gets the next die roll and saves it in current_roll   */
 9 /*                                                          */
10 /* If the number of sides is not specified, 6 is used.      */
11 /*                                                          */
12 /* It has only 1 copy of the Random number generator object  */
13 /*                                                          */
14 /**************************************************************/
15
16 class Die {
17
18 public:
19  static const int DefaultNumSides; // = 6 used if not given
20  static const int MinimumNumSides; // = 4 the smallest allowed
21
22  static Random random; // one copy of the actual number generator
23                        // to service all dice roll requests
24
25  const int numberSides;    // number of sides for this die
26        int currentRoll;    // the current die roll value
27
28 public:
29         // construct a die, default to 6 sides
30         Die (int sides = DefaultNumSides);
31
32         // throw the die, save result in currentRoll
33 Die&   Toss (); // allows for chaining of events
34
35         // returns value last rolled
36 int    GetRollValue () const;
37
38         // returns the number of sides of this die
39 int    GetNumberSides () const;
40 };
```

In the **Die** implementation, notice how the constant **static** members are coded and given their values of 4 and 6 respectively. Also notice how the constant instance member, **number_sides**, is initialized in the constructor.

```
Class Die Implementation

 1  #include "die.h"
 2
 3  /*****************************************************************/
 4  /*                                                             */
 5  /* Die Class: simulates the action of rolling a die of sides>=4*/
 6  /*                                                             */
 7  /*****************************************************************/
 8
 9  // all static data members must be defined in the cpp file
10  // so the compiler can create space for them in the exe file
11  // we can initialize them here
12
13  const int  Die::DefaultNumSides = 6; // used if number not given
14  const int  Die::MinimumNumSides = 4; // min allowed number sides
15     Random  Die::random;         // one copy of the number generator
16
17
18  /*****************************************************************/
19  /*                                                             */
20  /* Die: construct a die with a given number of sides           */
21  /*      must be 4 or more                                      */
22  /*                                                             */
23  /*****************************************************************/
24
25  Die::Die (int sides) : numberSides (sides < MinimumNumSides ?
26                          DefaultNumSides : sides) {
27   // constant data members must be initialized PRIOR to ctor block
28   // entry - do a preparatory die roll - not really needed, but it
29   // ensures that currentRoll also has a value
30   Toss ();
31  }
32
33  /*****************************************************************/
34  /*                                                             */
35  /* Toss: emulates the effect of rolling the die                */
36  /*       result is in currentRoll                              */
37  /*                                                             */
38  /*****************************************************************/
39
40  Die&      Die::Toss () {
41   currentRoll = random.GetRandom (numberSides);
42   return *this; // permits chaining Die events by the user
43  }
44
45  /*****************************************************************/
46  /*                                                             */
```

```
47 /* GetRollValue: returns the current die roll value           */
48 /*                                                             */
49 /***************************************************************/
50
51 int       Die::GetRollValue () const {
52  return currentRoll;
53 }
54
55 /***************************************************************/
56 /*                                                             */
57 /* GetNumberSides: returns the number of sides of this die     */
58 /*                                                             */
59 /***************************************************************/
60
61 int    Die::GetNumberSides () const {
62  return numberSides;
63
```

Now we can define a **Dice** class to encapsulate a bunch of dice. The Dice class needs to store how many die objects it holds and an array of the Die objects. It is much simpler if we dynamically allocate the array and store Die pointers instead of Die objects in the array. Hence the data member is

```
Die* *dieArray; // an array of pointers to the Die objects
```

Further, the collection of dice may not all have the same number of sides. The easy way to handle this is to let the constructor just set the array to NULL or 0. A member function, **AddDie()**, is then called by the client to add in a number of dice of the same number of sides. In AddDie(), we just grow the array by allocating a new array as big as it needs to be, copying the pointers of the previously added die objects into this larger array, and then allocating and adding in the new requested Die objects. This will give us a production version of these classes, one that you can use in your games.

For operations, we can provide several methods of obtaining the results. After a **Roll()** is finished, **GetTotal()** returns the sum of all the individual die values. Often this is all that is required. However, the **Display()** function makes a nice printout such as $1 + 3 + 5 = 9$ for the user to clearly see what the roll produced. In other situations, the caller may desire to have an array of integers filled with the actual numerical value of each **Die**. **GetDieValues()** does this. To avoid overwriting memory should the passed user array of integers to be filled be too small to hold all of the values, the user must specify the maximum array bounds of the array they pass.

Additionally, we can provide a function to return the number of Die in the array and another to return the number of sides of each die, should the client need such. Finally, once this set of dice has been created, it would be illegal to make duplicates of it; that's called cheating. Hence, we can make the copy constructor private along with the assignment operator. However, although we have not yet discussed this function, the assignment function, I have included it here on line 22 so that the class is complete as it stands. You may take this function prototype on faith for a short while.

205

```
Class Dice Definition

 1 #pragma once
 2 #include "Die.h"
 3
 4 /******************************************************************/
 5 /*                                                                */
 6 /* Dice: simulates rolling a collection of dice                   */
 7 /*        the array of die is growable                            */
 8 /*        so that any number of any kind can be housed            */
 9 /*                                                                */
10 /******************************************************************/
11
12 class Dice {
13
14 protected:
15
16  int    numberOfDice;  // this instance's number of dice
17  Die*   *dieArray;     // the growable array of die*
18
19 public:
20          // creates an empty array of dice
21          Dice ();
22          ~Dice ();
23
24 private: // don't allow any copying of any instance of this class
25          Dice (const Dice& d) {}
26          Dice& operator= (const Dice& d) {return *this;}
27
28 public:
29          // add numDie of this die sides to the array
30  bool   AddDie (int numDie, int numSides = Die::DefaultNumSides);
31
32          // roll the dice - allows chaining
33  Dice&  Roll ();
34
35          // retrieve total value of all dice
36  int    GetTotal () const;
37
38              // displays each die value
39  const Dice&  Display (ostream& os = cout) const;
40
41          // fills users array of count ints with the die results
42  void   GetDieValues (int die[], int count) const;
43
44          // gets the number of die in the array
45  int    GetNumberOfDice () const;
46
47          // fills users array of the number of sides on each die
48  void   GetDieSides (int dieSides[], int count) const;
49 };
```

In the constructor, the number of dice in the collection and the pointer to the array are set to 0.

Next, examine AddDie(); this is the most complex of the functions of the class. The caller invokes this function to add, for example, a pair of six-sided dice to the collection. First, abort the request if the number of sides is below the minimum of four. Then, allocate a larger array, storing it in a temporary pointer.

```
Die** temp = new (std::nothrow) Die* [numberOfDice + numDie];
```

Now, we must copy in all of the existing Die elements, if any. Notice that if the array is empty, the loop does not execute.

```
for (i=0; i<numberOfDice; i++) {
  temp[i] = dieArray[i];
}
```

Next, we allocate the required number of new Die objects of the number of sides requested, adding these onto the end of the array. However, if part way through allocating these new Die objects, we run out of memory, then let's delete those new ones that we have allocated, keeping the original array intact. Notice that j becomes the subscript of the first empty slot in the new array we are filling.

```
for (i=0, j=numberOfDice; i<numDie; i++, j++) {
  temp[j] = new (std::nothrow) Die (numSides);
  if (!temp[j]) {
    cerr << "Error out of memory in Dice - allocating die\n";
    for (int k=numberOfDice; k<j; k++) {
      if (temp[k]) delete temp[k];
    }
    delete [] temp;
    return false;
  }
}
```

When the loop finished allocating and adding in the new Die objects, then we simply delete the old array of pointers and assign our member variable this new temporary address and add in the number of new dice added.

```
delete [] dieArray;
dieArray = temp;
numberOfDice += numDie;
return true;
```

In the destructor, we first loop through each element in the array and delete that Die object. Only then can we safely delete the array of pointers to Die objects. The remainder of the coding is straightforward.

```
Class Dice Implementation

1 #include <iostream>
2 using namespace std;
3 #include "Dice.h"
4
5 /*************************************************************/
6 /*                                                          */
7 /* Dice: simulates rolling a collection of dice             */
```

```
 8 /*                                                                        */
 9 /***************************************************************************/
10
11 /***************************************************************************/
12 /*                                                                        */
13 /* Dice: construct an empty growable array of die                         */
14 /*                                                                        */
15 /***************************************************************************/
16
17 Dice::Dice () {
18   dieArray = 0;
19   numberOfDice = 0;
20 }
21
22          // add a die of this type to the array
23 bool   Dice::AddDie (int numDie, int numSides) {
24   if (numSides < Die::MinimumNumSides)
25     numSides = Die::MinimumNumSides;
26
27   if (numDie < 0) {
28     cerr << "Error: trying to add too few new dice\n";
29     return false;
30   }
31
32   // allocate a new array of Die pointers to hold numDie more
33   Die** temp = new (std::nothrow) Die* [numberOfDice + numDie];
34   if (!temp) {
35     cerr << "Error: out of memory making the Die array in Dice\n";
36     return false;
37   }
38
39   int i, j;
40   // copy existing Die pointers into the larger array
41   for (i=0; i<numberOfDice; i++) {
42     temp[i] = dieArray[i];
43   }
44   // allocate and store all newly added dice
45   for (i=0, j=numberOfDice; i<numDie; i++, j++) {
46     temp[j] = new (std::nothrow) Die (numSides);
47     if (!temp[j]) {
48       // ran out of memory, so remove only those we've added
49       cerr << "Error out of memory in Dice - allocating die\n";
50       for (int k=numberOfDice; k<j; k++) {
51         if (temp[k]) delete temp[k];
52       }
53       delete [] temp;
54       return false;
55     }
56   }
57
58   // delete old array and reset new one and its count
59   delete [] dieArray;
60   dieArray = temp;
```

208

```
 61   numberOfDice += numDie;
 62   return true;
 63 }
 64
 65 /******************************************************************/
 66 /*                                                              */
 67 /* ~Dice: remove the allocated die_array and individual dice    */
 68 /*                                                              */
 69 /******************************************************************/
 70
 71 Dice::~Dice () {
 72   for (int i=numberOfDice-1; i>=0; i--) delete dieArray[i];
 73   delete [] dieArray;
 74 }
 75
 76 /******************************************************************/
 77 /*                                                              */
 78 /* Roll: roll all the dice at one time - use GetTotal, Display */
 79 /*       or GetDieValues to retrieve the results of this roll   */
 80 /*                                                              */
 81 /******************************************************************/
 82
 83 Dice&     Dice::Roll () {
 84   if (!numberOfDice) {
 85     cerr << "No Dice have been allocated!\n";
 86   }
 87   else {
 88     for (int i=0; i<numberOfDice; i++) dieArray[i]->Toss ();
 89   }
 90   return *this;
 91 }
 92
 93 /******************************************************************/
 94 /*                                                              */
 95 /* GetTotal: returns the sum of all the dice in this roll       */
 96 /*                                                              */
 97 /******************************************************************/
 98
 99 int       Dice::GetTotal () const {
100   int total = 0;
101   for (int i=0; i<numberOfDice; i++) {
102     total += dieArray[i]->GetRollValue ();
103   }
104   return total;
105 }
106
107 /******************************************************************/
108 /*                                                              */
109 /* Display: show the results like this: 2 + 4 + 5 = 11          */
110 /*                                                              */
111 /******************************************************************/
112
113 const Dice&  Dice::Display (ostream& os) const {
```

```
114  if (!numberOfDice) {
115   os << "No Dice have been allocated";
116   return *this;
117   }
118
119   for (int i=0; i<numberOfDice; i++) {
120    os << dieArray[i]->GetRollValue ();
121    if (i < numberOfDice -1) os << " + ";
122   }
123   os << " = " << GetTotal ();
124   return *this;
125  }
126
127  /*****************************************************************/
128  /*                                                               */
129  /* GetDieValues: fill up the user's array with the individual   */
130  /*               die roll values but avoid overwriting memory   */
131  /*               if user's array is too small                   */
132  /*                                                               */
133  /*****************************************************************/
134
135  void      Dice::GetDieValues (int die[], int count) const {
136   int num_to_do = count < numberOfDice ? count : numberOfDice;
137   for (int i=0; i<num_to_do; i++)
138    die[i] = dieArray[i]->GetRollValue ();
139  }
140
141  /*****************************************************************/
142  /*                                                               */
143  /* GetNumberOfDice: returns the number of dice in the array    */
144  /*                                                               */
145  /*****************************************************************/
146
147  int    Dice::GetNumberOfDice () const {
148   return numberOfDice;
149  }
150
151  /*****************************************************************/
152  /*                                                               */
153  /* GetDieSides:  fill up the user's array with the individual  */
154  /*               die number of sides, avoid overwriting memory */
155  /*               if user's array is too small                   */
156  /*                                                               */
157  /*****************************************************************/
158
159  void   Dice::GetDieSides (int dieSides[], int count) const {
160   int num_to_do = count < numberOfDice ? count : numberOfDice;
161   for (int i=0; i<num_to_do; i++)
162    dieSides[i] = dieArray[i]->GetNumberSides ();
163  }
```

Finally, here is a small tester program that illustrates the actions and its output.

```
 1 #include <iostream>
 2 using namespace std;
 3
 4 #include "Dice.h"
 5
 6 #include <crtdbg.h> // for memory leak checking
 7
 8 void ShowSides (int a[], int num);
 9 void ShowDieValues (int a[], int num);
10
11
12 int main () {
13   {
14   int a[20];
15
16   Dice d;  // empty set
17   cout << "Should get empty array error message\n";
18   d.Roll ();
19   cout << endl;
20   d.AddDie (2, 6);
21   d.GetDieSides (a, sizeof (a));
22   ShowSides (a, d.GetNumberOfDice());
23   d.Roll ();
24   cout << "Should see 2 6-sided dice\n";
25   d.Display ();
26   cout << "\nThe total of this roll is: " << d.GetTotal() << endl;
27   d.GetDieValues (a, sizeof (a));
28   ShowDieValues (a, d.GetNumberOfDice());
29   cout << endl;
30
31   cout << endl;
32   d.AddDie (4, 8);
33   d.GetDieSides (a, sizeof (a));
34   ShowSides (a, d.GetNumberOfDice());
35   d.Roll ();
36   cout << "Should see 2 6-sided + 4 8-sided dice\n";
37   d.Display ();
38   cout << "\nThe total of this roll is: " << d.GetTotal() << endl;
39   d.GetDieValues (a, sizeof (a));
40   ShowDieValues (a, d.GetNumberOfDice());
41   cout << endl;
42   }
43
44   // check for memory leaks
45   if (_CrtDumpMemoryLeaks())
46     cerr << "Memory leaks occurred!\n";
47   else
48     cerr << "No memory leaks.\n";
49
```

```
50  return 0;
51 }
52
53 void ShowSides (int a[], int num) {
54  cout << "Number of dice: " << num  << endl << "Sides: ";
55  for (int i=0; i<num; i++)
56   cout << a[i] << " ";
57  cout << endl;
58 }
59
60 void ShowDieValues (int a[], int num) {
61  for (int i=0; i<num; i++) {
62   cout << a[i] << (i < num -1? " + " : "\n");
63  }
64 }
```

```
Output of the Small Tester Program

 1 Should get empty array error message
 2 No Dice have been allocated!
 3
 4 Number of dice: 2
 5 Sides: 6 6
 6 Should see 2 6-sided dice
 7 3 + 4 = 7
 8 The total of this roll is: 7
 9 3 + 4
10
11
12 Number of dice: 6
13 Sides: 6 6 8 8 8 8
14 Should see 2 6-sided + 4 8-sided dice
15 2 + 4 + 8 + 4 + 4 + 4 = 26
16 The total of this roll is: 26
17 2 + 4 + 8 + 4 + 4 + 4
18
19 No memory leaks.
```

Making Production Libraries, Example 2

We now have a set of classes that ought to be put into production. When a class is fully operational, it is often put into production in a shared library of classes. The file extension of these is .lib. Users or client programs are given the header file and the lib file which with to link. The Visual C++ compiler can make such a lib file for us. When you choose File-New Project, after choosing Win32 Console Application, in the options, check **Win32 Static Library**. (In the series of dialogs that appear, do not check Pre-compiled Header or MFC Support.)

Make the folder as usual and then copy the header and implementation files that you desire to be part of the library package into that project folder. Right click on the project in Project View and choose Add Existing Files to Project. Build the project. Then use Explorer to examine the Debug or Release folders of the project. There you will find the .lib file. I did just this in Pgm05DiceLib

When you build these production libraries, make both a Release Build as well as a Debug Build. This way, while the client is debugging his code, he can use your debug versions of the production classes. Later, when he switches to a release build, your release versions are used. Shortly, we will see just how this works in practice.

Pgm05DiceLib does all of the above, making a library our of Random, Die, and Dice classes. I made both a Release and a Debug build. Open and examine that project, check the Project Properties as well.

Next, one would make the actual Production Libraries. For example, you might create the following folders.
D:\Production
D:\Production\Include
D:\Production\Lib
D:\Production\Lib\Debug
D:\Production\Lib\Release
One would then copy the header files only from your Lib project and paste them into the Include folder. Next, one would copy the release .lib file into the Release folder and the debug .lib file into the Debug folder.

Another approach which handles the situation of no control over where the client installs the sample programs is to create a Production folder under the Samples-2005 folder. Then, use the DOS syntax of ..\Production meaning go to the parent of the current folder and from there find the Production subfolder. Here is where I have copied all the relevant files. Use the Explorer to view what is where under the Production folder of your samples for this text.

I then made a new Project, Pgm05DiceLibTest and copied the little tester program into it.

Next, we need to see how a project can now access these production classes. Pgm05DiceLibTest illustrates how this is done, using our original simple tester program. First, make a new project and install your main cpp file. Next, click on the project icon in the Solution Explorer and choose Properties. In the C++ tab and General section, the first line is Additional Include Directories. Here is where you specify the location of your production include library. You can use the tiny browse button to navigate to where it is located or you can just type it in the box. You can have a fully qualified file specification or a partial one. If one had it setup as D:\Production\Include, then that is what I would enter in the edit control.

However, so that these projects will compile and run no matter where you chose to install the samples, I am using a relative path. Recall that I placed my Production folder directly beneath the

Samples folder. Thus, the Production folder is always beneath the parent of the current sample program folder, here Pgm05DiceLibTest. I used the DOS relative path method. The ..\\ means go to the parent of the current project folder, which is Samples. Then, from there find the Production subfolder and then the Include one. Figure 5.2 shows this setting.

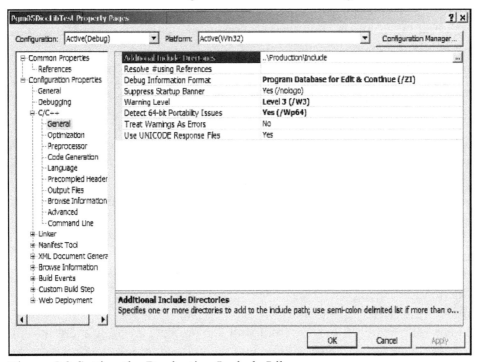

Figure 5.2 Setting the Production Include Library

Once you set the additional include property, the program will compile. However, it will not link because the compiler cannot find the .lib files which contain the object code. Another setting must be made. However, this setting must be made differently, depending upon which type of build the client selects. Select the Linker tab and then the General tab. Notice at the bottom is Additional library directories. Then look at the Input tab just below the General tab and the notice the Additional Dependencies on the top line on that one. There are the two places we need to modify.

Notice in the upper left of the properties window is a combobox called Configuration. It has settings for Debug and Release. Active Debug might be the current one if you have just made a new project. Set the configuration to Debug or Active Debug. Go to the General tab and the Additional Library directories. Here, enter the path to the debug version of your production .lib files. I entered a relative path of ..\\Production\\Lib\\Debug. Next, click on the Input tab and go to the Additional Dependencies edit control. Here, enter the name of the .lib file. I entered Pgm05DiceLib.lib.

Now repeat these steps to set the version to use when making a Release Build. First, at the very top, select Release. First, go to the C++ tab and General section. On the first line of Additional Include Directories, specify once more the location of your production include library. Then, click on Linker-General and enter the path to the release version in the Additional Libraries line. Finally, go to the Input tab and enter the Pgm05DiceLib.lib as Additional Dependencies. Click Ok and you are all set. The following two figures show these settings.

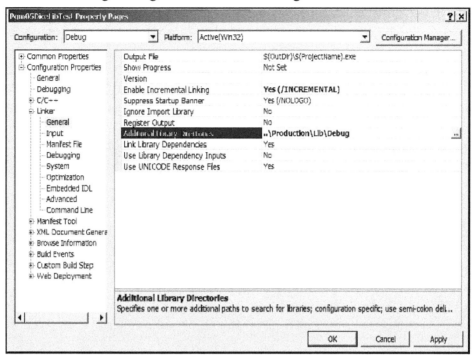

Figure 5.2 Setting the Production Lib Folder

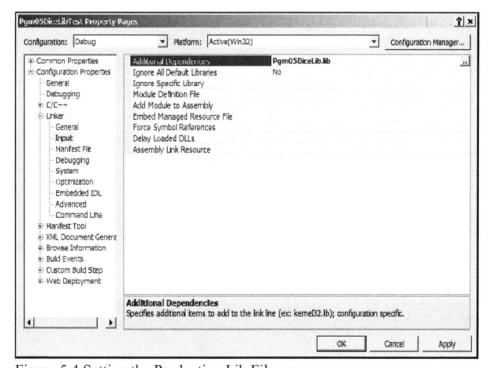

Figure 5.4 Setting the Production Lib Filename

215

Okay, now you try it. Make yourself your personal Production libraries where you desire them. Next, make a new project and copy Pgm05DiceLibTest.cpp into that new project folder. Now add it to the project. Next, make the three new project settings for the Debug version and then the three for the Release Build. Now verify you can build both a Debug and Release version and that it does run.

There is one slight glitch when using this method. If you do not actually include the production headers in the Solution Explorer for the project, as you would normally, then Intellisense does not work. True, the project will compile fine, but there is no Intellisense help available. What I often do is temporarily Add Existing Item and add the specific Production header file to the project so that Intellisense works. Later, one can delete that header from the Solution Explorer project.

Review Questions

1. Why is **#ifndef**/**#define** logic used in header files? Show an example of circular headers that absolutely must have this logic in them or **main.cpp** will not compile.

2. Explain why a class might wish to have an instance of some other class as one of its data members.

3. What is a forward reference? If, in the definition of class A, an instance of class B is used as a data member or as a parameter copy, can a forward reference be used? Why or why not. If in the definition of class A a reference to an instance of class B is used as a parameter, can a forward reference be used?

4. Under what circumstances does the class definition of class B have to be included in the definition file for class A?

5. What is the **this** pointer? How does it get a value? What value does it get?

6. What use is the **this** parameter to us as we code our member functions? When would we absolutely need the **this** parameter?

7. What is a class **enum**? Why are they useful? How does a class **enum** differ from an ordinary **enum**?

8. What is a friend function? Does a friend function have a **this** parameter? Is a friend function a class member function?

9. What is meant by constant data members? Give an example of a constant data member in some class not mention in this chapter.

10. By what point in the constructor coding must all constant data members have their values?

11. What is meant by the term base class and member initialization mechanism? When can it be used? What purpose does it serve at this point in our studies of OOP?

12. What is a copy constructor? Give three situations in which it is called by the compiler.

13. How can we make certain constructors unavailable for client programs to use?

14. Why would a class need or desire a reference member variable? How can a constructor initialize a reference variable?

15. What is a **static** data member? Under what circumstances would a **static** data member be useful for a class?

16. If 100 instances of a class are created which also has a **static** data member, how many instances of the **static** data member are created? If there are no instances yet created of that same class, how many instances are there of that **static** data member?

17. Can a member function access a **static** data member?

18. What is a **static** member function? What purpose do **static** member functions serve? Do they have a this parameter? Can a **static** member function access instance data of an instance of the class?

19. What is an inline function? Why do inlined functions execute more quickly? What is the price that one pays for having inline functions? Why cannot you use the debugger to step through the instructions in an inline function?

20. What is meant by implicit type conversion that the compiler performs? How is it useful? How can it be confusing when debugging a program that has errors in it?

21. What is meant by a lib project? How are production libraries of OOP classes useful?

22. What happens if the client program codes the following?
```
    Point p;
    this->SetCoordinates (42,10);
```

23. Write a class **enum** called **Month** for use in a **Date** class. The **enum** values contain three letter abbreviations for the 12 month names such as Jan for example.

Stop! Do These Exercises Before Programming

1. Look over the **Dice** series of three classes. These three classes are not robust or bulletproof. That is, client programs can easily still perform "illegal" actions with them. List all of the potential error situations that could create program crashes or illegal operations with a set of dice.

2. A programmer decided to implement a class called **Line**. He began with a simple header file shown below. What is syntactically wrong with it and what is non-optimum about the header file? Show how these can be corrected.

Line.h
```
struct Point {
  double x;
  double y;
}
class Line {
protected
  Point left;
  Point right;
public
  Line ();
  Line (const Point& l, const Point r);
}
```

3. A different programmer decided to implement a class called **Line** in an alternate way. He began with the following. What is syntactically wrong with it and what is non-optimum about the header files? Show how these can be corrected.

Point.h
```
class Point {
  double x;
  double y;
}
```
Line.h
```
class Line {
protected
  Point left;
  Point right;
public
  Line ();
  Line (const Point& l, const Point r);
}
```

4. A third programmer tried his hand at creating a more optimum design and coded it this way. What is wrong with this version and how can it be corrected?

Point.h
```
class Point {
  double x;
```

```
     double y;
    }
```
Line.h
```
    class Line {
    protected
     Point& left;
     Point& right;
    public
     Line ();
     Line (const Point& l, const Point r);
    }
```

5. A programmer tried to implement the **Point** class constructor but it does not compile. Show four different approaches to making it work, only one of which should use the base class and member initialization mechanism.
```
    Point::Point (int x, int y) {
     x = x;
     y = y;
    }
```

6. Write a definition for a **Client** class that defines a class **enum ClientType** to store the values **SmallBusiness**, **Corporation**, and **Chain**. In the class, define an instance of this type. Code the prototype for a constructor that takes such an **enum**. Code the prototype for a function **GetClientType()** which returns the corresponding member variable. Then, write a **main()** function that creates three instances of the **Client** class each with a different type.

7. Assume the definition of the **Point** class given at the beginning of this chapter. Write a **Compare()** member function that returns true if the two points are equal, that is, if both their x and y values match each other. Then write a **compare()** friend function to do the same thing. Show the prototypes and then the function bodies. Show how a client could call each of the two comparison functions.

8. Write the class definition and inline the constructor function as described below. The class is called Car. It has two data members. One is the constant long integer vinNumber and the other is its speed. The constructor function takes a long number and the integer current speed.

9. In the class definition in question 8 above, show how one could prevent a client program from car cloning by coding
```
    Car a (123445, 42);
    Car b (a);
```

10. Modify the **Point** class given at the very start of this chapter. Add a static data member called **counter** whose initial value is 0. Add a static member function called **GetPointInstances()** which returns this counter's value. Modify the constructors to increment this counter and add a destructor to decrement this count. Show the modified header and definition files. Also show how a client program can track how many **Point** instances are in existence at any point in time.

219

Programming Problems

Problem Pgm05-1 —A Date Class—II

Modify the **Date** class of Problem **Pgm04-1** as follows to make it more efficient and useful.

Modifications to the Interface for the Date Class

Create 3 constructors:
>   One version takes 3 integers for month, day, and year in that order
>   One takes a constant character string of the form "9/1/1997" (meaning September 1, 1997)
>   A default constructor with no arguments

The default ctor initializes the date to the current computer system date. There is a short example at the end of these specifications that shows you how to access the local time on your PC. Note that, if you wish to use a constructor that takes a **long** serial date, it must be made private. It is not required that you have a constructor that takes a **long**, however.

Compare function:
>   This function, **Compare()**, takes another **Date** object and compares it to this date.
>   It returns a positive integer when this date is greater than the passed date, 0 if
>   the same, and a negative integer if less. Neither date is altered by this function.

usage: `int result = mydate.Compare (otherdate);`

Difference function:
>   This function, **Difference()**, returns the **long** number of days from the this date to
>   the passed date. It is negative when this date is before the passed date. Neither
>   this date nor the passed date are altered.

usage: `long diff = mydate.Difference (otherdate);`

Add function:
>   This function, **Add()**, allows one to add a **long** number of days onto this date,
>   returning the new date. It does not alter the date object itself.

usage: `Date z = mydate.Add (100L); // add 100 days to this date`

Subtract function:
>   This function, **Subtract()**, allows one to subtract a **long** number of days from this
>   date, returning the new date. It does not alter the date object itself.

usage: `Date z = mydate.Subtract (100L); // subs 100 from this date`

Note that for both Add and Subtract, the passed **long** could be positive or negative.

Input function:

This function, **Input()**, takes a reference to an **istream** and inputs a date of the form mm/dd/yy or mm/dd/yyyy. It should return a reference to the passed **istream**. Again, if the year is of the form 99, add 1900 to it. Ignore the fact that this is not year 2000 compliant.

Output function:

This function, **Output()**, takes a reference to an **ostream** and outputs the formatted date: 01/01/1997 for example. It should return a reference to the passed **ostream**. Always print 2 digits for the month and day and 4 digits for the year with a slash between them.

Remember that **Date** arguments should be passed by reference. Decide on how to use the **const** qualifier.

Here is how you can get the current date from your PC:
```
#include <ctime>
...
time_t now;
tm    *ptrtime;
now = time (NULL);
ptrtime = localtime (&now);

int mo, da, yr;
mo = ptrtime->tm_mon + 1;
da = ptrtime->tm_mday;
yr = ptrtime->tm_year + 1900;
```

I would suggest you write a simple testing main program to test the **Date** class until you feel it is working. Then, try to add in the provided **main()** program below. The source is in the **TestDataForAssignments** folder.

Test your class by running the provided **Pgm05-1.cpp** tester **main()** program. It inputs the file **Pgm05-1.txt** and writes a results file, **Pgm05-1Output.txt**. The correct output should be as follows:

```
 DATE  1          DATE  2          DIFFERENCE

01/01/1996       01/01/1996              0
01/02/1996       01/01/1996              1
01/02/1995       01/01/1996           -364
02/01/1996       01/01/1996             31
02/01/1995       01/01/1996           -334
03/01/1996       01/01/1996             60
03/01/1995       01/01/1996           -306
12/31/1996       01/01/1996            365
12/31/1995       01/01/1996             -1
```

```
01/01/1997    01/01/1996         366
01/01/1994    01/01/1996        -730
03/01/1997    01/01/1996         425
03/01/1994    01/01/1996        -671
06/15/1997    01/01/1996         531
06/15/1994    01/01/1996        -565
09/20/1999    01/01/1996        1358
09/20/1993    01/01/1996        -833
01/01/2000    01/01/1996        1461
01/01/1990    01/01/1996       -2191
04/21/2000    01/01/1996        1572
04/21/1990    01/01/1996       -2081
12/31/2400    01/01/1996      147923
12/31/1601    01/01/1996     -143906
01/01/1900    01/01/1900           0
12/31/2400    01/01/1601      292193
01/01/2000    12/31/1899       36525
01/01/2000    12/31/2400     -146462
07/01/2049    01/01/1900       54603
07/01/1750    01/01/1900      -54605
01/01/1601    12/31/2100     -182620


conDateA  =  12/31/1899
conDateB  =  01/01/2000
date_1    =  12/31/1899
date_2    =  01/01/2000
```

Problem Pgm05-2 —The Piggy Bank Class

Write a class to encapsulate a child's piggy bank. Allow for pennies, nickels, dimes, quarters, half dollars and dollar coins. Also allow for unknown type coins because children often insert any kind of coin token into their piggy banks. Create a class **enum** called **CoinType** that defines a coin's type (dime, nickel and so on). The **PiggyBank** class needs to keep track of the number of each type of coin in the bank. Thus, you can make a **Coin** structure that contains the coin type, number of those coins and string name of the coin type and store an array of these in the **PiggyBank** class. Or you can design a class **Coin** that encapsulates this same information and store an array of **Coin** objects in the **PiggyBank** class.

Next, decide what member functions the **PiggyBank** class would need to have. Certainly it must have an **AddCoin()** function and some means of displaying the entire contents of the **PiggyBank**. There must also be some way to remove a coin from the **PiggyBank**. See what other functions a **PiggyBank** ought to have.

After writing the class, create a testing oracle. Then write a client program to thoroughly test your **PiggyBank** class.

Problem Pgm05-3—A Checkbook Class

With electronic checking becoming more popular, design a **Checkbook** class to manage an account electronically.

Assume that a check contains the person's name and account number, the check number, to whom the check is written, the date, and the amount. A deposit slip contains the person's name and account number, the deposit number, the date, and the amount.

The default constructor, **Checkbook()**, initializes all fields to reasonable defaults, such as zero. Additionally, no other operations on an account whose account number is 0 are permitted until **Setup()** is called. **Setup()** is passed the person's name, account number, and the initial deposit. Provide an overloaded constructor that takes the person's name, account number, and the initial deposit.

With all financial type operations, a transaction's log is essential to maintain an account's history. Thus, the overloaded constructor and **Setup()** must take an additional parameter, the name of this customer's transaction log file. The first line in the log file should contain the information passed to **Setup()** or the overloaded constructor. Thus, after initializing the member data, these functions should open the transaction's log file and write that first line of data and then close the file.

Assume check and deposit numbers begin with number 100. Member operational functions consist of **GetBalance()**, **MakeDeposit()** and **WriteCheck()**. These functions should perform the indicated actions. In addition, **MakeDeposit()** and **WriteCheck()** must also reopen the transaction's log and append an additional line with the relevant deposit or check information.

Another operation is **DisplayHistory()**. This function opens the transaction log file and displays a report of the initial state and the account activities.

Write a tester program that thoroughly tests the **Checkbook** class.

Problem Pgm05-4—A Distance Class—II

Review Problem **Pgm04-5—A Distance Class—I**. We are going to make a number of revisions to it in Part A.

Part A. Revise the Distance class as follows.

1. Create two public class **enums**. The first is called **Type** whose values are **Metric** and **English**. The second **enum** is **ShowAs** whose values are **Mm, Feet, Meter, Miles**.

2. The default constructor remains unchanged. However, change all the other constructors to accept the **enum Type** as the **first** parameter. The other constructors and their **additional** parameters are now to be

      accept a **double** number of millimeters

      accept a **double** representing miles—careful with this one

      accept a **long** meters, **long** centimeters, and **double** millimeters (it was 3 **longs**). Also,
           default the millimeters parameter to 0

      accept a **long** feet and **double** inches, defaulting inches to 0 (it was 2 **ints**)

3. Modify member functions:

      GetDistance() is now passed the **Type enum** and based on its value returns the
           distance as a **double** millimeters or inches.

      SetDistance() is now passed the **Type enum** as a first parameter and then a **double**
           which represents either mm or inches according to the **enum** value.

      Paint() is now passed the **enum ShowAs** instead of the **char** and is used to
           determine how to print the distance. Default it to display in millimeters.

4. Remove **MtoE()** and **EtoM()** as class member functions. They are now to be stand-alone C style utility or helper functions.

      MtoE() is passed a **double** millimeters measurement and returns that value
           converted into a **double** inches.

      MtoE() is passed a reference to a **Distance** object. It returns the object's distance
           as a **double** inches.

      EtoM() is passed a **double** inches measurement and returns that value converted to
           a **double** millimeters.

      EtoM() is passed a reference to a **Distance** object and a **double** inches. After converting
           the inches into millimeters, it stores that measurement in the **Distance** object and
           returns the millimeters as a **double**.

5. Once again, decide which upon where the **const** keyword should be applied on both functions and parameters.

6. Create a main program to **thoroughly** test the **Distance** class. Be sure to illustrate **EtoM()** actually alters the passed **Distance** object.

Part B. Construct a class Path Class that Has Distance Objects as Data Members

We wish to construct a **Path** class that encapsulates a trajectory a moving object might take. For now, ignore the starting point and direction of travel. Instead, just store the line segment distances traveled along the path of movement.

1. The two private data members consist of an integer count of the number of **Distance** objects in the array and the array **path** which is a dynamically allocated array of **Distance** objects, for example

```
Distance *path;
int       count;
```

2. The **Path()** constructor sets **path** to NULL and the **count** to 0.

3. The **destructor** deletes the array of **Distances**, if any.

4. The public member function, **AddPath()**, allocates a new array of **count + 1 Distance** objects using the **new** operator, storing the pointer in say **temp**. Then, for each of the original **Distance** objects in the original array, it copies the original data into the new array's objects. Then, it copies the new **Distance** object's values into the last array object. The old array (which is pointed to by **path**) is then deleted and **path** is assigned the new array (**temp**) and **count** is incremented. (Yes, there are other far better ways of avoiding this awkward copying, but save them for later on. For now, you are after the experience of working with arrays, **new**, and **delete**.) Note that this is basically a growable array type of data structure.

The prototype for **AddPath()** is

```
        void AddPath (Distance &d);
```

5. The last member function of **Path** is **ShowPath()** which takes no parameters. It should display a series of messages that trace the complete path array of distance. If there were three distances in the path array, your output might be

```
        Tracing this path of 3 segments
           Segment 1: 45 mm
           Segment 2: 105 mm
           Segment 3: 9 mm
```

6. Your first main tester program should look something of the order of this

```
int main () {
 Distance d[3];
 d[0].SetDistance (Distance::Metric, 45);
 d[1].SetDistance (Distance::Metric, 105);
 d[2].SetDistance (Distance::Metric, 9);
   { // allow destructor to be called before main ends
```

```
        Path p;
        p.AddPath (d[0]);
        p.AddPath (d[1]);
        p.AddPath (d[2]);
        p.ShowPath ();
    }
  return 0;
}
```

7. Once you have this basic main testing program working, then run the **Pgm05-4.cpp** testing main program I have provided. Be very alert for memory leaks, that is, failing to free allocated memory. Note that you will need to insert compiler specific memory leak check coding at the indicated location in the tester program.

Turn in the test runs from both main programs (from Step 6 and 7). Your output from **Pgm05-4** should appear as:

```
Displaying Path1 Results:
Tracing this path of 6 segments
Segment 0: Distance is =            1000.50 millimeters
Segment 1: Distance is =      1610152055.90 millimeters
Segment 2: Distance is =          100086.30 millimeters
Segment 3: Distance is =            1181.10 millimeters
Segment 4: Distance is =           10010.00 millimeters
Segment 5: Distance is =            1524.00 millimeters


Displaying Path2 Results:
Tracing this path of 5 segments
Segment 0: Distance is =            1000.50 millimeters
Segment 1: Distance is =            1000.00 millimeters
Segment 2: Distance is =            1000.00 millimeters
Segment 3: Distance is =            1000.00 millimeters
Segment 4: Distance is =              42.00 millimeters
```

Pgm05-5—An Employee Class I (Using the Date Class)

The purpose of this assignment is to write and use a class which has a member variable from another class. Specifically, it uses the Date II class from **Pgm05-1** above.

The Employee Class Interface

Design an **Employee** class to contain the employee name, identification number and date hired. The id number is a one- to nine-digit integer; the name is a maximum of 20 characters; the date hired is in mm/dd/yyyy format. Note that you should have a **Date** object for the hired date as one of the three **Employee** data members.

226

Create the following public member functions:

The **default constructor** sets the id number to 0, the name to a null string ("") and the date hired to 01/01/2400.

The **Input()** function is passed a reference to any kind of input stream and returns that reference. The data order is id number followed by name and then the date hired. The name is enclosed in quote marks ("") so that blanks can be part of the name. Do not retain the quote marks in the name member variable. Typical invocations might be as follows.

```
emp.Input (infile);
```

The **OutputToFile()** function is passed a reference to any kind of output stream and it returns that reference. It displays on the output stream the contents of the employee record. Show the id number first with leading 0's as needed for a length of 9 digits (use the **setfill()** function). Then, have one blank separating the id number from the employee name. Surround the outputted employee name with leading and trailing quote marks. Lastly, display the date hired beginning in column 34 always. Display the date in the usual format mm/dd/yyyy. Typical invocations might be as follows.

```
emp.Output (outfile);
```

The **CompareDate()** function is passed another **Employee** object and returns an **int** that is 0 if the two hire dates are the same. It returns a positive integer if this employee's hire date is greater than the passed date; a negative integer if less than. Typical invocations might be as follows.

```
if (emp.CompareDate (other_emp)) ...
```

The **GetId()** function returns the employee's identification number.

```
long id = emp.GetId ();
```

The **GetName()** function returns the employee's name as a **const char***.

```
const char *name = emp.GetName ();
```

The **GetHireDate()** function returns the employee's hire date.

```
Date hiredate = emp.GetHireDate ();
```

There are **no** other public member functions. You may have any protected or private member functions you wish. Create a separate **Employee.h** and **Employee.cpp** set of files. Include the **Date.h** file as needed. Notice that in the **Employee** class, you will have an instance of the **Date** class as a member variable.

The Main Program Client

Create the main client program that uses the **Employee** class. All functions described below belong in the **main.cpp** file and **not** in the **Employee** class.

1. Call a load array function that inputs a file of employee data (**employee1.txt**) into an array. The file is in the test data folder as usual.

2. Call an output file function that outputs the array (via calls to the **Employee**'s **OutputToFile()**) to a file on disk called **employee_new.txt**. Output the 9-digit id number first followed by 1 blank, followed by the name surrounded by quote marks. Start the date field in column 34 always. When done, do a file compare of the original data with your new file—they should be the same.

```
c:>fc  employee1.dat   employee_new.dat
```

3. Now make a **Date** object to hold the report date of December 31, 2010. Make a printed report (output redirection is ok) with appropriate column headings as shown in the attached printout. Put the report date at the top. Calculate the years hired and display that in the fourth column on the report. Convert the report date and the hired date into days and subtract to find the total days of employment. Then divide by 365.25 to get the years employed. Your report should be similar to the sample output shown below.

Turn in a screen shot of your file compare along with the printed report from step 3.

```
Report Date: 12/31/2010

ID Number   Employee Name          Date Hired      Years
                                                    Employed

333445555   AILSHIE, LARRY         01/01/1990      21.00
444662000   ANDERSON, J. DENNIS    11/16/1985      25.12
555770001   BENSON, JAMES          12/04/1982      28.07
000008888   BOLDEN, EDWARD         01/05/1977      33.98
011111111   BRAHAM, JOSEPH         08/19/1986      24.37
444562001   BROWN, CLAYTON         03/07/1988      22.82
000002001   CALLAM, LARRY          10/15/1991      19.21
666779003   COPELAND, LINDA        01/02/1994      16.99
000000011   DARNELL, FREDERICK     07/22/1975      35.44
444561001   FREY, WILLIAM          05/29/1986      24.59
444562000   HANNAH, CAROL          04/28/1987      23.68
000666666   HERLAN, WILLIAM        02/28/1995      15.84
000000001   HOOP, JEANETTE         05/16/1968      42.63
445660001   JARETT, PAUL           09/14/1992      18.29
000667777   LACEY, JAMES           02/06/1989      21.90
444557000   MCCLEARY, JANE         12/31/1988      22.00
000007777   NOBEL, WILLIAM         04/01/1979      31.75
666778888   NOONCASTER, BRENDA     07/18/1987      23.46
555777777   NUTTING, TERESA        11/03/1983      27.16
666778889   RAINTREE, VICTORIA     06/17/1988      22.54
444560002   REEVES, WILLA          08/23/1993      17.36
555777778   RICHARDSON, O. SUSAN   10/02/1984      26.25
000779001   SEVERNS, JERRY         03/04/1992      18.83
445661000   STEARNS, KENNETH       06/21/1995      15.53
000778888   TYNER, CHARLES         09/10/1985      25.31
666779000   WATASHE, KENNETH       04/05/1991      19.74
000000099   WOOD, STEVEN           07/22/1972      38.44
444556667   WOODS, REBECCA JANIE   01/02/1995      15.99
666779002   YOUNG, RICHARD         02/03/1993      17.91
```

Chapter 6—Operator Overloading

Introduction

The C++ operators, such as +, -, [], ==, >>, and <<, can be overloaded just as ordinary functions can be overloaded. These are called **operator overloaded** functions. The syntax is a bit unusual because of the "name of the function" is + for example. Assume that the **Point** class has two protected data members **x** and **y**. By providing overloaded operator functions, we can extend the functionality of the **Point** class. Here are some likely operations a client program might desire.

```
Point a, b, c;
c = a + b;
a++;
c = a;
if (a == b) ;
cin >> a;
cout << b;
```

While each of the above do not look like function calls, they are, in fact, operator overloaded function calls. The general syntax of these unusual looking functions is as follows.

```
return type  classname::operatorZ (argument list);
```

where "Z" is the operator. The name of the functions in the above **Point** examples are

operator+, **operator++**, **operator==**, **operator=**, **operator>>**, and **operator<<**

The return type is most frequently the class for which the function is defined, such as **Point** in this case. However, you can return most anything desired. In fact, the implementation is totally up to the programmer. That is, one can define **operator+** for the **Point** class to actually add 42 to both coordinates, plot this point on a graph, output this point's distance from the origin while returning the square root of that distance!

However, a cardinal rule applies to OOP operator overloading.

Rule: Always maintain the spirit of the C++ operator.

When implementing the operator overloaded function, the actions it performs should parallel what would occur if the intrinsic C++ operator was being invoked on intrinsic types. That is, when implementing **operator+**

```
c = a + b;
```

the actions you take for the **Point**'s **operator+** should parallel that that would occur if the data types of the three variables were **int**. Maintain the spirit of C++ usage of operators when overloading them.

Which operators in the C++ language can be overridden? It is easier to state which operators cannot be overridden. The only operators that cannot be overridden are **. :: ? :** and any of the

229

preprocessor directives. Yes, **[]** and even **()** function call operators can be overridden! Even **new** and **delete** can be overridden.

> **Rule: The precedence of C++ operators neither can be altered nor can the number of parameters an operator requires be altered.**

> **Corollary: Thus, operator overloaded functions cannot have default arguments.**

Examine the series of operations on the three **Point** objects above. Notice the similarities. The operator overloaded functions break down into two categories: **binary operators** and **unary operators**. A binary operator function has two parameters; a unary operator has only one. In the above examples with the three **Point** objects, only the increment operator is a unary operator. The others are binary in nature. One cannot say the following.

```
c = a *
a /
a =
a -
```

The compiler as well as the reader says multiply **a** by what? Divide **a** by what? Assign what to **a**? Subtract what from **a**?

First, let's examine the overloading of the binary operators and then the unary operators.

Overloading Binary Operators

Overloading the Math Binary Operators (such as + and –)

Suppose our **Point** class is defined this way.

```
class Point {
protected:
  int x;
  int y;
public:
  Point () : x(0), y(0){}
  Point (int xx, int yy) {x = xx; y = yy;}
  Point (const Point& p) : x(p.x), y(p.y) {}
};
```

We want to be able to write such operations as these.

```
Point a (5, 10), b (10, 20), c;
c = a + b;
c = c + 42;
c = 42 + c;
```

> **Rule: When overloading binary operators, there is only one parameter—the item that is to the right of the operator! It is the object on the left of the operator**

that generates the function call. The *this* parameter is used to pass the left side object to the function.

In the above desired addition operation,
```
c = a + b;
```
it is object **a** that invokes the **operator+** function passing object **b** as a parameter to the **operator+** function. So in the **Point::operator+** function, *this* points to object **a**. Thus, we would expect to need a prototype of the following.
```
Point    operator+ (Point b);
```

In the second case,
```
c = c + 42;
```
here object **c** is passed with the *this* parameter and the **42 int** is passed as the single argument. We would expect to need a prototype of the following.
```
Point    operator+ (int i);
```

In the third case,
```
c = 42 + c;
```
the integer class's **operator+** is invoked passing object **c** as its parameter; immediately we have a problem! There is no integer class **operator+** function! In this case we have no choice but to write an ordinary C style nonmember function that is a friend of the **Point** class.

Let's look at each of these in turn. Let's take them in order. The simplest case is
```
Point    operator+ (Point p);
```
for
```
c = a + b;
```
However, we know passing copies of objects is slow and inefficient, especially if the class has dynamically allocated memory or contains a lot of member data. We can immediately try this variation.
```
Point    operator+ (Point& p);
```
But wait a moment. If the three objects were integers, would the value of integer **b** be altered in the statement? No. Thus, we should pass a constant reference.
```
Point    operator+ (const Point& p);
```

Further, if the three objects were integers, would integer **a** be changed by the instruction? Nope. And since object **a** is providing the *this* parameter, the function itself should be constant indicating that it is not changing the **this** object.
```
Point    operator+ (const Point& p) const;
```

Now what about the return data type? Consider the following line.
```
c = d = e = a + b;
```
If these were integers, we know that **c**, **d**, and **e** are all being assigned the same value. Chaining the assignment operator must therefore be considered at all times. This is why we must always try to return an instance of the class data type, here **Point**. But can we return a reference to a Point in order to make it more efficient? Remember, the object that the reference is pointing to must exist after the

function terminates and returns. Specifically, we cannot return a reference to a temporary automatic (or stack) instance that is defined within the operator function. Since neither **a** or **b** are being changed, we must construct a temporary **Point** object within the **operator+** function to hold the sum result. Thus, a reference cannot be returned.

These are the three considerations you must always make when creating the operator overloaded function prototype.

Can it be passed a constant reference to the parameter?
Can the entire function be constant?
Can it return an object or a reference to an object?

Thus, our prototype is

```
Point    operator+ (const Point& p) const;
```

Now how can it be implemented? The answer is that there are many ways it can be done, assuming that the addition of two points means to add the corresponding coordinate values. Let's examine several implementations. Here is the simplest way.

```
Point    Point::operator+ (const Point& p) const {
  Point ret;
  ret.x = x + p.x;
  ret.y = y + p.y;
  return ret;
}
```

It could also be implemented this way by making use of existing constructor functions.

```
Point    Point::operator+ (const Point& p) const {
  Point ret (x, y);
  ret.x += p.x;
  ret.y += p.y;
  return ret;
}
```

But we could also go a bit farther by coding only this.

```
Point    Point::operator+ (const Point& p) const {
  Point ret (x + p.x, y + p.y);
  return ret;
}
```

And finally, we could shorten it to just this.

```
Point    Point::operator+ (const Point& p) const {
  return Point (x + p.x, y + p.y);
}
```

Here, we are constructing an unnamed temporary **Point** object and initializing it to the desired two values and returning it to the caller.

Let's also examine an error version. What would this have done?

```
Point    Point::operator+ (const Point &p) { // error!
```

```
x = x + p.x;
y = y + p.y;
return *this;
}
```

In this case the *this* object is **altered**. Coding **c = a + b;** yields both **c** and **a** now containing the sum of **a + b**! However, coding **c = c + b;** would have first altered **c** to being **c + b** and then copied that value back into **c**, clearly redundant.

Now consider the second case.

```
c = a + 42;
```

What is the prototype this time?

```
Point operator+ (int j) const;
```

What does it mean to add a single integer to a **Point** object? If the user defines this operation as meaning "add the integer to both coordinates," we can then implement it very straightforwardly this way.

```
Point   Point::operator+ (int j) const {
 Point ret;
 ret.x = x + j;
 ret.y = y + j;
 return ret;
}
```

Again, we can shorten it by making use of the constructor functions we already have.

```
Point   Point::operator+ (int j) const {
 Point ret (x, y);
 ret.x += j;
 ret.y += j;
 return ret;
}
```

Or even shorter this way.

```
Point   Point::operator+ (int j) const {
 Point ret (x + j, y + j);
 return ret;
}
```

Or even shorter this way.

```
Point   Point::operator+ (int j) const {
 return Point (x + j, y + j);
}
```


However, there is also another way we can implement this one. Notice that we already have written the function to add two point objects. Can that coding be reused? Yes, all we need to do is to construct a **Point** object from the integer and call the existing function.

```
Point   Point::operator+ (int j) const {
 Point p (j, j);
 Point ret = *this + p;
 return ret;
}
```

Here I use ***this** to obtain a **Point** object to use. However, it could be shortened to just this.

```
Point   Point::operator+ (int j) const {
 return *this + Point (j, j);
}
```

So what is the significant difference between writing two separate implementations versus reusing an existing implementation? Speed of execution and complexity of the implementation are the two design considerations. In both methods, a constructor for **Point** is called to create the return **Point** object. However, the code reuse second version has the additional overhead of making a second function call to the original **operator+** function with its additional constructor call, not to mention the copying of the returned objects. If the design of the class requires that these **operator+** functions execute as quickly as possible, then the second version that reuses the original **operator+** function will run more slowly. However, sometimes the addition process is quite complex, requiring many lines of coding to carry it out. In such a case, writing the lengthy addition code once and then reusing it makes good sense.

Using Friend Functions to Handle Overloading Normal Data Types

This handles the first two cases of addition above. But we must still deal with the third version.
```
    a = 42 + b;
```
As it stands, it appears that the integer addition operator is called passing an instance of **b**. This is, of course, an impossibility, We solve this circumstance by using a friend function. In the class definition, add a new public prototype.
```
    friend Point operator+ (int j, const Point &p);
```
Its implementation can also be done several ways. Here is the simplest.
```
    Point operator+ (int j, Point const &p) {
     Point ret;
     ret.x = p.x + j;
     ret.y = p.y + j;
     return ret;
    }
```

It can be shortened this way by making use of the constructor.
```
    Point operator+ (int j, const Point &p) {
     Point ret (p.x + j, p.y + j);
     return ret;
    }
```
Or just
```
    Point operator+ (int j, const Point &p) {
     return Point (p.x + j, p.y + j);
    }
```

It can also be implemented by reusing the addition of two points member function this way.
```
    Point operator+ (int j, const Point &p) {
     Point q (j, j);
     Point ret = p + q;
```

```
    return ret;
  }
```

Or even simpler

```
Point operator+ (int j, const Point &p) {
  return p + Point (j, j);
}
```

The Subtraction Operator

With subtraction, three cases arise.

```
c = a - b;
c = a - 42;
c = 42 - a;
```

In the first and second lines, the **this** parameter points to **a**'s instance. Neither objects involved in the subtraction are altered by the subtraction process. Thus, the parameter **Point** reference and the member function are constant. Here it the first subtraction prototype.

```
Point operator- (const Point& p) const;
```

It can be implemented in several ways. The simplest is this.

```
Point Point::operator- (const Point &p) const {
  Point ret;
  ret.x = x - p.x;
  ret.y = y - p.y;
  return ret;
}
```

It can be shortened by using another constructor.

```
Point Point::operator- (const Point &p) const {
  Point ret (x - p.x, y - p.y);
  return ret;
}
```

Or even

```
Point Point::operator- (const Point &p) const {
  return Point (x - p.x, y - p.y);
}
```

The function to subtract an integer from a point would have the following prototype.

```
Point operator- (int j) const;
```

And it can be implemented this way.

```
Point   Point::operator- (int j) const {
  Point ret;
  ret.x = x - j;
  ret.y = y - j;
  return ret;
}
```

Or shorter

```
Point    Point::operator- (int j) const {
```

```
      Point ret (x - j, y - j);
      return ret;
    }
```
Or just
```
    Point    Point::operator- (int j) const {
      return Point (x - j, y - j);
    }
```
Or in terms of the existing subtraction of two points, it can be done this way.
```
    Point operator- (int j, const Point &p) {
      return p - Point (j, j);
    }
```

However, the third case of subtracting a point from an integer must be done with a friend function.
```
    friend Point operator- (int j, const Point &p);
```
Its implementation can also be done several ways. Here is the simplest.
```
    Point operator- (int j, const Point &p) {
      Point ret;
      ret.x = j - p.x;
      ret.y = j - p.y;
      return ret;
    }
```
Or
```
    Point operator- (int j, const Point &p) {
      Point ret (j - p.x, j - p.y);
      return ret;
    }
```
Or
```
    Point operator- (int j, const Point &p) {
      return Point (j - p.x, j - p.y);
    }
```
Or
```
    Point operator- (int j, const Point &p) {
      return Point (j, j) - p;;
    }
```
What about the other math operators such as multiplication, division, and the remainder operator? They are overloaded in a similar manner. However, always design first. What would it mean to multiply or divide two points? Nothing. These are most likely undefined operations for a **Point** class, since they have no meaning unless you consider the dot and cross products operations.

Overloading the += and Similar Operators

Suppose that the client wanted to have the following be supported.

```
a += 5;
a += b;
```

The **Point** object to the operator's left supplies the *this* parameter and the parameter to the function lies to the right of the operator. In this case, the *this* object is being modified while the parameter object is not. Here are the two prototypes.

```
Point& operator+= (int j);
Point& operator+= (const Point& p);
```

Notice this time I am returning a reference to a **Point** object. The *this* object is changed but it does not go out of scope. Hence, a reference to it can be returned.

Here is a way these two can be implemented.

```
Point& Point::operator+= (int j) {
  x += j;
  y += j;
  return *this;
}
```

and

```
Point& Point::operator+= (const Point& p) {
  x += p.x;
  y += p.y;
  return *this;
}
```

Notice how the *this* pointer is turned into a reference by coding ***this**.

The other similar operators, such as —=. *=, /=, and %=, are coded in parallel ways. But again, they are provided only if they have some meaning. Certainly *= for **Point** objects has no meaning. How would you multiply a point times a point, for example?

Overloading the Relational Operators

The six relational operators, ==, !=, <, >, <=, and >=, can easily be overloaded so that client programs can do comparisons such as these.

```
if (a == b)
```

where both **a** and **b** are **Point** instances. Again, the object to the left of the operator provides the *this* parameter while the object to the right of the operator becomes the parameter. In a comparison operation, neither operand is modified, so both are constant. Here is the prototype for the equality relational operator.

```
bool operator== (const Point& p) const;
```

It is easily implemented by checking for identical coordinates.

```
bool Point::operator== (const Point& p) const {
```

```
    return x == p.x && y == p.y;
}
```

The not equals operator is similarly coded. However, what would it mean to say
```
if (a > b)
```
or is one point larger than another point? Sometimes a class does not have to support all of the relational operators. In this case, the client's specifications might say that one point is larger than another if its distance from the origin of the coordinate system is greater than the other point.

Overloading the Insertion and Extraction Operators—<< and >>

Again, assuming we are dealing with instances of the **Point** class, client programs greatly desire to be able to code the following.
```
cin >> a;
cout << a;
infile >> a;
outfile << a;
```
Following the guidelines, the item to the left of the operator provides the *this* parameter and the item to the right of the operator is passed as the parameter. So in this case, the **operator<<** function belongs in the **istream** class because **cin** or **outfile** is to the left! Oops. The only way that these functions can be implemented is by once again using an ordinary C nonmember function that is granted friendship with the class so that it can access the protected data members. Here are the two required prototypes.
```
friend istream& operator>> (istream& is, Point& p);
friend ostream& operator<< (ostream& os, const Point& p);
```
Notice that outputting a **Point** object should not alter its value, so it has been made a constant reference.

How do we implement the functions? Well, that depends upon how the client wishes the output of a point to appear and what is desired for input. Suppose that the specifications call for a point to be displayed this way.
```
(10, 541)
```
Then, it is our task to implement **operator<<** to provide this format. Here is how it can be accomplished.
```
ostream& operator<< (ostream& os, const Point& p) {
 os << "(" << p.x << ", " << p.y << ")";
 return os;
}
```
Or it could be shortened to just this.
```
ostream& operator<< (ostream& os, const Point& p) {
 return os << "(" << p.x << ", " << p.y << ")";
}
```

Suppose that on input, the point data also was in the same format. Then, the **operator>>** function could be done this way.

```
istream& operator>> (istream& os, Point& p) {
  char c;
  is >> c >> p.x >> c >> p.y >> c;
  return is;
}
```

The first character in **c** is the leading (; the second is the comma; the third is the trailing).

The Assignment Operator

The assignment **operator=** overloaded function can be quite useful, especially when the class needs to dynamically allocate memory for member variables or has constant data members. Continuing with the **Point** examples, the client may wish to do the following.

```
a = b;
a = b = c;
```

In this example of **Point** objects, is an overloaded **operator=** really needed? No. The compiler automatically can do a shallow copy by making a duplicate copy of the data members. In this case, that is perfectly fine. However, let's see how we could implement it. Here is the prototype.

```
Point&  operator= (const Point &p);
```

Here is its implementation. When dynamic memory is involved, we must take additional precautions. But that is discussed in the next chapter.

```
Point&  Point::operator= (const Point &p) {
  x = p.x;
  y = p.y;
  return *this;
}
```

Notice that the return value is a reference and ***this** is used. This is done so one can chain multiple assignments. Also, the reference is needed to prevent making a copy of the right side of the assignment.

Overloading the Unary Operators

With unary operators, there are no parameters passed to the functions except the hidden *this* parameter.

Overloading the Inc and Dec Operators

The increment and decrement operators are very often overloaded to add or subtract one from the object. With the **Point** objects, the client desires the ability to write the following.

```
a++;
++a;
```

The first problem is to be able to distinguish between these two functions. Following the guidelines for constructing prototypes, we have the following.

```
Point operator++ ();
Point operator++ ();
```

Oops. Both of these have the same prototype! Hence, the C++ language steps in to provide a means of distinguishing between prefix increment and postfix increment. Here are the correct versions.

```
Point operator++ ();        // ++a;
Point operator++ (int x); // a++
```

Note that the parameter **x** will always be 0. To avoid compiler warnings about unused parameter variables, it is often not coded as shown below in the implementations.

However, there is still a subtle difference in return values that we are overlooking. Certainly in both cases the object being incremented is in fact incremented or changed. But with the after (postfix) increment, the function must return the previous value of the **Point**, not the new one. We must save the initial point contents so that they can be returned in a temporary **Point** object. With the before (prefix) increment, the function must return the new value. Thus, we could return a reference to the **Point**. Here are the revised prototypes.

```
Point& operator++ ();        // ++a;
Point  operator++ (int); // a++
```

Here are the two implementations.

```
Point& Point::operator++ () { // ++a;
 x++;
 y++;
 return *this;
}

Point Point::operator++ (int) { // a++
 Point ret (*this);
 x++;
 y++;
 return ret;
```

```
// or even fancier just: return Point (x++, y++);
    }
```

The decrement operator is handled similarly.

Overloading the Unary – Operator

To handle the negation of a **Point** object, the prototype is

```
    Point operator- () const;
```

where the client writes

```
    c = -a;
```

And it is implemented this way, since **a**'s values are not changed.

```
    Point Point::operator- () const {
     Point ret(-x, -y);
     return ret;
    }
```

or

```
    Point Point::operator- () const {
     return Point(-x, -y);
    }
```

The Time Class—A Complete Programming Example

In order to fully illustrate many of these operator overloaded functions, I have used one of the classes from my World War II game, the **Time** class. Since the basic turn interval is in minutes, in my game, time is tracked only in minutes since midnight. Further, since there are likely to be a huge number of **Time** instances used throughout the game, I wanted to keep the actual memory requirements for these instances as small as possible. Thus, the **Time** class stores only a single 24-hour time in a **short** representing the number of minutes since midnight. Obviously, a large number of operations can then be performed upon a time instance.

The game also has a **Date** class and a combined **DateTime** class. When a time in incremented past the 24-hour limit, another day is added to the **DateTime** instance and the **Time** instance is rolled back into the required 24-hour period of the next day. Similarly, if a **Time** instance is decremented past midnight (that is, it goes negative), the **DateTime** day is decremented and the **Time** instance is rolled back into the proper range for the previous day. However, in this sample program, only the **Time** class is used to illustrate the many operator overloaded functions.

Here is the **Time** class definition. Notice how I have grouped the various function definitions into sections for ease and clarity of reading. The copy constructor and assignment operator are not really needed in this class, but are shown to illustrate how they can be coded.

```
The Time Class Definition

 1 #pragma once
 2 #include <iostream>
 3 using namespace std;
 4
 9 /*******************************************************************/
10 /*                                                               */
11 /* Class: Time - chronometer class handling time in minutes      */
12 /*                                                               */
13 /*******************************************************************/
14
15
16 class Time {
17
18   /*****************************************************************/
19   /*                                                             */
20   /* Data Member: stores the number of minutes from midnight     */
21   /*                                                             */
22   /*****************************************************************/
23
24 protected:
25
26   short time;   // the time in minutes
27
28   /*****************************************************************/
29   /*                                                             */
```

```
30  /* Functions:                                                    */
31  /*                                                               */
32  /****************************************************************/
33
34 public:
35
36        Time (long hrs, long mns);
37        Time (short hrs, short mns);
38        Time (double t);
39        Time ();
40        Time (const Time &t);
41
42      ~Time () {}
43
44 void  SetTime (long t);
45 void  SetTime (short t);
46 void  SetTime (long hrs, long mns);
47 void  SetTime (short hrs, short mns);
48 void  SetTime (double t);
49
50 short GetTime () const;
51 void  GetTime (short &h, short &m) const;
52 void  GetTime (double &t) const;
53
54        Time& operator=  (const Time &t);
55
56        bool  operator== (const Time &t) const;
57        bool  operator>  (const Time &t) const;
58        bool  operator<  (const Time &t) const;
59        bool  operator>= (const Time &t) const;
60        bool  operator<= (const Time &t) const;
61        bool  operator!= (const Time &t) const;
62
63        Time  operator+  (long n) const;
64        Time  operator+  (const Time& t) const;
65  friend Time  operator+  (long n, const Time &t);
66
67        Time  operator-  (long n) const;
68        Time  operator-  (const Time &t) const;
69  friend Time  operator-  (long n, const Time &t);
70
71        Time& operator+= (long n);
72        Time& operator+= (const Time& t);
73        Time& operator-= (long n);
74        Time& operator-= (const Time& t);
75
76        Time& operator++ ();
77        Time  operator++ (int);
78        Time& operator-- ();
79        Time  operator-- (int);
80
81        void  FormatHM (char *string, int maxlen) const;
82        void  FormatH  (char *string, int maxlen) const;
```

243

```
83
84 friend  ostream& operator<< (ostream& os, const Time& t);
85 friend  istream& operator>> (istream& is, Time& t);
86
87 protected:
88         void  RollIt (); // get a time back into a 24-hour range
89 };
90
```

The **FormatHM()** function converts the short time into a client provided character string in the format of hh:mm. The client must also pass the length of its string so that I can avoid overwriting memory should the string be too small to hold all of the characters. Similarly, the **FormatH()** function converts it into a string in the decimal format of hh.hhh.

As you look over these definitions, make sure you understand the use of the **const** keyword both on the parameters and on the member functions. These are critical. Likewise, observe which functions return a **Time** copy versus which are able to return a **Time** reference.

Here is the implementation of the **Time** class. Notice that most all of the functions are actually quite simple. Whenever a time value is altered, **RollIt()** is called to force that value back into the proper range for a 24-hour time.

```
The Time Class Implementation
```

```
 1 // file TIME.CPP
 2 #include <iostream>
 3 #include <strstream>
 4 #include <iomanip>
 5 #include "time.h"
 6 using namespace std;
 7
 8 /***************************************************************/
 9 /*                                                           */
10 /* Time implementation: tracks minutes since midnight        */
11 /*                                                           */
12 /* RollIt() forces time back into 24 hour range              */
13 /*                                                           */
14 /***************************************************************/
15
16 // the constructor series
17
18 Time::Time (long hrs, long mns) {
19   time = (short) (hrs * 60 + mns);
20   RollIt ();
21 }
22
23 Time::Time (short hrs, short mns) {
24   time = (short) (hrs * 60 + mns);
25   RollIt ();
```

```
26 }
27
28 Time::Time (double t) {
29  long h = (long) t;
30  time = (short) ((t - h) * 60.+ .5 + h * 60);
31  RollIt ();
32 }
33
34 Time::Time () {
35  time = 0;
36 }
37
38 Time::Time (const Time &t) { // copy ctor
39  time = t.time;
40 }
41
42
43 // the modifications series
44
45 void   Time::SetTime (long t) {
46  time = (short) t;
47  RollIt ();
48 }
49
50 void   Time::SetTime (short t) {
51  time = t;
52  RollIt ();
53 }
54
55 void   Time::SetTime (long hrs, long mns) {
56  time = (short) (hrs * 60 + mns);
57  RollIt ();
58 }
59
60 void   Time::SetTime (short hrs, short mns) {
61  time = (short) (hrs * 60 + mns);
62  RollIt ();
63 }
64
65 void   Time::SetTime (double t) {
66  int h = (long) t;
67  time = (short) ((t-h) * 60.+ .5 + h * 60.);
68  RollIt ();
69 }
70
71
72 // retrieval series
73
74 short int Time::GetTime () const {
75  return time;
76 }
77
78 void       Time::GetTime (short &h, short &m) const {
```

```
 79  h = (short) (time / 60);
 80  m = (short) (time % 60);
 81  }
 82
 83  void       Time::GetTime (double &t) const {
 84  t = time / 60.;
 85  }
 86
 87
 88  // the assignment operator - not really needed...
 89
 90  Time&  Time::operator=  (const Time &t) {
 91  if (*this == t)
 92    return *this;
 93  time = t.time;
 94  return *this;
 95  }
 96
 97
 98  // the relational operator series
 99
100  bool   Time::operator== (const Time &t) const {
101  return time == t.time;
102  }
103
104  bool   Time::operator> (const Time &t) const {
105  return time >  t.time;
106  }
107
108  bool   Time::operator< (const Time &t) const {
109  return time <  t.time;
110  }
111
112  bool   Time::operator>= (const Time &t) const {
113  return time >= t.time;
114  }
115
116  bool   Time::operator<= (const Time &t) const {
117  return time <= t.time;
118  }
119
120  bool   Time::operator!= (const Time &t) const {
121  return time != t.time;
122  }
123
124
125  // time addition series
126
127  Time   Time::operator+ (long n) const {
128  Time t  (*this);
129  t.time = (short) (t.time + n);
130  t.RollIt ();
131  return t;
```

```
132 }
133
134 Time    Time::operator+ (const Time &tt) const {
135   Time t;
136   t.time = (short) (time + tt.time);
137   t.RollIt ();
138   return t;
139 }
140
141 Time    operator+ (long n, const Time &t) {
142   Time tt;
143   tt.time = (short) (t.time + n);
144   tt.RollIt ();
145   return tt;
146 }
147
148
149 // time subtraction series
150
151 Time    Time::operator- (long n) const {
152   Time t;
153   t.time = (short) (time - n);
154   t.RollIt ();
155   return t;
156 }
157
158 Time    Time::operator- (const Time &t) const {
159   Time tt;
160   tt.time = (short) (time - t.time);
161   tt.RollIt ();
162   return tt;
163 }
164
165 Time    operator- (long n, const Time &t) {
166   Time tt;
167   tt.time = (short) (n - t.time);
168   tt.RollIt ();
169   return tt;
170 }
171
172
173 // the += and -= series
174
175 Time&  Time::operator+= (long n) {
176   time = (short) (time + n);
177   RollIt ();
178   return *this;
179 }
180
181 Time&  Time::operator+= (const Time& t) {
182   time = (short) (time + t.time);
183   RollIt ();
184   return *this;
```

```
185 }
186
187 Time&  Time::operator-= (long n) {
188  time = (short) (time - n);
189  RollIt ();
190  return *this;
191 }
192
193 Time&  Time::operator-= (const Time& t) {
194  time = (short) (time - t.time);
195  RollIt ();
196  return *this;
197 }
198
199
200 // the inc and dec series
201
202 Time&  Time::operator++ () { // before inc
203  time++;
204  RollIt ();
205  return *this;
206 }
207
208 Time   Time::operator++ (int) { // after inc
209  Time t = *this;
210  time++;
211  RollIt ();
212  return t;
213 }
214
215 Time&  Time::operator-- () { // before dec
216  time--;
217  RollIt ();
218  return *this;
219 }
220
221 Time   Time::operator-- (int) { // after dec
222  Time t = *this;
223  time--;
224  RollIt ();
225  return t;
226 }
227
228
229 // the fancy formatting series
230
231
232 void   Time::FormatHM (char *string, int maxlen) const {
233  // display as hh:mm
234  short int h, m;
235  GetTime (h, m);
236  ostrstream os (string, maxlen);
237  os << setfill ('0') << setw (2) << h << ":" << setw (2)
```

```
238      << m << ends;
239  if (maxlen < 6) // guard against too small a client string
240    string[maxlen-1] = 0;
241  }
242
243 void   Time::FormatH  (char *string, int maxlen) const {
244  // display as nn.nnn
245  double x;
246  GetTime (x);
247  ostrstream os (string, maxlen);
248  os << fixed << setw (6) << setprecision (3) << x << ends;
250  if (maxlen < 7) // guard against too small a client string
251    string[maxlen-1] = 0;
252  }
253
254
255 // the I/O series
256
257 ostream& operator<< (ostream& os, const Time& t) {
258  char msg[8];
259  t.FormatHM (msg, sizeof (msg));
260  return os << msg;
261  }
262
263 istream& operator>> (istream& is, Time& t) {
264  char c;
265  long h, m;
266  is >> h >> c >> m;
267  if (!is)
268    return is;
269  t.SetTime (h, m);
270  return is;
271  }
272
273
274 // RollIt() forces an out of range time back into a 24 hour range
275 void   Time::RollIt () {
276  if (time < 0)
277    time = (short) (1440 + (time % 1440));
278  else if (time >= 1440)
279    time = time % (short) 1440;
280  }
```

Next, we need a thorough tester program to guarantee that all functions are working properly. This is a major undertaking because of the volume of operator overloaded functions as well as the use of **const** and the use of **Time** and **Time&** return values. Each of these must be tested.

My philosophy when testing classes is to have the output set up so that at a glance I can tell if things are correct or not. So I tend to display messages such as this.

"Such and such should be this and it is that"

One quick glance at the output tells all.

With this many functions and variations to test, it is best to do it methodically from top to bottom, testing each function in the **Time** definition. A couple functions are automatically tested by the other functions: **RollIt()** and **FormatHM()**. Most of the tests are obvious and straightforward—insert a unique time into an object and add to it and display the results.

However, there are several circumstances that are not necessarily obvious that must be tested and which are often overlooked in testing. The first of these is the subtle difference between the prefix and postfix inc and dec operators. Assume that **a** is a **Time** instance storing 1 minute. What should the output from the following two lines be?

```
cout << ++a << " " << a;
cout << a++ << " " << a;
```

In the first line, the prefix inc takes place before any use of the object is made. Thus, 00:02 00:02 should be displayed. However, the postfix inc is done after usage is made of the current object's value. Thus, it should display 00:01 00:02.

The two formatting functions also have some special testing requirements. What happens if the client provides too small a string? Only those characters that can fit should be in the string along with a null terminator. So this situation is tested as well.

Finally, several constant **Time** objects are created and all of the possible **Time** functions that can be called using constant objects are invoked. Here is **Pgm06a** and its output.

```
Pgm06a - Tester Program for the Time Class

 1  #include <iostream>
 2  #include <iomanip>
 3  using namespace std;
 4  #include "Time.h"
 5
 6  /*****************************************************************/
 7  /*                                                             */
 8  /*  Tester Program for Time Class                              */
 9  /*                                                             */
10  /*****************************************************************/
11
12  int main () {
13    short shrs = 1;
14    short smin = 42;
15    Time a;
16    Time b (1L, 42L);
17    Time c (shrs, smin);
18    Time d (1.5);
19    Time e (d);
20    Time f (48L, 42L);
21    Time g (-72L, -2L);
22    cout << "Testing constructors\n";
23    cout << "a = 00:00 and is: " << a << endl;
```

250

```
24  cout << "b = 01:42 and is: " << b << endl;
25  cout << "c = 01:42 and is: " << c << endl;
26  cout << "d = 01:30 and is: " << d << endl;
27  cout << "e = 01:30 and is: " << e << endl;
28  cout << "\nTesting RollIt ()\n";
29  cout << "f = 00:42 and is: " << f << endl;
30  cout << "g = 23:58 and is: " << g << endl;
31
32  cout << "\nTesting SetTime()\n";
33  a.SetTime (1.5);
34  cout << "a = 01:30 and is: " << a << endl;
35  a.SetTime (1L, 30L);
36  cout << "a = 01:30 and is: " << a << endl;
37  a.SetTime (shrs, smin);
38  cout << "a = 01:42 and is: " << a << endl;
39  a.SetTime (102L);
40  cout << "a = 01:42 and is: " << a << endl;
41  a.SetTime ((short) 102);
42  cout << "a = 01:42 and is: " << a << endl;
43
44  cout << "\nTesting GetTime\n";
45  cout << "a = 102 and is: " << a.GetTime() << endl;
46  a.GetTime (shrs, smin);
47  cout << "a = 1:42 and is: " << shrs << ":" << smin << endl;
48  double td;
49  d.GetTime (td);
50  cout << "d = 1.5 and is " << td << endl;
51
52  cout << "\nTesting Assignment\n";
53  a = f;
54  cout << "a = 00:42 and is: " << a << endl;
55
56  cout << "\nTesting relational operators\n";
57  cout << (a == f ? "a is == f\n" : "error: a == f\n");
58  cout << (b > a ? "b is > a\n" : "error: b > a\n");
59  cout << (b >= a ? "b is >= a\n" : "error: b >= a\n");
60  cout << (a < c ? "a is < c\n" : "error: a < c\n");
61  cout << (a <= f ? "a is <= f\n" : "error: a <= f\n");
62  cout << (a != c ? "a is != c\n" : "error: a != c\n");
63
64  cout << "\nTesting Addition operators\n";
65  a.SetTime (1.0);
66  b.SetTime (1.0);
67  c.SetTime (1.0);
68  c = a + 30;
69  cout << "c = 01:30 and is " << c << endl;
70  c = a + b;
71  cout << "c = 02:00 and is " << c << endl;
72  c = 30 + a;
73  cout << "c = 01:30 and is " << c << endl;
74
75  cout << "\nTesting Addition operators\n";
76  a.SetTime (1.0);
```

```
 77   b.SetTime (1.0);
 78   c = a + 30;
 79   cout << "c = 01:30 and is " << c << endl;
 80   c = a + b;
 81   cout << "c = 02:00 and is " << c << endl;
 82   c = 30 + a;
 83   cout << "c = 01:30 and is " << c << endl;
 84
 85   cout << "\nTesting Subtraction operators\n";
 86   a.SetTime (1.0);
 87   b.SetTime (1.0);
 88   c = a - 30;
 89   cout << "c = 00:30 and is " << c << endl;
 90   c = a - b;
 91   cout << "c = 00:00 and is " << c << endl;
 92   c = 30 - a;
 93   cout << "c = 23:30 and is " << c << endl;
 94
 95   cout << "\nTesting += and -= operators\n";
 96   c.SetTime (0L, 42L);
 97   a += 42;
 98   cout << "a = 01:42 and is " << a << endl;
 99   a -= c;
100   cout << "a = 01:00 and is " << a << endl;
101   a += c;
102   cout << "a = 01:42 and is " << a << endl;
103   a -= 42;
104   cout << "a = 01:00 and is " << a << endl;
105
106   cout << "\nTesting inc and dec operators\n";
107   a++;
108   cout << "a = 01:01 and is " << a << endl;
109   ++a;
110   cout << "a = 01:02 and is " << a << endl;
111   a--;
112   cout << "a = 01:01 and is " << a << endl;
113   --a;
114   cout << "a = 01:00 and is " << a << endl;
115   cout << "old a = 01:00 and new a = 01:01 - old a is "
116       << a++ << " and new a is " << a << endl;
117   a--;
118   cout << "old a = 01:01 and new a = 01:01 - old a is "
119       << ++a << " and new a is " << a << endl;
120
121   cout << "\nTesting FormatH and FormatHM\n";
122   a.SetTime (1.567);
123   char msg[10];
124   a.FormatH (msg, sizeof (msg));
125   cout << "a = 1.567 and is " << msg << endl;
126   char msg2[4];
127   a.FormatH (msg2, sizeof (msg2));
128   cout << "a is 1. and is " << msg2 << endl;
129   d.FormatHM (msg, sizeof (msg));
```

```
130   cout << "d is 01:30 and is " << msg << endl;
131   d.FormatHM (msg2, sizeof (msg2));
132   cout << "d is 01: and is " << msg2 << endl;
133
134   const Time ca (10L, 30L);
135   const Time cb (5L, 30L);
136   cout << "\nTesting GetTime on constant objects\n";
137   cout << "ca = 630 and is: " << ca.GetTime() << endl;
138   ca.GetTime (shrs, smin);
139   cout << "ca = 10:30 and is: " << shrs << ":" << smin << endl;
140   cb.GetTime (td);
141   cout << "cb = 5.5 and is " << td << endl;
142
143   cout << "\nTesting relational ops on constant objects\n";
144   cout << (ca == cb ? "error ca is != f\n" : "ca is != cb\n");
145   cout << (ca > cb ? "ca is > cb\n" : "error: ca > cb\n");
146   cout << (ca >= cb ? "ca is >= cb\n" : "error: ca >= cb\n");
147   cout << (cb < ca ? "cb is < ca\n" : "error: cb < ca\n");
148   cout << (cb <= ca ? "cb is <= ca\n" : "error: cb <= ca\n");
149   cout << (ca != cb ? "ca is != cb\n" : "error: ca != cb\n");
150
151   cout << "\nTesting op+ and op- on constant objects\n";
152   c = ca + 30;
153   cout << "c is 11:00 and is " << c << endl;
154   c = ca + cb;
155   cout << "c is 16:00 and is " << c << endl;
156   c = 30 + ca;
157   cout << "c is 11:00 and is " << c << endl;
158   c = ca - 30;
159   cout << "c is 10:00 and is " << c << endl;
160   c = ca - cb;
161   cout << "c is 05:00 and is " << c << endl;
162   c = 640 - ca;
163   cout << "c is 00:10 and is " << c << endl;
164
165   cout << "\nTesting FormatH and FormatHM on constant objects\n";
166   ca.FormatH (msq, sizeof (msq));
167   cout << "ca = 10.500 and is " << msg << endl;
168   ca.FormatHM (msg, sizeof (msg));
169   cout << "ca is 10:30 and is " << msg << endl;
170
171   return 0;
172 }
```

```
Output of the Tester Program for the Time Class

  1 Testing constructors
  2 a = 00:00 and is: 00:00
  3 b = 01:42 and is: 01:42
  4 c = 01:42 and is: 01:42
  5 d = 01:30 and is: 01:30
  6 e = 01:30 and is: 01:30
```

```
 7
 8 Testing RollIt ()
 9 f = 00:42 and is: 00:42
10 g = 23:58 and is: 23:58
11
12 Testing SetTime()
13 a = 01:30 and is: 01:30
14 a = 01:30 and is: 01:30
15 a = 01:42 and is: 01:42
16 a = 01:42 and is: 01:42
17 a = 01:42 and is: 01:42
18
19 Testing GetTime
20 a = 102 and is: 102
21 a = 1:42 and is: 1:42
22 d = 1.5 and is 1.5
23
24 Testing Assignment
25 a = 00:42 and is: 00:42
26
27 Testing relational operators
28 a is == f
29 b is > a
30 b is >= a
31 a is < c
32 a is <= f
33 a is != c
34
35 Testing Addition operators
36 c = 01:30 and is 01:30
37 c = 02:00 and is 02:00
38 c = 01:30 and is 01:30
39
40 Testing Addition operators
41 c = 01:30 and is 01:30
42 c = 02:00 and is 02:00
43 c = 01:30 and is 01:30
44
45 Testing Subtraction operators
46 c = 00:30 and is 00:30
47 c = 00:00 and is 00:00
48 c = 23:30 and is 23:30
49
50 Testing += and -= operators
51 a = 01:42 and is 01:42
52 a = 01:00 and is 01:00
53 a = 01:42 and is 01:42
54 a = 01:00 and is 01:00
55
56 Testing inc and dec operators
57 a = 01:01 and is 01:01
58 a = 01:02 and is 01:02
59 a = 01:01 and is 01:01
```

```
60 a = 01:00 and is 01:00
61 old a = 01:00 and new a = 01:01 -
62      old a is 01:00 and new a is 01:01
63 old a = 01:01 and new a = 01:01 -
64      old a is 01:01 and new a is 01:01
65
66 Testing FormatH and FormatHM
67 a = 1.567 and is  1.567
68 a is 1. and is  1.
69 d is 01:30 and is 01:30
70 d is 01: and is 01:
71
72 Testing GetTime on constant objects
73 ca = 630 and is: 630
74 ca = 10:30 and is: 10:30
75 cb = 5.5 and is 5.5
76
77 Testing relational ops on constant objects
78 ca is != cb
79 ca is > cb
80 ca is >= cb
81 cb is < ca
82 cb is <= ca
83 ca is != cb
84
85 Testing op+ and op- on constant objects
86 c is 11:00 and is 11:00
87 c is 16:00 and is 16:00
88 c is 11:00 and is 11:00
89 c is 10:00 and is 10:00
90 c is 05:00 and is 05:00
91 c is 00:10 and is 00:10
92
93 Testing FormatH and FormatHM on constant objects
94 ca = 10.500 and is 10.500
95 ca is 10:30 and is 10:30
```

Review Questions

1. What is meant by operator overloading? Why is operator overloading an important feature of a class?

2. Why cannot a programmer overload the operator+ and have it output the object to a disk file? Is there anything in the language prohibiting it?

3. Which operators cannot be overloaded?

4. Can the precedence of C++ operators be modified to better suit a class design when needed?

5. What is the difference between a binary operator and a unary operator? Give an example of each.

6. Why should operator overloaded functions be passed a constant reference to objects whenever possible instead of a totally safe copy of that object?

7. When would an operator overloaded member function be a constant function?

8. Under what circumstances should an operator overloaded function return a copy of an object instead of a reference to an object?

9. Write the prototype for the multiply operator function in the **Point** class such that the client can write
```
c = a * 10;
```
where **c** and **a** are **Point** instances.

10. Why must the insertion and extraction operator overloaded functions be friend functions and not member functions?

Stop! Do These Exercises Before Programming

This series of exercises uses a **Date** class. In my World War II game, a date is stored as a **short** number of days since the war began on 1 September 1939. The class definition begins as follows.
```
class Date {
protected:
  short days;
public:
...
```

1. Write the function prototype and then the function header and body to implement **operator+** such that all of the following are valid.
```
date2 = date1 + 42;
date2 = 42 + date;
```

2. Write the function prototype and then the function header and body to implement **operator+=** such that the following is valid.
```
date2 += 42;
```

3. Write the function prototype and then the function header and body to implement **operator==** and **operator<** such that all of the following are valid.
```
if (date2 == date1)...
while (dateNow < dateEnd) {
```

4. Write the function prototype and then the function header and body to implement **operator++** such that all of the following are valid.

```
date2 = date1++;
date2 = ++date1;
```

5. Write the function prototype and then the function header and body to implement **operator=** such that all of the following are valid. Note that the assignment operator is not really necessary for this class.

```
date2 = date1;
date2 = date2;
```

6. Write the function prototype and then the function header and body to implement **operator>>** such that all of the following are valid.

```
cin >> date2 >> date3;
while (infile >> date2) {
```

On input, the date is in the form of mm/dd/yyyy. There is a helper function called **Serial()** that is passed three integers, month, day, and year, and it returns the short number of days since September 1, 1939. You do not need to code the **Serial()** function, just use call it.

7. Write the function prototype and then the function header and body to implement **FormatDate()** which is passed a client's string and its length. There is a helper function called **GetDate()** that is passed three integer references (month, day, and year) and it fills these references with the calendar date this short date represents. You do not need to code the **GetDate()** function, rather call it. The string should contain a date in the form of mm/dd/yyyy. Avoid overwriting memory if the passed string is too small to hold all of the characters. Under all circumstances the string should be null terminated.

8. Write the function prototype and then the function header and body to implement **operator<<** such that all of the following are valid.

```
cout << date2;
outfile << date2;
```

Reuse your **FormatDate()** function from question 7 above to assist in displaying the string date on the output stream.

Programming Problems

Problem Pgm06-1—A Date Class—III

Modify the **Date** class of Problem **Pgm05-1** as follows to make it more efficient and useful.

Modifications to the Interface for the Date Class

Remove the **Add()**, **Subtract()**, **Difference()**, **Compare()**, **Input()**, and **Output()** functions from the **Date** class and add in new operator functions to make the class much easier to use.

Alterations to the Date Class

For the following discussion, assume the following variables have been defined in **main()**.

```
Date date, olddate, newdate;
long  n;
```

1. Replace the **Input()** function with the extraction (>>) operator, deleting the old function. Typical use now is as follows.

```
cin >> date;
```

2. Replace the **Output()** function with the insertion operator (<<), deleting the old function. Typical use now is as follows.

```
cout << date;
```

3. Replace the **Add()** function with **operator+**, deleting the old function. The following addition instructions should work.

```
newdate = date + n;
newdate = n + date:
```

4. Replace the **Subtract()** function with **operator–**, deleting the old function. The following is a typical subtraction.

```
olddate = date - n;
```

5. Replace the **Difference()** function with **operator–**, deleting the old function. The following is typical use.

```
n = newdate - date;
```

6. Provide support for comparisons by adding the operators: ==, !=, >, >=, <, <=. Each operator returns a **bool** which is **true** when the condition is true. If you wish, you may keep and use the old **Compare()** function. Typical use might be as shown.

```
if (date == newdate)
if (newdate < olddate)
```

7. Add support for **operator++**. Both prefix and postfix forms are required so that either of these two are valid.

```
newdate = date++;
newdate = ++date;
```

8. Add support for **operator--**. Both forms are required so that either of these two are valid.

```
olddate = date--;
olddate = --date;
```

9. Add support for **operator+=**. Typical use is as shown.

```
newdate += n;
```

10 Add support for **operator-=**. Typical use is as shown.

```
olddate -= n;
```

11. Provide three access functions for retrieving the date components. All return an integer: **GetMonth()**, **GetDay()**, and **GetYear()**. Typical use is as follows.

```
int month = date.GetMonth ();
```

Remember to watch for the use of **const**. Note that there is no public function to create a **Date** object from a **long** serial date number, because that conversion from **long** back into a date is an implementation detail subject to change.

Test your class using the provided pair of programs and test data, **Pgm06-1A.cpp** and **Pgm06-1B.cpp** which use **Pgm06-1A.txt** and **Pgm06-1B.txt** test data files respectively. Build a project for each of these. Both programs create no screen output; all results are written to disk files, namely **Pgm06-1A-results.txt** and **Pgm06-1B-results.txt**. You should get the results shown in the next two figures, Figure 6.1 and Figure 6.2.

```
   DATE  1            DATE  2          DIFFERENCE

01/01/1996         01/01/1996               0
01/02/1996         01/01/1996               1
01/02/1995         01/01/1996            -364
02/01/1996         01/01/1996              31
02/01/1995         01/01/1996            -334
03/01/1996         01/01/1996              60
03/01/1995         01/01/1996            -306
12/31/1996         01/01/1996             365
12/31/1995         01/01/1996              -1
01/01/1997         01/01/1996             366
01/01/1994         01/01/1996            -730
03/01/1997         01/01/1996             425
03/01/1994         01/01/1996            -671
06/15/1997         01/01/1996             531
06/15/1994         01/01/1996            -565
09/20/1999         01/01/1996            1358
09/20/1993         01/01/1996            -833
01/01/2000         01/01/1996            1461
01/01/1990         01/01/1996           -2191
04/21/2000         01/01/1996            1572
04/21/1990         01/01/1996           -2081
12/31/2400         01/01/1996          147923
12/31/1601         01/01/1996         -143906
01/01/1900         01/01/1900               0
12/31/2400         01/01/1601          292193
01/01/2000         12/31/1899           36525
01/01/2000         12/31/2400         -146462
07/01/2049         01/01/1900           54603
07/01/1750         01/01/1900          -54605
01/01/1601         12/31/2100         -182620

conDateA = 12/31/1899
conDateB = 01/01/2000
date_1   = 12/31/1899
date_2   = 01/01/2000
```

Figure 6.1 Output from Pgm06-1A

DATE 1	DATE 2	DIFFERENCE
01/01/1996	01/01/1996	0
01/02/1996	01/01/1996	1
01/02/1995	01/01/1996	-364
02/01/1996	01/01/1996	31
02/01/1995	01/01/1996	-334
03/01/1996	01/01/1996	60
03/01/1995	01/01/1996	-306
12/31/1996	01/01/1996	365
12/31/1995	01/01/1996	-1
01/01/1997	01/01/1996	366
01/01/1994	01/01/1996	-730
03/01/1997	01/01/1996	425
03/01/1994	01/01/1996	-671
06/15/1997	01/01/1996	531
06/15/1994	01/01/1996	-565
09/20/1999	01/01/1996	1358
09/20/1993	01/01/1996	-833
01/01/2000	01/01/1996	1461
01/01/1990	01/01/1996	-2191
04/21/2000	01/01/1996	1572
04/21/1990	01/01/1996	-2081
12/31/2400	01/01/1996	147923
12/31/1601	01/01/1996	-143906
01/01/1900	01/01/1900	0
12/31/2400	01/01/1601	292193
01/01/2000	12/31/1899	36525
01/01/2000	12/31/2400	-146462
07/01/2049	01/01/1900	54603
07/01/1750	01/01/1900	-54605
01/01/1601	12/31/2100	-182620
12/31/1899	01/01/1900	-1
03/01/1900	02/28/1900	1
10/31/1999	10/30/1999	1
02/29/2000	02/28/2000	1
07/01/1995	06/30/1995	1

Figure 6.2 Output from Pgm06-1B

Problem Pgm06-2—Distance Class—III

This problem modifies **Pgm05-4—Distance Class II**.

Modifications to the Interface for the Distance Class

1. Add two friend functions, **operator<<** and **operator >>** so that we can input a distance object and output a distance object. The extraction operator displays a prompt to **cout** and then uses **cin** to input the distance as follows.

```
Enter a distance in millimeters: 3.456
```

The insertion function displays the following format on the passed output stream.

```
Distance is nnnnnn.nn millimeters
```

Always use a precision of two digits and a total width of 12 bytes.

2. Add operator functions so that the following are valid (all numbers are in millimeters)

```
Distance a, b, c;
c = a + b;
c = a + xxx;    // where xxx is an int, long or double
c = xxx + a;    // where xxx is an int, long or double
c = a;          // make an assignment operator
if (a == b)     // also valid are !=, <, >, <=, and >=
c++; and  ++c;
c--; and  --c;
```

Create a main program to thoroughly test the **Distance** class similar to **Pgm06a Time Class Tester**.

Chapter 7—Classes with Dynamic Memory Allocation

Introduction

When a class has dynamically allocated data members, that class should define three specific functions: the destructor, the copy constructor, and the assignment operator. Failure to do so most likely leads to memory leaks at best and client program crashes at worst. During normal construction or at any other point in the class operations, memory gets dynamically allocated. When the class instance goes out of scope, the destructor is called. The destructor's task is to delete that dynamically allocated memory. However, if during client program operations a copy of an instance is made, without the copy ctor and the assignment operator implementations, the compiler just makes a shallow copy, copying only the memory addresses. Thus, two or more instances point to the same memory. The client program crashes when the second destructor tries to delete the already deleted memory.

A String Class to Illustrate the Problem of a Shallow Copy

To illustrate these principles, let's examine the start of a **String** class designed to make operations with character strings easier for client programs. The class has a single data member, the pointer to the string. When working with classes with dynamic memory data members, it is most convenient to guarantee that under all situations, the pointer does point to something. So the default constructor allocates a null string—that is, a string of one byte containing the null terminator. This is quite different from a null pointer—that is, a pointer whose value is zero. Why?

If the string pointer always points to some kind of null terminated string, then all other class operations can proceed knowing that it does point to a valid string. If, on the other hand, the pointer could itself be zero, then all of the other member functions must begin their coding by querying the existence of the pointer before attempting to use it.

```
if (!string) {
 // oops it does not yet exist - so now what?
}
else {
 // do the requested operations on the string
}
```

Here is the start of the **String** class definition.
```
class String {
protected:
 char* string;
public:
 String ();
```

```
String (const char* str);
~String ();
};
```

The three functions can be implemented this way. Notice that some method must be provided to handle the out of memory situation. The approach here is to display an error message on **cerr** and abort the program. In a later chapter on C++ Error Handling, we will examine alternative methods.

```
String::String () {
 string = new (std::nothrow) char[1];
 if (!string) {
  cerr << "Error: out of memory in String ctor\n";
  exit (1);
 }
 string[0] = 0;
}

String::String (const char* str) {
 if (!str) {
  string = new (std::nothrow) char[1];
  if (!string) {
   cerr << "Error: out of memory in String ctor\n";
   exit (1);
  }
  string[0] = 0;
  return;
 }
 string = new (std::nothrow) char [strlen (str) + 1];
 if (!string) {
  cerr << "Error: out of memory in String ctor\n";
  exit (1);
 }
 strcpy (string, str);
}

String::~String () {
 if (string)
  delete [] string;
}
```

With this simple start, let's examine the copy constructor and assignment operator needs. Suppose that the client program did the following.

```
String Fun (String s); // prototype
...
String s1 ("Hello World");
String s2 ("Good-Bye");
String s3 (s1); // the copy ctor
String s4 = s1; // the copy ctor
String s5;
```

```
s5 = s1; // the assignment operator
String s6;
s6 = Fun (s1); // s1 is passed by copy ctor and returned by
               // copy ctor and assignment op to s6
}
...
String Fun (String s) {
 String ret (s); // copy ctor
 return ret;      // copy ctor
}
```

Figure 7.1 illustrates all of the instances of the **String** class just prior to the end brace of the function **Fun()** before the return value is assigned to **s6.** The moment the end brace is executed, troubles begin because the compiler then begins to call the destructors for the instances that go out of scope. The destructor for **ret** is called first, followed by the destructor for the parameter **s** which tries to delete the same memory as **ret**.

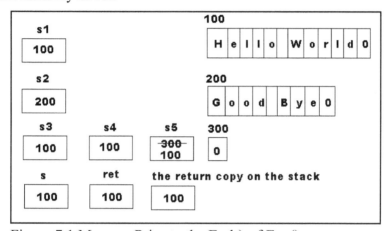

Figure 7.1 Memory Prior to the End } of Fun()

If the end brace of the **main()** function were to also execute, then the compiler would be attempting to delete the string at memory location 100 eight times, including **s6.** Further, because of the shallow copy to **s5**, memory is leaked at location 300. This leads to the following two rules.

> **Rule: Both the copy constructor and operator= must duplicate the data that is dynamically allocated.**

> **Rule: Operator= must first delete the dynamically allocated memory before it makes the duplicate copy.**

Coding the Copy Constructor and the Operator= Functions

The first thing to notice about these two functions is that both are making a duplicate copy of the passed object, including any dynamic memory allocated items. Rather than code these actions twice, once within each function, a protected helper function ought to be used, called say **Copy()**.

With the copy constructor, the *this* instance does not yet exist so there is nothing to delete yet. It can simply invoke the **Copy()** helper function. The **operator=()** must first delete any dynamically allocated memory that the *this* instance points to before it can call the **Copy()** helper function. However, there is a further situation that must be examined with **operator=()**. Suppose the client codes this.

```
String s1 ("Hello World");
String s2 ("Good Bye");
s1 = s1; // oops, the client meant s2 = s1;
```

If **operator=()** begins by deleting the memory pointed to by the passed parameter, which is the instance to the right of the equal sign, then, when the copy operation begins, there is no string left to copy. It has just been deleted!

The prototype for **operator=()** is this.
```
String& operator= (const String& s);
```
So the very first thing the function must do is guard against silly user errors such as the above assignment to itself. In this case, the *this* parameter contains the memory address of **String s1** while the parameter reference variable also contains the memory address of **String s1**. We need to verify that *this* and **s1** are not the same object. This is done by comparing the two memory addresses.

```
if (this == &s1)
   return *this;
```

What would result if we coded the test this way?

```
if (*this == s1)
   return *this;
```

*this now is a **String** object. Thus, the compiler attempts to call the **operator==** function to find out if the two objects are equivalent. Notice equivalent objects are not necessarily the **same** object! We must determine if these two are in fact the same object.

Here are how the copy constructor and the **operator=** functions can be implemented for the **String** class.

```
class String {
protected:
 char* string;
public:
 String ();
 String (const char* str);
 String (const String& s);
 String& operator= (const String& s);
 ~String ();
protected:
 void Copy (const String& s);
};

String::String (const String& s) {
 Copy (s);
}
```

```
String& String::operator= (const String& s) {
 if (this == &s)
  return *this;
 delete [] string;
 Copy (s);
 return *this;
}

void String::Copy (const String& s) {
 string = new (std::nothrow) char [strlen (s.string) + 1];
 if (!string) {
  cerr << "Error: out of memory in String Copy\n";
  exit (1);
 }
 strcpy (string, s.string);
}
```

Overloading the [] Operator

The array subscript operator can also be overloaded. With our **String** class, this would be a prudent operator to provide since it then allows the client programs to directly access individual characters within the array. The **operator[]** is a binary operator and thus has one parameter the value the client has coded within the brackets. With subscripts, this is usually an integer but it does not have to be so. But before we try to write the prototype, let's examine the slight problem the operator presents.

A client program can write either of the following statements.
```
String s1 ("Hello World");
char c = s1[0];
s1[0] = 'J';
```
Can you see the difficulty? The first usage is simply copying the indicated character while the second is replacing that character with the letter J. If our **operator[]** function returns the character at the indicated subscript location, then the first usage in the above coding works well; the letter H is stored in variable **c**. However, if we just return the indicated character, then the second usage fails because the letter J cannot be stored back into the string. However, if instead we return a reference to the indicated character, then the second usage works as expected because the compiler now has the memory location of the first element in the string and can replace the letter H with the letter J. Further, in the first usage, the compiler can dereference the reference character to get the actual letter H to store into variable **c**.

Rule: When overloading the operator[], always return a reference to the data so that the operator can be used either as a l-value or a r-value.

Here is the prototype for the **String** class **operator[]**.
```
char& operator[] (int j);
```
Its implementation is done this way. Notice how we can protect from subscript out of range errors.

267

```
char& String::operator[] (int j) {
 if (j < 0 || j >= (int) strlen (string)) {
  cerr << "Error: subscript out of range: " << j << endl;
  exit (2);
 }
 return string[j];
}
```

Overloading the & Address Operator

The address & operator can be overloaded. Why would anyone want to do so? Let's consider the following coding a client can make using our **String** class.

```
String s1 ("Hello World");
if (_stricmp (s1, "Hello World")...
```

Here, the string function requires a pair of **const char*** parameters. **s1** is a **String** object and so the compiler generates an error on this instruction. So next, the client tries the following.

```
if (_stricmp (&s1, "Hello World")...
```

But now **&s1** is a constant pointer to a **String** object not **const char*** and again issues a compiler error.

Certainly, we could provide an access function to return the needed address for the user.

```
const char* GetString () const {
 return string;
}
```

But this forces some awkward coding in the client program.

```
if (_stricmp (s1.GetString(), "Hello World")...
```

Here is a good situation where overloading the address operator is valuable. It is a unary operator and thus takes no parameters.

const char* operator& () const;

And it is very simply implemented as follows.

```
const char* String::operator& () const {
 return string;
}
```

Notice that the return value must be constant. If it were not constant, the client could store data into the string and could possibly overwrite memory, for example, by storing more characters than there is space available.

There is a side effect to overloading the address operator. Suppose that we have provided the above address operator overloaded function that returns the string's location. What then occurs when the client program does the following?

```
String* ptrstring = &s1;
```

This now fails as the address operator is now returning a **const char*** not a **const String***! In other words, the client programs can never again take the address of the **String** object itself! We cannot fix this by making a second version whose prototype is this.

```
const String* operator& () const;
```

Why? Overloaded functions cannot differ only in return data type. So if you expect that client programs would like to take the address of **String** objects, then you cannot overload the address operator. Instead, use the **GetString()** access function above to provide the **const char***. However, there is another way around this.

Operator Conversion Functions

An operator conversion function is a function that is used to convert from some user-defined type, such as a class instance, into some other user defined type or into an intrinsic data type. With instances of our **String** class, client programs most certainly would like to be able to insert them to an output stream. While we could provide the insertion operator friend function in the **String** class, we can also provide an operator conversion function to convert a **String** class instance into a **const char*** instance, which points to the **string** data member.

The syntax for operator conversion function prototypes is **operator** followed by the type to which it is to be converted. Such functions take no parameters. Since the instance is being converted to the indicated data type, there is also no return data type coded. Here is the **String** operator **const char*** conversion function prototype.

```
operator const char* () const;
```
It is implemented this way.
```
String::operator const char* () const {
  return string;
}
```

While this looks promising, in fact when client programs use it, the syntax is awful. Here is how the client can insert an instance of our **String** class to **cout**.

```
cout << s1.operator const char*() << endl;
```
This is not elegant coding for the client programs.

However, this concept does have a singularly powerful usage. Recall how we usually utilize the extraction operator when reading a set of data.

```
while (cin >> x) {
```
We know that this is saying while the stream is still okay do the body of the loop. But how is this accomplished? We also know the extraction operator returns a reference to the original input stream. So the above becomes the following once the extraction is complete.

```
while (cin) {
```
How does this actually work?

The compiler calls an operator conversion function. It is coded within the **ios** class this way.

```
ios::operator void* () {
  return fail () ? 0 : this;
}
```

In other words, the compiler calls a conversion function to try to convert the **cin** instance into a void pointer. And the compiler can test the pointer to obtain the **bool** value, **true** if the pointer is not 0. (The fail bit is on if any kind of non-good event has occurred.)

Can we make use of this with our **String** class? Perhaps. Unlike the futile attempt to allow a conversion to a **const char***, we can readily convert to a **void***. Suppose that the client programs frequently wished to know if a given **String** instance contained a null string, that is, a string of length 1 containing only the null terminator. We could have this operator **void*** return this state.

```
operator void* () const;

String::operator void* () const {
  return string[0] == 0 ? 0 : string;
}
```

Clients could now test for null strings this way.

```
if (!s1) ...
```

This approach of using a **void*** conversion function can be useful in certain circumstances in which clients wish to somehow "test" an instance of a class for some purpose.

Pgm07a—String Class Thus Far

Here is the **String** class to this point in its design.

```
String Class Definition

 1 #pragma once
 2
 3 /*******************************************************/
 4 /*                                                     */
 5 /* String Class: encapsulate a character string        */
 6 /*                                                     */
 7 /*******************************************************/
 8
 9 class String {
10 protected:
11  char* string; // the client's string
12
13 public:
14  String ();                              // makes a null string
15  String (const char* str);               // copies the passed string
16  String (const String& s);               // copies a String object
17  String& operator= (const String& s);    // assigns a String object
18  ~String ();                             // deletes the string array
```

```
19
20   const char* GetString () const; // returns ptr to the string
21   char& operator[] (int j);        // handles array subscripting
22   operator void* () const;  // true if string is not a null string
23
24 protected:
25   void Copy (const String& s); // performs deep copy of the String
26 };
```

```
String Class Implementation
```

```
 1 #include <iostream>
 3 #include <string>
 4 using namespace std;
 5 #include "String.h"
 6
 7 /******************************************************************/
 8 /*                                                                */
 9 /* String: allocates a null string, aborts if out of memory       */
10 /*                                                                */
11 /******************************************************************/
12
13 String::String () {
14   string = new (std::nothrow) char[1];
15   if (!string) {
16     cerr << "Error: out of memory in String ctor\n";
17     exit (1);
18   }
19   string[0] = 0;
20 }
21
22 /******************************************************************/
23 /*                                                                */
24 /* String: stores passed string, aborts if out of memory          */
25 /*                                                                */
26 /******************************************************************/
27
28 String::String (const char* str) {
29   if (!str) {
30     string = new (std::nothrow) char[1];
31     if (!string) {
32       cerr << "Error: out of memory in String ctor\n";
33       exit (1);
34     }
35     string[0] = 0;
36     return;
37   }
38   string = new (std::nothrow) char [strlen (str) + 1];
39   if (!string) {
40     cerr << "Error: out of memory in String ctor\n";
41     exit (1);
42   }
```

```
43  strcpy_s (string, strlen (str) + 1, str);
44 }
45
46 /****************************************************************/
47 /*                                                              */
48 /* ~String: deletes the array of char                          */
49 /*                                                              */
50 /****************************************************************/
51
52 String::~String () {
53   if (string)
54     delete [] string;
55 }
56
57 /****************************************************************/
58 /*                                                              */
59 /* String: copy ctor duplicates the passed string              */
60 /*                                                              */
61 /****************************************************************/
62
63 String::String (const String& s) {
64   Copy (s);
65 }
66
67 /****************************************************************/
68 /*                                                              */
69 /* operator=: assigns passed string to this instance           */
70 /*                                                              */
71 /****************************************************************/
72
73 String& String::operator= (const String& s) {
74   if (this == &s)
75     return *this;
76   delete [] string;
77   Copy (s);
78   return *this;
79 }
80
81 /****************************************************************/
82 /*                                                              */
83 /* Copy: actually duplicates the passed string, abort if out   */
84 /*                                              of memory       */
85 /*                                                              */
86 /****************************************************************/
87
88 void String::Copy (const String& s) {
89   string = new (std::nothrow) char [strlen (s.string) + 1];
90   if (!string) {
91     cerr << "Error: out of memory in String Copy\n";
92     exit (1);
93   }
94   strcpy_s (string, strlen (s.string) + 1, s.string);
95 }
```

```
 96
 97 /***************************************************************/
 98 /*                                                             */
 99 /* GetString: returns the address of the stored string         */
100 /*                                                             */
101 /***************************************************************/
102
103 const char* String::GetString () const {
104  return string;
105 }
106
107 /***************************************************************/
108 /*                                                             */
109 /* operator[]: provides access to jth element of the array     */
110 /*             aborts if subscript is out of range             */
111 /*                                                             */
112 /***************************************************************/
113
114 char& String::operator[] (int j) {
115  if (j < 0 || j >= (int) strlen (string)) {
116   cerr << "Error: subscript out of range: " << j << endl;
117   exit (2);
118  }
119  return string[j];
120 }
121
122 /***************************************************************/
123 /*                                                             */
124 /* operator void* - returns 0 if string is a null string       */
125 /*                  or addr of string is it is not null        */
126 /*                                                             */
127 /***************************************************************/
128
129 String::operator void* () const {
130  return string[0] == 0 ? 0 : string;
131 }
```

Pgm07a tests these functions that we have coded thus far. One of the programming assignments will extend this class by adding many very useful operator functions.

```
Pgm07a String Class Tester

 1 #include <iostream>
 2 #include <iomanip>
 3 #include <string>
 4 #include <crtdbg.h>
 5 using namespace std;
 6 #include "String.h"
 7
 8 /***************************************************************/
 9 /*                                                             */
```

```
10 /* Pgm07a: String Tester Program                              */
11 /*                                                            */
12 /************************************************************/
13
14 String Fun (String s);
15
16 int main () {
17  {
18  String s1 ("Hello World");
19  String s2 ("Good-Bye");
20  String s3 (s1); // the copy ctor
21  String s4 = s1; // the copy ctor
22  String s5;
23  s5 = s1; // the assignment operator
24  String s6;
25  s6 = Fun (s1); // s1 is passed by copy ctor and returned by
26                 //  copy ctor and assignment op to s6
27  String s7;
28
29  cout << "s1 should be |Hello World| and is\n"
30       << "              |" << s1.GetString() << "|\n\n";
31  cout << "s2 should be |Good-Bye| and is\n"
32       << "              |" << s2.GetString() << "|\n\n";
33  cout << "s3 should be |Hello World| and is\n"
34       << "              |" << s3.GetString() << "|\n\n";
35  cout << "s4 should be |Hello World| and is\n"
36       << "              |" << s4.GetString() << "|\n\n";
37  cout << "s5 should be |Hello World| and is\n"
38       << "              |" << s5.GetString() << "|\n\n";
39  cout << "s6 should be |Hello World| and is\n"
40       << "              |" << s6.GetString() << "|\n\n";
41  cout << "s7 should be || and is\n"
42       << "              |" << s7.GetString() << "|\n\n";
43
44  if (s7)
45   cout << "s7 is not null - error\n";
46  else
47   cout << "s7 is null and is correct\n";
48
49  if (s2)
50   cout << "s2 is not null and is correct\n";
51  else
52   cout << "s2 is null - error\n";
53
54  cout << "\nFirst character of s1 should be H and is "
55       << s1[0] << endl;
56  s1[0] = 'J';
57  cout << "\nFirst character of s1 should be J and is "
58       << s1[0] << endl;
59  }
60
61  // check for memory leaks
62  if (_CrtDumpMemoryLeaks())
```

```
63   cerr << "Memory leaks occurred!\n";
64  else
65   cerr << "No memory leaks.\n";
66
67  return 0;
68 }
69
70 String Fun (String s) {
71  String ret (s); // copy ctor
72  return ret;     // copy ctor
73 }
```

```
Output of Pgm07a String Class Tester

 1 s1 should be |Hello World| and is
 2              |Hello World|
 3
 4 s2 should be |Good-Bye| and is
 5              |Good-Bye|
 6
 7 s3 should be |Hello World| and is
 8              |Hello World|
 9
10 s4 should be |Hello World| and is
11              |Hello World|
12
13 s5 should be |Hello World| and is
14              |Hello World|
15
16 s6 should be |Hello World| and is
17              |Hello World|
18
19 s7 should be || and is
20              ||
21
22 s7 is null and is correct
23 s2 is not null and is correct
24
25 First character of s1 should be H and is H
26
27 First character of s1 should be J and is J
28 No memory leaks.
```

Designing a Generic Growable Array Class

A **container class** is a data structure which holds items for the user. In this case, the container is an array that grows in size as the number of items are added. The limit, as before, is the amount of memory available. The key feature is reusability. While one could easily envision a class devoted to holding an array of cost records, inventory records and so on, such would not be portable to the next programming project that needed an array of other items. I am always in favor of writing something once and then being able to use it in many different programs.

What should the specifications of an array class be? Obviously, there are going to be two data members of the class, the array of items and the count of the number of elements in the array. But what should be the data type of the array? This is the critical design aspect. If we make the array of some specific data type, such as a **CostRec** structure, then at once the container class cannot be reused except in another program that deals with cost records.

However, there is one type of data that is independent of data type and that is a **void***, a pointer to **void**. Such pointers cannot be dereferenced. However, if all that our class is doing is maintaining an array of such pointers and providing access to those pointers, we do not need to dereference such pointers. Thus, to make the array reusable, our class stores a resizeable array of **void** pointers. Note that our member data type is thus

```
void** array; // an array of void*
```

When a user wishes to gain access to a specific element and calls say **GetAt (i)** to acquire the ith one, our function returns to the user a **void***. For the user to be able to do anything with that data, he or she must typecast the pointer back to the specific data type to which it is pointing. The user, of course, knows what kind of data to which it is supposed to be pointing. This, of course, places an extra burden on the programmer. However, the benefits of using a generic array container are many. We can also implement **operator[]** as an alternative method to accessing elements.

There is also a significant side effect of storing only **void** pointers. To see the impact of that side effect, let's examine the alternative approach, say storing an array of **CostRec** structures. The class name might be **CostRecArray** and its data members might be as shown.

```
CostRec* array;
long     numElements:
```

When the user wants to add a new instance to the array, he or she calls our **Add()** function which might be coded as follows.

```
void CostRecArray::Add (const CostRec& crec) {
 CostRec* temp = new (std::nothrow) CostRec [numElements + 1];
 if (!temp) {
  cerr << "Array: Add Error - out of memory\n";
  return;
 }
 for (long i=0; i<numElements; i++) {
  temp[i] = array[i];
 }
```

```
temp[numElements] = crec;
numElements++;
delete [] array;
array = temp;
}
```

The sequence is simple: allocate space for a new array of **CostRec** structures that is one element larger than the current array. Then copy all of the **CostRec** structures in the old array into the new array. Next, copy the new one into the last element. After incrementing the number of elements in the array, delete the old array and assign the address of the new array to our **array** member.

When the destructor is called, we must delete all of the **CostRec** structures we are storing. Since we are storing an array of them, it is a simple task.

```
if (array) delete [] array;
```

Thus, the programmers never have to concern themselves with any clean up activities. The class handles the destruction of the array and its contents.

Okay. So what is the side effect of having the class store **void** pointers? The programmer must allocate the items they wish the container to store and they must delete those items before any class destructor is called. When the programmer calls the **Add()** function, they must pass the address of the item to be stored. Frequently, they will have already dynamically allocated that item and filled it up with relevant data. Later, **before** any destructor of the **Array** class is called, they must traverse all elements in the array, retrieve each pointer from the **Array** and then delete the memory occupied by that item.

Another side effect is copying of the array. The copy ctor and the assignment operator now have no way to actually make a deep copy of a passed array because the data items are **void** pointers. So in this case, these two functions will make a duplicate copy of the array of pointers, but not the client's data that is being stored. It is then up to the client to traverse the array, acquiring and then deleting each of the objects the array is storing before the destructor is called.

When designing the **Array** class, what member functions are needed? The default constructor sets the array pointer to zero along with the number of elements in the array. The destructor should delete the array. How would a client want to add elements to an array? If the data is coming from a file, most likely, the programmer would just want to add the next item at the end of the array. Let's call that the **Add()** function.

However, a programmer might wish to add an item at the beginning or after some specific index. Let's call that function **InsertAt()**. Certainly, the need the ability to get at an item located at a specific index, function **GetAt()** and **operator[]**. On the removal side, they might wish to remove an item at a specific index or perhaps empty the array to reuse it; this gives us **RemoveAt()** and **RemoveAll()**. A client program certainly must be able to find out the number of elements currently in the array—the **GetNumberOfElements()** function.

Finally, if there are any errors, let's display them to the **cerr** device. Here is the **Array** class definition. Notice the extensive use of comments alerting the programmer to class usage notes. It is sometimes helpful to insert a bit of client coding in the comments to illustrate what a client program must do that might not be clear to all programmers. I did just this to illustrate how a client program should clean up the array before the destructor gets called. I also documented the expected behavior of certain functions such as **InsertAt()**, **GetAt()** and **RemoveAt()**.

Here are the **Array** class definition and implementation files.

```
Growable Array Class Definition

 1 #pragma once
 2
 3 /********************************************************/
 4 /*                                                      */
 5 /*  Array: container for growable array of void* items  */
 6 /*         it can store a variable number of elements   */
 7 /*                                                      */
 8 /*         since elements stored are void*, they can    */
 9 /*         point to anything desired, intrinsic types,  */
10 /*         structures, other classes, for example      */
11 /*                                                      */
12 /*   limited by amount of memory and swap drive size    */
13 /*                                                      */
14 /*   errors are logged to cerr device                   */
15 /*                                                      */
16 /*   Note on destruction: before calling RemoveAt or    */
17 /*   RemoveAll or the destructor, the user is responsible */
18 /*   for the actual deletion of the items the void*     */
19 /*   pointers are actually pointing to                  */
20 /*                                                      */
21 /*   Typical clean up coding might be as follows:       */
22 /*   MyData* ptrd;                                      */
23 /*   for (i=0; i<array.GetNumberOfElements(); i++) {    */
24 /*    ptrd = (MyData*) array.GetAt (i);                 */
25 /*    if (ptrd)                                         */
26 /*      delete ptrd;                                    */
27 /*   }                                                  */
28 /*   array.RemoveAll ();                                */
29 /*                                                      */
30 /********************************************************/
31
32 class Array {
33
34   /********************************************************/
35   /*                                                      */
36   /* class data                                           */
37   /*                                                      */
38   /********************************************************/
39
40 protected:
```

```
41  void** array;
42  long  numElements;
43
44  /*******************************************************/
45  /*                                                     */
46  /* class functions                                     */
47  /*                                                     */
48  /*******************************************************/
49
50 public:
51    // default constructor - makes an empty array
52    Array ();
53
54    // be sure to delete what the void* are pointing to before
55    // the destructor is called
56    ~Array ();
57        // add the element to array end, returns true if successful
58    bool Add (void* ptrNewElement);
59
60        // adds this element at subscript i
61        // if i < 0, it is added at the front
62        // if i >= numElements, it is added at the end
63        // otherwise, it is added at the ith position
64        // returns true if successful
65    bool InsertAt (long i, void* ptrNewElement);
66
67        // returns element at the ith pos
68        // if i is out of range, it returns 0
69    void* GetAt (long i) const;
70
71        // returns element at the ith pos, if out of range
72    void* operator[] (long i);
73
74        // removes the element at subscript i, element actually
75        // pointed to is not deleted
76    bool RemoveAt (long i);
77
78        // removes all elements - what is pointed to is not deleted
79    void RemoveAll ();
80
81        // returns the number of elements in the array
82    long GetNumberOfElements () const;
83
84    // copy constructor duplicates the array, but not the items
85    Array (const Array& a);
86
87        // duplicates the array, but not the items
88    Array& operator= (const Array& a); //
89
90 protected:
91        // performs the actual deep copy
92    void Copy (const Array& a);
93  };
```

279

Growable Array Class Implementation

```
 1 #include <iostream>
 2 using namespace std;
 3 #include "Array.h"
 4
 5 /*****************************************************/
 6 /*                                                   */
 7 /* Array: constructs an empty array                  */
 8 /*                                                   */
 9 /*****************************************************/
10
11 Array::Array () {
12  numElements = 0;
13  array = 0;
14 }
15
16 /*****************************************************/
17 /*                                                   */
18 /* ~Array: deletes dynamically allocated memory      */
19 /*         It is the client's responsibility  to delete */
20 /*         what the void* are pointing to before the */
21 /*         destructor is called                      */
22 /*                                                   */
23 /*****************************************************/
24
25 Array::~Array () {
26  RemoveAll ();
27 }
28
29 /*****************************************************/
30 /*                                                   */
31 /* Add: Adds this new element to the end of the array  */
32 /*      if out of memory, displays error message to cerr */
33 /*                                                   */
34 /*****************************************************/
35
36 bool Array::Add (void* ptrNewElement) {
37  // allocate new temporary array one element larger
38  void** temp = new (std::nothrow) void* [numElements + 1];
39
40  // check for out of memory
41  if (!temp) {
42   cerr << "Array: Add Error - out of memory\n";
43   return false;
44  }
45
46  // copy all existing elements into the new temp array
47  for (long i=0; i<numElements; i++) {
48   temp[i] = array[i];
```

```
 49  }
 50
 51  // copy in the new element to be added
 52  temp[numElements] = ptrNewElement;
 53
 54  numElements++;  // inc the number of elements in the array
 55  if (array) delete [] array; // delete the old array
 56  array = temp;   // point out array to the new array
 57  return true;
 58  }
 59
 60  /***********************************************************/
 61  /*                                                         */
 62  /*  InsertAt: adds the new element to the array at index i*/
 63  /*   if i is in range, it is inserted at subscript i       */
 64  /*   if i is negative, it is inserted at the front         */
 65  /*   if i is greater than or equal to the number of        */
 66  /*      elements, then it is added at the end of the array*/
 67  /*                                                         */
 68  /*   if there is insufficient memory, an error message     */
 69  /*      is displayed to cerr                               */
 70  /*                                                         */
 71  /***********************************************************/
 72
 73  bool Array::InsertAt (long i, void* ptrNewElement) {
 74   void** temp;
 75   long j;
 76   // allocate a new array one element larger
 77   temp = new (std::nothrow) void* [numElements + 1];
 78
 79   // check if out of memory
 80   if (!temp) {
 81    cerr << "Array: InsertAt - Error out of memory\n";
 82    return false;
 83   }
 84
 85   // this case handles an insertion that is within range
 86   if (i < numElements && i >= 0) {
 87    for (j=0; j<i; j++) { // copy all elements below insertion
 88     temp[j] = array[j];  // point
 89    }
 90    temp[i] = ptrNewElement; // insert new element
 91    for (j=i; j<numElements; j++) { // copy remaining elements
 92     temp[j+1] = array[j];
 93    }
 94   }
 95
 96   // this case handles an insertion when the index is too large
 97   else if (i >= numElements) {
 98    for (j=0; j<numElements; j++) { // copy all existing elements
 99     temp[j] = array[j];
100    }
101    temp[numElements] = ptrNewElement; // add new one at end
```

281

```
102  }
103
104  // this case handles an insertion when the index is too small
105  else {
106   temp[0] = ptrNewElement;        // insert new on at front
107   for (j=0; j<numElements; j++) { // copy all others after it
108    temp[j+1] = array[j];
109    }
110  }
111
112  // for all cases, delete current array, assign new one and
113  // increment the number of elements in the array
114  if (array) delete [] array;
115  array = temp;
116  numElements++;
117  return true;
118 }
119
120 /***************************************************************/
121 /*                                                           */
122 /* GetAt: returns the element at index i                     */
123 /*        if i is out of range, returns 0                    */
124 /*                                                           */
125 /***************************************************************/
126
127 void* Array::GetAt (long i) const {
128  if (i < numElements && i >=0)
129   return array[i];
130  else
131   return 0;
132 }
133
134 /***************************************************************/
135 /*                                                           */
136 /* operator[]: returns the element at index i                */
137 /*             if i is out of range, returns 0               */
138 /*                                                           */
139 /***************************************************************/
140
141 void* Array::operator[] (long i) {
142  if (i < numElements && i >=0)
143   return array[i];
144  else
145   return 0;
146 }
147
148 /***************************************************************/
149 /*                                                           */
150 /* RemoveAt: removes the element at subscript i              */
151 /*                                                           */
152 /* If i is out of range, an error is displayed on cerr       */
153 /*                                                           */
154 /* Note that what the element actually points to is not      */
```

```
155 /*        deleted                                           */
156 /*                                                          */
157 /***********************************************************/
158
159 bool Array::RemoveAt (long i) {
160  void** temp;
161  if (numElements > 1) {
162   if (i >= 0 && i < numElements) { // if the index is in range
163    // allocate a smaller array
164    temp = new (std::nothrow) void* [numElements - 1];
165    long j;
166    for (j=0; j<i; j++) {            // copy all elements up to
167     temp[j] = array[j];            // the desired one to be
168    }                               // removed
169    for (j=i+1; j<numElements; j++) { // copy all the elements
170     temp[j-1] = array[j];          // that remain
171    }
172    numElements--;            // dec the number of elements
173    delete [] array;          // delete the old array
174    array = temp;             // and assign the new one
175    return true;
176   }
177  }
178  else if (numElements == 1 && i == 0) {
179   delete [] array;
180   numElements = 0;
181   array = 0;
182   return true;
183  }
184  cerr << "Array: RemoveAt Error - element out of range\n"
185       << "        It was " << i << " and numElements is "
186       << numElements << endl;
187  return false;
188 }
189
190 /***********************************************************/
191 /*                                                          */
192 /* RemoveAll: empties the entire array, resetting it to   */
193 /*            an empty state ready for reuse               */
194 /*                                                          */
195 /* Note that what the elements actually points to are     */
196 /*      not deleted                                       */
197 /*                                                          */
198 /***********************************************************/
199
200 void Array::RemoveAll () {
201  if (array) delete [] array; // remove all elements
202  numElements = 0;            // reset number of elements
203  array = 0;                  // and reset array to 0
204 }
205
206 /***********************************************************/
207 /*                                                          */
```

283

```
208 /* GetNumberOfElements: returns the number of elements    */
209 /*                       currently in the array            */
210 /*                                                         */
211 /***********************************************************/
212
213 long Array::GetNumberOfElements () const {
214  return numElements;
215 }
216
217 /***********************************************************/
218 /*                                                         */
219 /* Array: copy constructor, makes a duplicate copy of a    */
220 /*                                                         */
221 /* Note: what the elements actually point to are not       */
222 /* duplicated only our pointers are duplicated             */
223 /*                                                         */
224 /***********************************************************/
225
226 Array::Array (const Array& a) {
227  Copy (a);
228 }
229
230 /***********************************************************/
231 /*                                                         */
232 /* operator=: makes a duplicate array of passed array a    */
233 /*                                                         */
234 /* Note: what the elements actually point to are not       */
235 /* duplicated only our pointers are duplicated             */
236 /*                                                         */
237 /***********************************************************/
238
239 Array& Array::operator= (const Array& a) {
240  if (this == &a) // avoids silly a = a assignemnts
241   return *this;
242  if (array) delete [] array; // remove existing array
243  Copy (a);                   // duplicate array a
244  return *this;        // return us for chaining assignments
245 }
246
247 /***********************************************************/
248 /*                                                         */
249 /* Copy: helper function to actual perform the copy        */
250 /*                                                         */
251 /***********************************************************/
252
253 void Array::Copy (const Array& a) {
254  if (a.numElements) { // be sure array a is not empty
255   numElements = a.numElements;
256   // allocate a new array the size of a
257   array = new (std::nothrow) void* [numElements];
258
259   // check for out of memory condition
260   if (!array) {
```

```
261     cerr << "Array: Copy function - Error out of memory\n";
262     numElements = 0;
263     return;
264   }
265
266   // copy all of a's pointers into our array
267   for (long i=0; i<numElements; i++) {
268     array[i] = a.array[i];
269   }
270 }
271 else { // a is empty, so make ours empty too
272   numElements = 0;
273   array = 0;
274 }
275 }
```

Next, we must thoroughly test the **Array** implementation. To avoid the extra complexity of the tester program allocating and deleting all of the items, I have chosen a simpler route. I allocate an automatic storage array of integers. Each element is given an increasing value from zero on up. What is stored in the **Array** instances are the addresses of specific elements in this integer array. This makes the testing an easier proposition to implement. Before you look at my tester program's detailed coding, sketch out what kind of tests you think should be done to ensure **Array** works perfectly. Then, check to see if I tested for them. See if I missed any situations. (Hint, I did, in fact, fail to test thoroughly.)

Here are the tester program and its output. Please note how I created a uniform **PrintArray()** function that prints a test id string along with the theoretical output that we should see and the actual contents of the **Array** at this point. This way, errors are trivial to spot.

```
Pgm07b Tester of the Array Class

 1 #include <iostream.h>
 2 #include <iomanip.h>
 3 #include <crtdbg.h> // for memory leak checking
 4
 5 #include "Array.h"
 6
 7 // common results display function
 8 void PrintArray (const Array& a, const char* title,
 9                  const char* shouldBe);
10
11 // function to test passing a copy and returning a copy
12 Array Fun (Array f);
13
14 /***********************************************************/
15 /*                                                         */
16 /* Pgm07b: tester program to test the Array class          */
17 /*                                                         */
18 /***********************************************************/
```

```
19
20  int main () {
21   // an array of some items whose addresses can be stored in the
22   // growable array - this avoids our having to constantly
23   // allocate and delete items as they are added and removed
24   int test[50];
25   int i;
26   for (i=0; i<50; i++) {
27    test[i] = i;
28   }
29
30   // wrap the Array processing in a block so that the destructors
31   // are called before we check for memory leaks
32   {
33    Array a;
34
35    // Add testing
36    for (i=0; i<10; i++)  {
37     a.Add (&test[i+1]);
38    }
39    PrintArray (a, "Testing Add", "1 2 3 4 5 6 7 8 9 10");
40
41    // InsertAt testing
42    a.InsertAt (0, &test[0]);
43    a.InsertAt (11, &test[12]);
44    a.InsertAt (11, &test[11]);
45    a.InsertAt (1, &test[49]);
46    PrintArray (a, "Testing InsertAt",
47                   "0 49 1 2 3 4 5 6 7 8 9 10 11 12");
48
49    // RemoveAt testing
50    a.RemoveAt (0);
51    a.RemoveAt (a.GetNumberOfElements()-1);
52    a.RemoveAt (5);
53    PrintArray (a, "Testing RemoveAt", "49 1 2 3 4 6 7 8 9 10 11");
54
55    // RemoveAll testing
56    a.RemoveAll ();
57    PrintArray (a, "Testing RemoveAll", "empty ");
58
59    // some special cases of RemoveAt and RemoveAll
60    a.RemoveAt (42);
61    a.RemoveAll ();
62    PrintArray (a, "Testing Empty Array", "empty ");
63
64    // InsertAt the beginning test with negative subscript
65    for (i=0; i<10; i++)  {
66     a.InsertAt (-1, &test[i]);
67    }
68    PrintArray (a, "Testing InsertAt", "9 8 7 6 5 4 3 2 1 0");
69
70    // InsertAt the beginning test with constant 0 subscript
71    a.RemoveAll ();
```

```
 72    for (i=0; i<10; i++)   {
 73      a.InsertAt (0, &test[i]);
 74    }
 75    PrintArray (a, "Testing InsertAt", "9 8 7 6 5 4 3 2 1 0");
 76
 77    // InsertAt the end test with out of bounds high subscript
 78    a.RemoveAll ();
 79    for (i=0; i<10; i++)   {
 80      a.InsertAt (42, &test[i]);
 81    }
 82    PrintArray (a, "Testing InsertAt", "0 1 2 3 4 5 6 7 8 9");
 83
 84    // testing copy constructors
 85    Array b (a);
 86    PrintArray (b, "Testing Copy Ctor", "0 1 2 3 4 5 6 7 8 9");
 87
 88    Array c = a;
 89    PrintArray (c, "Testing Copy Ctor", "0 1 2 3 4 5 6 7 8 9");
 90
 91    // testing assignment operator
 92    Array d;
 93    d = a;
 94    PrintArray (d, "Testing Assignmment", "0 1 2 3 4 5 6 7 8 9");
 95
 96    // testing passing and returning copies of the array
 97    Array e = Fun (a);
 98    PrintArray (e, "Testing Returned Array", "1 2 3 4 5 6 7 8 9");
 99
100    // testing dumb assignment
101    e = e;
102    PrintArray (e, "Testing e = e assignment",
103               "1 2 3 4 5 6 7 8 9");
104
105    // testing assignment of empty arrays
106    Array h, j;
107    j = h;
108    PrintArray (h,
109        "Testing assignment of empty arrays - Original Array",
110        "empty");
111    PrintArray (j,
112        "Testing assignment of empty arrays - Duplicate Array",
113        "empty");
114
115  }
116
117  // check for memory leaks
118  if (_CrtDumpMemoryLeaks())
119    cerr << "Memory leaks occurred!\n";
120  else
121    cerr << "No memory leaks.\n";
122
123  return 0;
124 }
```

```
125
126 /***********************************************************/
127 /*                                                         */
128 /* PrintArray: helper function to create a standard        */
129 /*             display of results                          */
130 /*                                                         */
131 /***********************************************************/
132
133 void PrintArray (const Array& a, const char* title,
134                  const char* shouldBe) {
135  cout << endl << title << endl
136       << "Should Be:   " << shouldBe << endl
137       << "Actually Is: ";
138  int* ptrInt;
139  long i;
140  if (a.GetNumberOfElements () == 0) {
141   cout << "empty\n";
142   return;
143  }
144  for (i=0; i<a.GetNumberOfElements (); i++) {
145   ptrInt = (int*) a.GetAt (i);
146   if (!ptrInt)
147    cout << "Error Invalid ptr at" << i << endl;
148   else
149    cout << *ptrInt << " ";
150  }
151  cout << endl;
152 }
153
154 /***********************************************************/
155 /*                                                         */
156 /* Fun: function that is passed a copy of an Array and     */
157 /*                that returns a copy of an Array           */
158 /*                                                         */
159 /***********************************************************/
160
161 Array Fun (Array f) {
162  PrintArray (f, "Testing Fun's Parameter Copy of Array",
163              "0 1 2 3 4 5 6 7 8 9");
164  Array g;
165  g = f;
166  g.RemoveAt (0);
167  PrintArray (g, "Testing Fun's To Be Returned Array",
168              "1 2 3 4 5 6 7 8 9");
169  return g;
170 }
171
```

```
Output of the Pgm07b Tester of the Array Class Program

 1
 2 Testing Add
```

```
 3 Should Be:    1 2 3 4 5 6 7 8 9 10
 4 Actually Is: 1 2 3 4 5 6 7 8 9 10
 5
 6 Testing InsertAt
 7 Should Be:    0 49 1 2 3 4 5 6 7 8 9 10 11 12
 8 Actually Is: 0 49 1 2 3 4 5 6 7 8 9 10 11 12
 9
10 Testing RemoveAt
11 Should Be:    49 1 2 3 4 6 7 8 9 10 11
12 Actually Is: 49 1 2 3 4 6 7 8 9 10 11
13
14 Testing RemoveAll
15 Should Be:    empty
16 Actually Is: empty
17 Array: RemoveAt Error - element out of range
18         It was 42 and numElements is 0
19
20 Testing Empty Array
21 Should Be:    empty
22 Actually Is: empty
23
24 Testing InsertAt
25 Should Be:    9 8 7 6 5 4 3 2 1 0
26 Actually Is: 9 8 7 6 5 4 3 2 1 0
27
28 Testing InsertAt
29 Should Be:    9 8 7 6 5 4 3 2 1 0
30 Actually Is: 9 8 7 6 5 4 3 2 1 0
31
32 Testing InsertAt
33 Should Be:    0 1 2 3 4 5 6 7 8 9
34 Actually Is: 0 1 2 3 4 5 6 7 8 9
35
36 Testing Copy Ctor
37 Should Be:    0 1 2 3 4 5 6 7 8 9
38 Actually Is: 0 1 2 3 4 5 6 7 8 9
39
40 Testing Copy Ctor
41 Should Be:    0 1 2 3 4 5 6 7 8 9
42 Actually Is: 0 1 2 3 4 5 6 7 8 9
43
44 Testing Assignmment
45 Should Be:    0 1 2 3 4 5 6 7 8 9
46 Actually Is: 0 1 2 3 4 5 6 7 8 9
47
48 Testing Fun's Parameter Copy of Array
49 Should Be:    0 1 2 3 4 5 6 7 8 9
50 Actually Is: 0 1 2 3 4 5 6 7 8 9
51
52 Testing Fun's To Be Returned Array
53 Should Be:    1 2 3 4 5 6 7 8 9
54 Actually Is: 1 2 3 4 5 6 7 8 9
55
```

```
56 Testing Returned Array
57 Should Be:    1 2 3 4 5 6 7 8 9
58 Actually Is: 1 2 3 4 5 6 7 8 9
59
60 Testing e = e assignment
61 Should Be:    1 2 3 4 5 6 7 8 9
62 Actually Is: 1 2 3 4 5 6 7 8 9
63
64 Testing assignment of empty arrays - Original Array
65 Should Be:    empty
66 Actually Is: empty
67
68 Testing assignment of empty arrays - Duplicate Array
69 Should Be:    empty
70 Actually Is: empty
71 No memory leaks.
```

Review Questions

1. Looking over **Pgm07b**, what did I fail to test in the **Array** class? How could the tester program be modified to test for these situations?

2. Why must a class that has dynamic memory allocation occurring within its data members always provide the copy ctor and the assignment operator functions? Is a destructor function really needed? Why?

3. Why should a function that is dynamically allocating a data member take some kind of action when the returned pointer from the **new** function is 0?

4. Assume the following definition for a class **Fun**. What is the inherent design glitch?
```
class Fun {
protected:
  int* x;
public:
  Fun () : x(0) {}
...
```

5. Why must a **operator=** function first check to see it this instance is the same as the passed instance? Why doesn't this work to do so?
```
    if (*this == s)
```
where **s** is the passed object to be copied.

6. What are the benefits of using a **Copy()** function when implementing the copy ctor and assignment operator functions?

290

7. A programmer coded the following prototype for **operator[]** to access a specific element in an array of integers. What is wrong with this definition and how can it be fixed?
```
int operator[] (int i);
```

8. If one overloads the address operator for a class **Fun** to return the address of the start of an array of integers, why does the following then fail?
```
        Fun array;
        Fun* ptrThisOne = &array;
```

9. What is the purpose of coding an operator conversion function to convert a class into a **void*** ?

Stop! Do These Exercises Before Programming

1. Consider this class definition for a complex number array class.
```
class Cmplx {
protected:
 double* realPart;
 double* imagPart;
 long count;
public:
 Cmplx (double* realArray, double* imagArray, long num);
 Cmplx&  operator= (const Cmplx& c);
...

Cmplx::Cmplx (double* realArray, double* imagArray, long num) {
 realPart = new double [count];
 inagPart = new double [count];
 count = num;
 for (long j=0; j<num; j++) {
  realPart[j] = realArray[j];
  imagPart[j] = imagArray[j];
 }
}

Cmplx& Cmplx::operator= (const Cmplx& c) {
 realPart = new double [c.count];
 inagPart = new double [c.count];
 count = c.count;
 for (long j=0; j<count; j++) {
  realPart[j] = c.realPart[j];
  imagPart[j] = c.imagPart[j];
 }
}
```
What is wrong with the design of the **operator=** function and how can it be fixed?

2. Code a copy constructor for the above **Cmplx** number class.

3. Code an **operator[]** function for the above **Cmplx** number class. It should be able to handle both l-values and r-values. Display an error message to **cerr** if the subscript is out of range and abort the program.

4. Code an operator conversion **void*** function for the above **Cmplx** number class. It returns 0 if the array contains no elements. Otherwise, it returns the address of the realPart array.

Programming Problems

Problem Pgm07-1—Extensions to the String Class

Modify the **String** class of **Pgm07a** in this chapter as follows to make it more efficient and useful.

Add support for **operator+=** which should concatenate the passed string onto the end of the string data member.

Add support for the insertion and extraction operators to input or display a string. Assume that the maximum length of any string on input is 100.

Add support for **operator+** in which the passed parameter is a **const char***. Usage would be similar to this.
```
s1 = s2 + "Hello";
```

Add support for **operator+** in which the passed parameter is another **String** object. Usage would be similar to this.
```
s1 = s2 + s3;
```

Extend the tester program, **Pgm07a**, to include thorough testing of all the new functions.

Problem Pgm07-2—BigInt—A Class for Big Unsigned Integers

Currently, the largest unsigned long integer that can be used is 4,294,967,295. When dealing with numbers larger than this, floating point numbers are often used. This is inadequate for two reasons: speed and the number of digits of accuracy. Floating point operations usually execute more slowly and there can be only 15 digits of accuracy with a **double**—hence, the need for a **BigInt** class.

Write a **BigInt** class that can handle a large range of unsigned integers. The limit on the maximum number of digits is only determined by the amount of memory on the computer.

The BigInt Class Interface

The name of the class is **BigInt**. The smallest unsigned integer is 0.

The Four Construction Functions

```
BigInt (unsigned long n);// construct from an unsigned long
BigInt (const char *string); // construct from a string
BigInt ();                   // use a default of 0 as the number
BigInt (const BigInt &copy); // copy the existing number
```

```
The following are valid.
unsigned long n = 123456789ul;
char string[10] = "1234567889";
BigInt a;
BigInt b(n);
BigInt c(123456789ul);
BigInt d (string);
BigInt e ("1235456789");
BigInt f (b);
```

Operator=

Also, create the assignment operator= so that the compiler and user can write
```
d = b;
```

The I/O Functions

Create an extraction operator>> to input a **BigInt** so that the following is valid.
```
BigInt a;
cin >> a;
```
The input rules are as follows. Skip over white space to the first digit. Input all digits up to the first non-digit character. Note the non-digit could be EOF, a non-integer digit such as the letter 'A', or white space. Leave the non-digit **in the** input stream. Use **peek()** or **putback()** functions. You may also use the **ws** manipulator to handle white space if you like. The longest integer that can be input is arbitrarily assumed to be 100 characters long; this is an "arbitrary" so that you can perform the input operation more easily. This 100-character limit applies **only** to this extraction operator

function. In other words, your extraction operator is following the normal extraction rules for any unsigned integer.

Assuming that **stream** is any valid input stream and **c** is a **char**, then the following should work.

```
stream >>ws;          // skips over white space
c = stream.get();     // inputs a character
stream.putback (c);   // replaces a character you don't want
                      // back into the input stream to be
                      // retrieved by the next input operation
```

Create an insertion operator<< to output a **BigInt** so the following is valid. Print only the significant digits of the number or 0 if the number is 0. That is, no leading 0's are printed and no leading or trailing blanks are printed.

```
cout << a;
```

Utility Functions

Create a function called **length()** that returns the integer number of digits in the number. The following is valid.

```
BigInt a (123456789ul);
int num_digits = a.length ();   // here it returns 9 digits
```

Create a **compare()** function so that two **BigInt**s can be compared. This eliminates the need for a bunch of comparison operator functions. The compare function returns a –1 negative integer when the host is less than the passed argument; 0 when they are the same; and a positive 1 integer when the host is larger than the passed value. The following is valid.

```
BigInt a, b;
int  result  =  a.compare (b);
```

Math Operators

The **add (+)** and **subtract (–)** operators are supported. You should be able to add a pair of **BigInt**s, or a **BigInt** and an **unsigned long** (in any order). The result of the addition or subtraction does not alter either of the numbers but returns the result as a **BigInt**. Note that since **BigInt** is an unsigned number, a subtraction should produce the absolute value of the difference of the numbers. (Hint, subtract the smaller from the larger number.) When adding or subtracting a **BigInt** and an **unsigned long**, the operands can be in any order. The following are valid.

```
BigInt a, b, c;
unsigned long num;
a = b + c;
a = b + num;
a = num + b;
a = b - c;
a = num - b;
a = b - num;
```

Implementation Details

How you store the big integer is completely up to you, as well as how you implement the math operations. There are a number of different approaches that can be used. Some ideas will be discussed in class. I strongly urge that you implement it in stages, beginning with the five constructor functions, moving sequentially through the problem as given above, handling the math steps last.

Testing Main Programs

I have provided two versions of the main testing programs—one set for the Borland users and one for the Visual C++ users. Use the correct version. The Visual C++ versions are called **Pgm07-2Vx** where 'x' is a letter, A through F. The Borland versions are called **Pgm07-2Bx**.

The correct output is shown on the next series of pages. There should be no memory leaks or corruption.

Pgm07-2Ba and Pgm07-2Va

This program tests the **BigInt** constructors, destructor, assignment operator, the insertion operator, and the length function. You may run this program without having defined or implemented the extraction or comparison or math functions. This program does not read in any files and outputs to the screen and the debug output window. Specifically, you can develop, test and debug the functions in this order (note just comment out those tests you are not ready for.)
1. String constructor, destructor, insertion operator, and length function
2. unsigned long constructor
3. default constructor
4. copy constructor
5. assignment operator

Pgm07-2Bb and Pgm07-2Vb

These programs test the extraction operator and depend on the functions from version **a** above working properly, that is, the default constructor, destructor, insertion operator and the length function. It does not read in any file and writes to the screen.

Pgm07-2Bc and Pgm07-2Vc
These programs test the compare function and require a properly working default constructor, destructor, insertion operator, extraction operator, and the length function. It uses the test data file **Pgm07-2c.txt** and reads it as a file.

Pgm07-2Bd and Pgm07-2Vd
These programs test the addition operator and depend on all the class functions except the subtraction operator. It reads the file **Pgm07-2d.txt** and produces the output shown below.

Pgm07-2Be and Pgm07-2Ve

These programs also test all the functions except subtraction and it tests the speed of your solution. The program takes one or more command line arguments. Each command line argument is a number. With Visual C++, enter the command line values in the Project Settings–Debug Tab. The program finds the factorial of each number. For example,

```
C>Pgm12Be  5 7
```
will result in the calculation of 5! and then 7!

```
    Test your program with three test runs:
C>Pgm12Be 7  1  10  0  50
C>Pgm12Be 100 250
C>Pgm12Be 500
```

Yes, it is going to calculate 500! which is a huge number indeed. It will end up calling your **BigInt** add operator some 124,750 times and your assignment operator some 125,249 times. With debug options on, under Borland on a 120-MHz Pentium, it should take less than a minute. With Visual C++, it may take less than 2 minutes since more debugging actions are occurring under the hood. It yours takes longer than these times, you should revise your implementation. If in doubt, see your instructor.

For testing purposes, both compilers permit you to enter command line arguments and then run the debugger from the development platform. For Borland BC5, use Options—Environment—Debugger—Arguments edit control: enter the numbers such as 7 1 10 0 50. For Visual C++6, use Project Settings—Debug tab—Category: General—Program Arguments edit control: enter the numbers such as 7 1 10 0 50

Pgm07-2Bf and Pgm07-2Vf

These programs test your subtraction operator and also use all the other **BigInt** functions as well. It reads the data file **Pgm07-2f.txt** and produces the results shown below.

Output from Pgm07-2Va
```
Testing string constructor
--------------------------
1234567890
0
9876543210987654321 0
999999888888777777666666555555444444333333222222111111000000

Testing unsigned long constructor
---------------------------------
0
12345
987654321
1234567890
```

```
4294967295

Testing default constructor
----------------------------
0 0 0

Testing copy constructor
----------------------------
987654321   0   1234567890987654321012345678 90
987654321   0   1234567890987654321012345678 90
987654321   0   1234567890987654321012345678 90

Testing assignment operator
----------------------------
123456789   5   9876543210123456789098765432 10
123456789   5   9876543210123456789098765432 10
123456789   5   9876543210123456789098765432 10
123456789   5   9876543210123456789098765432 10

Ok, no memory leaks
```

Output from Pgm07-2Vb

```
Testing extraction operator
----------------------------
12345 @ 12345
12345 # 6
12345 $ 0
12345 @ 345678909876543210123456789098765 43210
6 @ 12345
6 # 6
6 $ 0
6 @ 345678909876543210123456789098765432 10
0 @ 12345
0 # 6
0 $ 0
0 @ 3456789098765432101234567890987654 3210
3456789098765432101234567890987654 3210 @ 12345
3456789098765432101234567890987654 3210 # 6
3456789098765432101234567890987654 3210 $ 0
3 4 5 6 7 8 9 0 9 8 7 6 5 4 3 2 1 0 1 2 3 4 5 6 7 8 9 0 9 8 7 6 5 4 3 2 1 0      @
3456789098765432101234567890987654 3210

Testing extraction operator recognition of eof
-----------------------------------------------
Ok

Ok, no memory leaks
```

Output from Pgm07-2Vc
```
123456788 < 123456789

123456780 > 99999999

9876543210123456789 == 9876543210123456789

1999999999 < 2000000000

1234567892123456789 > 1234567891123456789

987654321 < 9876543210

123456789012345678901234 == 123456789012345678901234

123456789012345 < 123456789012346

98765123456789012345 > 98765123456789012344

123456789012345 < 223456789012345

323456789012345 > 223456789012345

12345678901234567890 > 12345677901234567890

123455789012345 < 123456789012345

1111111111111111111111111 > 99999999999999999999999

199999999999999 < 200000000000000


Ok, no memory leaks
```

Output from Pgm07-2Vd
```
  4132024431
+ 3854963512
------------
  7986987943


  6034132024431
+    3854963512
---------------
  6037986987943
```

```
    5748296375
 +  3854963517
 ------------
    9603259892


     7748296375
 +   3854963517
 ------------
    11603259892


    19999999999999999999
 +                     1
 ----------------------
    20000000000000000000


    12345678901234567890
 +             3615221105
 ----------------------
    12345678904849788995


                 67523
 + 987654321031242
 -----------------
    987654321098765


                          1
 +   99999999999999999999999
 ---------------------------
    100000000000000000000000000


    108254950016237591310191 62757
 + 11263129401072191977021 5405133
 -----------------------------------
    12345678901234567890123 4567890


    3
 +  4
 ---
    7


    199999999999999999999999
```

```
+ 456789123456789012345678
--------------------------
  656789123456789012345677


  123456789012345678901111 1
+                     1234
--------------------------
  123456789012345678012345


     56789012345678012345678
+    78453989879642099887675 7
  --------------------------
  135243002225321001122243 5


  12345678901236
+ 111111110111109
----------------
  123456789012345


               9
+ 123456789012346
----------------
  123456789012355


  3456789012345678901
+ 8888889888888888989
--------------------
  12345678901234567890


  234567891
+ 999999999
-----------
  1234567890
```

```
Ok, no memory leaks
```

Output from Pgm07-2Ve—Note the line wrap on the longer lines may be different than shown below.

First Run: Pgm072e 7 1 10 0 50

```
7! = 5040
```

```
Elapsed time (HH:MM:SS) = 00:00:00

1! = 1

Elapsed time (HH:MM:SS) = 00:00:00

10! = 3628800

Elapsed time (HH:MM:SS) = 00:00:00

0! = 1

Elapsed time (HH:MM:SS) = 00:00:00

5                 0                !                                    =
30414093201713378043612608166064768844377641568960512000000000000

Elapsed time (HH:MM:SS) = 00:00:00


Ok, no memory leaks
```

Second Run: Pgm072e 100 250
```
1              0              0              !                          =
93326215443944152681699238856266700490715968264381621468592963895
21759999322991560894146397615651828625369792082722375825118521091
6864000000000000000000000
00000

Elapsed time (HH:MM:SS) = 00:00:00

2              5              0              !                          =
32328562609091077323208145520243684709948437176737806667479424271
12823747555111209488817915371028199450928507353189432926730931712
80899082279103027907128192167652724018926473321804118626100683292
53651336789390895699357135301750405131787600772479330654023390061
64825552248819436572586057399222641254832982204849137721776650641
27685880715312897877767295191399084437747870258917297325515028324
17873206581884820624785826598088488255488000000000000000000000000
00000000000000000000000000000000000000000000

Elapsed time (HH:MM:SS) = 00:00:02


Ok, no memory leaks
```

Third Run: Pgm072e 500
```
5              0             0             !                                    =
12201368259911100687012387854230469262535743428031928421924135883
85845373153881997605496447502203281863013616477148203584163378722
07817720048078520515932928547790757193933060377296085908627042917
45478824249127263443056701732707694610628023104526442188787894657
54777149863494367781037644274033827365397471386477878495438489595
53753799042324106127132698432774571554630997720278101456108118837
37095310163563244329870295638966289116589747695720879269288712817
80070265174507768410719624390394322536422605234945850129918571501
24870696156814162535905669342381300885624924689156412677565448188
65065938479517753608940057452389403357984763639449053130623237490
66445048824665075946735862074637925184200459369692981022263971952
59719094521782333175693458150855233282076282002340262690789834245
17120062077146409794561161276291459512372299133401695523638509428
85592018727433795173014586357570828355780158735432768888680120399
88238470215146760544540766353598417443048012893831389688163948746
96588175045069263653381750554781286400000000000000000000000000000
00000000000000000000000000000000000000000000000000000000000000000
000000000000000000000000000000000
```

Elapsed time (HH:MM:SS) = 00:00:13

Ok, no memory leaks

Output from Pgm07-2Ve

```
  12345678901234567890
+           3615221105
----------------------
  12345678904849788995


  987654321098765
-          67523
----------------
  987654321031242


  999999999999999999999999
+                        1
-------------------------
  1000000000000000000000000


  12345678901234567890123456789
- 1082549500162375913101 9162757
```

```
--------------------------------
    11263129401072191977 0215405133


    100000000000000
-                 1
-----------------
     99999999999999


    199999999999999999999999
+                          1
-------------------------
    200000000000000000000000


    7
-   3
---
    4


    199999999999999999999999
+   456789123456789012345678
-------------------------
    656789123456789012345677


    123456789012345678901 2345
-   123456789012345678901 1111
-------------------------
                         1234


    56789012345678901 2345678
+   78453989879642099 8876757
-------------------------
    135243002225321001 1222435


    123456789012345
-    12345678901236
-----------------
    111111110111109


    123456789012355
-   123456789012346
-----------------
```

9

```
   12345678901234567890
-   3456789012345678901
----------------------
     888888988888888989


   1234567890
-   234567891
------------
    999999999


   123456789012345678901234567890
- 123456789012345678901234567890
-------------------------------
                                0
```

Ok, no memory leaks

Chapter 8—Inheritance

Introduction

One of the most powerful features of OOP is inheritance—the ability to derive a new class from an existing class, forming a hierarchy of classes. Inheritance is the process by which a class is derived from a base or parent class so that it can inherit the data and functions of that base class to avoid "re-inventing the wheel" and to add or expand upon the base class functionality. In the real world of OOP programming, once you have created a terrific class, someone else will undoubtedly see it also as valuable and wish to reuse it by extending it a bit further to solve their problems.

The nomenclature that is used with these interdependent classes is as follows.

```
base class      derived class
parent class    child class
super class     sub class
```

In this text, I will use the terms base class and derived class exclusively.

Let's take an example from my WWII game. Assume that we have a complete implementation for a **Vehicle** class that encapsulates the movement of a basic vehicle. Now we can derive a **Car** class from the **Vehicle** class and inherit all of the data members and member functions of the **Vehicle** class. That is, all of those can be reused as is in the **Car** class. Of course, a **Car** class would add in some additional member data such as the size of the gas tank, the number of gallons of gas, the miles per gallon the car gets, and whether or not the engine is started. The **Car** class would also define additional member functions, if only to provide access to these new properties. However, should the base **Vehicle** class functions no longer provide the exact implementation, they can be overridden by a similarly named member function in the **Car** class. This certainly would be the case with the **SetSpeed()** function because one cannot have the car moving along at 50 miles per hour unless the car is started and has gas.

Now once the **Car** class is operational, what is a truck but a car with cargo carrying capacity? So now we can derive a **Truck** from a **Car** class and add in a new data member, the cargo capacity. Further, what is an armored car but a **Car** with a gun? So we can derive the **ArmoredCar** class from the **Car**. Similarly, a **Halftrack** class can be derived from the **Truck** class, adding in a machine gun and ammunition. Likewise, we can derive class **Tank** from the **Halftrack** by adding in a big gun.

Ah, but what is an airplane? Is it also not a vehicle that moves? So we can define class **Plane** from the **Vehicle**. And from class **Plane** we can extend to class **Fighter** and **Bomber**. Likewise, a boat is a **Vehicle** that moves on water. So class **Boat** can be derived from a **Vehicle**. And from **Boat**, we can derive **AircraftCarrier**, **Battleship**, **Cruiser**, **Destroyer**, and **Submarine**. Even class **Infantry** can be derived from the **Vehicle** class!

In short, every item used in an "army" in the war game can ultimately be derived from the lowly **Vehicle** class! You see, we can provide the basic implementation of movement activities and then inherit that functionality in every one of the additional classes. Of course, there will be times that we need to provide a replacement function because the **Vehicle** implementation does not apply, as with the motored vehicles.

Besides the large amount of code reuse, there is another terrifically important ability that this class hierarchy provides us. Suppose that our task is to manage a fleet of company vehicles. The company's fleet certainly would have instances of a **Car** and **Truck** class, but would also likely have instances of classes **Limo** and **Bus**. If a program must maintain a fleet of such vehicles, then the main function would need to define the following fields.

```
Car cars[100];
Truck trucks[100];
Limo limos[100];
Bus buses[100];
int numCars;
int numTrucks;
int numLimos;
int numBuses;
```

What would the prototype for a **FillFleetWithGas()** function look like? It would have to be passed all four arrays and the current number in each array. This becomes very awkward indeed.

However, since each of these new classes is derived from a lowly **Vehicle**, one could define the fleet this way.

```
Vehicle* fleet[1000];
int numFleet;
```

The eight variables have been reduced to a single array of pointers to **Vehicle** objects and the number in that array. One would then allocate individual vehicles as needed.

```
fleet[0] = new Car;
fleet[1] = new Truck;
fleet[2] = new Limo;
fleet[3] = new Bus;
numFleet = 4;
```

Operations can then be performed using the pointer operator. For example,

```
fleet[0]->SetSpeed (42);
```

Rule: A pointer declared as a pointer to a base class can also be used to point to any class derived from that base class.

This is indeed where we are headed with inheritance. By storing an array of pointers to the base class, a tremendous reduction in client programming complexity is removed.

Principles of Inheritance

The syntax to derive a new class from an existing class is as follows.
```
class derived : access base_class {
};
```
where *access* is **public**, **protected**, or **private**.

Protected access allows one to retain the base class access types for all base class data and member functions. Yet, these base class items are still accessible directly within the derived class. In other words, if an item is public in the base class, it remains public in the derived class. If it is protected, it is still protected in the derived class though the derived class only can directly access it. If it is private in the base class, it remains private in the derived class which means the derived class cannot directly access it.

The following table 8.1 illustrates the options and their effects.

Table 8.1 The Derivation Table

derived from base class as:	access qualifier for base class data and functions		
	public:	protected:	private:
public	public	protected	inaccessible
protected	protected	protected	inaccessible
private	private	private	inaccessible

The most common derivation used is public. If one derives **Car** publically from **Vehicle**, then whatever is public in the **Vehicle** class remains public in the **Car** class. Whatever was protected remains protected. And private **Vehicle** items remain inaccessible both in the derived class as well as the client programs.

On the other hand, if you derive **Car** protected or private from **Vehicle**, then all those public items in the **Vehicle** class cannot be used by the client programs anymore! That is, the client programs can no longer call **GetSpeed()** or **SetSpeed()** unless the **Car** class writes replacement functions that are public in access. This is generally way too severe an approach to take. Hence, the vast majority of the time, a class derives itself publically from the base class.

Here is the basic **Vehicle** class from which we can derive other classes.
Vehicle.h
```
class Vehicle {
protected:
  bool isMoving;
```

307

```
int   speed;

public:
      Vehicle ();
      Vehicle (bool move, int sped);
    ~Vehicle ();
 bool IsMoving  () const;
 void SetMoving ();
 int  GetSpeed  () const;
 void SetSpeed  (int);
 void SetSpeed  (bool mov, int sped);
};
```

We can then derive the **Car** class from it as follows.

Car.h

```
#include "Vehicle.h"

class Car : public Vehicle {
protected:
 bool   isStarted;
 double mpg;
 double gallons;

 public:
    Car ();
    Car (bool move, int sped, bool start,
         double mpgs, double gals);
   ~Car ();
 ...
};
```

Here the new **Car** class defines three additional data members in addition to the two in the **Vehicle** class that it inherits. **Car** also inherits the five **Vehicle** access functions for getting and setting the speed and is moving state.

What about the base class constructors and destructors? Notice that both the base and derived classes have constructors and may also have a destructor function as well.

Rule: The constructors are always executed in the order of the derivation.

Here the base class **Vehicle** constructor must be called first and then the derived class **Car** constructor.

Rule: Destructors should always be executed in the reverse order; the derived class destructor is called first then the base class.

308

A special syntax is used to force the proper order of constructor calls. It is the base class and member initialization sequence which we have already been using to initialize constant data members.

```
derived_constructor (arg_list) : base_constructor (arg_list) {
}
```

For the **Car** constructor, whose prototype is

```
Car (bool move, int sped, bool start, double mpgs, double gals);
```

we must code the following.

```
Car::Car (bool move, int sped, bool start, double mpgs,
          double gals)  : Vehicle (move, sped) {
  isStarted = start;
  mpg = mpgs;
  gallons = gals;
}
```

Or code it this way.

```
Car::Car (bool move, int sped, bool start, double mpgs,
          double gals)  : Vehicle (move, sped),
          isStarted(start), mpg(mpgs), gallons(gals) {}
```

This sequence guarantees that the base class constructor is called before the implementation of the derived class constructor.

The **Car** default constructor is called this way.

```
Car::Car ()  : Vehicle (), isStarted(false), mpg(20),
          gallons(10) {}
```

With destructor functions, the compiler automatically called the class destructors in reverse sequence for us. Even though the destructors for the **Vehicle** and **Car** classes have nothing to do, here is how they are coded.

```
Vehicle::~Vehicle () {}
Car::~Car () {}
```

Notice that we make no reference to the base class destructor in the **Car** class. The compiler handles it for us.

Rule: Constructors and destructor functions are never inherited.

Rule: Constructors must be explicitly called by the derived class constructors in the base class and member initialization list.

Rule: Destructors are called in the reverse order of derivation automatically by the compiler.

All other functions are inherited. Friend functions are never inherited. A friend of yours is not necessarily a friend of mine, even though we may be friends.

Next, let's derive class **Truck** from the **Car** class. Here is how it might be done.
Truck.h
```
#include "Car.h"
class Truck : public Car {
protected:
 double cargo;
public:
 Truck ();
 Truck (bool move, int sped, bool start,
        double mpgs, double gals, double cargos);
~Truck ();
 ...
};
```

Here is the implementation of the two constructor functions and the destructor.
```
Truck::Truck () : Car (), cargo(4000) {}
Truck::Truck (bool move, int sped, bool start,
              double mpgs, double gals, double cargos)
     : Car (move, sped, start, mpgs, gals), cargo(cargos) {}
Truck::~Truck () {}
```

Now, let's derive the **Bus** class from the **Car** class.
Bus.h
```
#include "Car.h"
class Bus : public Car {
protected:
 int passengers;
public:
 Bus ();
 Bus (bool move, int sped, bool start,
        double mpgs, double gals, int pass);
~Bus ();
 ...
};
```

Here is the implementation of the two constructor functions and the destructor.
```
Bus::Bus () : Car (), passengers(10) {}
Bus::Bus (bool move, int sped, bool start,
            double mpgs, double gals, int pass)
  : Car (move, sped, start, mpgs, gals), passengers(pass) {}
Bus::~Bus () {}
```

Figure 8.1 illustrates what memory looks like in a client program that has allocated an instance of each of these classes.

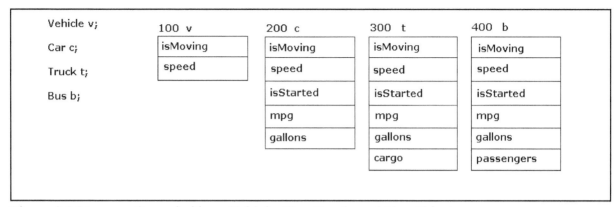

Figure 8.1 Memory Occupied by a Vehicle, Car, Truck, and Bus Object

Notice how memory is laid out. In all cases, the storage for the **Vehicle** base class data items is first. This is then followed by all the data members for the **Car** class. And these are followed by that of the **Truck** and **Bus** classes. This figure clearly shows why we must involve the base class constructors first. The **Truck** instance is built upon the **Car** portion which is built upon the **Vehicle** portion. When the Truck constructor is called, the base class initialization list gets executed before the compiler executes the rest of the Truck ctor coding.

```
Truck::Truck () : Car (), cargo(4000) {}
```
But when it gets to the **Car** ctor, it must first call the **Vehicle** ctor.
```
Car::Car () : Vehicle (), isStarted(false), mpg(20),
              gallons(10) {}
```
Thus, the **Vehicle** ctor actually executes first building the **Vehicle** data members properly. When **Vehicle::Vehicle()** returns, then the remainder of the **Car** initialization is finished. When **Car::Car()** then returns, the remainder of the **Truck** initialization is done.

It's like building a house. The basement (**Vehicle**) must be built first before the first floor (**Car**) can be added which must be done before the second floor (**Truck**) can be built. You cannot build the second floor hanging in space and then try to build the first floor beneath it and then try adding a basement below that.

Working With Inherited Member Functions

In this example, the **Car** class inherits five access functions from the **Vehicle** class:
IsMoving(), **SetMoving()**, **GetSpeed()**, **SetSpeed(int)**, and **SetSpeed (bool, int)**. Thus, as it stands at this point, any **Car** member function and or the client program can call these five functions on a **Car** object.

```
Car c;
c.SetSpeed (42);
cout << c.GetSpeed();
```

However, with the addition of a motor and a gas tank, the **Car** class may wish to modify the behavior involved with setting the car's speed. That is, the speed can be set only if the motor is running and there is gas in the tank.

> **Rule: If one or more functions of the base class are re-declared in the derived class, all functions with that name in the base class become hidden and not directly accessible in the derived class. (Virtual functions, see below, are an exception.)**

This is saying that if we declare this version of **SetSpeed(int)** in the **Car** class, that the other version of **SetSpeed(bool, int)** is hidden.

```
class Car : public Vehicle {
...
 void SetSpeed (int);
}
```

In the client program,

```
Car c;
c.SetSpeed (42); // works
c.SetSpeed (true, 42); // fails - it is hidden
```

Or

```
void Car::SetSpeed (int sped) {
 if (gallons) {
  isStared = true;
  SetSpeed (true, sped); // fails - it is hidden
 }
}
```

There are two ways around this hidden rule.
1. Re-declare the hidden versions of that function in the derived class
2. Explicitly call the hidden function using the base class qualifier.
Using way 2, we could implement the **SetSpeed()** function this way.

```
void Car::SetSpeed (int sped) {
 if (gallons) {
  isStared = true;
  Vehicle::SetSpeed (true, sped);
 }
}
```

312

This concept of hiding base class functions is useful when the base class function has no meaning for a derived class object. One then just hides these meaningless base class functions. The new implementation could output an error message, for example. Usually, when a derived class reimplements a base class function, it also reimplements the other variations of that function. So realistically, in the **Car** class, we would be reimplementing both versions of **SetSpeed()**.

Copy Constructors

How are copy constructors handled? Since a copy ctor is another version of the constructor, the same rules apply. If we added copy constructors to each of these four classes, their implementation parallels the other ctor functions.

```
Vehicle::Vehicle (const Vehicle& v)
          : speed(v.speed), isMoving(v.isMoving) {}

Car::Car (const Car& c) : Vehicle (c),
          isStarted(c.isStarted), mpg(c.mpg),
          gallons(c.gallons) {}

Truck::Truck (const Truck& t) : Car(t), cargo(t.cargo) {}

Bus::Bus (const Bus& b) : Car(b), passengers(b.passengers){}
```

The Assignment Operator Implementation

The assignment operator must make a duplicate copy of an object. Thus, it too must follow the same sequence of handling the base class first.

>**Rule: The operator=() must first invoke the base class assignment before it can copy the derived class items.**

You must explicitly call that base class **operator=()** function. This yields a rather strange-looking syntax. Suppose that we implemented **operator=()** for the **Vehicle** class.

```
Vehicle& Vehicle::operator= (const Vehicle& v) {
  if (this == &v)
   return *this;
  // nothing to delete
  isMoving = v.isMoving;
  speed = v.speed;
  return *this;
}
```

Now consider the **Car operator=()** function. It begins like this.

```
Car& Car::operator= (const Car& c) {
  if (this == &c)
```

```
      return *this;
    // nothing to delete
```
Now how do we call the base class function?
```
      Vehicle::operator= (c);
```
Or alternatively one can code this.
```
      *((Vehicle*) (this)) = c;
```
Personally, I prefer the first approach, directly invoking the base class function. The remainder of the assignment function is as follows.
```
      isStarted = c.isStarted;
      mpg = c.mpg;
      gallons = c.gallons;
      return *this;
    }
```

The **Truck operator=()** function is coded this way.
```
Truck& Truck::operator= (const Truck& t) {
  if (this == &t)
    return *this;
  // nothing to delete
  Car::operator= (t);
  cargo = t.cargo;
  return *this;
}
```

The **Bus operator=()** function is coded this way.
```
Bus& Bus::operator= (const Bus& b) {
  if (this == &b)
    return *this;
  // nothing to delete
  Car::operator= (b);
  passengers = b.passengers;
  return *this;
}
```

Problems When Client Programs Use Base Class Pointers

Let's return to the client program that must perform operations on a company's fleet of vehicles. We had originally written the following.
```
      Vehicle* fleet[1000];
      int numFleet;
      fleet[0] = new Car;
      fleet[1] = new Truck;
      fleet[2] = new Bus;
      numFleet = 3;
      for (int i=0; i<numFleet; i++)
        cout << fleet[i]->GetSpeed() << endl; // works fine
```

314

```
fleet[i]->SetSpeed (42); // oops calls Vehicle::SetSpeed
delete fleet[i];         // oops calls Vehicle::~Vehicle
}
```

The function calls to **GetSpeed()** work fine because neither of the three derived classes redeclared the **GetSpeed()** function. The **fleet[i]** pointer is a base class pointer and it only knows about base class, **Vehicle**, functions. Thus, the calls to **SetSpeed()** end up going to the base class function and not to the **Car::SetSpeed()** which is to replace it. Since the Truck and Bus classes have not redeclared **SetSpeed()**, they inherit and expect to use **Car**'s **SetSpeed()** function. When it is time to destroy the objects, the delete only deletes the **Vehicle** portion of the objects because it is a **Vehicle*** and only knows about the base class. Clearly we are in big trouble with our implementation at this point.

What is needed is a mechanism in which a base class pointer or reference knows what kind of object it is pointing to so that the correct derived class functions can be called. This is the virtual function mechanism.

Virtual Functions

We saw earlier that a pointer declared as a pointer to a base class can also be used to point to any class derived from that base class.

> **Rule: The base class pointer or reference variable, when used to point to the derived class, can only access those members inherited from the base class; it knows nothing of new items added in the derived class.**

A **virtual** function is a class member function that is declared **virtual** in a base class and then later redefined by the derived class without changing parameters or return type.

> **Rule: A base class pointer or reference variable can be used to access functions that are declared to be virtual in the base class. Calls go to the derived class, overridden virtual function.**

Let's examine a very simple situation. Here is a base and derived class.
```
class base {
public:
int fun ();
};

class derived : public base {
public:
int fun (); // redeclared version of fun()
};
```
In the client program, we can code the following.

315

```
base     b;
derived d;
base     *ptrbase = &b;
derived *ptrderived = &d;

ptrbase->fun();      // invokes base class fun
ptrderived->fun ();  // invokes derived class fun
ptrbase = &d;
ptrbase->fun();      // invokes base class fun => error!
```

We have an error on the last call to function **Fun()**; it should go to the derived class version but does not because of the first rule above. Yet by making the base class function **Fun() virtual**, the problem is rectified.

```
class base {
public:
virtual int fun ();
};


class derived : public base {
public:
int fun ();
};
```

Now in the client, we have the same coding as before.

```
base     b;
derived d;

base     *ptrbase = &d;
ptrbase->fun();              // invokes derived class fun()
```

This is known as **run-time polymorphism**. In other words, at run time, the compiler determines which **virtual** function to call based on what the object really is!

Rule: Virtual functions must have the same prototypes in the base and derived classes! If not, they represent overloaded functions.

Rule: Virtual functions are hierarchical in order of inheritance.

Rule: If a derived class does not override a base class virtual function, then the base class implementation is used in its place.

Let's examine these three rules. Consider the following hierarchy of derived classes from **Pgm08a**. I defined a base class with five functions, **Fun1()** through **Fun5()**. Notice that I forgot the **virtual** keyword on **Fun5()**. Then, I created a **Derived1** class from **Base** and a **Derived2** class from **Derived1**.

```
Base and Derived Class Definitions
```

```
 1 #include <iostream>
 2 using namespace std;
 3 class Base {
 4 public:
 5 virtual void Fun1 () {cout << "Base::Fun1\n";}
 6 virtual void Fun2 (int) {cout << "Base::Fun2\n";}
 7 virtual void Fun3 (int, int) {cout << "Base::Fun3\n";}
 8 virtual void Fun4 (double) {cout << "Base::Fun4\n";}
 9         void Fun5 (short) {cout << "Base::Fun5\n";}
10 };
11
12 class Derived1 : public Base {
13 public:
14 virtual void Fun1 () {cout << "Derived1::Fun1\n";}
15 virtual void Fun2 (double) {cout << "Derived1::Fun2\n";}
16 virtual void Fun4 (double) {cout << "Derived1::Fun4\n";}
17 virtual void Fun5 (short) {cout << "Derived1::Fun5\n";}
18 };
19
20 class Derived2 : public Derived1 {
21 public:
22  void Fun1 () {cout << "Derived2::Fun1\n";}
23  void Fun2 (int) {cout << "Derived2::Fun2\n";}
24  void Fun3 (int, int) {cout << "Derived2::Fun3\n";}
25  void Fun5 (short) {cout << "Derived2::Fun5\n";}
26 };
```

Now consider a client program that uses a base class pointer to invoke all five functions. Certainly when the base pointer is set to the address of the **Base** object, all five of the **Base** class functions are invoked. However, see if you can predict which versions are called when the base pointer is set to the address of the **Derived1** object and then to that of **Derived2.** Finally, I created a **Derived1** pointer and invoked the five functions and then used that pointer to point to the **Derived2** object and called them again.

```
Pgm08a - Illustrates Virtual Functions

 1 #include <iostream>
 2 #include <iomanip>
 3 #include "Base.h"
 4 using namespace std;
 5 int main () {
 6  short s = 10;
 7  Base      b;
 8  Derived1  d1;
 9  Derived2  d2;
10  Base*     ptrbase;
11  Derived1* ptrd1;
12
13  cout << "ptrbase-> where it is the address of Base b\n";
14  ptrbase = &b;
```

```
15  ptrbase->Fun1 ();
16  ptrbase->Fun2 (42);
17  ptrbase->Fun3 (42, 42);
18  ptrbase->Fun4 (42.);
19  ptrbase->Fun5 (s);
20  cout << endl;
21
22  cout << "ptrbase-> where it is the address of Derived1 d1\n";
23  ptrbase = &d1;
24  ptrbase->Fun1 ();
25  ptrbase->Fun2 (42);
26  ptrbase->Fun3 (42, 42);
27  ptrbase->Fun4 (42.);
28  ptrbase->Fun5 (s);
29  cout << endl;
30
31  cout << "ptrbase-> where it is the address of Derived2 d2\n";
32  ptrbase = &d2;
33  ptrbase->Fun1 ();
34  ptrbase->Fun2 (42);
35  ptrbase->Fun3 (42, 42);
36  ptrbase->Fun4 (42.);
37  ptrbase->Fun5 (s);
38  cout << endl;
39
40  cout << "ptrd1-> where it is the address of Derived1 d1\n";
41  ptrd1 = &d1;
42  ptrd1->Fun1 ();
43  ptrd1->Fun2 (42);
44  ptrd1->Fun3 (42, 42);
45  ptrd1->Fun4 (42.);
46  ptrd1->Fun5 (s);
47  cout << endl;
48
49  cout << "ptrd1-> where it is the address of Derived2 d2\n";
50  ptrd1 = &d2;
51  ptrd1->Fun1 ();
52  ptrd1->Fun2 (42);
53  ptrd1->Fun3 (42, 42);
54  ptrd1->Fun4 (42.);
55  ptrd1->Fun5 (s);
56  cout << endl;
57
58  return 0;
59 }
```

Here is the output showing which exact functions are invoked in each case.

```
Output of Pgm08a - Illustrates Virtual Functions

 1 ptrbase-> where it is the address of Base b
```

```
 2 Base::Fun1
 3 Base::Fun2
 4 Base::Fun3
 5 Base::Fun4
 6 Base::Fun5
 7
 8 ptrbase-> where it is the address of Derived1 d1
 9 Derived1::Fun1
10 Base::Fun2
11 Base::Fun3
12 Derived1::Fun4
13 Base::Fun5
```

Derived1 does reimplement **Fun2()** but uses a different parameter type, so this **Fun2()** is not the virtual one. Thus, it uses **Base::Fun2()**. **Derived1** does not implement **Fun3()** so **Base::Fun3()** is invoked. Having forgotten the **virtual** on **Base::Fun5()**, it is not virtual so it does not call the **Derived1::Fun5()** version.

```
14
15 ptrbase-> where it is the address of Derived2 d2
16 Derived2::Fun1
17 Derived2::Fun2
18 Derived2::Fun3
19 Derived1::Fun4
20 Base::Fun5
```

Derived2's **Fun1()** reimplements **Fun1()** and is called. It also implements **Fun2()** with the same prototype as the **Base** class and so **Derived2::Fun2()** called. Even though **Derived1** did not reimplement **Fun3()**, since **Derived2** did so, **Derived2::Fun3()** is then called. Since **Derived2** did not reimplement **Fun4()**, **Derived1::Fun4()** is then called. Again, having forgotten the **virtual** on **Base::Fun5()**, it is not virtual so it does not call the **Derived2::Fun5()** version.

```
21
22 ptrd1-> where it is the address of Derived1 d1
23 Derived1::Fun1
24 Derived1::Fun2
25 Base::Fun3
26 Derived1::Fun4
27 Derived1::Fun5
```

Using a **Derived1** pointer causes all of the **Derived1** versions to be called directly. However, since there is no provided **Derived1::Fun3()** function, the inherited **Base::Fun3()** is used as usual.

```
28
29 ptrd1-> where it is the address of Derived2 d2
30 Derived2::Fun1
31 Derived1::Fun2
32 Derived2::Fun3
33 Derived1::Fun4
34 Derived2::Fun5
```

319

Finally, using the **Derived1** pointer with a **Derived2** object calls the **Derived2::Fun1()** as expected. Since **Derived1**'s **Fun2()** function has a different prototype from **Base** and **Derived2** class versions, it is **Derived1::Fun2()** that is invoked. Now even though there is no reimplemented **Fun3()** in the **Derived1** class, there is one in **Base**, so thus **Derived2::Fun3()** is called. **Derived2** does not reimplement **Fun4()** and so **Derived1::Fun4()** is called.

If you understand these situations, you will have no trouble with virtual functions.

I/O Operations with Derived Classes Demand Virtual Functions

When one has a hierarchy of classes, handling I/O operations for all situations requires careful design and must utilize virtual functions. Let's see how this comes about. Let's add the ability to input and output **Vehicle**, **Car**, **Truck**, and **Bus** objects. This means that we must add friend **operator>>()** and **operator<<()** functions to all four classes. Skeletally, we have the following.

```cpp
class Vehicle {
  ...
  friend istream& operator>> (istream& is, Vehicle& v);
  friend ostream& operator<< (ostream& os, const Vehicle& v);
};

class Car : public Vehicle {
  ...
  friend istream& operator>> (istream& is, Car& v);
  friend ostream& operator<< (ostream& os, const Car& v);
};

class Truck : public Car {
  ...
  friend istream& operator>> (istream& is, Truck& v);
  friend ostream& operator<< (ostream& os, const Truck& v);
};

class Bus : public Car {
  ...
  friend istream& operator>> (istream& is, Bus& v);
  friend ostream& operator<< (ostream& os, const Bus& v);
};
```

But before you charge ahead and implement these eight functions, consider how the client programs can perform the I/O operations. Certainly these operators are all called in the following client program situations.

```cpp
Vehicle v;
Car c;
Truck t;
Bus b;
Vehicle* ptrv = &v;
Car* ptrc = &c;
Truck* ptrt = &t;
Bus* ptrb = &b;
cin >> v >> c >> t >> b >> *ptrv >> *ptrc >> *ptrt >> *ptrb;
```

However, suppose that the client program was written this way.

```cpp
Vehicle* fleet[100];
```

```
fleet[0] = new Vehicle;
fleet[1] = new Car;
fleet[2] = new Truck;
fleet[3] = new Bus;
for (j=0; j<4; j++) {
  cin >> *fleet[j];
  cout << *fleet[j];
}
```

Now we are in big trouble. In all cases, since ***fleet[j]** is a **Vehicle**, only the **Vehicle** insertion and extraction functions are called! Our design must be able to handle the fleet situation, using a base class pointer or reference to input or output the derived class object.

How do we get this insertion and extraction operator situation to work properly? Actually, this is an extremely important detail, vital to inheritance programming. The key is to notice what the two operator functions are given as the second parameter. In all eight cases, the functions are presented with a **reference** to an object. Virtual functions take effect when pointers or references are used. True, if we are using the **Vehicle** base class reference with which to input or output a derived class object, the **Vehicle** insertion or extraction operator function is what is directly called by the compiler. However, when we implement these functions, because a reference to that object is given to the function, our implementation must then use that reference to invoke a **virtual** function of the **Vehicle** class so that the virtual function mechanism then invokes the proper derived class function.

Often these virtual functions are called **Input()** and **Output()**. When these are added to the classes, we have the following revisions.

```
class Vehicle {
  ...
 virtual istream& Input (istream& is);
 virutal ostream& Output (ostream& os) const;
 friend istream& operator>> (istream& is, Vehicle& v);
 friend ostream& operator<< (ostream& os, const Vehicle& v);
};

class Car : public Vehicle {
  ...
 virtual istream& Input (istream& is);
 virutal ostream& Output (ostream& os) const;
 friend istream& operator>> (istream& is, Car& c);
 friend ostream& operator<< (ostream& os, const Car& c);
};

class Truck : public Car {
  ...
 virtual istream& Input (istream& is);
 virutal ostream& Output (ostream& os) const;
 friend istream& operator>> (istream& is, Truck& t);
 friend ostream& operator<< (ostream& os, const Truck& t);
};
```

322

```
class Bus : public Car {
 ...
 virtual istream& Input (istream& is);
 virutal ostream& Output (ostream& os) const;
 friend istream& operator>> (istream& is, Bus& b);
 friend ostream& operator<< (ostream& os, const Bus& b);
};
```

Notice how the insertion and extraction operator functions for the **Vehicle** class are implemented. They must only invoke the **Input()** or **Output()** member functions using the reference that is passed.

```
        istream& operator>> (istream& is, Vehicle& v) {
         return v.Input (is);
        }

        ostream& operator<< (ostream& os, const Vehicle& v) {
         return v.Output (os);
        }

        istream& Vehicle::Input (istream& is) {
         is >> speed;
         if (is)
          isMoving = speed ? true : false;
         else {
          speed = 0;
          isMoving = false;
         }
         return is;
        }

        ostream& Vehicle::Output (ostream& os) const {
         if (isMoving)
          os << "Vehicle is moving at " << speed << " mph\n";
         else
          os << "Vehicle is not moving\n";
         return os;
        }
```

Notice that if the reference is really to a **Vehicle** object, the insertion operator correctly calls **Vehicle::Output()** and the extraction operator correctly calls **Vehicle::Input()**. However, it the reference is to a derived class, the **Vehicle** insertion and extraction operator ends up calling the redeclared derived class **Input()** and **Output()** functions instead, assuming that these functions are present.

Now, let's examine the **Car** implementation of these.

```
istream& operator>> (istream& is, Car& c) {
 return c.Input (is);
}
```

323

```
ostream& operator<< (ostream& os, const Car& c) {
 return c.Output (os);
}
```

The insertion and extraction friend functions again call the virtual pair of functions. If this is a **Car** object, then the **Car** versions are called. However, if this reference is that of a **Truck** or **Bus** object, then those classes' virtual functions are invoked, if present.

To implement the **Car**'s pair, notice that I first call the **Vehicle** base class versions of these functions to input or output the basic **Vehicle** data. Then, I input or output the additional **Car** properties. This reuses the coding already present in the base class. Sometimes, however, one might not desire the input or output format delivered by the base class. In this case, do not call the base class versions; instead, input all of the data members here.

```
istream& Car::Input (istream& is) {
 Vehicle::Input (is);
 is >> mpg >> gallons;
 isStarted = (speed > 0 && gallons > 0) ? true : false;
 return is;
}

ostream& Car::Output (ostream& os) const {
 Vehicle::Output (os);
 if (!isStarted)
  os << "Car with " << gallons
     << " gallons of gas and that gets " << mpg
     << " miles per gallon is not started\n";
 else
  os << "Car with " << gallons
     << " gallons of gas and that gets " << mpg
     << " miles per gallon is started\n";
 return os;
}
```

In this case, one might not like the resulting output because the first line talks of a **Vehicle** moving or not moving and this is a **Car**. So one does not have to call that base class function. It could be done this way without reusing the **Vehicle::Output()** function.

```
ostream& Car::Output (ostream& os) const {
 if (!isStarted)
  os << "Car with " << gallons
     << " gallons of gas and that gets " << mpg
     << " miles per gallon is not started\n";
 else
  os << "Car with " << gallons
     << " gallons of gas and that gets " << mpg
     << " miles per gallon is started and is moving at "
     << speed << " miles per hour\n";
 return os;
}
```

The **Truck** is derived from a **Car**. Notice how its functions are implemented.

```
istream& operator>> (istream& is, Truck& t) {
 return t.Input (is);
}

ostream& operator<< (ostream& os, const Truck& t) {
 return t.Output (os);
}

istream& Truck::Input (istream& is) {
 Car::Input (is);
 if (is)
  is >> cargo;
 return is;
}

ostream& Truck::Output (ostream& os) const {
 Car::Output (os);
 os << "The Truck can carry " << cargo << " pounds\n";
 return os;
}
```

Notice that the operator functions invoke the **Input()** and **Output()** virtual functions. If the object **t** is a **Truck**, then the **Truck**'s functions are actually invoked. However, if this **t** object is a **Halftrack**, then the **Halftrack**'s versions are called instead.

The implementation of the **Input()** and **Output()** functions call the immediate base class versions, **Car**. If this is a **Truck** object, then **Car::Input()** is called first which in turn calls **Vehicle::Input()** to input the **speed** data. When the Vehicle function is done, it returns to **Car::Input()** which then inputs the **mpg** and **gallons** and sets the **isStarted bool**. **Car::Input()** then returns to **Truck::Input()** which finally inputs the **cargo** property.

Similarly **Truck::Output()** calls **Car::Output()** which immediately calls **Vehicle::Output()** which outputs the speed and moving properties. It returns to **Car::Output()** which then displays the **Car** portions and returns to **Truck** which then displays the cargo information.

Given this situation, can you figure out how to implement the **Bus** versions of these functions? They are the topic of a Review Question below.

Destructors

If a class is going to be used as a base class, then, since a client program could be using pointers to the base class to store dynamically allocated derived class objects (as in the fleet array of **Vehicles**), when the destructor is called using the base class pointer, the compiler must know to call the derived class destructor before calling the base class destructor. Hence, we have the following rule.

Rule: The destructor function should always be a virtual function if this class is used as a base class.

Failure to do so causes the compiler to bypass the derived class destructor function. This can cause problems if the derived class destructor actually has some tasks to perform, such as deleting dynamic memory allocations.

How the Virtual Function Mechanism Is Implemented

Just how can the compiler generate code that, given an unknown pointer or reference at run time, determines which virtual function is to be called? It is done by using what is called a **Virtual Function Table**, or **v-table** for short. The compiler cannot know at compile time what kind of object a given pointer or reference will be at run time. So it creates a table of all possibilities, the v-table.

The v-table contains an array of function addresses to call. With a **Car** instance, there is a **Vehicle** base class v-table that contains an array of if this virtual function is called, then actually use this **Car** function instead. Pictorially, the **Vehicle** base class v-table for a **Car** object looks like this.

```
If calling this function    Use this function
Input()                     Car::Input()
Output()                    Car::Output()
```

The v-table for a **Truck** instance is more complex because not only can virtual functions be called using a **Vehicle** pointer but also a **Car** pointer. Thus, there are two sections of the v-table, depending upon which base class pointer is being used. The v-table for the **Truck** appears this way.

```
Vehicle*  If calling this function    Use this function
          Input()                     Truck::Input()
          Output()                    Truck::Output()

Car*      If calling this function    Use this function
          Input()                     Truck::Input()
          Output()                    Truck::Output()
```

Thus, depending upon which base class pointer is used, at runtime, the compiler can loop up in the v-table which function should be actually be called.

Caution. As the size of the v-table grows, the amount of time at execution that is required to look up and find the correct function to call increases. Thus, if you have 200 member functions in a base class, do not make them all virtual. If you do, then the v-table look up process significantly slows down the program execution. Further, notice that the v-table is carried along with each instance of the class. So if one allocates 1,000 Truck objects, then each of those objects has a v-table as part of the instance data! With 200 virtual functions, the memory requirements for each object increases sharply.

Early Binding and Late Binding

When the compiler knows what function to call at compile-time, it creates a direct call to that function. Such is the case for normal functions, overloaded functions and operators and friend functions—that is, anything without the virtual tag. This is the most efficient method and is called **early binding**.

Late binding occurs when the compiler does not necessarily know what is to be actually called at compile time. This is the case with virtual functions. When a virtual function is accessed via a base pointer, the compiler can only figure out which function to call at run time. The advantage of late binding is greater flexibility; the price paid is greater overhead in making the call. The compiler maintains a virtual table look up mechanism to facilitate dynamic translation.

Animals: An Example with Dynamic Memory Allocation and Virtual Functions, Pgm08b

When dynamic memory allocations are part of the inheritance picture, virtual destructor functions are needed to ensure that the derived class destructor gets called when deleting the object using a base class pointer. To illustrate the effect of virtual functions as well as inheritance, let's examine another series of classes. This time, we pick on animals. Our pets are often dogs and cats. While one could easily write **Dog** and **Cat** classes as totally separate classes, they both share some animal properties. Hence, frequently both pet classes are derived from a base **Animal** class.

What kinds of properties could an **Animal** class contain? Rather, what properties do all animals share in common? If these classes were for a veterinarian, the list might be rather extensive. Sex, age, weight, color, height, its name, the sound it makes, and even the type of animal could be some such properties. But to keep these classes from mushrooming in size, let's just have the **Animal** class store a string that identifies the type of animal, such as "Dog" or "Cat." The derived **Dog** and **Cat** classes will store the sound that they make, such as "Ruff! Ruff!" Both of the strings will be dynamically allocated to use mo more memory than is needed to hold each specific string. Memory is, then, going to be allocated in both the base and the derived classes.

Here is the start of the **Animal** class definition. Notice that there are now a copy ctor, a destructor, and an assignment operator—all required because of the dynamic allocation of the **name** member.

```
class Animal {
protected:
 char* name;  // the name of the animal, such as Dog or Cat

public:
          Animal ();                  // default ctor - "Unknown"
          Animal (const char* n);   // make specific animal
          Animal (const Animal& a); // copy ctor duplicate animal

 Animal& operator= (const Animal& a); // assignment op

 virtual ~Animal ();                  // delete name
```

Here is the start of the derived **Dog** class. It allocates the string to store the sound that the dog makes. Notice that it also has a copy ctor, a destructor, and an assignment operator.

```
class Dog : public Animal {
protected:
 char* sound; // the sound it makes, such as "Ruff! Ruff!"

public:
          Dog ();                // default dog
          Dog (const char* s);   // dog with a specific sound
          Dog (const Dog& d);    // copy ctor
```

```
Dog& operator= (const Dog& d);  // assignment op

virtual ~Dog ();                //  dtor to remove sound
```

Here is the start of the **Cat** class. It closely parallels the **Dog**.

```
class Cat : public Animal {
protected:
 char* sound;  // the sound that a cat makes

public:
        Cat ();            // default cat "Meow! Meow!"
        Cat (const char* s);  // cat with specific sound
        Cat (const Cat& c);  // copy ctor duplicate Cat
 Cat& operator= (const Cat& c);  // assignment op

 virtual ~Cat ();               //  removes sound string
```

Before we get too involved with virtual functions and the I/O situation, let's see how just this much can be implemented. For the **Animal** class, it is fairly straightforward. The default ctor is problematical because **name** should point to a string and not be initialized to a null pointer or 0. Otherwise, every time a member function wanted to access the string, it would first have to check if **name** was not 0. So I choose to install the string "Unknown" because no one should be allocating an instance of the base class. Look over the coding. All of the **Animal** implementation should be familiar or as you would expect to see it at this point.

```
Animal::Animal () {
 name = new (std::nothrow) char[8];
 strcpy_s (name, 8 "Unknown");
}

Animal::Animal (const char* n) {
 if (!n) {                              // guard against 0 being passed
  name = new (std::nothrow) char[8]; // make default Unknown
  strcpy_s (name, 8, "Unknown");
 }
 else {                                 // make name be passed name
  name = new (std::nothrow) char[strlen(n) + 1];
  // should check for error
  strcpy_s (name, strlen(n) + 1, n);
 }
}

Animal::Animal (const Animal& a) {
 name = new (std::nothrow) char[strlen(a.name) + 1];
  // should check for error
 strcpy_s (name, strlen(a.name) + 1, a.name);
}

Animal& Animal::operator= (const Animal& a) {
```

329

```
if (this == &a)      // guard against a = a;
 return *this;
delete [] name;                      // remove current name
name = new (std::nothrow) char[strlen(a.name) + 1];
// should check for error
strcpy_s (name, strlen(a.name) + 1, a.name);
 return *this;
}


Animal::~Animal () {
 delete [] name;
}
```

Now we must implement the two derived classes. The **Dog** default ctor passes the string "Dog" on to the default **Animal** ctor. Once the base class is constructed, the default dog **sound** string is created.

```
Dog::Dog () : Animal ("Dog") {
 sound = new (std::nothrow) char [12];
 // should check for error
 strcpy_s (sound, 12, "Ruff! Ruff!");
}


Dog::Dog (const char* s) : Animal ("Dog") {
 if (!s) {                          // guard against 0 sound
  sound = new (std::nothrow) char [12];
  // should check for error
  strcpy_s (sound, 12, "Ruff! Ruff!");
 }
 else {                             // store the new sound
  sound = new (std::nothrow) char [strlen(s) + 1];
  // should check for error
  strcpy_s (sound, strlen(s) + 1, s);
 }
}
```

Notice how the **Dog** object **d** is passed to the **Animal** copy ctor. Since it is expecting a reference to an **Animal** and since a **Dog** is an **Animal**, the compiler passes the address of the base class.

```
Dog::Dog (const Dog& d) : Animal (d) {
 sound = new (std::nothrow) char [strlen(d.sound) + 1];
 // should check for error
 strcpy_s (sound, strlen(d.sound) + 1, d.sound);
}
```

With the assignment operator, things get a bit trickier. The **Animal** base class must first be given a chance to make its copy. Since the **Animal** assignment operator is expecting a reference to an **Animal**, the address of the base class is passed. Once the base class performs its copy, then the **Dog** class can remove the old sound string, allocate and copy the new one.

```
Dog& Dog::operator= (const Dog& d) {
 if (this == &d)                // guard against a = a;
```

330

```
 return *this;
 Animal::operator= (d);        // copy Animal portion of dog
 delete [] sound;              // remove old sound
 sound = new (std::nothrow) char [strlen(d.sound) + 1];
 // should check for error
 strcpy_s (sound, strlen(d.sound) + 1, d.sound);  // new sound
 return *this;
}


Dog::~Dog () {
 delete [] sound;
}
```

Notice that the destructor for **Dog** only deletes **Dog** items. The compiler first calls the **Dog** destructor and when it returns, the compiler then calls the **Animal** destructor. The Cat implementation is nearly identical except the default for the sound a cat makes is "Meow! Meow!"

Next, let's examine how a dog or cat could be input. Remember that a client can do either of these.

```
 Dog d;
 cin >> d;
```

or

```
 Animal* ptrpet = new (std::nothrow) Dog;
 cin >> *ptrpet;
```

In the first situation, the compiler calls the **Dog**'s friend **operator>>()** function. In the second case, the compiler calls **Animal**'s friend **operator>>()** function. Hence, to make both work for client programs, a virtual **Input()** function is needed.

In the **Animal** class, add these two prototypes.
```
 virtual istream& Input (istream& is);
 friend istream& operator>> (istream& is, Animal& a);
```
In the **Dog** class, add these two prototypes. The **Cat** class is similar.
```
 virtual istream& Input (istream& is);
 friend istream& operator>> (istream& is, Dog& d);
```

The implementation of the extraction operators are parallel. All call the virtual **Input()** function using the reference variable. Here is the **Animal** extraction implementation.
```
istream& operator>> (istream& is, Animal& a) {
 return a.Input (is); // invoke virtual Input
}
```
And here is the **Dog** version. The **Cat** version parallels the **Dog** implementation.
```
istream& operator>> (istream& is, Dog& d) {
 return d.Input (is); // call the virtual Input()
}
```

Now how do we actually implement the **Input()** functions? Here is where novice OOP programmers sometimes fail. The input of a **Dog**, **Cat** or **Animal** object must always input the name string. The actual input of the name string should be done one time in the **Animal::Input()** function.

It should **not** be done three times, once in each of the **Input()** functions. Code it once and reuse it. At this point, we must know of what the input is to consist. In this overly simplified case, I assume that the first item input is the name string and that it contains no blanks so it can easily be extracted. Further, I assume that no animal name can exceed 99 characters. There must be a real array of characters in which to store the data being extracted, a temporary string. Of course, we could also run into the end of file situation as well. If it is EOF, I store the usual "Unknown" as the name string. Finally, do not forget to delete the current **name** string before allocating space for the new **name**! To get to this function, the compiler has had to already call a constructor which has already allocated a **name** string.

```
istream& Animal::Input (istream& is) {
 char n[100];                    // arbitrary maximum length of name
 is >> n;                        // input the new name
 delete [] name;                 // remove current name
 if (!is) {                      // if failed to input, make unknown
  name = new (std::nothrow) char[8];
  // should check for error
  strcpy_s (name, 8, "Unknown");
 }
 else {                          // allocate and copy the new name
  name = new (std::nothrow) char[strlen(n) + 1];
  // should check for error
  strcpy_s (name, strlen(n) + 1, n);
 }
 return is;
}
```

With the **name** input successfully, the derived class can input the **sound** that the critter makes. The **sound** string is assumed to be enclosed in double quote marks. Here is the **Dog::Input()** function. Notice that first it calls back to the **Animal::Input()** to input the common name string. If the stream is still in the good state, the **sound** is extracted. Again, do not forget to delete the old **sound** string before allocating a new string. The **Cat** is done similarly.

```
istream& Dog::Input (istream& is) {
 if (!Animal::Input (is))  // attempt to input the name portion
  return is;               // if fails, abort
 char s[100];              // arbitrary max length of dog's sound
 char c;
 is >> c;                  // input the "
 if (!is)
  return is;
 is.getline (s, sizeof(s), '\"');  // input the sound it makes
 delete [] sound;                  // remove old sound
 sound = new (std::nothrow) char [strlen(s) + 1]; // copy new one
 // should check for error
 strcpy_s (sound, strlen(s) + 1, s);
 return is;
}
```

Finally, we can turn our attention to the output of a critter. Suppose that the output should be like this.

```
The Dog says Ruff! Ruff!
The Cat says Meow! Meow!
```

Just as with the input operations, the client has two ways to output instances.

```
Dog d;
cout << d;
```

or

```
Animal* ptrpet = new (std::nothrow) Dog;
cout << *ptrpet;
```

This once again dictates that a friend **operator<<()** function must be found in both the base and derived classes. It also implies that all must call a virtual **Output()** function using the passed reference variable instance so that the correct version of **Output()** is called.

However, thinking ahead, when additional members are added, such as height and weight, other types of output may be required than the "speak" line. So I added a third function, one that handles the speech aspect. Here are the **Animal** class prototypes.

```
virtual ostream& Speak (ostream& os) const;
virtual ostream& Output (ostream& os) const;
friend ostream& operator<< (ostream& os, const Animal& a);
```

The corresponding ones for the **Dog** class are these. The **Cat** is similar.

```
virtual ostream& Speak (ostream& os) const;
virtual ostream& Output (ostream& os) const;
friend ostream& operator<< (ostream& os, const Dog& d);
```

The **Animal** insertion operator just calls the virtual **Output()** function as does the **Dog** and **Cat**.

```
ostream& operator<< (ostream& os, const Animal& a) {
  return a.Output (os); // invoke virtual Output
}
ostream& operator<< (ostream& os, const Dog& d) {
  return d.Output (os); // call the virtual Output
}
```

The **Animal Output()** function displays a generic identification that can be used with several types of output. The generic message, "The Dog," can be followed by its weight and height or by its age and sex or, in this case by "says Ruff! Ruff!"

```
ostream& Animal::Output (ostream& os) const {
  return os << "The " << name;
}
```

The **Dog Output()** function controls the action by choosing to use the **Speak()** version. It calls **Animal Output()** to begin the message and then calls **Speak()** to display the dog's sound.

```
ostream& Dog::Output (ostream& os) const {
  Animal::Output (os); // display The dog says portion
  return Speak (os);   // display the sound
}
ostream& Dog::Speak (ostream& os) const {
  return os << " says " << sound << endl;
```

333

}

The **Cat** is done similarly.

Finally, we need a client program to thoroughly test all of this coding. **Pgm08b** does this. It creates numerous instances of the **Dog** and **Cat** classes, outputs them and then reads a small file of objects. Here is the output from **Pgm08b**.

```
Output of Pgm08b Animals Tester Program

 1 The Dog says Ruff! Ruff!
 2 The Dog says Bark! Bark!
 3 The Dog says Bark! Bark!
 4 The Dog says Bark! Bark!
 5
 6 The Cat says Meow! Meow!
 7 The Cat says Prrrrrrrr
 8 The Cat says Prrrrrrrr
 9 The Cat says Prrrrrrrr
10
11 The Dog says Ruff!! Ruff!!
12 The Cat says Pfssssttttt!
13 No memory leaks
```

Lines 11 and 12 are coming from the input file which consists of the following two lines.
d Dog "Ruff!! Ruff!!"
c Cat "Pfssssttttt!"

The importance of the input file is great. It is designed to show you a very common technique that is used when the client program wishes to use only pointers to the base class to do the processing, such as the fleet of vehicles. In this case, we could have an array of animals. Here is the client program, **Pgm08b**.

```
Pgm08b Animals Tester Program

 1 #include <iostream>
 2 #include <iomanip>
 3 #include <fstream>
 4 #include <string>
 5 #include <cctype>
 6 #include <crtdbg.h>
 7 using namespace std;
 8 #include "Dog.h"
 9 #include "Cat.h"
10
11 /************************************************************/
12 /*                                                        */
13 /* Tester for the Animals Series of Classes               */
14 /*                                                        */
15 /************************************************************/
16
```

```
17 int main () {
18  {
19  Dog d1;
20  Dog d2 ("Bark! Bark!");
21  Dog d3 (d2);
22  Dog d4;
23  d4 = d2;
24  cout << d1 << d2 << d3 << d4 << endl;
25
26  Cat c1;
27  Cat c2 ("Prrrrrrr");
28  Cat c3 (c2);
29  Cat c4;
30  c4 = c2;
31  cout << c1 << c2 << c3 << c4 << endl;
32
33  ifstream infile ("animals.txt");
34  if (!infile) {
35   cerr << "Error: cannot open file animals.txt\n";
36   return 1;
37  }
38  char type;
39  Animal* ptranimal;
40  while (infile >> type) {
41   type = toupper (type);
42   if (type == 'D')
43    ptranimal = new Dog;
44   else
45    ptranimal = new Cat;
46   infile >> *ptranimal;
47   cout << *ptranimal;
48   delete ptranimal;
49  }
50  infile.close ();
51  }
52
53  // check for memory leaks
54  if (_CrtDumpMemoryLeaks())
55   cerr << "Memory leaks occurred!\n";
56  else
57   cerr << "No memory leaks.\n";
58
59  return 0;
60
```

Pay particular attention to lines 38 through 49. The input loop is controlled by an attempt to input the animal type character. If a letter was input, then the body of the loop executes. Notice how the **ptranimal** gets one of two addresses assigned to it on line 43 or 45. It stores either a new dog or a new cat object. Then, notice line 46 and 47 to see how that base class pointer is turned into a reference to an **Animal** and passed to the **Animal** extraction or insertion operators. This is a very common method to handle this type of situation.

For your reference, here are the complete definitions and implementation of the three classes. Since we have to repeatedly allocate strings, check for errors and copy in the new string, I made a protected helper function in the Animal class, **AllocString()**. To make it general purpose and usable for all the different string members, I passed a reference to the string so that when I assign the new string address to it, that address is stored in the caller's pointer. As you examine the coding, notice how helpful this function actually is.

```
Animal Class Definition

 1 #pragma once
 2 #include <iostream>
 3 using namespace std;
 4
 5 /*****************************************************************/
 6 /*                                                               */
 7 /* Animal: stores name of the animal and provides I/O ops        */
 8 /*                                                               */
 9 /*****************************************************************/
10
11 class Animal {
12 protected:
13  char* name;  // the name of the animal, such as Dog or Cat
14
15 public:
16         Animal ();                   // default ctor - "Unknown"
17         Animal (const char* n);   // make specific animal
18         Animal (const Animal& a); // copy ctor duplicate animal
19
20  Animal& operator= (const Animal& a); // assignment op
21
22  virtual ~Animal ();                  // delete name
23
24  // displays "The 'name' says "
25  virtual ostream& Speak (ostream& os) const;
26
27  virtual istream& Input (istream& is);
28  virtual ostream& Output (ostream& os) const;
29
30  friend istream& operator>> (istream& is, Animal& a);
31  friend ostream& operator<< (ostream& os, const Animal& a);
32
33 protected:
34  void AllocString (char*& dest, const char* src,
35                    const char* errmsg);
36 };
```

```
Animal Class Implementation
```

```
 1 #include <iostream>
 2 #include <iomanip>
 3 #include <string>
 4 using namespace std;
 5 #include "Animal.h"
 6
 7 /*****************************************************************/
 8 /*                                                               */
 9 /* AllocString: dyn allocate new string and copy in src          */
10 /*                                                               */
11 /*****************************************************************/
12 void Animal::AllocString (char*& dest, const char* src,
13                           const char* errmsg) {
14  dest = new (std::nothrow) char[strlen (src) + 1];
15  if (!dest) {
16   cerr << "Error - out of memory in " << errmsg << endl;
17   exit (1);
18  }
19  strcpy_s (dest, strlen (src) + 1, src);
20 }
21
22 /*****************************************************************/
23 /*                                                               */
24 /* Animal: create a default "Unknown" animal                     */
25 /*                                                               */
26 /*****************************************************************/
27
28 Animal::Animal () {
29  AllocString (name, "Unknown", "Animal Constructor");
30 }
31
32 /*****************************************************************/
33 /*                                                               */
34 /* Animal: create an animal with this name                       */
35 /*                                                               */
36 /*****************************************************************/
37
38 Animal::Animal (const char* n) {
39  if (!n)                        // guard against 0 being passed
40   AllocString (name, "Unknown", "Animal Constructor");
41  else                          // make name be passed name
42   AllocString (name, n, "Animal Constructor");
43 }
44
45 /*****************************************************************/
46 /*                                                               */
47 /* Animal: duplicate an animal object                            */
48 /*                                                               */
49 /*****************************************************************/
50
51 Animal::Animal (const Animal& a) {
52  AllocString (name, a.name, "Animal Copy Constructor");
```

```
 53  }
 54
 55  /*****************************************************************/
 56  /*                                                               */
 57  /*  Operator= copy passed animal into this one                   */
 58  /*                                                               */
 59  /*****************************************************************/
 60
 61  Animal& Animal::operator= (const Animal& a) {
 62   if (this == &a)    // guard against a = a;
 63    return *this;
 64   delete [] name;                        // remove current name
 65   AllocString (name, a.name, "Animal Operator =");
 66   return *this;
 67  }
 68
 69  /*****************************************************************/
 70  /*                                                               */
 71  /*  ~Animal: remove the name array                               */
 72  /*                                                               */
 73  /*****************************************************************/
 74
 75  Animal::~Animal () {
 76   delete [] name;
 77  }
 78
 79  /*****************************************************************/
 80  /*                                                               */
 81  /*  Speak: placeholder for derived classes - shouldn't be called*/
 82  /*                                                               */
 83  /*****************************************************************/
 84
 85  ostream& Animal::Speak (ostream& os) const {
 86   return os << "nothing\n"; // oops - so display a goof message
 87  }
 88
 89  /*****************************************************************/
 90  /*                                                               */
 91  /*  Input: input the animal's name from the input stream         */
 92  /*                                                               */
 93  /*****************************************************************/
 94
 95  istream& Animal::Input (istream& is) {
 96   char n[100];                 // arbitrary maximum length of name
 97   is >> n;                     // input the new name
 98   delete [] name;              // remove current name
 99   if (!is)                     // if failed to input, make unknown
100    AllocString (name, "Unknown", "Animal Input");
101   else                        // allocate and copy the new name
102    AllocString (name, n, "Animal Input");
103   return is;
104  }
105
```

```
106 /**************************************************************/
107 /*                                                            */
108 /* Output: display "The 'name' says " string                  */
109 /*                                                            */
110 /**************************************************************/
111
112 ostream& Animal::Output (ostream& os) const {
113   return os << "The " << name;
114 }
115
116 /**************************************************************/
117 /*                                                            */
118 /* extraction: input an animal                                */
119 /*                                                            */
120 /**************************************************************/
121
122 istream& operator>> (istream& is, Animal& a) {
123   return a.Input (is); // invoke virtual Input
124 }
125
126 /**************************************************************/
127 /*                                                            */
128 /* insertion: display an animal                               */
129 /*                                                            */
130 /**************************************************************/
131
132 ostream& operator<< (ostream& os, const Animal& a) {
133   return a.Output (os); // invoke virtual Output
134 }
```

```
Cat Class Definition

 1 #pragma once
 2 #include "Animal.h"
 3
 4 /**************************************************************/
 5 /*                                                            */
 6 /* class Cat                                                  */
 7 /*                                                            */
 8 /**************************************************************/
 9
10 class Cat : public Animal {
11 protected:
12   char* sound;  // the sound that a cat makes
13
14 public:
15         Cat ();                 // default cat "Meow! Meow!"
16         Cat (const char* s);  // cat with specific sound
17         Cat (const Cat& c);   // copy ctor duplicate Cat
18   Cat& operator= (const Cat& c); // assignment op
19
20   virtual ~Cat ();                 // removes sound string
```

339

```
21
22  // displays the entire output line
23  virtual ostream& Speak (ostream& os) const;
24
25  virtual istream& Input (istream& is);
26  virtual ostream& Output (ostream& os) const;
27
28  friend istream& operator>> (istream& is, Cat& c);
29  friend ostream& operator<< (ostream& os, const Cat& c);
30  };
```

Cat Class Implementation

```
 1 #include <iostream>
 2 #include <iomanip>
 3 #include <string>
 4 using namespace std;
 5 #include "Cat.h"
 6
 7 /*****************************************************************/
 8 /*                                                             */
 9 /* Cat: make a default cat with sound Meow! Meow!              */
10 /*                                                             */
11 /*****************************************************************/
12
13 Cat::Cat () : Animal ("Cat") {
14  AllocString (sound, "Meow! Meow!", "Cat Constructor");
15 }
16
17 /*****************************************************************/
18 /*                                                             */
19 /* Cat: make a cat with this sound                             */
20 /*                                                             */
21 /*****************************************************************/
22
23 Cat::Cat (const char* s) : Animal ("Cat") {
24  if (!s)        // guard against 0 sound
25   AllocString (sound, "Meow! Meow!", "Cat Constructor");
26  else           // otherwise use this new sound
27   AllocString (sound, s, "Cat Constructor");
28 }
29
30 /*****************************************************************/
31 /*                                                             */
32 /* Cat: duplicate the passed cat                               */
33 /*                                                             */
34 /*****************************************************************/
35
36 Cat::Cat (const Cat& c) : Animal (c) {
37  AllocString (sound, c.sound, "Cat Copy Constructor");
38 }
39
```

340

```
40 /**************************************************************/
41 /*                                                          */
42 /* Operator= copy cat c into this cat                       */
43 /*                                                          */
44 /**************************************************************/
45
46 Cat& Cat::operator= (const Cat& c) {
47  if (this == &c) // guard against a = a;
48   return *this;
49  Animal::operator= (c);            // copy Animal base portion
50  delete [] sound;                  // remove old sound
51  AllocString (sound, c.sound, "Cat Operator =");
52  return *this;
53 }
54
55 /**************************************************************/
56 /*                                                          */
57 /* ~Cat: delete the sound array                             */
58 /*                                                          */
59 /**************************************************************/
60
61 Cat::~Cat () {
62  delete [] sound;
63 }
64
65 /**************************************************************/
66 /*                                                          */
67 /* Speak: output the Cat's sound                            */
68 /*                                                          */
69 /**************************************************************/
70
71 ostream& Cat::Speak (ostream& os) const {
72  return os << " says " << sound << endl;
73 }
74
75 /**************************************************************/
76 /*                                                          */
77 /* Input: input a Cat object                                */
78 /*                                                          */
79 /**************************************************************/
80
81 istream& Cat::Input (istream& is) {
82  if (!Animal::Input (is)) // try to input the name portion
83   return is;                 // here it failed, so abort
84  char s[100];                // arbitrary sound string max length
85  char c;
86  is >> c;                    // input the leading "
87  if (!is)
88   return is;
89  is.getline (s, sizeof(s), '\"');  // get the sound
90  delete [] sound;                  // remove old sound
91  AllocString (sound, s, "Cat Input");
92  return is;
```

```
 93 }
 94
 95 /*****************************************************************/
 96 /*                                                             */
 97 /* Output: display a Cat                                       */
 98 /*                                                             */
 99 /*****************************************************************/
100
101 ostream& Cat::Output (ostream& os) const {
102  Animal::Output (os); // display "The Cat says" part
103  return Speak (os);   // display its sound
104 }
105
106 /*****************************************************************/
107 /*                                                             */
108 /* extraction: input a Cat                                     */
109 /*                                                             */
110 /*****************************************************************/
111
112 istream& operator>> (istream& is, Cat& c) {
113  return c.Input (is); // invoke virtual Input
114 }
115
116 /*****************************************************************/
117 /*                                                             */
118 /* insertion: display a Cat                                    */
119 /*                                                             */
120 /*****************************************************************/
121
122 ostream& operator<< (ostream& os, const Cat& c) {
123  return c.Output (os); // invoke virtual Output
124 }
```

Dog Class Definition

```
 1 #pragma once
 2 #include "Animal.h"
 3
 4 /*****************************************************************/
 5 /*                                                             */
 6 /* Class Dog:                                                  */
 7 /*                                                             */
 8 /*****************************************************************/
 9
10 class Dog : public Animal {
11 protected:
12  char* sound; // the sound it makes, such as "Ruff! Ruff!"
13
14 public:
15          Dog ();                  // default dog
16          Dog (const char* s); // dog with a specific sound
17          Dog (const Dog& d);   // copy ctor
```

```
18  Dog& operator= (const Dog& d); // assignment op
19
20  virtual ~Dog ();                 // dtor to remove sound
21
22  // Speak displays the entire output line
23  virtual ostream& Speak (ostream& os) const;
24
25  virtual istream& Input (istream& is);
26  virtual ostream& Output (ostream& os) const;
27
28  friend istream& operator>> (istream& is, Dog& d);
29  friend ostream& operator<< (ostream& os, const Dog& d);
30 };
```

Dog Class Implementation

```
 1 #include <iostream>
 2 #include <iomanip>
 3 #include <string>
 4 using namespace std;
 5 #include "Dog.h"
 6
 7 /***************************************************************/
 8 /*                                                           */
 9 /* Dog: make a default dog with the sound Ruff! Ruff!        */
10 /*                                                           */
11 /***************************************************************/
12
13 Dog::Dog () : Animal ("Dog") {
14  AllocString (sound, "Ruff! Ruff!", "Dog Constructor");
15 }
16
17 /***************************************************************/
18 /*                                                           */
19 /* Dog: make a dog with this specific sound                  */
20 /*                                                           */
21 /***************************************************************/
22
23 Dog::Dog (const char* s) : Animal ("Dog") {
24  if (!s)       // guard against 0 sound
25  AllocString (sound, "Ruff! Ruff!", "Dog Constructor");
26  else          // store the new sound
27  AllocString (sound, s, "Dog Constructor");
28 }
29
30 /***************************************************************/
31 /*                                                           */
32 /* Dog: duplicate this dog                                   */
33 /*                                                           */
34 /***************************************************************/
35
36 Dog::Dog (const Dog& d) : Animal (d) {
```

```
37  AllocString (sound, d.sound, "Dog Copy Constructor");
38  }
39
40  /*************************************************************/
41  /*                                                         */
42  /* Operator= copy the passed dog into this dog             */
43  /*                                                         */
44  /*************************************************************/
45
46  Dog& Dog::operator= (const Dog& d) {
47   if (this == &d)                // guard against a = a;
48     return *this;
49   Animal::operator= (d);        // copy Animal portion of dog
50   delete [] sound;              // remove old sound
51   AllocString (sound, d.sound, "Dog Operator =");
52   return *this;
53  }
54
55  /*************************************************************/
56  /*                                                         */
57  /* ~Dog: remove sound array                                */
58  /*                                                         */
59  /*************************************************************/
60
61  Dog::~Dog () {
62   delete [] sound;
63  }
64
65  /*************************************************************/
66  /*                                                         */
67  /* Speak: display the sound the dog makes                  */
68  /*                                                         */
69  /*************************************************************/
70
71  ostream& Dog::Speak (ostream& os) const {
72   return os << " says " << sound << endl;
73  }
74
75  /*************************************************************/
76  /*                                                         */
77  /* Input: input a dog                                      */
78  /*                                                         */
79  /*************************************************************/
80
81  istream& Dog::Input (istream& is) {
82   if (!Animal::Input (is))   // attempt to input the name portion
83     return is;               // if fails, abort
84   char s[100];               // arbitrary max length of dog's sound
85   char c;
86   is >> c;                   // input the "
87   if (!is)
88     return is;
89   is.getline (s, sizeof(s), '\"');  // input the sound it makes
```

344

```
 90  delete [] sound;                        // remove old sound
 91  AllocString (sound, s, "Dog Input");
 92  return is;
 93 }
 94
 95 /***********************************************************/
 96 /*                                                        */
 97 /* Output: display the dog says 'sound'                   */
 98 /*                                                        */
 99 /***********************************************************/
100
101 ostream& Dog::Output (ostream& os) const {
102  Animal::Output (os); // display The dog says portion
103  return Speak (os);   // display the sound
104 }
105
106 /***********************************************************/
107 /*                                                        */
108 /* extraction: input a dog object                         */
109 /*                                                        */
110 /***********************************************************/
111
112 istream& operator>> (istream& is, Dog& d) {
113  return d.Input (is); // call the virtual Input()
114 }
115
116 /***********************************************************/
117 /*                                                        */
118 /* insertion: output a dog object                         */
119 /*                                                        */
120 /***********************************************************/
121
122 ostream& operator<< (ostream& os, const Dog& d) {
123  return d.Output (os); // call the virtual Output
124 }
```

Review Questions

1. Suppose that you were a botanist and needed a program to help classify a number of vegetables. How could inheritance assist you?

2. Assume that you have created a base Plant class and then derived Tree, Grass, and Flower classes from Plant. Why would a client program consider operations using an array of Plant pointers? How does this impact the design of the Plant class? How would it impact the Tree class if one then derived Oak, Maple, and Ash from the Tree class?

3. What is the impact on member functions if a pointer to a base class is used to point to any instance of a derived class?

345

4. What is the impact on the Tree class if it is derived privately from the Plant class? Be specific in the analysis.

5. Why must the constructor functions be executed in the order of derivation? What would happen if they were not so executed? What mechanism guarantees that they are so executed? Can a programmer violate this rule? If so, how?

6. Why must the destructor functions be executed in the reverse order, from derived to base? What mechanism guarantees that this occurs? Can a programmer violate this rule? If so, how?

7. What does the rule "Constructors and destructor functions are never inherited" mean? How is this different from ordinary member functions?

8. If a base class defines three versions of function **Fun()** that take an integer, **long**, and a **double** respectively and if a derived class defines a new version of **Fun()** that takes an integer, can a client program that has an instance of the derived class call the **double** version of **Fun()**? If not, why not?

9. When making copies of a derived class, why must the copy ctor and the assignment operator explicitly invoke the base class ctor? At what point in the coding sequence must it do so?

10. Assume that a base class defines a function **Fun()** and the derived class also redefines **Fun()**. If a client program uses a pointer to the base class of a derived object to invoke **Fun()**, which version of **Fun()** is invoked? If the derived class version of **Fun()** was made **virtual**, would that impact which was called? If the base class version of **Fun()** was made **virtual**, would that impact which was called?

11. What does the rule that "virtual functions must have the same prototypes in the base and derived classes" mean? What does it mean that if not, they represent overloaded functions?

12. What does it mean that virtual functions are hierarchical in order of inheritance mean?

13. What happens if a derived class does not override a virtual base class function?

14. When implementing the insertion and extraction operators in base and derived classes, what is the impact of a client program using a pointer to the base class of a derived class to invoke the insertion and extraction operator have on the design? What would happen in this case if there were no virtual functions involved? Show an example of this.

15. Explain how the virtual **Input()** and **Output()** functions work with the insertion and extraction operators of a base and derived class.

16. What is meant by the terms "early binding" and "late binding?" Is there any execution time difference between these two methods?

Stop! Do These Exercises Before Programming

1. Revise the **Animal**, **Dog**, and **Cat** classes as follows. In the **Animal** class, add two new members, **height** and **weight**, both doubles. Modify the input operations to accept these new items after the name field. Then, add a new **bool** member called **showSound** to the **Animal** class and add a **SetSound()** function that sets the **showSound** to the passed **bool**. Modify the derived **Dog** and **Cat** classes to output either of the following depending upon the **showSound bool**.

```
The Dog says "Ruff! Ruff!"
```
or
```
The Dog weighs 40.5 pounds and is 44.5 inches tall
```

2. Write a base class called **Plant** that stores the dynamically allocated name of the plant string and its **double** height in inches. Provide a default ctor that sets the height to zero and the name to "Unknown." Provide another ctor that is passed these two values. Provide a copy ctor and an assignment operator along with a destructor.

3. For class **Plant**, provide an **Input()** function that input the plant's name which is surrounded by double quote marks and the plant's height. Write an **Output()** function that displays "The name is height inches tall" where name and height are the data values being stored. Provide appropriate insertion and extraction operator functions that call these two functions.

4. Write class **Tree** that is derived from **Plant**. Add a new **double** data member called **girth**. Provide a default ctor that sets the **girth** to zero. Provide another ctor that is passed the necessary three values. Provide a copy ctor and an assignment operator along with a destructor.

5. For class **Tree**, provide an **Input()** function that input the tree's name which is surrounded by double quote marks, the tree's height and girth. Write an **Output()** function that displays "The name is height inches tall and girth inches around" where name, height, and girth are the data values being stored. Provide appropriate insertion and extraction operator functions that call these two functions.

6. Make the **Tree** class insertion and extraction operations work when a client program uses a **Plant** pointer with the insertion and extraction operators.

Programming Problems

Problem Pgm08-1—Distance Class IV

Part A.

Revise the Distance class from Pgm06-2—Distance III as follows.

Look over the **Distance** class members and functions. Decide which should be private, protected and public and make the requisite changes. We are going to be deriving from this class.

The Derived Ruler Class

Now derive a **Ruler** class from the **Distance** class. The only **Ruler** data member is just the **Type** (**English** or **Metric**); the base class holds the actual distance. There are two constructors

```
Ruler ();
Ruler (Distance::Type, double length);
```
The default is to use **Metric** of length 1 meter.

Create two friend functions operator << and >>. The input dialog in the Ruler extraction operation is as follows.

```
Enter Ruler Type E or M: x
Enter Ruler Length:      y
```
where x is either E, e, M, or m. If it is neither, re-prompt until the user gets it right. The output dialog from the Ruler insertion operation appears this way.

```
The Ruler is nnn.nn units long.
```
where nnn.nn has a width of 12 and 2 decimals. The "units" is either inches or millimeters.

The Tester Program

Write a main tester program that creates a yardstick and a meter stick and any other test cases you deem needed to thoroughly test the **Ruler** class. Ignore the inherent problems of all of the **Distance** math operators working on a Ruler instance. Only consider input and output of **Ruler** objects.

Part B.

In this part, we are going to make the **Distance::Paint()** function virtual and move the **Ruler** display actions into a **Ruler::Paint()** function.

Modifications to the Interface for the Distance Class

1. Revise the Distance class to make its **Paint** function virtual.
Modifications to the Interface for the Ruler Class

348

Add a **Paint** function to the **Ruler** class, overriding the inherited virtual **Paint**. **Ruler::Paint()** should take the same parameters as **Distance::Paint()**.

Ruler's **Paint**, based on **ShowAs**, will now say: "The Ruler is nnn.nn units long" where "units" is either millimeters or inches.

In the testing main program construct several instances of **Distance** and **Ruler** objects with known lengths you can debug.

Now define in the main program a pointer to a **Distance** object.

```
Distance *ptrbase;
```

Assign it an instance of one of the **Distance** objects and then call its **Paint** function.

```
Distance a;
...
ptrbase = &a;
ptrbase->Paint (Distance::Mm);
```

Assign it an instance of one of the **Ruler** objects and test its **Paint** function.

```
Ruler r (Distance::Metric, 1000.);
...
ptrbase = &r;
ptrbase->Paint (Distance::Mm);
```

Repeat for other **Distance** and **Ruler** objects to verify the virtual function works as expected. Be sure to check for some constant objects.

Problem Pgm08-2—Planets

Create a base class called **Planet** which has the following data members.

```
double mass;
double radius;
double distance;
char*  name;
```

Provide a default ctor, a ctor that is passed these four parameters, a copy ctor, a destructor, and an assignment operator. Default all parameters to zero except the name which defaults to the string "Unknown."

Create three derived classes called **Asteroid**, **Jovian**, **Terrestrial**. The Asteroid class adds a new member called **minerals** which is a dynamically allocated string such as "Iron and Platinum". The **Jovian** class adds a new member called **gasType** which is a dynamically allocated character string, such as "Ammonia and Methane". The **Terrestrial** class adds two new **double** members called **percentOcean** and **temperature**.

For the derived classes, create the appropriate constructors and destructor functions as well as the assignment operator.

Finally, add support for insertion and extraction operators. The client program can perform any of these operations for example.

```
Planet* ptrPlanet;
Jovian jupiter ();
Asteroid eros ();
Terrestrial earth ();
cin >> jupiter >> earth >> eros;
cout << jupiter << earth << eros;
ptrPlanet = &jupiter;
cin >> *ptrPlanet;
ptrPlanet = earth;
cout >> *ptrPlanet;
```

Create a tester program to fully test these classes.

Problem Pgm08-3—Bank Accounts

Part A.

Create a base class called **BankAccount**. The class has two data members, the **long** account number and the **double** balance. The default ctor sets these two to zero. An overloaded ctor accepts these two arguments and assigns the data members accordingly. However, if the ctor is passed an account number that is less than or equal to zero, display an error message to **cerr** and assign 0 to the account number. If the passed balance is below zero, also display an error message to **cerr** and assign zero to the balance.

Next, provide access functions to get the account number and get the balance. There are no Set... type of functions for these.

Next, write an **Input()** function to input a bank account. The account number is input first followed by the balance. Then write an **Output()** function to display the account number and balance. The account number is displayed with a width of 9 while the balance is displayed with a width of 9 and a precision of 2.

Write a **Deposit()** function that is passed the new amount to be deposited. If the amount to be deposited is less than zero, display an error message on **cerr** and return the integer called **INVALID_AMOUNT**. Otherwise, update the balance and return the integer **SUCCESSFUL**.

Write a **Withdraw()** function that is passed the amount to withdraw. If the amount to be withdrawn is less than 0, return **INVALID_AMOUNT**. If there are insufficient funds in the account, return the integer **INSUFFICIENT_FUNDS**. Otherwise, withdraw the funds and return **SUCCESSFUL**.

Finally, write a **GetMessage()** function that is passed the return code from **Deposit()** and **Withdraw()** and it returns a **const char*** pointer to the correct message for that passed integer:
SUCCESS return ""
INVALID_AMOUNT return "Invalid amount"
INSUFFICIENT_FUNDS return "Insufficient funds"
Otherwise, return "Unknown outcome code"

Part B.

Derive a **BankAccountWithInterest** class from **BankAccount**. It contains a new **double** member the year to date interest earned. The class also has a **static double** called **AnnualInterestRate** and a **static** member function **SetRate()** to set that rate to a value between 0 and .20. Also provide a **static** member function **GetRate()** to retrieve that rate.

The default ctor sets the year to date interest to 0. The second ctor which is passed the account number and initial amount also sets the year to date interest to 0.

The **Input()** function should input the year to date interest after the account number and balance fields. The **Output()** function should display the year to date interest with a width of 8 and precision of 3 and display it after the account number and balance.

Additionally, create an **EarnInterest()** function that is passed the number of **days** and a reference to the amount of **interest** earned this time. If the number of days is less than or equal to zero, return **INVALID_DAYS**. Otherwise calculate the earned interest as follows.

```
double dailyRate = AnnualRate / 365;
interest = days * dailyRate * GetBalance();
balance += interest;
year to date interest += interest;
return SUCCESS;
```

You need to modify the **GetMessage()** function to also return the new message:
INVALID_DAYS return "Invalid days"

Part C.

Write a **BankAccountWithCompoundInterest** class derived from **BankAccountWithInterest**. This type of account earns compounded interest. It has no new data members. It has one new member function, **EarnInterest()**. When this function is called, it is passed the number of **days** that have elapsed and a reference to **interest** earned this time. If the number of days is less than or equal to zero, return **INVALID_DAYS**. Otherwise calculate the earned compounded interest as follows.

```
double dailyRate = AnnualInterestRate / 365;
interest =  pow ( 1. + dailyRate, days ) - 1 ) * GetBalance();
balance += interest;
year to date interest += interest;
return SUCCESS;
```

Part D.

Write a tester program to ensure these classes are working correctly. When they are working, then do the final part.

Part E.

Write a tester program to determine the effects of a compound interest versus simple interest on two bank accounts. Create a bank account with interest and one with compound interest for two customers. Their account numbers and initial balances are shown below.
123456789 5000.00
333333333 5000.00

Apply the **transactions.txt** file to each of these two accounts. The first character of each transaction line contains a letter type code, W for withdrawal, D for deposit, and I for calculate interest. The next field on each line is the account number and that is followed by the amount to be deposited or withdrawn or it represents the number of days for this interest calculation.

The output should display the running effects of the transactions on the account and a final line outputting the total year to date interest earned on that account. One can then compare the resulting corresponding interest amounts earned to decide which type account is best for them.

Chapter 9—Abstract Base Classes

Abstract Base Class—Shapes—a Complete Example

Sometimes, a base class wants to provide the framework for derived class functionality, yet has no idea of how to implement that functionality. Such a base class cannot stand alone—that is, because it has no idea of how to implement a function, it really cannot itself be instantiated. Only classes derived from it which can provide an implementation for that function can be instantiated. Such functions in the base class are called **pure virtual functions** and the class that define pure virtual functions is known as an **abstract base class**, abstract, because no instances of that base class can ever be allocated.

To create a pure virtual function, add = 0; to the end of its declaration:
```
virtual double GetArea () = 0;
```

The main purpose of a pure virtual function is to force the derived class to implement it and not overlook it by accident. If so, a compiler error results. Let's examine in detail just such a situation.

The Abstract Base Class Shape and Its Derived Classes Development Steps

Geometric shapes are commonly encapsulated in a series of hierarchical classes which make extensive use of virtual functions. The base class called **Shape** provides the basic model from which to derive common geometrical shapes. This discussion will be evolutionary in that I present a basic framework at first and then see what changes are needed for additional operations and so on. This way, you can better see the need and the usage of virtual functions and see why abstract base classes can be very useful.

Also, I implement all member functions inline as we go along. This is done for two reasons. It conserves pages and it makes the total implementation picture easier to follow because far less physical space is needed to see what is going on. The final version contained on disk and shown at the end of the chapter contains no inlined functions.

An abstract shape will contain two dimensions called **x** and **y**. Constructors are needed to initialize the two members. Thus, initially the **Shape** class begins as follows.
```
class Shape {
protected:
  double x;
  double y;
```

```
public:
 Shape (double xx, double yy) : x(xx), y(yy) {}
 Shape () : x(0), y(0) {}
 Shape (const Shape& s) : x(s.x), y(s.y) {}
};
```

Next, a **Rectangle** class can be easily derived from **Shape** as follows. No new data members are required. However, we do need to document which base class data members correspond to the height and width which define the rectangle.

```
class Rectangle : public Shape {
// x = height, y = width
public:
 Rectangle (double height, double width) : Shape(height, width){}
 Rectangle () : Shape () {}
 Rectangle (const Rectangle& r) : Shape (r.x, r.y) {}
};
```

Now, a **Triangle** class can be derived from **Shape**. This time, a third variable is added because the three sides are to be stored.

```
class Triangle : public Shape {
// x = side1, y = side2
protected:
 double side3;
public:
 Triangle (double s1, double s2, double s3)
   : Shape (s1, s2), side3(s3) {}
 Triangle () : Shape (), side3(0) {}
 Triangle (const Triangle& t)
   : Shape (t.x, t.y), side3(t.side3) {}
};
```

A **Square** can be similarly derived. It could come from a **Shape** or even from a **Rectangle**. Let's derive it from **Rectangle**. Since a square has only one dimension, either we can store it in say **x** and ignore **y** or we can save it in both **x** and **y** and reuse more of the **Rectangle** operational functions later on. I intentionally chose to do the latter.

```
class Square : public Rectangle {
// x = side, y = side
public:
 Square (double side) : Rectangle (side, side) {}
 Square () : Rectangle () {}
 Square (const Square& s) : Rectangle (s.x, s.y) {}
};
```

Now we can create a **Circle** also derived from **Shape** and use the **x** member to store the radius.

```
class Circle : public Shape {
// x = radius
```

```
public:
 Circle (double radius) : Shape (radius, 0) {}
 Circle () : Shape () {}
 Circle (const Circle& c) : Shape (c.x, c.y) {}
};
```

Finally, a **Sphere** can be derived from a **Circle**. No new data members are required.

```
class Sphere : public Circle {
// x = radius
public:
 Sphere (double radius) : Circle (radius) {}
 Sphere () : Circle () {}
 Sphere (const Sphere& s) : Circle (s.x) {}
};
```

So far so good. Now let's define some operations that a client might wish to perform on these. Two actions come to mind at once, obtaining the area of the shape and the perimeter of the shape. Certainly, we can add these two functions to all of the classes except **Shape** because they have meaning for these classes. However, these two functions have no real method of implementation for the rather abstract **Shape** class. Consider what can happen if we do not put these functions in the base **Shape** class.

If a client program manages an array of geometric shapes, it is highly likely that an array of base class pointers will be used instead of numerous arrays of each specific type. Thus, calls to these two operational functions would fail unless they are defined as virtual in the **Shape** base class. Okay. So we can define **GetArea()** and **GetPerimeter()** in the **Shape** class as virtual functions. But then how do we implement them? Well, we could just display an error message such as "You should not be doing this", but that is rather tacky. We could have them return the area and perimeter assuming that the abstract **Shape** was a rectangle, but that would create mostly working software. Someone might actually call them and use their results! We could display an error message and abort the program, but that is quite drastic. No, the best possible solution is to make these two functions pure virtual functions. **Shape** becomes an abstract base class.

If **GetArea()** and **GetPerimeter()** are pure virtual, then the **Shape** class becomes an abstract class. No instances of **Shape** could ever be allocated. But that is fine, no one should be allocating an abstract shape in the first place. So here is the revised **Shape** class.

```
class Shape {
protected:
 double x;
 double y;

public:
 Shape (double xx, double yy) : x(xx), y(yy) {}
 Shape () : x(0), y(0) {}
 Shape (const Shape& s) : x(s.x), y(s.y) {}
 virtual double GetArea () const = 0;
```

356

```
virtual double GetPerimeter () const = 0;
};
```
Each derived class must provide an implementation for both these functions.

> **Rule: If a derived class fails to implement a pure virtual function, then that derived class also becomes an abstract base class; no instances of it can be created.**

In a complex hierarchy of classes, there could be several layers of abstract base classes providing a range of functionality for further classes.

The **Rectangle** class implements these as follows. Since I expect to derive another class from this one, I made the two functions virtual here as well.
```
class Rectangle : public Shape {
// x = height, y = width
public:
 Rectangle (double height, double width) : Shape(height, width){}
 Rectangle () : Shape () {}
 Rectangle (const Rectangle& r) : Shape (r.x, r.y) {}
 virtual double GetArea () const {return x * y;}
 virtual double GetPerimeter () const {return 2*x + 2*y;}
};
```

The **Triangle** implements these two functions as follows. To figure the area based upon the lengths of the three sides, first calculate the semi perimeter which is ½ the sum of the three sides. Since this class is not derived from, the two functions are not virtual.
```
class Triangle : public Shape {
// x = side1, y = side2
protected:
 double side3;
public:
 Triangle (double s1, double s2, double s3)
   : Shape (s1, s2), side3(s3) {}
 Triangle () : Shape (), side3(0) {}
 Triangle (const Triangle& t)
   : Shape (t.x, t.y), side3(t.side3) {}
 double GetArea () const {
      double s = .5 * (x + y + side3); // semiperimeter
      return sqrt (s * (s-x) * (s-y) * (s-side3));}
 double GetPerimeter () const {return x + y + side3;}
};
```

The **Square** does not have to implement either of these functions because it is derived from a **Rectangle** and since we stored the side length in both **x** and **y**, the **Rectangle** calculations totally handle the **Square**. **Square** is unchanged.
```
class Square : public Rectangle {
// x = side, y = side
```

357

```
public:
 Square (double side) : Rectangle (side, side) {}
 Square () : Rectangle () {}
 Square (const Square& s) : Rectangle (s.x, s.y) {}
 // uses Rectangle's GetArea() and GetPerimeter()
};
```

Here is the **Circle**'s implementation. Note **acos(–1.)** is PI. The area is PI times the radius^2 while the circumference is 2 times PI times the radius.

```
class Circle : public Shape {
// x = radius
public:
 Circle (double radius) : Shape (radius, 0) {}
 Circle () : Shape () {}
 Circle (const Circle& c) : Shape (c.x, c.y) {}
 virtual double GetArea () const {return acos(-1.) * x * x;}
         double GetPerimeter () const {return 2 * acos(-1.) * x;}
};
```

Finally, the **Sphere** area formula is 4 PI radius^2. The circumference is the same as the circle. So only the area function is defined here. Notice how I choose to reuse the base class calculation. Further, since **Sphere** is not being used as a base class, it is not virtual.

```
class Sphere : public Circle {
// x = radius
public:
 Sphere (double radius) : Circle (radius, 0) {}
 Sphere () : Circle () {}
 Sphere (const Sphere& s) : Circle (s.x) {}
 double GetArea () const {return 2 * Circle::GetArea();}
};
```

Now how do we handle inputting and outputting of these objects? Each of the classes must define the insertion and extraction operators because clients can be expected to directly input and output these objects. However, because the client could also use a base class pointer with the insertion and extraction operations, virtual functions must be implemented in all the classes, just like was done with the vehicle series of classes. So each class must define the virtual **Input()** and **Output()** functions and have the insertion and extraction friend operator functions call them. However, how would one implement these for a Shape? Once again, **Shape**'s virtual **Input()** and **Output()** functions will be pure virtual in nature.

But before we charge forward implementing all of these functions, let's give some thought to the client output being produced. Here is a possible report produced by a client program.

Shape	Side(s)			Area	Perimeter
Rectangle	10.0	20.0		200.0	60.0
Triangle	40.0	50.0	60.0	992.2	150.0
Square	10.0			100.0	40.0
Circle	10.0			314.2	6.3
Sphere	10.			628.4	6.3

Can you spot the new detail? Each object ought to be able to identify itself by producing the string naming its shape type, such as **Rectangle**. How can we implement this?

One solution would be to define a string member in each of the derived classes and provide a pure virtual **GetName()** function in the **Shape** class. It would have to be a virtual function in **Shape** so that base class pointers would call the correct derived class **GetName()** function. However, and this is a major however, each of the five classes would end up coding roughly the same coding to input the name and to output the name. This would be repetitive, redundant coding! OOP to the rescue. There is no reason why **Shape** cannot implement the inputting and outputting of the string name of the shape. This way, we write it once and the other derived classes reuse it.

To keep this simple, **Shape** defines the actual array of characters for the name. The first ctor is passed the string name. The default ctor simply assigns it a null string. An access function, **GetName()** is provided to retrieve the name. I also added the virtual destructor.

```cpp
class Shape {
protected:
 double x;
 double y;
 char name[10];

public:
 Shape (double xx, double yy, const char* n) : x(xx), y(yy) {
    strcpy (name, n);}
 Shape () : x(0), y(0) {name[0] = 0;}
 Shape (const Shape& s) : x(s.x), y(s.y) {strcpy (name, s.name);}
 virtual ~Shape () {}
 const char* GetName () const {return name;}
 virtual double GetArea () const = 0;
 virtual double GetPerimeter () const = 0;
};
```

The **Rectangle** class implements these changes by passing the name string to the base class as follows. Since **Rectangle** is being derived from, the destructor is added as well as a default third parameter. Square is going to be calling this base ctor and needs to pass it the string "Square". By defaulting the third parameter to the string "Rectangle" clients can still construct a rectangle from two dimensions.

```cpp
class Rectangle : public Shape {
// x = height, y = width
public:
 Rectangle (double height, double width,
          const char* n = "Rectangle")
    : Shape(height, width, n){}
 Rectangle () : Shape (0, 0, "Rectangle") {}
 Rectangle (const Rectangle& r) : Shape (r.x, r.y, r.name){}
 virtual ~Rectangle () {}
 virtual double GetArea () const {return x * y;}
 virtual double GetPerimeter () const {return 2*x + 2*y;}
};
```

The **Triangle** is coded as follows. It is simpler because it is not being used as an additional base class.

```
class Triangle : public Shape {
// x = side1, y = side2
protected:
 double side3;
public:
 Triangle (double s1, double s2, double s3)
    : Shape (s1, s2, "Triangle"), side3(s3) {}
 Triangle () : Shape (0, 0, "Triangle"), side3(0) {}
 Triangle (const Triangle& t)
    : Shape (t.x, t.y, t.name), side3(t.side3) {}
 double GetArea () const {
        double s = .5 * (x + y + side3); // semiperimeter
        return sqrt (s * (s-x) * (s-y) * (s-side3));}
 double GetPerimeter () const {return x + y + side3;}
};
```

The **Square** is coded this way. Notice that the default and copy ctors now call a different **Rectangle** ctor.

```
class Square : public Rectangle {
// x = side, y = side
public:
 Square (double side) : Rectangle (side, side, "Square") {}
 Square () : Rectangle (0, 0, "Square") {}
 Square (const Square& s) : Rectangle (s.x, s.y, s.name) {}
 // uses Rectangle's GetArea () and GetPerimeter ()
};
```

Circle's implementation parallels that of **Rectangle** because **Sphere** is derived from it.

```
class Circle : public Shape {
// x = radius
public:
 Circle (double radius, const char* n = "Circle")
        : Shape (radius, 0, n) {}
 Circle () : Shape (0, 0, "Circle") {}
 Circle (const Circle& c) : Shape (c.x, c.y, c.name) {}
 virtual ~Circle () {}
 virtual double GetArea () const {return acos(-1.) * x * x;}
 virtual double GetPerimeter () const {return 2 * acos(-1.) * x;}
};
```

Finally, the **Sphere** is simple and parallels the **Square**.

```
class Sphere : public Circle {
// x = radius
public:
 Sphere (double radius) : Circle (radius, "Sphere") {}
 Sphere () : Circle (0, "Sphere") {}
```

360

```
Sphere (const Sphere& s) : Circle (s.x, s.name) {}
double GetArea () const {return 2 * Circle::GetArea();}
};
```

Does the assignment operator need to be provided? No, there are no dynamically allocated memory items or constant data members. So now we can proceed to implement the I/O functions. Let's begin with **Shape**. On input, the input format will be similar to the following. [Rectangle 10 20] or [Circle 10]. So **Shape**'s **Input()** must extract what it can, namely the beginning angle bracket and the name. The **Output()** function just displays the name.

```
class Shape {
protected:
 double x;
 double y;
 char name[10];

public:
 Shape (double xx, double yy, const char* n) : x(xx), y(yy) {
    strcpy (name, n);}
 Shape () : x(0), y(0) {name[0] = 0;}
 Shape (const Shape& s) : x(s.x), y(s.y) {strcpy (name, s.name);}
 virtual ~Shape () {}
 const char* GetName() const {return name;}
 virtual double GetArea () const = 0;
 virtual double GetPerimeter () const = 0;
 virtual istream& Input (istream& is) {
        char c;
        is >> c >> name;
        return is;}
 virtual ostream& Output (ostream& os) const {
        os.setf (ios::left, ios::adjustfield);
        os << setw(12) << name;
        os.setf (ios::right, ios::adjustfield);
        return os;}
 friend istream& operator>> (istream& is, Shape& s) {
        return s.Input (is);}
 friend ostream& operator<< (ostream& os, const Shape& s) {
        return s.Output (os);}
};
```

The **Rectangle** class implements these changes by having its insertion and extraction operator friend functions invoke the virtual **Input()** and **Output()** functions. Within these functions, the base class is invoked first to input and output the name.

```
class Rectangle : public Shape {
// x = height, y = width
public:
 Rectangle (double height, double width,
            const char* n = "Rectangle")
    : Shape(height, width, n){}
```

361

```
Rectangle () : Shape (0, 0, "Rectangle") {}
Rectangle (const Rectangle& r) : Shape (r.x, r.y, r.name){}
virtual ~Rectangle () {}
virtual double GetArea () const {return x * y;}
virtual double GetPerimeter () const {return 2*x + 2*y;}
virtual istream& Input (istream& is) {
        char c;
        Shape::Input (is);
        if (!is) return is;
        return is >> x >> y >> c;}
virtual ostream& Output (ostream& os) const {
        Shape::Output (os);
        return os << setw (6) << x << setw(6) << y;}
friend istream& operator>> (istream& is, Rectangle& r) {
        return r.Input (is);}
friend ostream& operator<< (ostream& os, const Rectangle& r) {
        return r.Output (os);}
};
```

The **Triangle** is coded as follows.

```
class Triangle : public Shape {
// x = side1, y = side2
protected:
 double side3;
public:
 Triangle (double s1, double s2, double s3)
   : Shape (s1, s2, "Triangle"), side3(s3) {}
 Triangle () : Shape (0, 0, "Triangle"), side3(0) {}
 Triangle (const Triangle& t)
   : Shape (t.x, t.y, t.name), side3(t.side3) {}
 double GetArea () const {
        double s = .5 * (x + y + side3); // semiperimeter
        return sqrt (s * (s-x) * (s-y) * (s-side3));}
 double GetPerimeter () const {return x + y + side3;}
 virtual istream& Input (istream& is) {
        char c;
        Shape::Input (is);
        if (!is) return is;
        return is >> x >> y >> side3 >> c;}
 virtual ostream& Output (ostream& os) const {
        Shape::Output (os);
        return os <<setw(6)<< x <<setw(6)<< y <<setw(6)<< side3;}
 friend istream& operator>> (istream& is, Triangle& t) {
        return t.Input (is);}
 friend ostream& operator<< (ostream& os, const Triangle& t) {
        return t.Output (os);}
};
```

The **Square** cannot reuse the **Rectangle Input()** and **Output()** functions and is coded this way.

```cpp
class Square : public Rectangle {
// x = side, y = side
public:
 Square (double side) : Rectangle (side, side, "Square") {}
 Square () : Rectangle (0, 0, "Square") {}
 Square (const Square& s) : Rectangle (s.x, s.y, s.name) {}
 // uses Rectangle's GetArea() and GetPerimeter()
 virtual istream& Input (istream& is) {
        char c;
        Shape::Input (is);
        if (!is) return is;
        is >> x >> c;
        y = x;
        return is;}
 virtual ostream& Output (ostream& os) const {
        Shape::Output (os);
        return os <<setw(6)<< x;}
 friend istream& operator>> (istream& is, Square& s) {
        return s.Input (is);}
 friend ostream& operator<< (ostream& os, const Square& s) {
        return s.Output (os);}
};
```

Here is **Circle**'s implementation.

```cpp
class Circle : public Shape {
// x = radius
public:
 Circle (double radius, const char* n = "Circle")
        : Shape (radius, 0, n) {}
 Circle () : Shape (0, 0, "Circle") {}
 Circle (const Circle& c) : Shape (c.x, c.y, c.name) {}
 virtual ~Circle () {}
 virtual double GetArea () const {return acos(-1.) * x * x;}
        double GetPerimeter () const {return 2 * acos(-1.) * x;}
 virtual istream& Input (istream& is) {
        char c;
        Shape::Input (is);
        if (!is) return is;
        return is >> x >> c;}
 virtual ostream& Output (ostream& os) const {
        Shape::Output (os);
        return os <<setw(6) << x;}
 friend istream& operator>> (istream& is, Circle& c) {
        return c.Input (is);}
 friend ostream& operator<< (ostream& os, const Circle& c) {
        return c.Output (os);}
};
```

Finally, the **Sphere** derived from a **Circle** can, in fact, simply reuse **Circle**'s **Input()** and **Output()** functions because there are no new data members. It still must implement the friend insertion and extraction operators, though.

```
class Sphere : public Circle {
// x = radius
public:
 Sphere (double radius) : Circle (radius, "Sphere") {}
 Sphere () : Circle (0, "Sphere") {}
 Sphere (const Sphere& s) : Circle (s.x, s.name) {}
 double GetArea () const {return 2 * Circle::GetArea();}
 friend istream& operator>> (istream& is, Sphere& s) {
        return s.Input (is);}
 friend ostream& operator<< (ostream& os, const Sphere& s) {
        return s.Output (os);}
};
```

The Actual Implementation of Shape and Its Derived Classes

While every function in all of these classes could be inlined as given above, it's not practical to do so. First, if every function is inlined, then the client program's file size is much larger than needed because every time any of these functions is called, all of the coding is present in the client at that point. Second, the client must include the header file. With everything in it, the header takes longer to compile and the client gets to see all of your implementation coding.

Okay. So we split the definition and implementation into a header and cpp file. Now do we create six headers and six cpp files, one for each of the classes? Well, that all depends. In this particular case, each of the classes is quite small and they are very closely related. Thus, I chose to have only one header and one cpp file. The benefit for client programs is that only one header file must be included to gain access to any and all of the various shape classes.

Here are the definition and implementation files that are really used by client programs.

```
Shape Classes Definitions

 1 #pragma once
 2 #include <iostream>
 3 using namespace std;
 4
 5 /*****************************************************************/
 6 /*                                                             */
 7 /* Shape class - abstract base class holds 2 dimensions & name */
 8 /*                                                             */
 9 /* derived classes must implement GetArea, GetPerimeter        */
10 /*                                                             */
11 /*****************************************************************/
12
```

```
13 class Shape {
14 protected:
15  double x;
16  double y;
17  char name[10];
18
19 public:
20                    Shape (double xx, double yy, const char* n);
21                    Shape ();
22                    Shape (const Shape& s);
23  virtual           ~Shape ();
24
25  const char*       GetName() const;
26
27  virtual double    GetArea () const = 0;
28  virtual double    GetPerimeter () const = 0;
29
30  virtual istream&  Input (istream& is);
31  virtual ostream&  Output (ostream& os) const;
32
33  friend  istream& operator>> (istream& is, Shape& s);
34  friend  ostream& operator<< (ostream& os, const Shape& s);
35 };
36
37
38 /********************************************************************/
39 /*                                                                  */
40 /* Rectangle class                                                  */
41 /*                                                                  */
42 /********************************************************************/
43
44
45 class Rectangle : public Shape {
46 // x = height, y = width
47 public:
48                    Rectangle (double height, double width,
49                            const char* n = "Rectangle");
50                    Rectangle ();
51                    Rectangle (const Rectangle& r);
52  virtual           ~Rectangle ();
53
54  virtual double    GetArea () const;
55  virtual double    GetPerimeter () const;
56
57  virtual istream&  Input (istream& is);
58  virtual ostream&  Output (ostream& os) const;
59
60  friend  istream& operator>> (istream& is, Rectangle& r);
61  friend  ostream& operator<< (ostream& os, const Rectangle& r);
62 };
63
64
65 /********************************************************************/
```

```
 66 /*                                                             */
 67 /* Triangle class                                              */
 68 /*                                                             */
 69 /*****************************************************************/
 70
 71
 72 class Triangle : public Shape {
 73 // x = side1, y = side2
 74 protected:
 75  double side3;
 76 public:
 77                    Triangle (double s1, double s2, double s3);
 78                    Triangle ();
 79                    Triangle (const Triangle& t);
 80  virtual          ~Triangle ();
 81
 82         double    GetArea () const;
 83         double    GetPerimeter () const;
 84
 85  virtual istream& Input (istream& is);
 86  virtual ostream& Output (ostream& os) const;
 87
 88  friend  istream& operator>> (istream& is, Triangle& t);
 89  friend  ostream& operator<< (ostream& os, const Triangle& t);
 90 };
 91
 92
 93 /*****************************************************************/
 94 /*                                                             */
 95 /* Square class                                                */
 96 /*                                                             */
 97 /*****************************************************************/
 98
 99
100 class Square : public Rectangle {
101 // x = side, y = side
102 public:
103                    Square (double side);
104                    Square ();
105                    Square (const Square& s);
106  virtual          ~Square ();
107
108  // uses Rectangle's GetArea() and GetPerimeter()
109
110  virtual istream& Input (istream& is);
111  virtual ostream& Output (ostream& os) const;
112
113  friend  istream& operator>> (istream& is, Square& s);
114  friend  ostream& operator<< (ostream& os, const Square& s);
115 };
116
117
118 /*****************************************************************/
```

```
119 /*                                                               */
120 /* Circle class                                                  */
121 /*                                                               */
122 /******************************************************************/
123
124
125 class Circle : public Shape {
126 // x = radius
127 public:
128                    Circle (double radius, const char* n="Circle");
129                    Circle ();
130                    Circle (const Circle& c);
131  virtual          ~Circle ();
132
133  virtual double   GetArea () const;
134          double   GetPerimeter () const;
135
136  virtual istream& Input (istream& is);
137  virtual ostream& Output (ostream& os) const;
138
139  friend  istream& operator>> (istream& is, Circle& c);
140  friend  ostream& operator<< (ostream& os, const Circle& c);
141 };
142
143
144 /******************************************************************/
145 /*                                                               */
146 /* Sphere class                                                  */
147 /*                                                               */
148 /******************************************************************/
149
150
151 class Sphere : public Circle {
152 // x = radius
153 public:
154                    Sphere (double radius);
155                    Sphere ();
156                    Sphere (const Sphere& s);
157  virtual          ~Sphere ();
158
159          double   GetArea () const;
160  // uses Circle's GetPerimeter
161  // uses Circle's Input and Output
162
163  friend  istream& operator>> (istream& is, Sphere& s);
164  friend  ostream& operator<< (ostream& os, const Sphere& s);
165 };
166
```

```
Shape Classes Implementations
```

```
1 #include <iostream>
```

```cpp
 2 #include <iomanip>
 3 #include <string>
 4 #include <cmath>
 5 using namespace std;
 6 #include "Shape.h"
 7
 8 /**************************************************************/
 9 /*                                                          */
10 /* Shape Implementation                                     */
11 /*                                                          */
12 /**************************************************************/
13
14 Shape::Shape (double xx, double yy, const char* n)
15       : x(xx), y(yy) {
16  strcpy_s (name, sizeof(name), n);
17 }
18
19 Shape::Shape () : x(0), y(0) {
20  name[0] = 0;
21 }
22
23 Shape::Shape (const Shape& s) : x(s.x), y(s.y) {
24  strcpy_s (name, sizeof(name), s.name);
25 }
26
27 Shape::~Shape () {
28 }
29
30 const char* Shape::GetName() const {
31  return name;
32 }
33
34 istream& Shape::Input (istream& is) {
35  char c;
36  is >> c >> name; // inputs the leading [ and the name
37  return is;
38 }
39
40 ostream& Shape::Output (ostream& os) const {
41 return os << left << setw(12) << name << right;
45 }
46
47 istream& operator>> (istream& is, Shape& s) {
48  return s.Input (is);
49 }
50
51 ostream& operator<< (ostream& os, const Shape& s) {
52  return s.Output (os);
53 }
54
55
56 /**************************************************************/
57 /*                                                          */
```

```
 58 /* Rectangle Implementation                                            */
 59 /*                                                                      */
 60 /************************************************************************/
 61
 62 Rectangle::Rectangle (double height, double width, const char* n)
 63            : Shape(height, width, n) {
 64 }
 65
 66 Rectangle::Rectangle () : Shape (0, 0, "Rectangle") {
 67 }
 68
 69 Rectangle::Rectangle (const Rectangle& r)
 70            : Shape (r.x, r.y, r.name) {
 71 }
 72
 73 Rectangle::~Rectangle () {
 74 }
 75
 76 double Rectangle::GetArea () const {
 77  return x * y;
 78 }
 79
 80 double Rectangle::GetPerimeter () const {
 81  return 2*x + 2*y;
 82 }
 83
 84 istream& Rectangle::Input (istream& is) {
 85  char c;
 86  Shape::Input (is); // input [Rectangle portion
 87  if (!is)
 88   return is;
 89  return is >> x >> y >> c; // input h w] portion
 90 }
 91
 92 ostream& Rectangle::Output (ostream& os) const {
 93  Shape::Output (os);
 94  return os << setw (8) << x << setw(8) << y;
 95 }
 96
 97 istream& operator>> (istream& is, Rectangle& r) {
 98  return r.Input (is);
 99 }
100
101 ostream& operator<< (ostream& os, const Rectangle& r) {
102  return r.Output (os);
103 }
104
105
106 /************************************************************************/
107 /*                                                                      */
108 /* Triangle Implementation                                             */
109 /*                                                                      */
110 /************************************************************************/
```

```
111
112 Triangle::Triangle (double s1, double s2, double s3)
113         : Shape (s1, s2, "Triangle"), side3(s3) {
114 }
115
116 Triangle::Triangle () : Shape (0, 0, "Triangle"), side3(0) {
117 }
118
119 Triangle::Triangle (const Triangle& t)
120         : Shape (t.x, t.y, t.name), side3(t.side3) {
121 }
122
123 Triangle::~Triangle () {
124 }
125
126 double Triangle::GetArea () const {
127  // calculate the semi-perimeter
128  double s = .5 * (x + y + side3);
129  // now calc the area using semi-perimeter
130  return sqrt (s * (s-x) * (s-y) * (s-side3));
131 }
132
133 double Triangle::GetPerimeter () const {
134  return x + y + side3;
135 }
136
137 istream& Triangle::Input (istream& is) {
138  char c;
139  Shape::Input (is); // input [Triangle portion
140  if (!is)
141    return is;
142  return is >> x >> y >> side3 >> c;
143 }
144
145 ostream& Triangle::Output (ostream& os) const {
146  Shape::Output (os);
147  return os <<setw(8)<< x <<setw(8)<< y <<setw(8)<< side3;
148 }
149
150 istream& operator>> (istream& is, Triangle& t) {
151  return t.Input (is);
152 }
153
154 ostream& operator<< (ostream& os, const Triangle& t) {
155  return t.Output (os);
156 }
157
158
159 /****************************************************************/
160 /*                                                              */
161 /* Square Implementation                                        */
162 /*                                                              */
163 /****************************************************************/
```

```
164
165 Square::Square (double side)
166         : Rectangle (side, side, "Square") {
167 }
168
169 Square::Square () : Rectangle (0, 0, "Square") {
170 }
171
172 Square::Square (const Square& s)
173         : Rectangle (s.x, s.y, s.name) {
174 }
175
176 Square::~Square () {
177 }
178
179 istream& Square::Input (istream& is) {
180  char c;
181  Shape::Input (is); // input [Square portion
182  if (!is)
183   return is;
184  is >> x >> c;
185  y = x;
186  return is;
187 }
188
189 ostream& Square::Output (ostream& os) const {
190  Shape::Output (os);
191  return os <<setw(8)<< x;
192 }
193
194 istream& operator>> (istream& is, Square& s) {
195  return s.Input (is);
196 }
197
198 ostream& operator<< (ostream& os, const Square& s) {
199  return s.Output (os);
200 }
201
202
203 /****************************************************************/
204 /*                                                              */
205 /* Circle Implemenation                                         */
206 /*                                                              */
207 /****************************************************************/
208
209 Circle::Circle (double radius, const char* n)
210         : Shape (radius, 0, n) {
211 }
212
213 Circle::Circle () : Shape (0, 0, "Circle") {
214 }
215
216 Circle::Circle (const Circle& c) : Shape (c.x, c.y, c.name) {
```

```
217 }
218
219 Circle::~Circle () {
220 }
221
222 double Circle::GetArea () const {
223  return acos(-1.) * x * x;
224 }
225
226 double Circle::GetPerimeter () const {
227  return 2 * acos(-1.) * x;
228 }
229
230 istream& Circle::Input (istream& is) {
231  char c;
232  Shape::Input (is); // input [Circle portion
233  if (!is)
234    return is;
235  return is >> x >> c;
236 }
237
238 ostream& Circle::Output (ostream& os) const {
239  Shape::Output (os);
240  return os <<setw(8) << x;
241 }
242
243 istream& operator>> (istream& is, Circle& c) {
244  return c.Input (is);
245 }
246 ostream& operator<< (ostream& os, const Circle& c) {
247  return c.Output (os);
248 }
249
250
251 /*****************************************************************/
252 /*                                                             */
253 /* Sphere Implementation                                       */
254 /*                                                             */
255 /*****************************************************************/
256
257 Sphere::Sphere (double radius) : Circle (radius, "Sphere") {
258 }
259
260 Sphere::Sphere () : Circle (0, "Sphere") {
261 }
262
263 Sphere::~Sphere () {
264 }
265
266 Sphere::Sphere (const Sphere& s) : Circle (s.x, s.name) {
267 }
268
269 double Sphere::GetArea () const {
```

```
270  // 4 PI r squared - so 2 * circle's area
271  return 2 * Circle::GetArea();
272 }
273
274 istream& operator>> (istream& is, Sphere& s) {
275  return s.Input (is);
276 }
277
278 ostream& operator<< (ostream& os, const Sphere& s) {
279  return s.Output (os);
280 }
```

Writing the Client Tester Program Pgm09a

Now let's turn our attention to how a client program can make excellent usage of these classes. Two subtle key issues are raised. See if you can spot them. Here is the input file of shapes that the client program must input. It is followed by the report that is generated.

```
Input to Pgm09a Shapes Tester

 1 [Rectangle 50 50]
 2 [Circle    15]
 3 [Circle    10]
 4 [Square    42]
 5 [Circle     7]
 6 [Circle     5]
 7 [Triangle  35 20 20]
 8 [Triangle  15 30 40]
 9 [Sphere     10]
10 [Triangle 15 20 30]
11 [Triangle  30 30 30]
12 [Rectangle  15 30]
13 [Rectangle  20 5]
14 [Square     88]
15 [Rectangle 10 20]
16 [Sphere    100]
17 [Rectangle  20 15]
18 [Circle     12]
19 [Triangle  5 5 5 ]
20 [Triangle  50 50 50 ]
```

```
Output from Pgm09a Shapes Tester

 1 Shape Type  <-----  Dimensions ----->      Area    Perimeter
 2
 3 Rectangle       50.00   50.00           2500.00      200.00
 4 Circle          15.00                    706.86       94.25
 5 Circle          10.00                    314.16       62.83
```

```
 6 Square           42.00                              1764.00      168.00
 7 Circle            7.00                               153.94       43.98
 8 Circle            5.00                                78.54       31.42
 9 Triangle         35.00     20.00     20.00           169.44       75.00
10 Triangle         15.00     30.00     40.00           191.11       85.00
11 Sphere           10.00                               628.32       62.83
12 Triangle         15.00     20.00     30.00           133.32       65.00
13 Triangle         30.00     30.00     30.00           389.71       90.00
14 Rectangle        15.00     30.00                     450.00       90.00
15 Rectangle        20.00      5.00                     100.00       50.00
16 Square           88.00                              7744.00      352.00
17 Rectangle        10.00     20.00                     200.00       60.00
18 Sphere          100.00                             62831.85      628.32
19 Rectangle        20.00     15.00                     300.00       70.00
20 Circle           12.00                               452.39       75.40
21 Triangle          5.00      5.00      5.00            10.83       15.00
22 Triangle         50.00     50.00     50.00          1082.53      150.00
23 No memory leaks.
```

The first detail is how can the client input the file of shapes? Recall that the **Shape::Input()** function inputs the leading [and the name, such as "[Rectangle". Certainly, the client program can input the shape data into an array of base class pointers.

```
        Shape* shapes[MAX]; // the array of shapes
```
and
```
        infile >> *shapes[i];   // input the shape
```
But the problem facing the client is **shapes[i]** must already contain an instance of the correct derived class for which the line to be inputted represents. The client must know in advance which kind of shape is coming. In earlier examples, this can be done by having a single character code as the first item on the line, identifying what kind of shape the line contains. But that is not the way the input file is structured in this case.

The client program can input the first three characters of the line. Why three? The first is the useless leading [. In order to determine which shape is on the line, two characters are needed because of **Sp**here and **Sq**uare. If the client inputs these first three characters to determine what kind of shape is coming, then, if nothing else is done, the **Shape::Input()** function does not have the proper data in the stream for it to input!

The input stream has another function, **putback()**, that puts back into the input stream the character that it is passed. In other words, after the client has extracted the first three characters of a line, it can put those characters just read back into the stream so that **Shape::Input()** can actually input them properly!

Thus, the client's main loop can be written like this.
```
while (infile >> b >> c >> d) { // ie. input [Re of [Rectangle
  infile.putback (d);           // and put those chars back
  infile.putback (c);           // into the stream so they can
  infile.putback (b);           // be extracted by Shape::Input
```

374

And here it can switch on the character **c** and use character **d** to assist in sorting out **Sphere** and **Square** objects. It can now dynamically allocate the correct new shape and store that pointer in the base class pointer array, **shapes**.

The second hurdle is the output formatting. Examine the report to be generated as shown above once again. Can you spot this new difficulty? Consider what happens when one of the **Output()** function is called. Compare the output results of **Triangle::Output()** and **Circle::Output()**. What is the difference? The triangle output contains three numerical side values while the circle only has one. So the problem is one of columnar alignment of all fields after the dimensions of the shape are displayed. We must force the area field to be aligned in a specific column.

This can be done in a clever way. If we make up an **ostrstream** wrapped around a sufficiently large character string and pass that stream to the shape's **Output()** functions, then the output fills up the string. We can then display that resultant string left justified in a sufficiently wide width to get good column alignment. We can use coding like this.

```
ostrstream os (leftPart, sizeof (leftPart));
os << fixed << setprecision (2) << *shapes[i] << ends;

// now display that string left adjusted in wide field
cout << left << setw (36) << leftPart << right;

// and display the area and perimeter columns
cout << setw(12) << shapes[i]->GetArea()
     << setw(12) << shapes[i]->GetPerimeter() << endl;
```

Here is the complete **Pgm09a** tester program. Since memory is dynamically allocated, I included memory leak checking as usual.

```
Pgm09a Shapes Tester

 1 #include <iostream>
 2 #include <iomanip>
 3 #include <fstream>
 4 #include <string>
 5 #include <ctype>
 6 #include <strstream>
 7 #include <crtdbg.h>
 8 #include "Shape.h"
 9 using namespace std;
10 const int MAX = 100;
11
12 int main () {
13 {
14 // setup floating point output format
15 cout << fixed << setprecision (2);
18
19 // open input file od shapes
20 ifstream infile ("testdata.txt");
21 if (!infile) {
```

```
22    cerr << "Error: cannot open testdata.txt file\n";
23    return 1;
24    }
25
26    Shape* shapes[MAX]; // the array of shapes
27    int numShapes;       // number of shapes currently in array
28    int i = 0;
29    char b, c, d;        // stores first three chars of each line
30
31    while (infile >> b >> c >> d) { // ie. input [Re of [Rectangle
32     infile.putback (d);            // and put those chars back
33     infile.putback (c);            // into the stream so they can
34     infile.putback (b);            // be extracted by Shape::Input
35
36     c = toupper(c);                // remove case sensitivity
37     d = toupper(d);
38     shapes[i] = 0;                 // initialize this Shape pointer
39
40     switch (c) {                   // allocate a new shape based on
41      case 'R':                     // what type it is
42       shapes[i] = new Rectangle;
43       break;
44      case 'T':
45       shapes[i] = new Triangle;
46       break;
47      case 'S':
48       if (d == 'Q') {
49        shapes[i] = new Square;
50        break;
51       }
52       else if (d == 'P') {
53        shapes[i] = new Sphere;
54        break;
55       }
56      case 'C':
57       shapes[i] = new Circle;
58       break;
59     };
60
61     if (shapes[i] == 0) {  // check for unknown shape type error
62      cerr << "Error: unknown shape encountered on input: "
63           << c << d << endl;
64      infile.close ();
65      return (2);
66     }
67
68     infile >> *shapes[i];  // input the shape
69     i++;
70    }
71    numShapes = i; // save number of shapes in the array
72    infile.close ();
73
74    // display report heading
```

```
75  cout << "Shape Type  <-----  Dimensions ----->"
76       << "         Area    Perimeter\n\n";
77
78  char leftPart[80];
79
80  for (i=0; i<numShapes; i++) {
81   // build the basic shape output string portion
82   ostrstream os (leftPart, sizeof (leftPart));
83   os << fixed << setprecision (2)<< *shapes[i] << ends;
87
88   // now display that string left adjusted in wide field
89   cout << left << setw (36) << leftPart << right;
92   // and display the area and perimeter columns
93   cout << setw(12) << shapes[i]->GetArea()
94        << setw(12) << shapes[i]->GetPerimeter() << endl;
95  }
96
97  // clean up action - remove all shapes that were allocated
98  for (i=0; i<numShapes; i++) {
99   delete shapes[i];
100  }
101  }
102
103  // check for memory leaks
104  if (_CrtDumpMemoryLeaks())
105   cerr << "Memory leaks occurred!\n";
106  else
107   cerr << "No memory leaks.\n";
108
109  return 0;
110  }
```

Multiple Inheritance

It is possible for a derived class to have more than one immediate base class. This is known as **multiple inheritance**. For example going back to the **Vehicle** class, the **Tank** class could be derived from a **Truck** class to get **Vehicle** aspects and also be derived from a **Gun** class to inherit gun properties and methods.

```
class Tank : public Truck, public Gun {
```

The syntax for multiple inheritance is

```
class derived : access base1, access base2, ... access basen {
```

The constructor functions must then invoke all of the base classes.

```
Tank::Tank () : Truck(), Gun() {
```

When a tank is constructed, the **Truck** base class is called first, followed by the **Gun** base class ctor, followed by the **Tank** constructor's body. When the tank destructors are called, first ~**Tank()** is called, then ~**Gun()** is called and finally ~**Truck()** is invoked—the reverse order of construction.

Multiple base classes offer powerful class design capabilities as you can imagine with the **Tank** class. However, there is one small catch that sometimes can arise. Let's see how this can occur.

The **Gun** class could also be derived from a **Vehicle** because a gun can be moved. Small caliber machine guns can be carried by a squad of men. Smaller field pieces can be manhandled by the gun crew for short distances if needed. Thus, we might have the following pictorial derivation, Figure 9.1.

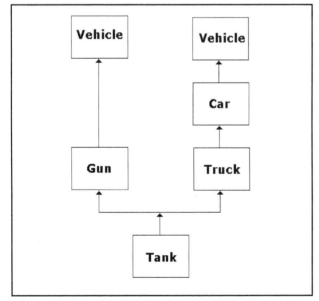

Figure 9.1 Multiple Inheritance of Tank

Notice that two copies of the **Vehicle** base class are included in a **Tank** object. This causes ambiguity when a member of **Vehicle** is referenced by **Tank**. This problem is resolved by another C++ mechanism, a **virtual base class**.

By adding the virtual keyword before the access qualifier in the derivation, only a single copy of such virtual base classes is included in the derived class. If we code the class definitions as follows, then only a single copy of the **Vehicle** class is included in class **Tank**.

```
class Gun : virtual public Vehicle { ...
class Car : virtual public Vehicle { ...
class Truck : virtual public Car { ...
class Tank : public Gun, public Truck { ...
```

Adding Multiple Base Classes to Shapes

Returning to the series of geometrical shape classes, each object would also likely have an origin point or center coordinates in two-dimensional space. That origin point could be defined by a class called **Point**.

```
class Point {
protected:
  int coordx;
  int coordy;
  ...
};
```

Given this definition of **Point**, the **Rectangle** class could be defined this way. Assume for input the x and y coordinates precede the height and width values and similarly for output.

```
class Rectangle : public Shape, public Point {
// x = height, y = width
public:
 Rectangle (double height, double width, int x, int y,
         const char* n = "Rectangle")
     : Shape(height, width, n), Point (x, y) {}
 Rectangle () : Shape (0, 0, "Rectangle"), Point (0,0) {}
 Rectangle (const Rectangle& r) : Shape (r.x, r.y, r.name),
         Point (r.coordx, r.coordy) {}
virtual ~Rectangle () {}
virtual double GetArea () const {return x * y;}
virtual double GetPerimeter () const {return 2*x + 2*y;}
virtual istream& Input (istream& is) {
       char c;
       Shape::Input (is);
       if (!is) return is;
       return is >> coordx >> coordy >> x >> y >> c;}
 virtual ostream& Output (ostream& os) const {
```

379

```
        Shape::Output (os);
        return os << setw (4) << coordx << setw (4) << coordy
                  << setw (6) << x << setw(6) << y; }
  friend istream& operator>> (istream& is, Rectangle& r) {
        return r.Input (is); }
  friend ostream& operator<< (ostream& os, const Rectangle& r) {
        return r.Output (os); }
};
```

The use of multiple base classes can add a new dimension in class design and corresponding hierarchy.

Review Questions

1. What is meant by an abstract base class? If class **Plant** is an abstract base class, what ramifications does this have on client programs?

2. What is a pure virtual function? How does one differ from an ordinary virtual function?

3. If a class has just one pure virtual function defined in it, what impact does that have on that class?

4. In class derivations, when should one consider using a pure virtual function?

5. What does multiple inheritance involve? How can it be effectively used?

6. What is the problem with having two or more copies of the same base class in a multiple inheritance derived class? How can one force only one instance of a specific base class being included?

Stop! Do These Exercises Before Programming

1. Acme sells appliances and services them. They need a billing program to display a customer's bill. Excited about inheritance, management decided to give multiple inheritance a try. Create a base class called **BillItem** that contains a 30-character **description** string and a double **amount** field. If this item was a new refrigerator, the **description** string would contain "refrigerator" and the **amount** would represent its total cost, $750.00. If this item was a service call, then the **description** string would contain "Service Call" and the **amount** would represent total charges, such as $90.00. Create appropriate constructors, a destructor, and a **Print()** function. Since this class does not know how the bill is to be printed, **Print()** is a pure virtual function.

2. Create a derived class called **ServiceCall** that encapsulates a service repairman's charges. It is derived from **BillItem** and contains one new data member, the hours worked. Its **Print()** function outputs a line such as this.

```
Service Call      2.5 hours labor      $90.00
```

3. Create a derived class called **Appliance** that encapsulates the sale of an appliance. It is derived from **BillItem** and contains one new member, the quantity sold. Its **Print()** function outputs a line such as this.

```
Acme Refrigerator quantity 1          $750.00
```

4. Create a derived class called **Installation** that encapsulates the sale of a new appliance and the service charge for setting it up. It is derived from **Appliance** and from **ServiceCall**. Only a single **BillingItem** instance should be contained in the derived class. Its **Print()** function should look like this.

```
Purchase and Install 1 Refrigerator  $800.00
```

Programming Problems

Problem Pgm09-1—Employee Class II—Using Derived Classes

The Employee Payroll Program

In the **Employee** class from **Pgm05-5—Employee Class I**, remove the **Date** object data member for the date hired and remove all traces of that object from the class. Remove the **GetHireDate()** and **CompareDate()** functions. The **Input()** and **Output()** functions may be kept as utility functions as you see fit.

The Larger Picture

Employees of the Acme Company are paid either an hourly wage, a piece-rate, or a fixed salary. Thus, there are three kinds of employee classifications. Common to all employee classifications is the need for the employee name and social security number. All other retained employee compensation details vary by the class they are in.

Thus, the **Employee** class becomes the base class encapsulating the basic functionality and the name and social security number. Three other classes are to be derived from the **Employee** class, **HourlyEmp**, **PieceRateEmp**, and **SalariedEmp**.

The actual implementation is broken down into three smaller sections that can be compiled and run and tested in smaller units so you do not have to implement the entire project at one time. There should be a single header file, Employee.h and a single cpp file that contain all four classes. In reality, these classes are tightly coupled and are very small in size.

The other three classes require additional information. The hourly wage employees are paid for each hour worked and are paid "time and a half" for all overtime hours (any hours above 40). Salaried employees are paid a fixed annual rate; thus, their pay is found by dividing the yearly amount by 52 weeks and then multiplying by the number of weeks in the pay period. The piece-rate employees are paid based on the number of pieces produced; they are paid a fixed amount on each piece made up to their production quota and then a bonus rate for each piece above that quota. Thus, each of the three employee classes stores different additional information beyond the base class's name and id number.

On this programming assignment, I am minimizing the "specifications" so that you may have a greater level of creativity. Your fundamental design rule is simple: make your classes work with the three provided main programs without altering the three main programs. Pay particular attention to what functions must be virtual. Your header file should define the four classes and your cpp file should implement the four classes.

Pgm09-1A: Tests the constructors and operator<<

The **HourlyEmp** class constructor takes the long ID, the employee name, and the hourly pay rate. The id number may be up to nine digits long and the name may be up to 25 characters long.

The **PieceRateEmp** class constructor takes the ID number, employee name, the base rate, the bonus rate, and the production quota.

The **SalariedEmp** class constructor takes the ID number, employee name, and the annual salary.

All constructor parameters have a 0 as their default value. Pgm09-1A uses no input file.

The **operator<<()** function prints the ID number as a zero-filled nine-digit integer followed by one blank space. The employee name is printed enclosed within a pair of double quote marks and there are sufficient blank spaces after the trailing double quote marks to complete a total of 28 columns. The next item output maybe hourly pay rate, the base piece rate or the annual salary, depending upon the employee class. In each case, the number is printed in an 8-column field with two decimal digits after the decimal point. For piece-rate employees, there are two more fields printed, the bonus rate and then the production quota. The bonus rate is printed in a five-column field preceded with one blank space; it is printed with two digits after the decimal point. The production quota is a whole number and is printed with one preceding blank space in a three-column field.

Finally, **do not write repetitive coding**. That is, there should only be a single function to input the employee's name and id. That coding should not be in three different functions. It belongs only in the base class. **Pgm09-1A.cpp** is found in the test data folder under **Pgm09-1**. Here is what that tester program looks like.

```
// Pgm09-1A.CPP
#include <iostream>
#include <iomanip>
```

```
using namespace std;
#include "employee.h"

main()
   {
   HourlyEmp
      hEmp1 (333456789L, "JONES, W.", 7.25),
      hEmp2 (45698L, "BROWN, SARA L.", 10.50);
   PieceRateEmp
      prEmp1(123445566L, "MILLER, ROBERT JONATHON", 1.5, .1, 50),
      prEmp2(2L, "ROW, ANN", 3.0, .75, 30);
   SalariedEmp
      sEmp1 (3549876L, "ABERNATHY, ALEXANDER", 28000.0);

   Employee
      *pEmp[] = { &hEmp1, &prEmp2, &sEmp1, &hEmp2, &prEmp1 };
   int count = sizeof(pEmp) / sizeof(pEmp[0]);

   cout << "EMPLOYEE LISTING\n\n";

   for (int i = 0; i < count; i++)
      cout << *pEmp[i] << '\n';
   return 0;
   }
```

The output of **Pgm09-1A** should be as shown in Figure 9.2.

```
333456789 "JONES, W."                        7.25
000000002 "ROW, ANN"                         3.00 0.75   30
003459876 "ABERNATHY, ALEXANDER"
000045698 "BROWN, SARA L."                   10.5
123445566 "MILLER, ROBERT JONATHON"         1.50 0.10   50
Figure 9.2 Output from Pgm09-1A
```

Pgm09-1B: Tests operator>>

This program inputs the **Pgm09-1.txt** data file. On input, the ID number can be nine digits long and represents the social security number. This can be entered in one of two ways. It can be a series of nine digits or as 999-99-9999 where a dash is the separator.

On input, the employee name is always enclosed in double quote marks to handle the presence of blanks in the name field. Do not store the leading and trailing double quote marks. It is up to 25 characters long, not counting the two double quote marks. The data following the name depends upon the employee class. If this is a salaried employee, the next field is the annual pay. For hourly employees, the next field is the hourly pay rate. For piece-rate employees, there is the base rate, the bonus rate and then the production quota.

When testing your program, run the program against the provided **Pgm09-1.txt** data file. Save the display output to a file. You can then input the output as the input and produce the exact same output as from using **Pgm09-1.txt**. In other words the output of **Pgm09-1B** is compatible with the input file for this program.

```
// Pgm09-1B.CPP
#include <iostream>
#include <iomanip>
using namespace std;
#include "employee.h"

enum { HOURLY = 'H', SALARIED = 'S', PIECE_RATE = 'P' };

main()
    {
    ifstream infile ("Pgm09-1.txt", ios::in | ios::nocreate);
    if (!infile) {
     cerr << "Error: unable to open file Pgm09-1.txt\n";
     return 1;
    }

    Employee *emp;
    char type;

    while (infile >> type)
        {
        switch (type)
            {
            case HOURLY:       emp = new(HourlyEmp);    break;
            case PIECE_RATE:   emp = new(PieceRateEmp); break;
            case SALARIED:     emp = new(SalariedEmp);  break;
            default:           cerr << "Bad employee type\n";
                               return 1;
            }
        infile >> *emp;
        infile.ignore(100, '\n');
        cout << type << ' ' << *emp << '\n';
        delete emp;
        }

    infile.close ();
    return 0;
    }
```

Notice that **Pgm09-1B** inputs the employee type as a character, H, S or P.

Pgm09-1C: The full implementation of the Employee Pay Program

Now that you have the constructors and I/O operators working, you can add in the payroll calculation portion. **Pgm09-1C** inputs the data similarly to **Pgm09-1B** but adds in another field, **work_amount**. For salaried employees, **work_amount** is the number of weeks in the pay period. For hourly workers, this field contains the number of hours worked. For piece-rate employees, this represents the number of items made.

Provide two new functions, **id()** and **name()**, that return the employee's id and name. Note that the name string returned should be **const char***. Finally create the **pay()** function which is passed the **work_amount** field and returns the employee's pay. Here is what **Pgm09-1C** looks like.

```cpp
// Pgm09-1C.CPP
#include <iostream>
#include <iomanip>
#include <fstream>
using namespace std;
#include "employee.h"

enum { HOURLY = 'H', SALARIED = 'S', PIECE_RATE = 'P' };

main()
    {
    Employee *emp;
    char type;
    float work_amount;

    ifstream infile ("Pgm09-1.txt", ios::in | ios::nocreate);
    if (!infile) {
     cerr << "Error: unable to open file Pgm09-1.txt\n";
     return 1;
    }

    cout << fixed << setprecision(2);

    cout << "   ID                    NAME                    PAY\n\n";

    while (infile >> type)
        {
        switch (type)
            {
            case HOURLY:      emp = new(HourlyEmp);     break;
            case PIECE_RATE:  emp = new(PieceRateEmp); break;
            case SALARIED:    emp = new(SalariedEmp);  break;
            default:          cerr << "Bad employee type\n";
                              return 1;
            }
        infile >> *emp >> work_amount;
        cout << setfill('0') << setw(9) << emp->id() << "       "
            << setfill(' ') << left << setw(30) << emp->name() << right
            << '$' << setw(7) << emp->pay(work_amount) << '\n';
        delete emp;
        }

    infile.close ();
    return 0;
    }
```

Figure 9.3 shows the output your program should produce.

```
|  ID            NAME                        PAY       |
|                                                      |
| 333456789    DARNELL, FREDERICK       $  961.54      |
| 456123456    NOBEL, WILLIAM           $  510.00      |
| 111223333    WOOD, STEVEN             $  735.81      |
| 345671234    NUTTING, TERESA ELAINE   $  100.00      |
| 123456789    HOOP, JEANETTE           $2307.69       |
| 678654321    BOLDEN, EDWARD D.        $  272.70      |
| 555667777    MCCLEARY, JANE           $  486.06      |
| 004556666    HERLAN, WILLIAM BART     $  384.62      |
| 001020003    ANDERSON, J. DENNIS      $  437.50      |
| 777889999    HANNAH, CAROL            $  323.20      |
| 888990000    RAINTREE, VICTORIA LYNN  $  461.54      |
| 467010002    NOONCASTER, BRENDA       $  240.00      |
| 321456789    YOUNG, RICHARD           $1750.00       |
| 333040005    FRESH, GAIL              $1076.92       |
| 234854321    KINGSLEY, JACKIE         $  550.00      |
| 012998877    BRAHAM, JOSEPH           $  512.50      |
```

Figure 9.3 Output from Pgm09-1C

Problem Pgm09-2—A Revised Shapes Set of Classes

Revise the sample shapes' classes given in this chapter to use multiple base classes. The **Point** base class has two members, **coordx** and **coordy**, both integers. Create appropriate constructor functions as desired. Create an **Input()** function that extracts two integers from the input stream. Create an **Output()** function that displays the coordinates as follows.

(100, 100)

The format is a leading (followed by the **coordx** value with a width of four digits followed by a comma and one blank followed by the **coordy** value with a width of four digits followed by a trailing).

The **Shape** class is unchanged. Derive all of the remaining classes from both **Shape** and **Point**. Modify their **Input()** functions to input the coordinates before the remaining dimensions of the shape. Modify their **Output()** functions to display the location after the name and before the dimensions.

Rewrite the tester program **Pgm09a** to now display the point locations after the name and before the dimensions. Note that you will need to add some testing x and y values after the names and before the dimensions in the input test file.

386

Chapter 10—Applications of OOP

Introduction

Sometimes, a picture is worth a thousand words. That is what this chapter is all about—examples of OOP in action. Let's begin by seeing just how **cin** is defined.

The Microsoft I/O Stream Classes

At this point in our studies of OOP, we know enough to grasp the basics of how Microsoft defines the I/O stream classes—that is, if advanced complexities are removed from the files and if we examine the Old Style streams. In the following two listings, I have removed a large number of complex #defines and other items, leaving a more understandable definition. The objective of this section is to gain a better overall understanding of the stream classes, not an in depth understanding. Further, these are the older iostreams not the current ones because the current ones utilize templates which we have not discussed as yet and are more complex for beginners to understand.

In the definition of the **ios** class below, notice that there is also a forward reference for another class, **streambuf**, line 16. Essentially, **streambuf** handles the actual keyboard character buffer in which DOS places incoming characters from the keyboard. For our purposes of gaining an initial overview of the stream classes, this is as far as we will go with how characters are actually extracted or inserted into the buffers and so on.

Line 19 defines the **ios** class proper. And the first items in it are a number of public **enum**s for all of the **ios::** identifiers that we have been using. First come **io_state** and **open_mode**, lines 22 through 34. Notice the notation of the values, such as 0x01. The 0x prefix specifies that the following value is in hexadecimal. For example,

```
enum open_mode { in        = 0x01,
                 out       = 0x02,
                 ate       = 0x04,
                 app       = 0x08,
                 trunc     = 0x10,
                 nocreate  = 0x20,
                 noreplace = 0x40,
                 binary    = 0x80 };
```

We know that these are the various flag values that we OR together when defining or opening a file or stream, such as

```
ifstream infile ("test.txt", ios::in | ios::nocreate);
```

This example illustrates a very common coding technique of flags. Suppose that some function could be passed any number of flag values—say six were possible. Rather than making that function take six parameters, one for each possible flag setting, by carefully specifying individual flag values, it is possible to pass a single flag parameter that contains those six flag values. To see how this is done, let's examine the eight bits within a byte value.

```
The 8 Bits           Decimal Value    Hex Value
0 0 0 0    0 0 0 1         1            0x01
0 0 0 0    0 0 1 0         2            0x02
0 0 0 0    0 1 0 0         4            0x04
0 0 0 0    1 0 0 0         8            0x08
0 0 0 1    0 0 0 0        16            0x10
0 0 1 0    0 0 0 0        32            0x20
0 1 0 0    0 0 0 0        64            0x40
1 0 0 0    0 0 0 0       128            0x80
```

If each bit position represents a single flag value (true/false), then a single byte could contain eight different flags as shown below.

```
1 1 1 1    1 1 1 1
```

Since the values are passed as a **long** or 32-bit value, theoretically, one **long** could contain up to thirty-two different flag values!

This concept is further illustrated by the next anonymous enumerated series in the **ios** class beginning on line 38. Here we find the actual definition of most all of the other values we have been using, such as **ios::left**, **ios::right**, and **ios::fixed**.

Next notice that the definitions of **basefield**, **adjustfield**, and **floatfield** (lines 55 through 57) are storing whether numbers with leading zeroes are to be considered decimal or octal, left or right justification is in force, and how floating point numbers are to be displayed (scientific or fixed). These fields are **static**; one setting services all class instances.

Line 59 defines the single constructor function that is passed a pointer to the stream buffer instance that holds the actual characters to be input or output. What about other possible constructor functions? Look down to line 94. Here are several other constructor functions including the copy ctor and the assignment operator. However, these others are all protected. This prevents someone from trying to do the following.

```
istream myIn = cin;
```

For if this were allowed, we would now effectively have two keyboards and total confusion!

The group of member function prototypes beginning on line 62 defines many of the familiar functions that we have used, such as **setf()**. Notice in particular the two functions defined on lines 84 through 87. These functions are called when we write

```
while (cin)
if (!infile)
```

These functions test the state of the stream. Remember that the fail bit is on if there is bad data encountered, it is EOF, or there has been a physical I/O error.

C++ Object Oriented Programming

Finally, notice how Microsoft handles the inlining of functions. The **inline** keyword appears before the prototype. And after the class definition, the functions are implemented here in the header file. If a function is to be implemented here in the header file, the function header must have the **inline** keyword before it.

```
Modified Microsoft ios.h Header File

 1 /***
 2 *ios.h - definitions/declarations for the ios class.
 3 *
 4 *         Copyright (c) 1990-1997, Microsoft Corporation.
 5 *   All rights reserved.
 6 *
 7 *Purpose:
 8 *         This file defines the classes, values, macros, functions
 9 *         used by the ios class.
10 *         [AT&T C++]
11 *
12 *         [Public]
13 *
14 ****/
15 ...
16 class streambuf;
17 class ostream;
18
19 class ios {
20
21 public:
22     enum io_state {  goodbit = 0x00,
23                      eofbit  = 0x01,
24                      failbit = 0x02,
25                      badbit  = 0x04 };
26
27     enum open_mode { in        = 0x01,
28                      out       = 0x02,
29                      ate       = 0x04,
30                      app       = 0x08,
31                      trunc     = 0x10,
32                      nocreate  = 0x20,
33                      noreplace = 0x40,
34                      binary    = 0x80 };
35
36     enum seek_dir { beg=0, cur=1, end=2 };
37
38     enum {  skipws    = 0x0001,
39             left      = 0x0002,
40             right     = 0x0004,
41             internal  = 0x0008,
42             dec       = 0x0010,
43             oct       = 0x0020,
44             hex       = 0x0040,
45             showbase  = 0x0080,
```

389

```
46              showpoint  = 0x0100,
47              uppercase  = 0x0200,
48              showpos    = 0x0400,
49              scientific = 0x0800,
50              fixed      = 0x1000,
51              unitbuf    = 0x2000,
52              stdio      = 0x4000
53                                  };
54
55      static const long basefield;        // dec | oct | hex
56      static const long adjustfield;      // left | right | internal
57      static const long floatfield;       // scientific | fixed
58
59      ios(streambuf*);                    // differs from ANSI
60      virtual ~ios();
61
62      inline long flags() const;
63      inline long flags(long _l);
64
65      inline long setf(long _f,long _m);
66      inline long setf(long _l);
67      inline long unsetf(long _l);
68
69      inline int width() const;
70      inline int width(int _i);
71
72      inline ostream* tie(ostream* _os);
73      inline ostream* tie() const;
74
75      inline char fill() const;
76      inline char fill(char _c);
77
78      inline int precision(int _i);
79      inline int precision() const;
80
81      inline int rdstate() const;
82      inline void clear(int _i = 0);
83
84      operator void *() const {
85                  if(state&(badbit|failbit) ) return 0;
86                  return (void *)this; }
87      inline int operator!() const;
88
89      inline int  good() const;
90      inline int  eof() const;
91      inline int  fail() const;
92      inline int  bad() const;
93 ...
94 protected:
95      ios();
96      ios(const ios&);                     // treat as private
97      ios& operator=(const ios&);
98      void init(streambuf*);
```

```
 99
100     int     state;
101     long    x_flags;
102     int     x_precision;
103     char    x_fill;
104     int     x_width;
105 ...
106 };
107
108
109
110 inline long ios::flags() const { return x_flags; }
111 inline long ios::flags(long _l) {
112                 long _l0; _l0 = x_flags;
113                 x_flags = _l; return _l0; }
114
115 inline long ios::setf(long _l,long _m) {
116                 long _l0; lock(); _l0 = x_flags;
117                 x_flags = (_l&_m) | (x_flags&(~_m));
118                 unlock(); return _l0; }
119 inline long ios::setf(long _l) {
120                 long _l0; lock(); _l0 = x_flags;
121                 x_flags |= _l; unlock(); return _l0; }
122 inline long ios::unsetf(long _l) {
123                 long _l0; lock(); _l0 = x_flags;
124                 x_flags &= (~_l); unlock(); return _l0; }
125
126 inline int ios::width() const { return x_width; }
127 inline int ios::width(int _i) {
128                 int _i0; _i0 = (int)x_width;
129                 x_width = _i; return _i0; }
130
131 inline char ios::fill() const { return x_fill; }
132 inline char ios::fill(char _c) {
133                 char _c0; _c0 = x_fill;
134                 x_fill = _c; return _c0; }
135
136 inline int ios::precision(int _i) {
137         int _i0; _i0 = (int)x_precision;
138         x_precision = _i; return _i0; }
139 inline int ios::precision() const { return x_precision; }
140
141 inline int ios::operator!() const{return state&(badbit|failbit);}
142
143 inline int  ios::bad() const { return state & badbit; }
144 inline void ios::clear(int _i){ lock(); state = _i; unlock(); }
145 inline int  ios::eof() const { return state & eofbit; }
146 inline int  ios::fail() const {return state &(badbit | failbit);}
147 inline int  ios::good() const { return state == 0; }
```

With class **ios** defined, the **istream** class is derived from it as shown in line 16 below in the **istream.h** file.

```
class istream : virtual public ios {
```

(The **virtual** keyword is used with multiple base classes to ensure only a single copy of **ios** is included in derived classes.) Line 19 defines the only constructor that is allowed, one that is passed a pointer to the actual stream buffer containing the characters coming from the keyboard.

This is followed by a huge number of extraction operator overridden functions. Here we can actually see what function is being called when we write

```
double x;
int y;
cin >> x >> y;
```

Remember the operator overloaded function rule. The item to the left of the operator >> provides the **this** parameter and the item to the right becomes the single parameter to the function. The above example first calls the **operator>>()** function that is passed a **double&** and then calls the **operator>>()** function that is passed an **int&**.

Next, beginning on line 41 the various overloaded forms of the **get()** and **getline()** functions are defined. Notice how the last parameter is defaulted to a newline code.

Finally, on line 120, class **istream_withassign** is defined, derived from **istream**. And on line 131 comes the actual definition of **cin** as an instance of **istream_withassign**. Notice that it is in the global namespace and would be included in any file that includes **iostream.h** which in turn includes **istream.h**. This is reason that **cin** seems to be available everywhere we need it – it is a global variable.

```
Modified Microsoft istream.h Header File

 1 /***
 2 *istream.h - definitions/declarations for the istream class
 3 *
 4 *        Copyright (c) 1990-1997, Microsoft Corporation.
 5 *   All rights reserved.
 6 *
 7 *Purpose:
 8 *        This file defines the classes, values, macros, functions
 9 *        used by the istream class.
10 *        [AT&T C++]
11 *
12 *        [Public]
13 *
14 ****/
15
16 class istream : virtual public ios {
17
18 public:
19     istream(streambuf*);
20     virtual ~istream();
```

```
21
22      istream& operator>>(char *);
23      inline istream& operator>>(unsigned char *);
24      inline istream& operator>>(signed char *);
25      istream& operator>>(char &);
26      inline istream& operator>>(unsigned char &);
27      inline istream& operator>>(signed char &);
28      istream& operator>>(short &);
29      istream& operator>>(unsigned short &);
30      istream& operator>>(int &);
31      istream& operator>>(unsigned int &);
32      istream& operator>>(long &);
33      istream& operator>>(unsigned long &);
34      istream& operator>>(float &);
35      istream& operator>>(double &);
36      istream& operator>>(long double &);
37      istream& operator>>(streambuf*);
38
39      int get();
40
41      inline istream& get(        char *,int,char ='\n');
42      inline istream& get(unsigned char *,int,char ='\n');
43      inline istream& get(  signed char *,int,char ='\n');
44
45      istream& get(char &);
46      inline istream& get(unsigned char &);
47      inline istream& get(  signed char &);
48
49      istream& get(streambuf&,char ='\n');
50      inline istream& getline(        char *,int,char ='\n');
51      inline istream& getline(unsigned char *,int,char ='\n');
52      inline istream& getline(  signed char *,int,char ='\n');
53
54      inline istream& ignore(int =1,int =EOF);
55      istream& read(char *,int);
56      inline istream& read(unsigned char *,int);
57      inline istream& read(signed char *,int);
58
59      int gcount() const { return x_gcount; }
60      int peek();
61      istream& putback(char);
62
63      istream& seekg(streampos);
64      istream& seekg(streamoff,ios::seek_dir);
65      streampos tellg();
66
67      void eatwhite();
68
69 protected:
70      istream();
71      istream(const istream&);    // treat as private
72      istream& get(char *, int, int);
73
```

393

```
 74  private:
 75      istream(ios&);
 76      int getint(char *);
 77      int getdouble(char *, int);
 78  };
 79
 80      inline istream& istream::operator>>(unsigned char * _s) {
 81                            return operator>>((char *)_s); }
 82      inline istream& istream::operator>>(  signed char * _s) {
 83                            return operator>>((char *)_s); }
 84
 85      inline istream& istream::operator>>(unsigned char & _c) {
 86                            return operator>>((char &) _c); }
 87      inline istream& istream::operator>>(  signed char & _c) {
 88                            return operator>>((char &) _c); }
 89
 90      inline istream& istream::get(         char * _b, int _lim,
 91                            char _delim) {
 92        return get(         _b, _lim, (int)(unsigned char)_delim); }
 93      inline istream& istream::get(unsigned char * _b, int _lim,
 94                            char _delim) {
 95        return get((char *)_b, _lim, (int)(unsigned char)_delim); }
 96      inline istream& istream::get(signed   char * _b, int _lim,
 97                            char _delim) {
 98        return get((char *)_b, _lim, (int)(unsigned char)_delim); }
 99
100      inline istream& istream::get(unsigned char & _c) {
101                            return get((char &) _c); }
102      inline istream& istream::get(  signed char & _c) {
103                            return get((char &) _c); }
104
105      inline istream& istream::getline(         char * _b,int _lim,
106                            char _delim) {...
107      inline istream& istream::getline(unsigned char * _b,int _lim,
108                            char _delim) {...
109      inline istream& istream::getline(  signed char * _b,int _lim,
110                            char _delim) {...
111
112      inline istream& istream::ignore(int _n,int _delim) {...
113
114      inline istream& istream::read(unsigned char * _ptr, int _n) {
115                            return read((char *) _ptr, _n); }
116      inline istream& istream::read(  signed char * _ptr, int _n) {
117                            return read((char *) _ptr, _n); }
118
119
120  class istream_withassign : public istream            {
121          public:
122              istream_withassign();
123              istream_withassign(streambuf*);
124              ~istream_withassign();
125      istream& operator=(const istream& _is) {
126                  return istream::operator=(_is); }
```

394

```
127       istream& operator=(streambuf* _isb) {
128                return istream::operator=(_isb); }
129 };
130
131 extern istream_withassign cin;
```

If you examine the actual source files provided with your compiler, you will find that there is more complexity wrapped around these definitions. But the above simplified view is sufficient to get us familiar with the streams. (The newer I/O streams are implemented as template classes. Templates are covered in chapter 12.)

Putting OOP to Use—the Double Linked List Data Structure

The subject of data structures is all about ways and means of storing and organizing data, often large volumes of data. One of these techniques is a linked list of items. A list is a data structure that is accessed sequentially. The first item in the list is located at the **head** of the list, while the last item in the list is located at the **tail**. Each item in the list points to the next item in the list by some means. These are known as **single linked lists**. In other lists, each item also points to the previous item in the list. These are known as **double linked lists.** There usually is no arbitrary maximum number of items in a list.

Each item in the list is called a **node**. A node contains the client's data in some manner and the physical linking mechanism forward to the next node in the list and is known as **chaining**. Figure 10.1 shows the general nature of a single linked list.

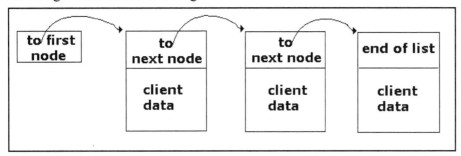

Figure 10.1 General Single Linked List

A way to find the first node in the list must always exist. A number of mechanisms are available for tracking the next node. Likewise there are different ways that the client's data can be stored. I focus solely on using pointers to handle the "to next node" situation and use dynamic memory allocation to create the nodes. This specific choice does not introduce an arbitrary upper limit to the number of nodes in the list and makes the list very flexible and extensible.

Typical implementations of a list data structure maintain a pointer, often called **headptr**, that points to the first node in the list. Each node in the list contains a pointer, often called **fwdptr**, that points to the next node in the list. When a node's **fwdptr** is 0, there are no further items in the list. Figure 10.2 illustrates the pointer mechanism for chaining.

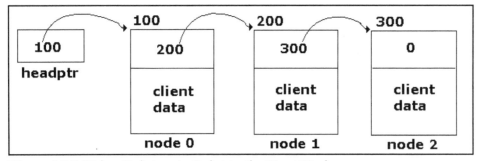

Figure 10.2 Using Pointers to Point to the Next Node

In order to iterate sequentially through a list, the list data structure must maintain a pointer to the current node in the list, for example, called **currentptr**. This current node in the list pointer is called a **cursor**, something that marks a current location. The cursor can also be called an **iterator** in the literature.

The single linked list provides basic support for simple lists of items. Each node in the list contained a forward pointer to the next node in the list. Thus, one can traverse the list in the forward direction, beginning with the first node that is pointed to by the head of the list pointer. However, there is no way to easily traverse in the reverse direction; that is, to get the previous node to the current one.

A **double linked list** contains both a forward and a back pointer. Any node then points both forward to the next node in the list and points backwards to the previous node in the list. When either of these pointers are null or 0, such indicates that there is no previous or no next node. We are either at the beginning of the list or the end.

The class that implements a double linked list would have both a head pointer as well as a tail pointer that points to the last node in the list. The current pointer member can be used to traverse the list in either direction. This general situation is shown in Figure 10.3.

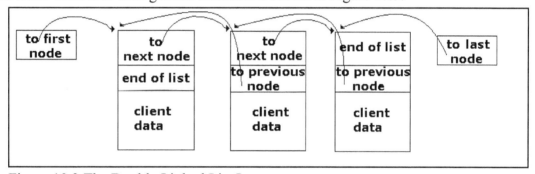

Figure 10.3 The Double Linked List Layout

Designing a Double Linked List Class

The data members of a double linked list class are obvious. Such a class would have a head pointer, a tail pointer and a current node pointer for iteration purposes. These pointers are of the data type of the "node." The class could also maintain a count of the number of nodes in the list for convenience. However, specification of the client's data that is to be stored in a node is the variable factor. Let's begin by exploring some possibilities for storing that client's data in the node.

Methods of Storing the Client Data in a Node

The client program's data could be anything. In a list that contains numbers, the data could be an int. Often, the client's data consists of a structure of data or even class instances. First, let's examine how we can store the client's data as a **Student** structure.

Method A. Storing a Copy of the Client's Data in the Node

Here is the first approach that can be used. The client's data is stored in either a structure or class instance, here called **Student**.

```
struct Student {   // or class Student {
    ...
};
```

The **LinkNode** definition that defines the nodes can be either a structure or a class. Since the **LinkNode** has no member functions, it is more often just a structure. Notice the instance of the client's data within the **LinkNode**.

```
struct LinkNode {
    LinkNode* fwdptr;
    LinkNode* backptr;
    Student s;
};
```
or
```
class  LinkNode {
public:
    LinkNode* fwdptr;
    LinkNode* backptr;
    Student s;
};
```

The benefits of hardwiring the link node to the client's data is that many client-specific functions can be provided by the **LinkedList** class itself. Since **LinkedList** class knows all about the client's data, functions to find or match on a specific field, such as student id, can be included. Other functions, such as load the list from a file, write the list to a file, display the contents of the list—all can be provided by the **LinkedList** class itself. Very specific functions can be included, such as **DeleteStudentWithIdNumber()**. This can occur because the **LinkedList** class is completely aware of what the client's data actually is. In other words, we can move a good deal of list-processing complexity from the client program into the **LinkedList** class. This results in smaller, easier to maintain client programs. Additionally, lists can easily be copied, unless there are dynamically allocated memory items within the **Student** structure or **Student** class itself.

Since we are storing copies of the client's data, there is no need for the client to dynamically allocate **Student** instances to pass into the **LinkedList** class to store. Thus, there are no clean up activities that the client programs must perform.

Are there any penalties or drawbacks of this method? Consider for a moment the memory requirements of a larger client data structure. Suppose that it had two dozen fields that occupied nearly 4k of memory. Each node would then be over 4k in size! Worse still, consider the impact at runtime for the compiler to make all the necessary copy structure operations. This penalty of size and runtime speed is a serious one indeed on larger client data structures and lengthy lists.

What about reusability of the **LinkedList** class when written using this method? There is none! If another application needed to store a list of boats, the entire class would have to be rewritten and then debugged. The next method handles the performance penalty but not the reusability issue.

Method B. Storing a Pointer to the Client's Data in the Node

To reduce any memory and speed of execution penalties, the **LinkNode** can store a pointer to the client's data instead. We change the structure or class as follows.

```
struct LinkNode {
    LinkNode* fwdptr;
    LinkNode* backptr;
    Student*  dataptr;
};
```

How many bytes does this structure occupy independently of however large the **Student** structure actually is? **LinkNode** consists of three pointers which are each four bytes in size. Each node occupies twelve bytes. How fast can the assignment of the client's data be done? All that **LinkedList** must do is copy a pointer. Thus, any speed and memory requirements are removed, from the viewpoint of the **LinkedList** class proper.

This method retains all of the benefits of Method A in which specific functions to assist client programs can be included as part of the class itself. This is because the **LinkedList** class still knows all about the client's data, **Student** in this case. We can still provide an easy copy list operation duplicating each node by dynamically allocating new instances of the **Student** structure or class and copying the data from the pointer to the old list structure.

However, by storing pointers to the client's data in the nodes, we have introduced an additional complexity level for all client programs. The client program must now dynamically allocate instances of the data and pass a pointer to this memory instance to the **LinkedList** class to be stored in the nodes. However, since we know the data type of these pointers, we can provide for their removal when **EmptyList()** or the destructor is called. We can specifically call the **delete** function for each **dataptr** in each node. Hence, forcing client programs to dynamically allocate each data instance is not too terrible a price to pay in the client programs.

Of course, this method does nothing to address the reusability factor. Both Method A and B are closely tied to the client's data and are not reusable without a total rewrite.

Method C. Storing a void Pointer to the Client's Data in the Node

To reduce any memory and speed of execution penalties as well as to make a reusable double linked list class, the **LinkNode** can store a **void** pointer to the client's data instead. We change the structure or class as follows.

```
struct LinkNode {
    LinkNode* fwdptr;
    LinkNode* backptr;
    void*     dataptr;
};
```

Once again, the **LinkNode** structure consists of three pointers which are each four bytes in size. Any speed and memory requirements are once again removed, from the viewpoint of the **LinkedList** class proper.

By storing **void** pointers to the client's data, we have removed all dependencies upon client data. Thus, we can write a single implementation of the double linked list that can be used to store any kind of client data. This is the approach the **Pgm10a** follows. I am a firm believer in writing code once and then being able to just plug it into another application, as is with no changes.

Once more, by storing **void** pointers to the client's data, we are normally forcing the client program to dynamically allocate instances of their data to be stored in the list. However, now we no longer know the data type of the client's data. And this factor does indeed impact the client programming significantly. Let's see how.

One of the more significant results of using **void** pointers is that the linked list class can no longer be responsible for the deletion of the client's data portions whenever **EmptyList()** or the destructor is called. All that the linked list class can do is delete the **LinkNode** instances. Thus, it becomes the full responsibility of the client program to traverse the list and delete all of the client's data **before** the client program calls **EmptyList()** or a linked list destructor!

There is another major impact on client programs. When copying lists either by use of the copy constructor or the assignment operator, a deep copy cannot be performed. The linked list class can only make duplicate copies of the **LinkNode** instances. Each of these new copies will contain the original client's data pointers. There is no way we can make duplicate copies of the actual client's data in the list. This is generally not a serious problem as long as the client program is aware of this side effect.

Thus, by placing a bit more of the burden on the client programs, we are able to write a reusable double linked list class. There are other methods of writing a linked list class. One of these is to use a template class. Templates are covered in chapter 12 and there we will revisit this same problem and see how the link list could be written using a template class. I would point out that such a template container class could store specific instances of the client's data in the nodes. This approach allows for tight coupling with client data while still having a reusable class.

Method D. Storing a Pointer to a Common Base Class from which the Client's Data Is Derived

With **void** pointers, we lose all capacity to find or locate specific instances of client data within the list. This forces us to make the client provide call back functions to assist us in finding specific instances within the list. That is a high price to pay. OOP to the rescue.

Suppose that we forced all client data to be class instances that are derived from some abstract base class. We can then store a pointer to this base class in the node. This abstract base class can then provide the basic functionality we desire for finding and locating specific instances. If we are going to make this requirement, then we must minimize the contents of this common base class so that virtually any client class could be derived from it without seriously impacting the client's design.

This **BaseObj** class then only contains two pure virtual functions to assist us in finding items in the list.

```cpp
class BaseObj {

public:
  virtual bool MatchObject (const void* ptrtarget) const = 0;
  virtual int  operator== (const void* ptrtarget) const = 0;
  virtual ~BaseObj () {}
};
```

Thus, this approach removes many of the inherent problems associated with storing a **void** pointer to the client's data.

Next, let's examine two ways the double linked list class can be designed. The first approach is to use Method C, storing **void** pointers to the client's data. The second approach is to use Method D, storing pointers to a base class **BaseObj**.

Designing the Double Linked List Class Storing void Pointers

The actual **LinkNode** structure comes from Method C above and is repeated here.

```cpp
struct LinkNode {
    LinkNode* fwdptr;
    LinkNode* backptr;
    void*     dataptr;
};
```

The four private data members are as follows.

```cpp
 LinkNode* headptr;       // points to first node in list
 LinkNode* currentptr;    // points to the current node
 LinkNode* tailptr;       // points to last node in list
 long      count;         // the number of nodes in list
```

The class should have a constructor and destructor, the latter of which calls the usual **EmptyList()** function which could also be called by client programs. What kinds of add new node functions are needed? Because the list has both a head and a tail pointer, additions can be made at both locations; these are called **AddAtHead()** and **AddAtTail()**. With the current pointer marking the current node in the list, the user may wish to add either before or after this specific node. This is often the case when they wish to maintain a sorted list. We have then another pair of functions: **InsertAfterCurrentNode()** and **InsertBeforeCurrentNode()**.

We should also provide a means of deleting the current node, **DeleteCurrentNode()**. We can add some convenience functions such as **GetSize()**, which returns the number of items in the list, **IsHead()**, which returns **true** if the current pointer is pointing to the first item in the list, and **IsTail()**, which returns **true** if the current pointer is pointing to the last item in the list.

What iterator functions are required for list traversal? They include **ResetToHead()**, **ResetToTail()**, **Next()**, **Previous()** and **GetCurrentNode()**. Thus, a client program can move both forward and backwards through the list.

Providing a Find Matching List Item Function

Look over the functionality that the linked list class provides. Is anything missing? Well, yes, as a matter of fact, there is something missing. How would a client program find a specific item in the list? Suppose that the list contained instances of a **Student** structure. How could a client program find the student whose id number was 123456789? As the class design currently stands, the client program would have to manually iterate sequentially through the list from either end looking for a matching id number in the list.

Can we provide a **FindNode()** function to assist client programs in locating a specific item? Yes, however, this single function poses a major problem in design. Certainly, we can iterate sequentially through the list, setting **currentptr** as we go along. But how do we compare the current node's user data with the user's matching criteria when we know nothing about the client's data? In fact, we cannot. Instead, we must rely on the user to notify our **FindNode()** function if a specific node matches their criteria. The user criteria can be anything so **FindNode()** must accept that criteria using a constant **void** pointer. The user can typecast it back into the actual matching criteria data type. For each node in the list, we must call a function back in the client program and give it the current user data and the criteria in use on this search. This is known as a **call back function** because our function (which is viewed as "system" coding by the client program) must repeatedly call a function back in the client program to perform the actual comparison list item by list item. This process is diagramed in Figure 10.4 below.

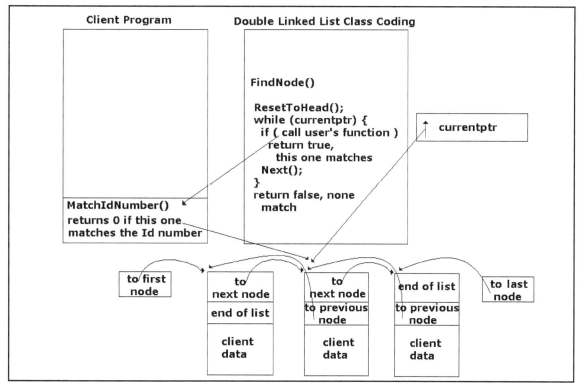

Figure 10.4 The Callback Function Process

403

What would the user call back function prototype be? It is given two constant **void** pointers, the pointer to the specific criteria for matching and the pointer current node's item. For example, suppose that the client program needed to match on student id numbers. They would have coded the function **MatchOnId()**.

```
int MatchOnId (const void* ptrmatchData,
               const void* ptrthis);
```

On the other hand, suppose the client program wanted to match on the student's name. The matching function prototype is

```
int MatchOnName (const void* ptrmatchData,
                 const void* ptrthis);
```

Sample client coding to perform these actions might be as follows.
```
long idToFind;
char nameToFind[NAMELEN];
...
if (roster.FindNode (&idToFind, MatchOnId)) {
...
if (roster.FindNode (&nameToFind, MatchOnName) {
...
```
Notice how the client must pass the address of the matching data item as the first parameter. However, it is the second parameter that causes the complexity. The client must pass into our **FindNode()** function the function for us to actually use.

This raises a most interesting question. What is the data type of the name of a function? We need this information to code our own prototype for **FindNode()**. The data type of the name of a function is a pointer to a function that has the same prototype. In the following prototype of the matching function, the parentheses around the * are required.
```
int (*FINDFUNCT) (const void* ptrmatchData, const void* ptrthis);
```
This reads, **FINDFUNCT** is a pointer to a function that returns an **int** and is passed two constant **void** pointers. If the parentheses (*) are omitted as in this next one,
```
int *OOPS (const void* ptrmatchData, const void* ptrthis);
```
This says that **OOPS** is a function that returns a pointer to an **int**!

Okay. Then how do we code our **FindNode()** prototype. The easiest way is to use the **typedef** statement to define **FINDFUNCT** as a new kind of data, one that is a pointer to a function that returns an **int** and is passed two constant **void** pointers.
```
typedef int (*FINDFUNCT) (const void* ptrmatchData,
                          const void* ptrthis);
```
Then, the **FindNode()** prototype in our class is simply
```
bool  FindNode (const void* ptrmatchData, FINDFUNCT Find);
```
Within **FindNode()**, how do we actually call the passed function pointer, **Find()**?

Okay. Now how do we actually call this passed function pointed to by parameter **Find**? Normally, to get to the value pointed to by a pointer, we dereference the pointer; again the parentheses are required.
```
(*Find) (x, y); // the hard way to invoke the Find function
```

If we had coded it as
```
*Find (x, y); // error
```
The dereference operator is applied to the return value of the **Find()** function, a **bool** in this case, causing a compile-time error.

But wait a minute. All names of all functions in C/C++ are pointers to the coding that they represent. We never do the following.
```
x = (*sqrt (z));
y = (*sin (angle));
```
The compiler automatically performs function pointer dereference for us. Thus, we can call the passed **Find()** function by coding just this.
```
Find (x, y); // the easy way to invoke the Find function
```

In reality, by having the **typedef** for the call back function, the **FindNode()** function is easily implemented. Here is the shell of our generic **DoubleLinkedList** class showing the implementation of **FindNode()**.
```
typedef int (*FINDFUNCT) (const void* ptrmatchData,
                          const void* ptrthis);
class DoubleLinkedList {
 bool  FindNode (const void* ptrmatchData, FINDFUNCT Find);
...
bool  DoubleLinkedList::FindNode (const void* ptrmatchData,
                                  FINDFUNCT Find) {
 if (!count)      // is the list is empty
  return false;   // yes, so leave doing nothing with no match
 ResetToHead (); // begin at the first node in the list
 while (currentptr) { // for each node, see if it matches
  if (Find (ptrmatchData, currentptr->dataptr) == 0)
   return true; // yes, this one matches, return true to caller
  Next ();       // move to the next item in the list
 }
 return false;  // here no item matched the user's criteria
}
```

Handling the Insertions into the List

Now let's examine how items are added to the list with the four functions. The functions **AddAtHead()** and **AddAtTail()** are the simpler ones to implement because we are always at one end of the list, never in the middle. Adding at the head of the list presents only two circumstances—either the list is empty or there are one or more items already in the list. Figures 10.5 and 10.6 illustrates what must be done to insert a new node at the head. For both cases, allocate a new node and fill it as shown.

```
LinkNode* ptrnew = new LinkNode;
ptrnew->dataptr = ptrdata;  // copy the passed client pointer
ptrnew->backptr = 0;        // back pointer is 0 because at head
count++;                    // increment total number of nodes
```

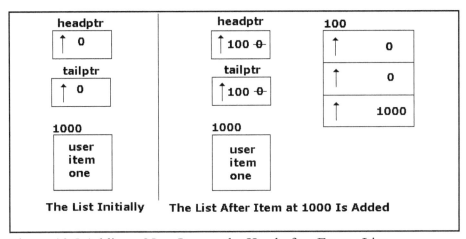

Figure 10.5 Adding a New Item at the Head of an Empty List

For an empty list, we just set the head and tail pointers to the new node.
```
headptr = tailptr = ptrnew; // this new node
ptrnew->fwdptr = 0;         // and no forward nodes yet
```

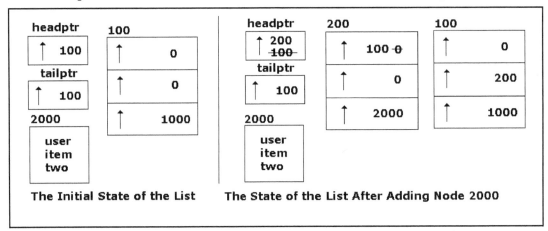

Figure 10.6 Adding a New Item at the Head with Items Already in the List

If there are items in the list, we must set the new node's forward pointer to the previous node that was at the front of the list. We must also set the previous first node's back pointer to point to the new first node. And **headptr** now stores the new node's address.

```
ptrnew->fwdptr = headptr; // fwdptr contains the previous one
headptr->backptr = ptrnew;// prev node's backptr is us now
headptr = ptrnew;         // set headptr to newly added node
```

When adding at the tail, once again, two cases arise: an empty list and a list with items in it. The situation of an empty list is the same as it is with adding at the head when the list is empty. When there are items in the list, adding at the tail is shown in Figure 10.7.

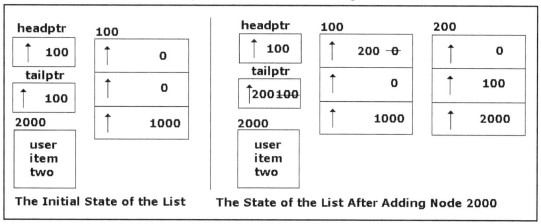

Figure 10.7 Adding a Node at the Tail of the List When There Are Items in the List

The current last node's forward pointer must now point to the new one being added at the tail. The new one being added must have its backwards pointer pointing to the previous last node. And the **tailptr** is updated to point to the new one being added at the tail.

```
tailptr->fwdptr = ptrnew; // yes, prev tail node points to us
ptrnew->backptr = tailptr;// us points back to the prev node
tailptr = ptrnew;         // tail is now us
```

Handling the insertion either before or after the current node raises additional complexities because a node could exist on either side of the insertion point. If the list is empty, **headptr** is 0, then reuse the **AddAtHead()** function. If the current pointer is 0, then I chose to also call **AddAtHead()**. However, one could signal an insertion error in this case if you so desire or even add at the tail. That leaves two remaining possibilities.

If we are inserting after the current node, then there must be a previous node from the viewpoint of this new one we are adding. If the current pointer is actually the last node in the list, then in effect we are adding at the tail and I chose to simple call **AddAtTail()** to carry out the insertion. That leaves only the one remaining possibility, we are inserting between two nodes. Figure 10.8 shows this more complicated case. Notice carefully how the forward and back chains on the list must be broken as the new node is inserted in between them. The code begins by allocating a new node and storing the user's data pointer and incrementing the count of the number of items in the list.

```
LinkNode* ptrnew = new LinkNode;
```

```
ptrnew->dataptr = ptrdata;
count++;
```

The new node must point forward to the node on the right and back to the node on the left of it. The node to its left must point forward to this new node while the node to its right must point back to the new node.

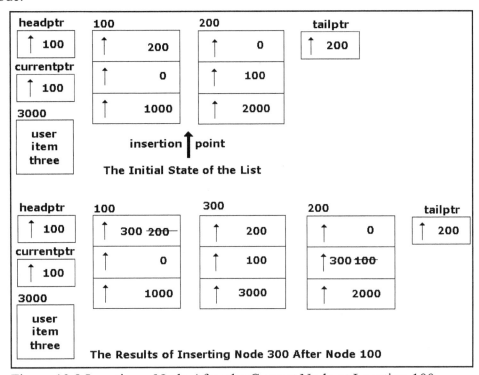

Figure 10.8 Inserting a Node After the Current Node at Location 100

The first two assignments are easy. Remember that **currentptr** is pointing to the node just before the new node.

```
ptrnew->backptr = currentptr;
ptrnew->fwdptr = currentptr->fwdptr;
```

The next two lines break the existing chain, inserting the new node into the chain.

```
currentptr->fwdptr = ptrnew;
ptrnew->fwdptr->backptr = ptrnew;
currentptr = ptrnew;
```

The insert before the current node is handled in a similar fashion. If the list is empty or the current pointer is 0, I call **AddAtHead()** to insert the new node. This leaves two remaining cases to handle. Since we are inserting before the current node, then there will always be a node to the new node's right. But if the current node is actually the first node, then there is no node to its left and we are in effect adding at the head once again. The coding begins the same way as before. Allocate a new node, copy the user's pointer and increment the number of items in the list.

```
LinkNode* ptrnew = new LinkNode;
ptrnew->dataptr = ptrdata;
count++;
```

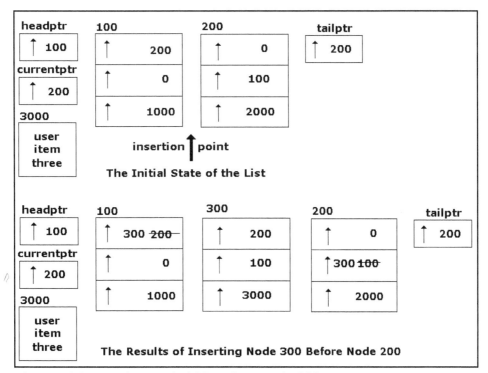

Figure 10.9 Inserting Node 300 Before Node 200

The new node's forward pointer is set to **currentptr** while the new node's back pointer is set to the current node's back pointer. This is shown in Figure 10.9.

```
ptrnew->backptr = currentptr->backptr;
ptrnew->fwdptr = currentptr;
```

Then, the current pointer's back pointer must be set to point to the new node. And the previous node's forward pointer must now point to the new node.

```
currentptr->backptr = ptrnew;
ptrnew->backptr->fwdptr = ptrnew;
currentptr = ptrnew;
```

Deleting the Current Node

When we wish to delete the current node, five situations arise. If the current node is 0, then there is nothing to do. The function should return **false** to alert the client program. Next, suppose that there is only one node in the list which is the current one to delete. This case is easy, we simply delete the node and reset all pointers and the count to 0. The remaining three cases deal with the location of the current node to delete in the list. The current node to delete could be the first node or the last node or one in the middle. Let's examine each of these three remaining cases in detail beginning with the node to delete being the first node in the list. Figure 10.10 illustrates the deletion process for the first node in the list.

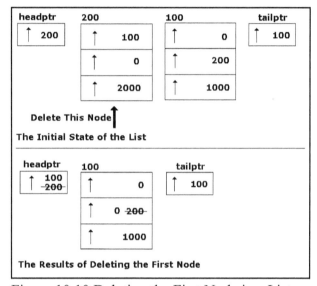

Figure 10.10 Deleting the First Node in a List

To delete the first node in the list, we must set the next node's back pointer to 0 and the **headptr** to the next node in order to remove the first node from the chain.

```
LinkNode* ptrtodelete = currentptr;
if (IsHead()) {                          // deleting first node? if so,
  currentptr->fwdptr->backptr = 0;// set next node's back to none
  headptr = currentptr->fwdptr;   // set head to next node
  currentptr = headptr;           // and current to next node
}
```

Next, suppose we are deleting the last node in the list. Figure 10.11 shows the situation. We must set the previous node's forward pointer to 0 and reset the tail pointer to that one.

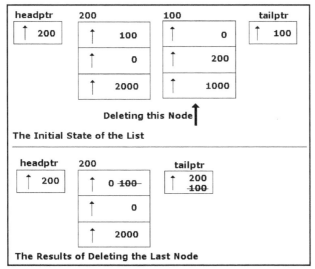

Figure 10.11 Deleting the Last Node in a List

```
else if (IsTail()) {                 // deleting last one, if so,
 currentptr->backptr->fwdptr = 0;// set prev node's fwd to none
 tailptr = currentptr->backptr;  // set tail to prev node
 currentptr = tailptr;           // set current to prev node
}
```

The final situation is deleting a node that is in the middle with a node on either side. Figure 10.12 illustrates how the chain of pointers must be adjusted to remove a middle node.

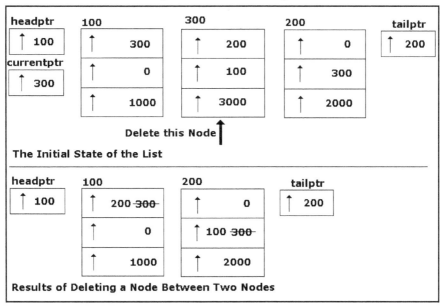

Figure 10.12 Deleting a Node from the Middle of the List

411

Examine the following two key coding lines and compare them to the above figure. Make sure you understand how the node at 300 is removed from the forward and back chains.

```
else { // here the node to delete is in the middle
  // set next node's back to previous node
  currentptr->fwdptr->backptr = currentptr->backptr;
  // set previous node's fwd to next node
  currentptr->backptr->fwdptr = currentptr->fwdptr;
  // leave current pointing to previous node
  currentptr = currentptr->backptr;
}
delete ptrtodelete; // now delete the requested node
return true;
```

The Generic DoubleLinkedList Class Storing void Pointers

Here is the header file for our generic **DoubleLinkedList** class. Notice that I placed numerous comments and some coding samples for the users in the header file.

```
Double Linked List Class Definition

 1 #pragma once
 2 #include <iostream>
 3 using namespace std;
 4
 5 /*****************************************************/
 6 /*                                                   */
 7 /* DoubleLinkedList Class: a reusable double linked list */
 8 /*                                                   */
 9 /*****************************************************/
10
11 // LinkNode: the link list node structure
12 struct LinkNode {
13   LinkNode* fwdptr;  // points to the next node in the list
14   LinkNode* backptr; // points to the previous node
15   void*     dataptr; // points to the client data stored
16 };
17
18 typedef int (*FINDFUNCT) (const void* ptrmatchData,
19                           const void* ptrthis);
20
21 class DoubleLinkedList {
22
23 private:
24   LinkNode* headptr;     // points to first node in list
25   LinkNode* currentptr;  // points to the current node
26   LinkNode* tailptr;     // points to last node in list
27   long      count;       // the number of nodes in list
28
29 public:
```

```
30          // constructs an empty list
31          DoubleLinkedList ();
32
33          // deletes the list but not the user's items stored
34        ~DoubleLinkedList ();
35
36          // removes all nodes, but not the user's items stored
37   void   EmptyList ();
38   /* Note: client program must ensure that all client data are
39    deleted before calling EmptyList() or the destructor
40    Example: suppose the list contains CostRec structures
41    list.ResetToHead();
42    CostRec* ptrdata = (CostRec*) list.GetCurrentNode();
43    while (ptrdata) {
44     delete ptrdata;
45     list.Next();
46     ptrdata = (CostRec*) list.GetCurrentNode();
47    }
48    list.EmptyList();*/
49
50          // add user's data at the head
51   void   AddAtHead (void* ptrdata);
52
53          // add user's data at the tail
54   void   AddAtTail (void* ptrdata); // add node at the tail
55
56          // add it after the current node - if current node is 0,
57          // it is added at the head
58   void   InsertAfterCurrentNode (void* ptrdata);
59
60          // add it before the current node - if the current
61          // node is 0, it is added at the head
62   void   InsertBeforeCurrentNode (void* ptrdata);
63
64          // deletes the current node, but not the user's data
65          // returns false if there is no current node
66   bool   DeleteCurrentNode ();
67
68          // sets the current pointer to the node whose data matches
69          // the matching criteria set by the caller
70   bool   FindNode (const void* ptrmatchData, FINDFUNCT Find);
71   /* example of usage. Suppose that user data are double pointers
72    client's prototype is:
73     int MatchDbl(const void* ptrmatchData, const void* ptrthis);
74    double findThis = 2;
75    if (test.FindNode (&findThis, MatchDbl)) {
76     double* ptrMatched = (double*) test.GetCurrentNode();
77     cout << "Found: " << *ptrMatched << " should find 2\n";
78    }
79    and the user's function is coded:
80    int MatchDbl (const void* ptrmatchData, const void* ptrthis){
81     double* ptrMatchThisOne = (double*) ptrmatchData;
82     double* ptrQuery = (double*) ptrthis;
```

413

```
83      if (*ptrQuery == *ptrMatchThisOne) return 0;
84      if (*ptrQuery > *ptrMatchThisOne) return -1;
85      return +1;
86    } */
87          // returns the number of items in the list
88   long  GetSize () const;
89
90          // returns true if current pointer is list at the start
91   bool  IsHead () const;
92
93          // returns true if current pointer is list at the tail
94   bool  IsTail () const;
95
96          // set current pointer to start of the list
97   void  ResetToHead ();
98
99          // set current pointer to the end of the list
100  void  ResetToTail ();
101
102           // moves current pointer to the next item
103  void  Next ();
104
105          // moves current pointer to the previous item
106  void  Previous ();
107
108          // returns user data stored in the current node, 0 if none
109  void* GetCurrentNode () const;
110
111  // makes a copy of this list, but not the user's data stored
112  DoubleLinkedList (const DoubleLinkedList& r);
113
114      // makes a copy of this list, but not the user's data stored
115  DoubleLinkedList& operator= (const DoubleLinkedList& r);
116
117  protected:
118   // duplicates the list
119   void  CopyList (const DoubleLinkedList& r);
120  };
121
```

Here is the actual implementation. The major coding has already been discussed. You should look over the smaller functions as well as the more complex ones.

```
Double Linked List Class Implementation

1 #include <iomanip>
2 using namespace std;
3 #include "DoubleLinkedList.h"
4
5 /********************************************************/
6 /*                                                    */
```

```
 7 /* DoubleLinkedList: constructs an empty list              */
 8 /*                                                          */
 9 /************************************************************/
10
11 DoubleLinkedList::DoubleLinkedList () {
12  headptr = tailptr = currentptr = 0;
13  count = 0;
14 }
15
16 /************************************************************/
17 /*                                                          */
18 /* ~DoubleLinkedList: destructor to remove all nodes        */
19 /*                                                          */
20 /************************************************************/
21
22 DoubleLinkedList::~DoubleLinkedList () {
23  EmptyList ();
24 }
25
26 /************************************************************/
27 /*                                                          */
28 /* EmptyList: remove all nodes from the list                */
29 /*                                                          */
30 /************************************************************/
31
32 void  DoubleLinkedList::EmptyList () {
33  if (!headptr) return;
34  LinkNode* ptrnext = headptr; // pointer to traverse the list
35  LinkNode* ptrdel;            // the node to delete
36  // traverse the list - ends when there are no more nodes
37  while (ptrnext) {
38   ptrdel = ptrnext;        // save the current one to be deleted
39   ptrnext = ptrnext->fwdptr;// point to the next node
40   delete ptrdel;           // and delete the previous node
41  }
42  headptr = currentptr = tailptr = 0;
43  count = 0;
44 }
45
46 /************************************************************/
47 /*                                                          */
48 /* AddAtHead: insert new node at the beginning of list      */
49 /*                                                          */
50 /************************************************************/
51
52 void  DoubleLinkedList::AddAtHead (void* ptrdata) {
53  // allocate a new node and fill it up
54  LinkNode* ptrnew = new (std::nothrow) LinkNode;
55  if (!ptrnew) {
56   cerr << "DoubleLinkedList::AddAtHead - out of memory\n";
57   exit (1);
58  }
59  ptrnew->dataptr = ptrdata; // copy the passed client pointer
```

415

```
 60   ptrnew->backptr = 0;        // back pointer is 0 because at head
 61   count++;                    // increment total number of nodes
 62   // now chain this one into the list
 63   if (headptr) {              // if headptr exists, then the new
 64    ptrnew->fwdptr = headptr; // fwdptr contains the previous one
 65    headptr->backptr = ptrnew;// prev node's backptr is us now
 66    headptr = ptrnew;         // set headptr to newly added node
 67   }
 68   else {                      // empty list, so all ptrs point to
 69    headptr = tailptr = ptrnew; // this new node
 70    ptrnew->fwdptr = 0;       // and no forward nodes yet
 71   }
 72   currentptr = ptrnew; // leave the current one at the new one
 73  }
 74
 75  /****************************************************************/
 76  /*                                                            */
 77  /* AddAtTail: insert new node at the end of the list      */
 78  /*                                                            */
 79  /****************************************************************/
 80
 81  void  DoubleLinkedList::AddAtTail (void* ptrdata) {
 82   LinkNode* ptrnew = new (std::nothrow) LinkNode;
 83   if (!ptrnew) {
 84    cerr << "DoubleLinkedList::AddAtTail - out of memory\n";
 85    exit (1);
 86   }
 87   count++;                    // increment total number of nodes
 88   ptrnew->dataptr = ptrdata; // store the client pointer in node
 89   ptrnew->fwdptr = 0;        // at end, cannot be forward node
 90   if (tailptr) {              // is there anything in the list yet?
 91    tailptr->fwdptr = ptrnew; // yes, prev tail node points to us
 92    ptrnew->backptr = tailptr;// us points back to the prev node
 93    tailptr = ptrnew;         // tail is now us
 94   }
 95   else {                      // no - list is empty,
 96    headptr = tailptr = ptrnew; // so set all to point to us
 97    ptrnew->backptr = 0;      // and there is no prev node
 98   }
 99   currentptr = ptrnew;       // leave with current node set to us
100  }
101
102  /****************************************************************/
103  /*                                                            */
104  /* InsertAfterCurrentNode: add new node after the        */
105  /*                      current node                        */
106  /*                                                            */
107  /****************************************************************/
108
109  void  DoubleLinkedList::InsertAfterCurrentNode (void* ptrdata) {
110   if (!headptr)            // list is empty so add at head
111    AddAtHead (ptrdata);
112   else if (!currentptr) // current ptr is 0, so also add at head
```

```
113   AddAtHead (ptrdata);
114  else if (IsTail())     // current ptr is the last node, so
115   AddAtTail (ptrdata); // reuse add at the tail
116  else {                 // here we are inserting in the middle
117   LinkNode* ptrnew = new (std::nothrow) LinkNode;
118   if (!ptrnew) {
119    cerr << "DoubleLinkedList::InsertAfterCurrentNode -"
120         << "out of memory\n";
121    exit (1);
122   }
123   ptrnew->dataptr = ptrdata;
124   count++;
125   // set new node's back pointer to current node to insert us
126   ptrnew->backptr = currentptr;
127   // set new node's forward ptr to the next node to the right
128   ptrnew->fwdptr = currentptr->fwdptr;
129   // set current's forward ptr to us to insert us
130   currentptr->fwdptr = ptrnew;
131   // set the node to the right of us to point back to us
132   ptrnew->fwdptr->backptr = ptrnew;
133   currentptr = ptrnew; // make the newly added node the current
134  }
135 }
136
137 /************************************************************/
138 /*                                                          */
139 /* InsertBeforeCurrentNode: add new node before current   */
140 /*      node.                                               */
141 /*                                                          */
142 /************************************************************/
143
144 void  DoubleLinkedList::InsertBeforeCurrentNode (void* ptrdata) {
145  if (!headptr)          // no nodes in list - so add at head
146   AddAtHead (ptrdata);
147  else if (!currentptr)// no current ptr, so add at head too
148   AddAtHead (ptrdata);
149  else if (IsHead())    // current ptr is the last node - so
150   AddAtHead(ptrdata); // add this one at the tail
151  else {                 // here we are adding in the middle of list
152   LinkNode* ptrnew = new (std::nothrow) LinkNode;
153   if (!ptrnew) {
154    cerr << "DoubleLinkedList::InsertBeforeCurrentNode -"
155         << "out of memory\n";
156    exit (1);
157   }
158   ptrnew->dataptr = ptrdata;
159   count++;
160   // set new node's back ptr to pcurrents back
161   ptrnew->backptr = currentptr->backptr;
162   // set new node's forward ptr to current node
163   ptrnew->fwdptr = currentptr;
164   // set current node's back ptr to point to us
165   currentptr->backptr = ptrnew;
```

```
166    // set prevous node's forward ptr to point to us
167    ptrnew->backptr->fwdptr = ptrnew;
168    currentptr = ptrnew; // set current pointer to the new node
169    }
170  }
171
172  /****************************************************************/
173  /*                                                            */
174  /* DeleteCurrentNode: removes the current node               */
175  /*     returns false if there is no current node             */
176  /*                                                            */
177  /****************************************************************/
178
179  bool  DoubleLinkedList::DeleteCurrentNode () {
180   if (!currentptr) // if no current node, abort
181    return false;
182   count--;
183   if (!count) { // will list now be empty? if so reset to 0
184    delete currentptr;
185    headptr = tailptr = currentptr = 0;
186    return true;
187   }
188   LinkNode* ptrtodelete = currentptr;
189   if (IsHead()) {                    // deleting first node? if so,
190    currentptr->fwdptr->backptr = 0;// set next node's back to none
191    headptr = currentptr->fwdptr;   // set head to next node
192    currentptr = headptr;           // and current to next node
193   }
194   else if (IsTail()) {               // deleting last one, if so,
195    currentptr->backptr->fwdptr = 0;// set prev node's fwd to none
196    tailptr = currentptr->backptr;  // set tail to prev node
197    currentptr = tailptr;           // set current to prev node
198   }
199   else { // here the node to delete is in the middle
200    // set next node's back to previous node
201    currentptr->fwdptr->backptr = currentptr->backptr;
202    // set previous node's fwd to next node
203    currentptr->backptr->fwdptr = currentptr->fwdptr;
204    // leave current pointing to previous node
205    currentptr = currentptr->backptr;
206   }
207   delete ptrtodelete; // now delete the requested node
208   return true;
209  }
210
211  /****************************************************************/
212  /*                                                            */
213  /* GetSize: returns the number of nodes in the list          */
214  /*                                                            */
215  /****************************************************************/
216
217  long  DoubleLinkedList::GetSize () const {
218   return count;
```

418

```
219 }
220
221 /*****************************************************/
222 /*                                                 */
223 /* IsHead: returns true if current node is the first node*/
224 /*                                                 */
225 /*****************************************************/
226
227 bool  DoubleLinkedList::IsHead () const {
228  return currentptr == headptr;
229 }
230
231 /*****************************************************/
232 /*                                                 */
233 /* IsTail: returns true if current node is the last one  */
234 /*                                                 */
235 /*****************************************************/
236
237 bool  DoubleLinkedList::IsTail () const {
238  return currentptr == tailptr;
239 }
240
241 /*****************************************************/
242 /*                                                 */
243 /* ResetToHead: sets current pointer to start of list  */
244 /*                                                 */
245 /*****************************************************/
246
247 void  DoubleLinkedList::ResetToHead () {
248  currentptr = headptr;
249 }
250
251 /*****************************************************/
252 /*                                                 */
253 /* ResetToTail: sets current pointer to last node in list*/
254 /*                                                 */
255 /*****************************************************/
256
257 void  DoubleLinkedList::ResetToTail () {
258  currentptr = tailptr;
259 }
260
261 /*****************************************************/
262 /*                                                 */
263 /* Next: move forward one node in the list           */
264 /*                                                 */
265 /*****************************************************/
266
267 void  DoubleLinkedList::Next () {
268  if (currentptr)
269    currentptr = currentptr->fwdptr;
270 }
271
```

```
272 /***********************************************************/
273 /*                                                         */
274 /* Previous: backs up one node in the list                 */
275 /*                                                         */
276 /***********************************************************/
277
278 void  DoubleLinkedList::Previous () {
279  if (currentptr)
280    currentptr = currentptr->backptr;
281 }
282
283 /***********************************************************/
284 /*                                                         */
285 /* GetCurrentNode: returns user data at current node or 0 */
286 /*                                                         */
287 /***********************************************************/
288
289 void* DoubleLinkedList::GetCurrentNode () const {
290  return currentptr ? currentptr->dataptr : 0;
291 }
292
293 /***********************************************************/
294 /*                                                         */
295 /* DoubleLinkedList: copy constructor - duplicate a list */
296 /*                                                         */
297 /***********************************************************/
298
299 DoubleLinkedList::DoubleLinkedList (const DoubleLinkedList& r) {
300  CopyList (r);
301 }
302
303 /***********************************************************/
304 /*                                                         */
305 /* operator=: Make a duplicate copy of a list             */
306 /*                                                         */
307 /***********************************************************/
308
309 DoubleLinkedList& DoubleLinkedList::operator= (
310                  const DoubleLinkedList& r) {
311  if (this == &r) return *this; // avoid a = a; situation
312  EmptyList ();  // remove all items in this list
313  CopyList (r);  // make a copy of r's list
314  return *this;
315 }
316
317 /***********************************************************/
318 /*                                                         */
319 /* CopyList: Make a duplicate copy of a list              */
320 /*                                                         */
321 /***********************************************************/
322
323 void  DoubleLinkedList::CopyList (const DoubleLinkedList& r) {
324    // handle the empty list first
```

```
325  if (!r.headptr) {
326   headptr = currentptr = tailptr = 0;
327   return;
328  }
329  count = r.count;
330  LinkNode* ptrRcurrent = r.headptr;
331  // previousptr tracks our prior node so we can set its
332  // forward pointer to the next new one
333  LinkNode* previousptr = 0;
334  // prime the loop so headptr can be set one time
335  currentptr = new (std::nothrow) LinkNode;
336  if (!currentptr) {
337   cerr << "DoubleLinkedList::CopyList - out of memory\n";
338   exit (1);
339  }
340  headptr = currentptr;  // assign this one to the headptr
341
342  // traverse list r's nodes
343  while (ptrRcurrent) {
344   // copy r's student info into our new node
345   currentptr->dataptr = ptrRcurrent->dataptr;
346   currentptr->fwdptr = 0;  // set our forward ptr to 0
347   currentptr->backptr = 0; // set our back ptr to 0
348   // if previous node exists, set its forward ptr to the new one
349   if (previousptr) {
350    previousptr->fwdptr = currentptr;
351    currentptr->backptr = previousptr;
352   }
353   // save this node as the prevous node
354   previousptr = currentptr;
355   // and get a new node for the next iteration
356   currentptr = new (std::nothrow) LinkNode;
357   if (!currentptr) {
358    cerr << "DoubleLinkedList::CopyList - out of memory\n";
359    exit (1);
360   }
361   // move to r's next node
362   ptrRcurrent = ptrRcurrent->fwdptr;
363  }
364  tailptr = previousptr; // save tail
365  delete currentptr; // delete the extra unneeded node
366  // leave list at the beginning
367  ResetToHead ();
368 }
369
370 /******************************************************/
371 /*                                                    */
372 /* FindNode: find the node whose data matches users   */
373 /*           specifications - calls user's Find Function */
374 /*                                                    */
375 /******************************************************/
376
377 bool  DoubleLinkedList::FindNode (const void* ptrmatchData,
```

421

```
378                                    FINDFUNCT Find) {
379  if (!count) // empty list => not found
380   return false;
381  ResetToHead ();         // begin at the start of the list
382  while (currentptr) {   // examine each node in turn
383   if (Find (ptrmatchData, currentptr->dataptr) == 0)
384    return true;          // return true if this one matches
385   Next ();               // move to the next node in the list
386  }
387  return false;           // did not find it in whole list
388 }
```

Writing Client Programs that Use the Double Linked List

With our generic class written and tested, let's turn our attention to how client programs are written using this generic list class. Now we get to deal with the client side dynamic memory allocation of items to be stored in the list.

Acme has a contract to produce an inquiry/update type of program to process telephone directory information. Initially, the directory should contain the person's first and last names, the area code and phone number. If the concept proves acceptable to their client, then the additional fields that a phone directory has will be added. The specifications call for drawing a text box graphic around the actual listing. A sample is shown below.

My Phone Directory

Record Number	First Name	Last Name	Area Code	Phone Number
1	Tom	Jones	(309)	699-9999
2	Betsy	Smith	(309)	699-4444
3	Annie	Cringle	(309)	696-4242
4	Henry	Albright II	(309)	694-5555
5	Lorri Ann	Spieldt	(309)	676-6666
6	Harry	Durch	(309)	688-4325
7	Rusty	Earls	(309)	676-5551
8	Jennifer	Smallville	(309)	688-5321

The ASCII codes to use when drawing the box are from the upper ASCII sequence and thus must be defined as **unsigned char**. Each of these displays one character, such as the upper left corner angle.

```
unsigned char upleft = 218;
unsigned char upright = 191;
unsigned char botleft = 192;
unsigned char botright = 217;
unsigned char horiz = 196;
unsigned char vert = 179;
```

```
unsigned char leftright = 195;
unsigned char rightleft = 180;
unsigned char cross = 197;
unsigned char topdown = 194;
unsigned char botup = 193;
```

The program, upon startup, loads the current test file of directory entries and displays the above report. Next, the main menu is shown as follows.

```
Friends Phone Book

1 Add new friend
2 Delete an entry
3 Display the phone listing
4 Display phone listing to a file
5 Save into a new file
6 Exit

Enter the number of your choice: 1
```

The program should only accept a valid menu choice. The entry of a non-numeric character should not halt the program but be rejected and the menu re-shown.

When "Add new friend" is chosen, the following is a sample of the conversational dialog required.

```
Enter first name (10 characters):  Jenny
Enter last name (20 characters):   Heart-Smith
Enter the area code (3 numbers):   309
Enter the phone number (999-9999): 699-7777
Addition was successful
```

When "Delete an entry" is chosen, a new problem arises. How should the user indicate which directory entry is to be deleted? Rather than asking the user to enter the person's name (first and last), the program should maintain a record number id that begins at one. Thus, when the original file is loaded, as the records are being added to the list, the program adds a consecutive numerical id to each directory record. Thus, to delete an entry, the user is prompted to enter the record number id. The conversational dialog is shown below.

```
Enter the number of the phone book entry to delete: 8
Confirm deletion of the following entry
   8   Jennifer    Smallville            (309)   688-5321

Enter Y to confirm deletion or N to abort: y

Record deleted
```

If a matching list entry matches the user's number, that directory entry is then displayed and a "confirm deletion" query is made. The only acceptable reply is Y or N; the user is re-prompted until either y or n is entered. When the deletion is made, a new problem arises with the record numbers. To avoid a "hole" in the numbers, all records that come after the deleted one in the list must be renumbered.

423

When "Display phone listing to a file" is chosen, prompt the user for the filename. However, the program should accept long filenames and filenames that contain blanks. To handle the blanks, force the user to surround the filename with double quote marks.

```
Enter the filename on which to display the report
If there are blanks in the filename,
place double quotemarks around the whole filename.
for example, "My Phone Book.txt"
"My Phone Book.txt"

Report written to: My Phone Book.txt
```

When "Save into a new file" is chosen, use a similar dialog to obtain the new filename.

```
Enter the new filename to use
If there are blanks in the filename,
place double quotemarks around the whole filename.
for example, "My Phone Book.txt"
NewPhoneBook.txt
File Saved
```

Finally, if any changes have been made to the original data, then any attempt to exit the program should force a query of the user as shown below.

```
Note: you have made changes to the phone database
and have not yet saved those changes
Do you want to quit and discard those changes?
Enter Y or N: n
```

Again, accept only y or n and re-prompt until a valid entry is made. If the user does not want to quit, re-show the main menu.

I began the solution to the problem by using Top-down design to functionally decompose the problem into functional modules. Figure 10.13 shows the design I used.

Here is the completed **Pgm10a**, Update Phone Directory program. Examine the **main()** function first to see how the instance of the list is created. Next, look over the **LoadPhoneBook()** and **EmptyPhoneBook()** functions to see how **PhoneDirectory** structures are dynamically allocated, inserted into the list and finally deleted prior to program termination to avoid memory leaks.

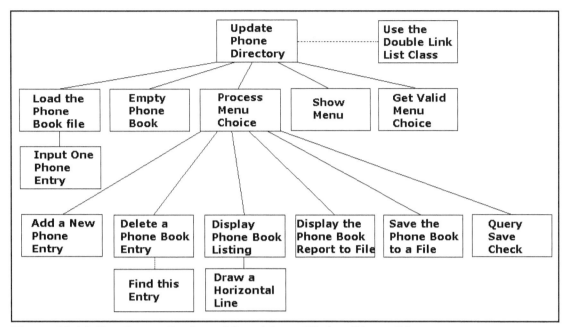

Figure 10.13 Top-Down Design of Pgm10a — Update Phone Directory

Next, examine **DeleteEntry()** and its call back function **FindEntry()** to see how entries are found and deleted from the list. If you are interested in how the box is drawn around the reports, study the function **DisplayPhoneListing()**.

```
Pgm10a - Update Phone Directory Program

 1 #include <iostream>
 2 #include <iomanip>
 3 #include <fstream>
 4 #include <string>
 5 using namespace std;
 6 #include <crtdbg.h>
 7 #include "DoubleLinkedList.h"
 8
 9 /****************************************************************/
10 /*                                                            */
11 /* Pgm10a: Maintaining a Phone Directory Application     */
12 /*                                                            */
13 /****************************************************************/
14
15 const int MAX_FNAME_LEN = 11;
16 const int MAX_LNAME_LEN = 21;
17
18 // Phone Directory Information
19 struct PhoneDirectory {
20  int  recordNumber; // these are added by the pgm for id purposes
21  char firstName[MAX_FNAME_LEN];
22  char lastName[MAX_LNAME_LEN];
23  char areaCode[4];
24  char phoneNumber[9];
```

425

```
25 };
26
27 // the prototypes
28 bool LoadPhoneBook (DoubleLinkedList& pb, const char* filename);
29 istream& InputPhoneData (istream& is, PhoneDirectory& pd);
30
31 ostream& DisplayPhoneListing (DoubleLinkedList& pb, ostream& os);
32 void DrawLine (ostream& os, unsigned char c, int count);
33 void DisplayPhoneBookToFile (DoubleLinkedList& pb);
34
35 void EmptyPhoneBook (DoubleLinkedList& pb);
36
37 void ShowMenu ();
38 int  GetMenuChoice ();
39 bool ProcessMenuChoice (DoubleLinkedList& pb, int choice,
40                         bool& needToSave, ostream& os);
41
42 void AddEntry (DoubleLinkedList& pb, bool& needToSavePb);
43 void DeleteEntry (DoubleLinkedList& pb, bool& needToSavePb);
44 int  FindEntry (const void* ptrmatchData, const void* ptrthis);
45 void SavePhoneBook (DoubleLinkedList& pb, bool& needToSavePb);
46 bool SaveCheck (DoubleLinkedList& pb, bool needToSavePb);
47
48
49 int main () {
50  {
51   DoubleLinkedList phoneBook; // create the phonebook list
52
53   // load the book from a file
54   if (!LoadPhoneBook (phoneBook, "phoneBook.txt"))
55    return 1;
56   // display the listing using fancy box drawing characters
57   DisplayPhoneListing (phoneBook, cout);
58
59   bool needToSavePb = false; // true when data has been changed
60   bool quit = false;         // true when it is safe to quit
61
62   // main loop shows a menu, gets a valid choice and process it
63   while (!quit) {
64    quit = ProcessMenuChoice (phoneBook, GetMenuChoice (),
65                              needToSavePb, cout);
66   }
67
68   // remove all items from list
69   EmptyPhoneBook (phoneBook);
70  }
71
72  if (_CrtDumpMemoryLeaks ())
73   cout << "\nOops! Memory Leaks!!\n";
74  else
75   cout << "\nNo Memory Leaks\n";
76
77  return 0;
```

```
 78 }
 79
 80 /**********************************************************/
 81 /*                                                        */
 82 /* LoadPhoneBook: loads the list from a database file     */
 83 /*                                                        */
 84 /**********************************************************/
 85
 86 bool LoadPhoneBook (DoubleLinkedList& pb, const char* filename) {
 87  ifstream infile (filename);
 88  if (!infile) {
 89   cerr << "Error: unable to open file: " << filename << endl;
 90   return false;
 91  }
 92
 93  int i = 1; // this will be the record id number value
 94
 95  // allocate a new phone directory structure
 96  PhoneDirectory* ptrpd = new PhoneDirectory;
 97
 98  // for each set of input data, insert the id number, add to list
 99  // and allocate another phone directory structure for the next
100  // input opperation
101  while (InputPhoneData (infile, *ptrpd)) {
102   ptrpd->recordNumber = i++;
103   pb.AddAtTail (ptrpd);
104   ptrpd = new PhoneDirectory;
105  }
106
107  delete ptrpd;   // delete the unneeded structure - eof was found
108  infile.close ();
109  return true;
110 }
111
112 /**********************************************************/
113 /*                                                        */
114 /* InputPhoneData: input a single phone directory entry   */
115 /*                                                        */
116 /**********************************************************/
117
118 istream& InputPhoneData (istream& is, PhoneDirectory& pd) {
119  char c;
120  is >> c;  // input the leading " of first name
121  if (!is)
122   return is;
123  is.getline (pd.firstName, sizeof (pd.firstName), '\"');
124  is >> c; // get leading " of last name
125  is.getline (pd.lastName, sizeof (pd.lastName), '\"');
126  is >> pd.areaCode >> pd.phoneNumber;
127  return is;
128 }
129
130 /**********************************************************/
```

```
131 /*                                                      */
132 /* DisplayPhoneListing: display in a fancy fashion the   */
133 /*                   complete phone listing              */
134 /*                                                      */
135 /*****************************************************/
136
137 ostream& DisplayPhoneListing (DoubleLinkedList& pb, ostream& os){
138   // the text graphics codes to draw fancy boxes
139   unsigned char upleft = 218;
140   unsigned char upright = 191;
141   unsigned char botleft = 192;
142   unsigned char botright = 217;
143   unsigned char horiz = 196;
144   unsigned char vert = 179;
145   unsigned char leftright = 195;
146   unsigned char rightleft = 180;
147   unsigned char cross = 197;
148   unsigned char topdown = 194;
149   unsigned char botup = 193;
150
151   os << "                    My Phone Directory\n\n";
152
153   // draws the top line
154   os << upleft;
155   DrawLine (os, horiz, 6);
156   os << topdown;
157   DrawLine (os, horiz, 12);
158   os << topdown;
159   DrawLine (os, horiz, 22);
160   os << topdown;
161   DrawLine (os, horiz, 7);
162   os << topdown;
163   DrawLine (os, horiz, 10);
164   os << upright << endl;
165
166   // display a pair of column heading lines
167   os << vert << "Record" << vert << " First       " << vert
168      << " Last                " << vert << " Area  "
169      << vert << " Phone    " << vert << endl;
170   os << vert << "Number" << vert << " Name        " << vert
171      << " Name               " << vert << " Code  "
172      << vert << " Number   " << vert << endl;
173
174   // display another horizontal line
175   os << leftright;
176   DrawLine (os, horiz, 6);
177   os << cross;
178   DrawLine (os, horiz, 12);
179   os << cross;
180   DrawLine (os, horiz, 22);
181   os << cross;
182   DrawLine (os, horiz, 7);
183   os << cross;
```

```
184  DrawLine (os, horiz, 10);
185  os << rightleft << endl;
186
187  // for each set of data, display all values within the boxes
188  pb.ResetToHead ();
189  PhoneDirectory* ptrpd = (PhoneDirectory*) pb.GetCurrentNode ();
190  while (ptrpd) {
191   os << vert << ' ' << setw(4) << ptrpd->recordNumber << ' '
192      << vert << ' ' << left
194      << setw(10) << ptrpd->firstName << ' ' << vert << ' '
195      << setw(20) << ptrpd->lastName << ' ' << vert << " ("
196      << setw(3) << ptrpd->areaCode << ") " << vert << ' '
197 << setw(8) << ptrpd->phoneNumber << ' ' << vert << endl << right;
199   pb.Next ();
200   ptrpd = (PhoneDirectory*) pb.GetCurrentNode ();
201  }
202
203  // display the bottom line of the box
204  os << botleft;
205  DrawLine (os, horiz, 6);
206  os << botup;
207  DrawLine (os, horiz, 12);
208  os << botup;
209  DrawLine (os, horiz, 22);
210  os << botup;
211  DrawLine (os, horiz, 7);
212  os << botup;
213  DrawLine (os, horiz, 10);
214  os << botright << endl;
215  os << endl;
216  return os;
217 }
218
219 /************************************************************/
220 /*                                                          */
221 /* DrawLine: helper function to draw a horizontal line     */
222 /*                                                          */
223 /************************************************************/
224
225 void DrawLine (ostream& os, unsigned char c, int count) {
226  // displays character c count times to the stream
227  for (int i=0; i< count; i++) {
228   os << c;
229  }
230 }
231
232 /************************************************************/
233 /*                                                          */
234 /* ShowMenu: displays the main menu of choices             */
235 /*                                                          */
236 /************************************************************/
237
238 void ShowMenu () {
```

429

```
239  cout << "\n\n"
240       << "Friends Phone Book\n\n"
241       << "1 Add new friend\n"
242       << "2 Delete an entry\n"
243       << "3 Display the phone listing\n"
244       << "4 Display phone listing to a file\n"
245       << "5 Save into a new file\n"
246       << "6 Exit\n"
247       << "\nEnter the number of your choice: ";
248  }
249
250  /***********************************************************/
251  /*                                                       */
252  /* GetMenuChoice: gets a valid menu choice               */
253  /*                                                       */
254  /***********************************************************/
255
256  int GetMenuChoice () {
257  // get only a valid number between 1 and 6
258  int choice = 7;
259  while (choice < 1 || choice > 6) {
260   ShowMenu ();
261   cin >> choice;
262   if (!cin) {      // check for non-numeric data entered
263    cin.clear (); // yes, so reset cin state flags to good
264    char c;
265    cin.get(c);   // and get the offending character
266   }
267  }
268  cout << endl;
269  return choice;  // choice is a number between 1 and 6
270  }
271
272  /***********************************************************/
273  /*                                                       */
274  /* ProcessMenuChoice: driver to process that menu choice */
275  /*                                                       */
276  /***********************************************************/
277
278  bool ProcessMenuChoice (DoubleLinkedList& pb, int choice,
279                        bool& needToSavePb, ostream& os) {
280   switch (choice) {
281    case 1:
282     AddEntry (pb, needToSavePb);
283     return false;
284    case 2:
285     DeleteEntry (pb, needToSavePb);
286     return false;
287    case 3:
288     DisplayPhoneListing (pb, os);
289     return false;
290    case 4:
291     DisplayPhoneBookToFile (pb);
```

```
292     return false;
293   case 5:
294     SavePhoneBook (pb, needToSavePb);
295     return false;
296   case 6:
297     return SaveCheck (pb, needToSavePb);
298   };
299   return false;
300 }
301
302 /*****************************************************/
303 /*                                                   */
304 /* AddEntry: Adds a new person to the phone directory   */
305 /*                                                   */
306 /*****************************************************/
307
308 void AddEntry (DoubleLinkedList& pb, bool& needToSavePb) {
309   PhoneDirectory* ptrpd = new PhoneDirectory;
310   char c;
311   cin.get (c); // eat the crlf from the previous cin
312
313   // acquire the data on the new person to be added
314   cout << "Enter first name (10 characters):  ";
315   cin.get (ptrpd->firstName, sizeof(ptrpd->firstName));
316   cin.get (c);
317   cout << "Enter last name (20 characters):   ";
318   cin.get (ptrpd->lastName, sizeof(ptrpd->lastName));
319   cin.get (c);
320   cout << "Enter the area code (3 numbers):   ";
321   cin.get (ptrpd->areaCode, sizeof(ptrpd->areaCode));
322   cin.get (c);
323   cout << "Enter the phone number (999-9999): ";
324   cin.get (ptrpd->phoneNumber, sizeof(ptrpd->phoneNumber));
325   cin.get (c);
326
327   // set its record id to one larger than is in the list
328   ptrpd->recordNumber = pb.GetSize() + 1;
329
330   // and add it to the list
331   pb.AddAtTail (ptrpd);
332
333   // set the data has been modified flag
334   needToSavePb = true;
335   cout << "Addition was successful\n";
336 }
337
338 /*****************************************************/
339 /*                                                   */
340 /* DeleteEntry: removes a person from the phone directory */
341 /*    Note: use the record id number as the key id field  */
342 /*                                                   */
343 /*****************************************************/
344
```

```
345 void DeleteEntry (DoubleLinkedList& pb, bool& needToSavePb) {
346  char c;
347  cout << "Enter the number of the phone book entry to delete: ";
348  int num;
349  cin >> num;
350
351  // now see if that number is in the list
352  if (pb.FindNode (&num, FindEntry)) {
353
354   // here we found the number in the list, so get that set
355   // and display it to the user and get a verification that
356   // they really do want to delete this one
357   PhoneDirectory* ptrpd = (PhoneDirectory*) pb.GetCurrentNode ();
358   cout << "Confirm deletion of the following entry\n";
359   cout << setw(4) << ptrpd->recordNumber << "   ";
360   cout << left << setw(10) << ptrpd->firstName << "  "
362        << setw(20) << ptrpd->lastName << "  ("
363        << setw(3) << ptrpd->areaCode << ")  "
364        << setw(8) << ptrpd->phoneNumber << endl << right;
366
367   // do not accept anything but a Y or N
368   c = ' ';
369   while (c != 'Y' && c != 'N') {
370    cout << endl << "Enter Y to confirm deletion or N to abort: ";
371    cin >> c;
372    c = toupper (c);
373   }
374   if (c == 'N')
375    cout << endl << "Nothing done\n";
376   else {
377    // here it has been verified as the one to delete, so do it
378    delete ptrpd;
379    pb.DeleteCurrentNode ();
380    // now handle renumbering all list items....
381    if (pb.IsHead()) // if deleted first one,
382     num = 1;         // renumbering begins at 1
383    else              // if we have not deleted the first one,
384     pb.Next ();      // move current to the first that may need it
385
386    // get current next one after the deleted one, if any
387    ptrpd = (PhoneDirectory*) pb.GetCurrentNode ();
388    while (ptrpd) { // for each phone directory, change its record
389     ptrpd->recordNumber = num++; // id number down one
390     pb.Next ();
391     ptrpd = (PhoneDirectory*) pb.GetCurrentNode ();
392    }
393    cout << endl << "Record deleted\n";
394    // set the data has been modified flag
395    needToSavePb = true;
396   }
397  }
398  else
399   cout << endl
```

```
400              << "No such number in the phone book - try again\n";
401 }
402
403 /**********************************************************/
404 /*                                                        */
405 /* FindEntry: call back function to see if this one       */
406 /*            the one we are looking for                  */
407 /*                                                        */
408 /**********************************************************/
409
410 int FindEntry (const void* ptrmatchData, const void* ptrthis) {
411  int* ptrnum = (int*) ptrmatchData;
412  PhoneDirectory* ptrpd = (PhoneDirectory*) ptrthis;
413  if (*ptrnum == ptrpd->recordNumber)
414   return 0;
415  if (*ptrnum > ptrpd->recordNumber)
416   return 1;
417  return -1;
418 }
419
420 /**********************************************************/
421 /*                                                        */
422 /* DisplayPhoneBookToFile: displays report to a file      */
423 /*            Note: can handle long filenames and those   */
424 /*            with blanks in them                         */
425 /*                                                        */
426 /**********************************************************/
427
428 void DisplayPhoneBookToFile (DoubleLinkedList& pb) {
429  char filename[_MAX_FNAME];
430  char c;
431  cin.get(c); // eat the crlf from previous cin
432
433  cout << "Enter the filename on which to display the report\n";
434  cout << "If there are blanks in the filename,\n"
435       << "place double quotemarks around the whole filename.\n"
436       << "for example, \"My Phone Book.txt\" \n";
437  cin.get (filename, sizeof(filename));
438
439  // check for long filename with quotemarks
440  if (filename[0] == '\"') {// doesn't check for required ending "
441   int len = (int) strlen (filename) - 2;
442   strncpy_s (filename, sizeof(filename), &filename[1], len);
443   filename[len] = 0;
444  }
445
446  // attempt to open the file
447  ofstream outfile (filename);
448  if (!outfile) {
449   cerr << "Error: cannot open output file: " << filename << endl;
450   return;
451  }
452
```

```
453  // now display the fancy report to this file
454  DisplayPhoneListing (pb, outfile);
455  outfile.close();
456  cout << endl << "Report written to: " << filename << endl;
457  }
458
459  /******************************************************/
460  /*                                                    */
461  /* SavePhoneBook: saves the list to a new phone book file */
462  /*                Note: it allows long filenames with    */
463  /*                blanks as part of the filename         */
464  /*                                                    */
465  /******************************************************/
466
467  void SavePhoneBook (DoubleLinkedList& pb, bool& needToSavePb) {
468   char filename[_MAX_FNAME];
469   char c;
470   cin.get(c); // eat crlf from previous cin
471
472   cout << "Enter the new filename to use\n";
473   cout << "If there are blanks in the filename,\n"
474        << "place double quotemarks around the whole filename.\n"
475        << "for example, \"My Phone Book.txt\" \n";
476   cin.get (filename, sizeof(filename));
477
478   // check for leading "
479   if (filename[0] == '\"') {          // this code doesn't check for
480    int len = (int) strlen (filename) - 2; // required trailing "
481    strncpy_s (filename, sizeof(filename), &filename[1], len);
482    filename[len] = 0;
483   }
484
485   // attempt to open the file
486   ofstream outfile (filename);
487   if (!outfile) { // here we cannot, bad name or possibly bad path
488    cerr << "Error: cannot open output file: " << filename << endl;
489    return;
490   }
491
492   // now save all data, but do not save the record Id number
493   pb.ResetToHead ();
494   PhoneDirectory* ptrpd = (PhoneDirectory*) pb.GetCurrentNode ();
495   while (ptrpd) {
496    outfile << "\"" << ptrpd->firstName << "\" "
497            << "\"" << ptrpd->lastName  << "\" "
498            << ptrpd->areaCode << " "
499            << ptrpd->phoneNumber << endl;
500    pb.Next ();
501    ptrpd = (PhoneDirectory*) pb.GetCurrentNode ();
502   }
503
504   pb.ResetToHead ();        // leave list at a valid location
505   outfile.close ();
```

434

```
506  needToSavePb = false;  // turn off any need to save the data
507  cout << "File Saved\n";
508 }
509
510 /*****************************************************/
511 /*                                                   */
512 /* SaveCheck: query the user - saving the data on exit  */
513 /*                                                   */
514 /*****************************************************/
515
516 bool SaveCheck (DoubleLinkedList& pb, bool needToSavePb) {
517  if (needToSavePb) { // has the data been modified and not saved?
518   char yn = ' ';      // yes, so ask user if they want to quit
519   while (yn != 'Y' && yn != 'N') {
520    cout << "Note: you have made changes to the phone database\n"
521         << "and have not yet saved those changes\n"
522         << "Do you want to quit and discard those changes?\n"
523         << "Enter Y or N: ";
524    cin >> yn;
525    yn = toupper (yn);
526   }
527   return yn == 'Y' ? true : false;
528  }
529  else // here it has not changed, so it is safe to quit
530   return true;
531 }
532
533 /*****************************************************/
534 /*                                                   */
535 /* EmptyPhoneBook: removes out phone directory items   */
536 /*                 before the list gets destroyed      */
537 /* Note: once this function is done, the list is trashed */
538 /*                                                   */
539 /*****************************************************/
540
541 void EmptyPhoneBook (DoubleLinkedList& pb) {
542  pb.ResetToHead ();
543  PhoneDirectory* ptrpd = (PhoneDirectory*) pb.GetCurrentNode ();
544  while (ptrpd) {
545   delete ptrpd;
546   pb.Next ();
547   ptrpd = (PhoneDirectory*) pb.GetCurrentNode ();
548  }
549 }
```

Notice how awkward it is for the client program to handle clean up operations by manually traversing the list and deleting each **PhoneDirectory** structure that the list contains. Should the programmer forget to do this, all of the memory these structures occupied is leaked! Further notice how clumsy the Find process actually is with the unusual call back function. Method D which uses a derived class pointer instead of the **void** pointer removes both of these complexities totally.

Designing a Double Linked List Class That Stores BaseObj Pointers

Method D offers a much cleaner and easier approach for client programs as long as the client's data to be stored in the list can be derived from the **BaseObj** class we provide. Specifically, since the **BaseObj** class provides for implementation of comparison operations, the Find process can be totally handled without the use of any complex call back functions. Additionally, since the **BaseObj** class provides a virtual destructor, the link list class can now delete the client's data instances that it is storing. This eliminates all such clean up coding from the client programs as well as reducing any chance for accidental memory leaks.

Here is the **BaseObj** class definition from which client data classes must derive.

```
The Base Class BaseObj Definition

 1 #pragma once
 3
 4 // abstract base class for LinkList Node objects
 5
 6 // both functions return true if the target matches the
 7 // this object
 8
 9 class BaseObj {
10
11 public:
12   virtual  bool MatchObject (const void* ptrtarget) const = 0;
13   virtual  bool operator==  (const void* ptrtarget) const = 0;
14   virtual  ~BaseObj () {}
15 };
```

The virtual destructor guarantees that when we delete an object using a **BaseObj** pointer, the derived class destructors are called, if present. What is the difference between the **operator==()** function and the **MatchObject()** function? None, really. It is done for convenience. Sometimes, forcing the use of the **operator==()** function is awkward, as it is in this linked list implementation.

```
        if (*(currentptr->dataptr) == ptrmatchData)
```

This can be done much more easily as follows.

```
        if (currentptr->dataptr->MatchObj (ptrmatchData))
```

However, we must now redesign the client to actually have a **PhoneDirectory** class that is derived from **BaseObj**. The data items that were in the structure now become the data members. A series of **Get/Set** access functions are provided to retrieve and change their values. To avoid overwriting memory when copying in the user data strings, I provided a protected helper function, **CopyString()**. We must provide the implementations for the two pure virtual functions as well. Here are the new client **PhoneDirectory** class definition and its implementation.

```
Phone Directory Class Definition
```

```
 1 #pragma once
 2 #include <iostream>
 3 #include <string>
 4 #include <fstream>
 5 using namespace std;
 6 #include "BaseObj.h"
 7
 8 const int MAX_FNAME_LEN = 11;
 9 const int MAX_LNAME_LEN = 21;
10 const int MAX_AREA_LEN = 4;
11 const int MAX_PHNUM_LEN = 9;
12
13 /************************************************************/
14 /*                                                          */
15 /* class PhoneDirectory - encapsulates a Phone Book entry */
16 /*                                                          */
17 /************************************************************/
18
19 class PhoneDirectory : public BaseObj {
20
21 protected:
22  int  recordNumber; // these are added by the pgm for id purposes
23  char firstName[MAX_FNAME_LEN];
24  char lastName[MAX_LNAME_LEN];
25  char areaCode[MAX_AREA_LEN];
26  char phoneNumber[MAX_PHNUM_LEN];
27
28 public:
29  PhoneDirectory ();
30  PhoneDirectory (const char* first, const char* last,
31                  const char* area, const char* pnum, int num = 0);
32
33  // the access functions
34  int         GetRecordNumber () const;
35  const char* GetFirstName () const;
36  const char* GetLastName () const;
37  const char* GetAreaCode () const;
38  const char* GetPhoneNumber () const;
39
40  void SetRecordNumber (int num);
41  void SetFirstName (const char* first);
42  void SetLastName (const char* last);
43  void SetAreaCode (const char* area);
44  void SetPhoneNumber (const char* phnum);
45
46  // provide implementations of the pure virutal functions
47  bool MatchObject (const void* ptrtarget) const;
48  bool operator==  (const void* ptrtarget) const;
49
50 protected:
51  // helper function to copy strings and avoid overlaying memory
52  void CopyString (char* des, const char* src, unsigned int max);
53 };
```

437

```
54
55 #endif
```

PhoneBook Class Implementation

```
 1 #include <string>
 2 #include "PhoneDirectory.h"
 3 using namespace std;
 4 /*******************************************************/
 5 /*                                                     */
 6 /* PhoneDirectory: default ctor                        */
 7 /*                                                     */
 8 /*******************************************************/
 9
10 PhoneDirectory::PhoneDirectory () {
11   recordNumber = 0;
12   firstName[0] = 0;
13   lastName[0] = 0;
14   areaCode[0] = 0;
15   phoneNumber[0] = 0;
16 }
17
18 /*******************************************************/
19 /*                                                     */
20 /* PhoneDirectory: make an instance from these values  */
21 /*                                                     */
22 /*******************************************************/
23
24 PhoneDirectory::PhoneDirectory (const char* first,
25                 const char* last, const char* area,
26                 const char* pnum, int num) {
27   recordNumber = num;
28   CopyString (firstName, first, MAX_FNAME_LEN);
29   CopyString (lastName, last, MAX_LNAME_LEN);
30   CopyString (areaCode, area, MAX_AREA_LEN);
31   CopyString (phoneNumber, pnum, MAX_PHNUM_LEN);
32 }
33
34 /*******************************************************/
35 /*                                                     */
36 /* CopyString: copy a string into member string without */
37 /*             overlaying memory                       */
38 /*             if src is too big, copies what will fit */
39 /*                                                     */
40 /*******************************************************/
41
42 void PhoneDirectory::CopyString (char* des, const char* src,
43                                  unsigned int max) {
44   if (strlen (src) >= max) {
45     strncpy (des, src, max-1);
46     des[max-1] = 0;
47   }
```

```
48  else
49    strcpy (des, src);
50  }
51
52  /***********************************************************/
53  /*                                                       */
54  /* The Get... access functions                           */
55  /*                                                       */
56  /***********************************************************/
57
58  int        PhoneDirectory::GetRecordNumber () const {
59    return recordNumber;
60  }
61
62  const char* PhoneDirectory::GetFirstName () const {
63    return firstName;
64  }
65
66  const char* PhoneDirectory::GetLastName () const {
67    return lastName;
68  }
69
70  const char* PhoneDirectory::GetAreaCode () const {
71    return areaCode;
72  }
73  const char* PhoneDirectory::GetPhoneNumber () const {
74    return phoneNumber;
75  }
76
77  /***********************************************************/
78  /*                                                       */
79  /* The Set... Access functions                           */
80  /*                                                       */
81  /***********************************************************/
82
83  void PhoneDirectory::SetRecordNumber (int num) {
84    recordNumber = num;
85  }
86
87  void PhoneDirectory::SetFirstName (const char* first) {
88    CopyString (firstName, first, MAX_FNAME_LEN);
89  }
90
91  void PhoneDirectory::SetLastName (const char* last) {
92    CopyString (lastName, last, MAX_LNAME_LEN);
93
94  }
95
96  void PhoneDirectory::SetAreaCode (const char* area) {
97    CopyString (areaCode, area, MAX_AREA_LEN);
98  }
99
100 void PhoneDirectory::SetPhoneNumber (const char* phnum) {
```

439

```
101  CopyString (phoneNumber, phnum, MAX_PHNUM_LEN);
102  }
103
104  /*******************************************************/
105  /*                                                     */
106  /* MatchObject: return true if this object matches target */
107  /*                                                     */
108  /*******************************************************/
109
110  bool PhoneDirectory::MatchObject (const void* ptrtarget) const {
111   return recordNumber == *((int*) ptrtarget);
112  }
113
114  /*******************************************************/
115  /*                                                     */
116  /* operator== return true if this object matches target  */
117  /*                                                     */
118  /*******************************************************/
119
120  bool PhoneDirectory::operator== (const void* ptrtarget) const {
121   return recordNumber == *((int*) ptrtarget);
122  }
```

As you can see, it is a very simple class indeed. The two matching functions just compare record numbers. The Double Linked List class definition now makes use of the **BaseObj** class. I have bold faced the minor changes. Other coding has been removed since this class can now delete the client's data directly.

```
Double Linked List Definition

 1  #pragma once
 2  #include <iostream>
 3  using namespace std;
 4  #include "BaseObj.h"
 5
 6  /*******************************************************/
 7  /*                                                     */
 8  /* DoubleLinkedList Class                              */
 9  /*                                                     */
10  /* A double linked list that stored objects derived from */
11  /* class BaseObj                                       */
12  /*                                                     */
13  /*******************************************************/
14
15  /*******************************************************/
16  /*                                                     */
17  /* LinkNode: the link list node structure              */
18  /*                                                     */
19  /*******************************************************/
20
21  struct LinkNode {
```

```
22  LinkNode* fwdptr;  // points to the next node in the list
23  LinkNode* backptr; // points to the previous node
24  BaseObj*  dataptr; // points to the client data stored
25  };
26
27  class DoubleLinkedList {
28
29  /***********************************************************/
30  /*                                                       */
31  /* class data                                            */
32  /*                                                       */
33  /***********************************************************/
34
35  private:
36  LinkNode* headptr;     // points to first node in list
37  LinkNode* currentptr;  // points to the current node
38  LinkNode* tailptr;     // points to last node in list
39  long      count;       // the number of nodes in list
40
41  /***********************************************************/
42  /*                                                       */
43  /* class functions                                       */
44  /*                                                       */
45  /***********************************************************/
46
47  public:
48        DoubleLinkedList (); // constructs an empty list
49       ~DoubleLinkedList (); // deletes the total list
50  void  EmptyList ();        // removes all items from the list
51
52  // the add new node functions
53  void  AddAtHead (BaseObj* ptrdata); // add node at the head
54  void  AddAtTail (BaseObj* ptrdata); // add node at the tail
55
56  // add node after the current node - if current node is 0,
57  // it is added at the head
58  void  InsertAfterCurrentNode (BaseObj* ptrdata);
59
60  // add node before the current node - if the current node is 0,
61  // it is added at the head
62  void  InsertBeforeCurrentNode (BaseObj* ptrdata);
63
64  // deletes the current node. If there is no current node,
65  // it returns false; otherwise it returns true.
66  bool  DeleteCurrentNode ();
67
68  // sets the current pointer to the node whose data matches
69  // the criteria set by the caller.
70  bool  FindNode (const void* ptrmatchData);
71
72  long  GetSize () const; // get number of items in the list
73  bool  IsHead () const;  // is list at the start?
74  bool  IsTail () const;  // is list at the end?
```

441

```
75
76  // list iterator functions
77  void  ResetToHead ();   // set current back to start of the list
78  void  ResetToTail ();   // set current to the end of the list
79  void  Next ();          // moves current to the next item
80  void  Previous ();      // moves current to  previous item
81
82  // returns user data stored in the current node, 0 if none
83  BaseObj* GetCurrentNode () const;
84
85  // functions to copy or assign this list
86  DoubleLinkedList (const DoubleLinkedList& r);
87 DoubleLinkedList& operator= (const DoubleLinkedList& r);
88
89 protected:
90  void  CopyList (const DoubleLinkedList& r); // duplicate list
91 };
92
93 #endif
```

Here is the Double Linked List class implementation using **BaseObj**. Notice the bold faced changes.

```
Double Linked List Implementation

 1 #include <iomanip>
 2 #include "DoubleLinkedList.h"
 3 using namespace std;
 4 /**************************************************/
 5 /*                                                */
 6 /* DoubleLinkedList: constructs an empty list     */
 7 /*                                                */
 8 /**************************************************/
 9
10 DoubleLinkedList::DoubleLinkedList () {
11  headptr = tailptr = currentptr = 0;
12  count = 0;
13 }
14
15 /**************************************************/
16 /*                                                */
17 /* ~DoubleLinkedList: destructor to remove all nodes   */
18 /*                                                */
19 /**************************************************/
20
21 DoubleLinkedList::~DoubleLinkedList () {
22  EmptyList ();
23 }
24
25 /**************************************************/
26 /*                                                */
```

```
27 /* EmptyList: remove all nodes from the list            */
28 /*                                                       */
29 /*********************************************************/
30
31 void  DoubleLinkedList::EmptyList () {
32  if (!headptr) return;
33  LinkNode* ptrnext = headptr; // pointer to traverse the list
34  LinkNode* ptrdel;            // the node to delete
35  BaseObj*  ptrdatadel;        // pointer to the data to delete
36  // traverse the list - ends when there are no more nodes
37  while (ptrnext) {
38   ptrdatadel = ptrnext->dataptr; // save client's data to delete
39   ptrdel = ptrnext;         // save the current one to be deleted
40   ptrnext = ptrdel->fwdptr; // point to the next node
41   delete ptrdel;            // and delete the previous node
42   delete ptrdatadel;        // and delete the client's data
43  }
44  headptr = currentptr = tailptr = 0;
45  count = 0;
46 }
47
48 /*********************************************************/
49 /*                                                       */
50 /* AddAtHead: insert new node at the beginning of list   */
51 /*                                                       */
52 /*********************************************************/
53
54 void  DoubleLinkedList::AddAtHead (BaseObj* ptrdata) {
55  // allocate a new node and fill it up
56  LinkNode* ptrnew = new LinkNode;
57  ptrnew->dataptr = ptrdata; // copy the passed client pointer
58  ptrnew->backptr = 0;       // back pointer is 0 because at head
59  count++;                   // increment total number of nodes
60  // now chain this one into the list
61  if (headptr) {             // if headptr exists, then the new
62   ptrnew->fwdptr = headptr; // fwdptr contains the previous one
63   headptr->backptr = ptrnew;// prev node's backptr is us now
64   headptr = ptrnew;         // set headptr to newly added node
65  }
66  else {                     // empty list, so all ptrs point to
67   headptr = tailptr = ptrnew; // this new node
68   ptrnew->fwdptr = 0;       // and no forward nodes yet
69  }
70  currentptr = ptrnew; // leave the current one at the new one
71 }
72
73 /*********************************************************/
74 /*                                                       */
75 /* AddAtTail: insert new node at the end of the list     */
76 /*                                                       */
77 /*********************************************************/
78
79 void  DoubleLinkedList::AddAtTail (BaseObj* ptrdata) {
```

443

```
 80   LinkNode* ptrnew = new LinkNode;
 81   count++;                     // increment total number of nodes
 82   ptrnew->dataptr = ptrdata;  // store the client pointer in node
 83   ptrnew->fwdptr = 0;          // at end, cannot be forward node
 84   if (tailptr) {               // is there anything in the list yet?
 85    tailptr->fwdptr = ptrnew;  // yes, prev tail node points to us
 86    ptrnew->backptr = tailptr; // us points back to the prev node
 87    tailptr = ptrnew;           // tail is now us
 88   }
 89   else {                       // no - list is empty,
 90    headptr = tailptr = ptrnew; // so set all to point to us
 91    ptrnew->backptr = 0;        // and there is no prev node
 92   }
 93   currentptr = ptrnew;         // leave with current node set to us
 94  }
 95
 96  /***********************************************************/
 97  /*                                                         */
 98  /* InsertAfterCurrentNode: add new node after the          */
 99  /*                         current node                    */
100  /*                                                         */
101  /***********************************************************/
102
103  void DoubleLinkedList::InsertAfterCurrentNode(BaseObj* ptrdata){
104   if (!headptr)          // list is empty so add at head
105    AddAtHead (ptrdata);
106   else if (!currentptr) // current ptr is 0, so also add at head
107    AddAtHead (ptrdata);
108   else if (IsTail())    // current ptr is the last node, so
109    AddAtTail (ptrdata); // reuse add at the tail
110   else {                // here we are inserting in the middle
111    LinkNode* ptrnew = new LinkNode;
112    ptrnew->dataptr = ptrdata;
113    count++;
114    // set new node's back pointer to current node to insert us
115    ptrnew->backptr = currentptr;
116    // set new node's forward ptr to the next node to the right
117    ptrnew->fwdptr = currentptr->fwdptr;
118    // set current's forward ptr to us to insert us
119    currentptr->fwdptr = ptrnew;
120    // set the node to the right of us to point back to us
121    ptrnew->fwdptr->backptr = ptrnew;
122    currentptr = ptrnew; // make the newly added node the current
123   }
124  }
125
126  /***********************************************************/
127  /*                                                         */
128  /* InsertBeforeCurrentNode: add new node before current    */
129  /*       node.                                             */
130  /*                                                         */
131  /***********************************************************/
132
```

```
133 void DoubleLinkedList::InsertBeforeCurrentNode(BaseObj* ptrdata){
134  if (!headptr)          // no nodes in list - so add at head
135   AddAtHead (ptrdata);
136  else if (!currentptr)// no current ptr, so add at head too
137   AddAtHead (ptrdata);
138  else if (IsHead())    // current ptr is the last node - so
139   AddAtHead(ptrdata);  // add this one at the tail
140  else {                // here we are adding in the middle of list
141   LinkNode* ptrnew = new LinkNode;
142   ptrnew->dataptr = ptrdata;
143   count++;
144   // set new node's back ptr to current's back
145   ptrnew->backptr = currentptr->backptr;
146   // set new node's forward ptr to current node
147   ptrnew->fwdptr = currentptr;
148   // set current node's back ptr to point to us
149   currentptr->backptr = ptrnew;
150   // set prevous node's forward ptr to point to us
151   ptrnew->backptr->fwdptr = ptrnew;
152   currentptr = ptrnew; // set current pointer to the new node
153  }
154 }
155
156 /**************************************************************/
157 /*                                                          */
158 /* DeleteCurrentNode: removes the current node              */
159 /*    returns false if there is no current node             */
160 /*                                                          */
161 /**************************************************************/
162
163 bool  DoubleLinkedList::DeleteCurrentNode () {
164  if (!currentptr) // if no current node, abort
165   return false;
166  BaseObj* ptrdatadel;
167  count--;
168  if (!count) { // will list now be empty? if so reset to 0
169   ptrdatadel = currentptr->dataptr;
170   delete currentptr;
171   delete ptrdatadel;
172   headptr = tailptr = currentptr = 0;
173   return true;
174  }
175  LinkNode* ptrtodelete = currentptr;
176  ptrdatadel = currentptr->dataptr;
177  if (IsHead()) {                      // deleting first node? if so,
178   currentptr->fwdptr->backptr = 0;// set next node's back to none
179   headptr = currentptr->fwdptr;   // set head to next node
180   currentptr = headptr;            // and current to next node
181  }
182  else if (IsTail()) {              // deleting last one, if so,
183   currentptr->backptr->fwdptr = 0;// set prev node's fwd to none
184   tailptr = currentptr->backptr;  // set tail to prev node
185   currentptr = tailptr;            // set current to prev node
```

445

```
186  }
187  else { // here the node to delete is in the middle
188   // set next node's back to previous node
189   currentptr->fwdptr->backptr = currentptr->backptr;
190   // set previous node's fwd to next node
191   currentptr->backptr->fwdptr = currentptr->fwdptr;
192   // leave current pointing to previous node
193   currentptr = currentptr->backptr;
194  }
195  delete ptrtodelete; // now delete the requested node
196  delete ptrdatadel;  // delete the client's data too
197  return true;
198  }
199
200  /*************************************************************/
201  /*                                                         */
202  /* GetSize: returns the number of nodes in the list        */
203  /*                                                         */
204  /*************************************************************/
205
206  long  DoubleLinkedList::GetSize () const {
207   return count;
208  }
209
210  /*************************************************************/
211  /*                                                         */
212  /* IsHead: returns true if current node is the first node*/
213  /*                                                         */
214  /*************************************************************/
215
216  bool  DoubleLinkedList::IsHead () const {
217   return currentptr == headptr;
218  }
219
220  /*************************************************************/
221  /*                                                         */
222  /* IsTail: returns true if current node is the last one    */
223  /*                                                         */
224  /*************************************************************/
225
226  bool  DoubleLinkedList::IsTail () const {
227   return currentptr == tailptr;
228  }
229
230  /*************************************************************/
231  /*                                                         */
232  /* ResetToHead: sets current pointer to start of list      */
233  /*                                                         */
234  /*************************************************************/
235
236  void  DoubleLinkedList::ResetToHead () {
237   currentptr = headptr;
238  }
```

```
239
240 /************************************************************/
241 /*                                                          */
242 /* ResetToTail: sets current pointer to last node in list*/
243 /*                                                          */
244 /************************************************************/
245
246 void  DoubleLinkedList::ResetToTail () {
247  currentptr = tailptr;
248 }
249
250 /************************************************************/
251 /*                                                          */
252 /* Next: move forward one node in the list                  */
253 /*                                                          */
254 /************************************************************/
255
256 void  DoubleLinkedList::Next () {
257  if (currentptr)
258    currentptr = currentptr->fwdptr;
259 }
260
261 /************************************************************/
262 /*                                                          */
263 /* Previous: backs up one node in the list                  */
264 /*                                                          */
265 /************************************************************/
266
267 void  DoubleLinkedList::Previous () {
268  if (currentptr)
269    currentptr = currentptr->backptr;
270 }
271
272 /************************************************************/
273 /*                                                          */
274 /* GetCurrentNode: returns user data at current node or 0 */
275 /*                                                          */
276 /************************************************************/
277
278 BaseObj* DoubleLinkedList::GetCurrentNode () const {
279  return currentptr ? currentptr->dataptr : 0;
280 }
281
282 /************************************************************/
283 /*                                                          */
284 /* DoubleLinkedList: copy constructor - duplicate a list */
285 /*                                                          */
286 /************************************************************/
287
288 DoubleLinkedList::DoubleLinkedList (const DoubleLinkedList& r) {
289  CopyList (r);
290 }
291
```

```
292 /***********************************************************/
293 /*                                                         */
294 /* operator=: Make a duplicate copy of a list             */
295 /*                                                         */
296 /***********************************************************/
297
298 DoubleLinkedList& DoubleLinkedList::operator= (
299                  const DoubleLinkedList& r) {
300  if (this == &r) return *this; // avoid a = a; situation
301  EmptyList ();   // remove all items in this list
302  CopyList (r);   // make a copy of r's list
303  return *this;
304 }
305
306 /***********************************************************/
307 /*                                                         */
308 /* CopyList: Make a duplicate copy of a list              */
309 /*                                                         */
310 /***********************************************************/
311
312 void  DoubleLinkedList::CopyList (const DoubleLinkedList& r) {
. . .
345 }
346
347 /***********************************************************/
348 /*                                                         */
349 /* FindNode: find the node whose data matches users       */
350 /*           specifications - calls user's Find Function  */
351 /*                                                         */
352 /***********************************************************/
353
354 bool  DoubleLinkedList::FindNode (const void* ptrmatchData) {
355  if (!count) // empty list => not found
356   return false;
357  ResetToHead ();        // begin at the start of the list
358  while (currentptr) {  // examine each node in turn
359   if (*(currentptr->dataptr) == ptrmatchData)
360    return true;        // return true if this one matches
361   Next ();             // move to the next node in the list
362  }
363  return false;         // did not find it in whole list
364 }
```

Finally, here is the revised client program **Pgm10b** that uses **PhoneDirectory** class instances. Notice how much more streamlined it is with no Find type functions and no clean up activities to handle. However, it must use the access functions to get and set the instance data.

```
Pgm10b - Update Phone Directory Program

 1 #include <iostream>
 2 #include <iomanip>
```

```
 3 #include <fstream>
 4 #include <crtdbg.h>
 5 #include <string>
 6 using namespace std;
 7 #include "PhoneDirectory.h"
 8 #include "DoubleLinkedList.h"
 9
10 /************************************************************/
11 /*                                                          */
12 /* Pgm10b: Maintaining a Phone Directory Application     */
13 /*                                                          */
14 /************************************************************/
15
16 // the prototypes
17 bool LoadPhoneBook (DoubleLinkedList& pb, const char* filename);
18 istream& InputPhoneData (istream& is, PhoneDirectory& pd);
19
20 ostream& DisplayPhoneListing (DoubleLinkedList& pb, ostream& os);
21 void DrawLine (ostream& os, unsigned char c, int count);
22 void DisplayPhoneBookToFile (DoubleLinkedList& pb);
23
24 void ShowMenu ();
25 int  GetMenuChoice ();
26 bool ProcessMenuChoice (DoubleLinkedList& pb, int choice,
27                         bool& needToSave, ostream& os);
28
29 void AddEntry (DoubleLinkedList& pb, bool& needToSavePb);
30 void DeleteEntry (DoubleLinkedList& pb, bool& needToSavePb);
31 int  FindEntry (const void* ptrmatchData, const void* ptrthis);
32 void SavePhoneBook (DoubleLinkedList& pb, bool& needToSavePb);
33 bool SaveCheck (DoubleLinkedList& pb, bool needToSavePb);
34
35
36 int main () {
37  {
38   DoubleLinkedList phoneBook; // create the phonebook list
39
40   // load the book from a file
41   if (!LoadPhoneBook (phoneBook, "phoneBook.txt"))
42    return 1;
43   // display the listing using fancy box drawing characters
44   DisplayPhoneListing (phoneBook, cout);
45
46   bool needToSavePb = false; // true when data has been changed
47   bool quit = false;         // true when it is safe to quit
48
49   // main loop shows a menu, gets a valid choice and process it
50   while (!quit) {
51    quit = ProcessMenuChoice (phoneBook, GetMenuChoice (),
52                              needToSavePb, cout);
53   }
54  }
55
```

449

```
56  if (_CrtDumpMemoryLeaks())
57    cout << "\nOops! Memory Leaks!!\n";
58  else
59    cout << "\nNo Memory Leaks\n";
60
61  return 0;
62 }
63
64 /******************************************************/
65 /*                                                    */
66 /* LoadPhoneBook: loads the list from a database file */
67 /*                                                    */
68 /******************************************************/
69
70 bool LoadPhoneBook (DoubleLinkedList& pb, const char* filename) {
71  ifstream infile (filename);
72  if (!infile) {
73   cerr << "Error: unable to open file: " << filename << endl;
74   return false;
75  }
76
77  int i = 1; // this will be the record id number value
78
79  // allocate a new phone directory structure
80  PhoneDirectory* ptrpd = new PhoneDirectory;
81
82  // for each set of input data, insert the id number, add to list
83  // and allocate another phone directory structure for the next
84  // input opperation
85  while (InputPhoneData (infile, *ptrpd)) {
86   ptrpd->SetRecordNumber (i++);
87   pb.AddAtTail (ptrpd);
88   ptrpd = new PhoneDirectory;
89  }
90
91  delete ptrpd;   // delete the unneeded structure - eof was found
92  infile.close ();
93  return true;
94 }
95
96 /******************************************************/
97 /*                                                    */
98 /* InputPhoneData: input a single phone directory entry */
99 /*                                                    */
100 /******************************************************/
101
102 istream& InputPhoneData (istream& is, PhoneDirectory& pd) {
103  char c;
104  is >> c;  // input the leading " of first name
105  if (!is)
106   return is;
107  char str[80];
108  is.getline (str, sizeof(str), '\"');
```

```
109  pd.SetFirstName (str);
110  is >> c; // get leading " of last name
111  is.getline (str, sizeof(str), '\"');
112  pd.SetLastName (str);
113  is >> str;
114  pd.SetAreaCode (str);
115  is >> str;
116  pd.SetPhoneNumber (str);
117  return is;
118  }
119
120  /**********************************************************/
121  /*                                                        */
122  /* DisplayPhoneListing: display in a fancy fashion the    */
123  /*                      complete phone listing            */
124  /*                                                        */
125  /**********************************************************/
126
127  ostream& DisplayPhoneListing (DoubleLinkedList& pb, ostream& os){
128   // the text graphics codes to draw fancy boxes
129   unsigned char upleft = 218;
130   unsigned char upright = 191;
131   unsigned char botleft = 192;
132   unsigned char botright = 217;
133   unsigned char horiz = 196;
134   unsigned char vert = 179;
135   unsigned char leftright = 195;
136   unsigned char rightleft = 180;
137   unsigned char cross = 197;
138   unsigned char topdown = 194;
139   unsigned char botup = 193;
140
141   os << "                   My Phone Directory\n\n";
142
143   // draws the top line
144   os << upleft;
145   DrawLine (os, horiz, 6);
146   os << topdown;
147   DrawLine (os, horiz, 12);
148   os << topdown;
149   DrawLine (os, horiz, 22);
150   os << topdown;
151   DrawLine (os, horiz, 7);
152   os << topdown;
153   DrawLine (os, horiz, 10);
154   os << upright << endl;
155
156   // display a pair of column heading lines
157   os << vert << "Record" << vert << " First     " << vert
158      << " Last               " << vert << " Area  "
159      << vert << " Phone    " << vert << endl;
160   os << vert << "Number" << vert << " Name        " << vert
161      << " Name               " << vert << " Code  "
```

451

```
162        << vert << " Number   " << vert << endl;
163
164  // display another horizontal line
165  os << leftright;
166  DrawLine (os, horiz, 6);
167  os << cross;
168  DrawLine (os, horiz, 12);
169  os << cross;
170  DrawLine (os, horiz, 22);
171  os << cross;
172  DrawLine (os, horiz, 7);
173  os << cross;
174  DrawLine (os, horiz, 10);
175  os << rightleft << endl;
176
177  // for each set of data, display all values within the boxes
178  pb.ResetToHead ();
179  PhoneDirectory* ptrpd = (PhoneDirectory*) pb.GetCurrentNode ();
180  while (ptrpd) {
181   os << vert << ' ' << setw(4) << ptrpd->GetRecordNumber() << ' '
182      << vert << ' ' << left << setw(10) << ptrpd->GetFirstName()
183      << ' ' << vert << ' ' << setw(20) << ptrpd->GetLastName()
184      << ' ' << vert << " (" << setw(3) << ptrpd->GetAreaCode()
185      << ") " << vert << ' ' << setw(8) << ptrpd->GetPhoneNumber()
186      << ' ' << vert << endl << right;
187   pb.Next ();
188   ptrpd = (PhoneDirectory*) pb.GetCurrentNode ();
189  }
190
191  // display the bottom line of the box
192  os << botleft;
193  DrawLine (os, horiz, 6);
194  os << botup;
195  DrawLine (os, horiz, 12);
196  os << botup;
197  DrawLine (os, horiz, 22);
198  os << botup;
199  DrawLine (os, horiz, 7);
200  os << botup;
201  DrawLine (os, horiz, 10);
202  os << botright << endl;
203  os << endl;
204  return os;
205 }
206
207 /************************************************************/
208 /*                                                          */
209 /* DrawLine: helper function to draw a horizontal line    */
210 /*                                                          */
211 /************************************************************/
212
213 void DrawLine (ostream& os, unsigned char c, int count) {
214  // displays character c count times to the stream
```

452

```
215  for (int i=0; i< count; i++) {
216   os << c;
217  }
218 }
219
220 /***************************************************************/
221 /*                                                           */
222 /* ShowMenu: displays the main menu of choices               */
223 /*                                                           */
224 /***************************************************************/
225
226 void ShowMenu () {
227  cout << "\n\n"
228       << "Friends Phone Book\n\n"
229       << "1 Add new friend\n"
230       << "2 Delete an entry\n"
231       << "3 Display the phone listing\n"
232       << "4 Display phone listing to a file\n"
233       << "5 Save into a new file\n"
234       << "6 Exit\n"
235       << "\nEnter the number of your choice: ";
236 }
237
238 /***************************************************************/
239 /*                                                           */
240 /* GetMenuChoice: gets a valid menu choice                   */
241 /*                                                           */
242 /***************************************************************/
243
244 int GetMenuChoice () {
245  // get only a valid number between 1 and 6
246  int choice = 7;
247  while (choice < 1 || choice > 6) {
248   ShowMenu ();
249   cin >> choice;
250   if (!cin) {      // check for non-numeric data entered
251    cin.clear (); // yes, so reset cin state flags to good
252    char c;
253    cin.get(c);   // and get the offending character
254   }
255  }
256  cout << endl;
257  return choice;  // choice is a number between 1 and 6
258 }
259
260 /***************************************************************/
261 /*                                                           */
262 /* ProcessMenuChoice: driver to process that menu choice */
263 /*                                                           */
264 /***************************************************************/
265
266 bool ProcessMenuChoice (DoubleLinkedList& pb, int choice,
267                            bool& needToSavePb, ostream& os) {
```

453

```
268  switch (choice) {
269   case 1:
270    AddEntry (pb, needToSavePb);
271    return false;
272   case 2:
273    DeleteEntry (pb, needToSavePb);
274    return false;
275   case 3:
276    DisplayPhoneListing (pb, os);
277    return false;
278   case 4:
279    DisplayPhoneBookToFile (pb);
280    return false;
281   case 5:
282    SavePhoneBook (pb, needToSavePb);
283    return false;
284   case 6:
285    return SaveCheck (pb, needToSavePb);
286   };
287   return false;
288  }
289
290  /****************************************************************/
291  /*                                                            */
292  /* AddEntry: Adds a new person to the phone directory         */
293  /*                                                            */
294  /****************************************************************/
295
296  void AddEntry (DoubleLinkedList& pb, bool& needToSavePb) {
297   PhoneDirectory* ptrpd = new PhoneDirectory;
298   char c;
299   cin.get (c); // eat the crlf from the previous cin
300
301   char str[80];
302   // acquire the data on the new person to be added
303   cout << "Enter first name (10 characters):  ";
304   cin.get (str, sizeof (str));
305   ptrpd->SetFirstName (str);
306   cin.get (c);
307   cout << "Enter last name (20 characters):   ";
308   cin.get (str, sizeof (str));
309   ptrpd->SetLastName (str);
310   cin.get (c);
311   cout << "Enter the area code (3 numbers):   ";
312   cin.get (str, sizeof (str));
313   ptrpd->SetAreaCode (str);
314   cin.get (c);
315   cout << "Enter the phone number (999-9999): ";
316   cin.get (str, sizeof (str));
317   ptrpd->SetPhoneNumber (str);
318   cin.get (c);
319
320   // set its record id to one larger than is in the list
```

```
321  ptrpd->SetRecordNumber (pb.GetSize() + 1);
322
323  // and add it to the list
324  pb.AddAtTail (ptrpd);
325
326  // set the data has been modified flag
327  needToSavePb = true;
328  cout << "Addition was successful\n";
329  }
330
331  /***********************************************************/
332  /*                                                         */
333  /* DeleteEntry: removes a person from the phone directory */
334  /*     Note: use the record id number as the key id field */
335  /*                                                         */
336  /***********************************************************/
337
338  void DeleteEntry (DoubleLinkedList& pb, bool& needToSavePb) {
339   char c;
340   cout << "Enter the number of the phone book entry to delete: ";
341   int num;
342   cin >> num;
343
344   // now see if that number is in the list
345   if (pb.FindNode (&num)) {
346    // here we found the number in the list, so get that set
347    // and display it to the user and get a verification that
348    // they really do want to delete this one
349    PhoneDirectory* ptrpd = (PhoneDirectory*) pb.GetCurrentNode ();
350    cout << "Confirm deletion of the following entry\n";
351    cout << setw(4) << ptrpd->GetRecordNumber() << "    "
352         << left << setw(10) << ptrpd->GetFirstName() << "  "
353         << setw(20) << ptrpd->GetLastName() << "  ("
354         << setw(3) << ptrpd->GetAreaCode() << ")  "
355         << setw(8) << ptrpd->GetPhoneNumber() << endl << right;
356
357    // do not accept anything but a Y or N
358    c = ' ';
359    while (c != 'Y' && c != 'N') {
360     cout << endl << "Enter Y to confirm deletion or N to abort: ";
361     cin >> c;
362     c = toupper (c);
363    }
364    if (c == 'N')
365     cout << endl << "Nothing done\n";
366    else {
367     // here it has been verified as the one to delete, so do it
368     pb.DeleteCurrentNode ();
369     // now handle renumbering all list items....
370     if (pb.IsHead()) // if deleted first one,
371      num = 1;         // renumbering begins at 1
372     else              // if we have not deleted the first one,
373      pb.Next ();      // move current to the first that may need it
```

455

```
374
375    // get current next one after the deleted one, if any
376    ptrpd = (PhoneDirectory*) pb.GetCurrentNode ();
377    while (ptrpd) { // for each phone directory, change its record
378     ptrpd->SetRecordNumber (num++); // id number down one
379     pb.Next ();
380     ptrpd = (PhoneDirectory*) pb.GetCurrentNode ();
381    }
382    cout << endl << "Record deleted\n";
383    // set the data has been modified flag
384    needToSavePb = true;
385   }
386  }
387  else
388   cout << endl
389        << "No such number in the phone book - try again\n";
390 }
391
392 /**********************************************************/
393 /*                                                        */
394 /* DisplayPhoneBookToFile: displays report to a file      */
395 /*            Note: can handle long filenames and those   */
396 /*                  with blanks in them                   */
397 /*                                                        */
398 /**********************************************************/
399
400 void DisplayPhoneBookToFile (DoubleLinkedList& pb) {
401  char filename[_MAX_FNAME];
402  char c;
403  cin.get(c); // eat the crlf from previous cin
404
405  cout << "Enter the filename on which to display the report\n";
406  cout << "If there are blanks in the filename,\n"
407       << "place double quotemarks around the whole filename.\n"
408       << "for example, \"My Phone Book.txt\" \n";
409  cin.get (filename, sizeof(filename));
410
411  // check for long filename with quotemarks
412  if (filename[0] == '\"') {// doesn't check for required ending "
413   int len = (int) strlen (filename) - 2;
414   strncpy_s (filename, sizeof(filename), &filename[1], len);
415   filename[len] = 0;
416  }
417
418  // attempt to open the file
419  ofstream outfile (filename);
420  if (!outfile) {
421   cerr << "Error: cannot open output file: " << filename << endl;
422   return;
423  }
424
425  // now display the fancy report to this file
426  DisplayPhoneListing (pb, outfile);
```

456

```
427  outfile.close();
428  cout << endl << "Report written to: " << filename << endl;
429  }
430
431  /****************************************************************/
432  /*                                                            */
433  /* SavePhoneBook: saves the list to a new phone book file */
434  /*                Note: it allows long filenames with        */
435  /*                blanks as part of the filename             */
436  /*                                                            */
437  /****************************************************************/
438
439  void SavePhoneBook (DoubleLinkedList& pb, bool& needToSavePb) {
440   char filename[_MAX_FNAME];
441   char c;
442   cin.get(c); // eat crlf from previous cin
443
444   cout << "Enter the new filename to use\n";
445   cout << "If there are blanks in the filename,\n"
446        << "place double quotemarks around the whole filename.\n"
447        << "for example, \"My Phone Book.txt\" \n";
448   cin.get (filename, sizeof(filename));
449
450   // check for leading "
451   if (filename[0] == '\"') {          // this code doesn't check for
452    int len = (int) strlen (filename) - 2; // required trailing "
453    strncpy_s (filename, sizeof(filename), &filename[1], len);
454    filename[len] = 0;
455   }
456
457   // attempt to open the file
458   ofstream outfile (filename);
459   if (!outfile) { // here we cannot, bad name or possibly bad path
460    cerr << "Error: cannot open output file: " << filename << endl;
461    return;
462   }
463
464   // now save all data, but do not save the record Id number
465   pb.ResetToHead ();
466   PhoneDirectory* ptrpd = (PhoneDirectory*) pb.GetCurrentNode ();
467   while (ptrpd) {
468    outfile << "\"" << ptrpd->GetFirstName() << "\" "
469            << "\"" << ptrpd->GetLastName()  << "\" "
470            << ptrpd->GetAreaCode() << " "
471            << ptrpd->GetPhoneNumber() << endl;
472    pb.Next ();
473    ptrpd = (PhoneDirectory*) pb.GetCurrentNode ();
474   }
475
476   pb.ResetToHead ();      // leave list at a valid location
477   outfile.close ();
478   needToSavePb = false;  // turn off any need to save the data
479   cout << "File Saved\n";
```

```
480 }
481
482 /******************************************************/
483 /*                                                    */
484 /*  SaveCheck: query the user - saving the data on exit  */
485 /*                                                    */
486 /******************************************************/
487
488 bool SaveCheck (DoubleLinkedList& pb, bool needToSavePb) {
489  if (needToSavePb) { // has the data been modified and not saved?
490    char yn = ' ';      // yes, so ask user if they want to quit
491    while (yn != 'Y' && yn != 'N') {
492     cout << "Note: you have made changes to the phone database\n"
493          << "and have not yet saved those changes\n"
494          << "Do you want to quit and discard those changes?\n"
495          << "Enter Y or N: ";
496     cin >> yn;
497     yn = toupper (yn);
498    }
499    return yn == 'Y' ? true : false;
500  }
501  else // here it has not changed, so it is safe to quit
502    return true;
503 }
```

Review Questions

1. Explain the concept of a double linked list. How does it work? Illustrate your answer with a drawing of how it operates.

2. What are the benefits of using a double linked list over a single linked list? Give two examples of applications in which a double linked list is more desirable than a single linked list.

3. What is the impact on client programs when the linked list class stores a copy of the client's data in the link nodes versus storing only a **void*** to that data? Be specific.

4. If a linked list class is storing only **void** pointers to the user's data, how can the linked list class ever be able to find any node that matches the user's criteria? Illustrate your answer with a drawing showing how this works.

5. What is meant by a call back function?

6. Describe how a new node can be inserted between two existing nodes. What pointers must be reset? Show an illustration of this process.

7. Describe how a node that lies between two other nodes can be removed from the list. What pointers must be reset? Show an illustration of this process.

8. When loading data from a file into a linked list, what is the difference between always calling **AddAtHead()** versus always calling **AddAtTail()**?

9. When using a linked list class that stores only **void** pointers to the client's data, how does the client program manage to avoid memory leaks when the list class instance is destroyed?

10. How does the use of a **BaseObj** type of class improve client program coding of linked list applications?

11. A **FolderOperations()** function must be passed two strings and a **long** flag field. Based on the flag settings various operations are performed on the folder string that was passed. The flag should indicate one or more of the following activities to perform.

    List the folder's contents
    Make a new folder
    Rename the folder
    Delete the folder
    Create a subfolder beneath this folder
    Mark the folder as read-only
    Mark the folder as read and write

Create an **enum** that could be used with this function. Notice that several of these can be used in combination. The combined flag is created by ORing one or more of these **enum** values together.

Stop! Do These Exercises Before Programming

1. This time our programmer decided to be wise and use our **DoubleLinkedList** class as his container class in his latest programming project. He thought, "What can possibly go wrong this time?" His application needs to perform real time inquiry and update of automobile parts for Acme's Finest Cars Company. He created an initial test data file, corresponding structure and then attempted to load the input file into the array. The following coding failed miserably. Why? How can it be repaired so that it works?

```
...
struct PARTS {
 long partNum;
 int qtyOnHand;
 double cost;
};

int main () {
 DoubleLinkedList parts;
 ifstream infile ("parts.txt", ios::in | ios::nocreate);
 PARTS part;
```

```
while (infile >> part.partNum >> part.qtyOnHand >> part.cost) {
 parts.AddAtTail (&part);
}

parts.ResetToHead();
PARTS* ptrp = parts.GetCurrentNode ();
while (ptrp) {
 cout << ptrp->partNum << " " << ptrp->qtyOnHand << endl;
 parts.Next();
 ptrp = parts.GetCurrentNode ();
}
return 0;
}
```

2. With your assistance, he now has encapsulated the loading of the file in a function and gotten it to load properly and display fine. However, he now finds that he has a memory leak. He tried to fix it as follows. It did not work. Help the programmer out—correct his errors.

```
int main () {
 DoubleLinkedList parts;
 LoadParts (parts, "parts.txt");
 DisplayParts (parts);
 parts.EmptyList ();
 return 0;
}
```

3. Having gotten his program to load, display and clean up properly, he now has written the main menu and has embarked upon implementing the various menu choices. He has written the following for his **FindAPart()** function. It does not work and he begs you for assistance once more. Find his errors so that this function works properly.

```
int main () {
 DoubleLinkedList parts;
...
 FindAPart (parts);
...
 parts.EmptyList ();
 return 0;
}

void FindAPart (DoubleLinkedList p) {
 char c;
 long num;
 cout << "Enter the number of the part to find: ";
 cin >> num;
 if (p.FindNode (&num, FindPart)) {
  PARTS* ptrpart = (PARTS*) p.GetCurrentNode ();
  cout ... this ptrpart fields...
 }
 else
```

```
  cout << "Error: part not found\n";
}

int FindPart (const void* ptrmatch, const void* ptrthis) {
 LinkNode* ptrpart = (LinkNode*) ptrthis;
 long* ptrnum = (long*) ptrmatch;
 if (ptrnum == ptrpart->ptrdata)
  return 0;
 else
  return 1;
}
```

4. With the find operation now working, he decided to make a very fancy display of the items in the list. He now has an infinite loop. Please help him out and fix his code so that it does not run forever.
```
void FancyDisplay (DoubleLinkedList& p) {
 p.ResetToHead ();
 PARTS* ptrpart = (PARTS*) p.GetCurrentNode ();
 while (ptrpart) {
  cout << ...fancy display of ptrpart items;
  ptrpart = (PARTS*) p.GetCurrentNode ();
 }
}
```

5. Claiming that it was sure a silly mistake in Problem 4, he now embarks on an ambitious method of adding items to the list such that all items in the list are in increasing numerical order on part number. His **AddSortedItem()** function does not work. After much experimentation, he again asks for your assistance. Correct his function so that items are added to the list in the proper order.
```
void AddSortedItem(PARTS* ptrp, DoubleLinkedList& p) {
 long matchNum = ptrp->partNum;
 p.ResetToHead ();
 PARTS* ptrlist = (PARTS*) p.GetCurrentNode ();
 while (ptrlist && ptrlist->partNum > matchNum) {
  p.Next ();
  ptrlist - (PARTS*) p.GetCurrentNode ();
 }
 p.InsertAfterCurrentNode (ptrp);
}
```

461

Programming Problems

Problem Pgm10-1—The Revised Update Phone Directory Program

Use Pgm10b as the beginning point for this problem. Acme wishes to add an "Undo" feature to all actions that can be performed on the Phone Book list. Add another item to the main menu, "Undo previous changes." To handle the undo process, Acme decided to create a second instance of the **DoubleLinkedList** class called **Undos**. Each time a change is made to the list, the original **PhoneDirectory** structure is copied and placed at the head of the **Undos** list.

When the user chooses the "Undo previous changes" menu item, begin at the head of the undo list and display each original **PhoneDirectory** instance in turn. Ask the user if they wish to revert this change. If yes is entered, go ahead and undo that change in the main phonebook list. Continue showing successive undo instances until the user chooses to quit the undo process.

Also add another menu choice "Update a phone entry." This option first asks the user for the record id number and then finds that record in the list. If the record is in the list, display it on the screen and ask if they want to change any of this information. If yes is chosen, allow the user to change any of the four main fields but not the record id number.

Thoroughly test your program.

Problem Pgm10-2—The Acme Music Store's Sheet Music in Stock

Acme Music Store carries a wide line of sheet music, much of which is always in stock. They desire a program to allow them to perform real time inquiries while the customer is waiting.

Each piece of sheet music carries their stock number on it. They maintain a data base of sheet music in stock called **music.txt** located in the **TestDataForAssignments chapter10** folder. Each line contains the stock number (4 numerical digits), composer's name (21 characters), the title (31 characters), the quantity in stock at the moment and the cost of the music.

When the program begins, it should allocate an instance of the **DoubleLinkedList** class from **Pgm10b**. Make no changes in that class. Input the file of music in stock into that linked list instance, always adding at the tail. Then display the main menu.

```
Acme Music Store - Sheet Music Inventory Program

1. Check on availability of a piece of music by stock number
2. Find a piece of music given the composer
3. Find a piece of music given the title
4. Exit the program

Enter the number of your choice: _
```

When choice 1 is made, prompt the user to enter the four-digit stock number and then look it up in the list. If the item is found, display its information nicely formatted on the screen. If it is not found, so state.

When choice 2 or 3 is made, prompt the user to enter the composer or music title. Then search the list for any matches. The search should be case insensitive. If one is found, display that item's information nicely formatted along with an option to continue the search. Remember, that there can be more than one piece of music written by any specific composer and some works may have duplicate titles.

Thoroughly test your program. You may add additional data to the music.txt file to ensure that your program is working perfectly.

Problem Pgm10-3—The Sorted List Class

Sometimes, a sorted list is a preferable container for the client's items. Add a new function to the void pointer version of the **DoubleLinkedClass** called **AddSortedAscending()** that is passed a **void** pointer to the new client's data to be added to the list along with a **void** pointer to the client's sorting criteria and and the client's **Find()** call back function to use.

The **void** pointer to the client's sorting criteria and the prototype of the call back function are used exactly the same as in the **FindNode()** function. Traverse the list, calling **Find()** on each passing it the criteria pointer and the user's data contained in that node. When the user's call back function tells you that this current node's value is greater than his matching criteria, insert this new node before the current node. To test your new function, use Pgm10b and its data file as a starting point. Load the file of phone directory entries into the list in alphabetical order on last name. Then display the list to verify that the entries are in the proper order.

Chapter 11—C++ Error Handling

Introduction

C++ adds a new methodology toward the handling of error situations that arise during a program's execution. This chapter's purpose is to examine this new approach with emphasis on how we can best handle error situations that develop while a program is running. The discussion begins with an examination of typecasting.

Typecasting—Static and Dynamic

Undoubtedly you have used typecasting in programming probably from the beginning of your C++ training. It is often used to force a conversion into the proper data type so that a calculation can be done correctly or to remove warning messages. Consider the following two situations.

```
int points;
int number;
float grade = (float) points / number;

double dollars;
int pennies = (int) (dollars * 100 + .5);
```

In the first equation, the typecast is required in order to obtain the correct result while in the second equation, the possible loss of precision warning is being eliminated. These are called static casts. A **static cast** always performs the indicated conversion no matter whether or not it makes any sense as long as the conversion is actually possible. I jokingly call a static cast the "idiot cast."

In **Pgm10b**, a static cast was used to convert the **BaseObj** pointer into a **PhoneDirectory** pointer.

```
PhoneDirectory* ptrpd = (PhoneDirectory*) pb.GetCurrentNode();
```

A static cast was also used in **Pgm10a** to convert the **void** pointer into a **PhoneDirectory** structure pointer.

```
PhoneDirectory* ptrpd = (PhoneDirectory*) pb.GetCurrentNode();
```

What would result if the pointer in the list was not a **PhoneDirectory** pointer but instead was actually a **double** pointer or a **CostRecord** pointer? The static cast assumes that you know what you are doing and it goes ahead and makes the assignment. As soon as the program makes use of **ptrpd**, any number of runtime errors occur, especially if the program attempts to assign values to **PhoneDirectory** members pointed to by **ptrpd**!

What is needed is a way to make an intelligent cast, one that fails to make the cast if the source pointer is not of the correct data type. This type of cast is called a **dynamic cast**. A dynamic cast is made at runtime, not at compile time as the static cast. If the source pointer is not of the correct data type, the dynamic cast assigns 0 or NULL to the resulting pointer.

The syntax is a bit awkward.

```
dynamic_cast<desired pointer datatype>(pointer to typecasted)
```

The **PhoneDirectory** cast could be done this way using a dynamic cast.

```
PhoneDirectory* ptrpd;
ptrpd = dynamic_cast<PhoneDirectory*> (pb.GetCurrentNode());
if (!ptrpd) {
  cerr << "Pointer in list is not a PhoneDirectory pointer\n";
}
```

Incidentally, the static cast can be coded in a similar manner as the dynamic cast.

```
static_cast<desired pointer datatype>(pointer to typecasted)
```

However, it is far easier to use the **(datatype*)** format.

Invoking Derived Class Functions That Are Not Virtual or Defined in the Base Class

The dynamic cast also provides a way for us to get a pointer to the derived class from a pointer to a base class. Consider the fleet array of **Vehicle** pointers from chapter 9.

```
Vehicle* fleet[100];
```

It is unlikely that any pointer in the array is actually a **Vehicle***. Rather, the elements are **Car***, **Truck***, **Limo***, **Bus***, and so on. Further, only virtual or **Vehicle** base class functions can be invoked using the **fleet[i]** pointer. Thus, if the **Truck** class had a function called **LoadCargo()**, it could not be called this way

```
fleet[i]->LoadCargo(); // error
```

unless **LoadCargo()** was present in the **Vehicle** base class, which it is highly unlikely to so be.

However, if the **fleet[i]** pointer was actually a **Truck***, then the following would work well.

```
Truck* ptrt = dynamic_cast<Truck*> (fleet[i]);
if (ptrt) {
  ptrt->LoadCargo();
```

This is a vital detail, for it now permits us to safely get a pointer to the derived class from a pointer to a base class.

With the .NET 2005 compiler, the default is setup to enable the dynamic casts automatically.

465

To Use dynamic_cast with the Older Microsoft VC6.0 Compiler

In order to use the dynamic cast with Microsoft's VC6 compiler, a project setting must be made. Go to Project Settings—C/C++ tab—C++ Language combo box choice—check the box entitled "Enable Run-Time Type Information."

Run-Time Type Information

Run-Time Type Information is a new feature which obtains the object's data type at runtime. It is often used with base class pointers in order to find out what kind of object that pointer is really pointing to at this instant. However, this mechanism can be used with any kind of data, including the built-in data types, such as a **double**. In order to use run-time type information, the **<typeinfo.h>** header file must be included when using the Old Style headers or **<typeinfo>** when using the New Style headers with **namespace std**.

To get the data type of an item, use the **typeid()**. The syntax is simple.

```
typeid (object)
```

typeid() returns a reference to an instance of **type_info** that is used to describe the object. This class has three commonly used member functions: **name()**, **operator==()**, and **operator!=()**. The **name()** function returns the character string name of the data type. For example,

```
double cost;
Vehicle v;
Car c;
cout << "The data type of cost is " << typeid(cost).name ()
     << endl;
cout << "The data type of v is " << typeid(v).name ()
     << endl;
cout << "The data type of c is " << typeid(c).name ()
     << endl;
```

gives this output.

```
The data type of cost is double
The data type of v is class Vehicle
The data type of c is class Car
```

When dealing with base class pointers, the data type returned is that of the derived class, if any. Further, since **typeid()** requires an object, pointers must be dereferenced. For example, the following sequence produces the indicated output.

```
Vehicle* ptrv;
Car c;
Truck t;
ptrv = &c;
cout << "The data type of ptrv is " << typeid(*ptrv).name ()
     << endl;
ptrv = & t;
```

```
cout << "The data type of ptrv is " << typeid(*ptrv).name ()
     << endl;
```

the output:

```
The data type of ptrv is class Car
The data type of ptrv is class Truck
```

What happens if the pointer is 0 or NULL? The class throws a **bad_typeid** exception. Thus, we must examine next the new C++ error handling system and find out what these exceptions are all about.

The C++ Error Handling System

Let's establish the groundwork for the need of a new method for handling error situations detected at run time. Suppose that we have written an **Image** class that encapsulates a graphical image such as a bitmap or JPG file. We would expect one of the constructor functions to be passed the filename to open and load into this class instance. Consider the following snippet of coding.

main:

```
Image pic ("MyImage.bmp");
pic.Display();
```

Image.h

```
class Image {
...
Image (const char* file) {
 ifstream infile (file);
 if (!infile) {
   // oops! Now what do we do????
```

The constructor is in big trouble if the file that is to be loaded cannot be opened. What does the ctor do next? If it only displays an error message, what then happens when **main()** then calls the **Display()** function? Disaster strikes.

This is the very common problem constructor functions have—a constructor function cannot return any value, not even **void**. Thus, it has no way to indicate that it failed to construct the object in question! We arrive at the same situation if the constructor must dynamically allocate some memory and the system cannot provide the necessary memory.

One common solution to the situation is to maintain an **isValid bool** member variable. One might implement it this way.

Image.h

```
class Image {
protected:
 bool isValid;
public:
bool IsValid () const { return isValid; }
```

467

. . .

```
Image (const char* file) {
 ifstream infile (file);
 if (!infile) {
  cerr << ....
  isValid = false;
 }
 ...
 isValid = true;
}

void Display () {
 if (!IsValid())
  return;
 ...
```

The ctor sets **isValid** to **true** or **false**. Then, every other function must first test **isValid** before it attempts any operations on the image. While this is effective, when there are a large number of functions in the class, it is awkward to have to check **isValid** at the start of every function body!

Indeed the C++ error handling system provides a much better way to handle error situations that can occur at run time. However, a new philosophy for handling errors must be observed. The philosophy is this:

A. a function checks for errors and signals their presence

B. the caller then decides what to do about those errors

In other words, the function that detects that an error has occurred does NOT attempt to handle the error. Rather, the function merely signals the C++ system and thereby the caller that an error of a specific nature has occurred. It is totally up to the caller to decide what to do about that error—whether to abort the program or attempt some kind of recovery process. Should the caller choose to ignore the error, then the standard C++ error system handles it for the caller and terminates and aborts the program.

The function signals the presence of errors by using the **throw** statement, while the caller checks and handles the errors using the **try-catch** statements. Let's examine these within a simple context first. Consider the following **Quadratic()** function. What types of run time errors could occur?

```
double Quadratic (double a, double b, double c) {
 double determinant = b * b - 4 * a * c;
 return ( - b + sqrt (determinant) ) / (2 * a);
}
```

Suppose that **a** contains 0? What happens if the determinant is less than zero? These are the two situations that can arise at run time. If they should occur, what action should this function take? Obviously, this function is totally ignorant of the program logic of which it is a part. There is no way that this function could "handle" these two error situations. Instead, it can signal their presence and let the caller make the determination about what to do about the errors.

The **throw** statement syntax is very simple.

```
throw item;
```

Here item can be any intrinsic data type (variable or constant) or any instance of any user defined data type, such as a structure or class instance. For example, consider the following statements.

```
throw 0;        // throws an int whose value is 0
throw 42.;      // throws a double whose value is 42.
throw "This is an error."; // throws a const char* string
char message[80];
throw message; // throws a char* string
class Error {
...
};
Error e;
throw e;        // throws an instance of class Error
```

When a function intends to use the throw statement, it should notify the compiler what data types it intends to throw. These are added to the function header using the keyword **throw** followed by a parentheses list of data types that could be thrown separated by a comma.

```
void fun () throw (int, double, const char*, Error) {
```

Here **fun()** is defined as possibly throwing an **int**, **double**, **const char***, and an instance of the **Error** class.

The **Quadratic()** function can be rewritten this way.

```
double Quadratic (double a, double b,
                  double c) throw (int, const char*) {
 if (a == 0)
  throw 0;
 double determinant = b * b - 4 * a * c;
 if (determinant < 0)
  throw "Imaginary Roots";
 return ( - b + sqrt (determinant) ) / (2 * a);
}
```

What happens if a function should throw an exception that is not in the indicated series in the header? That is, what would happen if **Quadratic()** threw 42.—a **double**? When a function throws something that was not expected, the C++ Error Handler in turn throws the "Unexpected Exception" exception. And these unexpected exceptions can also be checked for in the caller.

The caller must wrap the possible instructions that could raise an exception within a **try-catch** block. Wrapping the instructions within a **try** block notifies the compiler that this caller function wishes to be notified of thrown exceptions that these instructions might raise. The syntax of the **try-catch** block is

```
try {
 1 or more statements that could raise an exception
}
catch (item1) {
```

469

```
   ...
   }
catch (item2) {
   ...
   }
   ...
```

If a statement is outside of the **try** block and if that statement in turn raises an exception, then the C++ Error Handler does not notify it of the exceptions. Instead, the Error Handler looks to the caller of this function for possible handling.

Here is how **main()** could be coded.

main:
```
double a, b, c, ansr;
// get a set of a, b, c values
...
try {
 ansr = Quadratic (a, b, c);
}
catch (int num) {
 if (num == 0)
   cerr << "a's value is 0 which results in division by 0\n";
 else
   cerr << "Unknown integer error value raised\n";
}
catch (const char* msg) {
   cerr << msg << endl;
}
// get next set of a, b, c values
```

Notice that if an operation could result in several different error situations, using different values of an integer to identify each type is common practice. That is, in this situation, **Quadratic()** could have thrown 1 instead of the string error message when the determinant was less than zero.

The other common method is to have all exceptions throw a string error message. This then simplifies the caller's reporting of the error. That is, **Quadratic()** could have thrown "Division by 0" instead of the integer value 0. Then, the single **catch (const char* msg)** could have displayed both messages.

If a caller does not have a catch block for something that was thrown, then the Error Handler looks on up the calling sequence to see if the caller of the caller wishes to handle this exception. If the Error Handler can find no one in the calling sequence that wishes to handle a given exception, then the Error Handler calls the **terminate()** and **abort()** functions to shut the program down.

Consider this sequence of function calls and where each of **Quadratic()**'s exceptions would be handled.
main:

```
try {
 ansr = funA ();
}
catch (const char* msg) {
  cerr << msg << endl;
}
```

funA:

```
double funA () {
 double a, b, c, ansr;
 // get a set of a, b, c values
 ...
 try {
  ansr = Quadratic (a, b, c);
 }
 catch (int num) {
  if (num == 0)
   cerr <<"a's value is 0 which results in division by 0\n";
  else
   cerr << "Unknown integer error value raised\n";
 }
 return ansr;
}
```

If **Quadratic()** throws a zero integer, then it is handled in function **funA()**'s **catch** block. However, if the **const char*** message is thrown, then the Error Handler looks to see if **funA()** wishes to handle it. It does not. So then the Error Handler looks to see if the caller of **funA()**, **main()** wishes to handle it. Again, if no one handles it, then the Error Handler calls the **terminate()** and **abort()** functions to shut the program down.

Sometimes, one might not be sure what all a subsystem of function calls can **throw**. In this case, there is the ellipsis form of the **catch** statement that can **catch** any thrown exception.

```
catch (...) {
 // catches all throws here
}
```

However, note that the catch statements are searched in the order that they are coded. What would be the result of this sequence?

```
try {
 ansr = Quadratic (a, b, c);
}
catch (...) {
 cerr << "An Error Occurred\n";
}
catch (const char* msg) {
  cerr << msg << endl;
}
```

The **catch** of the string would never be called because **catch (...)** already caught it. Reserve **catch (...)** as the last item for which to check.

Details of the try-catch-throw Mechanism

The code that you wish to monitor for errors must be wrapped in a **try-catch** block. Exceptions thrown by that code are then possibly caught by the **catch** statements that immediately follow the end of the **try** block. The statements to be monitored can be as simple or as vast in scope as desired. One can even wrap the entire **main()** function in a **try** block!

throw exception; this generates or raises the exception at the point of the **throw** statement. The Error Handler then looks back up the calling sequence function by function looking for a **catch** block that can handle what was thrown. If none are found, it calls **terminate()** or **unexpected()**.

When a **catch** block finishes execution, program flow then continues at the first line after all of the **try-catch** blocks. Control never is returned to the statement that threw the error in the first place.

When terminating a program, you can either call **abort()** or **exit()**. The **abort()** function does not return a return code back to DOS while **exit()** does return a value.

You can control what, if any, exceptions are thrown by including the **throw** clause on the function's header. In this example
```
void fun (int x) throw (double) {
```
fun() is restricted to only being able to **throw** a **double**. If it tries to **throw** any other type of exception, the system raises the Unexpected Exception exception instead.

However, if you code
```
void fun (int x){
```
fun() is not allowed to throw any kind of exception whatsoever.

Exceptions can be rethrown! For example, if a **catch** block decides that it does not have enough information with which to recover from the exception, it can rethrow the exception by simply coding **throw;** (with no item after the **throw** keyword). In effect, this **catch** block is passing the original exception on up the calling sequence to the next higher block. A **catch** may also **throw** a different exception as well. Consider the results of this sequence.
```
void funA (int x) throw (int) {
 if (!x)
  throw 0;
 ...
}

void funB (int x) throw (int) {
 try {
  int y = funA (x);
 }
 catch (int j) {
  // cannot handle it so pass it on up to main
```

```
      throw;
   }
   ...
}

int main () {
   int x;
   try {
      int z = funB (x);
   }
   catch (int) {
      cerr << ...
   }
   // get a new value for x and repeat
```

First, **main()** calls **funB()** and **funB()** calls **funA()**. If the passed integer is 0, then **funA()** throws an integer whose value is 0. Now **funB()**'s **catch** block gets control but it does not know what to do about it and merely rethrows the original exception, an integer whose value is 0. Finally, **main()**'s **catch** block is called to handle the original exception thrown in **funA()**.

Replacing the Default terminate() Function and the Default unexpected() Functions

In certain circumstances, one might desire to replace the default **terminate()** and **unexpected()** functions which display an error message and call the **abort()** function. Suppose that you intended to "borrow" or reuse a subsystem of functions that performed folder manipulation operations. Some of these functions could raise errors. If the system is well documented, great, go ahead and program in the **try-catch** blocks. However, if you do not have any ideas what can get thrown and you do not want the program automatically aborted when they are raised, then you can supply your own replacement functions for the **terminate()** and **unexpected()** functions.

To provide replacement functions, use the prototypes for these two functions.
```
void terminate ();
void unexpected ();
```
Two functions are provided to allow you to install your replacement functions.
```
set_terminate (your replacement function name);
set_unexpected (your replacement function name);
```
Commonly, the last line of your replacement functions should invoke **abort();** if the program is to terminate.

This first example shows how to replace the **terminate()** function.
```cpp
#include <iostream>
using namespace std;
void myTerminate () {
 cerr << "Error - in my terminate function\n";
 abort ();
}

int main () {
 set_terminate (myTerminate);
 throw 1;
 return 0;
}
```
This second example shows how to replace the **unexpected()** function.
```cpp
#include <iostream>
using namespace std;
void myUnexpected () {
 cerr << "Error - in my unexpected throw function\n";
 terminate ();
}

void fun () throw (int) {
 throw "Error Message"; // throws const char* instead
}

int main () {
```

```
set_unexpected (myUnexpected);
try {
 fun ();
}
catch (int x) {
 ...
}
return 0;
}
```

Overloading the new and delete Functions

The **new** and **delete** dynamic memory allocation functions can also be overloaded. However, their behavior differs between the Old Style and New Style headers. In the Old Style headers, if memory could not be allocated, the **new** function returned a 0 or NULL value for the pointer. However, in the New Style, the **new** function raises the **bad_alloc** exception when it fails. The header file **<new>** must be included to gain access to **bad_alloc**.

Historical note: exactly what the exception is called that is raised when **new** fails has changed frequently over time as the compiler manufacturers scrambled to meet the ever changing C++ guidelines before the language was finally standardized. One earlier name for this exception was **xalloc**.

Thus, when checking on dynamic memory allocations, the method used should match the style of headers in use.

Old Style
```
#include <iostream.h>
int main () {
 double* array = new double [1000];
 if (!array)
 cerr << ...
```
New Style
```
#include <iostream>
#include <new>
using namespace std;
int main () {
 double* array;
 try {
  array = new double [1000];
 }
 catch (bad_alloc bad) {
  cerr << ...
 }
```
Finally, if you wish the New Style new function to behave as it does in the Old Style, that is, return a 0 for the memory address if it fails instead of throwing an exception, you can pass the new function another option, **nothrow**. When you pass **nothrow**, the New Style **new** function does not

raise the **bad_alloc** exception but returns 0 instead. This is useful when reworking older C or C++ coding that is not making use of try-catch logic.

New Style

```
#include <iostream>
#include <new>
using namespace std;
int main () {
 double* array = new (nothrow) double [1000];
 if (!array)
  cerr << ...
```

What are the prototypes of new and delete should one want to overload them?

```
void* operator new (size_t size) {
 void* ptrMemory;
 // you allocate memory as you wish
 // the compiler will subsequently call any class ctor needed
 return ptrMemory;
}
void operator delete (void* ptrObject) {
 // you free up the memory pointed to by ptrObject
 // and class dtor will automatically be called by the compiler
}
```

Why would you want to overload them? In a large project that uses the New Style headers, not all programmers are familiar with exception handling or have coding that allows for exception processing. Further, it is hard to guarantee that all calls to **new** are passed **nothrow**. Thus, you could rewrite **new** to return 0 when it fails instead of throwing the exception. Or perhaps your program must continue to operate even when the computer is out of memory. In this case you could detect this situation and allocate memory from disk and use it in place of real memory. In fact, this is very easy to do in Windows C++ programming; there are some API functions that allow your program to create its own "swap" drive as "real" memory. In this manner, a program could act as if it had access to 40G or more of memory. (I'll show you how this is done in the next book in this series, Windows Programming.)

Finally, when overloading **new** and **delete**, if you make these functions global in scope, they replace the C++ default **new** and **delete**. However, if you make these functions member functions of a class, then they are only used in conjunction with allocation/deletion of instances of that class.

Throwing Class Instances

Up to this point, we have examined throwing intrinsic items, such as an **int** or **char*** (string). In reality, these are very easy to use and **int** or **char*** items are by far the most commonly thrown items. A program could throw thousands of different integer values representing the numerous run time errors that that program could generate. Thrown integer values can be switched upon and alternative recovery implemented. Or even easier, strings can be thrown. Strings have the advantage that the **catch** block can simply display the thrown error message. However, in more advanced situations, class instances can be thrown. This approach is often found in larger systems, such as the Microsoft Foundation C++ Windows Classes (the MFC).

When class instances are thrown, quite often the actual instance thrown is a derived class instance. Then the **catch** block catches a reference to the base class. In this manner, a single **catch** block can catch all of the possible items thrown. To see how this clever approach works, let's return to the **Quadratic()** function example.

What functionality would be desirable in the base class say called **Quad_Error**? Certainly, it should store the error message so that catch blocks can easily display the error message. Additionally, it might be very useful to client programs if the negative value of the discriminant was also automatically displayed. Thus, the base class should hold an error message and provide a means to display that message. The derived class can add in the discriminant value. Here are the base class definition and implementation.

```cpp
class QuadError {
private:
 char message[256];
public:
 QuadError (const char* msg);
 virtual ostream& Display (ostream& os = cerr) const;
 friend ostream& operator<<(ostream &os, const QuadError& qe);
};
```

Notice that the **catch** block will be getting a reference to this base class and will call either the **Display()** function or attempt to directly output the **QuadError** reference using the insertion operator.

```cpp
QuadError::QuadError (const char* msg) {
 strcpy (message, msg);
}

ostream& QuadError::Display (ostream& os) const {
 return os << message;
}

ostream& operator<< (ostream &os, const QuadError& qe) {
 return qe.Display (os);
}
```

Notice too that the insertion operator of this base class calls the **virtual Display()** function which then will invoke the derived class's **Display()** function.

Next, here is the first of the two derived classes, **NonQuadError**. This class handles the division by zero error situation. Since no additional information must be stored beyond the division by zero message, then the ctor only has to pass the message on down to the base class which in turn copies the message ("division by zero") into the base class **message** member. I also implement the

477

virtual **Display()** function. However, the **NonQuadError** version of **Display()** does nothing more than the base class. In fact, **Display()** does not even need to be defined or implemented for **NonQuadError!**

```
class NonQuadError : public QuadError {
public:
  NonQuadError (const char* msg) : QuadError (msg) {}
  virtual ostream& Display (ostream& os = cerr) const;
};

ostream& NonQuadError::Display (ostream& os) const {
  return QuadError::Display (os);
}
```

Here is the second derived class, **ImagRootsError**. This class must store the double discriminant value and also display it. Thus, this class must reimplement the **Display()** function.

```
class ImagRootsError : public QuadError {
private:
 double discriminant;
public:
 ImagRootsError (const char* msg, double d) :
     QuadError (msg), discriminant (d) {}
 virtual ostream& Display (ostream& os = cerr) const;
};

ostream& ImagRootsError::Display (ostream& os) const {
 return QuadError::Display (os) << "\nDiscriminant = "
        << discriminant << endl;
}
```

Given these three classes, here is how **Quadratic()** can be rewritten to **throw** instances of these derived classes.

```
double Quadratic (double a, double b, double c)
                   throw (QuadError) {
 if (!a)
  throw NonQuadError ("Non-quadratic equation");
 double discriminant = b*b - 4*a*c;
 if (discriminant < 0)
  throw (ImagRootsError ("Imaginary roots", discriminant));
 return (-b + sqrt (discriminant)) / (2*a);
}
```

Notice that within the **throw** statement itself, a new instance of either **NonQuadError** or **ImagRootsError** is created and then thrown.

Finally, here is how **main()** can utilize these.

```
int main () {
 double a, b, c;
 cout << "Enter the three coefficients: ";
```

```
while (cin >> a >> b >> c) {
  try {
    double x = Quadratic (a, b, c);
    cout << "The first root is at " << x << endl;
  }
  catch (const QuadError& qe) {
    cout << qe << endl;
    // the following show how to use the dynamic cast
    QuadError* p = (QuadError*) &qe;
    NonQuadError* pn = dynamic_cast<NonQuadError*> (p);
    if (pn) cout << "yes it is really a NonQuadError!!!\n";
    cout << typeid(qe).name () << endl;
  }
  cout << "Enter the three coefficients: ";
}

return 0;
}
```

This complete example is contained in **Pgm11** in the **Samples** folder. I have not included a complete listing for it here since the above coding is it. Here is a sample test run.

```
Output From Pgm11a - Quadratic() Errors

 1 Enter the three coefficients: 1 2 3
 2 Imaginary roots
 3
 4 Discriminant = -8
 5
 6 Enter the three coefficients: 0 1 2
 7 Non-quadratic equation
 8
 9 Enter the three coefficients: 1 9 1
10 The first root is at -0.112518
11 Enter the three coefficients: ^Z
```

One footnote. When compiling **Pgm11a**, the warning "warning C4290: C++ Exception Specification ignored" is generated. This is because Microsoft .NET2005 does not yet fully implement standardized C++. This warning will be eliminated in the future when they do in fact follow the standard for C++. The warning is on the line

```
double Quadratic (double a, double b, double c)
                    throw (QuadError) {
```

Handling Error Situations Where Multiple Dynamic Memory Allocations Exist

The final situation to be examined is what must be done when a constructor must dynamically allocate several data members, any one of which could fail. Care must be taken so that all memory that has been previously allocated just before the failing allocation is deleted. To illustrate this, suppose that we need a **BigArray** class which is to encapsulate two large arrays of x and y integers.

The class begins in this manner.
```cpp
class BigArray {
protected:
  int* x;
  int* y;
  int  xcount;
  int  ycount;

public:
  BigArray (int xc = 0, int yc = 0) throw (const char*);
  BigArray (const BigArray&) throw (const char*);
  ~BigArray ();
  BigArray& operator= (const BigArray& b);
```
The constructor must allocate two arrays containing **xcount** and **ycount** number of elements. The assignment operator must also allocate the two arrays, of course after deleting any existing arrays.

The problem arises when the second allocation fails. Suppose that we implemented the ctor this way.
```cpp
BigArray::BigArray (int xc, int yc) throw (const char*) {
 xcount = xc;
 ycount = yc;
 x = new (std::nothrow) int [xcount];
 y = new (std::nothrow) int [ycount];
 if (!x || !y)
   throw "Out of memory";
}
```
Back in the caller function, we then have the following **try-catch** logic.
```cpp
 try {
  BigArray big (100000, 100000);
 }
 catch (const char* msg) {
  cerr << msg << endl;
 }
```
If the system obtains memory for array **x** and then runs out of memory for array **y**, the exception is raised. However, all memory for array **x** is leaked. The destructor for **big** has never been called.

Certainly, we must free up unneeded memory before the exception is thrown. And since this same process is needed in two constructor functions and the assignment operator, I chose to add two protected helper functions, **Allocate()** and **Release()** and **Copy()**. Notice that **Allocate()** is passed the error string to throw if it cannot obtain the required memory. If the allocation for array **y** is unsuccessful, before throwing the string exception, memory just allocated for array **x** is deleted.

```cpp
void BigArray::Allocate (const char* msg) throw (const char*) {
 x = new (std::nothrow)  int[xcount];
 if (!x) throw msg;
 y = new (std::nothrow) int[ycount];
 if (!y) {
  if (x) delete [] x;
  throw msg;
 }
}

void BigArray::Release () {
 if (x) delete [] x;
 if (y) delete [] y;
}

void BigArray::Copy (const BigArray& b) {
 int i;
 for (i=0; i<b.xcount; i++) x[i] = b.x[i];
 for (i=0; i<b.ycount; i++) y[i] = b.y[i];
}
```

Given these helper functions, then the implementation of the remaining member functions is straightforward. Each of the functions passes to **Allocate()** a string that identifies where the error arose.

```cpp
BigArray::BigArray (int xc, int yc) throw (const char*) :
                  x(0), y(0), xcount (xc), ycount (yc) {
 Allocate ("Default constructor failed");
}

BigArray::BigArray (const BigArray& b) throw (const char*) :
             x(0), y(0), xcount(b.xcount), ycount(b.ycount) {
 Allocate ("Copy constructor failed");
 Copy (b);
}

BigArray::~BigArray () {
 Release ();
}

BigArray& BigArray::operator= (const BigArray& b)
                                  throw (const char*) {
 if (this == &b)
  return *this;
 Release ();
 x = y = 0;
```

481

```
xcount = b.xcount;
ycount = b.ycount;
Allocate ("Assignment operator failed");
Copy (b);
return *this;
}
```

The **Pgm11b** tester program is very simple—just ask for more memory than exists.

```
int main () {
  try {
    BigArray g (1000000000, 1000000000);
  }
  catch (const char *msg) {
    cout << msg << endl;
  }
  ...
```

This tester displays the message "Default constructor failed." Complete coding is contained in the **Pgn11b** folder under the **Samples** folder.

Review Questions

1. How does a dynamic cast differ from a static cast?

2. Consider an array of void pointers. When the elements are assigned their values, statements such as this are used.

```
CostRec* ptrrec = new CostRec;
array[i] = ptrtrec;
```

What is inherently wrong with later retrieval statements such as this?

```
ptrrec = (CostRec*) array[i];
```

How can a dynamic cast remedy the deficiency? Code an appropriate dynamic cast for the above.

3. Consider the Shapes program discussed in chapter 9. If the client program stored all the derived shape class instances in an array of type **Shape***, how could dynamic casting assist the client program in accessing the ith shape?

4. What is meant by RTTL—Run-Time Type Information? How can RTTL be utilized in programs? What is its value in an application that utilizes many derived classes with pointers to their base classes?

5. What is meant by the philosophy of C++ Error Handling?

6. Consider function **Fun1()**. If the passed parameter contains 0, what occurs?

```
int Fun1 (int num) throw (int) {
  if (!num)
```

```
    throw 42;
    ...
  }
```

7. Consider function **Fun2()**. If the passed parameter contains 0, what occurs?

```
    int Fun2 (int num) throw (int) {
     if (!num)
      throw 42.;
     ...
    }
```

8. Consider function **Fun3()**. If the passed parameter contains 0, what occurs?

```
    int Fun3 (int num) {
     if (!num)
      throw 42;
     ...
    }
```

9. Consider function **Fun4()**. If the passed parameter contains 0, what occurs?

```
    int Fun4 (int num) throw (int, const char*) {
     if (!num)
      throw "Error: num is 0";
     ...
    }
```

10. Assume **Fun1()** is defined as given in question 6 above and that its parameter is 0. What occurs in the following code? What is displayed?

```
    try {
     int y = Fun1 (x);
    }
    catch (int) {
     cerr << "An error has occurred\n";
     y = 0;
    }
    cout << y << endl;
```

11. Assume **Fun1()** is defined as given in question 6 above and that its parameter is 0. What occurs in the following code? What is displayed?

```
    try {
     int y = Fun1 (x);
    }
    catch (const char* msg) {
     cerr << msg;
     y = 0;
    }
    cout << y << endl;
```

12. Assume **Fun1()** is defined as given in question 6 above and that its parameter is 0. What occurs in the following code? What is displayed?

```
try {
  int y = Fun1 (x);
}
catch (...) {
  cerr << "An error has occurred\n";
  y = 0;
}
cout << y << endl;
```

13. When would a **catch** block ever rethrow the same exception? Give an example. When might a **catch** block desire to **throw** a different exception? Give an example.

14. When might an application desire to supply its own terminate handler?

15. How can the New Style **new** function be directed to return a NULL pointer instead of throwing an exception? How can this behavior change be valuable in an application?

16. When a constructor function must allocate three member arrays and the third allocation fails due to lack of memory, what must that function do before any exceptions are raised?

Stop! Do These Exercises Before Programming

1. Consider the function **ReciprocalSum()**. This function is passed an integer representing the maximum value to be used in the summation of reciprocals. For example, if the function is passed 5, then it returns the sum of $1/1 + 1/2 + 1/3 + 1/4 + 1/5$. Determine what errors could possibly occur. Then design and code this function, checking for and throwing appropriate errors. You may determine what is thrown when.

2. The constructor for the **PhoneBookArray** class is passed a filename. The class stores an array of **PhoneBook** structures. The array size is a constant, **MAXNUM**. The constructor opens the file and fills the array. Consider what events could go wrong in this possibility and create a series of exceptions that can be thrown. The class begins in this manner.

```
const int MAXNUM = 42;
class PhoneBookArray {
protected:
  PhoneBook array[MAXNUM];
  int count;
public:
  PhoneBookArray (const char* filename);
```

Alter the constructor to throw your chosen exceptions. Then write the shell coding of the constructor, throwing the exceptions as they are detected. Finally, show how a **main()** function could call this ctor.

3. A programmer attempted to utilize C++ exceptions with the **Image** class discussed at the start of this chapter. He has coded the following.

main.cpp

```
Image pic ("MyImage.bmp");
pic.Display();
```

Image.h

```
class Image {
unsigned char* imageData;
...
Image (const char* file);
}
```

Image.cpp

```
Image::Image (const char*file) {
 ifstream infile (file);
 if (!infile) {
  throw 1;
 }
 ...
 // size contains the number of bytes in the image file
 imageData = new unsigned char [size];
 if (!imageData)
  throw 2;
 ...
}
```

Correct all syntax errors so that the C++ exceptions are properly handled in all three files.

4. A program maintains various shapes by storing a pointer to the **Shape** base class. Write a block of coding to convert **ptrshape,** which is a **Shape** pointer, into either a **Rectangle***, **Square***, **Triangle***, or a **Circle*** depending upon what the true derived class actually is.

Programming Problems

Problem Pgm11-1—The Vehicle-Car-Truck-Limo Program

This is fundamentally a design problem.

Step One. Use the basic shell coding for the **Vehicle** class given in chapter 9. It maintains a **double speed** and **bool isMoving** members. Create **virtual** access functions for these members.

Step Two. Create a **Car** class derived from **Vehicle**. The **Car** class maintains a **bool isStarted**, **double gallons**, and **double mpg**. Provide **virtual** access functions for these as well. Override the SetSpeed access function to do nothing is the car is not started.

Step Three. Create a **Truck** class derived from **Car**, adding the double cargo data member and corresponding access functions.

Step Four. Create a **Limo** class derived from **Car**, adding the integer number of possible passengers and a **bool isTV_On**. Also, provide access functions for these.

Step Five. Write a **main()** function that has an array of 4 **Vehicle** pointers called **fleet**. Dynamically allocate one each of the four classes and store them in the **fleet** array. The design problem to overcome is this. For each of the four elements in the **fleet** array, invoke each of the corresponding access functions. Note, do NOT provide pure **virtual** or **virtual** functions for all of these derived class access functions down in the **Vehicle** class. Keep **Vehicle** down to its minimum number of functions required to manipulate a **Vehicle** object. This means, at run time, you need to discover what derived class each **fleet** element actually is and dynamically cast each **fleet** element pointer back into the appropriate derived class pointer and use that pointer to call the derived class functions.

Problem Pgm11-2—The LoadArray Function with Exceptions

The **LoadArray()** function is passed an array of **CostRecord** structures and the integer maximum array size and a **const char*** filename. **LoadArray()** opens the passed filename, inputs the cost records, closes the file, and returns the number of records now actually in the array. A **CostRecord** structure can be of your own design, but it should include at least the item number, character string description, a quantity, and a cost.

Consider what errors can possibly occur within **LoadArray()**—there are several. For each of the possible errors that can occur, throw an exception at the appropriate point within the actual function coding. Thus, you must add the **throw ()** list to the prototype and header of **LoadArray()**. When you have written **LoadArray()**, it should return the number in the array or throw an exception. Thus, the only direct way back to the calling program is when all goes well and no errors occur.

Now write a **main()** function to call **LoadArray()**. Wrap this call in a **try-catch** block. Be sure that you **catch** all of the error situations and display an appropriate error message stating the exact cause of the error. All displays of error messages must occur from within a **catch** block in **main()**. That is, no error messages are ever displayed from within **LoadArray()**.

Finally, thoroughly test the program using as many test files as needed to trigger each of the errors that can occur.

Chapter 12—Templates

Introduction to Template Functions

A **template** is a model or blueprint for the compiler to follow when the compiler needs to create a function or a class. The idea is to write a generic model for a function or even a whole class and then let the compiler use this model to create specific instances tailored to the specific data types that the compiler encounters in a program.

Footnote: the syntax for templates is just awful. In the industry, programmers either love or detest templates. There seems to be no middle ground. My personal opinion is that templates are hideous in nature and a nightmare to debug and get working. They are definitely an advanced C++ topic. However, I will do my best to present templates in an understandable manner and to effectively illustrate their need and uses.

To see the need for templates, let's examine an extremely simple C function, **max()**, which returns the larger of two values. Suppose first that your application needed to obtain the maximum of two integers and this capability was needed in numerous places within the application. One would not hesitate a moment to create a **max()** function such as this.

```
int max (int x, int y) {
  return x>y ? x : y;
}
```

Now later on, the data types change and you find that you need **max()** written for a pair of doubles. So you code

```
double max (double x, double y) {
  return x>y ? x : y;
}
```

And then you need one for a pair of long values and then unsigned short values and then a pair of char values and then for a pair of strings. So you write these additional versions of **max()**.

```
long max (long x, long y) {
  return x>y ? x : y;
}
unsigned short max (unsigned short x, unsigned short y) {
  return x>y ? x : y;
}
char max (char x, char y) {
  return x>y ? x : y;
}
char* max (char* x, char* y) {
  return x>y ? x : y;
}
```

Oops. With strings, we cannot compare memory addresses. It must be rewritten as follows.

488

```
char* max (char* x, char* y) {
  return stricmp (x, y) > 0 ? x : y;
}
```

There is really no problem doing this repetitive coding; functions can be overloaded. So when a **max()** function is needed for **CostRecord** structures, we go ahead and write yet another version.

```
CostRecord& max (CostRecord& x, CostRecord& y) {
  return x.qty > y.qty ? x : y;
}
```

With the exception of the last two versions of **max()**, the coding of the function bodies is identical. Only the data types have changed. This is where a template **max()** function shines. The objective is to write a model for compiler to follow and let it build the actual function for the specified data types it encounters in this particular program. The syntax of a template function is as follows.

```
template<list of generic types>
the function header using these generic types
  and the corresponding function body implemented using
  these generic types
```

The generic type is called **name** after the keyword class "name"—often it is coded as T. If there are more than one generic type of data, then the subsequent types are usually called U, V and so on. In the syntax notation found with templates, the keyword **class** means type of data and has absolutely nothing to do with OOP classes. (I find this most confusing for beginners.) Thus, the "list of generic types" becomes

```
class T, class U, int, double
```

Generic types can be interspersed with intrinsic types or even hard-coded classes and structures.

To implement **max()** as a template function, in the header file we code the following.

```
template <class T>
const T& max (const T& x, const T& y) {
  return x>y ? x : y;
}
```

The first line says that here comes a single template function. This function has one generic data type, **T**. The second line is the function header written in terms of this generic type **T**. Notice that constant references are used. Why? Because when the compiler creates specific instances of this function, any kind of data can be passed. It is more efficient in the long run to use constant references unless you know for certain that only intrinsic built-in types such as **char**, **short**, **int**, or **long** will ever be used. The third line then provides the implementation written in terms of the parameters. However, other variables could have been defined within the body, including those of type **T**.

Now in the cpp files, such as the **main()** function, the programmer codes the following.

```
int a, b, c;
c = max (a, b);

double d, e, f;
f = max (d, e);
```

The compiler looks over all known prototypes to find one for a function **max()** that takes two integer parameters. It does not find one. However, it does find a template version of **max()**. Here the program is passing **max()** two integer parameters. So the compiler examines the template version to see what it is passed. It also is passed two items of the same data type, **T**. Thus, if the compiler substitutes **int** for **T**, it can generate the required **max()** function and so does. Next, the compiler encounters another version of **max()** which is passed two **doubles**. Again, it makes a **double** version of **max()** by substituting **double** for **T** in the template version.

All template definitions must be in a header file. The template statement must precede each and every function definition. The function body follows the template function's definition.

One can instruct the compiler to use a particular form of a function by coding the data type(s) to be substituted for the template parameters by coding the data types desired separated by commas inside a pair of angle brackets. In the following line, the compiler is told to generate a **double** version of **max()**.

```
f = max<double>(d, e);
```

This variation is useful when the actual parameters differ. It is also required when at least one of the types is not a formal argument and cannot therefore be deduced. This usually happens when that type is used as the return data type. Consider the following template for a **compare()** function.

```
template <class T, class U>
T  compare (const U& a, const U& b) {
 return a < b ? -1 : a > b;
}
```

The return data type is the province of the compiler for it can often convert a result into many different data types. If the user codes the following,

```
int res;
double a, b;
res = compare(a, b); // error T = kind???
res = compare<int, double>(a, b);
```

then in the first case, the compiler cannot tell what the return data type is to be and thus generates the error message. However, by explicitly telling the compiler what the data types for **T** and **U** are to be, the compiler can successfully generate and use the function.

Since these are models, the template functions must be made available where the compiler can find them. Thus, they are in the header files not cpp files. Note that there is no actual code in them; they are blueprints only. The actual code is generated by the compiler when it encounters their use within a cpp file. Thus, if we were to actually implement **max()**, we would have the following. File: max.h

```
#pragma once
template <class T>
const T& max (const T& x, const T& y) {
 return x>y ? x : y;
}
```

One can mix parameterized and non-parameterized items within the formal argument list. For example, consider this version of a **largest()** function which returns the largest element within an array of type **T**. Such a function must also be passed the number of elements in the array.

```
template <class T>
const T& largest (const T* array, unsigned int size) {
 unsigned int answer = 0, i;
 for (i=1; i<size; i++) {
  if (array[i] >  array[answer])
    answer = i;
 }
 return array[answer];
}
```

Specializing a Template

A single template function usually cannot handle all possible types of data. This is often true when pointers are being passed. Consider this next need for function **max()**.

```
char* s1 = "A";
char* s2 = "B";
const char* s3 = max (s1, s2);
// error: this compares pointer values not strings
```

The way around this dilemma is to provide specialized version of **max()** in the header file. add to max.h

```
template <>
const char* max (const char* s1, const char* s2) {
 return stricmp (s1, s2) > 0 ? s1 : s2;
}
```

Now the user can successfully code the following.

```
cout << max (s1, s2);
```

Another form of trouble can arise when the parameters actually being passed differ in type. Consider this case.

```
long a;
unsigned int b;
cout << max (a, b); // error
```

No version of **max()** can take two different data types. However, just declaring and not defining a version of **max()** permits the compiler to handle data conversion. If we add this one line to the header, the compiler can use it.

```
inline const long& max (const long& x, const long& y);
```

This one now allows the compiler to convert **unsigned int** to **long** and then to create a **max()** that is passed two **long** parameters. Caution. Since references are being passed, it is going to pass a reference to the temporary **long** that into which it converted the **unsigned int**; if the temporary **long** is the larger, its address is returned. Addresses of temporary variables are very short in duration. One may end up with a reference to memory that has already been destroyed.

Template Classes

An entire class can be templatized. Such classes must have at least one parameterized type. Template classes are often used with abstract container types such as link lists, queues, stacks, and arrays. The New Style I/O stream classes are also template classes.

To illustrate a template class, let's consider how a class can be constructed to encapsulate a complex number. Recall from mathematics that a complex number has two portions, a real part and an imaginary part. Such numbers are often notated this way.

1.5 + 3.9i

x + y i

where i represents the square root of −1.

A complex number class would have two numerical members, the real and imaginary parts. Certainly both parts would be of the same data type. Often doubles are used, but longs or ints may work as well, depending upon the application. It is this data type to which the class **T** in the template refers. Here is the class definition portion.

```
template <class T>
class ComplexNumber {
protected:
 T realpart;
 T imagpart;
 static int counter;
public:
 ComplexNumber (const T& = T(), const T& = T());
 ComplexNumber (const ComplexNumber&);
same as
 ComplexNumber<T>(const T& = T(), const T& = T());
 ComplexNumber<T>(const COmplexNumber<T>&);
};
```

Note first that the class qualifier is now technically **ComplexNumber<T>**. However, since we expect to code the class qualifier many times, the compiler allows a short cut of just **ComplexNumber**. Next, note how the default values are coded. For example, in a non-template version, one might desire to code a constructor prototype like this.

```
ComplexNumber (double x = 0, double y = 0);
```

The syntax **= T()** is used to indicate the insertion of the 0 value for this data type **T** whatever **T** actually is.

When a template class is written, the header file as usual contains the class definition. However, it also must include the template member functions as well. In other words, the entire class and its template implementation must be in the header file! Thus, after the above **ComplexNumber** definition come all of the following.

```
template <class T>
ComplexNumber<T>::ComplexNumber (const T& r, const T& i) :
```

```
                    realpart (r), imagpart (i) {}

template <class T>
ComplexNumber<T>::ComplexNumber (const ComplexNumber& c) :
            realpart (c.realpart), imagpart (c.imagpart) {}

int ComplexNumber<T>::counter = 0;
```

I used the **static** member variable to illustrate how **static** data members are handled in a template class.

In the **main()** function, entire instances of the entire **ComplexNumber** class can be created this way.

```
ComplexNumber<int> c1 (1,2);
ComplexNumber<double> c2 (42., 99.);
```

Because the syntax is awful and since these class instances are likely to be passed to functions, to avoid constant use of ComplexNumber<double>, a **typedef** is nearly always used to streamline the syntax.

```
typedef ComplexNumber<double> ComplexDouble;
ComplexDouble c3 (42., 99.);
```

Pgm12a—a Practical Example of a Template Class

To see how this all works, I chose to rewrite **Pgm10b** using a template class for the Double Linked List class. The data type that **main()** will use is **PhoneDirectory**, the class instance the list is to store. The **LinkNode** becomes as follows.

```
template<class T>
class DoubleLinkedList {

/*******************************************************/
/*                                                     */
/* LinkNode: the link list node structure              */
/*                                                     */
/*******************************************************/

struct LinkNode {
 LinkNode* fwdptr;   // points to the next node in the list
 LinkNode* backptr;  // points to the previous node
 T*  dataptr;        // points to the client data stored
};
```

There are many ramifications to using this template version. First, the actual data type of the object to be stored in the list is known, type **T**. Thus, this class can now be smart in its handling of the client's data. This means that the class can perform a **deep** copy because it can allocate new instances this way.

```
        dataptr = new (std::nothrow) T;
```

The user is not required to clean up stored instances of type **T** because the **EmptyList()** function can delete them directly. The user now, when they wish access to the data of a node, no longer must perform a typecast to get it back. The **GetCurrentNode()** function returns a **T***. Further, the client's data class does not have to be derived from **BaseObj** anymore. It still must provide matching functions, though.

In short, by using a template double linked list class, we gain all of the benefits associated with knowing precisely what kind of data the client is storing in the list! Further, the class can be used to store any kind of data. It is reusable. Well, reusable in the sense that we write the template class once. Then, for each type of client data to be stored, the compiler generates the entire class and all its functions for us. If a client program needed six lists to store six different kinds of objects, with the template version, there would be six total classes with all of their functions included in the executable file. However, with the generic void pointer version, there would only be one set of class functions in the executable, all shared by the six different instances. So the price of using templates in a program is that of a larger executable file along with the huge size of the header files.

Here is the complete template Double Linked List class. In this example, I did not use the std::nothrow parameter to the new function. Hence, if the application should run out of memory, a C++ exception is thrown, but not caught, terminating the program.

Template Double Linked List Class

```
 1 #pragma once
 2 #include <iostream>
 3 using namespace std;
 4
 5 /**************************************************************/
 6 /*                                                          */
 7 /* DoubleLinkedList Template Class                          */
 8 /*                                                          */
 9 /* A double linked list that stores objects                */
10 /*                                                          */
11 /**************************************************************/
12
13 template<class T>
14 class DoubleLinkedList {
15
16 /**************************************************************/
17 /*                                                          */
18 /* LinkNode: the link list node structure                  */
19 /*                                                          */
20 /**************************************************************/
21
22 struct LinkNode {
23  LinkNode* fwdptr;  // points to the next node in the list
24  LinkNode* backptr; // points to the previous node
25  T*  dataptr;       // points to the client data stored
26 };
27
28  /**************************************************************/
29  /*                                                          */
30  /* class data                                              */
31  /*                                                          */
32  /**************************************************************/
33
34 private:
35  LinkNode* headptr;      // points to first node in list
36  LinkNode* currentptr;   // points to the current node
37  LinkNode* tailptr;      // points to last node in list
38  long      count;        // the number of nodes in list
39
40  /**************************************************************/
41  /*                                                          */
42  /* class functions                                         */
43  /*                                                          */
44  /**************************************************************/
45
46 public:
47         DoubleLinkedList (); // constructs an empty list
48        ~DoubleLinkedList (); // deletes the total list
49  void  EmptyList ();         // removes all items from the list
50
51  // the add new node functions
```

495

```
 52  void   AddAtHead (T* ptrdata); // add node at the head
 53  void   AddAtTail (T* ptrdata); // add node at the tail
 54
 55  // add node after the current node - if current node is 0,
 56  // it is added at the head
 57  void   InsertAfterCurrentNode (T* ptrdata);
 58
 59  // add node before the current node - if the current node is 0,
 60  // it is added at the head
 61  void   InsertBeforeCurrentNode (T* ptrdata);
 62
 63  // deletes the current node. If there is no current node,
 64  // it returns false; otherwise it returns true.
 65  bool   DeleteCurrentNode ();
 66
 67  // sets the current pointer to the node whose data matches
 68  // the criteria set by the caller.
 69  bool   FindNode (const void* ptrmatchData);
 70
 71  long   GetSize () const; // get number of items in the list
 72  bool   IsHead () const;  // is list at the start?
 73  bool   IsTail () const;  // is list at the end?
 74
 75  // list iterator functions
 76  void   ResetToHead ();   // set current back to start of the list
 77  void   ResetToTail ();   // set current to the end of the list
 78  void   Next ();          // moves current to the next item
 79  void   Previous ();      // moves current to  previous item
 80
 81  // returns user data stored in the current node, 0 if none
 82  T* GetCurrentNode () const;
 83
 84  // functions to copy or assign this list
 85  DoubleLinkedList (const DoubleLinkedList& r);
 86 DoubleLinkedList& operator= (const DoubleLinkedList& r);
 87
 88 protected:
 89  void   CopyList (const DoubleLinkedList& r); // duplicate list
 90 };
 91
 92
 93 /*****************************************************/
 94 /*                                                   */
 95 /* DoubleLinkedList: constructs an empty list        */
 96 /*                                                   */
 97 /*****************************************************/
 98
 99 template<class T>
100 DoubleLinkedList<T>::DoubleLinkedList () {
101  headptr = tailptr = currentptr = 0;
102  count = 0;
103 }
104
```

```
105 /**********************************************************/
106 /*                                                        */
107 /* ~DoubleLinkedList: destructor to remove all nodes      */
108 /*                                                        */
109 /**********************************************************/
110
111 template<class T>
112 DoubleLinkedList<T>::~DoubleLinkedList () {
113  EmptyList ();
114 }
115
116 /**********************************************************/
117 /*                                                        */
118 /* EmptyList: remove all nodes from the list              */
119 /*                                                        */
120 /**********************************************************/
121
122 template<class T>
123 void  DoubleLinkedList<T>::EmptyList () {
124  if (!headptr) return;
125  LinkNode* ptrnext = headptr; // pointer to traverse the list
126  LinkNode* ptrdel;            // the node to delete
127  T*        ptrdatadel;        // pointer to the data to delete
128  // traverse the list - ends when there are no more nodes
129  while (ptrnext) {
130   ptrdatadel = ptrnext->dataptr; // save client's data to delete
131   ptrdel = ptrnext;           // save the current one to be deleted
132   ptrnext = ptrdel->fwdptr; // point to the next node
133   delete ptrdel;            // and delete the previous node
134   delete ptrdatadel;        // and delete the client's data
135  }
136  headptr = currentptr = tailptr = 0;
137  count = 0;
138 }
139
140 /**********************************************************/
141 /*                                                        */
142 /* AddAtHead: insert new node at the beginning of list    */
143 /*                                                        */
144 /**********************************************************/
145
146 template<class T>
147 void  DoubleLinkedList<T>::AddAtHead (T* ptrdata) {
148  // allocate a new node and fill it up
149  LinkNode* ptrnew = new LinkNode;
150  ptrnew->dataptr = ptrdata; // copy the passed client pointer
151  ptrnew->backptr = 0;       // back pointer is 0 because at head
152  count++;                   // increment total number of nodes
153  // now chain this one into the list
154  if (headptr) {             // if headptr exists, then the new
155   ptrnew->fwdptr = headptr; // fwdptr contains the previous one
156   headptr->backptr = ptrnew;// prev node's backptr is us now
157   headptr = ptrnew;         // set headptr to newly added node
```

```
158  }
159  else {                     // empty list, so all ptrs point to
160   headptr = tailptr = ptrnew; // this new node
161   ptrnew->fwdptr = 0;        // and no forward nodes yet
162  }
163  currentptr = ptrnew; // leave the current one at the new one
164 }
165
166 /************************************************************/
167 /*                                                          */
168 /* AddAtTail: insert new node at the end of the list        */
169 /*                                                          */
170 /************************************************************/
171
172 template<class T>
173 void  DoubleLinkedList<T>::AddAtTail (T* ptrdata) {
174  LinkNode* ptrnew = new LinkNode;
175  count++;                      // increment total number of nodes
176  ptrnew->dataptr = ptrdata; // store the client pointer in node
177  ptrnew->fwdptr = 0;        // at end, cannot be forward node
178  if (tailptr) {                // is there anything in the list yet?
179   tailptr->fwdptr = ptrnew; // yes, prev tail node points to us
180   ptrnew->backptr = tailptr;// us points back to the prev node
181   tailptr = ptrnew;          // tail is now us
182  }
183  else {                     // no - list is empty,
184   headptr = tailptr = ptrnew; // so set all to point to us
185   ptrnew->backptr = 0;       // and there is no prev node
186  }
187  currentptr = ptrnew;       // leave with current node set to us
188 }
189
190 /************************************************************/
191 /*                                                          */
192 /* InsertAfterCurrentNode: add new node after the           */
193 /*                     current node                         */
194 /*                                                          */
195 /************************************************************/
196
197 template<class T>
198 void DoubleLinkedList<T>::InsertAfterCurrentNode(T* ptrdata){
199  if (!headptr)            // list is empty so add at head
200   AddAtHead (ptrdata);
201  else if (!currentptr) // current ptr is 0, so also add at head
202   AddAtHead (ptrdata);
203  else if (IsTail())    // current ptr is the last node, so
204   AddAtTail (ptrdata); // reuse add at the tail
205  else {                  // here we are inserting in the middle
206   LinkNode* ptrnew = new LinkNode;
207   ptrnew->dataptr = ptrdata;
208   count++;
209   // set new node's back pointer to current node to insert us
210   ptrnew->backptr = currentptr;
```

```
211   // set new node's forward ptr to the next node to the right
212   ptrnew->fwdptr = currentptr->fwdptr;
213   // set current's forward ptr to us to insert us
214   currentptr->fwdptr = ptrnew;
215   // set the node to the right of us to point back to us
216   ptrnew->fwdptr->backptr = ptrnew;
217   currentptr = ptrnew; // make the newly added node the current
218  }
219 }
220
221 /****************************************************************/
222 /*                                                            */
223 /* InsertBeforeCurrentNode: add new node before current  */
224 /*      node.                                                 */
225 /*                                                            */
226 /****************************************************************/
227
228 template<class T>
229 void DoubleLinkedList<T>::InsertBeforeCurrentNode(T* ptrdata){
230  if (!headptr)         // no nodes in list - so add at head
231   AddAtHead (ptrdata);
232  else if (!currentptr)// no current ptr, so add at head too
233   AddAtHead (ptrdata);
234  else if (IsHead())   // current ptr is the last node - so
235   AddAtHead(ptrdata); // add this one at the tail
236  else {               // here we are adding in the middle of list
237   LinkNode* ptrnew = new LinkNode;
238   ptrnew->dataptr = ptrdata;
239   count++;
240   // set new node's back ptr to current's back
241   ptrnew->backptr = currentptr->backptr;
242   // set new node's forward ptr to current node
243   ptrnew->fwdptr = currentptr;
244   // set current node's back ptr to point to us
245   currentptr->backptr = ptrnew;
246   // set previous node's forward ptr to point to us
247   ptrnew->backptr->fwdptr = ptrnew;
248   currentptr = ptrnew; // set current pointer to the new node
249  }
250 }
251
252 /****************************************************************/
253 /*                                                            */
254 /* DeleteCurrentNode: removes the current node          */
255 /*     returns false if there is no current node        */
256 /*                                                            */
257 /****************************************************************/
258
259 template<class T>
260 bool  DoubleLinkedList<T>::DeleteCurrentNode () {
261  if (!currentptr) // if no current node, abort
262   return false;
263  T* ptrdatadel;
```

```
264  count--;
265  if (!count) { // will list now be empty? if so reset to 0
266   ptrdatadel = currentptr->dataptr;
267   delete currentptr;
268   delete ptrdatadel;
269   headptr = tailptr = currentptr = 0;
270   return true;
271  }
272  LinkNode* ptrtodelete = currentptr;
273  ptrdatadel = currentptr->dataptr;
274  if (IsHead()) {                        // deleting first node? if so,
275   currentptr->fwdptr->backptr = 0;// set next node's back to none
276   headptr = currentptr->fwdptr;   // set head to next node
277   currentptr = headptr;           // and current to next node
278  }
279  else if (IsTail()) {                   // deleting last one, if so,
280   currentptr->backptr->fwdptr = 0;// set prev node's fwd to none
281   tailptr = currentptr->backptr;  // set tail to prev node
282   currentptr = tailptr;           // set current to prev node
283  }
284  else { // here the node to delete is in the middle
285   // set next node's back to previous node
286   currentptr->fwdptr->backptr = currentptr->backptr;
287   // set previous node's fwd to next node
288   currentptr->backptr->fwdptr = currentptr->fwdptr;
289   // leave current pointing to previous node
290   currentptr = currentptr->backptr;
291  }
292  delete ptrtodelete; // now delete the requested node
293  delete ptrdatadel;  // delete the client's data too
294  return true;
295  }
296
297  /******************************************************/
298  /*                                                    */
299  /* GetSize: returns the number of nodes in the list   */
300  /*                                                    */
301  /******************************************************/
302
303  template<class T>
304  long  DoubleLinkedList<T>::GetSize () const {
305   return count;
306  }
307
308  /******************************************************/
309  /*                                                    */
310  /* IsHead: returns true if current node is the first node*/
311  /*                                                    */
312  /******************************************************/
313
314  template<class T>
315  bool  DoubleLinkedList<T>::IsHead () const {
316   return currentptr == headptr;
```

```
317 }
318
319 /***********************************************************/
320 /*                                                       */
321 /* IsTail: returns true if current node is the last one  */
322 /*                                                       */
323 /***********************************************************/
324
325 template<class T>
326 bool  DoubleLinkedList<T>::IsTail () const {
327  return currentptr == tailptr;
328 }
329
330 /***********************************************************/
331 /*                                                       */
332 /* ResetToHead: sets current pointer to start of list    */
333 /*                                                       */
334 /***********************************************************/
335
336 template<class T>
337 void  DoubleLinkedList<T>::ResetToHead () {
338  currentptr = headptr;
339 }
340
341 /***********************************************************/
342 /*                                                       */
343 /* ResetToTail: sets current pointer to last node in list*/
344 /*                                                       */
345 /***********************************************************/
346
347 template<class T>
348 void  DoubleLinkedList<T>::ResetToTail () {
349  currentptr = tailptr;
350 }
351
352 /***********************************************************/
353 /*                                                       */
354 /* Next: move forward one node in the list               */
355 /*                                                       */
356 /***********************************************************/
357
358 template<class T>
359 void  DoubleLinkedList<T>::Next () {
360  if (currentptr)
361    currentptr = currentptr->fwdptr;
362 }
363
364 /***********************************************************/
365 /*                                                       */
366 /* Previous: backs up one node in the list               */
367 /*                                                       */
368 /***********************************************************/
369
```

```
370 template<class T>
371 void  DoubleLinkedList<T>::Previous () {
372  if (currentptr)
373    currentptr = currentptr->backptr;
374 }
375
376 /************************************************************/
377 /*                                                        */
378 /* GetCurrentNode: returns user data at current node or 0 */
379 /*                                                        */
380 /************************************************************/
381
382 template<class T>
383 T* DoubleLinkedList<T>::GetCurrentNode () const {
384  return currentptr ? currentptr->dataptr : 0;
385 }
386
387 /************************************************************/
388 /*                                                        */
389 /* DoubleLinkedList: copy constructor - duplicate a list */
390 /*                                                        */
391 /************************************************************/
392
393 template<class T>
394 DoubleLinkedList<T>::DoubleLinkedList (
395                                    const DoubleLinkedList<T>& r) {
396  CopyList (r);
397 }
398
399 /************************************************************/
400 /*                                                        */
401 /* operator=: Make a duplicate copy of a list            */
402 /*                                                        */
403 /************************************************************/
404
405 template<class T>
406 DoubleLinkedList<T>& DoubleLinkedList<T>::operator= (
407                    const DoubleLinkedList& r) {
408  if (this == &r) return *this; // avoid a = a; situation
409  EmptyList ();  // remove all items in this list
410  CopyList (r);  // make a copy of r's list
411  return *this;
412 }
413
414 /************************************************************/
415 /*                                                        */
416 /* CopyList: Make a duplicate copy of a list             */
417 /*                                                        */
418 /************************************************************/
419
420 template<class T>
421 void  DoubleLinkedList<T>::CopyList (
422                                    const DoubleLinkedList<T>& r) {
```

```
423    // handle the empty list first
424    if (!r.headptr) {
425     headptr = currentptr = tailptr = 0;
426     return;
427    }
428    count = r.count;
429    LinkNode* ptrRcurrent = r.headptr;
430    // previousptr tracks our prior node so we can set its
431    // forward pointer to the next new one
432    LinkNode* previousptr = 0;
433    // prime the loop so headptr can be set one time
434    currentptr = new LinkNode;
435    headptr = currentptr;  // assign this one to the headptr
436
437    // traverse list r's nodes
438    while (ptrRcurrent) {
439     // copy r's student info into our new node
440     currentptr->dataptr = new T;
441     *(currentptr->dataptr) = *(ptrRcurrent->dataptr);
442     currentptr->fwdptr = 0;  // set our forward ptr to 0
443     currentptr->backptr = 0; // set our back ptr to 0
444     // if previous node exists, set its forward ptr to the new one
445     if (previousptr) {
446      previousptr->fwdptr = currentptr;
447      currentptr->backptr = previousptr;
448     }
449     // save this node as the prevous node
450     previousptr = currentptr;
451     // and get a new node for the next iteration
452     currentptr = new LinkNode;
453     // move to r's next node
454     ptrRcurrent = ptrRcurrent->fwdptr;
455    }
456    delete currentptr; // delete the extra unneeded node
457    // leave list at the beginning
458    ResetToHead ();
459    }
460
461    /******************************************************/
462    /*                                                    */
463    /* FindNode: find the node whose data matches users   */
464    /*           specifications - calls user's Find Function */
465    /*                                                    */
466    /******************************************************/
467
468    template<class T>
469    bool  DoubleLinkedList<T>::FindNode (const void* ptrmatchData) {
470     if (!count) // empty list => not found
471      return false;
472     ResetToHead ();        // begin at the start of the list
473     while (currentptr) {  // examine each node in turn
474      if (*(currentptr->dataptr) == ptrmatchData)
475       return true;        // return true if this one matches
```

503

```
476   Next ();                    // move to the next node in the list
477   }
478   return false;              // did not find it in whole list
479 }
```

Here are the revised **PhoneDirectory** class definition and implementation. Note that it no longer is derived from **BaseObj**.

```
Phone Directory Class Definition
```

```
 1 #pragma once
 4 #include <string>
 5 #include <fstream>
 3 using namespace std;
 7
 8 const int MAX_FNAME_LEN = 11;
 9 const int MAX_LNAME_LEN = 21;
10 const int MAX_AREA_LEN = 4;
11 const int MAX_PHNUM_LEN = 9;
12
13 /**********************************************************/
14 /*                                                        */
15 /* class PhoneDirectory - encapsulates a Phone Book entry */
16 /*                                                        */
17 /**********************************************************/
18
19 class PhoneDirectory {
20
21 protected:
22   int   recordNumber; // these are added by the pgm for id purposes
23   char firstName[MAX_FNAME_LEN];
24   char lastName[MAX_LNAME_LEN];
25   char areaCode[MAX_AREA_LEN];
26   char phoneNumber[MAX_PHNUM_LEN];
27
28 public:
29   PhoneDirectory ();
30   PhoneDirectory (const char* first, const char* last,
31                   const char* area, const char* pnum, int num = 0);
32
33   // the access functions
34   int         GetRecordNumber () const;
35   const char* GetFirstName () const;
36   const char* GetLastName () const;
37   const char* GetAreaCode () const;
38   const char* GetPhoneNumber () const;
39
40   void SetRecordNumber (int num);
41   void SetFirstName (const char* first);
42   void SetLastName (const char* last);
43   void SetAreaCode (const char* area);
```

504

```
44  void SetPhoneNumber (const char* phnum);
45
46  // provide implementations of the pure virutal functions
47  bool MatchObject (const void* ptrtarget) const;
48  bool operator==  (const void* ptrtarget) const;
49
50 protected:
51  // helper function to copy strings and avoid overlaying memory
52  void CopyString (char* des, const char* src, unsigned int max);
53 };
54
55 #endif
```

Phone Directory Class Implementation

```
 1 #include <string.h>
 2 #include "PhoneDirectory.h"
 3
 4 /*********************************************************/
 5 /*                                                     */
 6 /* PhoneDirectory: default ctor                        */
 7 /*                                                     */
 8 /*********************************************************/
 9
10 PhoneDirectory::PhoneDirectory () {
11  recordNumber = 0;
12  firstName[0] = 0;
13  lastName[0] = 0;
14  areaCode[0] = 0;
15  phoneNumber[0] = 0;
16 }
17
18 /*********************************************************/
19 /*                                                     */
20 /* PhoneDirectory: make an instance from these values  */
21 /*                                                     */
22 /*********************************************************/
23
24 PhoneDirectory::PhoneDirectory (const char* first,
25                 const char* last, const char* area,
26                 const char* pnum, int num) {
27  recordNumber = num;
28  CopyString (firstName, first, MAX_FNAME_LEN);
29  CopyString (lastName, last, MAX_LNAME_LEN);
30  CopyString (areaCode, area, MAX_AREA_LEN);
31  CopyString (phoneNumber, pnum, MAX_PHNUM_LEN);
32 }
33
34 /*********************************************************/
35 /*                                                     */
36 /* CopyString: copy a string into member string without */
37 /*             overlaying memory                        */
```

505

```
38 /*              if src is too big, copies what will fit   */
39 /*                                                        */
40 /**********************************************************/
41
42 void PhoneDirectory::CopyString (char* des, const char* src,
43                                   unsigned int max) {
44   if (strlen (src) >= max) {
45     strncpy_s (des, max, src, max-1);
46     des[max-1] = 0;
47   }
48   else
49     strcpy_s (des, max, src);
50 }
51
52 /**********************************************************/
53 /*                                                        */
54 /* The Get... access functions                           */
55 /*                                                        */
56 /**********************************************************/
57
58 int         PhoneDirectory::GetRecordNumber () const {
59   return recordNumber;
60 }
61
62 const char* PhoneDirectory::GetFirstName () const {
63   return firstName;
64 }
65
66 const char* PhoneDirectory::GetLastName () const {
67   return lastName;
68 }
69
70 const char* PhoneDirectory::GetAreaCode () const {
71   return areaCode;
72 }
73 const char* PhoneDirectory::GetPhoneNumber () const {
74   return phoneNumber;
75 }
76
77 /**********************************************************/
78 /*                                                        */
79 /* The Set... Access functions                           */
80 /*                                                        */
81 /**********************************************************/
82
83 void PhoneDirectory::SetRecordNumber (int num) {
84   recordNumber = num;
85 }
86
87 void PhoneDirectory::SetFirstName (const char* first) {
88   CopyString (firstName, first, MAX_FNAME_LEN);
89 }
90
```

```
 91 void PhoneDirectory::SetLastName (const char* last) {
 92  CopyString (lastName, last, MAX_LNAME_LEN);
 93
 94 }
 95
 96 void PhoneDirectory::SetAreaCode (const char* area) {
 97  CopyString (areaCode, area, MAX_AREA_LEN);
 98 }
 99
100 void PhoneDirectory::SetPhoneNumber (const char* phnum) {
101  CopyString (phoneNumber, phnum, MAX_PHNUM_LEN);
102 }
103
104 /**********************************************************/
105 /*                                                        */
106 /* MatchObject: return true if this object matches target */
107 /*                                                        */
108 /**********************************************************/
109
110 bool PhoneDirectory::MatchObject (const void* ptrtarget) const {
111  return recordNumber == *((int*) ptrtarget);
112 }
113
114 /**********************************************************/
115 /*                                                        */
116 /* operator== return true if this object matches target   */
117 /*                                                        */
118 /**********************************************************/
119
120 bool PhoneDirectory::operator== (const void* ptrtarget) const {
121  return recordNumber == *((int*) ptrtarget);
122 }
```

Finally, here is the revised client program, **Pgm12a**. Key changes are highlighted in bold face.

```
Pgm12a - Phone Directory Program Using Template Double Linked List

 1 #include <iostream>
 2 #include <iomanip>
 3 #include <fstream>
 4 #include <crtdbg.h>
 5 #include <string>
 6 using namespace std;
 7 #include "PhoneDirectory.h"
 8 #include "DoubleLinkedList.h"
 9
10 /**********************************************************/
11 /*                                                        */
12 /* Pgm12a: Maintaining a Phone Directory Application      */
13 /*                                                        */
```

```
14  /************************************************************/
15
16  typedef DoubleLinkedList<PhoneDirectory> DoubleLL;
17
18  // the prototypes
19  bool LoadPhoneBook (DoubleLL& pb, const char* filename);
20  istream& InputPhoneData (istream& is, PhoneDirectory& pd);
21
22  ostream& DisplayPhoneListing (DoubleLL& pb, ostream& os);
23  void DrawLine (ostream& os, unsigned char c, int count);
24  void DisplayPhoneBookToFile (DoubleLL& pb);
25
26  void ShowMenu ();
27  int  GetMenuChoice ();
28  bool ProcessMenuChoice (DoubleLL& pb, int choice,
29                          bool& needToSave, ostream& os);
30
31  void AddEntry (DoubleLL& pb, bool& needToSavePb);
32  void DeleteEntry (DoubleLL& pb, bool& needToSavePb);
33  int  FindEntry (const void* ptrmatchData, const void* ptrthis);
34  void SavePhoneBook (DoubleLL& pb, bool& needToSavePb);
35  bool SaveCheck (DoubleLL& pb, bool needToSavePb);
36
37
38  int main () {
39   {
40    DoubleLL phoneBook; // create the phonebook list
41
42    // load the book from a file
43    if (!LoadPhoneBook (phoneBook, "phoneBook.txt"))
44     return 1;
45    // display the listing using fancy box drawing characters
46    DisplayPhoneListing (phoneBook, cout);
47
48    bool needToSavePb = false; // true when data has been changed
49    bool quit = false;         // true when it is safe to quit
50
51    // main loop shows a menu, gets a valid choice and process it
52    while (!quit) {
53     quit = ProcessMenuChoice (phoneBook, GetMenuChoice (),
54                               needToSavePb, cout);
55    }
56   }
57
58   if (_CrtDumpMemoryLeaks())
59    cout << "\nOops! Memory Leaks!!\n";
60   else
61    cout << "\nNo Memory Leaks\n";
62
63   return 0;
64  }
65
```

```
 66 /***********************************************************/
 67 /*                                                         */
 68 /* LoadPhoneBook: loads the list from a database file      */
 69 /*                                                         */
 70 /***********************************************************/
 71
 72 bool LoadPhoneBook (DoubleLL& pb, const char* filename) {
 73  ifstream infile (filename);
 74  if (!infile) {
 75   cerr << "Error: unable to open file: " << filename << endl;
 76   return false;
 77  }
 78
 79  int i = 1; // this will be the record id number value
 80
 81  // allocate a new phone directory structure
 82  PhoneDirectory* ptrpd = new PhoneDirectory;
 83
 84  // for each set of input data, insert the id number, add to list
 85  // and allocate another phone directory structure for the next
 86  // input opperation
 87  while (InputPhoneData (infile, *ptrpd)) {
 88   ptrpd->SetRecordNumber (i++);
 89   pb.AddAtTail (ptrpd);
 90   ptrpd = new PhoneDirectory;
 91  }
 92
 93  delete ptrpd;   // delete the unneeded structure - eof was found
 94  infile.close ();
 95  return true;
 96 }
 97
 98 /***********************************************************/
 99 /*                                                         */
100 /* InputPhoneData: input a single phone directory entry    */
101 /*                                                         */
102 /***********************************************************/
103
104 istream& InputPhoneData (istream& is, PhoneDirectory& pd) {
105  char c;
106  is >> c;  // input the leading " of first name
107  if (!is)
108   return is;
109  char str[80];
110  is.getline (str, sizeof(str), '\"');
111  pd.SetFirstName (str);
112  is >> c; // get leading " of last name
113  is.getline (str, sizeof(str), '\"');
114  pd.SetLastName (str);
115  is >> str;
116  pd.SetAreaCode (str);
117  is >> str;
118  pd.SetPhoneNumber (str);
```

```
119  return is;
120 }
121
122 /*****************************************************************/
123 /*                                                             */
124 /* DisplayPhoneListing: display in a fancy fashion the         */
125 /*                      complete phone listing                 */
126 /*                                                             */
127 /*****************************************************************/
128
129 ostream& DisplayPhoneListing (DoubleLL& pb, ostream& os){
130   // the text graphics codes to draw fancy boxes
131   unsigned char upleft = 218;
132   unsigned char upright = 191;
133   unsigned char botleft = 192;
134   unsigned char botright = 217;
135   unsigned char horiz = 196;
136   unsigned char vert = 179;
137   unsigned char leftright = 195;
138   unsigned char rightleft = 180;
139   unsigned char cross = 197;
140   unsigned char topdown = 194;
141   unsigned char botup = 193;
142
143   os << "                          My Phone Directory\n\n";
144
145   // draws the top line
146   os << upleft;
147   DrawLine (os, horiz, 6);
148   os << topdown;
149   DrawLine (os, horiz, 12);
150   os << topdown;
151   DrawLine (os, horiz, 22);
152   os << topdown;
153   DrawLine (os, horiz, 7);
154   os << topdown;
155   DrawLine (os, horiz, 10);
156   os << upright << endl;
157
158   // display a pair of column heading lines
159   os << vert << "Record" << vert << " First     " << vert
160      << " Last              " << vert << " Area  "
161      << vert << " Phone    " << vert << endl;
162   os << vert << "Number" << vert << " Name       " << vert
163      << " Name             " << vert << " Code  "
164      << vert << " Number   " << vert << endl;
165
166   // display another horizontal line
167   os << leftright;
168   DrawLine (os, horiz, 6);
169   os << cross;
170   DrawLine (os, horiz, 12);
171   os << cross;
```

```
172  DrawLine (os, horiz, 22);
173  os << cross;
174  DrawLine (os, horiz, 7);
175  os << cross;
176  DrawLine (os, horiz, 10);
177  os << rightleft << endl;
178
179  // for each set of data, display all values within the boxes
180  pb.ResetToHead ();
181  PhoneDirectory* ptrpd = pb.GetCurrentNode ();
182  while (ptrpd) {
183   os << vert << ' ' << setw(4) << ptrpd->GetRecordNumber() << ' '
184      << vert << ' ' << left
186      << setw(10) << ptrpd->GetFirstName() << ' ' << vert << ' '
187      << setw(20) << ptrpd->GetLastName() << ' ' << vert << " ("
188      << setw(3) << ptrpd->GetAreaCode() << ") " << vert << ' '
189      << setw(8) << ptrpd->GetPhoneNumber() << ' ' << vert <<endl
190      << right;
191   pb.Next ();
192   ptrpd = pb.GetCurrentNode ();
193  }
194
195  // display the bottom line of the box
196  os << botleft;
197  DrawLine (os, horiz, 6);
198  os << botup;
199  DrawLine (os, horiz, 12);
200  os << botup;
201  DrawLine (os, horiz, 22);
202  os << botup;
203  DrawLine (os, horiz, 7);
204  os << botup;
205  DrawLine (os, horiz, 10);
206  os << botright << endl;
207  os << endl;
208  return os;
209  }
210
211  /*************************************************************/
212  /*                                                         */
213  /* DrawLine: helper function to draw a horizontal line    */
214  /*                                                         */
215  /*************************************************************/
216
217  void DrawLine (ostream& os, unsigned char c, int count) {
218   // displays character c count times to the stream
219   for (int i=0; i< count; i++) {
220    os << c;
221   }
222  }
223
224  /*************************************************************/
225  /*                                                         */
```

511

```
226 /* ShowMenu: displays the main menu of choices              */
227 /*                                                            */
228 /**************************************************************/
229
230 void ShowMenu () {
231  cout << "\n\n"
232       << "Friends Phone Book\n\n"
233       << "1 Add new friend\n"
234       << "2 Delete an entry\n"
235       << "3 Display the phone listing\n"
236       << "4 Display phone listing to a file\n"
237       << "5 Save into a new file\n"
238       << "6 Exit\n"
239       << "\nEnter the number of your choice: ";
240 }
241
242 /**************************************************************/
243 /*                                                            */
244 /* GetMenuChoice: gets a valid menu choice                    */
245 /*                                                            */
246 /**************************************************************/
247
248 int GetMenuChoice () {
249  // get only a valid number between 1 and 6
250  int choice = 7;
251  while (choice < 1 || choice > 6) {
252   ShowMenu ();
253   cin >> choice;
254   if (!cin) {      // check for non-numeric data entered
255    cin.clear (); // yes, so reset cin state flags to good
256    char c;
257    cin.get(c);   // and get the offending character
258   }
259  }
260  cout << endl;
261  return choice;  // choice is a number between 1 and 6
262 }
263
264 /**************************************************************/
265 /*                                                            */
266 /* ProcessMenuChoice: driver to process that menu choice */
267 /*                                                            */
268 /**************************************************************/
269
270 bool ProcessMenuChoice (DoubleLL& pb, int choice,
271                         bool& needToSavePb, ostream& os) {
272  switch (choice) {
273   case 1:
274    AddEntry (pb, needToSavePb);
275    return false;
276   case 2:
277    DeleteEntry (pb, needToSavePb);
278    return false;
```

```
279    case 3:
280     DisplayPhoneListing (pb, os);
281      return false;
282    case 4:
283     DisplayPhoneBookToFile (pb);
284      return false;
285    case 5:
286     SavePhoneBook (pb, needToSavePb);
287      return false;
288    case 6:
289      return SaveCheck (pb, needToSavePb);
290    };
291    return false;
292  }
293
294  /************************************************************/
295  /*                                                        */
296  /* AddEntry: Adds a new person to the phone directory     */
297  /*                                                        */
298  /************************************************************/
299
300  void AddEntry (DoubleLL& pb, bool& needToSavePb) {
301    PhoneDirectory* ptrpd = new PhoneDirectory;
302    char c;
303    cin.get (c); // eat the crlf from the previous cin
304
305    char str[80];
306    // acquire the data on the new person to be added
307    cout << "Enter first name (10 characters):  ";
308    cin.get (str, sizeof (str));
309    ptrpd->SetFirstName (str);
310    cin.get (c);
311    cout << "Enter last name (20 characters):   ";
312    cin.get (str, sizeof (str));
313    ptrpd->SetLastName (str);
314    cin.get (c);
315    cout << "Enter the area code (3 numbers):   ";
316    cin.get (str, sizeof (str));
317    ptrpd->SetAreaCode (str);
318    cin.get (c);
319    cout << "Enter the phone number (999-9999): ";
320    cin.get (str, sizeof (str));
321    ptrpd->SetPhoneNumber (str);
322    cin.get (c);
323
324    // set its record id to one larger than is in the list
325    ptrpd->SetRecordNumber (pb.GetSize() + 1);
326
327    // and add it to the list
328    pb.AddAtTail (ptrpd);
329
330    // set the data has been modified flag
331    needToSavePb = true;
```

```
332  cout << "Addition was successful\n";
333 }
334
335 /*****************************************************************/
336 /*                                                             */
337 /* DeleteEntry: removes a person from the phone directory */
338 /*    Note: use the record id number as the key id field  */
339 /*                                                             */
340 /*****************************************************************/
341
342 void DeleteEntry (DoubleLL& pb, bool& needToSavePb) {
343  char c;
344  cout << "Enter the number of the phone book entry to delete: ";
345  int num;
346  cin >> num;
347
348  // now see if that number is in the list
349  if (pb.FindNode (&num)) {
350   // here we found the number in the list, so get that set
351   // and display it to the user and get a verification that
352   // they really do want to delete this one
353   PhoneDirectory* ptrpd = pb.GetCurrentNode ();
354   cout << "Confirm deletion of the following entry\n";
355   cout << setw(4) << ptrpd->GetRecordNumber() << "   " << left
357       << setw(10) << ptrpd->GetFirstName() << "   "
358       << setw(20) << ptrpd->GetLastName() << "  ("
359       << setw(3) << ptrpd->GetAreaCode() << ")  "
360       << setw(8) << ptrpd->GetPhoneNumber() << endl << right;
362
363   // do not accept anything but a Y or N
364   c = ' ';
365   while (c != 'Y' && c != 'N') {
366    cout << endl << "Enter Y to confirm deletion or N to abort: ";
367    cin >> c;
368    c = toupper (c);
369   }
370   if (c == 'N')
371    cout << endl << "Nothing done\n";
372   else {
373    // here it has been verified as the one to delete, so do it
374    pb.DeleteCurrentNode ();
375    // now handle renumbering all list items....
376    if (pb.IsHead()) // if deleted first one,
377     num = 1;         // renumbering begins at 1
378    else               // if we have not deleted the first one,
379     pb.Next ();      // move current to the first that may need it
380
381    // get current next one after the deleted one, if any
382    ptrpd = pb.GetCurrentNode ();
383    while (ptrpd) { // for each phone directory, change its record
384     ptrpd->SetRecordNumber (num++); // id number down one
385     pb.Next ();
386     ptrpd = pb.GetCurrentNode ();
```

514

```
387      }
388      cout << endl << "Record deleted\n";
389      // set the data has been modified flag
390      needToSavePb = true;
391    }
392  }
393  else
394    cout << endl
395        << "No such number in the phone book - try again\n";
396  }
397
398  /************************************************************/
399  /*                                                        */
400  /* DisplayPhoneBookToFile: displays report to a file      */
401  /*          Note: can handle long filenames and those     */
402  /*          with blanks in them                           */
403  /*                                                        */
404  /************************************************************/
405
406  void DisplayPhoneBookToFile (DoubleLL& pb) {
407  char filename[_MAX_FNAME];
408  char c;
409  cin.get(c); // eat the crlf from previous cin
410
411  cout << "Enter the filename on which to display the report\n";
412  cout << "If there are blanks in the filename,\n"
413      << "place double quotemarks around the whole filename.\n"
414      << "for example, \"My Phone Book.txt\" \n";
415  cin.get (filename, sizeof(filename));
416
417  // check for long filename with quotemarks
418  if (filename[0] == '\"') {// doesn't check for required ending "
419    int len = (int) strlen (filename) - 2;
420    strncpy_s (filename, sizeof(filename), &filename[1], len);
421    filename[len] = 0;
422  }
423
424  // attempt to open the file
425  ofstream outfile (filename);
426  if (!outfile) {
427    cerr << "Error: cannot open output file: " << filename << endl;
428    return;
429  }
430
431  // now display the fancy report to this file
432  DisplayPhoneListing (pb, outfile);
433  outfile.close();
434  cout << endl << "Report written to: " << filename << endl;
435  }
436
437  /************************************************************/
438  /*                                                        */
439  /* SavePhoneBook: saves the list to a new phone book file */
```

```
440 /*                    Note: it allows long filenames with      */
441 /*                    blanks as part of the filename            */
442 /*                                                              */
443 /****************************************************************/
444
445 void SavePhoneBook (DoubleLL& pb, bool& needToSavePb) {
446  char filename[_MAX_FNAME];
447  char c;
448  cin.get(c); // eat crlf from previous cin
449
450  cout << "Enter the new filename to use\n";
451  cout << "If there are blanks in the filename,\n"
452       << "place double quotemarks around the whole filename.\n"
453       << "for example, \"My Phone Book.txt\" \n";
454  cin.get (filename, sizeof(filename));
455
456  // check for leading "
457  if (filename[0] == '\"') {          // this code doesn't check for
458   int len = (int) strlen (filename) - 2; // required trailing "
459   strncpy_s (filename, sizeof(filename), &filename[1], len);
460   filename[len] = 0;
461  }
462
463  // attempt to open the file
464  ofstream outfile (filename);
465  if (!outfile) { // here we cannot, bad name or possibly bad path
466   cerr << "Error: cannot open output file: " << filename << endl;
467   return;
468  }
469
470  // now save all data, but do not save the record Id number
471  pb.ResetToHead ();
472  PhoneDirectory* ptrpd = pb.GetCurrentNode ();
473  while (ptrpd) {
474   outfile << "\"" << ptrpd->GetFirstName() << "\" "
475           << "\"" << ptrpd->GetLastName()  << "\" "
476           << ptrpd->GetAreaCode() << " "
477           << ptrpd->GetPhoneNumber() << endl;
478   pb.Next ();
479   ptrpd = pb.GetCurrentNode ();
480  }
481
482  pb.ResetToHead ();     // leave list at a valid location
483  outfile.close ();
484  needToSavePb = false;  // turn off any need to save the data
485  cout << "File Saved\n";
486 }
487
488 /****************************************************************/
489 /*                                                              */
490 /* SaveCheck: query the user - saving the data on exit          */
491 /*                                                              */
492 /****************************************************************/
```

```
493
494 bool SaveCheck (DoubleLL& pb, bool needToSavePb) {
495  if (needToSavePb) { // has the data been modified and not saved?
496   char yn = ' ';      // yes, so ask user if they want to quit
497   while (yn != 'Y' && yn != 'N') {
498    cout << "Note: you have made changes to the phone database\n"
499         << "and have not yet saved those changes\n"
500         << "Do you want to quit and discard those changes?\n"
501         << "Enter Y or N: ";
502    cin >> yn;
503    yn = toupper (yn);
504   }
505   return yn == 'Y' ? true : false;
506  }
507  else // here it has not changed, so it is safe to quit
508   return true;
509 }
```

If you are interested in further studies of templates, examine the Standard Template Library (STL) that comes with the Microsoft VC compiler as well as examine the New Style I/O stream classes.

Review Questions

1. What are the potential benefits of using one or more template functions in a program?

2. What are the potential benefits of using a template class in a program?

3. Why must a statement like
```
template<class T>
```
appear before each template function header and body?

4. Why must all of the member functions of a template class also be in the header file and not in a cpp file included in the project?

5. How can a client program specify which version of a template function the compiler is to use in a specific case? When would the client program desire to do so?

6. Why must some versions of a template function be specialized and hard coded in the header file?

Stop! Do These Exercises Before Programming

1. Write a template **ReciprocalSum()** function that is passed one type T parameter representing the upper limit to which to sum. Thus, if the function is called and passed an integer of 5, then it returns the sum of $1/1 + 1/2 + 1/3 + 1/4 + 1/5$ as a double. It always does the division and summation using doubles. Show how the client program can use it with the parameter being an int, a long and a double.

2. Write a **FindMin()** template function that is passed an array of type **T** and the maximum number of elements in use in the array. The function returns the smallest value in the array. Show how a client could use it to find the smallest element in the following arrays.

```
double array1[100];
int count1;

long array2[100];
int count2;

double* array3[100];
int count3;
```

3. Add insertion and extraction operators for the **ComplexNumber<T>** class presented in this chapter. The output should appear in the form of x + yi. The input consists of numbers in one of two formats: either 2.5 + 6.5i or (4.4, 2.2). Of course, they could also be x - yi as well.

Programming Problems

Problem Pgm12-1—A Template Growable Array Container Class

In chapter 7, **Pgm7b** presented a growable array container class. It achieved this ability to grow and be reusable by storing void pointers to the client's data. Redesign this class to be a template class storing the client's data as type **T**. Test the program using a modified **Pgm07b** client program. Note that the new class should perform a deep copy not a shallow copy and the client program should not have to use typecasting to get pointers back nor should it have to manually delete all items being stored before the destructor of the class is called.

Chapter 13—Binary I/O and Manipulator Functions

Introduction

A **binary file** is a file of data which are stored in internal numeric format rather than in the ASCII text format. Traditionally, the concepts and usage of binary files either are not presented or are not well covered in traditional beginning programming courses. However, virtually all company master files are in the binary format; very few, if any, data files contain text that can be streamed in using the usual extraction operator. This chapter is an attempt to remedy this situation. This chapter begins with a thorough discussion of what binary files are, how they are commonly used and finally some significant processing methods employed with binary files.

Dealing with Binary Files

Normal files are text files usually with the txt file extension. Other names used for text files are ASCII files and DOS text files. These files contain only ASCII displayable or printable characters and are fully visible using Notepad, for instance. The end of the file is marked by a single byte that contains a ^Z (Ctrl-Z). This EOF byte is normally never visibly displayed by editors. Text files can be displayed on the screen or printed exactly as is.

For example, if a text file contained the line
```
ABC 1234<cr>
```
Then the file would contain ten bytes with the following ASCII decimal values.
```
65, 66, 67, 32, 49, 50, 51, 52, 13, 10 <- ASCII values
 A   B   C   b   1   2   3   4  CR  LF <- the text line
```
To input this line, we must define two variables as follows.
```
char name[10];
int qty;
```
Then, we can use **cin** to input the line.
```
cin >> name >> qty;
```
The **istream** must therefore perform internal data conversion to convert this line into the way the data is to be stored in these variables in memory as shown in Figure 13.1.

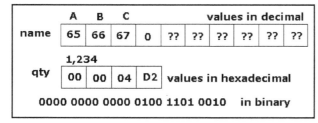

Figure 13.1 Internal Form of name and qty

In the above figure, the character string's contents are shown using the decimal values of the corresponding ASCII codes. The byte that contains the 0 is the null terminator. The integer **qty** occupies four bytes on a Win32 platform. I have shown the contents of each byte in the hexadecimal format which is usually used to show binary values. I also gave the contents of **qty** in binary. The leftmost 0 bit is the sign: 0 indicates a positive number. The 1 bit represents corresponding powers of 2. Or

$$1x2^1 + 1x2^4 + 1x2^6 + 1x2^7 + 1x2^{10} = 2 + 16 + 64 + 128 + 1024 = 1234$$

Notice then, that the **istream** must convert the ASCII digits into the binary number form before it can store the value into the integer. Likewise, on output, the internal forms must be converted back into a series of ASCII values. This data conversion is slow, particularly so for floating point types.

A binary file consists of data stored as a memory image of that data. Thus, if an **int** occupies four bytes and contains 00 00 04 D2 in hex, then, when written to a binary file, the binary file contains four bytes containing 00 00 04 D2 in hex.

Rule: No data conversion of any kind is ever done to binary files.

With binary files, data is transferred to and from memory precisely as it is/or will be in memory. The result is a tremendous increase in the speed of I/O operations.

Also, the end of file in a binary file is really tracked by the system and occurs when the file size number of bytes has been read into the computer.

Most all production data files will be binary files! Why? I/O speed is dramatically faster.

C++ Mechanics of Binary File Operations

When you open a binary file, you MUST tell the **iostreams** that this is a binary file. The **iostreams** default to a text file. All manner of ills will befall I/O operations if the binary file is opened as text and vice-versa. To tell the streams that this file is a binary file, OR in the **ios::binary** flag:

```
istream infile ("myfile.dat",
                ios::in | ios::binary);
ostream outfile ("newfile.dat", ios::out | ios::binary);
```

The input and output operations are much simpler. The **read()** and **write()** functions are used.

```
istream& read (char* inputarea, int number of bytes to input);
ostream& write (char* outputarea, int num of bytes to output);
```

If we are inputting or outputting something other than a string, we must use a typecast of the pointers.

```
infile.read ( (char*) &qty, sizeof (qty));
outfile.write ( (char*) &qty, sizeof (int));
```
Note that using the **sizeof (qty)** is better than **sizeof (int)** because, if you change its data type, it automatically gets the correct new size.

Suppose that we had an array of bounds 1000 which contained 950 elements and we wished to save that data to a binary file. The following writes all 950 elements in one write operation.
```
long array[1000];
int    count;
outfile.write ( (char*) array, sizeof (long) * count);
```

Character strings in a binary file are a bit peculiar. The binary file is a memory copy of the variable. So if **name** is defined to contain a maximum of 10 characters (including the null) and if it contains "Sam" (S, a, m, 0) at the moment, then, when written to a binary file, all ten bytes are written. When read in from a binary file, all ten bytes are input. However, C++ knows that the real contents of the string end at the null terminator.

Structures are commonly read or written to or from binary files. Suppose that we use the **CostRec** structure. Here is how an instance of this structure can be written and read.
```
struct CostRec {
 int itemno;
 short qty;
 char descr[21];
 double cost;
};
...
CostRec crec;
...
outfile.write ((char*) &crec, sizeof (crec));
                    // or sizeof (CostRec)
...
infile.read ((char*) &crec, sizeof (crec));
```

In this example, an array of cost records is loaded from a binary file.
```
int LoadArray (CostRec arec[], int limit) {
 ifstream infile("master.dat",
                ios::in | ios::binary);
 if (!infile) {
  cerr << "Error: Unable to open the input file!\n"
  exit (1);
 }
 int j = 0;
 while (j < limit &&
       infile.read ((char*) &arec[j], sizeof (CostRec))) {
  j++;
 }
 infile.close ();
```

```
    return j;
}
```

Physical I/O Versus Logical I/O Operations

The above examples have been logical I/O operations. That is, a program asks for the next cost record and the system "inputs" it into our designated input structure instance. However, in order to understand other I/O operations a program needs to make, the concepts of how the Windows/DOS system handles the physical I/O operations must be understood.

The smallest amount of data that the system will actually input or output to disk is called a **cluster**. The size of a cluster varies widely depending upon the size of the drive and the file system in use on that drive. Specifically, a cluster is **n** adjacent sectors of 512 bytes each. The number **n** varies depending upon the drive. For example, on the old 5¼ floppy disks, that held 360K of data, a cluster consisted of 2 adjacent sectors of data. Figure 13.2 shows the terminology of a track (a concentric circle of magnetic material that stores data) and a sector (a pie shaped section of a track).

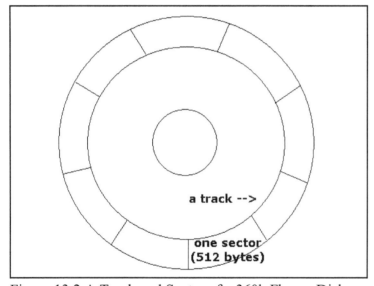

Figure 13.2 A Track and Sector of a 360k Floppy Disk

When running the FAT16 file system, Windows/DOS stores the number of clusters in an unsigned integer which is therefore limited to 65,536 clusters. The system identifies each cluster on the drive starting with cluster 0 and increases successive cluster numbers by one. On larger capacity drives, DOS must increase the number of sectors in a cluster to reduce the number of clusters to get their numbers to fit in range of the unsigned integer. Table 13.1 shows some cluster sizes for various disk drives or partitions.

Table 13.1 Cluster Sizes for Various Sized Partitions

Partition Size in MB	Type	Sectors Per Cluster	Cluster Size
16-127	FAT16	4	2K
128-255	FAT16	8	4K
256-511	FAT16	16	8K
512-1023	FAT16	32	16K
1024-2047	FAT16	64	32k
2048-4096	FAT16	128	64K
.256-8.01	FAT32	8	4K
8.02-16.02	FAT32	16	8K
16.03-32.04	FAT32	32	16K
>32.04	FAT32	64	32K

The cluster size is important. The significance is given by the following rule.

Rule: Windows/DOS physically inputs and outputs only clusters at a time.

In other words, DOS really only actually **physically** inputs or outputs a cluster. This is the smallest unit of I/O. Smaller requests are accumulated in a **buffer** staging area which is the size of a cluster. A buffer is a staging area for I/O operations. DOS stores smaller sized output requests in this buffer until it becomes full. When the buffer is full, DOS now actually writes that cluster. (When the file is closed, any partially filled buffers are also written. Also, there is a flush buffer instruction that a program may request.)

Suppose that you are running the FAT16 file system and have a 2G drive. The cluster size is 32K. Now suppose that you start writing a letter to me and get as far as entering the "D" (for Dear Vic) and then save the file. DOS reports that the file size is one byte. However, DOS can only write a cluster. So in fact this 1-byte file really occupies 32K of disk space!

I remember when I first got a large capacity drive and proceeded to copy all my data that was stored on several smaller drives onto this new big drive. The copy operation failed. The drive reported that there was 640M stored on a 1G drive! Most of the files were small C++ source files. I had wasted 360M of disk space because of the large cluster size.

Large cluster size also has a benefit—faster loading of data. For example, if Windows needed to load a system DLL file that was 64K in size, then only 2 physical I/O operations are required to input it if the cluster size is 32K. If I had a cluster size of say 4K instead of the 32K cluster size, then Windows would have to issue 16 I/O requests to load that same DLL file.

The vitally important fact is that a cluster is the smallest unit of information that Windows/DOS can physically I/O. Let's see how this physical I/O buffering operation works by following how the program that loads in cost records from a binary file on disk works. The main loop in **LoadArray()** was

```
int j = 0;
while (j < limit &&
       infile.read ((char*) &arec[j], sizeof (CostRec))) {
  j++;
}
```

Further, let's assume that the size of the **CostRec** structure is 100 bytes and that the cluster size of the drive holding the file is 2K or 2048 bytes. When the program issues its first read for the very first record, DOS must input the first cluster of data into its buffer and then copy the first 100 bytes into **arec[0]** as shown in Figure 13.3.

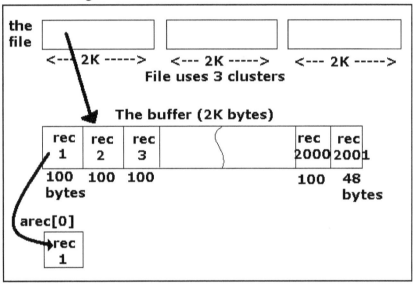

Figure 13.3 Input of the First Record

In order to input our first record, Windows/DOS inputs the first cluster into its internal buffer. Notice that there are 2000 complete 100 byte records and a partial last one of only 48 bytes. The remaining 52 bytes of the record 2001 are the first bytes in cluster 2. Next, the system copies the required 100 bytes from its buffer into our designated input area, here **arec[0]**.

However, when our program requests the next 1,999 records, Windows/DOS merely has to copy the required bytes from its buffer into our array elements. No physical I/O operations occur. However, when the program requests the 2001st record, after copying in the first 48 bytes of the data from its buffer, the system must again issue a physical I/O request to input the next cluster of data into its buffer. When that operation is complete, it can then move the remaining 52 bytes into our input area.

Note that smart disk cache controllers are highly likely to have (during some background processing time) already inputted the remaining clusters of the file and stored the data in cache memory. Thus, a real physical I/O operation might not need to be done. Instead, only a copy from cache memory is required in this case, speeding up the operation significantly.

As the system works its way through the buffer giving us our successive 100 byte records, DOS needs a pointer to keep track of where it is at in the buffer and file. This is called the **DOS File Offset Pointer** and is encapsulated by the **iostream** classes. The meaning of the DOS File Offset Pointer is this: the next input or output operation begins at this offset from the beginning of the file. And it is this DOS File Offset Pointer that we are vitally interested in understanding and using.

Figure 13.4 shows the DOS File Offset Pointer in operation during a series of successive input operations. Initially, when the file is first opened, the offset pointer is set to 0. In Figure 13.4, the first record has been input and stored in **arec[j]** and the file offset pointer has been incremented by the number of bytes just input. Figure 13.5 shows the situation after we input the second record.

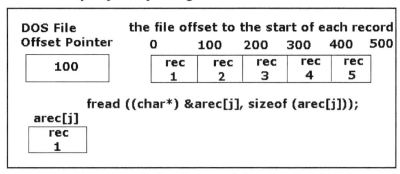

Figure 13.4 The File Offset Pointer After the First Read

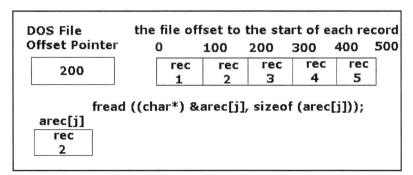

Figure 13.5 The File Offset Pointer After the Second Read

Now consider what would happen if somehow we placed 400 into the DOS file offset pointer and then issued another read instruction? Remember that the next file I/O operation will occur at this offset from the start of the file. We input record number 5. Further, what is the significance of the offset 500 in this example? It is the true DOS file size!

By adjusting the contents of the DOS file offset pointer, we can control which record in input by the next read instruction! Further, we can easily get the true file size of the file on disk. Finally, what results if we divide the file size by the size of the input record? This would be the number of records in the file! So this DOS file offset pointer is of vital importance when dealing with binary files.

Input streams have a pair of functions to read the contents of the DOS file offset pointer and to alter it. Output streams have a different pair of functions to read its contents and to alter it.
Input Streams:

```
pos_type tellg (); pos_type can be a long if filesize < 2G
istream& seekg (int offsetAmount, seekdir flag);
```
where the flag is
```
ios::beg - this offset from the beginning of the file
ios::cur - this offset from the current position in the file
ios::end - this offset from the end of the file
```

Output Streams:
```
pos_type tellp (); pos_type can be a long if filesize < 2G
istream& seekp (int offsetAmount, seekdir flag);
```
where the flag is the same as for input streams

The next series of examples illustrates some of the things we can do using binary files and the DOS file offset pointer.

Example 1: Reading and Writing Several Arrays to/from One Binary File

When the binary file contains several unrelated members, such as the contents of two different arrays that can contain differing number of elements, the current number in each array can be written first followed by that many elements of the corresponding array. Next, the number of elements in the second array is written followed by the second array.

```
long array1[1000];
int   count1;
double array2[2000];
int   count2;
...
outfile.write ((char*) &count1, sizeof (count1));
outfile.write ((char*) array1,  sizeof (long) * count1);
outfile.write ((char*) &count2, sizeof (count2));
outfile.write ((char*) array2,  sizeof (double) * count2);
```
To input the data, we code
```
infile.read ((char*) &count1, sizeof (count1));
infile.read ((char*) array1,  sizeof (long) * count1);
infile.read ((char*) &count2, sizeof (count2));
infile.read ((char*) array2,  sizeof (double) * count2);
```

Example 2: Processing an Array of Cost Records Blazingly Fast

Hard disks transfer data at very high rates. Some of today's faster disks transfer something like 120M per second or better. Let's say your drive can transfer 40M per second, roughly. How much data is 40M? To give you an appreciation for that volume, consider how many characters are in a large, fat novel. I wrote one once and it had 1,250,000 characters. How long would it take to type that many characters into the computer? Suppose that you can type as fast as the keyboard can accept data, 10 characters per second which corresponds to about 150 words per minute! This yields 125,000 seconds. How long is that? Well, let's divide by 50 seconds per minute (you need a breather each minute). This yields 2500 minutes. So let's divide by 50 minutes per hour (you will need a food break). This gives 50 hours or 2 days nonstop typing at 150 words per minute just to get the large novel entered. But in one second, the drive can give us 40M. Thus, if we had to type in that amount of data by hand, it would take us over 2 months continuously typing at 150 words per minute!

We can harness this incredible speed in our programs. There is no need for message boxes to pop up saying "10 seconds remaining" on copying a 10M file. It should take only a fraction of a second.

Here, the array **arec** can contain up to 100,000 records and **count** contains the current number in the array. To output the entire array of **count** elements, we code the following.

```
CostRec arec[100000];
long    count;
outfile.write ((char*) arec, sizeof (arec[0]) * count);
```

However, to input an array of an unknown number of cost records is more complex. We must find the number of elements that are actually in the binary file. We can use the **seekg()** and **tellg()** functions as follows.

```
// first, position file offset ptr to eof
infile.seekg (0, ios::end);
// get that offset and divide by size to get count
// note: if infile.tellg () % sizeof (CostRec) is not 0,
// then the file is somehow corrupt as we have a partial
// record in the file somewhere...
count = infile.tellg () / sizeof (CostRec);
// vitally important: reposition file offset to beginning!
infile.seekg (0, ios::beg);
// one read request inputs entire file at blazing speed
infile.read ((char*) arec, sizeof (CostRec) * count);
```

Just how fast is this going to be? It depends on the size of the file and available memory and the state of file fragmentation. But it will be a very dramatic speed up. I once had a student who was maintaining a production program that needed to input a very large two-dimensional array of long integers. It was a drafting type of program. However, every time the program needed to load the array, it took over three minutes! Likewise, when the user chose the save option, another three minutes elapsed. After this presentation, he rewrote the load operation to use the blazing fast approach. He wrapped a **cout** pair of messages around the new loading code: Starting the load and

End of load. This way, he figured he could time how long it now took to load. When he first ran it, the two messages went by almost instantaneously so he figured the data failed to load. But upon checking, it was all there! He ran it again to be sure. His three minute delay was cut down to virtually no observable time at all!

Example 3: Using Dynamic Allocation for an Array of Unknown Number of Records

Dynamic memory allocation is very often used to load arrays of unknown numbers of elements. The idea is to determine the file size and hence the number of elements actually present in the file. Then, allocate an array sufficiently large enough to hold that data. Finally, issue a single read to load the entire file in a blaze.

```
CostRec* arec;
int    count;
infile.seekg (0, ios::end);
count = infile.tellg () / sizeof (CostRec);
infile.seekg (0, ios::beg);
arec = new CostRec [count];
infile.read ((char*) arec, sizeof (CostRec) * count);
...
delete [] arec;
```

However, the above coding is mostly working. What happens if the amount of memory the program asks for is not available? What happens if the file is corrupt? We can insert a bit of error checking as follows.

```
count = infile.tellg () / sizeof (CostRec);
if (infile.tellg () % sizeof (CostRec) != 0) {
 cerr << "Error: the input file may be corrupt\n";
 infile.close();
 exit (2);
}
infile.seekg (0, ios::beg);
arec = new CostRec [count];
if (!arec) {
 cerr << "Error: insufficient memory to load the array\n";
 infile.close();
 exit (1);
}
infile.read ((char*) arec, sizeof (CostRec) * count);
```

Pgm13a—Speed Testing of Binary File Processing

The C language also has a set of binary file processing functions. Since some of you might not be familiar with these, here is a brief review of the pure C versions of these same functions. Once the review is complete, **Pgm13a** examines the relative speeds of the C versions versus the **iostream** versions and the impact of using a static input area versus dynamically allocating memory for the input area.

In C, a file is an instance of a **FILE** pointer. The **FILE** is a system structure that is created by the **fopen()** function and its address is returned by **fopen()**. This function is passed the character string file name which is in the same format as that for an **iostream**. It is also passed an options string. Typically, the options string is

"r"   for an ASCII text file opened for input only
"rb" for a binary file opened for input only
"w"   for an ASCII text file opened for output only
"wb" for a binary file opened for output only
"rb+" for a binary file opened for input and output - an update file

Here are two typical definitions and opens.

```
FILE *infile = fopen ("mybinaryfile.dat", "rb");
FILE *outfile = fopen ("mynewbinaryfile.dat", "wb");
```

If the file cannot be opened, **fopen()** returns a 0 or NULL pointer. This is usually tested this way.

```
if (!infile) {
  printf ("Error opening input file");
  return 1;
}
if (!outfile) {
  printf ("Error opening output file");
  return 1;
}
```

Handling the DOS File Offset Pointer is done with two functions similar to the **iostreams**. However, there is no difference between an input and an output file as there is with the streams. The two C functions are

```
fseek (FILE*, long offset, seek flag);
```

where the seek flag is

SEEK_END—seek offset number of bytes from the end of the file
SEEK_SET—seek offset number of bytes from the beginning of the file
SEEK_CUR—seek offset number of bytes from the current position

The content of the DOS File Offset Pointer is returned by the **ftell()** function.

```
long ftell (FILE*);
```

Typical coding to find the true DOS file size of a binary file is as follows.

```
fseek (infile, 0, SEEK_END);
```

529

```
filesize = ftell (infile);
fseek (infile, 0, SEEK_SET);
```

The C functions to input and output to a binary file are **fread()** and **fwrite()**. Their syntax is as follows using "thingy" as the item to be I/Oed.

```
NumberItemsRead    fread (void* addrOfThingy, sizeOfThingy,
                         numberOfThingys, FILE*);
fwrite (void* addrOfThingy, sizeOfThingy, numberOfThingys,
        FILE*);
```

For example to input and output a single **long** into the **quantity** variable, one can code this.

```
fread (&quantity, sizeof (quantity), 1, infile);
fwrite (&quantity, sizeof (quantity), 1, outfile);
```

To input and output the entire file, code this.

```
fread (buffer, filesize, 1, infile);
fwrite (buffer, filesize, 1, outfile);
```

Finally, **fclose()** is used to close the file.

```
fclose (infile);
fclose (outfile);
```

The C file handling functions are known for their speed of execution. On the other hand, the **iostreams** are much more convenient and easier to use. The extra ease of use costs a program a bit of execution speed. **Pgm13a** is going to explore the run time execution speed of these two file handling systems.

Suppose that the objective is to "copy" a file as fast as possible. The key variable is just how big is the file. For a copy operation, the file's type is not important; it can be a text or a binary file. This is true because the program is just going to copy all of the bytes and not attempt to make any sense of the meaning of the bytes in the file. The only thing that matters is the true DOS file size when the file is opened as if it were a binary file.

We could input 100 bytes at a time and output that 100 bytes and repeat that action until the entire file has been copied. If the file were large, this results in a large number of function calls. However, this is often the approach that programs take—input and output a "record" at a time until EOF is reached.

We can get a faster copy operation if we input the entire file at one time and then output it all at once. But to do this, an input/output area of sufficient size to hold the entire file must be available. Since we do not know the file size in advance, we can dynamically allocate the memory required once we obtain the true DOS file size. Alternatively, we could arbitrarily define a buffer that is sufficiently large enough—remember, on a WIN32 platform, a program can occupy up to 2G of memory. However, when the available free memory is exceeded, the program execution speed crashes because Windows then begins to make extensive usage of its swap drive to simulate the extra memory that is not physically available.

For this program, I have set an arbitrary maximum size for this I/O buffer area at 80M. And **Pgm13a** will abort the copy operation if the source file is larger than this 80M buffer. Since we wish our copy program to run as fast as possible, we cannot just define this buffer as automatic storage like this.

```
const long maxfilesize (81920000);
char buffer[maxfilesize];
```

Why? When is the memory for automatic storage allocated? Upon block entry. This will automatically cause the program to take a long time entering the block since the stack size default is usually around 2K and Windows must then resize memory to handle this sudden huge demand for automatic storage on the stack. (Note Windows 95 actually crashes when this much stack is requested.) A far better way is to make that buffer **static** so that the compiler creates space for it within the exe file itself. Thus, the buffer is really defined as **static**.

```
static char buffer[maxfilesize];
```

Pgm13a will time how long it takes to copy a large file using four methods:

> using a **static** buffer and the **iostreams** for the I/O,
> using **new** to dynamically allocate the buffer and **iostreams** for I/O,
> using a **static** buffer and the C style I/O functions,
> I/Oing as many 100 byte records as needed using the C style I/O functions

To track the time required by these methods, the **clock()** function is needed whose prototype is in **<ctime>**. Its prototype is

```
clock_t  clock (void);
```

where the data type **clock_t** is a **long**. This return value is the product of the amount of time that has elapsed since the start of a process and the value of the **CLOCKS_PER_SEC** constant.

The clock function tells how much processor time the calling process has used. The time in seconds is approximated by dividing the clock return value by the value of the **CLOCKS_PER_SEC** constant. In other words, clock returns the number of processor timer ticks that have elapsed. A timer tick is approximately equal to **1/CLOCKS_PER_SEC** second.

Thus, to time how long a sequence takes, we do the following.

```
clock_t start, end;
start = clock ();
... do the series to be timed
end = clock ();
double elapsedTime = ((double)(end - start))/CLOCKS_PER_SEC;
```

Thus, there are to be four programs to be run. However, when running timing series, it is wise to run the series a number of times and average the results. Thus, each of the four timing programs will append the seconds required on each run to an output text file. A fifth program will input these four result files and compute the four average times. Thus, there are five related programs that make up **Pgm13a**.

531

Multiple Projects in a Single Workspace

One could make five separate projects in five separate work spaces as we have been doing. However, these five are all related. Here it makes sense to make a single workspace that has five separate projects within it. Thus, if you examine the project folder, you will find **Pgm13a** folder and beneath it lie five other sub-project folders, **Pgm13a1**, **Pgm13a2**, **Pgm13a3**, **Pgm13a4**, and **Pgm13Avgs**.

To build one of these multi-program projects, select the solution icon in the Solution explorer, right click and add a new solution. Image 13.1 shows the complete **Pgm13a** workspace with its five sub-projects.

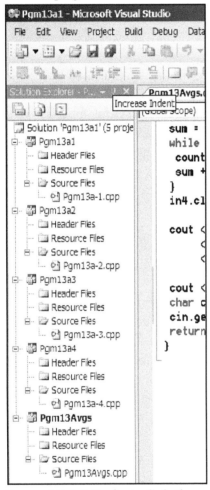

Image 13.1 5 Projects-Solution

To run a specific project, right click on the project and select "Set as startup project." when you set the Release Build, it sets such for all the projects at once. Rebuild Solution will then re-compile all the programs.

Here are the five programs in this timing package along with the batch command file I made to run them 10 times.

```
Pgm13a1
```

```cpp
 1 #include <iostream>
 2 #include <iomanip>
 3 #include <fstream>
 4 #include <stdio.h>
 5 #include <ctime>
 6 using namespace std;
 7 /***************************************************************/
 8 /*                                                             */
 9 /* Pgm13a: times the relative speed of several methods of      */
10 /*         copying a large file using binary I/O               */
11 /*                                                             */
12 /***************************************************************/
13
14 int main (int argc, char* argv[]) {
15
16  clock_t t0, t1;
17
18  // verify two filenames are passed on the DOS command line
19  if (argc != 3) {
20   cerr << "Error: enter 2 filenames on the command line";
21   return 1;
22  }
23
24  ifstream in;
25  ofstream out;
26  long filesize;
27  const long maxfilesize (81920000);
28
29  /***************************************************************/
30  /*                                                             */
31  /* begin timing the iostream sequence that dynamically         */
32  /* allocates memory for the actual size of the file            */
33  /*                                                             */
34  /***************************************************************/
35
36  t0 = clock ();
37  in.open (argv[1], ios::in | ios::binary);
38  if (!in.good ()) {
39   cerr << "Error opening input file " << argv[1] << endl;
40   return 1;
41  }
42
43  out.open (argv[2], ios::out | ios.binary);
44  if (!out.good ()) {
45   cerr << "Error opening output file " << argv[2] << endl;
46   return 1;
47  }
```

```
48
49  in.seekg (0, ios::end);      //find end of file
50  filesize = in.tellg ();      //store filesize
51  in.seekg (0, ios::beg);      //go to beginning of file
52
53  if (filesize > maxfilesize) {
54   cerr << "error: not able to go beyond 80M file\n";
55   return 1;
56  }
57
58  char *bufr = new char [filesize];
59  if (!bufr) {
60   cerr << "Unable to allocate memory";
61   return 1;
62  }
63
64  in.read (bufr, filesize);
65  out.write (bufr, filesize);
66
67  in.close ();
68  out.close ();
69  delete [] bufr;
70  t1 = clock ();
71
72  cout.setf (ios::fixed, ios::floatfield);
73  cout << setprecision (3);
74  // display the results
75  cout << "Time for newed  buffer and iostreams : " << setw (7)
76       << ((double)(t1-t0))/CLOCKS_PER_SEC << " seconds\n";
77
78  ofstream results ("a1.txt", ios::app);
79  results.setf (ios::fixed, ios::floatfield);
80  results << setprecision (3);
81  results << setw (7) << ((double)(t1-t0))/CLOCKS_PER_SEC << endl;
82  results.close ();
83
84  return 0;
85
```

Pgm13a2

```
 1 #include <iostream>
 2 #include <iomanip>
 3 #include <fstream>
 4 #include <stdio.h>
 5 #include <ctime>
 6 using namespace std;
 7 /***********************************************************/
 8 /*                                                         */
 9 /* Pgm13a: times the relative speed of several methods of  */
10 /*         copying a large file using binary I/O           */
11 /*                                                         */
```

```
12  /**************************************************************/
13
14  int main (int argc, char* argv[]) {
15
16   clock_t t0, t1;
17
18   // verify two filenames are passed on the DOS command line
19   if (argc != 3) {
20    cerr << "Error: enter 2 filenames on the command line";
21    return 1;
22   }
23
24   ifstream in;
25   ofstream out;
26   long filesize;
27   const long maxfilesize (81920000);
28   static char buffer[maxfilesize];
29
30   /**************************************************************/
31   /*                                                          */
32   /* begin timing the iostream sequence using a static 8M buffer*/
33   /*                                                          */
34   /**************************************************************/
35
36   t0 = clock ();
37   in.open (argv[1], ios::in | ios::binary);
38   if (!in.good ()) {
39    cerr << "Error opening input file " << argv[1] << endl;
40    return 1;
41   }
42
43   out.open (argv[2], ios::out | ios.binary);
44   if (!out.good ()) {
45    cerr << "Error opening output file " << argv[2] << endl;
46    return 1;
47   }
48
49   in.seekg (0, ios::end);      //find end of file
50   filesize = in.tellg ();      //store filesize
51   in.seekg (0, ios::beg);      //go to beginning of file
52
53   if (filesize > maxfilesize) {
54    cerr << "error: not able to go beyond 80M file\n";
55    return 1;
56   }
57
58   in.read (buffer, filesize);
59   out.write (buffer, filesize);
60
61   in.close ();
62   out.close ();
63   t1 = clock ();
64
```

535

```
65   cout.setf (ios::fixed, ios::floatfield);
66   cout << setprecision (3);
67   // display the results
68   cout << "Time for static buffer and iostreams : " << setw (7)
69        << ((double)(t1-t0))/CLOCKS_PER_SEC << " seconds\n";
70
71   ofstream results ("a2.txt", ios::app);
72   results.setf (ios::fixed, ios::floatfield);
73   results << setprecision (3);
74   results << setw (7) << ((double)(t1-t0))/CLOCKS_PER_SEC << endl;
75   results.close ();
76
77   return 0;
78
```

Pgm13a3

```
 1   #include <iostream>
 2   #include <iomanip>
 3   #include <fstream>
 4   #include <stdio.h>
 5   #include <ctime>
 6   using namespace std;
 7   /*************************************************************/
 8   /*                                                         */
 9   /* Pgm13a: times the relative speed of several methods of  */
10   /*         copying a large file using binary I/O           */
11   /*                                                         */
12   /*************************************************************/
13
14   int main (int argc, char* argv[]) {
15
16    clock_t t0, t1;
17
18   // verify two filenames are passed on the DOS command line
19   if (argc != 3) {
20     cerr << "Error: enter 2 filenames on the command line";
21     return 1;
22   }
23
24   long filesize;
25   const long maxfilesize (81920000);
26   static char buffer[maxfilesize];
27
28   /*************************************************************/
29   /*                                                         */
30   /* begin timing the C style sequence that uses a static 8M buf*/
31   /*                                                         */
32   /*************************************************************/
33
34    t0 = clock ();
35
```

```
36  FILE *input = fopen (argv[1], "rb");
37  FILE *output = fopen (argv[2], "wb");
38  if (!input) {
39   printf ("Error opening input file");
40   return 1;
41  }
42  if (!output) {
43   printf ("Error opening output file");
44   return 1;
45  }
46
47  fseek (input, 0, SEEK_END);
48  filesize = ftell (input);
49  fseek (input, 0, SEEK_SET);
50
51  if (filesize > maxfilesize) {
52   printf ("Error: not able to go beyond 80M file\n");
53   return 1;
54  }
55
56  fread (buffer, filesize, 1, input);
57  fwrite (buffer, filesize, 1, output);
58
59  fclose (input);
60  fclose (output);
61  t1 = clock ();
62
63  cout.setf (ios::fixed, ios::floatfield);
64  cout << setprecision (3);
65  // display the results
66  cout << "Time for static buffer and C style   : " << setw (7)
67       << ((double)(t1-t0))/CLOCKS_PER_SEC << " seconds\n";
68
69  ofstream results ("a3.txt", ios::app);
70  results.setf (ios::fixed, ios::floatfield);
71  results << setprecision (3);
72  results << setw (7) << ((double)(t1-t0))/CLOCKS_PER_SEC << endl;
73  results.close ();
74
75  return 0;
76
```

Pgm13a4

```
1 #include <iostream>
2 #include <iomanip>
3 #include <fstream>
4 #include <stdio.h>
5 #include <ctime>
6 using namespace std;
7 /**********************************************************/
8 /*                                                      */
```

```
 9  /* Pgm13a: times the relative speed of several methods of   */
10  /*          copying a large file using binary I/O            */
11  /*                                                           */
12  /*************************************************************/
13
14  int main (int argc, char* argv[]) {
15
16    clock_t t0, t1;
17
18    // verify two filenames are passed on the DOS command line
19    if (argc != 3) {
20      cerr << "Error: enter 2 filenames on the command line";
21      return 1;
22    }
23
24    /*************************************************************/
25    /*                                                           */
26    /* begin timing the C style sequence that pretends the file is*/
27    /* composed of 100 byte records and inputs and outputs each   */
28    /* record until eof is reached                                */
29    /*                                                           */
30    /*************************************************************/
31
32    char buf[100];
33
34    t0 = clock ();
35    FILE* input = fopen (argv[1], "rb");
36    FILE* output = fopen (argv[2], "wb");
37
38    if (!input) {
39      printf ("Error opening input file");
40      return 1;
41    }
42    if (!output) {
43      printf ("Error opening output file");
44      return 1;
45    }
46
47    long bytesToWrite;
48
49    while ((bytesToWrite = fread (buf, 1, sizeof (buf), input))
50      == sizeof (buf)) {
51      fwrite (buf, sizeof(buf), 1, output);
52    }
53    if (bytesToWrite)
54      fwrite (buf, bytesToWrite, 1, output);
55
56    fclose (input);
57    fclose (output);
58    t1 = clock ();
59
60    cout.setf (ios::fixed, ios::floatfield);
61    cout << setprecision (3);
```

```
62  // display the results
63  cout << "Time for 100 byte records and C style: " << setw (7)
64       << ((double)(t1-t0))/CLOCKS_PER_SEC << " seconds\n";
65
66  ofstream results ("a4.txt", ios::app);
67  results.setf (ios::fixed, ios::floatfield);
68  results << setprecision (3);
69  results << setw (7) << ((double)(t1-t0))/CLOCKS_PER_SEC << endl;
70  results.close ();
71
72  return 0;
73
```

Pgm13Avgs

```
 1 #include <iostream>
 2 #include <iomanip>
 3 #include <fstream>
 4 using namespace std;
 5 int main () {
 6
 7  cout << fixed << setprecision (3);
 9
10  double time;
11  double sum;
12  int count;
13
14  ifstream in1 ("a1.txt");
15  count = 0;
16  sum = 0;
17  while (in1 >> time) {
18   count++;
19   sum += time;
20  }
21  in1.close ();
22
23  cout << "Time for newed  buffer and iostreams : " << setw (7)
24       << sum / count << " seconds for " << setw (3) << count
25       << " runs\n";
26
27  ifstream in2 ("..\\a2.txt");
28  count = 0;
29  sum = 0;
30  while (in2 >> time) {
31   count++;
32   sum += time;
33  }
34  in2.close ();
35
36  cout << "Time for static buffer and iostreams : " << setw (7)
37       << sum / count << " seconds for " << setw (3) << count
38       << " runs\n";
```

```
39
40   ifstream in3 ("..\\a3.txt");
41   count = 0;
42   sum = 0;
43   while (in3 >> time) {
44    count++;
45    sum += time;
46   }
47   in3.close ();
48
49   cout << "Time for static buffer and C style   : " << setw (7)
50        << sum / count << " seconds for " << setw (3) << count
51        << " runs\n";
52
53   ifstream in4 ("..\\a4.txt");
54   count = 0;
55   sum = 0;
56   while (in4 >> time) {
57    count++;
58    sum += time;
59   }
60   in4.close ();
61
62   cout << "Time for 100 byte records and C style: " << setw (7)
63        << sum / count << " seconds for " << setw (3) << count
64        << " runs\n";
65
66   return 0;
67 }
```

```
Tester Bat File to Run The Series Ten Times

 1  Pgm13a1 a.dat b.dat
 2  Pgm13a4 a.dat b.dat
 3  Pgm13a2 a.dat b.dat
 4  Pgm13a3 a.dat b.dat
 5
 6  Pgm13a1 a.dat b.dat
 7  Pgm13a4 a.dat b.dat
 8  Pgm13a2 a.dat b.dat
 9  Pgm13a3 a.dat b.dat
10
11  Pgm13a1 a.dat b.dat
12  Pgm13a4 a.dat b.dat
13  Pgm13a2 a.dat b.dat
14  Pgm13a3 a.dat b.dat
15
16  Pgm13a1 a.dat b.dat
17  Pgm13a4 a.dat b.dat
18  Pgm13a2 a.dat b.dat
19  Pgm13a3 a.dat b.dat
20
```

```
21 Pgm13a1 a.dat b.dat
22 Pgm13a4 a.dat b.dat
23 Pgm13a2 a.dat b.dat
24 Pgm13a3 a.dat b.dat
25
26 Pgm13a1 a.dat b.dat
27 Pgm13a4 a.dat b.dat
28 Pgm13a2 a.dat b.dat
29 Pgm13a3 a.dat b.dat
30
31 Pgm13a1 a.dat b.dat
32 Pgm13a4 a.dat b.dat
33 Pgm13a2 a.dat b.dat
34 Pgm13a3 a.dat b.dat
35
36 Pgm13a1 a.dat b.dat
37 Pgm13a4 a.dat b.dat
38 Pgm13a2 a.dat b.dat
39 Pgm13a3 a.dat b.dat
40
41 Pgm13a1 a.dat b.dat
42 Pgm13a4 a.dat b.dat
43 Pgm13a2 a.dat b.dat
44 Pgm13a3 a.dat b.dat
45
46 Pgm13a1 a.dat b.dat
47 Pgm13a4 a.dat b.dat
48 Pgm13a2 a.dat b.dat
49 Pgm13a3 a.dat b.dat
50
51 cd Pgm13Avgs
52 pgm13avgs
53 cd ..
```

Of course, running these programs is a bit tricky. I copied all of the executables from the various **Release** subfolders into the main **Pgm13a** folder where the batch file is located. Here also is where I placed the large file to be copied, **a.dat**.

What are the results? Well, the exact results depend upon a wide variety of factors. Among these are the following. The type of CPU, the amount of available free memory, the cluster size, the state of file fragmentation, the total file size of the file to be copied, release or debug builds, and what other programs and events are also running at the time of the monitoring.

Debug builds tend to run much slower because of all the runtime checking that is occurring under the hood. One should time Release builds—they are highly optimized for speed.

If there is not enough free memory, then when copying large files, speed is lost rapidly as the system swaps things to the paging swap file.

One should time from a DOS prompt and not from running the program within the IDE. The VC IDE consumes a rather large amount of memory itself.

Files should be defragmented. Otherwise, the hard disk's read write heads must do a large amount of seeking to find each cluster scattered about the disk.

Here are some results that I obtained on a couple systems. I also manually timed a straight DOS copy operation.

C:\>copy a.dat b.dat

Plus I used the Explorer. With the file selected, I did an Edit-Copy followed by an Edit-Paste. With both of these, I manually watched the clock to obtain the durations.

Results on a 7M file using a Pentium 200 MHz with 64M RAM and running Windows 95b using a debug version run from the IDE:

```
Time for static buffer and iostreams : 3790 or    3.790 seconds
Time for newed  buffer and iostreams : 4340 or    4.340 seconds
Time for static buffer and C style   :  660 or    0.660 seconds
Time for 100 byte records and C style: 5270 or    5.270 seconds
```

Corresponding Release version run from a dos prompt:

```
Time for static buffer and iostreams : 3240 or    3.240 seconds
Time for newed  buffer and iostreams : 3620 or    3.620 seconds
Time for static buffer and C style   :  500 or    0.500 seconds
Time for 100 byte records and C style: 2300 or    2.300 seconds
```

Results on a 7M file using a PentiumII 333 MHz with 128M RAM and running Windows 2000 Pro using the same 7M file but with 80M buf

```
Time for newed  buffer and iostreams : 1.193 seconds for  10 runs
Time for static buffer and iostreams : 1.041 seconds for  10 runs
Time for static buffer and C style   : 0.768 seconds for  10 runs
Time for 100 byte records and C style: 0.737 seconds for  10 runs
```

Results on a 47M file using a PentiumII 333 MHz with 128M RAM and running Windows 2000 Pro with 80M buffer

```
Time for newed  buffer and iostreams : 8.051 seconds for  10 runs
Time for static buffer and iostreams : 8.267 seconds for  10 runs
Time for static buffer and C style   : 8.298 seconds for  10 runs
Time for 100 byte records and C style:14.176 seconds for  10 runs
Time for a DOS copy command          :13. seconds approximately
Time for Explorer Edit-Copy-Paste    :15. seconds approximately
```

Results on a 23M file on PentiumII 333 MHz with 128M RAM and running Windows 2000 Pro with 30M buffer

```
Time  for  newed   buffer  and  iostreams  :  3.600  seconds  for   10  runs
Time  for  static  buffer  and  iostreams  :  3.106  seconds  for   10  runs
Time  for  static  buffer  and  C  style   :  3.395  seconds  for   10  runs
Time  for  100  byte  records  and  C  style:  4.368  seconds  for   10  runs
```

The results are very interesting. The cluster size on Win95 system was 32K while the Win2000 system has a 4K cluster size. Note the interesting differences in these runs. The bottom line: using either the **iostreams** or C style functions to I/O the whole file at one time is significantly faster than either a DOS copy or the Explorer copy operations! Finally, a teaser. If you think this is fast I/O, there is another even faster method of I/O that is significantly faster than any of these. However, you will have to wait for the Windows programming text to find out about it, because it uses a series of Windows API functions calls.

Overview of Direct Access File Processing Operations

The ability to access the DOS file offset pointer becomes the basis for all types of direct access file processing operations. Direct access refers to the ability to input or output one specific record out of all others. In an Inquiry type of program, when the user enters some kind of key identification value, the program retrieves directly the record in the file that corresponds to that key. In a direct access update type of program, in addition to accessing a record with a specific identification key value, the program can rewrite just that corresponding record.

Direct access processing then differs from sequential access. The only way a sequential access operation could find a record that corresponded to a specific key identification value would be to input every record in turn looking for a match. With larger files, this is unworkable.

This section deals with the general theory of the more common methods that are employed.

The Relative Record Number Method

The most fundamental method of direct access is known as the relative record number method. Every record in the file must have the same length. The first record in the file is arbitrarily assigned relative record number of 0. Each successive record in the file has a relative record number that is one greater than the previous record. Figure 13.6 illustrates this with the five cost records. The key identifier value becomes the relative record number.

To access the cost record whose relative record number is 1, we must multiply the key by the size of the records, seek to that position from the beginning of the file and input that data.

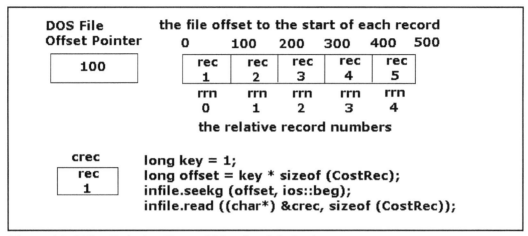

Figure 13.6 The Relative Record Number Method

Thus, given the key (which is the relative record number), one can directly access this data by the following.

```
CostRec crec;
long key;
long offset = key * sizeof (CostRec);
infile.seekg (offset, ios::beg);
infile.read ((char*) &crec, sizeof (crec);
```

The relative record number method is the fastest of all the methods for directly accessing a specific record in a binary master file. It is also the foundation of all the other more advanced methods. However, it has two serious drawbacks.

First, relative record numbers make terrible key identifier fields. Suppose your relative record number was 0. How many checks do you suppose you could cash if your account number was 0? These kinds of keys have nothing to do with real world identifiers, such as a person's social security number that is so often used as the key identifier.

Second, relative record numbers make deletion of records a total mess. Consider the following scenario as shown in Figure 13.7. Our company has five accounts. We use the relative record number as each account's id number. Now we delete Tom's account for failure to pay the balance due. What happens to the relative record numbers for those accounts that follow the deleted Tom account? They all change! Betsy's id, which was 3, now becomes 2. Fred's id, which was 4, now becomes 3. Thus, we have to issue new account numbers every time a record is deleted—reprint checks or issue a new plastic charge card and so forth.

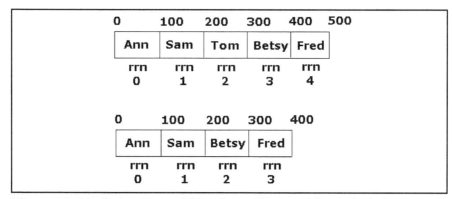

Figure 13.7 Relative Record Numbers Change After a Deletion

The Remainder Method

The remainder method is a vast improvement over the relative record number method because any numerical key can be used. Thus, one could use keys such as a person's social security number. With this method, one must know the absolute maximum number of records the binary master file is to contain. And a file containing this many records must be built. Initially all the records are dummies and contain dummy data. The procedure goes as follows.

1. Determine the maximum number of records.
2. Find the largest prime number that does not exceed this maximum number.
3. Let key equal the individual's key id number % this prime number.
4. The resulting key becomes the relative record number of that record on disk.

Suppose that we decide that our company will never have more than 3 clients. So the maximum number is three. The largest prime number that does not exceed 3 is 3. Now we decide to add Ann as a client. We assign her an id number of 1. The key becomes 1 % 3 or 1. Thus, her data goes into relative record number 1 in the file. This process is shown in Figure 13.8. In a similar manner, we add clients Tom (id = 2) and Betsy (id = 3).

Client	ID	Key (rrn)
		ID % 3
Ann	1	1
Tom	2	2
Betsy	3	0

0	100	200
Betsy	Ann	Tom
rrn	rrn	rrn
0	1	2

Figure 13.8 The Remainder Method in Action

So far, all is working perfectly. But what happens when we decide to expand and add another client, say Sam? We assign Sam the id number of 4. The remainder is 1 and so the relative record number is 1. However, there already is a record at that location, Ann. Oops. Now what do we do? This is the common problem of duplicate remainders. The solution is to store all duplicate remainder records sequentially in an overflow area that begins immediately after the maximum number of records. Figure 13.9 shows the situation after adding three more clients.

545

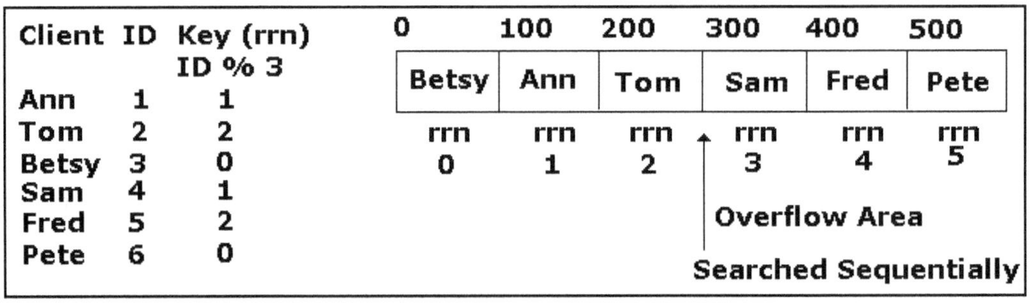

Client	ID	Key (rrn) ID % 3	0	100	200	300	400	500
			Betsy	Ann	Tom	Sam	Fred	Pete
Ann	1	1	rrn 0	rrn 1	rrn 2	rrn 3	rrn 4	rrn 5
Tom	2	2						
Betsy	3	0						
Sam	4	1				Overflow Area		
Fred	5	2						
Pete	6	0				Searched Sequentially		

Figure 13.9 Three Records in the Overflow Area

The coding to access a remainder method file is as follows.

```
long idNumber;            // the person's id number just input
long key = idNumber % Max; //Max is the max number of recs
long offset = key * sizeof (CostRec);
infile.seekg (offset, ios::beg);
infile.read ((char*) &crec, sizeof (crec);
if (crec.idNumber != idNumber) {
 // oops, the record must be in the overflow area
 infile.seekg (Max * sizeof(CostRec));
 while (idNumber != crec.idNumber && infile) {
  infile.read ((char*) &crec, sizeof (crec);
 }
 if (infile) {
 // here we have the desired record
 }
 else {
  cerr << "Error: record not found in data base\n";
 }
}
else {
 // here we have the desired record
}
```

Since the overflow area must be searched sequentially, the more records that are in the overflow area, the poorer the program's performance. Consider what would have occurred if I had used these clients' social security numbers as their identification keys. We might have had the following.

```
Ann      333 33 3333
Tom      333 33 3336
Betsy    333 33 3339
Sam      666 66 6666
Fred     999 99 9999
Pete     333 66 9999
```

All of these yield the same exact relative record number of 1!

To get the best results from the remainder method, one needs a good guess of the maximum number of records ever to be needed. Secondly, one should assign id numbers beginning with 1 up to that maximum number. This would avoid as many duplicate remainders as possible.

The Indexed Sequential Access Method (ISAM)

The Indexed Sequential Access Method, or ISAM for short, permits one to have any type of key identifiers desired, including characters as well as numerical digits. The ISAM scheme then stores a table of id keys versus the relative record number assigned to that record. Figure 13.10 illustrates this approach for our three clients.

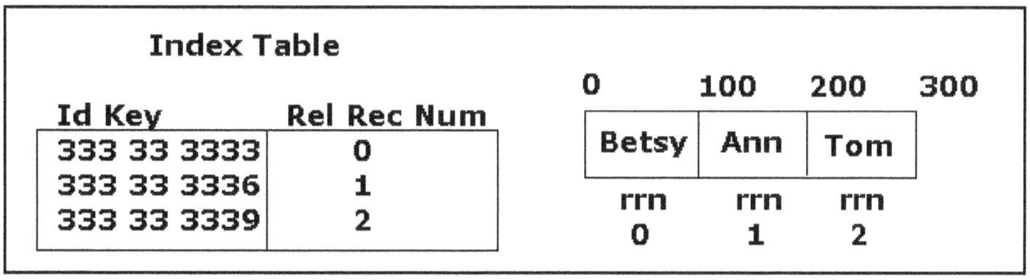

Figure 13.10 The ISAM Method with Three Clients

Notice that the key id numbers can be anything. To find any record, one searches the index table's Id Key array looking for an exact match. When found, the key to use becomes the corresponding relative record number. One would then proceed to input the data as before by finding the offset, seeking to that location and reading in the record.

Of course, one must save this index table on disk as well as the binary master file. Often the file extension .idx or .id is used. Sometimes the index file gets lost or accidentally deleted. Thus, the Id Key values must also be stored as a field within each record in the master file. Then, the index file can be recreated simply by reading in each record sequentially and adding another entry to the new index.

This method gets its name from the ability to read the file sequentially or by accessing a specific record directly. A monthly billing program certainly would access the file sequentially as it methodically printed a bill for each customer in turn.

However, of the three methods for direct access, the ISAM method is the slowest in execution because of the table lookup operation. Suppose that the Id Keys were actually character strings, such as part numbers AA-123-Z-42. How would the comparisons be done? We would have to use a **stricmp()** function call for each test! To speed up the searching operation when there are large numbers of records in the index, the index is maintained in a sorted manner, usually low to high. If the Id Keys are numeric and sorted, a binary search can be used to more rapidly find the matching entry.

Further, if the index is huge, then several layers of indices can be constructed. One might have a top-level index table such as shown below.

547

Master Index
Id Range   Use this index file next
100 00 0000 to 199 99 9999   Index1.idx
200 00 0000 to 299 99 9999   Index2.idx

...

900 00 0000 to 999 99 9999   Index9.idx
Then in the nine additional index tables, only the indicated range of id values are present.

Handling Variable Length Records

Implicit in the entire discussion thus far is the fact that all records must be fixed in length. That is, all records contain the same number of bytes so that we can calculate the file offset by multiplying the relative record number by the constant fixed size. However, in the real world, not all records are fixed in length. How can a binary file contain variable length records and still provide direct access to them?

When a variable length record is written to disk, uniformly across all platforms, the first two or four bytes of that record contain the total length of the record. Without some idea of the length of the current record, it is impossible to effectively input it.

A trick that is often used to provide a method of direct access to a set of varying length records in a binary master file is to modify the ISAM index table. Instead of storing the relative record number, let's store the actual file offset to get to that record. It is also valuable to store the length of that record in the table as well. For example, we could have the following index table.

```
Id Number       Offset Length
111 11 1111        0       50
122 34 4444       50      100
344 43 6456      150      200
344 55 5555      350       50
555 55 5555      400      100
```

Now when a match is found, we seek to that offset and input the length number of bytes.

Handling Update Files in C++

When a program is to perform a binary file update, a record with a specific key is read into memory, changes are made to its contents, and the record rewritten back to disk at the same location in the file. This means that we need a file stream that can be both read and written. Such streams are instances of the **fstream** class.

Further, we must use **seekg()** and **tellg()** on the input side and **seekp()** and **tellp()** on the output side. However, another problem is likely to occur. Suppose we are reading records and reach the end of file. The stream goes into the end of file state. No further I/O operations are allowed because it is at the end of file. After handling any processing required because the end of file was reached, we need a way to reset the file back into the good state so that further I/O operations can be performed. The **clear()** function does this for us. We pass it the flag **ios::good** as the state in which we wish the stream to be. For example,

```
file.clear (ios::good);
```

would reset all flags to the good state for the resumption of I/O operations.

Pgm13b—The Master File Update Program—Relative Record Method

Pgm13b is designed to illustrate the methods required to handle update files using **fstream** instances. Acme Credit Card Company has a master file of card holders. During the day, three types of transactions can occur. A new card holder can be added. An existing card holder can have an increase in their credit limit. An existing card holder's balance can be changed because of payments or additional charges.

Initially, the binary master file must be constructed from a text file. The file contains the person's name surrounded by double quote marks. This is followed by their balance and their credit limit. The id number of each client is the relative record number. Thus, the program begins by building the binary master file.

Next, a file of new transactions must be applied to the master file. The first character in the transaction's file determines what type of transaction this line contains. If the character is an "a", then this is an add new client request. The new client's name follows next and is surrounded by double quote marks. Then comes the balance and finally the limit for that client. If the character is a "b", then we are to modify the balance. In this case, the next number is the relative record number id field which is followed by the relative change in their balance, a positive or negative number. If the first character is an "l", then we are to change their credit limit. The client's id number again comes next followed by the relative change in their credit limit.

When the transactions have been processed, a new binary master file is written. Here is what the output from the program looks like.

```
Output from Pgm13b - Binary Master File Update Program

 1 File initially contains 4 records
 3
 4  Acme Credit Master File
 5
 6 Id Number   Name                   Balance   Limit
 7
 8     0        Annie Jones-Smith     4500.00   5000.00
 9     1        Betsy Smith           3000.00   4000.00
```

```
10       2        Samuel Spade           2500.42   3000.00
11       3        Thomas Dunhill         3500.00   4500.00
12
13
14 Transaction Log
15
16       4        Joe Smythe             4242.00   5000.00   Added
17       0        Annie Jones-Smith      4750.00   5000.00   Balance +250.00
18       2        Samuel Spade           2542.42   3000.00   Balance + 42.00
19       1        Betsy Smith            3000.00   6000.00   Limit + 2000.00
20       5        Henry P. Jones         4000.00   5000.00   Added
21
22
23 File now contains 6 records
24
25
26  Acme Credit Master File
27
28 Id Number  Name                       Balance   Limit
29
30       0        Annie Jones-Smith      4750.00   5000.00
31       1        Betsy Smith            3000.00   6000.00
32       2        Samuel Spade           2542.42   3000.00
33       3        Thomas Dunhill         3500.00   4500.00
34       4        Joe Smythe             4242.00   5000.00
35       5        Henry P. Jones         4000.00   5000.00
```

Here are the original **Accounts.txt** input file from which the master file is constructed and the **transactions.txt** file that defines the day's operations to be performed on the master file.

```
The Original Text Accounts Input File

1 "Annie Jones-Smith" 4500 5000
2 "Betsy Smith" 3000 4000
3 "Samuel Spade" 2500.42 3000
4 "Thomas Dunhill" 3500 4500
```

```
The TransactionsText File

1 a "Joe Smythe" 4242 5000
2 b 0 250
3 b 2 42
4 L 1 2000
5 a "Henry P. Jones" 4000 5000
```

In the **main()** function, notice how the update file is defined and opened.
```
fstream inout (masterfile, ios::in | ios::out | ios::binary);
```
Also, notice how the current number of records in the binary master file is obtained.
```
inout.seekg (0, ios::end);
maxCountOfRecs = inout.tellg () / sizeof (AccountRec);
```

```
cout << "File initially contains " << maxCountOfRecs
     << " records\n";
inout.seekg (0, ios::beg);
```

Remember to always keep the DOS file offset pointer at the beginning of the file. This is because **MakeReport()** reads the file sequentially from beginning to end. Also notice how the update file is passed to other functions. It is a reference to a **fstream** instance.

```
void MakeReport (fstream& inout);
void ProcessTransactions (fstream& inout, int& count);
```

Notice in the **MakeReport()** function, which reads the binary file sequentially until the end of file is signaled, that there must be a call to the **clear()** function to reset the EOF flag.

```
in.seekg (0, ios::beg);
// and clear the eof flag so more I/O to file can occur
in.clear (ios::goodbit);
```

To add a new record to the binary master file, we must position the file offset pointer to the end of the file so that the next write is appended to the end of the file.

```
inout.seekp (0, ios::end);
// and write new data at the current end of the file
inout.write ((char*) &rec, sizeof (rec));
```

The update sequence starts with the input of the id number, that is, the relative record number. This number is multiplied by the size of the records to obtain the offset for this record in the file. The file offset pointer is then set and the original data read. Once the changes have been made, the file offset pointer is repositioned back to the start of this record and the new data is written over the top of the old data in the file. If we did not reposition, then the rewrite would write over the next record after this one in the master file because the read operation adds the number of bytes just read to the file offset pointer.

```
infile >> findId >> num;
long offset = findId * sizeof (AccountRec);
inout.seekg (offset, ios::beg);
inout.read ((char*) &rec, sizeof (rec));
rec.creditBalance += num;
inout.seekp (offset, ios::beg);
inout.write ((char*) &rec, sizeof (rec));
```

Here is the complete **Pgm13b** update program.

```
Pgm13b - Master File Update Program - Relative Record Number

 1 #include <iostream>
 2 #include <fstream>
 3 #include <iomanip>
 4 #include <string>
 5 using namespace std;
 6
 7 /**********************************************************************/
 8 /*                                                                    */
 9 /* Pgm13b: Acme Credit Update - binary file update program           */
10 /*                                                                    */
```

```
11 /**************************************************************/
12
13 const int MaxNameLen = 42;
14
15 struct AccountRec {
16   int    idNum;
17   char   name[MaxNameLen];
18   double creditBalance;
19   double creditLimit;
20 };
21
22 void InitialBuildOfMasterFile (const char* filename);
23 void MakeReport (fstream& inout);
24 void ProcessTransactions (fstream& inout, int& count);
25
26 int main () {
27   // setup floating point output for dollars and cents
28   cout << fixed << setprecision (2);
31
32   int maxCountOfRecs;
33   const char* masterfile = "AcmeCredit.dat";
34
35   // one time only, build the binary master file from a text file
36   InitialBuildOfMasterFile (masterfile);
37
38   // open the binary master file as an updat file
39   fstream inout (masterfile, ios::in | ios::out | ios::binary);
40   // calculate the number of records in the master file
41   inout.seekg (0, ios::end);
42   maxCountOfRecs = inout.tellg () / sizeof (AccountRec);
43   cout << "File initially contains " << maxCountOfRecs
44        << " records\n";
45   inout.seekg (0, ios::beg);
46
47   // display a report of all clients - read the binary master file
48   MakeReport (inout);
49
50   // handle all additions and updates to master file
51   ProcessTransactions (inout, maxCountOfRecs);
52
53   // now recalculate the number of records in the file
54   inout.seekg (0, ios::end);
55   maxCountOfRecs = inout.tellg () / sizeof (AccountRec);
56   inout.seekg (0, ios::beg);
57   cout << "\n\nFile now contains " << maxCountOfRecs
58        << " records\n";
59
60   // display a report of all clients after the update process
61   MakeReport (inout);
62   inout.close ();
63   return 0;
64 }
65
```

```
 66  /****************************************************************/
 67  /*                                                              */
 68  /*  InitialBuildOfMasterFile: make binary master from txt file  */
 69  /*                                                              */
 70  /****************************************************************/
 71
 72  void InitialBuildOfMasterFile (const char* filename) {
 73   AccountRec rec;
 74   // open text and the binary file
 75   ofstream outfile (filename, ios::out | ios::binary);
 76   ifstream infile ("accounts.txt");
 77   if (!infile || !outfile) {
 78    cerr << "Error: cannot open files\n";
 79    exit (1);
 80   }
 81
 82   char c;
 83   int i = 0;
 84
 85   while (infile >> c && c == '\"') {
 86    infile.getline (rec.name, sizeof (rec.name), '\"');
 87    infile >> rec.creditBalance >> rec.creditLimit;
 88    rec.idNum = i++;
 89    if (infile)
 90     outfile.write ((char*) &rec, sizeof (rec));
 91   }
 92
 93   if (infile.good ()) {
 94    cerr << "Error inputting initial data\n";
 95    exit (2);
 96   }
 97
 98   infile.close ();
 99   outfile.close ();
100  }
101
102  /****************************************************************/
103  /*                                                              */
104  /*  MakeReport: read binary file sequentially to eof            */
105  /*                                                              */
106  /****************************************************************/
107
108  void MakeReport (fstream& in) {
109   AccountRec rec;
110   int count = 0;
111   cout << "\n\n Acme Credit Master File\n\n"
112        << "Id Number  Name                            Balance"
113           "  Limit\n\n";
114
115   while (in.read ((char*) &rec, sizeof (rec))) {
116    cout << setw (5) << rec.idNum << "       ";
117    cout.setf (ios::left, ios::adjustfield);
118    cout << setw (30) << rec.name;
```

```
119      cout.setf (ios::right, ios::adjustfield);
120      cout << setw (9) << rec.creditBalance << setw (9)
121          << rec.creditLimit << endl;
122    }
123
124    // here it is eof, so reset file offset pointer back to start
125    in.seekg (0, ios::beg);
126    // and clear the eof flag so more I/O to file can occur
127    in.clear (ios::goodbit);
128  }
129
130  /****************************************************************/
131  /*                                                              */
132  /* ProcessTransactions: add, update limit or update balance    */
133  /*                                                              */
134  /****************************************************************/
135
136  void ProcessTransactions (fstream& inout, int& count) {
137    AccountRec rec;
138    char transType;
139    char c;
140    double num;
141    int findId;
142
143    cout << "\n\nTransaction Log\n\n";
144
145    ifstream infile ("transactions.txt");
146    if (!infile) {
147     cerr << "Error: cannot open transactions file\n";
148     exit (3);
149    }
150
151    // handle all transactions in the file
152    while (infile >> transType) {
153     transType = toupper (transType);  // change code to upper case
154
155     if (transType == 'A') { // add a new record to master file
156      rec.idNum = count;
157      infile >> c;
158      infile.getline (rec.name, sizeof (rec.name), '\"');
159      infile >> rec.creditBalance >> rec.creditLimit;
160      // first point file offset pointer to eof mark
161      inout.seekp (0, ios::end);
162      // and write new data at the current end of the file
163      inout.write ((char*) &rec, sizeof (rec));
164      // display results of addition
165      cout << setw (5) << rec.idNum << "     ";
166      cout.setf (ios::left, ios::adjustfield);
167      cout << setw (30) << rec.name;
168      cout.setf (ios::right, ios::adjustfield);
169      cout << setw (9) << rec.creditBalance << setw (9)
170          << rec.creditLimit << " Added\n";
171      count++;
```

```
172     }
173     else if (transType == 'B') { // do a balance update
174       infile >> findId >> num;
175       // calculate the file offset of this id
176       long offset = findId * sizeof (AccountRec);
177       // position file offset pointer to this record's location
178       inout.seekg (offset, ios::beg);
179       // and input the record with this id
180       inout.read ((char*) &rec, sizeof (rec));
181       // update its balance
182       rec.creditBalance += num;
183       // reposition to this record in the master file
184       inout.seekp (offset, ios::beg);
185       // and rewrite this updated record
186       inout.write ((char*) &rec, sizeof (rec));
187       // display results
188       cout << setw (5) << rec.idNum << "        ";
189       cout.setf (ios::left, ios::adjustfield);
190       cout << setw (30) << rec.name;
191       cout.setf (ios::right, ios::adjustfield);
192       cout << setw (9) << rec.creditBalance << setw (9)
193           << rec.creditLimit << " Balance + " << num << endl;
194     }
195     else if (transType == 'L') { // here update credit limit
196       infile >> findId >> num;
197       // calculate the file offset for this id
198       long offset = findId * sizeof (AccountRec);
199       // position file offset to point to this record
200       inout.seekg (offset, ios::beg);
201       // input the record with this id
202       inout.read ((char*) &rec, sizeof (rec));
203       // update its credit limit
204       rec.creditLimit += num;
205       // reposition to this record in the master file
206       inout.seekp (offset, ios::beg);
207       // and rewrite this record in the master file
208       inout.write ((char*) &rec, sizeof (rec));
209       // display the results
210       cout << setw (5) << rec.idNum << "        ";
211       cout.setf (ios::left, ios::adjustfield);
212       cout << setw (30) << rec.name;
213       cout.setf (ios::right, ios::adjustfield);
214       cout << setw (9) << rec.creditBalance << setw (9)
215           << rec.creditLimit << " Limit + " << num << endl;
216     }
217     else {
218       cerr << "Error: invalid transaction code: " << transType
219           << endl;
220       exit (4);
221     }
222   }
223 }
```

Structure Alignment

When dealing with binary files, there is another architectural concern that must be understood and used. This is the principle of structure or data alignment in memory. Applications should align structure members and data values at addresses that are "natural" for the data type. A 4-byte type should be aligned on an address evenly divisible by 4. An 8-byte type should be aligned on an address evenly divisible by 8. The reason for this is how the circuitry fetches data from memory. No matter how you have the data stored in memory, the circuitry will retrieve that data. It is a matter of how efficiently it gets that data.

When inputting data from disk, remember that DOS first inputs an entire cluster of data into its internal buffer in memory. Then, it extracts what has been requested from the buffer and moves it into the destination variable. Thus, binary files on disk mirror this structure alignment.

Suppose that we wished to access a **long** whose 4-byte value began at memory location 2 in the DOS buffer, which is an address not evenly divisible by 4. The circuitry must fetch 2 4-byte memory locations and then extract the desired 4-byte long from the two 4-byte locations. This is shown in Figure 13.11. This is action causes a hardware fetch fault to occur. The hardware proceeds to get the two pieces from memory and join them into the 4-byte resulting **long** value. This faulting operation slows the memory accessing down significantly. But it guarantees that the requested data is retrieved. If the data is properly aligned, no fault occurs and the data is fetched normally and quickly.

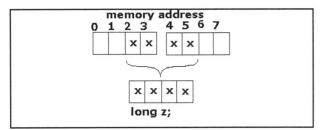

Figure 13.11 Fetching Unaligned Data

When you make a new project, Visual Studio sets the structure alignment to 8 bytes by default. The guideline is "a structure should begin on address boundaries of the worst type of data in the structure." In our case of **AccountRec** structure, the **double** is the worst type. Thus, each instance of the structure in memory should be aligned on 8-byte addresses.

However, how many bytes does our structure contain? It is 4 + 42 + 8 + 8 bytes or 62 bytes long. And this value is NOT evenly divisible by 8. If we look into the data file or the DOS internal buffer when that cluster containing the data has been input, successive records are not back to back in memory since 62 is not an even multiple of 8. If the structure alignment is 8 bytes, then the compiler adds some additional **gas** or **slack** or **pad** bytes to each structure instance so that the total size ends up a multiple of 8 bytes. That is, gas, pad, or slack bytes are added by the compiler to enforce the alignment.

On a computer with only 32-bit or 4-byte high speed registers, then the computer cannot fetch a 64-bit or 8-byte value directly from memory with one fetch: its registers are too small. In this case, 8-byte alignment becomes really 4-byte alignment. If however, you do have one of the new 64-bit PCs which has a 64-bit memory bus access, then the data will be aligned on an 8-byte boundary because the high speed work registers are indeed 8 bytes in size and can handle it.

I am running a 32-bit computer. Thus, the binary master file Pgm13b wrote is aligned on 4-byte addresses. Since each structure instance that was written to disk contained only 62 bytes, the compiler automatically inserts two additional gas fill bytes. When you ask for the size of the **AccountRec**, the compiler returns 64 bytes not 62 bytes! When one looks at the actual data stored in the binary file, each record has an additional 2 bytes appended to it containing garbage.

When you are going to input a binary file, you **must** know what the structure alignment was in the program that wrote the binary file in the first place. Your program must match that structure alignment. If the original data was aligned on a byte boundary and your program inputs it aligned on a 4-byte boundary, then your program will input scrambled data! In the case of the **AccountRec** structure, each input would result in 64 bytes being input while the actual byte aligned data on disk had only 62 bytes.

Structure alignment is set through the project settings—Project Settings—C++ tab—Code Generation Category combo box choice—struct member alignment combo box—make your choice.

Rule: if the data was created with older DOS programs, the data is very likely to have been only byte aligned.

Corollary: if an older DOS program will be reading the data your program creates, then make sure that your project uses 1-byte alignment or the older DOS program will be inputting scrambled data.

To view a binary file, one needs an editor that can display the bytes in hex. Figure 13.12 shows the binary master file made by Pgm13b using 8-byte structure alignment.

Each line in Figure 13.12 shows the precise contents of 16 bytes or 10 in hexadecimal. Each byte consists of two hexadecimal nibbles. Each line shows groups of 4 bytes separated by a blank column. On the far right side of each line are the corresponding ASCII equivalent characters if there are any. Notice that on the right side we can read the contents of the string name because those are ASCII characters. I also noted where the compiler inserted the two gas bytes, right after the end of the string in the structure. It added the gas bytes here so that the next two doubles would be aligned on an 8-byte boundary. I boxed in one record which occupies 64 bytes on disk.

Here is one final detail about structure alignment. Suppose that your structure was 9 bytes long and you saved the data to a binary file. Suppose further that there were 100,000 records in that file. If we used 1-byte structure alignment, how many bytes would the file occupy on disk? 900,000. However, if we used 8-byte alignment on a computer that could handle 8-byte aligned data, how many bytes would the file size report? Since 9 is not evenly divisible by 8, the compiler would add an additional 7 gas bytes to each structure instance. Now the file size on disk would be 1,600,000 bytes. This is a substantial difference in file size.

Hence, because of larger file sizes, many production applications that utilize large binary master files use 1-byte alignment to conserve disk space.

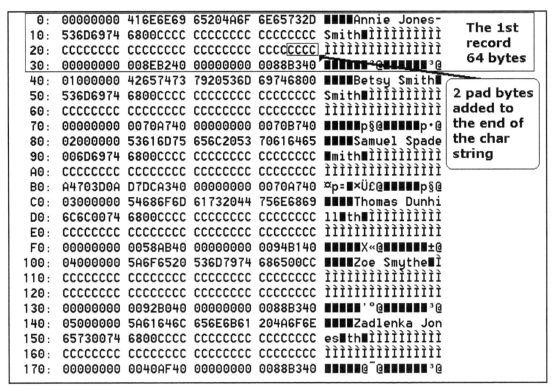

Figure 13.12 The Binary File (values in hex) Using 8-Byte Structure Alignment

In Figure 13.13, I rebuilt the project and binary master file using 1-byte alignment. Now each record is only 62 bytes long.

```
    0:  00000000 416E6E69 65204A6F 6E65732D  ████Annie Jones-   The 1st
   10:  536D6974 6800CCCC CCCCCCCC CCCCCCCC  Smith█ÌÌÌÌÌÌÌÌÌÌÌ   62-byte
   20:  CCCCCCCC CCCCCCCC CCCCCCCC CCCC0000  ÌÌÌÌÌÌÌÌÌÌÌÌÌÌ██    record
   30:  0000008E B2400000 00000088 B3400100  ████²@██████³@██
   40:  00004265 74737920 536D6974 6800536D  ██Betsy Smith█Sm
   50:  69746800 CCCCCCCC CCCCCCCC CCCCCCCC  ith█ÌÌÌÌÌÌÌÌÌÌÌÌ
   60:  CCCCCCCC CCCCCCCC CCCCCCCC 00000000  ÌÌÌÌÌÌÌÌÌÌÌÌ████
   70:  0070A740 00000000 0070B740 02000000  █p§@█████p·@████
   80:  53616D75 656C2053 70616465 006D6974  Samuel Spade█mit
   90:  6800CCCC CCCCCCCC CCCCCCCC CCCCCCCC  h█ÌÌÌÌÌÌÌÌÌÌÌÌÌÌ
   A0:  CCCCCCCC CCCCCCCC CCCCA470 3D0AD7DC  ÌÌÌÌÌÌÌÌÌÌ¤p=█×Ü
   B0:  A3400000 00000070 A7400300 00005468  £@█████p§@████Th
   C0:  6F6D6173 2044756E 68696C6C 00746800  omas Dunhill█th█
   D0:  CCCCCCCC CCCCCCCC CCCCCCCC CCCCCCCC  ÌÌÌÌÌÌÌÌÌÌÌÌÌÌÌÌ
   E0:  CCCCCCCC CCCCCCCC 00000000 0058AB40  ÌÌÌÌÌÌÌÌ█████X«@
   F0:  00000000 0094B140 04000000 5A6F6520  ██████±@████Zoe
  100:  536D7974 686500CC CCCCCCCC CCCCCCCC  Smythe█ÌÌÌÌÌÌÌÌÌ
  110:  CCCCCCCC CCCCCCCC CCCCCCCC CCCCCCCC  ÌÌÌÌÌÌÌÌÌÌÌÌÌÌÌÌ
  120:  CCCCCCCC CCCC0000 00000092 B0400000  ÌÌÌÌÌÌ█████'°@██
  130:  00000088 B3400500 00005A61 646C656E  ████³@████Zadlen
  140:  6B61204A 6F6E6573 00746800 CCCCCCCC  ka Jones█th█ÌÌÌÌ
  150:  CCCCCCCC CCCCCCCC CCCCCCCC CCCCCCCC  ÌÌÌÌÌÌÌÌÌÌÌÌÌÌÌÌ
  160:  CCCCCCCC 00000000 0040AF40 00000000  ÌÌÌÌ█████@ˉ@████
  170:  0088B340                             ██³@
```

Figure 13.13 The Binary Master File Using 1-Byte Structure Alignment

Writing Your Own Manipulator Functions

Manipulator functions are handy. Some are used with input streams while others are used with output streams. We have used **dec** and **ws** with input streams and have used **endl**, **setw()**, **setprecision()**, and **setfill()** with output streams, for example.

By now, you may have recognized numerous "repetitive" coding actions that you commonly use in program after program. Wouldn't be great if you could code those actions once and then have an easy way to reuse them in all of your programs? In fact, it is easy to write your own manipulator functions.

Manipulator functions break down into two different groups: those that take no parameters and those that take parameters. It is very easy to write parameterless manipulator functions. All parameterless manipulator functions have the same prototype.
stream& functionName (stream&);

Consider an input manipulator function called **quantityPrompt()** that prompts the user to input the quantity field, we would have the following definition and implementation.

```
istream& quantityPrompt (istream& is);
istream& quantityPrompt (istream& is) {
 cout << "Enter the quantity (or Ctrl-Z to quit): ";
 return is;
}
```

This convenience function can now be used this way.
```
cin >> quantityPrompt >> quantity;
```

Frequently, for dollar fields, we need to output a dollar sign and set the width to a specific amount before we display various currency fields. We could write the following **setForDollar()** manipulator function.
```
ostream& setForDollar (ostream& os);
ostream& setForDollar (ostream& os) {
 os << "$" << setw (10) << setprecision (2);
 return os;
}
```
And whenever we needed to output currency fields, we can code
```
cout << setForDollar << cost << "   "
     << setForDollar << totalCost << endl;
```

You can do just about any manipulations desired in these functions. The only requirement is to return a reference to the passed stream so that the caller can chain insertion and extraction operators. Also remember to include **iostream.h** and **iomanip.h** headers in your new manipulator files.

The manipulator functions that take parameters are coded differently. Suppose that we wished to make a **prompt()** input manipulator that took a string as its parameter and displayed that string on **cout**. We desire the user to code it this way.
```
cin >> prompt ("Enter quantity (Ctrl-Z to quit):") >> quantity;
```

At first glance, we would expect to see the prototype and implementation as follows.
```
istream& prompt (istream& is, const char* msg);
istream& prompt (istream& is, const char* msg) {
 cout << msg;
 return is;
}
```
However, the compiler cannot recognize this function when it is used as a manipulator function. Instead, each compiler maker has a special set of macros contained in **iomanip.h** that must be used to notify the compiler that this is a manipulator function. The **IMANIP** macro is used for input manipulator functions and the **OMANIP** macro is used for output ones. So in addition to defining our manipulator function as above, we must also include the following magic coding that permits the compiler to know this is an input manipulator function.
```
IMANIP (const char*) prompt (const char* msg);
IMANIP (const char*) prompt (const char* msg) {
 return IMANIP (const char*) (prompt, msg);
}
```

Similarly, our **setForDollar()** manipulator function would be even better if we could pass the width to set. Then, it could be used with any dollar field. For example
```
cout << setForDollar (8)  << cost << "   "
     << setForDollar (10) << totalCost << endl;
```

First, we write the function as we would expect it to be coded.

```
ostream& setForDollar (ostream& os, int num);
ostream& setForDollar (ostream& os, int num) {
 os << "$" << setw (num) << setprecision (2);
 return os;
}
```

Then, we add the magic coding to allow the compiler to recognize this as an output manipulator function.

```
OMANIP (int) setForDollar (int num);
OMANIP (int) setForDollar (int num) {
 return OMANIP (int) (setForDollar, num);
}
```

Review Questions

1. Explain the concept of a binary file. How does the storage of a **double** differ between a text file and a binary file? What would happen if you attempted to extract a **double** from a binary file? What would happen if you attempted to read in a **double** from a text file?

2. Under what circumstances is data conversion performed on data in a binary file?

3. How is a binary file opened in C++?

4. What functions can be used to I/O to or from a binary file? Under what circumstances can the insertion and extraction operator be used with a binary file?

5. How would an inventory structure be written to a binary file? How would it be read back in?

6. What is the most significant difference between the following two methods for outputting an array of **double**s? What will be in the file in both cases? Is there any significant benefit for using one of these in preference to another?

```
double array[10000];
for (i=0; i<10000; i++)
 outfile.write ((char*) array[i], sizeof (double));
```
and
```
outfile.write ((char*) array, sizeof (array));
```

7. What is a cluster? On a Windows/DOS platform, what is the significance of a cluster?

8. Explain what is meant by Physical I/O. Explain what is meant by Logical I/O.

9. What is the purpose of the DOS file offset pointer? How can a program make use of this pointer? What functions provide access to it?

10. Explain the instruction sequence required to obtain the DOS file size of a binary file.

11. Would there be any real benefit to inputting an entire text file in one I/O operation into an array of characters which is the same size as the binary file?

12. What is wrong with the following sequence to input a file of data?
```
infile.seekg (0, ios::end);
long sz = infile.tellg ();
char* buf = new char [sz];
infile.read (buf, sz);
```

13. Explain how the relative record number method for direct access of a specific record in a binary master file works. Why is this approach exceedingly fast at data retrieval?

14. Why do relative record numbers make poor values for client Id numbers?

15. A binary file is supposed to contain a series of **InventoryRec** structures. How can a program tell if the file either is corrupt or may contain other items besides these structure instances?

16. A direct access file uses the remainder method for locating where a record with a specific key id is located. Explain how this method works. Why does the file have to be pre-built with enough dummy records to equal the maximum number of records the file is designed to hold?

17. What kind of user id key fields can be used with a direct access type of file?

18. Explain how the ISAM method works. What kind of user id key fields can be used?

19. Why is the ISAM method slower at retrieving a specific record on disk?

20. What **iostream** class is used to create an update file—that is, a file instance that can be both read and written?

21. What is meant by structure alignment? How does it work? What is the impact of structure alignment on a program?

22. Program 1 writes a binary master file and uses 1-byte structure alignment. Program 2 inputs the data from that binary master file but uses 8-byte structure alignment. Explain what occurs at run time with Program 2 and why.

Stop! Do These Exercises Before Programming

1. Our programmer has been asked to write an inventory update program for Acme Manufacturing Corporation. The binary master file is an ISAM type of file that contains inventory records that are defined as follows.

```
const int PARTNO_LEN = 16;
const int DESCR_LEN = 46;
const int LOC_LEN = 11;
struct InvRec {
 char   partNo[PARTNO_LEN];
 char   description[DESCR_LEN];
 int    qtyOnHand;
 double unitCost;
 char   locationBin[LOC_LEN];
};
```

The key id field is the **partNo**. The master file itself is called **parts.dat** and was built using 8-byte structure alignment. The index file is called **parts.idx** and consists of instances of the structure **Index**.

```
struct Index {
 char partNo[PARTNO_LEN];
 long relRecNum;
};
```

The index records are stored in increasing ASCII sequence on the **partNo** field.

The programmer decided to implement the **FindRecord()** function whose purpose is to find the relative record number of the inventory record that corresponds to a given part number. Of course, he also had to write a **LoadIndex()** function to load the index file into an array. He also wrote a small driver program to test his new function. It fails completely. He has asked you for your assistance. Find his errors so that both the new function and driver work as expected. Is there anything grossly inefficient about his **FindRecord()** function?

```
const int NoMatch = -1;
int main () {
 InvRec rec;
 char partNo[PARTNO_LEN];
 fstream masterfile ("parts.dat", ios::in | ios::out);
 fstream indexfile ("parts.idx", ios::in | ios::out);
 long count;
 Index* index = LoadIndex (indexfile, count);
 while (cin >> partNo) {
  long relRecNum = FindRecord (index, count, partNo);
  if (relRecNum == NoMatch)
   cout << "Record not found - part number: " << partNo << endl;
  else {
   masterfile.seekg (relRecNum * sizeof (InvRec), ios::beg);
   masterfile.read ((char*) &rec, sizeof (rec));
```

```
    cout << "Found part number: " << rec.partNo << endl;
  }
 }
 ...
}

Index* LoadIndex (fstream& file, long& count) {
 file.seekg (0, ios::end);
 long size = file.tellg ();
 count = size / sizeof (Index);
 Index* index = new Index [count];
 file.read ((char*) index, count * sizeof (index));
 return index;
}

long FindRecord (Index index[], long count,
                 const char* findThis) {
 for (long j=0; j<count; j++) {
  if (findThis == index[j].partNo)
   return j;
 }
 return NoMatch;
}
```

2. The programmer, after singing praises to you for your assistance, embarks on a total rewrite of the **FindRecord()** function. He has decided to implement a binary search for the id value.

```
bool FindRecord (Index id[], long num,
                 const char* findId, long& foundIndex) {
 int firstidx = 0;
 int lastidx = num - 1;
 int middleidx;
 bool foundMatch = false;
 while (lastidx >= firstidx && !foundMatch) {
  middleidx = (firstidx + lastidx) / 2;
  if (findId < id[middleidx])
    lastidx = middleidx - 1;
  else if (findId > id[middleidx])
    firstidx = middleidx + 1;
  else foundMatch = true;
 }
 foundIndex = middleidx;
 return foundMatch;
}
```

He changed the call in **main()** to the following.

```
 long relRecNum;
 if (FindRecord (index, count, partNo, relRecNum)) {
```

When it runs, the program does not find any records. After spending hours debugging it, he humbly begs you for your assistance. Fix his function so that it correctly finds matching records.

3. His enthusiasm returns when you point out his errors; his find function is working properly. So next he embarks on writing the code to perform the updates of specific inventory records. The relevant parts of his tester program now appear as follows.

```
... performing an update of partNo record
... the needed new values have been input
long relRecNum;
if (FindRecord (index, count, partNo, relRecNum)) {
  masterfile.seekg (relRecNum * sizeof (InvRec), ios::beg);
  masterfile.read (&rec, sizeof (rec));
  // ... made changes to rec fields
  masterfile.write (&rec, sizeof (rec));
}
else
  cerr << "Error: unable to find part: " << partNo << endl;
```

Unfortunately, the above coding does not compile or work properly. Find his errors in syntax and the two major logic blunders.

4. After profusely apologizing for making such a stupid blunder, he then begins the design for the addition of new records to the master file. Now he encounters a new problem. While it will be easy to add the new record to the master file, the index is another matter entirely. The new part number must be inserted into the index table in sorted order. He decides that he must add the new record to the master file first so that he knows the new relative record number of that new record. This time, he writes only the couple of lines needed to store the new record in the master file. But when he tests it, he discovers that the new record is not where it should be located and has indeed wiped other data out!

```
// rec contains the new data, so write it at the end of the file
masterfile.seekg (0, ios::end);
masterfile.write ((char*) &rec, sizeof (rec));
```

After spending hours playing with this error, he comes to you once more stating the computer must be broken because these two simple lines of coding do not work! The record is not added at the end of the file! Point out his error and fix this error for him.

5. Humbled and in awe of your programming prowess, the programmer now attempts to update the index file. He is absolutely certain that he will bungle this one too. And his postulate holds. His coding does not work. Rescue the programmer once more, please. Fix this coding so that it properly adds a new entry to the index in the proper location.

```
long newRelRecNum; // contains the new relative record number
// for the added record while partNo contains its Id value
long newIndex; // the location in the index
if (!FindRecord (index, count, partNo, newIndex)) {
  // here, newIndex contains the location in index where this
  // partNo should be located. so move all entries from here
```

```
// down one slot and insert this new one
long j, k;
for (j=count-1; j>=newIndex; j--) {
 index[j] = index[j-1];
}
index[newIndex].partNo = partNo;
index[newIndex].relRecNum = newRelRecNum;
count++;
indexfile.write ((char*) index, sizeof (Index) * count);
}
```

In fact, just before he came to you this last time, his computer started doing funny things after he had run the program, forcing him to reboot.

Programming Problems

Problem Pgm13-1—The Duplicate File Finder Program

You have been collecting some terrific scenery jpg images from the Internet. However, you notice that there are what appears to be duplicate files in your collection. That is, different filenames, but what appears to be the same images. The objective is to find out if two specific files are identical or not.

Write a function called **IsDuplicate()** that takes two constant character string filenames and returns a bool, true if the two files are precisely identical. You do not need to know what the contents of the image file actually contain, just that they are identical byte for byte. The approach to take is to open each file as a binary file and get the DOS file size of each. If the file sizes do not match, return false as they cannot be byte-by-byte duplicates.

Next, dynamically allocate memory to hold each file's contents. Use arrays of unsigned char. Input both files into these two arrays. Make sure you are using binary I/O. Now compare the two arrays, byte-by-byte. At the first unequal byte result, return false as they do not match. Return true if the end of the two equal length arrays occurs as they are the same.

Verify that you have not leaked any memory. Be sure to close all opened files. Write a simple driver program to thoroughly test the function.

Problem Pgm13-2—the CD Stock Update Program

Acme Music Store wants a program written that they can use to maintain their stock inventory of CDs. The main menu consists of the following.

```
Acme CD Inventory Program

1. Display CD Inventory
2. Update CD Inventory
3. Add a New CD
4. Exit the Program

Enter the number of your choice: _
```

The file **CDinventory.dat** is located in the **Pgm13-2** folder of **TestDataForAssignments**. It is a binary file of the current inventory and was built using 8-byte structure alignment. The inventory record consists of

```
struct Inventory {
  char cdNum[11];
  char cdTitle[41];
  long qtyOnHand;
  double cost;
};
```

Initially, open this file using a **fstream** instance and open it for update operations. Before the main menu is displayed, construct an instance of a growable array container to store an array of **CD_to_RRN** structure instances. This structure stores the **cdNum** and its corresponding relative record number. So read each record in the master file and build this conversion array. When updates are done, the user provides the **cdNum** and you look it up in the **CD_to_RRN** array to obtain the relative record number of the data in the master file.

When Display CD Inventory is chosen, read the file sequentially displaying each item nicely formatted on the screen.

When Update a CD Inventory is chosen, prompt the user for the cd number. Then look it up in the **CD_to_RRN** to obtain the relative record number on disk. If that cd is not in the file, display an error message to the user. If it is, read in that cd's inventory data and display it onscreen. Prompt the user for any changes in quantity or cost. Then rewrite that record on disk.

When Add a New CD is chosen, prompt the user for the relevant information. Then, verify that the cd number is not already in the data base. If it is, display an error message to the user. If it is not in the file, then add this record to the master file and add a new entry to the **CD_to_RRN** array.

Thoroughly test your program.

567

Problem Pgm13-3—Building and Reading a Binary File

Write a program that inputs the text file **cd.txt** located in the **Pgm13-3** folder of **TestDataForAssignments**. It contains cd inventory records. Make a structure called **CD** as follows.

```
struct CD {
  char cdNum[11];
  char cdTitle[41];
  long qtyOnHand;
  double cost;
};
```

Input each record from the text file into a **CD** record and then write that record to a binary output file.

Then, open the binary output file and input each record and display all four fields onscreen in a nicely formatted report.

Problem Pgm13-4—A Blazingly Fast File Copy Program

The objective is to write a blazing file copy program for Windows 95/NT. Use **Pgm13a** as a model. The major problem of **Pgm13a** is that it has an arbitrary 80M maximum upper limit on the size of the file. Further a static 80M buffer consumes lots of memory. If one does not have that much memory on the system, performance greatly suffers.

Your program should pick up the two filenames from the command line. A sample might be as shown.
```
C:>pgm13-4    c:\student\test.dat    c:\work\test.dat
```
which is copying the file from **test.dat** in the **student** folder into the **work** folder.

Create an 8M **static** buffer. Input the entire file in a single read using binary I/O and write the entire file using binary I/O.
```
static char buf[8192000];
```

However, if the file size is greater than the 8M buffer, then proceed to bring in the first 8M and output that much. Then, input and output the next 8M and so on until all bytes have been copied. Be careful on the last portion, which is not likely to be 8M in total. Suppose the file was 17M in size. Your program should do two 8M I/O operations followed by the remaining 1M.

Make 2 versions of the program. Version 1 uses C functions only, **fopen**, **fseek**, **fread**, **fwrite**, **fclose**. Version 2 uses the **iostreams**, **ifstream** and **ofstream** and **read** and **write**.

Don't forget to test with a larger file, say one that is 20M. If you don't have such large files available, make one using the DOS copy command. Find the largest one you have, copy it to your testing area and call it a.dat. Then, use the /b binary option of the DOS copy command:

```
C>copy /b a.dat + a.dat + a.dat + a.dat        b.dat
```

This merges 4 copies of a.dat into b.dat.

Turn in test run results on a file that is about 1M in size and one that is about 20M in size. Also manually time how long a DOS copy command and the Explorer's Edit-Copy-Paste operation takes with the 20M file. Also note what CPU you are using, its speed in MHz, and the amount of memory on the machine.

To verify that your copy program works, use the file compare program of DOS. In the DOS prompt window, enter

```
C:\>FC   a.dat  b.dat
```

This says to file compare a.dat with b.dat. If all is well, you should see the message "No Differences." If there are differences you see screens of compare error messages.

Chapter 14—Persistent Data Objects

Introduction

Up to this point, all of the objects that we have created have resided only in memory. The next step is to find a mechanism by which to store an object in binary format on disk so that we may achieve a persistent data object—that is, so that we can easily load the object instance back from disk. This is a very tricky subject in general, but with some simplifications, there is a reasonable solution. Let's begin by examining some of the design considerations.

A First Attempt That Fails

Suppose that we derived our classes from some generic **Persistent** base class. The intention is to have the **Persistent** base class provide the underlying mechanism for saving and restoring our data to/from disk. Consider the following.

```
class Employee : public Persistent {

protected:
 long  employee_number;
 char* employee_name;
 char  department;

public:
               Employee (long num, char *name, char dept);
virtual        ~Employee ();
virtual double Pay (double hours);
};
```

Here it is assumed that we will be dynamically allocating the employee name string. Further, it is likely that other classes will be derived from this one, using the virtual function mechanism particularly with the **Pay()** function.

So far so good. But now what would the **Persistent** class look like? How would the **Persistent** class find all the relevant members of the **Employee** class in order to read and write them? How would the **Persistent** base class know how to construct the employee name string? How would it know how many data members the **Employee** class actually had? And how would it handle the **virtual** pointers that arise because of the **virtual** functions?

Answer: it cannot possibly do so. It cannot be written this way!

A Second Attempt That Fails

Suppose that we tried the following.

```
class Persistent {
protected:
 fstream of;
public:
          Persistent () { of.read (this, sizeof (*this)); }
virtual ~Persistent () { of.write (this, sizeof (*this)); }
};
```

Flaw: when the base class constructor (**Persistent**) executes, there is no **Employee** object in existence yet. Remember that the base class constructors are executed first! None of the derived class members have been initialized or set up as yet. Conversely, the **Persistent** destructor is executed **after** the derived class destructor has done its work. Hence, there are NO derived class data members left around for ~**Persistent()** to output!

Any persistent mechanism must wait for the derived objects to be fully constructed before it can input into their members. And the output must occur before the derived class destructors are executed.

Finally, the **sizeof()** operator is **not** polymorphic. That is, it returns the size of the base class, not the derived class.

A Third Attempt That Fails

Okay. We could add two functions to **Persistent**, **Read()** and **Write()**, and have them be called from the derived class constructor and destructor. This is shown as follows.

```
class Persistent {
protected:
 fstream of;
 int size;

public:
Persistent (int sz) : size (sz) {
    of.open ("data.dta", ios::in|ios::out|ios::binary);
}
virtual ~Persistent () {
    of.close ();
}
void Read ()  { of.read ((char*) this, size); }
void Write () { of.write ((char*) this, size); }
};
```

```
class Employee : public Persistent {
protected:
 long employee_number;
 char *employee_name;
 char department;

public:
 Employee () : Persistent (sizeof (*this)) { Read (); }
~Employee () { Write (); }
 virtual double Pay (double hours);
};
```

While this is getting better, we still have a serious problem with pointers. We are writing over the **char*** for an employee name, yielding a bogus pointer! Secondly, the **virtual** function pointer table is also overwritten, messing up those pointers as well!

Finally, many derived classes may have data members that do not need to be read or written, such as a "state" variables, like a **has_been_modified** flag.

Thus, making an object persistent is indeed a very tricky affair. However, in Windows programming, objects **must** be able to persist. Windows C++ libraries such as the MFC (Microsoft Foundation Classes) and OWL (Borland's Object Windows Library) have adopted another method to achieve object persistence. The MFC approach is the simplest. Although we cannot directly use the MFC C++ classes in a non-Windows application, the principles are extremely easy to adopt to a DOS C++ program.

Making a Class Persistent the MFC Way

There are three fundamental principles you must adhere to in order to achieve a persistent class in a straightforward manner.

1. You must provide a default constructor (one that takes no parameters). When streaming in an object from disk, this constructor is invoked to create a new empty object that will then be filled with the persistent data on disk.

2. Only the actual object itself can know what data needs to be read/written and how that is to be done. Thus, the streamable object must provide a member function to handle the I/O operations. I am using the MFC naming convention and calling it **Serialize()**. This function is passed a reference to a **fstream** and a **bool** which indicates whether it is a read or write operation.

3. Because programs and classes do get updated, a version number must be the first data item written/read to the disk stream. That way, newer versions of the program can input older versions of persistent data. Presumably, the newer version can plug some default values for the newer data members that were not present in the older versions.

Given these restrictions, we can proceed as follows. Let's make the **Animal**s' classes from chapter 8 into a set of persistent classes so that we can save the **Dog** and **Cat** instances. To do so, we must add a pure virtual function to the **Animal** base class, **Serialize()**. Here is the revised **Animal** definition. Notice that **Serialize()** is passed a **fstream** reference so that it can be used for either input or output. The actual implementation is unchanged, but for continuity, I have included it below as well.

```
Animal Class Definition

 1 #pragma once
 2 #include <iostream>
 3 #include <fstream>
 4 using namespace std;
 5
 6 /*****************************************************************/
 7 /*                                                               */
 8 /* Animal: stores name of the animal and provides I/O ops       */
 9 /*                                                               */
10 /*****************************************************************/
11
12 class Animal {
13 protected:
14   char* name;   // the name of the animal, such as Dog or Cat
15
16 public:
17         Animal ();                  // default ctor - "Unknown"
18         Animal (const char* n);   // make specific animal
19         Animal (const Animal& a); // copy ctor duplicate animal
```

```
20
21   Animal& operator= (const Animal& a); // assignment op
22
23   virtual ~Animal ();                   // delete name
24
25   // displays "The 'name' says "
26   virtual ostream& Speak (ostream& os) const;
27
28   virtual istream& Input (istream& is);
29   virtual ostream& Output (ostream& os) const;
30
31   friend istream& operator>> (istream& is, Animal& a);
32   friend ostream& operator<< (ostream& os, const Animal& a);
33   virtual bool Serialize (bool isstoring, fstream &ifs) = 0;
34
35 protected:
36   void AllocString (char*& dest, const char* src,
37                     const char* errmsg);
38 };
```

Animal Class Implementation - unchanged

```
 1 #include <iostream>
 2 #include <iomanip>
 3 #include <string>
 4 using namespace std;
 5
 6 #include "Animal.h"
 7
 8 /***************************************************************/
 9 /*                                                           */
10 /* AllocString: dyn allocate new string and copy in src      */
11 /*                                                           */
12 /***************************************************************/
13 void Animal::AllocString (char*& dest, const char* src,
14                           const char* errmsg) {
15  dest = new (std::nothrow) char[strlen (src) + 1];
16  if (!dest) {
17   cerr << "Error - out of memory in " << errmsg << endl;
18   exit (1);
19  }
20  strcpy_s (dest, strlen (src) + 1, src);
21 }
22
23 /***************************************************************/
24 /*                                                           */
25 /* Animal: create a default "Unknown" animal                 */
26 /*                                                           */
27 /***************************************************************/
28
29 Animal::Animal () {
30  AllocString (name, "Unknown", "Animal Constructor");
```

```
31 }
32
33 /*********************************************************************/
34 /*                                                                   */
35 /* Animal: create an animal with this name                           */
36 /*                                                                   */
37 /*********************************************************************/
38
39 Animal::Animal (const char* n) {
40   if (!n)
41     AllocString (name, "Unknown", "Animal Constructor");
42   else
43     AllocString (name, n, "Animal Constructor");
44 }
45
46 /*********************************************************************/
47 /*                                                                   */
48 /* Animal: duplicate an animal object                                */
49 /*                                                                   */
50 /*********************************************************************/
51
52 Animal::Animal (const Animal& a) {
53   AllocString (name, a.name, "Animal Copy Constructor");
54 }
55
56 /*********************************************************************/
57 /*                                                                   */
58 /* Operator= copy passed animal into this one                        */
59 /*                                                                   */
60 /*********************************************************************/
61
62 Animal& Animal::operator= (const Animal& a) {
63   if (this == &a)    // guard against a = a;
64     return *this;
65   delete [] name;                          // remove current name
66   AllocString (name, a.name, "Animal Operator =");
67   return *this;
68 }
69
70 /*********************************************************************/
71 /*                                                                   */
72 /* ~Animal: remove the name array                                    */
73 /*                                                                   */
74 /*********************************************************************/
75
76 Animal::~Animal () {
77   delete [] name;
78 }
79
80 /*********************************************************************/
81 /*                                                                   */
82 /* Speak: placeholder for derived classes - shouldn't be called*/
83 /*                                                                   */
```

```
 84 /****************************************************************/
 85
 86 ostream& Animal::Speak (ostream& os) const {
 87  return os << "nothing\n"; // oops - so display a goof message
 88 }
 89
 90 /****************************************************************/
 91 /*                                                            */
 92 /* Input: input the animal's name from the input stream       */
 93 /*                                                            */
 94 /****************************************************************/
 95
 96 istream& Animal::Input (istream& is) {
 97  char n[100];                // arbitrary maximum length of name
 98  is >> n;                    // input the new name
 99  delete [] name;             // remove current name
100  if (!is)                    // if failed to input, make unknown
101   AllocString (name, "Unknown", "Animal Input");
102  else                        // allocate and copy the new name
103   AllocString (name, n, "Animal Input");
104  return is;
105 }
106
107 /****************************************************************/
108 /*                                                            */
109 /* Output: display "The 'name' says " string                  */
110 /*                                                            */
111 /****************************************************************/
112
113 ostream& Animal::Output (ostream& os) const {
114  return os << "The " << name;
115 }
116
117 /****************************************************************/
118 /*                                                            */
119 /* extraction: input an animal                                */
120 /*                                                            */
121 /****************************************************************/
122
123 istream& operator>> (istream& is, Animal& a) {
124  return a.Input (is); // invoke virtual Input
125 }
126
127 /****************************************************************/
128 /*                                                            */
129 /* insertion: display an animal                               */
130 /*                                                            */
131 /****************************************************************/
132
133 ostream& operator<< (ostream& os, const Animal& a) {
134  return a.Output (os); // invoke virtual Output
135 }
```

Next, in the **Dog** class, we must define the new **Serialize()** function as well and then implement it.

```
Dog Class Definition

 1 #pragma once
 2 #include "Animal.h"
 3
 4 /*****************************************************************/
 5 /*                                                             */
 6 /* Class Dog:                                                  */
 7 /*                                                             */
 8 /*****************************************************************/
 9
10 class Dog : public Animal {
11 protected:
12   char* sound; // the sound it makes, such as "Ruff! Ruff!"
13
14 public:
15           Dog ();                   // default dog
16           Dog (const char* s);    // dog with a specific sound
17           Dog (const Dog& d);     // copy ctor
18   Dog& operator= (const Dog& d); // assignment op
19
20   virtual ~Dog ();                 // dtor to remove sound
21
22   // Speak displays the entire output line
23   virtual ostream& Speak (ostream& os) const;
24
25   virtual istream& Input (istream& is);
26   virtual ostream& Output (ostream& os) const;
27
28   friend istream& operator>> (istream& is, Dog& d);
29   friend ostream& operator<< (ostream& os, const Dog& d);
30
31   virtual bool Serialize (bool isstoring, fstream &ifs);
32 };
```

To implement **Serialize()**, first separate which I/O action is required. For output, the **Dog** class **version** level string is written first. Presumable all future **version** strings will be the same length. Thus, we can just write out the entire **version** string as is. However, for the **name** and **sound** dynamically allocated character strings, we must output the length of each string followed by the current contents of these strings. For convenience, I am also outputting the null terminator. That way, on input, a simple read operation also supplies the required null terminator.

```
bool Dog::Serialize (bool isstoring, fstream &ifs) {
  if (isstoring) { // write this Dog to disk
    // write version, length of name, name, length of sound,
    // and sound
```

```
        ifs.write (version, sizeof (version));
        long len = (int) strlen (name) + 1;// allow for null
        ifs.write ((char*)&len, sizeof (len));
        ifs.write (name, len);
        len = strlen (sound) + 1;
        ifs.write ((char*)&len, sizeof (len));
        ifs.write (sound, len);
        if (ifs.good ()) return true;
        return false;
    }
```

The input operation is the reverse action with one subtle difference. Remember that the class constructor, even if only the default ctor, has already been called. Both the **name** and **sound** strings exist and thus must be deleted and a new pair of strings of the proper length allocated before the data can be inputted.

```
    else {              // input this Dog
      char ver[9];
      ifs.read (ver, sizeof (ver));
      if (ifs.good() && strcmp (version, ver) == 0) {
        long len;
        ifs.read ((char*)&len, sizeof (len));
        delete [] name;
        name = new char [len];
        ifs.read (name, len);
        ifs.read ((char*)&len, sizeof (len));
        delete [] sound;
        sound = new char [len];
        ifs.read (sound, len);
        return ifs.good () ? true : false;
      }
      return false;
    }
  }
```

Here is the implementation of the **Dog** class followed by the parallel **Cat** class. Changes are in bold face.

```
Dog Class Implementation

 1 #include <iostream>
 2 #include <iomanip>
 3 #include <string>
 4 using namespace std;
 5 #include "Dog.h"
 6
 7 const char version[9] = "Dog V1.0";
 8
 9 /**********************************************************/
10 /*                                                      */
```

```
11 /* Dog: make a default dog with the sound Ruff! Ruff!                */
12 /*                                                                    */
13 /*********************************************************************/
14
15 Dog::Dog () : Animal ("Dog") {
16  AllocString (sound, "Ruff! Ruff!", "Dog Constructor");
17 }
18
19 /*********************************************************************/
20 /*                                                                    */
21 /* Dog: make a dog with this specific sound                          */
22 /*                                                                    */
23 /*********************************************************************/
24
25 Dog::Dog (const char* s) : Animal ("Dog") {
26  if (!s)       // guard against 0 sound
27  AllocString (sound, "Ruff! Ruff!", "Dog Constructor");
28  else          // store the new sound
29  AllocString (sound, s, "Dog Constructor");
30 }
31
32 /*********************************************************************/
33 /*                                                                    */
34 /* Dog: duplicate this dog                                           */
35 /*                                                                    */
36 /*********************************************************************/
37
38 Dog::Dog (const Dog& d) : Animal (d) {
39  AllocString (sound, d.sound, "Dog Copy Constructor");
40 }
41
42 /*********************************************************************/
43 /*                                                                    */
44 /* Operator= copy the passed dog into this dog                       */
45 /*                                                                    */
46 /*********************************************************************/
47
48 Dog& Dog::operator= (const Dog& d) {
49  if (this == &d)              // guard against a = a;
50   return *this;
51  Animal::operator= (d);       // copy Animal portion of dog
52  delete [] sound;             // remove old sound
53  AllocString (sound, d.sound, "Dog Operator =");
54  return *this;
55 }
56
57 /*********************************************************************/
58 /*                                                                    */
59 /* ~Dog: remove sound array                                          */
60 /*                                                                    */
61 /*********************************************************************/
62
63 Dog::~Dog () {
```

```
 64  delete [] sound;
 65 }
 66
 67 /******************************************************************/
 68 /*                                                              */
 69 /* Speak: display the sound the dog makes                       */
 70 /*                                                              */
 71 /******************************************************************/
 72
 73 ostream& Dog::Speak (ostream& os) const {
 74  return os << " says " << sound << endl;
 75 }
 76
 77 /******************************************************************/
 78 /*                                                              */
 79 /* Input: input a dog                                           */
 80 /*                                                              */
 81 /******************************************************************/
 82
 83 istream& Dog::Input (istream& is) {
 84  if (!Animal::Input (is))   // attempt to input the name portion
 85    return is;              // if fails, abort
 86  char s[100];              // arbitrary max length of dog's sound
 87  char c;
 88  is >> c;                  // input the "
 89  if (!is)
 90    return is;
 91  is.getline (s, sizeof(s), '\"');  // input the sound it makes
 92  delete [] sound;                  // remove old sound
 93  AllocString (sound, s, "Dog Input");
 94  return is;
 95 }
 96
 97 /******************************************************************/
 98 /*                                                              */
 99 /* Output: display the dog says 'sound'                         */
100 /*                                                              */
101 /******************************************************************/
102
103 ostream& Dog::Output (ostream& os) const {
104  Animal::Output (os); // display The dog says portion
105  return Speak (os);   // display the sound
106 }
107
108 /******************************************************************/
109 /*                                                              */
110 /* extraction: input a dog object                               */
111 /*                                                              */
112 /******************************************************************/
113
114 istream& operator>> (istream& is, Dog& d) {
115  return d.Input (is); // call the virtual Input()
116 }
```

580

```
117
118 /*****************************************************************/
119 /*                                                               */
120 /* insertion: output a dog object                                */
121 /*                                                               */
122 /*****************************************************************/
123
124 ostream& operator<< (ostream& os, const Dog& d) {
125   return d.Output (os); // call the virtual Output
126 }
127
128 /*****************************************************************/
129 /*                                                               */
130 /* Serialize: input or output this object to a binary file       */
131 /*                                                               */
132 /*****************************************************************/
133
134 bool Dog::Serialize (bool isstoring, fstream &ifs) {
135   if (isstoring) { // write this Dog to disk
136     // write version, length of name, name, length of sound, sound
137     ifs.write (version, sizeof (version));
138     long len = (int) strlen (name) + 1;// allow for null
139     ifs.write ((char*)&len, sizeof (len));
140     ifs.write (name, len);
141     len = (int) strlen (sound) + 1;
142     ifs.write ((char*)&len, sizeof (len));
143     ifs.write (sound, len);
144     if (ifs.good ()) return true;
145     return false;
146   }
147   else {            // input this Dog
148     char ver[9];
149     ifs.read (ver, sizeof (ver));
150     if (ifs.good() && strcmp (version, ver) == 0) {
151       long len;
152       ifs.read ((char*)&len, sizeof (len));
153       delete [] name;
154       name = new char [len];
155       ifs.read (name, len);
156       ifs.read ((char*)&len, sizeof (len));
157       delete [] sound;
158       sound = new char [len];
159       ifs.read (sound, len);
160       return ifs.good () ? true : false;
161     }
162     return false;
163   }
164 }
```

Cat Class Definition

```
 1 #pragma once
 2 #include "Animal.h"
 3
 4 /******************************************************************/
 5 /*                                                              */
 6 /* class Cat                                                    */
 7 /*                                                              */
 8 /******************************************************************/
 9
10 class Cat : public Animal {
11 protected:
12  char* sound;  // the sound that a cat makes
13
14 public:
15          Cat ();               // default cat "Meow! Meow!"
16          Cat (const char* s);  // cat with specific sound
17          Cat (const Cat& c);   // copy ctor duplicate Cat
18  Cat& operator= (const Cat& c); // assignment op
19
20  virtual ~Cat ();             // removes sound string
21
22  // displays the entire output line
23  virtual ostream& Speak (ostream& os) const;
24
25  virtual istream& Input (istream& is);
26  virtual ostream& Output (ostream& os) const;
27
28  friend istream& operator>> (istream& is, Cat& c);
29  friend ostream& operator<< (ostream& os, const Cat& c);
30
31  virtual bool Serialize (bool isstoring, fstream &ifs);
32 };
```

Cat Class Implementation

```
 1 #include <iostream>
 2 #include <iomanip>
 3 #include <string>
 4 using namespace std;
 5 #include "Cat.h"
 6
 7 const char version[9] = "Cat V1.0";
 8
 9 /******************************************************************/
10 /*                                                              */
11 /* Cat: make a default cat with sound Meow! Meow!               */
12 /*                                                              */
13 /******************************************************************/
14
15 Cat::Cat () : Animal ("Cat") {
16  AllocString (sound, "Meow! Meow!", "Cat Constructor");
```

```
17 }
18
19 /*****************************************************************/
20 /*                                                             */
21 /* Cat: make a cat with this sound                             */
22 /*                                                             */
23 /*****************************************************************/
24
25 Cat::Cat (const char* s) : Animal ("Cat") {
26  if (!s)        // guard against 0 sound
27   AllocString (sound, "Meow! Meow!", "Cat Constructor");
28  else           // otherwise use this new sound
29   AllocString (sound, s, "Cat Constructor");
30 }
31
32 /*****************************************************************/
33 /*                                                             */
34 /* Cat: duplicate the passed cat                               */
35 /*                                                             */
36 /*****************************************************************/
37
38 Cat::Cat (const Cat& c) : Animal (c) {
39  AllocString (sound, c.sound, "Cat Copy Constructor");
40 }
41
42 /*****************************************************************/
43 /*                                                             */
44 /* Operator= copy cat c into this cat                          */
45 /*                                                             */
46 /*****************************************************************/
47
48 Cat& Cat::operator= (const Cat& c) {
49  if (this == &c) // guard against a = a;
50   return *this;
51  Animal::operator= (c);          // copy Animal base portion
52  delete [] sound;                // remove old sound
53  AllocString (sound, c.sound, "Cat Operator =");
54  return *this;
55 }
56
57 /*****************************************************************/
58 /*                                                             */
59 /* ~Cat: delete the sound array                                */
60 /*                                                             */
61 /*****************************************************************/
62
63 Cat::~Cat () {
64  delete [] sound;
65 }
66
67 /*****************************************************************/
68 /*                                                             */
69 /* Speak: output the Cat's sound                               */
```

583

```
 70  /*                                                               */
 71  /****************************************************************/
 72
 73  ostream& Cat::Speak (ostream& os) const {
 74   return os << " says " << sound << endl;
 75  }
 76
 77  /****************************************************************/
 78  /*                                                               */
 79  /* Input: input a Cat object                                     */
 80  /*                                                               */
 81  /****************************************************************/
 82
 83  istream& Cat::Input (istream& is) {
 84   if (!Animal::Input (is)) // try to input the name portion
 85     return is;             // here it failed, so abort
 86   char s[100];             // arbitrary sound string max length
 87   char c;
 88   is >> c;                 // input the leading "
 89   if (!is)
 90     return is;
 91   is.getline (s, sizeof(s), '\"');  // get the sound
 92   delete [] sound;                   // remove old sound
 93   AllocString (sound, s, "Cat Input");
 94   return is;
 95  }
 96
 97  /****************************************************************/
 98  /*                                                               */
 99  /* Output: display a Cat                                         */
100  /*                                                               */
101  /****************************************************************/
102
103  ostream& Cat::Output (ostream& os) const {
104   Animal::Output (os); // display "The Cat says" part
105   return Speak (os);   // display its sound
106  }
107
108  /****************************************************************/
109  /*                                                               */
110  /* extraction: input a Cat                                       */
111  /*                                                               */
112  /****************************************************************/
113
114  istream& operator>> (istream& is, Cat& c) {
115   return c.Input (is); // invoke virtual Input
116  }
117
118  /****************************************************************/
119  /*                                                               */
120  /* insertion: display a Cat                                      */
121  /*                                                               */
122  /****************************************************************/
```

```
123
124 ostream& operator<< (ostream& os, const Cat& c) {
125  return c.Output (os); // invoke virtual Output
126 }
127
128 /***************************************************************/
129 /*                                                             */
130 /* Serialize: read or write a Cat object to a binary file      */
131 /*                                                             */
132 /***************************************************************/
133
134 bool Cat::Serialize (bool isstoring, fstream &ifs) {
135  if (isstoring) { // save this object
136   // write version, length of name, name, length of sound, sound
137   ifs.write (version, sizeof (version));
138   long len = (int) strlen (name) + 1; // allow for null
139   ifs.write ((char*)&len, sizeof (len));
140   ifs.write (name, len);
141   len = (int) strlen (sound) + 1;
142   ifs.write ((char*)&len, sizeof (len));
143   ifs.write (sound, len);
144   if (ifs.good ()) return true;
145   return false;
146  }
147  else { // input this object
148   char ver[9];
149   ifs.read (ver, sizeof (ver));
150   if (ifs.good() && strcmp (version, ver) == 0) {
151    long len;
152    ifs.read ((char*)&len, sizeof (len));
153    delete [] name;         // remove current name
154    name = new char [len];  // allocate a new string
155    ifs.read (name, len);   // fill it up
156    ifs.read ((char*)&len, sizeof (len));
157    delete [] sound;        // remove current sound
158    sound = new char [len]; // allocate new sound
159    ifs.read (sound, len);  // fill it up
160    return ifs.good () ? true : false;
161   }
162   return false;
163  }
164 }
```

Next, let's examine a client program that actually can build a binary file of **Animal** objects. The code that actually identifies what binary object is next in the input file must be able to sort out which derived class is present next in the input file, allocate a new one of that type and call its **Serialize()** function. While there are many ways to do this, perhaps the simplest is to store a letter code before each animal object that identifies which animal type is coming next. Thus, the client writes a 'C' or a 'D' followed by the binary **Cat** or **Dog** object. This makes input operations very easy. Here are the **Pgm14a** tester program and its output. Note that I am not using std::nothrow. Hence, if we run out of memory, a C++ exception is thrown and the program aborts.

```
Pgm14a Test Serialization of Animals
```

```
 1 #include <iostream>
 2 #include <iomanip>
 3 #include <fstream>
 4 #include <string>
 5 #include <cctype>
 6 using namespace std;
 7 #include <crtdbg.h>
 8
 9 #include "Dog.h"
10 #include "Cat.h"
11
12 /*******************************************************************/
13 /*                                                               */
14 /* Tester for the serialization of a set of Animals              */
15 /*                                                               */
16 /*******************************************************************/
17
18 int main () {
19   {
20   // input a text file series of animals and store each
21   // in a binary file of Animal objects
22   ifstream infile ("animals.txt");
23   if (!infile) {
24    cerr << "Error: cannot open file animals.txt\n";
25    return 1;
26   }
27   fstream inout;
28   inout.open ("animals.dat", ios::out | ios::binary);
29   char type;
30   Animal* ptranimal;
31   cout << "The original text inputted animals\n";
32   while (infile >> type) {
33    type = toupper (type);
34    if (type == 'D')
35     ptranimal = new Dog;
36    else
37     ptranimal = new Cat;
38    infile >> *ptranimal;
39    cout << *ptranimal;
40    inout.write (&type, sizeof (type));
41    ptranimal->Serialize (true, inout);
42    delete ptranimal;
43   }
44   infile.close ();
45   inout.close ();
46
```

```
47  // now input a binary file of Animals
48  cout << "\nBinary file of animals inputted now\n";
49  inout.open ("animals.dat", ios::in | ios::binary);
50  inout.read (&type, sizeof (type));
51  while (!inout.eof()) {
52   if (type == 'D')
53    ptranimal = new Dog;
54   else
55    ptranimal = new Cat;
56   ptranimal->Serialize (false, inout);
57   cout << *ptranimal;
58   delete ptranimal;
59   inout.read (&type, sizeof (type));
60  }
61  inout.close ();
62  cout << endl;
63  }
64
65  // check for memory leaks
66  if (_CrtDumpMemoryLeaks())
67   cerr << "Memory leaks occurred!\n";
68  else
69   cerr << "No memory leaks.\n";
70
71  return 0;
72
```

```
Output of Pgm14a Test Serialization of Animals

 1 The original text inputted animals
 2 The Dog says Ruff!! Ruff!!
 3 The Cat says Pfssssttttt!
 4 The Dog says Bark! Bark! Bark!
 5 The Cat says Prrrrrr. Meow
 6
 7 Binary file of animals inputted now
 8 The Dog says Ruff!! Ruff!!
 9 The Cat says Pfssssttttt!
10 The Dog says Bark! Bark! Bark!
11 The Cat says Prrrrrr. Meow
12
13 No memory leaks.
```

Thus, we have a very simple, yet effective, method by which we can store a binary image of an object in a disk file for later fast retrieval.

For a very detailed, alternative approach, see the book: C++ Database Development, Al Stevens, MIS Press, ISBN 1-55828-357-9. He presents a persistent, almost-relational, object database manager set of classes.

Review Questions

1. Explain the concept of a persistent data object.

2. Why would an application desire the ability to have persistent objects? Give some examples.

3. When using the MFC method, why must a class have a default constructor if the object is to be inputted from disk?

4. When using the MFC method, explain how a single function can handle both input and output operations to the same passed file stream?

5. When using the MFC method, why should a Version string be written as the very first item? Give an example in which its use is vital.

Stop! Do These Exercises Before Programming

1. Our programmer has been asked to create a serialization mechanism to the company's CustomerOrder class. The relevant sections of the class definition are as follows.

```
struct Date {
  short month;
  short day;
  short year;
};

class CustomerOrder {
protected:
  long   customerID;
  Date   orderDate;
  long   itemNumber;
  char*  itemDescription;
  long   quantityOrdered;
  double unitCost;
  char   stateCode;

public:
  CustomerOrder () {
        itemDescription = new char [1];
        itemDescription[0] = 0;
        customerID = quantityOrdered = stateCode = 0;
        unitCost = itemNumber = 0;
        orderDate.month = orderDate.day = orderDate.year = 0;
      }
  ~CustomerOrder () { delete [] itemDescription; }
    ...
```

```
};
```

The programmer added the following to the class definition. However, he feels that something is not right and has asked for your assistance. Correct his design errors.

```
class CustomerOrder {
protected:
 char    version[5] = "CO1.0";
 ...
bool Serialize (bool isStoring, ifstream& file) const;
```

2. The version string should be a static data member so that one a single instance of the string is needed to service all of the classes. This minimizes memory requirements. Redesign the class definition for the version information, if you have not already done so in question 1.

3. Next, the programmer has decided to see if he can implement only the file save operation. This is what he has written. It does not work and once again he calls upon you for assistance.

```
bool CustomerOrder::Serialize (bool isStoring,
        ifstream& file) const {
 if (isStoring) {
  file.write (version, sizeof (version));
  file.write (&customerID, sizeof (customerID));
  file.write (&orderDate, sizeof (orderDate));
  file.write (&itemNumber, sizeof (itemNumber));
  file.write (&itemDescription, sizeof (itemDescription));
  file.write (&quantityOrdered, sizeof (quantityOrdered));
  file.write (&unitCost, sizeof (unitCost));
  return true;
 }
else
 return true;
 }
```

4. Apologizing profusely for his many silly blunders in getting the data written, he then determinedly presses onward, writing the input operation portion of the **Serialize()** function. This is what he is trying to debug. Unsure of why it does not work and also unsure of what to do with the version string, he begs you for assistance one last time.

```
bool CustomerOrder::Serialize (bool isStoring,
        ifstream& file) const {
 if (isStoring) {
  ...
  return true;
 }
 else {
  file.read (version, sizeof (version));
  file.read ((char*)&customerID, sizeof (customerID));
  file.read ((char*)&orderDate, sizeof (orderDate));
  file.read ((char*)&itemNumber, sizeof (itemNumber));
  file.read (&itemDescription, sizeof (itemDescription));
```

```
    file.read ((char*)&quantityOrdered,
              sizeof (quantityOrdered));
    file.read ((char*)&unitCost, sizeof (unitCost));
    file.read ((char*)&stateCode, sizeof (stateCode));
    return true;
  }
}
```

Please fix up the many errors in his input section.

Programming Problems

Problem Pgm14-1—A Serializeable Rectangle Class

In chapter 4, **Pgm04b** defined a simple **Rectangle** class. Add the ability to serialize **Rectangle** objects to a binary file consisting only of other **Rectangle** objects. Create a tester program that inputs several rectangles and then stores them into a file called **Rectangles.dat**. Then, input that file of **Rectangle** objects into an array and produce a simple report that illustrates that these objects were successfully written and read back into the program.

Problem Pgm14-2—A Serializeable String Class

In chapter 7, **Pgm07a** defined a simple **String** class. Add the ability to serialize **String** objects to a binary file consisting only of other **String** objects. Create a tester program that inputs several strings and then stores them into a file called **Strings.dat**. Then, input that file of **String** objects produce a simple report that illustrates that these objects were successfully written and read back into the program.

Problem Pgm14-3—A Serializeable Shapes Set of Classes

In chapter 9, **Pgm09a** defined a set of shape classes. Add the ability to serialize the various **Shape** objects to a binary file consisting only of other **Shape** objects. Create a tester program that inputs several shapes, at least one of each kind, and then stores them into a file called **Shapes.dat**. Then, input that file of **Shape** objects produce a simple report that illustrates that these objects were successfully written and read back into the program. You may store a single character ahead of the binary shape object that identifies which kind of shape is coming next.

Appendix A — A Review of Array and Structure Processing

This appendix covers the basic principles of single dimensioned array processing, two-dimensional array processing and the use of structures in programming with which you should already be familiar.

A Review of Single Dimensioned Array Operations

This section is a general review of single dimensional array operations.

Using an Array for Direct Lookup Operations

When working with dates, one often needs to know how many days there are in a given month. Using an array can streamline such operations. Given the month number (1 through 12), the program can access directly the array element that contains the number of days in that month. If the month number is 1 for January, then **days_in_month[1]** should contain 31 days. When setting up the **days_in_month** array, since all arrays begin with element 0 and since 0 is not normally a month number, it is permissible to make the array one element larger, placing a dummy value in the never-to-be-used element 0. The array could be defined as follows

```
const int days_in_month[13] = {0, 31, 28, 31, 30, 31, 30,
                                   31, 31, 30, 31, 30, 31}
```

Notice also the usage of the **const** keyword. Once the array elements are given their initial values, they should never be changed. Making the array constant ensures that no accidental changes to these values can be made.

In this example, the month number is used as the subscript to directly access the correct number of days in that month. The following illustrates this.

```
int month;
cout << "Enter a month number: ";
cin >> month;
while (month < 1 || month > 12) {
 cout << "Invalid month number - please re-enter: ";
 cin >> month;
}
cout << "Month " << month << " contains "
     << days_in_month[month] << " days\n"
```

Parallel Arrays and Sequential Searches — Inquiry Programs

Consider two single-dimensioned arrays, one contains the student id number and the other contains his/her course grade. Clearly, the two arrays must be kept synchronized at all times. The grade stored in element 1 of the **grade** array corresponds to the student whose id is stored in element 1 of the **id** array. Once the information is loaded into the two arrays, then the inquiry operations can begin. An **inquiry program** is one in which the user is prompted to enter a specific id of some kind and the program then finds the corresponding data and displays it. Inquiry programs are widespread in the modern world. Checking on your bank account balance, credit card limit, and even the grade that you received in a course — all are inquiry type programs.

Let's first examine how the inquiry array is loaded and then how it is used or searched. Assume that each line of input contains a long student id number followed by the letter grade they received. The following loads both arrays

```
long id[MaxStudents];
char grade[MaxStudents];
int numberStudents;
int j = 0;
while (j < MaxStudents && cin >> id[j] >> grade[j]) {
 j++;
}
numberStudents = j;
```

Notice the **while** test condition checks first to see if there is still another available element and if so, attempts the input operation and if successful, increments the subscript for the next iteration. Assume that the following Illustration A.1 represents the arrays after all the data have been input. The variable **numberStudents** contains the number actually input into the arrays and is 5.

Illustration A.1 The Id and Grades Arrays

```
subscript     id array  grade array
     0        111111111      A
     1        444444444      B
     2        222222222      A
     3        555555555      C
     4        333333333      B
```

Next, the inquiry program prompts the user to enter the id of the student whose grade is to be found.

```
long studentId;
char studentGrade;
cout << "Enter student id number: ";
cin >> studentId;
```

Now the objective is to search the id array looking for a match on **studentId**, obtain the subscript of the matching id and use that subscript to get at that student's grade. Let's encapsulate the matching process in a function, **MatchId()**, whose header begins

```
int  MatchId (long id[], int num, long findId) {
```

MatchId() must be passed the array of id numbers and the current number in the array along with the id number to find, **findId**. It should return the subscript of that element of the id array that matched **findId**.

Look over Illustration A.1 above; suppose that the user enters an id number of 555555555. Counting down the array elements, the **MatchId()** function should return 3. But what would happen if the user asks **MatchId()** to find a student id of 666666666? That id number is not in the list. Thus, when **MatchId()** ends, if there is no match on the **findId**, **MatchId()** must have a way to notify the caller of that fact. Because no subscript can ever be a negative integer, we can adopt some negative number to return to indicate no match found. Commonly −1 is used for this purpose.

Following good programming practice, define a constant integer to represent it and place it in the global namespace above the **main()** function.

```
const int NoMatch = -1;
```

The logic of the **MatchId()** function is

```
int  MatchId (long id[], int num, long findId) {
 for (int j=0; j<num; j++) {
  if (findId == id[j])
    return j;
 }
 return NoMatch;
}
```

The **main()** program then invokes **MatchId()** as follows.

```
int match = MatchId (id, numberStudents, studentId);
if (match != NoMatch) {
 studentGrade = grade[match];
 cout << studentID << "received a grade of "
      << studentGrade << endl;
}
else {
 cout << "Error: invalid student id\n";
}
```

Inserting Another Element into an Unsorted Array

Suppose that a student with an id number of 666666666 takes a make-up exam and scores a grade of B. One could alter the input file to add this sixth line and rerun the program. However, in some applications, it is neither possible nor desirable to terminate the program and restart it just to reload the arrays. Instead, the new information is additionally inserted into the array. In an unsorted array, the new information added into the first empty element. Make sure that the total number of elements in the array is incremented. The following **InsertStudent()** function illustrates how this may be done.

```
bool  InsertStudent (long id[], char grade[],
                     int& num, int maxlimit,
```

```
                           long newid, char newgrade) {
if (num >= maxlimit) return false;
id[num] = newid;
grade[num] = newgrade;
num++;
return true;
}
```

Notice that the function returns **false** if there is no more room left in the array. Observe that the number in the array, **num**, must be passed by reference so that the number in **main()** can be incremented. The two arrays now appear as follows as shown in Illustration A.2.

Illustration A.2 Updated Id and Grade Arrays
numberStudents is 6 — **main()**'s variable

```
subscript    id array   grade array
    0        111111111       A
    1        444444444       B
    2        222222222       A
    3        555555555       C
    4        333333333       B
    5        666666666       B
```

Ordered (Sorted) Lists

One problem of unsorted lists is the time that it takes to search through the array sequentially looking for a matching value in the array. If there are only a few elements, the amount of time is negligible. However, suppose that these arrays contained a store's inventory numbers, quantity on hand and unit cost. Further, suppose that the store handles 100,000 separate items. If the item number desired was the last one in the list, a significant amount of time is needed to find that match. The answer is not "Get a faster computer" but rather devise a better algorithm. If the list is sorted into numerical or alphabetical order depending upon the type of data the array contains, then far faster searches can be devised. Returning to the student id and grades arrays, let's assume that the arrays have been sorted into increasing numerical order on the ids. The arrays appear as shown in Illustration A.3.

Illustration A.3 Sorted Id and Grade Arrays
numberStudents is 6 — **main()**'s variable

```
subscript    id array   grade array
    0        111111111       A
    1        222222222       A
    2        333333333       B
    3        444444444       B
    4        555555555       C
    5        666666666       B
```

The array of ids can still be matched sequentially. However, we can take advantage of the ordered nature to detect no matching id number more quickly. Suppose that the **findId** this time was

345678999. Notice that when we are at subscript 3 which contains id 444444444, we know for certain that this id is not in the array and can return **false** at once without having to check any further subscripts. The slight modification is in boldface.

```
int  MatchSortedId (long id[], int num, long findId) {
  for (int j=0; j<num && findId >= id[j]; j++) {
   if (findId == id[j])
     return j;
  }
  return NoMatch;
}
```

On the average, some increase in speed results. However, for items near the end of the array are still going to take a large number of iterations through the loop to find them.

The Binary Search Method

The **binary search** method uses a different searching algorithm, one that drastically reduces the number of comparisons that need to be done to find the match. Before looking at the coding for the search, let's examine in detail how the binary search works. Let N represent the number of ids in the array. The first subscript to use in the search is N/2 — the midpoint. We compare the **findId** to the element in the middle. If we are lucky, we have an exact match and are done. More likely it does not match, but if the **findId** is smaller than the one in the middle, we can eliminate the entire higher half of the array from further consideration. Likewise if the **findId** is greater than that in the middle, we can eliminate all those values in the lower half. Thus, on one test, we have eliminated one-half of the array from further consideration! Now that same process is repeated, halving the new interval and testing the one in the middle again, and so on until we find the match or run out of array, indicating no match.

Let's do a concrete example using the student data above in Illustration 2.4. Say the **findId** is 22222222. The first subscript to try is (0 + 5) / 2 or index 2 which stores id 333333333. The **findId** is smaller so if this one is in the array it must lie in the lower half, between indexes 0 and 1. The new index to try is halfway between. At subscript 1, we have our match.

The binary search function should be designed so that it returns **true** if it finds a match; the index of the match is stored in a reference parameter for use by the caller. However, if it does not find a match, the index stored in the passed reference parameter should be the index of where that value ought to have been if it was in the list. Why? Code reuse. True, for a simple query, match this id, just a return value of **false** for not present is sufficient. But the next feature one might need to implement is to add this id into the sorted list where it belongs. Thinking ahead, when an id is not in the list, it is a simple matter to also provide the index of where this element should be if it were in the list. Then only one **BinarySearch()** function need be written.

```
bool  BinarySearch (long id[], int num,
                    long findId, int& foundIndex) {
  int firstidx = 0;
  int lastidx = num - 1;
  int middleidx;
```

```
 bool foundMatch = false;
 while (lastidx >= firstidx && !foundMatch) {
  middleidx = (firstidx + lastidx) / 2;
  if (findId < id[middleidx])
    lastidx = middleidx - 1;
  else if (findId > id[middleidx])
    firstidx = middleidx + 1;
  else foundMatch = true;
 }
 foundIndex = middleidx;
 return foundMatch;
}
```

Inserting New Data into a Sorted List

Inserting new elements into a sorted array is more difficult. Consider the above **id** and **grade** arrays with the six elements currently in it, Illustration A.3. Suppose that a student id of 255555555 with a grade of B needs to be inserted. What would have to be done to actually insert this new student?

First, we would have to find the subscript where that id would be the proper sequence. In this case, 255555555 belongs in the element with a subscript of 2, between the values 222222222 and 333333333. Since element 2 is already occupied, that element and all others must be moved down one element. That is, the data at index 2 must be moved into subscript 3; 3 must be moved into index 4; 4 into 5 and 5 into the unoccupied 6.

Caution. The movement of elements must be done in reverse order. If we move 33333333 into the **id** array at subscript 3, it replaces the data that is there, id 444444444. Thus, the movement must be 5 into 6, 4 into 5, 3 into 4 and finally 2 into 3. Once the data in the element of index 2 has been copied into element 3, we can then copy in the new id of 255555555 into the element at index 2.

Of course, nothing can be inserted if all the elements are used. To be robust, the insert function should also make sure the requested id is not already in the list. Remember, too, when parallel arrays are involved, what is done to one array must be echoed in the other parallel array(s).

For this example, assume the following **const int** definitions are available in the global namespace.

```
const int InsertErrorBoundsExceeded = -1;
const int InsertErrorDuplicateId = -2;
const int InsertSuccess = 0;
```

Further assume that the new data to be inserted into the list are contained in the following **main()** program's variables.

```
long newId;
char newGrade;
```

The **main()** function invokes the **InsertStudent()** function as follows

```
int retcd = InsertStudent (id, grade, numberStudents,
                           MaxStudents, newId, newGrade);
```

596

```
if (retcd == InsertErrorBoundsExceeded) {
  cout << "Error: Cannot add more students\n"
       << "The list is full\n";
}
else if (retcd == InsertErrorDuplicateId) {
  cout << "Error: student id " << newId
       << " is already present in the list\n";
}
```

The coding for the robust **InsertStudent()** function is as follows.

```
int InsertStudent (long id[], char grade[],
                   int& num, int maxlimit,
                   long newId, char newGrade) {
  if (num >= maxlimit) // out of elements
    return InsertErrorBoundsExceeded;
  int index; // subscript where id belongs
  if (BinarySearch (id[], num, newId, index))
    return InsertErrorDuplicateId; // found this id
  if (index != num) {
  // move all items down one index
  for (int j=num-1; j >= index; j--) {
   id[j+1] = id[j];
   grade[j+1] = grade[j];
  }
  // copy new data into lists
  id[index] = newid;
  grade[index] = newgrade;
  num++;
  return InsertSuccess;
}
```

Review of Two-dimensional Array Processing

One common application of two-dimensional arrays is a spreadsheet. In a monthly budget spreadsheet, for example, the rows represent the income and expenses while the columns represent the monthly expenses. Consider the following budget.

```
item               June      July     August
income           1500.00   1550.00   1500.00
rent              500.00    500.00    500.00
utilities         200.00    200.00    200.00
phone              40.00     40.00     40.00
movies             20.00     30.00     25.00
```

All of the above numerical values are **double**s. While one could create five single-dimensioned arrays, each containing three elements to hold the sets of monthly values, a single two-dimensional array of five rows each with three columns greatly simplifies the programming logic.

Defining Multidimensional Arrays

The above budget two-dimensional array is defined as

```
double budget[5][3];
```

In general, the syntax is

```
datatype name[limit1][limit2][limit3]...[limitn];
```

The number of dimensions is unlimited; however, for practical purposes, the amount of memory available for a program to use on a specific platform becomes the limiting factor. How much memory does the above budget array occupy? Assuming that a **double** occupies 8 bytes, then budget takes 5 x 3 x 8 bytes, or 120 bytes.

When defining multidimensional arrays, each array bound or limit should be either a **#define** value or a **const int**. These limit values are likely to be used throughout the program. If a symbolic limit is used, it is easier to later modify the limits to allow for more data. The above budget array can be defined as follows.

```
const int NumberItems = 5;
const int NumberMonths = 3;
...
double budget[NumberItems][NumberMonths];
```

Consider another example. Suppose that we needed to accumulate the total sales from various cash registers located in three different stores and that each store had four departments each. We could define three separate total arrays, one for each store; each array would have four elements, one for each department. However, defining one two-dimensional array of three stores each with four departments greatly simplifies programming. The **totals** array could be defined as follows.

```
#define STORES 3
#define DEPTS 4
...
double totals[STORES][DEPTS];
```

Suppose further that, within each department, there are always two cash registers. Now the array would contain a third dimension.

```
#define REGS 2
...
double regtotals[STORES][DEPTS][REGS];
```

How are the individual elements within a multidimensional array accessed? By providing all the needed subscripts. Remember that all subscripts begin with element 0. The following are valid.

```
totals[0][1] = 5.;   // store 0, dept 1
totals[1][3] = 10.;  // store 1, dept 3
totals[0][0] = 0;    // the first element in the array
x = totals[2][3];    // the last element in the array
regtotals[1][2][0] = 42; // store 1, dept 2, reg 0
```

The following are invalid.

```
totals[0,1] = 5; // each subscript must be within []
totals[1] = 1;   // this only specifies row 1 -
```

```
                          // which has 4 columns
totals = 0;               // unfortunately not allowed either
```

Normally, the subscripts are variables and not constants. The subscripts may also be integer expressions. The following are valid.

```
totals[i][j]++;  // increments this specific total
totals[k][0] = 5;
totals[k+j][j/2] = 5;
```

The following are invalid.

```
totals[k++][0]; // incs k not the element in total
totals++[k][0]; // ++ op comes after the subscripts
totals[.5][.3] = 5; // subscripts must be integers
```

Physical Memory Layout Versus Logical Layout

The physical memory layout always follows the same sequence. In a two-dimensional array, all of the columns of row 0 come first followed by all the columns for row 1 and so on. This is called **row-major order**. Figure A.2 shows how memory is laid out for the **totals** array while Figure A.2 shows how the **regtotals** array is stored in memory.

Figure A.2 Memory Layout for **totals**

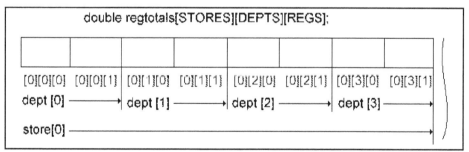

Figure A.3 Memory Layout for **regtotals**

Programmatically, two-dimensional arrays are often thought of as having rows and columns, rather like a table. It is more useful to take the following logical viewpoint of the **totals** array, where the x-axis represents the columns and the y-axis represent the rows. This is shown in Figure A.4.

In a similar manner, a three-dimensional array has the first or leftmost dimension on the z-axis (coming into or out of the page) and its second dimension is along the y-axis and the rightmost dimension is along the x-axis.

599

columns-> 0	1	2	3
r o w s 0 totals[0][0]	totals[0][1]	totals[0][2]	totals[0][3]
1 totals[1][0]	totals[1][1]	totals[1][2]	totals[1][3]
2 totals[2][0]	totals[2][1]	totals[2][2]	totals[2][3]

Figure A.4 The logical Rows and Columns View

Initialization of Multidimensional Arrays

The basic concept of single-dimensioned array initialization is extended in a similar fashion to multidimensional arrays. Consider the totals array of 3 rows by 4 columns. First, all of row 0 is initialized. However, since row 0 is an array of 4 columns, the array notation is used.

```
double totals[3][4] = { {1, 2, 3, 4}, {11. 12. 13. 14},
                          row 0              row 1

                        {21, 22, 23, 24} };
                         row 2
```

If all of the elements of a single-dimensioned array are not initialized, the default value of 0 is used for the remaining unspecified elements. Thus, if **totals** were to be initialized to 0, it could be done as follows.

```
double totals[3][4] = { {0}, {0}, {0} };
```

To initialize all the elements of **regtotals** to 0, one could do the following.

```
double regtotals[3][4][2] = { { {0}, {0}, {0}, {0} },
//                            dept 0    1    2    3
//                               -- store 0 ---------
  { {0}, {0}, {0}, {0} }, { {0}, {0}, {0}, {0} } };
// ----- store 1 -----        ----- store 2 -----
```

As the number of dimensions increases, the initialization syntax becomes awful! Frequently, it is much simpler just to write some loops to initialize the arrays at run time. The **regtotals** array can be initialized as follows.

```
for (int i=0; i< STORES; i++) {
  for (int j=0; j<DEPTS; j++) {
    for (int k=0; k<REGS; k++) {
      regtotals[i][j][k] = 0;
    }
  }
}
```

Passing Multidimensional Arrays to Functions

With single-dimensioned arrays, the name of the array is a constant pointer or memory address of the first element of the array. The same is true of a multidimensional array; its name is a constant pointer or memory address of the first element. If the **totals** array were to be passed to a function, say **calcs()**, the prototype is

```
void calcs (double totals[][DEPTS]);
```

It would not be wrong to provide all dimensions though, as in

```
void calcs (double totals[STORES][DEPTS]);
```

However, the compiler always ignores the leftmost dimension's value. However, all other dimensions must be specified. The **main()** function would then invoke the **calcs()** function by

```
calcs (totals);
```

The following is in error – why?

```
void calcs (double totals[][]);
```

To see why, suppose that within **calcs()** one coded the following.

```
totals[1][0] = qty * sales;
```

How does the compiler locate the specific element to assign the calculation result? The compiler finds the start of the 2nd row (subscript 1) by multiplying the number of elements in any row times the size of the data type of the array. This is called the **row offset** from the start of the array. It then finds the **column offset** by multiplying the column number by the size of the data type of the array. Finally, the compiler adds the starting address of the array with the row offset and then the column offset to yield the memory address of the requested element. Thus, to find the row offset, the compiler must know how many elements are in a row, that is, the second dimension.

Suppose that the array **regtotals** is to be passed to the **calcs2()** function. The prototype is

```
void calcs2 (double regtotals[][DEPTS][REGS]);
```

In all cases, it is permissible to omit only the leftmost dimension. However, it is always permissible to provide all the dimension limits; this is also less error prone.

```
void calcs2 (double regtotals[STORES][DEPTS][REGS]);
```

The **main()** function would then invoke **calcs2()** by the following.

```
calcs2 (regtotals);
```

Loading a Multidimensional Array from an Input File

Consider again the **budget** array with which the chapter began. It was defined as

```
double budget[NumberItems][ NumberMonths];
```

Suppose that the data were stored in a file called **budget.txt** and that a **LoadArray()** function is to read this data filling up the **budget** array. Recall with a single-dimensioned array, typically, not all potential elements were used in a given execution of a program. We commonly track the number of elements actually input with an integer, **numElements**, for example. The input of a multidimensional array presents some additional complications.

Suppose in true generality that not every column of every row was present. That is, for row 0, we might only have the first two columns; for row 1, all three columns are present; for row 2, only the first column's data is present; and so on. How could this be represented in the input data and worse still, how would the program know when accessing a specific row how many columns of data were actually in that row? True, we could input on a line by line basis and say all columns for a given row were on one line so that line breaks ended that row's input, but there is no easy way to "remember" how many elements each row has. If this needed to be done, a parallel second array of integer column counts would have to be constructed in which the number of elements actually in row 0 of the budget array was stored in element 0 of the counts array. Notice how fast the complexity is rising!

In reality, very often the input of multidimensional arrays is simplified to one of two approaches:

All elements of every row and all rows are entered

All elements of every row are entered, but not all rows are input

In other words, only the leftmost dimension can have a variable number input. For instance, with the **budget** array, we could store the number of rows of budget items actually input in the integer **numItems**. However, every row entered must have all three monthly values present.

The **main()** function calls **LoadBudget()** as follows.
```
int numItems = LoadBudget (budget, NumberItems,
                           NumberMonths);
```

Here is the **LoadBudget()** function that returns the number of items or rows actually input.
```
int LoadBudget (double budget[NumberItems][NumberMonths],
                int itemLimit, int monthLimit) {
 ifstream infile ("budget.txt");
 if (!infile) {
  cerr << "Error: cannot open budget.txt\n";
  exit (1);
 }
 int j = 0;
 int k;
 while (j<itemLimit && infile >> ws && infile.good()) {
  for (k=0; k<monthLimit; k++) {
   infile >> budget[j][k];
  }
  j++;
 }
 infile.close ();
 return j;
}
```

602

Working with Multidimensional Arrays

When working with two-dimensional arrays, a programmer is frequently called upon to sum the contents of an entire row (summing all the columns of that row) or to sum the contents of a specific column (summing that column in all the rows). Let's examine the straightforward approach to these two problems and then see what can be done to improve execution speed of the operations. The **main()** function defines the array to use and calls the simple **sumrow1()** function to sum all of the values in a row and display that sum.

```
#include <iostream.h>
const int NUMROWS = 3;
const int NUMCOLS = 4;

int sumrow1 (int x[][NUMCOLS], int whichrow);
int sumrow2 (int x[NUMCOLS]);

int sumcol1 (int x[][NUMCOLS], int whichcol);
int sumcol2 (int x[NUMCOLS], int whichcol);

int main() {
 int n;
 int array[NUMROWS][NUMCOLS] = { {1,2,3,4}, {11,12,13,14},
                                  {21,22,23,24} };
 // Method 1: normal sumrow function
 for (n=0; n<NUMROWS; n++) {
   cout << "sumrow1 = " << sumrow1(array,n) << endl;
 }
```

The function **sumrow1()** is straightforward.

```
int sumrow1 (int x[][NUMCOLS], int whichrow) {
 int i, sum = 0;
 for (i=0; i<NUMCOLS; i++) {
  sum += x[whichrow][i];
 }
 return sum;
}
```

How can this coding be speeded up at execution time? First of all, if the bounds are small and the sum is invoked only one time, there is no need to try to improve its efficiency. However, if the bounds are large and this function is to be invoked many times, then a speed up is in order. What is slowing down the **sumrow1()** function is the need for two subscripts. Remember that to find the current element to add to the sum, the compiler must first calculate the row offset and then the column offset and add those to values to the beginning memory address of the array in order to find the requested element. Both offset calculations involve multiplying by the size of the data type, the **sizeof** a **double** or 8 in this case. The multiplication machine instruction is fairly slow, though on the Pentium class chips, it has been drastically speeded up. If we can reduce the number of multiplies, the function executes more quickly.

When summing a row, all the columns of that row are in consecutive memory locations, that is, it can be thought of as a single-dimensioned array of four columns in this case. Thus, we pass only the current row **n** of four columns. The notation is

```
array[n]
```

Here I have provided only the first subscript of the two-dimensional array. The compiler assumes that I am specifying only the nth row, which is a single-dimensioned array of four **double**s.

The **main()** function now does the following.

```
// results in 25% less code, 4% faster execution
for (n=0; n<NUMROWS; n++) {
  cout << "sumrow2 = " << sumrow2(array[n]) << endl;
}
```

The **sumrow2()** function is now very simple indeed.

```
int sumrow2 (int x[NUMCOLS]) {
  int i, sum = 0;
  for (i=0; i<NUMCOLS; i++) {
    sum += x[i];
  }
  return sum;
}
```

The other common operation is summing columns. For a specific column, find the sum of that column by accumulating the sum of that column in every row. The **main()** function calls **sumcol1()** illustrating the straightforward approach. Note that no matter which vertical column whose sum is desired, the entire array is passed.

```
for (n=0; n<NUMCOLS; n++) {
  cout << "sumcol1 = " << sumcol1(array,n) << endl;
}
```

The basic **sumcol1()** function is as follows.

```
int sumcol1 (int x[][NUMCOLS], int whichcol) {
  int i, sum = 0;
  for (i=0; i<NUMROWS; i++) {
    sum += x[i][whichcol];
  }
  return sum;
}
```

If performance requires the **sumcol()** function to be more efficient, how can it be improved? The objective is once more to reduce the number of multiplication machine instructions it takes to find the desired element. In this case, we cannot just pass the needed row as an array of four column values; we need to go vertical through the rows summing the specific column in each row. However, there is a trick that we can use. Recall that the compiler never checks for the "subscript out of range" condition. Assume that we have passed only the very first row of the two-dimensional array, so that the **sumcol2()** function sees only a single-dimension array of four elements, those of row 0. Set the initial subscript to the desired column that we are to sum - for example column 2. Then, to get to the next row's corresponding column, to our subscript add the number of columns in a row. In this case there are four columns per row. The next subscript is 2 + 4 or 6 which is, in fact, really in column 2 of the next row.

```
// The results: it has 2% faster execution
for (n=0;n<NUMCOLS;n++) {
 cout << "sumcol2 = " << sumcol2(array[0],n) << endl;
}
```

The improved **sumcol2()** function is shown below.

```
int i, j = whichcol, sum = 0;
for (i=0; i<NUMROWS; i++) {
 sum += x[j];
 j = j + NUMCOLS;
}
```

A Review of Structures

A **structure** is a grouping of related fields of information into one group which is often called a record of data. Many convenient operations can be performed using this structure aggregate. The structure also provides means for us to access the individual member fields as needed.

Defining Structures

The starting point is to define the model or blueprint that the compiler uses when it needs to create an actual instance of the structure in memory. This model is called the **structure template** or definition. The template includes the keyword **struct** followed by the **structure tag** which is the name that is used to identify this structure from all others. This is followed by all of the member field definitions surrounded by braces {...} and ends with a semicolon.

Suppose that the program is to process cost records. Each cost record includes the item number, quantity on hand, product description and its cost. Here is what the structure template looks like.

```
const int DescrLen = 21; // max length of description

struct COSTREC {
   long    itemNum;        // item number
   short   qty;            // quantity on hand
   char    descr[DescrLen]; // item description
   double  cost;           // item cost
};
```

The structure tag, **COSTREC** in this case, is used to identify this particular structure. By convention, all structure tags either are wholly uppercase names (usually) or are capitalized.

The four data items contained between the braces { } are called the **structure members**. Each structure member is a normal variable data definition. Constant integers or **#define**s should be used for array bounds, but those definitions must precede the structure template, following the "defined before first use" rule.

When any instance of **COSTREC** is created or used, the member fields are always created and stored in the order shown in the template. For most problems, the fields can be in any order you choose.

Suppose that when recording weather statistics, data is measured and recorded every hour. A daily weather record might be defined as follows.

```
const int NumObs = 24;
const int StationLen = 21;

struct WEATHER {
  char  stationName[StationLen]; // reporting location
  float temps[NumObs];           // degrees Centigrade
  float humidity[NumObs];        // such as 50%
  float rainfall[NumObs];        // in millimeters
  float windspeed[NumObs];       // in m/s
};
```

Notice that a structure can contain arrays.

Creating Instances of a Structure

With the structure template defined, how are instances of it created? The data type precedes the desired name of the variable. Structure instances follow the same pattern. The data type is the structure tag in C++. The following creates a **structure variable** called **costRec** and a structure variable called **weaRec**. A structure variable is just an instance of a structure in memory.

```
COSTREC costRec;
WEATHER weaRec;
```

What does the structure variable **costRec** look like in memory when it is created by the compiler? Figure A.1 shows the memory layout of **costRec** and its member fields. Notice that the fields are in the same order as in the **COSTREC** template.

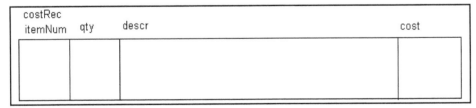

Figure A.1 The **costRec** Memory Layout

One can have arrays of structures as well. Suppose that the program needed to store a maximum of 1000 cost records and a maximum of 500 weather records. The following defines these two arrays and also shows the location of all the parts of the structure definitions.
File: CostRec.h

```
#ifndef COSTREC_H
#define COSTREC_H

#define MAXRECS 1000
const int DescrLen = 21;   // max length of description

struct COSTREC {
  long   itemNum;          // item number
  short  qty;              // quantity on hand
  char   descr[DescrLen];  // item description
  double cost;             // item cost
};
#endif
```

File: main.cpp
```
#include "CostRec.h"
int main () {
 COSTREC arec[MAXRECS];   // array of 1000 cost records
 ...
```

or

File: WeatherRec.h
```
#pragma once

#define LIMIT 500
const int NumObs = 24; // number observations per day
const int StationLen = 21; // max len of station

struct WEATHER {
 char  stationName[StationLen]; // reporting location
 float temps[NumObs];           // degrees Centigrade
 float humidity[NumObs];        // such as 50%
 float rainfall[NumObs];        // in millimeters
 float windspeed[NumObs];       // in m/s
};
```

File: main.cpp
```
#include "WeatherRec.h"
int main () {
 WEATHER weaArray[LIMIT];
```

A Structure Can Contain Instances of Other Structures

A structure can also contain instances of other structures and arrays of other structures. For example, consider a **DATE** structure which represents a calendar date. Using instances of a **DATE** structure would make passing dates very convenient. Further, consider an employee record that contained the employee's id number, his/her salary and the date that he/she was hired. The **EMPLOYEE** structure contains an instance of the **DATE** structure as shown below.

```
struct DATE {
```

607

```
    char month;
    char day;
    short year;
};

struct EMPLOYEE {
    long id;
    double salary;
    DATE hireDate;
};
```

Suppose that a **CARMAINT** structure must be defined to represent the periodic maintenance requirements for a new car. Here the **CARMAINT** structure contains an array of **DATE** structures.

```
const int numMaint = 10;
struct CARMAINT {
 bool maintenanceDone[numMaint];    // true if the work was done
 int  maintenanceCode[numMaint];    // manufacturer's maint. codes
 DATE maintenanceDueDate[numMaint];// date maintenance is due
};
```

How are Structure Instances Initialized?

An instance of a structure can be initialized when it is defined, just as any other variable. However, since a structure typically has a number of data members, the values are surrounded by braces {} as are single dimensioned arrays. The following structure represents a quarter coin initialized as it is defined within **main()**.

```
    const int MaxLen = 10;
    struct COIN {
     int denomination;
     char singular[MaxLen];
     char multiple[MaxLen];
    };
    int main () {
     COIN quarter = {25, "Quarter", "Quarters"};
```

How are Structure Members Accessed?

Having defined the structure template and created instance(s) of it, the next action is to utilize the members within the structure. This is done by using the **dot (.)** operator. To the left of the **dot** operator must be a **structure variable** and to the right must be a **member variable** of that structure.

To access the **qty** member of the **costRec** instance, one codes
```
costRec.qty
```
To calculate the **totalCost** using the **cost** and **qty** members of the **costRec** instance, do the following.
```
double totalCost = costRec.qty * costRec.cost;
```
To display the description, use
```
cout << costRec.descr;
```

To increment the **costRec**'s quantity member or add another variable to it, one can code

```
costRec.qty++;
costRec.qty += orderedQty;
```

To input a set of data into the **costRec** variable, there are a number of ways. Here is one.

```
cin >> costRec.itemNum >> costRec.qty >> ws;
cin.get (costRec.descr, DescrLen);
cin >> costRec.cost;
```

The above assumes that no description field in the input data contains all blanks. It also assumes that all descriptions contain **DescrLen − 1** number of characters.

As you look these over, notice that there are no differences at all on input or output of structure members, other than the requisite **dot** operator qualification with the structure variable.

Rules of Use for Structure Variables

Structure variables can be used for only five actions. These are the following.

A structure variable can be used to access structure members.

A structure variable or reference to one can be passed to a function.

A function can return a structure variable.

The address operator & returns the memory address of a structure variable

A structure variable can be assigned to another structure variable as long as they both have the same structure tag.

We have already examined the first one, using the structure variable to access the individual members, as in **costRec.qty**. The **address** operator & returns the address of the structure variable. If one codes

```
&costRec
```

then the compiler provides the memory location where the instance begins. Normally, the compiler does this automatically for us when we use reference variables.

Assume that the program also had defined another instance of the **COSTREC**.

```
COSTREC previousRec;
```

The fifth rule says that a complete copy of a structure variable can be done as follows.

```
previousRec = costRec;
```

This is very powerful indeed. Consider the alternative if this were not allowed. One would have to write an assignment for each of the three numeric fields and then use **strcpy()** to copy the string as shown below.

```
previousRec.itemNum = costRec.itemNum;
previousRec.qty = costRec.qty;
previousRec.cost = costRec.cost;
strcpy (previousRec.descr, costRec.descr);
```

Clearly, the ability to assign one structure variable to another instance can be a terrific operation when it is needed.

A structure variable can be passed to a function or a reference or pointer to one can be passed. Passing by reference is the best approach to take. However, passing by use of a pointer is also fine. Likewise, a function can return a copy of a structure. However, in reality, returning a structure and passing a structure and not using reference to a structure instance is generally avoided. Let's examine these two issues in detail.

Suppose that the **main()** program defined the cost record structure as we have been using it thus far. Suppose further that the **main()** function then wanted to call a **PrintRec()** function whose task is to print the data nicely formatted. The **main()** function does the following.

```
int main () {
COSTREC crec;
...
PrintRec (outfile, crec);
```
The **PrintRec()** function begins as follows.
```
void PrintRec (ostream& outfile, COSTREC crec) {
    outfile << crec.itemNum...
```

When the compiler generates the instructions to make the call to **PrintRec()**, it must make a new parameter instance of the **COSTREC** structure and then spend execution time to copy all the data from the **main()**'s **costRec** instance into **PrintRec()**'s **crec** parameter instance. For structures that contain a large number of members, this is wasteful of both memory (the parameter copy) and execution speed (making the copy every time the function is called).

A far better approach is to pass the structure variable by reference. A simple change to **PrintRec()** vastly improves both memory utilization and execution speed.
```
void PrintRec (ostream& outfile, const COSTREC& crec) {
    outfile << crec.itemNum...
```
Here the compiler actually passes only the memory address of **main()**'s **costRec**. **PrintRec()**'s **crec** parameter is now a reference variable (usually occupying 4 bytes of memory). No copy of the data is made. Further, since the print operation does not change the data, it is passed as a constant reference.

If the instance was passed using a pointer, the programmer must remember to carry out all the actions that the compiler does when a reference variable is used.
```
void PrintRec (ostream& outfile, const COSTREC* ptrcrec) {
    outfile << ptrcrec->itemNum...
```
and main() would call it this way
```
PrintRec (cout, &crec);
```

This brings up the **ReadRec()** function whose job it is to input the data and somehow fill up the **main()**'s **costRec** with that data. One way that the **ReadRec()** function can be defined is to have it return a **COSTREC** structure. This is not a good way to do it, but let's see how a function can return a structure instance. Then, we will see how to better design the **ReadRec()** function. If **ReadRec()** returns a structure, then **main()** would have to assign it to **main()**'s **costRec** variable. From a design point of view, since **main()** is passing **ReadRec()** a reference to the input stream,

ReadRec() lets the **main()** function decide on what to for I/O errors, bad data and EOF detection. The coding for **main()** is as follows.

```
int main () {
  COSTREC costRec;
  costRec = ReadRec (infile);
  // now check on infile's state
```

Now in **ReadRec()**, the coding can be done this way.

```
COSTREC ReadRec (istream& infile) {
  COSTREC temp = {0};
  if (infile >> ws && !infile.good()) {
    return temp;
  }
  infile >> temp.itemNum >> and so on
  return temp;
}
```

Here the structure variable **temp** is filled with the input file's next set of data and then a complete copy of **temp** is returned to **main()**. However, since EOF can occur as well as bad data and since we have to return an instance of the **COSTREC** structure, **temp** is initialized to zeros. Back in **main()**, when the function call to **ReadRec()** is completed, the compiler then must copy that returned copy of **temp** into **main()**'s **costRec** variable. If the structure contained a large number of member fields, memory is being wasted. In all cases, execution speed is going to suffer because of all the copying operations needed to move the data from **temp** into **costRec**.

While there can be times when this overhead cannot be avoided, usually the answer is to pass a reference to the **ReadRec()** function and have the function fill up **main()**'s **costRec** directly. This then frees up the return value for other uses. And by now returning a reference to the input stream being used for input, the caller of the **ReadRec()** function can make more effective use of the language.

Suppose that **ReadRec()** was rewritten to be passed a reference to the caller's **COSTREC** structure variable to be filled with the input data. The improved function is shown below.

```
istream& ReadRec (istream& infile, COSTREC& crec) {
  if (infile >> ws && !infile.good()) {
    return infile;
  }
  infile >> crec.itemNum >> and so on
  return infile;
}
```

Now the **main()** function has more ways that it can utilize the **ReadRec()** function. Here is the improved **main()** function.

```
int main () {
  COSTREC costRec;
  ...
  while (ReadRec (infile, costRec)) {
```

611

Certainly **main()** benefits from the change. The **while** clause is basically testing the goodness of the input stream after the input operations are complete. Also, **ReadRec()** now avoids both the extra memory overhead of returning a structure instance and the execution time needed to make the copies.